W9-BFH-738

Japan

a travel survival kit

Japan – a travel survival kit
Second edition

Published by
Lonely Planet Publications
PO Box 88, South Yarra, Victoria 3141, Australia
PO Box 2001A, Berkeley, California 94702, USA

Printed by
Colorcraft, Hong Kong

Photographs by
Ian McQueen

First published
October 1981

This edition
January 1986

Cover
front: Karamon gate in Nishi-Honganji temple, Kyoto
back: tea ceremony in a Kyoto temple

National Library of Australia Cataloguing in Publication Data

McQueen, Ian.
Japan, a travel survival kit.

2nd ed.
Includes index
ISBN 0 908086 70 9

1. Japan – Description and travel – 1945 – Guide-books. I. Title.

915'.04428

© Ian McQueen, 1986

All rights reserved. No part of this publication may be reproduced, stored in a retrieval system or transmitted in any form by any means, electronic, mechanical, photocopying, recording or otherwise, except brief extracts for the purpose of review, without the written permission of the publisher and copyright owner.

The Author

Ian L McQueen is a Canadian who has been living in Tokyo for many years. He spent his earlier years in the port city of Saint John, New Brunswick, later graduating from the University of New Brunswick. Travels to South America, Europe, Iceland and Trinidad were followed by trips through Japan, South-East Asia, Taiwan and Hong Kong. He then spent nearly five years in Australia where he completed graduate studies in Chemical Engineering at Melbourne University. He returned to Japan in 1978 to research the first edition of *Japan – a travel survival kit* and remained there through the preparation of this edition. Ian is also a co-author of Lonely Planet's *North-East Asia on a shoestring*.

Acknowledgements

Many individuals and organisations have given information or other forms of assistance in researching this book.

The Japan National Tourist Organisation, through both its head office and its Tourist Information Centres in Tokyo and Kyoto, have provided invaluable assistance of many kinds. The staff at the TICs deserve special thanks for their friendly helpfulness.

Grateful acknowledgement is made to the Australian-Japan Foundation for supporting the research of the first edition. I would like to make a special note of the kindness of Canon Inc for help in the preparation of the original manuscript and thank various colleagues on staff for their information and assistance, particularly K Sasaki, H Kawatsura and A Miyaji.

The following individuals deserve specific mention for their assistance; D Britton, D Green, T Kaihata, N J Kang, M Kira, K Matsumoto, R Morley, J Morris, N Nagayoshi, S Onda, J Pearce, D Petersen, H Suzuki, D Weber, W Wetherall, J Yamamoto, Dr G Zobel, and Ian N Lynas.

Gilles Pineau was an invaluable source for most of the detailed information on Okinawa and other islands of southern Japan.

The *Hibiya Park* cartoon in the Mt Fuji section, which was one of a series that delighted *Japan Times* readers for more than a year, was reprinted with the kind permission of 'Seton' (Brian Pringle).

My apologies for not being able to single out everyone who has supplied useful information.

FROM THE PUBLISHER

Thanks must go to all the travellers who used the first edition of this book and have written to us with information, comments and suggestions. They are: Joe Greenholtz (USA), Barbara Craver (Japan), Israel Moyston III (USA), William S Wier & J Gordon Wier (USA), Roger Landas (Japan), Goran & Catrine Fredrikson (Sweden), Melissa Hughes (Australia), Edna Phaneuf (Canada), Moshe Matsuba (Japan), Robert J Tatan, Conny van Manen (Holland), Robert Aronoff (USA), James Anderson (UK), Scott Shelley (USA), Barry Pither (Canada), D G W Malone (NZ), S Jackson (Australia), Stephen Brown (USA), John Norbury (Hong Kong), David Zoppetti (Switzerland), Allan Greenwood, Margaret L John (USA), Julie Meyer (USA),

Andrew Phillips (Australia), John Mulrey (UK), Ken Dickman (USA), Logan A McKoe (USA), Tammy & Shlomi Elad (Israel), Kevin Dwyer (USA), Ed Lyons (Japan), Ruthi Sondack & Beth Carter (Canada), Sue Brown (Japan), Richard Bean (Australia), Neil Gibson (Australia), Joe & Sylvia Weiss (Hong Kong), David Parry (Japan), Frank Pedley (UK), Paula Tavnapol & Bill Whitacre (USA), Karen Lybrand-Shimada (Japan), J Kurame (Japan), Elizabeth Nua (Philippines), Gary Tegg (Japan), Marcel Lemmens.

Last but by no means least elephant stamps must be awarded to Lindy Cameron for splendid organisational skills in the editorial department – for sifting, editing, proof reading, correcting, and several nb's; to Fiona Boyes, a warm and marvelous human being who fearlessly attacked the map situation and won; to Ann Logan – the best typesetter in the business; to young Todd Pierce for nine metric tons of bromiding and initiating the paste-up; to Richard Holt who finished it and proved to be the fastest paste-up artist in the southern hemisphere; to Mary, Andy and Jim for coping with the wall-climbing; and to those who must remain nameless for falling by the wayside.

AND A REQUEST
All travel guides rely on new information to stay up-to-date. Things change – prices go up, good places go bad, new places open up, nothing stays the same. So if you find things better, worse, cheaper, more expensive, recently opened or long ago closed please don't blame us but please do write and tell us about these changes. We love our letters from travellers out 'on the road' and, as usual, the best letters are rewarded with a free copy of the next edition, or another LP guide if you prefer.

LONELY PLANET NEWSLETTER
To make the most use out of all the information that comes in to Lonely Planet, we publish a quarterly newsletter with extracts from many of the letters we get from travellers 'on the road', plus other facts on air fares, visas, etc. It usually comes out in January, April, July and November. To subscribe, write to Lonely Planet in either Australia or California; a year's sub costs $7.50 (A$ in Australia, US$ in the US). Some back issues are available.

Contents

Introduction

It is sad but true that many travellers arrive in Japan not really knowing where to go, what to see, when to do things or how to see the most at the lowest cost. And most first-time visitors have pre-conceived ideas of this enigma of the Far East based on great shoguns, samurai warriors, geisha, cherry blossoms, Zen temples and Mt Fuji.

But today's Japan is much, much more – a complex mixture of the old and new. It is a modern, bustling, industrial nation steeped in history; its people, though still strictly governed by a social organisation and discipline that is hundreds of years old, have successfully embraced 20th century western technology and politics as if was their own invention.

It is a place where you can buy just about anything your heart desires; lose yourself in the neon-lit streets of densely populated cities where buildings seem to stretch as far as the eye can see; visit magnificent temples and ancient castles; climb sacred mountains to watch the sun rise; explore remote regions where you may be the first foreigner to ever pass that way; and meet the people themselves who are as fascinating and different as their country is surprising and beautiful.

Most of the population live on the scattered plains, the flatlands where rice fields have been fashioned broad and level to allow flood irrigation. The huge cities such as Tokyo and Osaka, sprang up on the edge of these agricultural areas and on the coast where fishing was the main industry. Japanese cities are a bit of a hodge-podge as city planning is still a foreign concept so light industry can be found everywhere and there is very little parkland. Most houses are very small, and are jumbled together with no yard or garden space to speak of. While these huge cities hold their own fascination there is very little beauty and anyone looking for the spirit exemplified by the beautiful traditional gardens is doomed to disappointment.

To find the traditional Japan, or what remains of it after the post-war prosperity, improved communications and TV, it is necessary to travel away from the big cities into the countryside, to the towns and the remote mountain regions where the settlements are smaller and the encroaching concrete and glass of the 20th century has taken less of a toll.

The best areas are Tohoku (northern Honshu), and Chubu (Central Japan). The Kyoto-Nara area has the largest number of historic remains, beautiful temples and gardens and should be on the top of any list of areas to visit. Hokkaido is superb for its wilderness scenery and splendid isolation and the Southern Islands offer a touch of the tropics.

Little remains of the traditional appearance of Japanese towns. The major industrial cities were severely damaged during WW II, earthquakes have struck most parts of the country at some time, and the Japanese have been systematically 'improving' what remains. The result is that there are relatively few old buildings, and these are scattered here and there. Towns that preserved unusually large numbers of old buildings are Kawagoe (Tokyo area), Kitakata and Kakunodate in Tohoku, the three old post towns of Narai, Tsumago and Magome in the Kiso river valley of Chubu, and the old castle town of Kanazawa. Many old thatched-roof houses may still be found in the Shirakawago-Gokayama area of northern Chubu and along the valley road between Imaichi and Aizu-Wakamatsu, just above Nikko. There are also collections of old buildings (generally wooden structures with thatched roofs) near Kawasaki, Takayama and Kanazawa, and a few in Sankei-en garden in Yokohama.

Having chosen a district to visit, a suggested way to travel is to book a room in a ryokan or minshuku for a day or two and take it from there. It is possible that you will be the first foreigner ever to stay there and the owners will go out of their way to make your visit a pleasure. After the first day or two you should feel confident enough to set out on your own. Because Japan is so far from most western countries and so expensive to get to it is impractical to make repeated trips to see what you missed the first time. It is hoped this book will help you make the best of your time in Japan.

Facts about the Country

Because Japanese records of history don't exist prior to the Nara era (600-784 AD), most knowledge of Japan before that time is based on Chinese records. Archeological excavations have found traces of settlement from 100,000 years ago, but nothing further until a few thousand years ago. The earliest civilisation about which much is known has been named the Jomon period, tentatively dated up to the second century BC. There is some evidence of a Polynesian/South-East Asian connection in these people and possible links between Japanese and Polynesian language structures may have been brought with them. There were probably northern Asian elements present in Japan at this time as well. It has also been hypothesised that the Jomon were in fact the Ainu people. Jomon pottery has been found in many areas of the country, as far north as Hokkaido, and the Ainu once lived throughout much or all of Japan.

The next civilisation that has been assigned a name is the Yayoi, identified by a clearly different type of pottery. It is likely that these people were closely related to (or belonged to) the peoples of southern Korea and that there were close ties of trade between the islands of Japan and the Korean peninsula, the nearest land mass to Japan. Bronze and iron were introduced into Japan at this time, although the bronze age was short lived. In the late fourth century settlements appear to have been conquered by warriors from Puyo (Korea); these were semi-nomadic, horse-riding people displaced from the Manchuria area who gradually conquered much of the Korean peninsula. Evidence for this is the sudden appearance of horses and armoured warriors, unknown in Japan in the third century, and the commencement of the construction of large tomb mounds in many areas of the country, a practice previously unknown in Japan but common in Korea.

The native Japanese probably became dominant around the end of the sixth century and developed into a loosely joined nation governed from Yamato (near present-day Nara). Culture from Korea and China flowed into the country during this time, including Buddhist teachings, the Chinese writing system and many new arts and crafts. This leads to the dawn of the Nara era (Nara-jidai).

Nara Era (600-784)
The most famous organiser of the early Japanese state was Prince Shotoku (shown on the now-obselete Y10,000 bill). In his lifetime (573-620) he introduced a constitution and concept of the state, promoted Buddhism as a state religion, greatly improved education and culture and set up an excellent system of state administration. Many temples were built in Nara under his direction, some of which still exist, such as Horyuji. Subsequent rulers continued his program of codification of laws and administration.

This period was the first time that the capital remained in the same location after the death of the ruler. It was a prosperous time and Nara grew to a large size, much greater than the present city. The Buddhist temples gained so much power and wealth that they were a threat to the ruler, so a later ruler (Kammu) moved the capital to Heiankyo (now Kyoto) in 794 where it remained until 1868.

The first four centuries of Kyoto rule are called the Heian Period (794-1192). The early days were ones of achievement, with cultural delegations from China, conquest of the Ezo (Ainu aboriginal people) in northern Honshu, and the blending of Buddhist beliefs with those of Shinto to make the former more acceptable

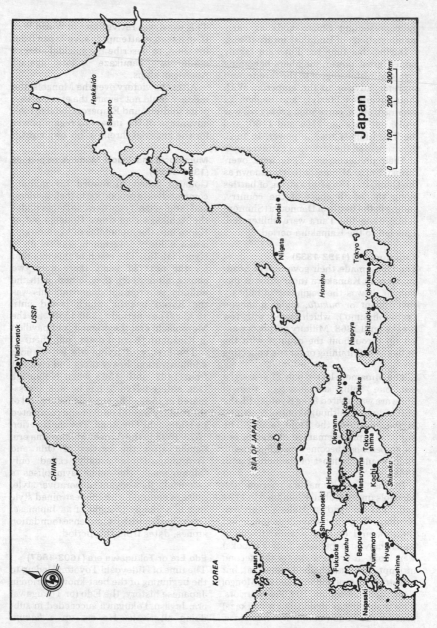

by representing Shinto gods as early manifestations of Buddhist incarnations.

During this time the Fujiwara family gained great power, members becoming Prime Minister, regent to the throne, and supreme advisor to the emperor. With their luxurious lifestyle and neglect of administration, corruption grew, civil war broke out between 1156 and 1160, and the Taira family rose to power. In turn, they repeated the luxurious extravagance of their predecessors. They were overthrown by the Minamoto (better known as the Genji) in 1185 after a string of battles along the south coast of the country, ending in the battle of Dannoura (Shimonoseki) when the Taira were obliterated. This led to the Kamakura period.

Kamakura Era (1192-1333)
The Genji made their government headquarters in Kamakura (near present-day Tokyo). It was the beginning of military government or *bakufu*, under a *shogun* ('generalissimo'), which lasted with few breaks until 1868. Military outposts were set up throughout the country with the duties of maintaining order and collecting taxes.

The Minamoto lasted only 27 years, the last one being assassinated, then a Fujiwara was invited from Kyoto to fill the post of *shogun*, although control remained in the hands of the Hojo family. The imperial capital remained at Kyoto, but the emperor had become a mere figurehead, as he would for most of the period until 1868.

During the Kamakura period the Mongols under Kublai Khan tried in 1174 and 1181 to land at Hakata (northern Kyushu). The first wave was fought off (barely), and defensive walls (traces of which may still be seen near Fukuoka) were built in preparation for the second attempt. The walls helped somewhat, but a destructive typhoon wrecked the Mongol fleet, decimating its 100,000 warriors. This typhoon was obviously a wind (kaze) sent by the gods (kami), or a *kamikaze*.

This word was revived late in World War II, in a second attempt to save Japan from invasion, to describe the suicidal attacks made by 'kamikaze' pilots against American ships.

After the victory over the Mongols, the military could not reward the expectations of its soldiers, and Emperor Godaigo took advantage of the unrest to regain power for the imperial throne in his own right.

Muromachi and Azuchi-Momoyama periods (1336-1598)
Godaigo failed to reward his military commanders in proportion to their services, and indulged his courtiers, so forces under the Ashikaga clan drove Godaigo out of Kyoto into the mountains of Yoshino and a new military government was set up in Kyoto (1336). The result of this was that for the next 57 years there were two courts, after which they joined, with the military government dominant; this was the Kyoto bakufu, which lasted until 1573. The period 1336-1573 is the Muromachi era; the original gold pavilion at Kinkakuji (Kyoto) dates from then.

The luxury of Kyoto life led to poor administration, heavy taxes and civil war from 1467 until 1568 when Nobunaga Oda entered Kyoto, but he was assassinated in 1582. The struggle for control of the country was taken over and completed by Hideyoshi Toyotomi. The short period 1573-1598 is the Azuchi-Momoyama era, named after the castles of Oda and Toyotomi. It is usually called only 'Momoyama'; the name symbolises a colourful, flamboyant decorative style, quite in contrast with the restrained style that is normally thought of as Japanese. Osaka castle, with its immense foundation stones, dates from this period.

Edo Era or Tokugawa era (1603-1867)
The time of Hideyoshi Toyotomi led up to the beginning of the best-known period in Japanese history, the Edo (or Tokugawa) era. Ieyasu Tokugawa succeeded in subduing all rivals. He set up a *bakufu*

Emperor Godaigo

government in Edo (Tokyo) while the emperor continued to reside in Kyoto, without power. The country was divided into nearly 270 fiefs, each under a *daimyo* (feudal lord) who owed their power and allegiance to the *shogun*, Tokugawa.

During this period contact by European traders and missionaries increased to the point where the government felt the foreign influences (particularly Christianity) were a threat to the stability of the country. Christianity was suppressed with the martyring of many thousands (especially in Kyushu, the centre of Catholicism). Only the Dutch were permitted to trade and only through Nagasaki on the southern island of Kyushu; the Portuguese were banned in 1639, and the English and Spanish had been excluded earlier. (The early days of the Tokugawa era is the period fictionalised in James Clavell's novel *Shogun*; the character 'Anjin' was patterned on an actual shipwrecked pilot, Will Adams.)

The following two centuries or so saw a Japan sealed as completely as possible from contact with the outside world. Japanese who left and returned were executed to prevent the introduction of outside ideas. Society was highly organised, with clearly defined classes (nobility, military, farmers and merchants) with little mobility between classes. Interestingly, the merchants were the lowest class. Incredibly detailed laws decreed every aspect of life, such as the type of clothing that might be worn, the kind of food one was allowed, place of residence, movement, even the position in which one might sleep! Orders of the military leaders were to be obeyed instantly; hesitation or expression of displeasure or question was likely to result in instant death. (This historic fact might give some explanation for the tendency to this day to show relatively little expression and to follow orders without much question.)

The isolation was brought to an end with the arrival of the Black Ships of Commodore Perry (US Navy) in 1853 with a demand that Japan open its doors to trade. Yokohoma and other ports were opened within a few years. The entry of the foreign barbarians was not universally welcomed and the Choshu clan, controlling Shimonoseki Strait, then closed it, resulting in a three-day bombardment and the destruction of the shore installations by British, American, French and Dutch ships in 1864. The Choshu then realised that the country had to be modernised to overcome Japan's powerless position.

Emperor Meiji had begun his reign in 1852, but was as powerless as his predecessors in the face of the Tokugawa. The Choshu joined with the Satsuma clan of Kagoshima (southern Kyushu) to press for the end of the Tokugawa government and the restoration of the emperor to full power. In the ensuing period of fighting and confusion the *shogun* stepped down and Emperor Meiji began his amazing reign in 1868. Fighting by elements loyal to the Tokugawa continued in several parts of the country and had to be put down by force but eventually the emperor was given full powers. This is called the Meiji Restoration.

The Meiji Era and Later (1868–)

During the Meiji era (1868-1912), Japan went from an isolated feudal agricultural nation to one of the world's most powerful and dynamic countries, with a modern navy and army (that defeated Russia in 1905), a network of railroads, industry of all kinds and a parliament. Every effort was made to modernise all aspects of Japanese life. This resulted in some excesses as many relics of the past were intentionally destroyed, including many picturesque castles and traditional objects like bronze lanterns. (The collection in the British Museum was rescued from a scrapyard by a ship's captain.)

Meiji was succeeded in 1912 by Emperor Taisho, but there is little record of his rule. It seems he was incompetent and mentally unstable – the result of inadvertent poisoning by a white lead compound while

Emperor Meiji

being suckled by a wet nurse. (The compound was commonly used by women to whiten their skin; its side effects, especially its effect on the brain, were not fully appreciated.) He was succeeded in 1926 by Hirohito.

The awakened national spirit and expansion of the Meiji era had far-reaching effects beyond the Taisho era and well into the present Showa era of Emperor Hirohito. The need for raw materials and markets for the growing industrial machine led to wars with China in 1894 and 1937; the former resulted in the ceding of Taiwan to Japanese control. Korea was invaded in 1910, providing the foundation for national antipathy towards Japan that persists to this day.

The world-wide economic depression of the 1930s gave the military the ability to expand its control over the country, resulting in conquests of many Asian countries. It led, however, to the ultimate disaster of World War II and the devastation of Hiroshima and Nagasaki – the first and only cities ever to be atom-bombed. It was also the first time in its recorded history that Japan had been conquered. Occupation by Allied forces (mainly American but including British and Australian) followed.

Post-war changes have been dramatic, with rejection of military values to such an extent that the armed forces are still held in low esteem. The right-wing militaristic mentality which promoted State Shinto as a national religion has largely disappeared. A small minority still supports it, and loud-speaker-laden trucks blaring national-istic music and slogans may be seen and heard on the streets of large cities, but are ignored by the general populace. One look at the immature young men strutting on the truck roofs in their uniforms explains why.

Prior to the war, the emperor had been revered as a living god by State Shinto. After Japan's defeat he renounced any claim to divinity. The present Emperor (Hirohito by name, but rarely referred to in this way by the Japanese) is a frail, bespectacled, kindly looking octogenarian whose main interest (according to inform-ation given out by the Imperial Household Agency) is marine biology about which he is knowledgable and has written books. One has the impression that his was a passive role during the pre-war period and that the military government carried out their actions in his name but without his active participation. Today he is basically a constitutional monarch, like the monarch of Great Britain. His present role is as a symbol of the Japanese state; although he is consulted and advised, he has no actual power in governing the country.

The use of war was renounced in the new constitution, although Japan is allowed a Self-Defence Force, which today is among the world's more powerful armed forces.

The country has an elected democratic government; the Diet has two chambers, the House of Representatives and the House of Councillors which enact laws, but the administrative arm (the civil service) is very powerful and controls many aspects of business. The conserv-ative Liberal-Democratic party has held power for nearly all the post-war period. It is a pro-free enterprise party (though the government gives much financial assist-ance and 'administrative guidance' to important or new industries), and the country is firmly and reliably in the western camp.

Interestingly, a peace treaty has never been signed with the USSR, partly because that country opportunistically siezed four islands off Hokkaido that had long been Japanese, by joining the war against Japan only a couple of weeks before the end and occupying the islands, even though there had never been any agreement among the Allies for this to happen.

The economic miracle that has taken place in Japan is well-known and needs little review. It is incredible to the visitor of today to think that all the major cities (except Kyoto, which was spared because of its historic treasures) lay in ruins 35 years ago, and that the Japanese people were on the edge of starvation for several years after the war. Now the country leads the world in many industries such as cars, steel, quality cameras and electronics.

Women were given the vote after the war and their place in society has been greatly elevated, although there is still blatant job discrimination in favour of men and male salaries are as much as double those of women. Women, by and large, are still expected to marry and raise children after a few years of work and forget any nonsense about careers.

GEOGRAPHY

Japan is made up of four main islands, Honshu, Hokkaido, Kyushu and Shikoku, and hundreds of smaller ones that stretch nearly 3000 km in the temperate and sub-tropical zones, between latitudes 20° and 45°. (Equivalent locations are from Morocco to Lyons or Milan; or from Miami to

Montreal.) Total land area is 377,435 sq km, about 85% of which is considered mountainous. Mountain ranges divide the country into four zones – the Japan Sea and Pacific Ocean sides of the north-east half; and the Japan Sea and Inland Sea sides of the south-west half – all of which have definite differences in patterns of both weather and customs of the people.

Japan is still geologically young and volcanic eruptions are not uncommon. The Pacific Plate, one of the huge areas of the earth's crust afloat on the mantle, is slowly forcing itself under the islands of Japan, causing frequent earthquakes, mostly harmless. The volcanoes, 67 of which are considered active, are part of the 'Ring of Fire' that follows a fault line (a junction of two plates) around the earth. Active volcanoes include *Usu-zan* on Hokkaido, and *Aso-zan* and *Sakurajima*, both on Kyushu. Other volcanoes on Honshu wake up from time to time; recently there was an eruption of one that had been thought dead. It is also theoretically possible for *Mt Fuji* to erupt again, although it hasn't since 1707, and shows no signs of doing so.

Japan is divided into administrative units that, for the most part, follow the natural boundaries. With the exception of Hokkaido and three other units, these smaller units are called *ken*, and are modelled on the French prefectural system. There are 43 ken.

Hokkaido was settled extensively only late in the 19th century and still has a small population relative to its size, so the entire island is a single *do*, or district; this is the last syllable of the name.

Tokyo is a *to* (metropolis), while Kyoto and Osaka and their surrounding regions are both *fu*; all three compare in size with the smaller ken. When writing the names of the latter cities in Japanese, they are 'Tokyo-to', 'Kyoto-fu' and 'Osaka-fu'.

In addition to the administrative units (ken) there are other traditional ways of dividing the country. The names of these regions, all based on geographical features, are still commonly used by the Japanese. For example the *Youth Hostel Handbook* is divided up according to one of the two traditional systems, as are most road maps that cover large regions of the country (such as the Hi-Power series referred to elsewhere). Large scale maps follow ken boundaries. Several brochures printed by the JNTO follow the old divisions as well, such as Hokuriku and Chubu.

Because the traditional divisions largely follow natural features, similar divisions are used for the chapters of this book. Also, prefectural boundaries are used for detailed description except where attractions overlap ken boundaries.

CLIMATE

Japan is a long country north to south, so the weather and climate vary widely; at any one time there can be a great difference in conditions from one part of the country to another and even in different parts of the same region, especially in the mountainous areas. There can be blizzard conditions on Hokkaido, sunny, crispy-cool weather in Tokyo and Kyoto, mild Mediterranean conditions on Kyushu and pleasant warmth on Okinawa.

The best time to visit Japan is from mid-September to mid-late November. By then the heat and humidity of summer have passed, as have the typhoons and rain. Starting in Hokkaido in the north, the weather cools and the leaves change colour in early October in a display of fiery autumn foliage that is among the best to be found anywhere in the world. The change of colour advances southward, earlier in high mountainous regions, more slowly along the coasts, and normally has reached Kyoto by the first half of November. This is the best two or three weeks of the year to visit Kyoto and it is well worth trying to get there then. However, the Japanese are also fully aware of the beauties of that season, and Kyoto is more crowded then than at any other time, so it is wise to book (even months ahead) for accommodation. Within the next couple of weeks the leaves will have fallen throughout the country, and the countryside will have faded to a dull brown, a far cry from the lush greens of summer or the almost iridescent green-gold of the rice paddies just before harvest.

Spring has long been touted as the ideal time to visit Japan. It seems that every brochure stresses the beauty of the cherry blossoms (*sakura*) as the symbol of Japan and gives the impression that this is the only time to visit. The fact is that anyone trying to see Japan at sakura time runs the risk of frustration and disappointment. True, the blossoms are beautiful, and when they're backdropped by or are part of a picturesque Japanese castle the effect is incomparably lovely. But the blossoms are fickle; the petals remain on the trees less than a week before fluttering to earth, prey to the wind and rain, both of which are prevalent at this time of the year. Fortunately, with the great diversity in climate from north to south, and from coast to mountain, the blossom season extends about six weeks nationwide, advancing in a wave of pink and white from Kyushu north to Hokkaido. Further fickleness of nature means the beginning of the blossom season can vary a few weeks from year to year.

Since sakura is an early blossoming species (though not the earliest, as plums come out in February), its appearance is followed by a period of several weeks while the rest of nature catches up and other greenery appears. This can be a season of windy and unsettled weather, with some beautiful days, some cloudy, some rainy. This leads up to the rainy season, or *tsuyu* (also called 'baiyu'), which normally begins in mid-June and may continue into early July, during which rain can be expected almost every day. Incidentally, it is a popular belief among the Japanese that there is no rainy season on Hokkaido, but foreign residents who have been there during that time report that a lot of water tends to fall out of the sky!

In general, spring begins chilly and clear in March and finishes warm to hot and humid in June. On Hokkaido, and in the highlands of Honshu, the temperatures are considerably lower, so that snow may remain on the ground as late as May or even June. There are some mountains where skiing is possible right into August. Spring is considered to begin on 1 March not the 21st as in North America.

Summer is hot and humidly uncomfortable in the coastal and lower regions, which includes most major cities. Even on Hokkaido, Sapporo has its hot days but not as many as Tokyo or Osaka, which can be very unpleasant. Despite the heat, summer can still be an enjoyable time to visit Japan. Birds and fantastically beautiful butterflies flitter around the lush green countryside and the air is filled with the shrill chorus of cicadas. On Hokkaido and in the highlands everywhere, summer is generally delightful, with low humidity and the temperature warm to hot. It is good weather for walking and enjoying the scenery (but a canteen of water will always be a welcome companion).

The summer officially lasts from 1 June to 1 September but the warm weather usually lasts well into October, and it is still pleasant in November. Despite the still scorching temperatures in the southern cities, swimming pools automatically close on the first day of September, and people abruptly cease going to the beach on the same date. (At one time in the past, the entire population even changed from the clothes of one season to those of the next on the same date, regardless of the weather on that day.) Visitors in summer should wear the lightest garments possible; wash-and-wear clothing is very useful. Japanese expect foreigners to be a little strange, so they look tolerantly on the summer 'fashions' worn by some western women whose acres of exposed flesh is a bit unusual. Japanese women rarely even expose their shoulders, so keep that in mind before becoming one of the sights for the locals.

Travellers who plan to spend several months travelling around Japan extensively would be wise to tour Hokkaido and northern Honshu through the hot season of July-August; the southern part of the country (Kyushu/Shikoku) between August and October; and the central part between September and November. For Kyoto aim to be there in mid-November; the period from from 10 to 20 November is generally the best. At that time Kyoto must rate as one of the most beautiful places in the world, with its gorgeous combination of beautiful temples set among brilliantly colourful leaves.

Winter is generally a time of clear air, bright sun and cool or cold weather. Snow covers much of Hokkaido, northern Honshu and the mountain highlands, often to a depth of several metres. Houses in the snow country may have a separate door at roof level for access during the winter. In lower regions, snow doesn't become a permanent feature until 100-200 km north of Tokyo. Tokyo and the other large southern cities are usually snow-free except for the occasional light falls that usually melt by midday. In 1978, though, a freak storm dumped 15 cm of snow on Tokyo.

For ordinary touring winter cannot be recommended very highly. Remember that when visiting temples and many other wooden-floored old buildings, it is necessary to remove your shoes and pad around in slippers so warm socks are a must! Houses are usually not centrally heated, as fuel is very expensive. Youth Hostels are often heated, especially in the colder regions, but an extra fee is levied to pay for the fuel. The large western-type hotels are invariably heated and comfortable while public buildings, such as stores and offices, are generally overheated to the point of being sweltering.

It is said that Kyushu is semi-tropical. While it is a few degrees warmer than Honshu, it is still no tropical paradise, just pleasant; and in the mountain areas it too will be cold and snowy in winter. Okinawa and the Ryukyu Islands are the warmest parts of Japan; their winter climate varies from cool to warm.

For skiers, winter is of course a good time to visit Japan; conditions and facilities have been described as good but not worth a special trip to Japan just for the skiing.

PEOPLE

The origins of the Japanese people are not known with any certainty. There are elements in the language that hint at a Polynesian/South-East Asian connection in very early times and it seems only logical to assume that various peoples immigrated across the relatively narrow Japan Sea from the Korean Peninsula, from Siberia via Sakhalin Island and from mainland Asia areas such as Manchuria and other parts of China. There are intriguing bits of evidence like tribes in the northern hills of India with several types of food, like sushi, identical to that in Japan.

There are many dialects spoken in Japan which were originally different languages. It can be proposed that the dialects developed through the immigration of numerous ethnic groups – each with their own original language or dialect and accompanying rhythm or cadence – was carried over into the vocabulary and grammar of standard Japanese as it established itself throughout the country (in the same way that numerous English accents developed).

The people of one region often look quite different from inhabitants of another region; Kyushu people would not be mistaken for Tohoku people for example. Although foreign visitors cannot identify accents they can notice the great variety of facial features around the country.

Many Japanese like to consider themselves as a unique race, different from other Asians, but the fact is there can be no such thing as an identifiable Japanese race. They have a national culture, but the present inhabitants of the Japanese islands are a mixture of many peoples of Asian origin. In their physical appearance many Japanese are clearly identifiable as such, but probably more than 40% of the population could be dropped into another country of the region, and would be indistinguishable from the local population. In appearance, not only do features differ from person to person and from region to region (for example some have narrow eyes, while others are almost as round-eyed as westerners) but there is also a large variety of skin colouring from as dark as Indonesians to whiter than a pale European. The Japanese however, do not remark on these differences because they want to believe they are all of the same race. Belonging to a group is very important to individual Japanese.

In addition to the 'mainstream' Japanese, there are also minority peoples. The Ainu (pronounced 'eye-noo') are now found only in Hokkaido though once they lived as far south as about 100 km north of Tokyo. Formerly a hunting and fishing people with an animistic culture, their way of life was destroyed through the centuries by the ethnic Japanese, and they now live much like other Japanese. No one knows the origin of the Ainu; their language seems unrelated to any other in the world, although native Siberian tribes have a similar bear cult. They are also said to be the most hirsute people on earth. Other lesser-known races or ethnic groups, each of only small numbers (Oroke, Gilyak, etc) are also found on Hokkaido.

There is another group who are ethnically Japanese but who, for some reason in history, were made outcasts and have been treated as such ever since. They were formerly called *eta*, and are now *burakujumin* (village people). The govern-

ment is taking steps to improve their lot in life, but they are discriminated against in housing, jobs and socially and most families of mainstream Japanese refuse to let their children marry one; prior to a marriage it is standard procedure to check the background of the other family.

Part of the belief still held regarding the 'uniqueness' of the Japanese is a legacy of the pre-war government promotion of Shinto. Myths regarding the origins of the Japanese, that they were descendants of the Sun Goddess *Amaterasu-Omikami*, were actually taught in schools. The purpose was to instill a feeling of nationalism. Japanese were encouraged to feel superior to, and separate from, other peoples; this served the ends of the militarists who were pushing Japan into conquest of other Asian countries.

At work and in other formal situations the Japanese may seem a stolid people with little spontaneity, personality, 'spark' or dynamism. Various explanations can be offered for this reticent behaviour. Either that it has long been a virtue in Japanese society to be self-effacing and stoic or that in the Tokugawa days a change in expression or hesitation of any kind when receiving an order could be grounds for death on the spot.

In contrast, Japanese (men especially) become boisterous when drinking and let this facade slip, as this is the only time they may voice their honest opinions without fear of retribution.

Although Japanese generally regard themselves as superior to all other peoples, they are extremely kind to foreigners of European extraction; far more so than they are to other Japanese, to non-Japanese Asians or to non-white races, such as Africans. On the other hand some newspapers and

children on a school excursion) seem very outgoing and may even want autographs. They have probably never had the opportunity to see or talk to anyone from another country and they are just curious. Keep this in mind if bombarded with a constant chorus of 'Aro' ('Hello') and try to keep smiling. Foreigners are frequently referred to as *gaijin*. This is generally said in complete innocence and is not meant to be offensive. This is another example of the Japanese tendency to divide everything into 'us' and 'them'. The 'us' can be a family, a school, a company or a department. The 'out' group is *gai*, so a foreign person is a *gai-jin*, an 'outside person'. It can be presumed that white foreigners receive their exalted status because during the Meiji era Japan received nearly all its knowledge from European people (including Americans). Also it was the Europeans who defeated the Japanese during the Pacific War and the Japanese respect a winner.

The self-indulgent, selfish side of the Japanese nature is recognised by the Japanese themselves; in one survey, they chose it as one category defining their nation, so it is no insult to mention it here. It is apparently an extension of the 'us' and 'them' mentality; everyone looks after one's own group and has little or no concern for others.

Behaviour in Japan is mainly situational, not determined by a universally applicable set of standards. Whereas the average westerner is generally guided by Jud Christian ethical values of behaviour (reflected in the 'common courtesy'), su principles do not ex society. One knows or that letely different verbs for use with people of different status. This seeking of information about another person is a possible explanation for the usual litany of questions that a foreigner tends to be asked on first meeting a Japanese, especially one with a limited knowledge of English. Japanese is not unique, by the way, in having multiple levels of politeness in the language; Korean has even more, and the language of Sunda (Indonesia) has a similar structure of formality.

One of the great achievements of Japanese society is the ability of large numbers of people to live in crowded conditions in peace with each other. Japan is certainly one of the safest countries in the world to live in and violence is quite uncommon, particularly in comparison with the USA. Japanese society is a system of interlocking obligations, conditioned social reflexes and formalised responses. This causes a lack of spontaneity but it provides a lubricant for social interactions to avoid interpersonal frictions. It is rare for Japanese to quarrel (outside the family); even if two people dislike each other, the facade is usually maintained with formally correct ways of speaking so they can get on with their work or their lives with a minimum of unpleasantness. One of the products of this formality is the 'Japanese smile' that can hide all real thoughts.

Despite the generally peaceable nature of most Japanese there exists the potential for violence. In the past decade student politics has flared up with occasional violence, mostly limited to radical leftist factions. However, the average Japanese remains an easy-going and relaxed person and not fanatical about anything, just a hard worker who looks forward to moving up the promotional ladder. (Even most student radicals appear to shed their views like a dirty shirt when they graduate and join a company to become a typical salaryman.)

One of the myths about Japanese behaviour that should be permanently laid to rest is their 'politeness'. As anyone who has travelled by commuter train can aver, the Japanese are not an excessively polite people. Any hint of manners vanishes in the attempt to get into or out of the train. When I return to Canada and travel on the subways of Montreal or Toronto I am always struck by the overall courtesy of the populace in comparision to the supposedly polite Japanese. I am astounded to see that western men still give up seats to women, a practice unheard of in Japan unless the woman is faced with imminent collapse.

The best summation of Japanese politeness is that 'Japanese are only polite with their shoes off', meaning they are exceedingly polite to people they know well enough to be indoors with (where shoes are removed).

Bowing to show respect is largely a conditioned reflex. Mothers push their children's heads down in a bow before they can even talk. The depth of a bow is more an indication of the rank or business importance of the recipient than a genuine measure of the bower's esteem. Advice to foreigners when respect is called for is to incline the head in a semi-bow, use normal western courtesy, and don't try to shake hands unless the Japanese person offers a hand first, as they are generally not accustomed to the habit.

In homes, one usually sits on the floor, an uncomfortable position for foreigners for extended periods. Try to keep your legs under you as long as possible; if it is necessary to stretch out, avoid pointing your feet at anyone (very rude). Most Japanese will realise that foreigners become uncomfortable and will make allowances for deviation from ideal Japanese manners.

An oft-heard cliche about the Japanese is their 'oneness with nature'. For the most part they (as a group) have no more appreciation of nature than any westerner. The average Japanese thoughtlessly drops cigarette packets, bottles and cans wherever he happens to be. A depressing number of gardens and other places that should be oases of beauty and tranquility for nature lovers have loudspeaker systems, or visitors bring portable tape-players. These can destroy any possibility of developing the contemplative mood intended when the structure was built.

The Japanese are also the worst offenders against the endangered species of the world. Pelts of rare animals are imported without qualm and ivory is easily obtainable, while most other countries have virtually banned their import. Japan is among the last countries in the world to hunt whales on a large scale, defending the practice on the specious grounds that it is a needed source of protein and that many people would lose their jobs if it were abolished.

Although there are many Japanese who practice ikebana (flower arrangement), enjoy the singing of crickets and refine their mind through the tea ceremony, there is so much publicity stressing these aspects that you get the impression that everyone is adept in the arts, which isn't true. The average Japanese is probably little more refined than a western counterpart, and westerners should avoid coming to Japan with a 'cultural cringe'; there is much to be admired and there are many things that westerners can learn from Japan, but it is important to remain objective.

RELIGION
Shinto

Shinto – 'Way of the Gods' – is the so-called native Japanese religion. It has no fixed ceremonies or scriptures and is basically an animistic belief largely concerned with obtaining the blessing of the gods for future events. Ceremonies are held to bless babies, children (*Shichigosan* festival), weddings and the start of new enterprises. Even large corporations take no chances and enlist the aid of a Shinto priest. It is not uncommon to see a ceremony for blessing a building site before construction begins.

Before the war, Shinto was glorified by the state and used to bestow a blessing from the gods on the militaristic line that the government was following. State aid was given to shrines throughout the country. After the war, however, all such aid was cut and Shinto reverted to its earlier, simpler form, supported only by donations from the faithful.

Before Shinto existed there was a shamanistic folk faith similar to that in many other Asian countries. It still exists in isolated parts of Japan, such as Osorezan in the very north of Tohoku, and is known as Minkan-Shinko. When Shinto was first introduced, many existing shamanistic deities were given new Shinto names in a (largely successful) attempt to supplant the older religion by absorbing its gods and ceremonies. (In the same way Christianity absorbed many ancient pagan festivals in Europe.)

Shinto shrines, called *jinja, taisha* or *jingu* are generally identifiable by a *torii* gate – two uprights and a double crossbar. There is often a thick braided rope made of rice straw suspended between the uprights of the torii; it is a *shimenawa* and is put up after the harvest season. There are normally carved stone *koma-inu* (guardian lions or dogs) at the entrance, similar to those seen at Chinese shrines. If portrayed correctly, the mouth of one lion is open, the other closed. This symbolises 'Ah' and 'Um', the sounds of birth and death, the Beginning and the End, from Hindu mythology. The distance between them is the Path of Life, a reminder to those walking between them of the shortness of their temporal existence. (Most Japanese however, are unaware of the significance.)

The shrine building is often very simple, although all incorporate customary design elements of symbolic importance. There is often a rope hanging down from a 'rattle' suspended in the eaves. Worshippers shake it to wake up the gods and get their attention and then clap their hands together before praying. This is almost a reflex action with most Japanese, even those who claim no religious faith.

It is common for people to follow both Shinto and Buddhist beliefs without any conflict in their minds, as each covers certain aspects of life not touched by the other. Buddhism, with its many sects and voluminous literature, appeals more to the intellectual side of the religious nature, while the simplicity of Shinto makes it instantly accessible to all.

Buddhism

Buddhism arrived in Japan, from China, in the middle of the sixth century. Through the centuries, the original teachings of the Buddha in India had already been modified by the Chinese to suit their temperament and culture, and

this derivative form which reached Japan was further moulded so that foreign Buddhists scarcely recognise the Japanese faith as being part of their own. Numerous Buddhist sects have developed in Japan since its introduction; even in recent decades there have been new ones, such as Soka Gakkai.

Most Japanese families have some ties with Buddhism, if in no other way than through burial by a Buddhist priest on temple grounds. The eldest son of most families is guardian of the family altar, an ornately gilded wooden structure in the household place of honour. In it are tablets with the names of deceased family members. Regular ceremonies honour these ancestors, ceremonies which have led to the mistaken belief that the Japanese actually worship their ancestors. During the annual O-bon season (July or August), it is believed that the souls of the deceased return to visit. It is a happy time with public dancing everywhere in the country.

The greatest manifestation of Buddhist belief is the beautiful temple buildings in Kyoto. The significance of the brilliantly gilded figures, altar fittings, etc, will be lost on those not familiar with Buddhist symbolism, but they can still be appreciated as works of art. Another symbol of Buddhism and of Japan itself is the Daibutsu, the great bronze statue of Buddha, at Kamakura.

NATIONAL HOLIDAYS

There are 12 national holidays; the following Monday is generally taken as the holiday if the day falls on a Sunday. On these days most offices, factories and businesses close, but most stores and restaurants remain open.

1 January
New Year's Day
15 January
Coming-of-Age Day
11 February
National Foundation Day
21 March
Vernal Equinox Day (may change some years)
29 April
Emperor's Birthday
1 May
May Day (semi holiday)
3 May
Constitution Memorial Day
5 May
Children's Day
15 September
Respect-for-the-Aged Day
24 September
Autumnal Equinox Day (date may change some years)

10 October
Physical Culture Day
3 November
Culture Day
23 November
Labour Thanksgiving Day

Two periods to avoid in Japan are around New Year, roughly 28 December to 5 January, and the week around early May. New Year is the biggest holiday season in Japan and many people try to return to their family home. Nearly all businesses and many restaurants are closed, busy cities like Tokyo are nearly deserted and most shops are shuttered, so it is the least interesting time to visit Japan unless you have personal connections. In the period from 29 April to 5 May there are no less than four holidays. It is known in Japan as 'Golden Week'; many businesses give their employees the entire week off and, because the weather is usually fine, everyone travels. Or tries to! It is very difficult to obtain reservations on trains and at hotels and train passengers without reserved seats will most likely have to stand for the full journey.

Although it is not a listed national holiday, be wary of the *Obon* season, a week in mid-August when all Japanese try to visit the graves of their ancestors. Again transport is difficult to obtain. This is, however, a lively and interesting time because there is dancing every night in almost every neighbourhood.

There are busy seasons also when school children go on excursions, but these mostly affect Youth Hostel accommodation in historic or nature areas and are mentioned in the Youth Hostel section.

Festivals

Japan has a huge number of festivals, many with a known history of hundreds of years and some that date back thousands, with evidence of religious and folk rites – such as the many fertility festivals.

The Tokyo Tourist Information Centre has free monthly listings of the festivals in Tokyo and the rest of the country. If you want an idea of what will be happening in the following month, staff can copy the info sheets of the previous year; many dates remain the same from year to year.

Festivals provide an insight into Japan that cannot be gained in any other way, and it is worthwhile planning an itinerary to take in as many as possible. With few exceptions they are occasions of joy and celebration. The men (and some of the older women) get gloriously drunk and happy, and often invite any foreigners present to join in the fun and sample the contents of the cask of sake just opened. (This can make taking pictures quite difficult after a while!) A feature of nearly every festival, especially those in the country, is the drumming. The amazingly primitive rhythm is executed with great skill and precision. The drumming is apparently a carry-over from long forgotten days of the earliest inhabitants of the islands.

Festivals give some of the most lasting memories of Japan as they are a reflection of the true spirit, a renewal of contact with their origins.

MEETING THE JAPANESE

It is unfortunate that most visitors to a foreign country such as Japan have little opportunity to meet the people who live there. They are always on the move and there is often a language barrier. Yet it is only through such contact, of course, that a visitor has a chance to learn of their daily life, work, pleasures and problems. Leaving Japan without meeting any of its people, other than hotel employees etc, is like wearing earplugs to Carnegie Hall or a blindfold to the Louvre. Because of the education system inflicted on the Japanese (they study to pass exams, not to learn), most of them have little ability to speak English despite untold hours of instruction at school. The emphasis is all on written, not spoken, work with the result that contact with most people in Japan can be difficult.

There are, however, a variety of programs aimed at introducing visitors to Japanese who do speak foreign languages. Because English is the most widely spoken language in the world it is the one that most Japanese learn. (This is a source of annoyance for many Europeans who encounter Japanese who think that everyone with 'white' skin speaks English.) Through several independent programs in operation around the country, you can visit a Japanese home for a couple of hours in the evening, meet Japanese people who are willing to act as guides and escorts at no charge, attend a wide variety of parties, excursions and cultural activities with Japanese people, simply chat over a cup of coffee or even stay with Japanese families in their homes around Japan, at no charge.

Home Visit System

The Home Visit System is a voluntary program through which Japanese families in several cities receive foreign visitors into their homes. The system is 'semi-official' in that it is publicised in a brochure issued by the semi-government Japan National Tourist Organisation (JNTO). Visits are normally arranged for a couple of hours in the evening. Food is not served, but green tea and sweets will usually be part of the evening. Hosts will show guests around the house, if desired, perhaps showing the finer points of Japanese house design (if it is not a modern western type!) and the garden, if there is space for one; Japanese houses are usually rather small. The homes open under this program are often those of well-to-do Japanese so they will tend to be more spacious and elegant than average. The Japanese usually do not receive guests at home because they consider their houses to small and humble.

There is no charge for a visit. It is customary among Japanese to take a small gift to the host or hostess whenever

visiting, even among close friends. Flowers, fruit or candy are suggestions. The Japanese participate in the program just for the pleasure it gives the guests and the international contact it gives them.

The program is operating in Tokyo, Yokohama, Nagoya, Kyoto, Otsu (near Kyoto), Osaka, Kobe and Kagoshima. Details about arranging visits are given in the sections covering each city. If possible, obtain a copy of the JNTO publication 'Home Visit System' which contains more information and useful tips. Most hosts speak English but in each city there are some who speak other languages.

Tescort

The TESCO company has facilities and programs of interest to foreign visitors and residents who wish to meet and talk with English-speaking Japanese. The primary business of TESCO is the production of English-language education programs, the purchase of which entitles the buyer to use the 15 International Community Services (ICS) Centres around the country. The centres have foreign language newspapers and magazines, give educational and social programs and organise weekend trips. Foreigners are welcome to use the facilities, talk to any members there and participate in any of the progams, including the trips, at reasonable cost.

Certain to be of even greater interest to short-term visitors (though open to all foreigners in Japan) is the Tescort program. The Japanese members of TESCO have little opportunity to practice speaking English with native speakers while many foreign visitors not only want to meet Japanese but need some travel assistance. The Tescort scheme solves both these problems at once. TESCO members participating in the scheme are willing to act as unpaid guides to accompany visitors on sightseeing trips, shopping expeditions or anything else within their ability that time will allow. Many Tescort volunteers are so anxious to speak English that they will take time off work to act as guides.

Those participating in the Tescort program come from all walks of life so this is an excellent chance to meet people from a variety of backgrounds. The more time the coordinator has to make arrangements though the better the chances of being introduced to someone with similar interests.

Visiting couples might be able to arrange for a Japanese couple to accompany them to a hotspring resort for a weekend, or some other overnight trip to an out-of-the-way place.

The volunteers are willing to pay their own expenses for reasonable amounts of travel and eating at reasonably priced places, though it would be appreciated if the overseas visitors subsidised some of these expenses occasionally.

To arrange a Tescort escort, phone one of the offices in the following list and ask for the Tescort coordinator. Supply details about yourself and when you'll be in the particular area. It is best to allow two or three days for arrangements to be made, if time allows.

Tokyo	(03)	234-8757
Sapporo	(011)	271-3611
Sendai	(0222)	23-2571
Niigata	(0252)	41-1081
Kanazawa	(0762)	65-5752
Shizuoka	(0542)	52-1059
Nagoya	(052)	581-1872
Osaka	(06)	311-2533
Okayama	(0862)	32-2351
Hiroshima	(082)	249-1920
Fukuoka	(092)	441-7720
Kumamoto	(0963)	24-3474
Nagasaki	(0958)	26-1137
Oita	(0975)	37-3946

To pre-arrange an escort before arriving in Japan, write to:

TESCO International Co
Tokyo ICS Centre
Landic Hirakawa-cho Bldg 2fl
2-6-2 Hirakawa-cho
Chiyoda-ku
Tokyo 102

International 3F Club

In Tokyo the International 3F Club offers a number of programs where visiting foreigners can meet and talk with English-speaking Japanese. Details are given in the chapter on Tokyo.

Clubs and Organisations

Several international organisations like Toastmasters and Lions International have affiliates in Japan. With prior preparation it should be possible to arrange to meet Japanese members who speak English.

Servas

Anyone who really wants yo get to know the Japanese more than superficially should look into the international organisation Servas. If accepted as members of Servas, travellers may stay at the homes of Japanese families in many parts of the country, both rural and urban, for up to three days at no charge, sharing the family's home and life. Anyone looking for a free ride should read no further. Servas travellers staying with Japanese families are expected to spend much of their time talking with their hosts and otherwise participating in their lives. Only people who have a sincere interest in learning about Japanese family life and exchanging views and experiences would be interested.

Servas was founded in 1948 as a private venture in international relations. Reasoning that person-to-person contact by people from countries around the world is a worthwhile goal, a network of volunteer hosts was put together. In addition to Japan, there are hosts in at least 70 other countries . If it is possible, travelling members are expected to act as hosts on their return to a settled life, although this is not compulsory. Many hosts have never travelled themselves, but open their doors to travellers as their contribution to world understanding and as a way to bring a little of the outside world to them.

It is preferable to join Servas in your

home country. Joining requires filling in an application form and appearing for a personal interview in order to ensure that the applicant is sincere in his interest in Servas and its ideals. Regional staff are voluntary, but there are staff and administrative expenses at the local, national and international level; for this reason a contribution of about US$30 (it varies from country to country) is required. For the address of the national offices in your country, write to the international president Mr Graham Thomas, Servas International Peace Secretary, 80 Bushwood, London E11; send an international reply coupon (or stamps if in the UK). If it is impossible to join Servas before reaching Japan, write as early as possible to Mr Masuo Amano, 21-22 6-chome, Todoroki, Setagaya-ku, Tokyo 158, giving the estimated date of arrival and port of entry and stating that you would like to participate in the Servas program. If you are accepted there is a joining fee of Y5000.

Communes

Few outsiders are aware of the existence of several communes in Japan. They have a long history; Itto-en commune in the Kansai area (near Kyoto) dates back to 1905. Travellers interested in communes should write to:

Kibbutz Akan
Shin Shizen Noen
Nakasetsuri
Tsurui-mura
Akan-gun
Hokkaido
Japan

They have published a book *Communes of Japan*, listed at Y1000. They also issue the *Journal of the Commune Movement* every month or two. Copies (not free) can be obtained from the above address.

If you have just arrived in Japan and haven't time to correspond with Kibbutz Akan, you could try a phone call to Itto-en Commune, (075) 581-3136. They should be able to give information on the movement and other communes around the country.

Teaching

One of the best ways to meet a cross section of Japanese people is by teaching English. The system of teaching English in schools is so poor in Japan that private schools are necessary to provide an opportunity to learn from native speakers. Teaching without a proper visa is not legal of course but it seems the Immigration office does not waste too much of its time tracking down illicit teachers.

The only problem with teaching is that you may get any level of student. It is difficult to carry on conversations about Japanese society and culture with beginners who have trouble just putting five words together correctly. However, in free conversation classes with advanced students it is possible to learn a great deal about Japan that doesn't appear in books. It is interesting that Japanese people will express very open and candid opinions in English (or another foreign language) that they will not say in Japanese; there are many constraints on behaviour in Japanese society which are reinforced by the very structure of the language. Through teaching you also have an opportunity to experience every type of personality, from very open (and contrary to the stereotyped image of the Japanese) to girls who are so painfully shy that they refuse to answer questions for fear of making a mistake.

MEN & WOMEN

One of the characteristics of the upbringing of Japanese women is subordination to males, beginning with her brothers. In a relationship, she generally looks after her man. (To many western men first exposed to this coddling it seems like paradise arrived and many are happy with this level of relationship.) Conversely Japanese males tend to be spoiled from childhood so the result is that Japanese men and western women tend not to be very compatible. This is reflected by the ratio of only one marriage of a Japanese male to a western female to every 10 of Japanese women to western men.

For some Japanese men there is prestige in dating a western woman. While this is not the general rule, some foreign women tend to wonder if they are being asked out for their company or for the prestige they bring. Incidently many Japanese men have a very distorted view of western women, especially their moral standards, and expect them to leap into bed with any man. Any woman who suspects this attitude in her Japanese friend and wishes to dispel it should easily be able to give a suitable hint in conversation.

There are various ways to meet Japanese of the opposite sex. In Tokyo, there are a few social clubs and coffee shops where people go to chat in English. There are several places in cities where people gather for drinks and conversation; in Tokyo, *Berni Inn, Henry Africa* and *Charleston* are examples. There are also many discos in the large cities; the Roppongi area of Tokyo has several. They are not cheap, generally about Y3000-4000 entrance charge which includes some drinks and eats. Their main drawback as meeting places is that the sound levels are so high it is almost impossible to talk; and many discos and clubs only admit couples.

After meeting a suitably charming young woman or man there comes the matter of future meetings. Some families are open-minded and have no objections if their daughter or son has an 'appointment' with a foreigner, but others, especially the wealthy and upper-class families, object strongly.

Japanese people in general, by the way, have a reputation for a lack of punctuality in keeping 'appointments'. Another incidental bit of information concerns twosomes. There is the distinct possibility that a girl who meets a man casually will keep a second date, but will show up with a girlfriend in tow. On further meetings she may appear alone once she knows there is no danger while others will continue to show up accompanied.

Couples in Japan who want privacy but have no place of their own to go to be alone have a great range of facilities. Many coffee shops have inky-dark rooms (often downstairs) with two-people booths, high partitions between booths and discreet waiters. These offer a modicum of privacy for nothing more than the cost of a coffee and reportedly quite amazing activities have been carried out in the cramped quarters. The next step up the ladder is also a type of coffee shop, but it has individual rooms with a couch and table in each and a door (unlocked). For a moderate fee, couples can stay until five am, and the table can be moved to block the door. Beyond this comes the love hotel – described in the Places to Stay section.

Marriage

Marriages in Japan result from love matches, where the couple have met by chance or informally through friends or from formal arranged introductions called *omi-ai*. Few, if any, result from families getting together and deciding the fate of their children as happens in some other societies.

Formal introductions may occasionally be seen in coffee shops or similar surroundings. The man and woman and their families sit on opposite sides of the table and attempt to make conversation, after which the two have a chance to meet without onlookers. If they think there might be the basis for a marriage they arrange to meet again. They soon decide if there is promise in continuing or if they should forget the idea and start over with someone else. Many people have 10 or more such introductions. The go-between may be a professional (nakado), a maiden aunt or someone else with extra time and many friends. Some Japanese women may begin to get a bit frantic after 26 and put their names before more and more remote acquaintances. Marriages resulting through arranged introductions appear to be as stable and lasting as love matches.

To westerners, the reasons for getting married in Japan sometimes seem rather trivial or shallow, more financial than romantic, somewhat akin to arranging a corporate merger rather than linking two lives. Many couples seem content with an arrangement whereby the husband brings in an income and the wife tends the house, and bears and rears the children, with apparently little affection between the couple. In some cases this may be accurate and in others the couple are not demonstrative but have developed an affection through the years. In most households, the husband dutifully hands over his entire pay packet and is doled out an allowance. Any westerner considering marriage to a Japanese woman should take note of this.

Foreign men and women marrying Japanese are affected differently by Japanese law. When two Japanese marry the wife's name is removed from her family's register and transferred to that of her husband's family. Because registry is tantamount to citizenship, foreign spouses may not be put in family registers. A foreign wife may remain in Japan as long as her husband resides there and sends a letter to Immigration authorities whenever her period of stay is due for renewal, stating that he wants her to remain. A foreign husband has no right of residence just because he is married to a Japanese woman. By Japanese law a wife is expected to reside in her husband's country. A foreign man must have an independent reason for remaining in Japan (work, study, etc, with appropriate visa), or else he can be deported with his children, who must take on his nationality by Japanese law. This unequal treatment is in conflict with a constitutional provision of sexual equality and is currently under legal challenge.

Children of mixed marriages often have a difficult time in Japan because their foreign blood sets them apart from the rest of the population in a society which values sameness and uniformity. They may also have difficulty deciding to which society they belong, Japanese or foreign; it is a problem trying to be both and such children often fail to fit in completely, not learning either language properly.

Unlike in nearby Korea, it is most unlikely that any Japanese girl would be trying to find a way out of the country by marrying a foreigner, so it isn't necessary to try to figure if the girl's affection is genuine or feigned only to catch a husband. However, one should give careful thought as to how well she would fit in back home.

SEX

Sex is an entertainment commodity in Japan. In addition to strip shows, that leave little to the imagination, sexual services of many types are readily available.

Prostitution was declared illegal in 1947. The former red-light districts are no longer official but after a history of hundreds of years brothels have just taken a different form. Today, a man with the yen for such things can have his desires accommodated in Toruko (mispronounced 'Turk' of 'Turkish baths'), in a 'Pink Saron', or by negotiating with an obliging hostess at a bar or club.

In early 1985 the Toruko throughout Japan were required, officially, to change the name of their establishments to *Soapland* following protests from the country's Turkish community. Apparently even the Turkish embassy was receiving phone calls from potential customers wanting a run-down on their 'services'.

Although most such establishments are intended for men, there are clubs for women where handsome young men give them total attention and offer similar services. However, they are reportedly very expensive. (For men contemplating this sort of work the ability to speak good Japanese is a prerequisite.)

There are hundreds of gay bars in areas like Shinjuku (Tokyo) and in other large cities. There is considerable prestige in having a western boyfriend, so a welcome is assured.

Note: Many clubs and their female employees are under control of gangsters. Foreigners with little knowledge of the language are very susceptible to being suckered into exorbitant bills for which payment is extorted by violence if necessary. Any club where large numbers of girls are available is not going to be cheap; even quite legitimate places can be exorbitantly expensive.

Toruko/Soapland

Although seemingly places for bathing and cleansing, 'soapland' establishments are designed to satisfy needs deeper than outward cleanliness. The 'attendant' soaps all of her customer's body, often applying the soap by first lathering her own nude body and acting like a human sponge.

The best-known Toruko/Soapland areas in Japan are the Horinouchi district of Kawasaki and the Sakae-cho district of Chiba (both in the Tokyo region), Gifu (near Nagoya), and Ogoto (on the western shore of Biwa-ko lake, in the Kyoto/Osaka area). Toruko are found throughout the country. They should not, be confused with *sento* (local public baths), *onsen* (hotspring resorts), or *sauna* – all legitimate massage establishments, although the onsen are also noted for catering to male desires. Toruko are for the well-heeled and can cost up to Y30,000 for high-class services. The help of a Japanese would be most essential in finding one and obtaining admission, as foreigners are often unwelcome at such facilities, largely because of the language problem that can give rise to many difficulties about charges.

Pink Saron

Obviously this is a mispronunciation of 'Pink Salon'. These are bars with hostesses. There is a flat fee for drinks and nibbles (say Y3000), but the tender ministrations of the hostess can become a lot more personal if extra money changes hands. This can run the gamut from a lapfull of underwearless hostess, to 'relief massage', or more.

Pink Sarons are plentiful in large cities and elsewhere, usually near large railway stations and identifiable by garish pink signs and touts standing outside. The interior is very dark to give the hostesses some privacy for their work. Although the touted price is in the Y3000, the full treatment will run considerably higher, generally Y8000-10,000.

Hostesses

Hostesses in bars and clubs are there to please their male customers by boosting their frail egos with flattery and attention. Although there are bars where the girls merely sit opposite their customers and do nothing more than pour drinks and make conversation, more usually the girls will allow the customer to become more physical and can often be induced to accompany him afterward. It is frequently necessary to pay the establishment a 'ransom' if leaving with a hostess before closing time.

Live sex shows

An amusement that has become popular in recent years at hotspring resort towns, but which may also be found in the larger cities, is live sex shows. A couple performs on stage before the delighted audience and in some cases members of the audience are invited to strip off and join in. As one newspaper expressed it, for the man who is able to function before a crowd, there's no cheaper way in Japan to get some action.

Because women of European origin are greatly preferred as partners for such shows, there is sure employment for anyone wishing to partake. Arrest and deportation is a risk of the business but it seems the police don't go far out of their way to stamp out such activities.

LANGUAGE

It is very useful to take a course in Japanese before travelling extensively in Japan as few people outside major cities can speak English and those that do never seem to be around when needed. However, even students with a year of Japanese under their belts will probably find that they understand very little of what is said as most language courses seem to bear little relationship to the spoken language. When studying, concentrate on the plain or informal forms of verbs; the formal or - *imasu* and *imashita* forms are seldom used among people in normal conversation.

There are various dialects in different parts of the country. Japanese taught in language courses is normally the Tokyo dialect (Tokyo-ben) which is considered to be the 'standard' dialect; it is taught in the nation's schools and used on national TV. It will be of negligible use in understanding people in some rural areas such as those who speak Tohoku-ben (northern Honshu) or Kagoshima-ben (southern Kyushu). But then the people of these areas find each other totally incomprehensible and inhabitants of Tokyo or Kyoto find it equally difficult.

Much is made of the supposed vagueness of Japanese. However, it is not the language itself that is vague but rather the way it is used. Japanese can be spoken just as precisely as English, but to do so would often be considered impolite; the correct thing to do is to speak in circumlocutions and avoid making direct statements of fact that would imply that the speaker has superior knowledge. Actual meanings are traditionally conveyed as much by gesture and tone of voice as by the words themselves although young Japanese are growing up without learning this older system of spoken communication.

Certainly the language is not simple

because of the multitude of verb forms and the many words needed to indicate social distinctions, but it is not difficult to learn a major proportion, perhaps 70 per cent of the language in *romaji* (the romanised form). You have to learn the written form for the rest because each character (*kanji*) has at least two pronunciations, *on* (Chinese) and *kun* (Japanese). These multiple readings for kanji cause much difficulty for travellers because names (especially place names) have many ways of being pronounced. As much as possible the correct local pronunciations of place names are used in this book; these may occasionally differ from names in literature printed in Tokyo as they may use Tokyo readings of the kanji. Place names in Hokkaido are the worst example of this. It all sounds silly but it's true; the average Japanese cannot pronounce the names of a large number of places on a road map.

Important words are written in *kanji* (Chinese characters) while grammatical endings are written in *hiragana*, a syllabary of all the vowel and consonant-plus-vowel sound combinations in the language. Yet another complete syllabary is used to transliterate foreign words. Unfortunately they use this method for writing English and so many learn incorrect pronunciations since the syllabary is deficient in l, f and some other letters.

The most valuable basic phrasebook is the *Tourist's Handbook*, available free from the Tourist Information Centres in Tokyo and Kyoto. It has the most often asked questions and a series of answers in both languages, so a Japanese person can point to the correct answer.

If you want to learn the rudiments of the language, one of the best books is *Japanese Made Easy* by Monane, published by Tuttle. For a comprehensive study of Japanese, *Beginning Japanese* by Jorden can be recommended. It is published by Yale University Press.

A few basic phrases are listed on the following pages.

Communicating with Japanese

Except with Japanese who have really mastered English, usually by living overseas, there will be problems with many questions requiring a 'yes' or 'no' answer. In Japanese a 'yes' answer will mean 'Yes, what you say is true', so it is essential to avoid asking negative questions, like 'Aren't you going?' A Japanese will answer 'yes' if he is *not* going, 'no' if he *is* going. It takes a while to get into the habit of asking unambiguous questions.

Another problem is an 'or' question. Even though Japanese has an exact equivalent, they seem to have insuperable difficulty recognising that there is a choice between A and B. The simplest way around the problem is to say 'Is it A? Is it B?', instead of 'Is it A or B?' The latter is almost sure to get 'yes' as a reply.

Generally, direct statements are not made in Japanese. Instead, the speaker alludes to or suggests a fact so as not to appear superior or presumptuous in suggesting he knows something the listener doesn't. Women use this suggestive form to a greater extent than men, which makes their statements less forceful or believable than a similar statement by a man. The existence of 'women's language' and 'men's language' is clearly sexist by western thinking, but is an inescapable fact. Its function is partly to keep women in an inferior position; a woman using stronger forms of expression sounds masculine and quite undesirable.

Because of the circumlocutions often required to bypass a direct statement, misunderstandings can easily occur, with the result that the Japanese language is excellent for maintaining social distinctions but poor for imparting information and knowledge. Younger Japanese today tend not to follow the older conventions of speech and are dropping many of the 'formula' phrases, with the result that the older people can have difficulty explaining what they want because the younger ones fail to pick up the cues.

It is surprising that young Japanese do

not speak English better than they do; most of them seem unable to put together more than one or two sentences of correct English. About 300 hours of instruction is given at junior high school level, nearly 500 hours in the senior school, and a further 300-600 hours at university is required to become an English teacher.

Unfortunately a very large proportion of teachers at all levels cannot carry on a conversation in English and have learned English in the same way as they are teaching it, as a field of academic study. Another problem is that English is mostly taught using the Japanese katakana syllabary to represent English sounds, a purpose for which it is entirely inadequate, having no distinction between the letters 'r' and 'l', and misrepresenting several other sounds, which explains the frequent interchange of these letters. (Often quoted is the banner strung across the Ginza when General MacArthur was being proposed for US President: 'We play for MacArthur's erection'.)

The Japanese must have a sense of humour. Why else would the car manufacturers choose the names that they do. Nearly every model has a name which Japanese cannot pronounce correctly, with a copious mix of r's and l's, such as 'Gloria', 'Corolla'. 'Tercel' or 'Starlet'.

Romanisation

As a (much appreciated) courtesy to visitors to Japan, many signs are written in romaji (Roman letters). As well as names on road signs, some other Japanese words may appear on signs. Unfortunately there may be difficulty in knowing how to pronounce them because there is more than one system of romanisation.

The most common is the Hepburn system, devised more than a century ago and still useful as an aid to English speakers in pronouncing Japanese correctly but it is of negligible use to speakers of other languages. The other systems are useful in formal studies of Japanese but they are not very useful for general application because you have to learn the conventions of the system.

The Hepburn system, with few changes, is used throughout this book. Either it or the Ministry of Education system may be seen on signs in Japan, sometimes both in the same sentence.

The following is a list of the major differences between the two systems; the Hepburn is pronounced like normal English.

Hepburn	Min of Education
shi	si
sha	sya
shu	syu
sho	syo
chi	ti
cha	tya
chu	tyu
cho	tyo
tsu	tu
fu	hu
ji	zyi
ja	zya
ju	zyu
jo	zyo

The use of the two systems of romanisation (both of which Japanese know) leads to mistakes as a result of carelessness or ignorance. One common mistake is interchanging 'a' and 'u' because they sound the same to the Japanese (compare the sounds of the vowels in 'a cup'). Because 'n' and 'm' are also interchangeable, the word 'damper' (meaning a shock absorber to British) gets written 'dunper'. Sometimes, also, one sees 'thu' instead of 'tsu', or 'tu'; thith a mithtake ath the 'th' thound doethn't exthitht in Japanethe.

Phrase List

Japanese is basically easy to pronounce. The consonants are pronounced much the same as in English (all 'hard' not soft), and the vowels are similar to those in Italian:

a	as the English indefinite article
e	as in the 'a' of ale
i	as in machine
o	as in oh
u	as in the 'oo' of hoot

The 'o' sound shifts when followed by 'n'. so the Japanese word *hon* rhymes with the English word *on*, not *own*.

Although there is a rhythm to the language, there is not nearly as much stress on individual syllables as in English, and each syllable is generally pronounced separately. Thus *Hiroshima* is 'hi ro shi ma', not 'hi rosh i ma'.

The following phrases may prove useful in daily travels. They are intended for survival, not as a language course. Therefore they are simplified and in some cases barely grammatical but should be understandable.

yes	*hai; ee*
no	*iie; chigau* (different); *nai/nai des* (not/it is not). All mean 'no' but most books only give *iie*; it is too abrupt and rude for use with friends (except as in 'No, you can't pay for this.') The other two forms are heard more often.
goodbye	*sayonara*

please	*kudasai*
thankyou (simple/ formal)	*domo/domo arigato gozaimasu*
how much?	*i'kura?*
how many?	*ikutsu?*
where? (is)	*doko? (des'ka)*
when?	*itsu?*
which one/way?	*dochira?*
where is . . .?	*. . . wa, doko des'ka?*
this . . .	*kono . . .*
that . . . (near you)	*sono . . .*
that . . . (over there)	*ano . . .*
this (thing)	*kore*
that (thing, near you)	*sore*
that (thing, yonder)	*are*
here	*koko*
there (near you)	*soko*
there (yonder)	*asoko*
right	*migi*
left	*hidari*
beyond	*saki*
this side of	*temae*
far, beyond	*muko*
in front of	*mae*
next to	*tonari*
straight ahead	*massugi; zuutto* (or *zuuuuuuto* when spoken by country people!)
today	*kyo*
tomorrow	*ash'ta*
day after tomorrow	*asatte*
yesterday	*kino*

Numbers

For numbers up to 10, the Japanese have one set of words which can be used alone and another for use only with a 'counter'. A counter is one of many words, depending on the shape or nature of the object. The with-counter numbers are used to make composite numbers above 10, and in expressions of time. There are too many counters to mention here, so use counterless numbers or write the number down.

The number goes after the word for the things. When requesting something put 'o' between the word for the object and the number; eg *Kore o futatsu kudasai* ('two of these, please').

	counterless	with-counter
0	*maru; re*	
1	*hitotsu*	*ichi*
2	*futatsu*	*ni*
3	*mittsu*	*san*
4	*yottsu*	*yon, shi (shi* is a homonym of 'death' so is often avoided.)
5	*itsutsu*	*go*
6	*muttsu*	*roku*
7	*nanatsu*	*nana, shichi*
8	*yattsu*	*hachi*
9	*kokonotsu*	*kyu*
10	*to*	*ju*
11		*ju-ichi*
12		*ju-ni*
20		*ni-ju*
30		*san-ju*
49		*yon-ju-kyu*
100		*hyaku*
200		*ni-hyaku*
1000		*sen*
5000		*go-sen*
10,000		*ichi-man.*(Not *ju-sen;* Japanese count by ten-thousands)
20,000		*ni-man*
25,000		*ni-man-go-sen*
100,000		*ju-man*
1,000,000		*hyaku-man*

Time

o'clock (one o'clock)	*-ji (ichi-ji)* (Use with-counter numbers for time.)
minute (for telling time)	*– pun*
second (duration)	*– byo*
hour (duration)	*– jikan*
year (date)	*– nen*
year (duration)	*– nenkan*

Telephone

hello	*moshi moshi* (The caller usually says this first.)
may I speak with . . .?	*. . . -san onegai shimasu? (-san =* Mr, Mrs, Miss etc)
isn't here	*imasen*
extension (eg ext 153)	*naisen (ichi-go-san)* (With-counter numbers are used here.)

Post Office

post office	*yubin kyoku*
stamps	*kitte*
poste restante (general delivery)	*kyoku dome yubin tome oki*
registered	*kaki tome*
special delivery	*soku tatsu*
air mail	*kohku bin*
sea mail	*funa bin*
aerogram	*kohku shokan*
money order	*yubin gawase*
stamped post card	*yubin hagaki*
parcel	*kozutsumi*
letter	*tegami*

Trains

ticket	*kippu*
one way	*katamichi*
return	*ohfuku, shuyuken*
express	*kyuko*
rapid	*kaisoku*
local	*kaku eki teisha*
reserved (seat)	*shite, (seki)*
unreserved	*jyuseki*
What track for . . . (station)?	*. . . (eki) wa, nan ban sen (des' ka)?*
next train/electric train	*sugi no kisha/densha*
basic charge (all trains)	*unchin*
limited express charge	*tokkyu ryokin*
green car (first class) charge	*gurin ryokin*
excursion ticket	*shuyuken*

Youth Hostel

I am a member.
Kai-in des.
membership card
kai-in sho
Are you a member?
Kai-in des'ka?
Do you have a membership card?
Kai-in sho arimas' ka?
Do you want meals?
Shokuji wa?
evening meal
yu-shoku
breakfast
cho-shoku
Do you have a sleeping sheet?
Shiitsu arimas'ka?
May I stay?
Tomare mas'ka?
full
Ippai
Is there a room available tomorrow/the day after tomorrow?
Ash'ta/asatte heya wa aitemas'ka?

Facts for the Visitor

ENTRY REQUIREMENTS

Everyone entering Japan must carry a passport with an appropriate visa. If you stay 90 days or more you will need to get an Alien Registration Card. Your passport or registration card must be carried at all times.

Entry to Japan is barred to certain categories of undesirable people, including lepers, paupers (or anyone with insufficient funds), drug users, prostitutes or anyone who may cause harm to the interests and security of Japan. The latter is a catch all and can be interpreted to suit the authorities.

Japan can deport aliens of some countries without notifying their embassies, but in fact the embassy is usually notified so as to get rid of the problem as quickly as possible.

VISAS

Everyone must, in principle, have a visa to visit Japan. However, to help tourism, bilateral agreements with some countries mean you don't need a visa if you are from western Europe, the UK or most English speaking countries, with the notable exceptions of the USA, Australia and South Africa.

Whether or not you need a visa, on arrival in Japan your fate is decided by the immigration inspector who has the final say on whether you are admitted. He may, for example, demand to see a return ticket or proof of adequate funds. He also decides what 'status of residence' to grant you, and your period of stay. The status of residence is identified by a string of numbers, eg 4-1-4; details are given later.

The following countries have reciprocal visa-waiving agreements with Japan: New Zealand (30 days); Canada, Denmark, France, Sweden and many others (90 days); UK, West Germany, Switzerland and others (180 days). These are nominal periods of stay. For example, Kiwis may get 60 days not 30, simply because the inspector didn't have a 30-day stamp that day.

Visas are waived for people from these countries only if they are entering for tourism. This can include sightseeing, recreation, attending meetings or conventions, inspection tours, participation in contests (athletic or others), visiting relatives or friends, learning cultural arts, goodwill visits and similar non-remunerative activities. Note that 'non-remunerative' excludes any activity that will result in earning income at a later date in another country, such as writing a travel book.

Visa-exempt tourists eligible for stays of 90 or 180 days may be granted either 4-1-4 or 4-1-16(3) status. The latter is preferred if you want to stay as long as possible since 4-1-4 status is valid for only 60 days, regardless of nationality. A period of stay can usually be extended twice, say from 60 days to 180 days, but the red tape can be time consuming so the fewer renewals you need the better.

Australians, Americans and other tourists who need visas must apply for them before arriving in Japan. On arrival they will usually get 4-1-4 status with a 60-day period of stay. Again this can usually be extended twice but after that you will have to leave the country (eg to Korea) and start again.

An exception is made for transit tourists. If you are on a cruise ship that will dock at two ports in Japan you may get a transit visa that is valid for up to 15 days for travel by a designated route through Japan to rejoin the ship. Also, sea and air passengers who have onward bookings and the required visa for the next country on their route can obtain up to 72 hours excursion time without a visa. In both cases ask your travel agent about the exact regulations and how to obtain landing permission, as the carrier or its representative must make the arrangements. In both cases an ordinary tourist visa could prevent you from being unnecessarily restricted.

When you apply for an extension of stay, the immigration official may ask for proof of a ticket out of the country, sufficient funds, and/or a letter of guarantee. Some offices may accept a letter from your bank certifying that you have arranged a line of credit for an amount adequate to guarantee your repatriation from Japan.

Long-Term Visas

For any long-term stay in Japan – more than six months, for example – there are two options. One is to leave Japan at the expiration of the period of stay and return on another tourist visa. This can be done once or twice without problem (although some ports, such as Shimonoseki and Fukuoka, have a reputation for being uncooperative) but it gets harder as the stamps in the passport accumulate. The simplest way around the problem is to obtain a long-stay visa. The type would depend on the purpose, but the most common types are cultural (study of traditional arts, eg tea ceremony, music or dancing, martial arts etc); or student (academic or non-academic). One can also obtain a working or teaching visa that will allow working full time. While it is generally possible to obtain permission to work part-time on a cultural or student visa, for full time work it might be better to get the appropriate visa.

In any case, it is usually difficult to arrange the foundation for a long-stay visa without actually coming to Japan to make the necessary arrangements in person.

Student and Cultural Visas

For language study, it is much easier to find a school once you get to Japan than by correspondence. For any course of study the institution has to provide letters of guarantee and other documents to satisfy the authorities and they prefer to see the person before committing themselves. An exception is study in a recognised academic course, especially at university level, where standards are similar internationally and entry is based on the applicant's academic record. Visas for such study can be arranged from abroad without too much trouble.

If you have to locate a school from within Japan, the usual procedure is to enter, giving 'travel-sightseeing' or 'cultural study' as the purpose of entry, thus obtaining either 4-1-4 or 4-1-16(3) status. Then find a school or teacher and make the arrangements. The school then prepares the necessary documentation which the student takes to a Japanese diplomatic mission in another country. The Japanese embassy in Seoul is most popular for this purpose. So many foreigners make similar applications that this embassy handles them as a matter of routine, and if all papers are in order, a study or cultural visa will usually be granted in one working day.

Since it is possible for 4-1-16(3) status to be extended up to three years, anyone eligible for that status could possibly obtain sufficient extensions, 90 days at a time, to complete a year or two of studies without the bother of collecting documents and trekking to Korea. But there is no guarantee this could be achieved. Like everything else involving Japanese bureaucracy, decisions are made case by case. Also there might be difficulty obtaining permission to work part-time under such an arrangement whereas part-time work is possible with a proper cultural or student visa.

Working Visa

In the case of working/teaching visas, it is usually very difficult to arrange employment with a Japanese company from outside Japan unless you are being transferred from another country. So give 'travel-sightseeing' as the reason for entry. Do not say you are looking for work as that is a prohibited activity on entry and you could be turned back at the port of entry.

Once you have found a job and obtained the required documents (described later), go to Korea and apply for the working visa. This takes six or eight weeks during which time you could travel around Korea or return to Japan on a tourist visa.

The embassy in Seoul will give you a receipt of your application but they will not normally inform you whether your application has been approved. You could try leaving a self-addressed card or offer to pay cable fees. Otherwise you must check regularly on the current status. If you remain in Korea, this means checking at the embassy from time to time. If you return to Japan, inquire at the Visa Section of the Ministry of Foreign Affairs (Gaimusho), either in person or by phone (tel (03) 5803311). With the receipt issued in Seoul, find out the file number being used in Japan (it will be different from the one used in Korea); this can make enquiries much easier. When making enquiries it helps to have the assistance of a Japanese person as the staff speak little English, and besides, foreigners never sound properly obsequious.

Once you have a work visa, remember you still have to pass the Immigration Inspector. An inspector at Shimonoseki (the main port of entry from Korea) once refused entry to a person on the grounds that he did not have enough money, even though he had a new work visa and a job in Tokyo. Shimonoseki has a bad reputation in such matters so it might be worth flying to Osaka or Tokyo where officials seem more reasonable.

Other Long-term Visas

Visas that enable a long stay may be issued for other purposes as well and may be useful to some readers, most particularly for press or commercial purposes. In this case it is possible to make all necessary arrangements before entering Japan.

STATUS OF RESIDENCE

The following table lists the main statuses and the nominal period of stay for each.

4-1-4	tourist – 60 days
4-1-5	commercial/management of business – 3 years
4-1-6	student (junior college level and up) – 1 year
4-1-7	lecturers/professors (academic) – 3 years
4-1-8	cultural/artistic/scientific – 1 year
4-1-9	entertainers – 60 days
4-1-10	missionary/religious – 3 years
4-1-11	journalist (radio/press) – 3 years
4-1-12	specialised skills/technicians – 3 years
4-1-13	specialised labour (eg specialty cooks) – 1 year
4-1-14	permanent resident – permanent
4-1-15	spouses and children of person in category 4-1-5/6/7/8/9/10/11/12/13 – same as spouse/parent
4-1-16(1)	short-term version of 4-1-5/10/11/12 – 180 days
4-1-16(3)	short-term version of all statuses – up to 3 years; (case by case)

The word 'nominal' is used to describe the period of stay because the actual allowable period may be longer or shorter. Thus a tourist (4-1-4) is given a nominal 60 days, but this can usually be extended for two further periods of 60 days each to a total of 180 days. Periods of stay listed as more than one year usually have to be renewed annually.

The proper term to use is 'extension of period of stay', not 'extension of visa'.

CHANGE OF STATUS

A person entering Japan may only engage in the activity allowed under his or her status, and permission must be obtained from an Immigration office to change activity – or even to engage in the same activity in a different place – or to change status.

For example, permission would be needed for a person with a student status, eg 4-1-6 or 4-1-16(3) who wanted to teach English; for a teacher who wanted to change to a different school; for a person on a cultural visa (4-1-8) studying pottery who wanted to take up lacquer-making; or a person wanting to change status from teaching (4-1-7 or 4-1-16(3)) to commercial (4-1-5 or 4-1-16(3)) so as to engage in business.

The good news is that the authorities seem to grant such requests in most cases.

In all cases, though, it is necessary to check before taking on the new activity. There is always the chance that the authorities will check whether the change has already been made, in which case, a letter of apology might be needed. But it is best to avoid problems in the first place. Failure to obtain prior permission may result in 'unfavourable consideration' of a future request for an extension, or possibly even outright deportation.

Change of status can be obtained in Japan without leaving the country only in the case of status 4-1-5/6/7/8 and 4-1-10/11/12. (Since 4-1-16(3) is frequently given for the same purpose as these it seems logical that holders of that status should also be able to change status, but this remains to be seen.)

A person holding 4-1-4 status definitely cannot change status, nor can holders of status other than those listed above.

Anyone who is leaving Japan to apply for status 4-1-6 (student), 4-1-7 (teaching), 4-1-12 (technical), or 4-1-13 (skilled labour) can speed up the procedure abroad by obtaining a 'Certificate of Eligibility for Status of Residence' from an Immigration Office in Japan. This procedure might be applicable to an application for a cultural visa as well.

RE-ENTRY PERMIT

If you have long-term status and wish to leave Japan for a short time and then return to take up the same activity, you should obtain a Re-entry Permit before leaving Japan. This is not a landing permit and you must still satisfy the Immigration Inspector at the port of entry, but it does facilitate re-entry and preservation of the original status category. Failure to obtain the permit will almost certainly result in cancellation of the original status.

A Re-entry Permit is valid for up to one year; it will be less if the balance of the permitted period is less. It must be used within six months of issue. Its period of validity (and that of the original visa) cannot be extended outside Japan; if it (or the visa) expires while the holder is abroad, a new visa must be obtained before returning to Japan.

LETTER OF GUARANTEE

For any type of long-term visa, and often for an extension of stay as a tourist, a Letter of Guarantee is required. An acceptable form of letter is shown below.

If possible the guarantor should be a Japanese citizen who has the financial resources to take on this obligation. To demonstrate this capability, the guarantor is usually required to supply a certificate of employment and recent certificate of tax payment.

For a working or language-teaching visa, the company or school can provide the letter, and for a press or commercial visa, the guarantee letter would of course be provided by the person's organisation.

The Japanese authorities always prefer to have a Japanese guarantor.

In one case, a foreign employee of a very large multinational corporation presented a letter of guarantee from his company, but was asked if he couldn't find a Japanese guarantor. So instead he asked his secretary if she would write a letter of guarantee for him. She did and it was accepted.

Form Letter of Guarantee
To: Consul-General (Ambassador) of Japan
　　　　　Letter of Guarantee
This serves to certify that . . . (name, date and place of birth, nationality, occupation etc) intends to enter into Japan for . . . (purpose of entry), for . . . (expected period of stay in Japan).

In this connection, I, the undersigned, guarantee the following:
1. Logistic support while he/she is in Japan.
2. Travelling expenses when he/she leaves Japan.
3. He/she will abide by all Japanese laws and regulations.
4. Any other information concerning . . . will gladly be given.

I should be much obliged if the visa application could be approved at your earliest convenience.

Yours faithfully
(Signature)

Guarantor's address in Japan.
Nationality
Date of Birth
Immigration status
Occupation
Relationship to applicant

Visa Information

Information on obtaining special visas, like student, working, teaching, etc, should be obtained from the Visa Section of the Ministry of Foreign Affairs of the Ministry of Foreign Affairs (Gaimusho). The immigration offices the period of residence, change of status etc.

Staff at the Visa Section are helpful. There is no need to fear asking questions regarding visas. They will give out photocopied sheets that list the exact documentation that is required when applying for any kind of visa at a Japanese representation overseas, and can check the documents to be sure that everything required is present.

The Visa Section office is easily reached from Kasumigaseki station (Hibiya, Marunouchi and Chiyoda subway lines) by taking exit A4 and walking a short distance along the street to the first entrance though the fence. The Visa Section is a small office on the right side of the left-hand building. The phone number is (03) 580-3311.

Information on documentation required for long-term visas should also be available at any Japanese diplomatic representation overseas. Generally you must send (in duplicate) an application form (Form 1C), a photo 45 x 45 mm, letter of guarantee, and documents showing why you wish to stay in Japan, school records, documentation on the institution where you will study/teach etc.

It is a good idea to take to Japan a 35 mm negative of your photo so that further prints can be made as required.

ALIEN REGISTRATION

All aliens, with the exception of diplomats and US military personnel, must register with the authorities and obtain an Alien Registration Card (ARC) if they remain in Japan for 90 days or more. This includes tourists!

The Alien Registration Card (or your passport) must be carried at all times. You can be asked by police or other authorities to produce it at any time. Failure to be able to show either document will most likely lead to several unpleasant hours in custody while someone else fetches it. The 'offender' is usually not allowed to go and get it, even in the company of an officer, or even if his/her residence is close by. If there is noone else who can get it, an impasse is reached. It is a needless annoyance, but one that could befall any foreigner in Japan.

Obtaining an ARC is simple and costs nothing but does require three photographs – about 5 x 5 cm. It is issued by the municipal office of the city, town or ward (ku) in which you are living. In the case of travellers, the address of a lodging place is acceptable.

An ARC is normally surrendered when you leave Japan. If you have long-term residence status and intend to return to Japan on a Re-entry Permit, the ARC can be taken with you.

Persons over 14 years of age who are granted a total stay of more than one year must be fingerprinted.

A change of residence within the district must be recorded at the original issuing office. A move to another district requires re-registration in the new district within 14 days.

Much unfavourable comment has been made over the years, observing (probably accurately) that Japan's control and treatment of aliens reflects an element of xenophobia that has existed in the country since it was first opened to foreigners in the 19th century, and probably much further back than that. The regulations requiring registration are said to be the strictest in the free world (and the most bothersome). They certainly emphasise the meaning of the Japanese word for foreigner, *gaijin*, which literally means 'outside person', and the omnipresent sense of 'us' and 'them' that prevails in Japanese society.

In 1979 Japan signed an international agreement that may eventually result in the abolition of the Alien Registration procedures, but at the time of publication this had not occured.

FURTHER INFORMATION

There are two books which give more detailed information on immigration procedures; one is comprehensive, while the other, though abridged, is more easily understood.

The more detailed of the two is *Immigration – A Guide to Alien Procedures in Japan*. It is published by the *Japan Times* in cooperation with the Ministry of Justice. It is available at a number of bookstores in Tokyo (and possibly elsewhere), eg Kinokuniya and Maruzen, as well as from the lunch counter in the Tokyo Immigration office. The cost is Y300.

It can be obtained by mail from:
The Japan Times
5-4 4-chome Shibaura
Minato-ku
Tokyo 108
Extra cost for surface postage is Y200 in Japan, or Y300 to any country.

Another source of information about immigration regulations is the booklet *Now You Live in Japan*. It is a goldmine of information regarding laws in Japan that affect aliens, such as marriage, divorce, citizenship, etc, and it has a good, though brief, coverage of immigration laws. It's available at bookstores or by mail from:
Research Committee for Bicultural Life in Japan
c/o The Japan Times Ltd
CPO Box 144
Tokyo 100-91
Cost is Y700; surface postage is Y200 extra in Japan, Y300 overseas.

IMMIGRATION OFFICES

The Tokyo Immigration office is located on the second and third floors of the Godochosha Dai-ichi Go-kan (across the street from the Mitsui Bussan building), near Otemachi subway stations (Marunouchi, Chiyoda, Tozai and Mita lines). The address is 1-3-1 Otemachi / Chiyoda-ku, tel 471-5111 or 986-2271.

Local immigration offices

Sapporo	(011) 261-9211
Sendai	(0222) 56-6076
Tokyo	(03) 471-5111
Narita	(0476) 32-6771
Yokohama	(045) 681-6801
Nagoya	(052) 951-2391
Osaka	(06) 941-0771
Kobe	(078) 391-6377
Takamatsu	(0878) 61-2555
Hiroshima	(0822) 21-4412
Shimonoseki	(0832) 23-1431
Fukuoka	(092) 281-7431
Kagoshima	(0992) 22-5658
Naha	(0988) 32-4185

WORKING IN JAPAN

Except for employees transferred by a foreign company, it is not usually possible to obtain work in ordinary fields of employment. An exception is a person with a skill not usually found in Japan, eg a cook trained in French cooking. For others, it is impossible to get a working visa.

The only jobs open to foreigners are those that require a skill, ability or quality that a Japanese cannot fill. One such example is modelling. Western models, especially girls with blonde hair, are widely used for modelling clothes for well-known department stores. Judging by billboards around the city extraordinary beauty is not necessary for such work.

Teaching English is the most popular occupation, and people with no training in the field are able to pick up work easily. It is a measure of the desperation of the Japanese to learn spoken English that even people who are not native speakers (often with atrocious accents) regularly find work teaching English.

By Japanese law, of course, you are required to have a visa to engage in any remunerative activity in Japan. However, it is no great secret that more than a few people have been known to teach without benefit of governmental blessing. From time to time, schools have been raided and some teachers deported. But there is the possibility that reality tempers enforcement, and the authorities take note of the fact that Japan is very dependent on citizens who are adept in foreign languages and that the educational system fails abysmally to produce them. Without the foreign teachers, there would be a gross insufficiency of native speakers; most Japanese teachers of English at schools are incapable of even an elementary conversation in the language they are teaching.

Pay at schools averages Y2000 per hour or better but the problem is that the schools seldom need teachers for more than a couple of consecutive hours. Work is mostly in the evening and it is often necessary to spend a lot of time travelling between schools.

The easiest place to find teaching work is at schools (private, not academic), though the pay is lower than for private lessons which take time and contacts to arrange. Advertisements for teachers appear regularly in the English-language newspapers, particularly the Monday *Japan Times*, and especially in September and January when new terms are beginning. The summer is the slackest time because many students are on vacation.

Teaching positions are more easily found in Tokyo than in other large cities. They are difficult to find in Kyoto because so many foreigners want to live in this historic and cultured city that there is often an over-supply of willing teachers. Those who do live in Kyoto often have to commute to Osaka, an hour away by train, or even Kobe, two hours away.

On the other hand, schools in smaller cities outside the metropolitan areas advertise fairly regularly. Since relatively few foreigners want to live in such places, away from the bright city lights, anyone who enjoys slower-paced provincial cities will have a much higher chance of landing a job, with the probability of lower living costs.

The preferred accents are first, North American (northern US and Canadian are best received), and second, British (no regional dialects please). Australians, Kiwis and South Africans, etc, will probably have some trouble obtaining work at the 'better' schools unless their accent is closer to British. Sorry, but that's the way it is.

There is a continual need for people who can write or re-write good English. Most translations are first done by Japanese people – from Japanese into 'Japlish'; it is the rewriter's job to put this into good readable English. There are many translation agencies that require rewriters, but this work is sporadic. People who turn out good work can often command higher rates once they have proved their worth. People with the combination of good technical knowledge and the ability to write clear and correct English are especially in demand particularly in the field of electronics and computers. Japan is very prominent in the computer field and thousands of pages of instruction manuals have to be translated and rewritten yearly.

Translators from Japanese, particularly those who have a technical background, should have no trouble finding steady work, even on a freelance basis.

Another type of work, best suited to attractive blonde women, is working as a hostess in clubs or nightclubs. They can make a good income just from their 'official' duties of talking with customers, but girls who have been hostesses uniformly remark that it is boring. They have to make small talk with men, mostly Japanese men who speak next to no English, and it is a continual battle to keep the men's hands in their laps – their own laps, that is.

Those prepared to give special attention outside working hours can make a bundle, so it is said. Apparently the going rate for outside activities can be as much as Y50,000 per night, so a girl can make a lot of money if she has no qualms about how she makes it.

Similar sums are rumoured to be made by westerners willing to perform in live sex shows. There is said to be more need for males, as it is easier to find females willing to participate.

Working holiday

In late 1980 an agreement was signed between the Japanese and Australian governments setting up a plan whereby young citizens (18-25; sometimes to 30) of their countries could arrange a working holiday for a period of up to a year, with extension at the option of the authorities. This is the first such agreement of the type entered into by Japan. Australians should obtain further information from Japanese diplomatic representatives. A similar plan for New Zealand is due to go into effect in late 1985 or early 1986.

STUDYING IN JAPAN

Studying in Japan can be broken into three broad categories: academic, cultural and religious.

Academic

Studies at Japanese universities leading to undergraduate or postgraduate degrees, or studies on an exchange basis, etc, at accredited educational institutions are usually arranged between the Japanese and foreign university. With the assistance of your home institution it will be possible to obtain a student visa prior to arriving in Japan.

Cultural

To study various aspects of Japanese society and culture, such as the tea ceremony, flower arranging, the Japanese language, the game of I-go, etc, it's usually extremely difficult to obtain a visa prior to arriving in Japan. The best procedure is described under the section on 'Long-term visas'.

A very useful source of information in Japan is the Information Centre, Association of International Education, 4-5-29 Komaba, Meguro-ku, Tokyo 153. Their book *ABC's of Study in Japan* probably has answers to most questions regarding study in the country.

Religious (Zen study and meditation)

One of the few things regarding Japan that most people outside the country seem to known about is Zen Buddhism. Contrary to popular belief, however, the general Japanese populace does not spend large amounts of time silently contemplating gardens or speculating the sound of one hand clapping. Zen is a little esoteric for the average Japanese. As a result, foreign visitors who wish to investigate Zen will not have a huge number of options open to them, and will have to seek out places to study.

Most temples and instruction centres in Japan will accept those who speak Japanese or who are already familiar with the practices of Zen meditation. Otherwise foreigners are generally not welcomed unless they have an introduction from a responsible Zen teacher.

Zen Sects There are two main Zen sects in Japan, Soto and Rinzai. Differences between them are minor. In zazen, Soto practitioners face a wall, while in Rinzai they face the room; Rinzai uses more koan (riddles) than Soto; and Soto sessions last longer, typically 40-50 minutes against 20 or so for Rinzai.

The Rinzai sect is more active in giving classes for laymen, but these are almost exclusively in Japanese; the Soto sect seems to have more programs in English.

Zen in Tokyo By far the best place to begin delving into Zen is Tokyo, as facilities are available for learning – in English – the fundamentals of belief, practice and zazen meditation. Two 'source people' are Ann Sargent (tel (03) 940-0979), and Gaynor Sekinori (tel (03) 891-8469) who can advise on classes and lectures, etc. Both are associated with the Soto sect.

Elsewhere in Japan *Eiheiji* temple is one of the two main temples of the Soto sect in Japan and is famous throughout the country. It is located near Fukui, which is on the east shore of Lake Biwa, not too far from Kyoto. Its magnificent, historic buildings and mountainside setting make it a target of thousands of sightseers each year, along with the many who wish to study Zen. Foreigners are invited to participate in the activities of the temple and may arrange accommodation there. It is necessary to organise this well in advance of a proposed visit so arrangements can be made. Contact: Sanzenkai, Eiheiji, Eiheiji-cho, Yoshida-gun, Fukui-ken.

Jofukuji on Shikoku is a small, local temple that also functions as a Youth Hostel (7404 in the YH Handbook). The younger priest is friendly and speaks good English. He welcomes visitors who wish to join him informally in meditation. It is a 'family'-type temple and no advance arrangements are needed for Zen participation although, like any hostel, it may be booked up at any time so it might be advisable to check first. The temple is located on the side of a valley, peaceful at

any time and very pretty in November when the leaves change colour. The address is: Jofukuji, 158 Ao, Otoyo-machi, Nagaoka-gun, Kochi-ken. Tel (07355) 2-0839.

Other temple youth hostels, where guests may participate in meditation, are listed in the YH Handbook.

There are no temples in Kyoto where foreigners can receive instruction in English. Several temples used to let foreigners join in, but too many became restless and disturbed others. An introduction from another priest would probably be the only way to obtain admission to temples in Kyoto. For further information contact the TIC in Kyoto; they may be able to help.

A good introduction to Zen is *Zen Mind, Beginner's Mind*, by Shunryo Suzuki, a Soto priest. You'll find a very large selection of Zen books at English book-stores in Japan, especially in Tokyo (Kinokuniya, Maruzen, etc).

CUSTOMS

Japanese Customs are quite generous in their allowances, especially for liquor. You can bring in three 760 ml bottles of alcoholic beverages. Other limits are: 400 cigarettes or 100 cigars or 500 g of tobacco, with a maximum combined weight of 500 g; two ounces of perfume; two watches valued no higher than Y30,000 each (including any in current use); and other goods with a total value of not more than Y100,000. Inspectors are generally lenient, allowing in anything that could be considered reasonable for a person's stay in Japan; luggage often isn't opened unless they are suspicious of the contents.

Even if you don't smoke, it might be worth bringing in foreign cigarettes (US or British are the best). They are very welcome gifts to Japanese smokers, and are a nice 'thankyou' for assistance or when hitch hiking, either the whole packet or one at a time. They are also appreciated by foreigners in Japan who think the local product is a bit rough. As for booze, it is expensive in Japan, so bring your limit if you like spirits or if you'll be visiting friends.

On arrival, a verbal declaration is usually sufficient if there is no unaccompanied baggage. You can send luggage separately (eg by mail) and declare it upon arrival on the form provided. A copy of the form, listing the number of packages that are coming is shown when they arrive, and it is unlikely that duty will be charged on the contents. Parcels arriving without such a customs declaration are subject to duty, although the inspectors are usually not too harsh. Packages of food and low-value items or gifts usually come through without trouble.

The Japanese authorities are very down on narcotics, marijuana and stimulant drugs. Anyone caught bringing any of these products into Japan can expect no sympathy from the law.

Firearms are very tightly controlled in Japan; anyone caught smuggling them or ammunition can expect an unpaid vacation.

Pornography is frowned on in Japan but what constitutes porn may seem rather laughable at times by western standards. The portrayal of pubic hair in any form is a complete no-no. Imported 'men's magazines' are completely sanitised before being offered for sale. Not only are offending areas of flesh disfigured by splotches of marking pen, but apparently the picture is actually abraded down to bare paper to prevent removal of the ink. Because of the enforced innocence of these magazines, the unexpurgated versions are good conversation/peering pieces. If you bring one in, keep it out of plain sight or fold the cover over.

Despite the strong censorship on nudity, in Japan you can buy 'comic' books that portray unbelievable scenes of brutality, sexual abuse and sadism, with scenes of sexual encounters painstakingly detailed, though often physiologically inaccurate.

Selling goods in Japan

Years ago there was a lucrative black market in bottles of foreign whisky, especially Johnnie Walker Black Label which sold then in shops for Y10,000 a bottle. Now the price has dropped to about Y4600 a bottle, so there is not so much profit to be made. In addition most Japanese are earning very good salaries and don't worry so much about saving a little money, especially if they don't know the seller. If you want to try selling a few bottles, bars and other drinking places are said to be good to try, both customers and the proprietors.

There also used to be a good market for gold Swiss watches (Rolex and Omega especially) but nowadays the Japanese travel abroad a lot and buy their own.

There are other items that would be saleable in Japan but the amount to be made is rather small. Unusual artefacts may find ready buyers; one person landed carrying a bundle of spears from Papua New Guinea and sold them easily. Top class world-famous goods may find buyers. One entrepreneur was bringing in Fender electric guitars (the latest models not yet available in Japan) and selling them at a good price. Several kinds of old model Japanese-made cameras sell for high prices in Japan, particularly Canon and Nikon range-finder models. Stores ask very high prices; what they would be willing to pay is another matter.

Some Japanese will pay large sums for expensive foreign-made cameras such as Leica, Hasselblad and Rollei, despite the fact that Japan makes the majority of high quality cameras. This seems to be part of a national inferiority complex that manifests itself in excessive adulation of foreign products simply because they are foreign. It seems the added prestige of having a foreign model slung around one's neck is worth the extra cost. If you bring one of these cameras into Japan in good condition you could probably sell it but it could take too long to be worth the effort. Professional photographers might provide one market.

MONEY

The name of the Japanese currency is the *yen* – which is about as much as anyone can say about it with any certainty. In the past few years the value of the yen in relation to one US dollar has ranged from Y178 to Y260. The Japanese economy is one of the most successful in the world today and the yen is increasingly becoming an international currency with its current value quoted in all major currency markets.

There are coins of 1, 5, 10, 50, 100 and 500 yen, and banknotes of 500, 1000, 5000 and 10,000 yen. For some time into the life of this edition there will be two types of Y1000, 5000 and 10,000 banknotes because the currency was changed in late 1984. There is speculation that the Y500 banknote will be phased and that a larger denomination one – Y50,000 or Y100,000 – will be introduced.

A$1 = Y150
US$1 = Y212
£1 = Y300

In terms of actual purchasing power in Japan, compared with what a US dollar will buy in the US, the 'true' exchange rate is closer to 350-500 yen to the dollar. Its official value is pushed up by continuing demand for the products of Japan's few really efficient industries such as electronics, cars, motorcycles, optical goods, ships and steel. Most other products including food are very expensive, the result of small-scale and inefficient production. Rice, for example, could be bought in the US or Australia for a fraction of the price charged in Japan. However, since it is the products in demand overseas that determine the demand for the yen, this knowledge will be only academic.

Only yen may be spent in Japan. It is against the law for foreign currencies to be used. Unlike many other countries in Asia, Japan doesn't accept US green-backs as a second currency; the average shopkeeper wouldn't even recognise one.

Foreign currencies can be changed only

at banks with a sign 'Authorised Foreign Exchange Bank', or at a few authorised stores that have a large tourist trade; they will have a similar sign posted. In metropolitan areas, authorised banks are thick on the ground, but don't get caught short of a yen out of town. Both cash and travellers' cheques may be exchanged at such banks. The currencies of the following countries may be exchanged in Japan: Australia, Austria, Belgium, Canada, Denmark, Netherlands, France, Germany, Hong Kong, Italy, Norway, UK, Portugal, Sweden, Switzerland and the USA. Travellers' cheques of the following countries can be exchanged: Australia, Canada, France, Germany, India, Italy, UK, Switzerland and the USA. While these currencies may be exchanged for yen, don't walk into a bank in a small city and try to exchange Canadian banknotes, for example. The bank will only accept them for clearance and send them to its head office, a process that would take several days.

The currency of Taiwan is worthless in Japan, so be sure to change everything to a convertible currency (Japanese, American, etc.) before leaving Taiwan. The currency of Korea is almost in the same boat, as it cannot be exchanged at the usual banks in Japan. However, if you have Korean won and have exchange certificates proving the money was changed through an authorised Korean Bank, you can convert them to yen, etc., at one of the three offices of the Korea Exchange Bank. They are located in Tokyo (in the Marunouchi financial district, quite close to the TIC), Osaka and Fukuoka.

If going to Korea, convert your yen to US$; they receive a premium on the black market (quite open in Seoul – just ask among other travellers), whereas Japanese money is worth little more than the official rate.

Travellers' cheques for yen are of little more use than foreign currency and there are many stories of clerks in bank branches outside the major cities who don't know what to do with yen travellers' cheques issued by their own bank. Banks are even more unwilling to cash the 'paper' of another bank, accepting them only for collection, so unless there is a branch of the bank that issued the yen cheques, you may have trouble trying to cash them. The major banks that issue travellers' cheques often don't have branches in the secondary cities, so check carefully where they can be cashed.

There are two ways to avoid carrying large amounts of cash. The first method, and probably the simplest, is to open a Post Office savings account. With such an account you can withdraw money from almost every post office in Japan, during normal business hours. Since there are far more post offices than banks, this method is most useful. An account can be opened at any but the smallest post office; certainly there is no problem at the central post office, Tokyo (near Tokyo station). The magic words are *Yubin chokin-o hajimetai*. That should be enough to open an account.

The other way to keep money in Japan is to open a passbook savings account with a large bank, one that has branches nationwide, such as Mitsubishi, Mitsui, Dai-ichi Kangyo, etc., and obtain a cashcard for the account. You will be able to withdraw funds at any branch of the bank with the passbook by the 'invisible signature' system; or from cash dispensing machines at almost any bank throughout the country (Y50 charge if the machine at a different bank is used). The latter gets around the problem that many large banks, like Mitsubishi, have few branches outside the largest cities. The staff at the Mitsubishi Bank's head office (near Tokyo station) speak enough English to open an account without difficulty.

It is not well known that it is possible to open a US dollar savings account in Japan. This is probably of greater use to residents rather than visitors. It allows easy transfer of money in and out of Japan without having to exchange it each time.

Banks might be unwilling to open an account for a stranger but by looking around there should be no trouble finding a branch willing to help. Interest rates paid on dollar accounts are usually higher than for yen accounts, but a tax may be imposed, and some banks deduct a handling fee of 1/10 of 1 per cent per transaction (or a minimum charge of Y750 to 100, whichever is greater.)

Transferring Money

Many travellers find it necessary to transfer money urgently from home while travelling. The path of transferring money to Japan can be smooth, or it can be fraught with difficulties, so it is useful to know what can go wrong.

If there is no rush to have money transferred the simplest way is to have a money order sent by mail. The money order should be payable in yen and could be bought in a bank or post office, depending on the country of origin. It can also be carried by hand and is a cheap way of transferring money to Japan without carrying a large amount of cash, and it saves the one per cent commission charged for travellers' cheques. While most mail gets through in Japan it would be safer to send a draft by registered mail, especially if it is to a Poste Restante (General Delivery) address.

Money can be sent directly from an overseas bank to its correspondent bank (or branch, if it has one), either by mail transfer (slower but cheaper) or by cable transfer (faster but at a price). It would be a good idea to talk with someone in your home bank before setting out, asking their advice on the best method of transferring money.

Despite the use of computers and other technology, the Japanese banking system is slow and inefficient in some fields. Transferring money to and from Japan is more expensive than in many other countries. Service charges seem to pop up out of nowhere; for example a few hundred yen can be taken out of a money order

received from overseas as a 'cashing charge'.

If remitting money out of the country, banks charge Y2000-2500 per money order, and preparing it will take several days, except at the bank's main branch. (Remittances to the USA are somewhat less costly and are prepared on the spot, at the Bank of America.) If you have an account with the Bank of America in the USA, you can deposit dollars in the Tokyo account by paying yen into the Tokyo branch. There is no transfer charge if you supply an encoded deposit slip for your account. Other foreign banks have a similar system.

In recent years the foreign exchange regulations have been relaxed greatly. For the amount of money that most travellers are likely to be dealing with, there are effectively no restrictions in changing money in either direction. An exchange receipt is given with each transaction. Up to Y3,000,000 may be exchanged without documentation, but if your exchange dealings are in this range it is wise to hold on to the receipts.

American banknotes may be purchased over the counter (though with the inevitable wait) as long as the bank has them in stock. This is generally true but I was once told that the bank had no notes available even though the woman ahead of me in the line was exchanging dollars for yen; when I requested those, I was told that they had to be sent to the New York office.

Bank hours

Banks are open Monday to Friday between 9 am and 3 pm; and on Saturdays (except the second Saturday of each month) from 9 am to midday. Cash dispensers are open from 8.45 am to 6 pm on weekdays; and from 9 am to 2 pm on the working Saturdays.

Credit Cards

Several international credit cards can be used in Japan. These include Diner's Club, American Express, Master Charge and Visa Card; inquire before leaving home if you have a card from another large credit card organisation. Establishments accepting credit cards have signs prominently displayed. Usually the places that accept them are high-priced, aimed at the expense account or wealthy traveller. When using a credit card you are unlikely to obtain a discount of any size because the shops must pay a commission to the card company.

TIPPING

Japan has the distinction of being one of the few developed countries where tipping is not generally expected, even at places like restaurants, hotels, etc. If a service charge is expected, it will automatically be added to your bill (another way of saying it is compulsory); this may be found at hotels and restaurants. Quite separate from the service charge, by the way, is the 10 per cent tax incurred if restaurant or bar bills exceed Y1200.

Only at expensive nightclubs, which are a western type of import, is tipping of waiters normal. Even nightclub hostesses do not expect tips if you pay the hostess charge and buy their drinks; this will amount to plenty in any case!

Porters at stations and airports (if you can find any) receive Y100-250 per piece of luggage, depending on the place and the size of the bags. At facilities frequented by foreigners, like international airports, there is often a sign in English stating the fee expected.

FOREIGN EMBASSIES

Following are the telephone numbers of the Tokyo offices of some foreign embassies.

Australia	453-0251
Austria	451-8281
Belgium	262-0191
Canada	408-2101
China	446-6781
Denmark	496-3001
Finland	583-7790
France	473-0171
W Germany	473-0151

Greece	403-0871
India	262-2391
Indonesia	441-4201
Ireland	263-0695
Italy	453-5291
Korea	452-7611
Malaysia	463-0241
Netherlands	431-5126
New Zealand	460-8711
Norway	440-2611
Pakistan	454-4862
Philippines	496-2731
Singapore	586-9111
Soviet Union	583-4224
Spain	583-8531
Sri Lanka	585-7431
Sweden	582-6981
Switzerland	473-0121
Taiwan *	583-8030
Thailand	441-7352
UK	265-5511
USA	583-7141

* See notes below

Taiwan

Since Japan recognised the People's Republic of China, Taiwan has been doing business in Tokyo under the name 'Association of East Asian Relations'; tel 583-8030. For visas it functions exactly as a consular office. To reach it, take the Hibiya subway to Kamiyacho, walk uphill along the major road (Sakurada-dori) toward Tokyo Tower, then across the large intersection at the top (keeping the Tower to your right). Continue downhill, on the right-hand side of the road. Look for the nine-storey brown T-shaped Heiwado Building. The visa office is located on the second floor. The postal address is: 39 Mori Bldg, 2-4-5 Azabudai, Minato-ku, Tokyo.

Korea

Many travellers go to Korea from Japan, both for sightseeing and for obtaining Japanese visas. Korean diplomatic representatives are located in the following cities.

Tokyo	(03) 452-7611
Sapporo	(011) 621-0288

Sendai	(0222) 21-2751
Niigata	(0252) 43-4771
Yokohama	(045) 621-4531
Nagoya	(052) 935-9221
Osaka	(06) 213-1401
Kobe	(078) 221-4853
Fukuoka	(092) 771-0461
Shimonoseki	(0832) 66-5341
Naha	(0988) 55-3381

In Tokyo, visas are not issued at the embassy, but at a separate building about 10 minutes away on foot. The easiest way to reach it is by bus. In all cases, get off at Ni-no-hashi bus stop; it has the same name on both sides of the road. Of the following buses, the first four let off passengers on the same side as the consulate building, the other three on the far side. The building is a tall white structure, about 100 m along in the direction taken by the first four buses after leaving the stop.

The following listing gives the bus number and the names of the starting and terminal JNR railway stations.

85	Shimbashi	Shibuya
10	Tokyo (S exit)	Meguro
91	Tokyo (N exit)	Shinagawa
70	Shinjuku (W exit)	Tamachi
10	Meguro	Tokyo (S exit)
85	Shibuya	Shimbashi
99	Gotanda	Shimbashi

Visas are granted on the spot within an hour except to Japanese who have to wait several days. Cost is the yen equivalent of US$1.50. One photo is required, nominally 6 x 6 cm (but smaller accepted).

INFORMATION
Japan National Tourist Organisation
The best single source for information on Japan is the JNTO. This is a semi-official body set up to distribute tourist information and otherwise encourage travel to Japan.

The JNTO has prepared a large number of excellent pamphlets and other publications that provide a great deal of useful information for travel in Japan, including info specially slanted for the budget traveller. JNTO publications are available by mail from their many overseas offices (listed at the end of this section).

Within Japan, the JNTO operates three Tourist Information Centres (TICs). Two are located in Tokyo, (in Yurakucho district and at Narita Airport), and one in Kyoto. In addition to the JNTO publications, the TIC have a large number of typewritten information sheets about various topics. These can be photocopied for anyone who is interested in a specific subject. Each TIC has an index of sheets available. Staff at the TICs are also goldmines of information.

Unfortunately the three Tourist Information Centres are the only places in Japan that are equipped to give a full range of travel information in foreign languages. Information offices in other cities are there to provide details on the local area only and there is usually no one who can speak any language but Japanese.

While TICs can provide information on any aspect of travel in any region of Japan, they do not make bookings or reservations. These services are provided by travel agencies. The best known travel agent is the Japan Travel Bureau, another semi-official organisation, which has offices in every major city throughout the country and branch offices overseas.

Publications
The following are useful general information booklets or other publications offered by the JNTO/TIC. The number in brackets is the JNTO code number, and the letter is the initial letter of the languages in which it is available: English, French, German, Spanish, Portuguese, Italian and Chinese.

Your Guide to Japan A 24-page booklet containing a wealth of general information about Japan – history, weather, geography, accommodation, transport, culture and the arts, and sightseeing. (101-E, F, G, S, P, I, C)

Japan Traveller's Companion A 24-page
booklet containing more specific inform-
ation than the above publication, with info
on transport, accommodation, sports and
embassies. (105-E)
The Tourist's Handbook A booklet of
useful phrases in an interesting layout
that makes communication less of a
problem.
Tokyo (2222-E,F,G,S,P,C)
Kyoto-Nara (224-E,F,G,S,P)
Nikko (221-E,F,G,S)
Northern Japan (Hokkaido and Tohoku)
(211-E)
Fuji-Hakone-Izu (223-E,F,G,S)
Central Japan (Kanto, Chubu, Kinki)
(214-E)
Western Japan (Chugoku, Shikoku) (212-
E)
Southern Japan (Kyushu, Okinawa) (213-
E)

Other JNTO publications on specific
topics such as accommodation and transport are listed in the appropriate sections
The JNTO-issued *Tourist Map of
Japan* is useful for overall itinerary
planning; it also has large scale maps of
many cities in Japan.

JNTO Telephone Info
Although there are JNTO TIC offices in
only two cities, Tokyo and Kyoto, TIC
information is easily available by phone
toll-free from anywhere in the country.
Except in Tokyo and Kyoto (03 and 075
area codes), use any yellow, blue or green
phone, put in a Y10 coin, and dial 106.
Say, in English, 'Collect call to TIC'. The
coin will be returned and the operator will
make the connection. In metro Tokyo call
502-1461; and Kyoto, tel 371-5649.

This service can be used to obtain travel
information (transport schedules, sightseeing advice, etc) and for assistance
when there is a language problem and no
one on hand who can help. The service
operates daily throughout the year from 9
am to 5 pm.

Other Sources
The commercial publication *Japan Visitor's
Guide* has some information and maps
that may be useful supplements to those
mentioned in this guide, but it is best to
wait till you get to Japan before obtaining
It is distributed free at the Tokyo TIC
and possibly at other tourist centres.

JNTO offices overseas
USA
45 Rockefeller Plaza, New York, N.Y.
10020. tel (212) Plaza 7-5640.
333 North Michigan Ave, Chicago, Ill.
60601. tel (312) 32-3975.
1420 Commerce St, Dallas, Texas 75201.
tel (214) 741-4931.
1737 Post St, San Francisco, Calif. 94115.
tel (415) 931-0700.
624 South Grand Ave, Los Angeles, Calif.
90017. tel (213) 623-1952.
2270 Kalakaua Ave, Honolulu, Hawaii
96815. tel (808) 923-7631.
Canada
165 University Ave, Toronto, Ont. M5H
3B8. tel (416) 366-7140.
England
1676 Regent St, London W.1. tel 734-
9638
Australia
115 Pitt St, Sydney, NSW 2000. tel 232-
4522.
Hong Kong
Peter Bldg, 58 Queen's Rd, Central. tel 5-
227913.
Thailand
56 Suriwong Rd, Bangkok. tel 233-5108.
Switzerland
Rue de Berne 13, Geneve. tel 318140.
Germany
Biebergasse 6-10, 6000 Frankfurt a/M. tel
292792.

BOOKS
The following short list of books can be
recommended as an introduction to
Japan, the country, people and language.
There are hundreds of books about Japan
available in Japan and a healthy number
in foreign countries; any competent bookstore would have listings and could order
what it didn't stock.

People and Society
The Japanese, Jack Seward (Lotus Press, Tokyo).
More about the Japanese, Jack Seward (Lotus Press, Tokyo).
The Tourist and the Real Japan, Boye de Mente (Charles E Tuttle).

All three books are getting on a bit in years, but their comments are still valid, except for costs and economic commentary.

Japanese Society, Chie Nakane (Penguin Books). Rather turgid and exhausting at times, it gives a thorough examination of the social structure of Japan.

The Chrysanthemum and the Sword, Ruth Benedict. The 'classic' book on Japanese society; although Japanese thinking has changed somewhat since this was written during WW II, it is still a good guide to what makes Japanese society function.

Japan: The Coming Economic Crisis, Jon Woronoff. An excellent dissection of the Japanese economy, how it works and potential problems.

The Land of the Rising Yen, George Mikes (Penguin Books). Although published in 1970, this book gives a witty and perceptive look at the country and people – better than any five sociology and history books combined.

A Look Into Japan (Japan Travel Bureau). This pocket-size book answers all those 'What is that?' questions asked by most travellers in Japan. Want to know the symbolism of the various positions of hands or feet on Buddhist statues; the names of the buildings in a temple/shrine; the parts making up the buildings; the parts of a room; the construction and movement of bunraku puppets . . . ? This book has the answers.

The Roads to Sata, Alan Booth (Weatherhill). Alan Booth walked from the top of Hokkaido to the bottom of Kyushu, then wrote about his experiences and the people he met. For anyone contemplating travel out in the boonies, this is a good introduction to the behaviour and reactions of typical Japanese when a non-Japanese

face shows up on their turf. It is realistic and candid, portraying both the great kindness and the subtle (and not-so-subtle) discrimination against a non-Japanese.

The Japanese Mind: The Goliath Explained, RC Christopher (Simon & Schuster). This book gives a very good overview of the country, the people and the culture in a very objective and incisive manner.

History
Japan from Prehistory to Modern Times, John Whitney Hall (Charles E Tuttle).
Tha Japanese, Reischauer.

Language
Japanese Made Easy, T.A. Monane (Charles E Tuttle).
Beginning Japanese (Parts 1 and 2), Eleanor Harz Jorden (Yale University Press).

The former is a normal-size paperback which gives adequate instruction for basic conversation as used for travel. The latter is a pair of larger paperbacks with much more detail in vocabulary and explanations of usage, so it is better suited to a formal course of study.

Bookshops
Tokyo has by far the largest number of stores selling foreign language books (mainly English) although at least one store in every major city should have a small selection. Two well-known chains of stores stocking foreign books are Kinokuniya and Maruzen.

GENERAL INFORMATION
TIME
All of Japan is in the same time zone, nine hours ahead of GMT. Because of its eastward position, day begins in Japan ahead of nearly all major populated areas except New Zealand and Australia. In mid-summer, the day begins excessively early, with sunrise at 4.30, and the evenings are very short. Japan does not use Daylight Saving Time.

When it is 12 noon in Tokyo the time in other places is:

Hong Kong	11 am
London	3 am
America, east coast	10 pm*
America, west coast	7 pm*
Hawaii, Alaska	5 pm*
Sydney, Melbourne	1 pm
New Zealand	3 pm

(* denotes previous day)

The 24-hour system is used for writing nearly all times in Japan, whether railway timetables or notices in restaurant windows. To convert a time later than 1300 (1 pm) to the 12-hour system, simply subtract 1200; thus 1730 hours is the same as 5.30 pm. For am times no arithmetic is necessary – 0900 simply means 9 am.

HEALTH
Food and water
It is very unlikely that anyone will become ill in Japan as the result of eating or drinking. Food sold is of high standard and tap water can be drunk anywhere in the country. The digestive troubles that you expect in most of Asia are virtually unknown. Food from mobile stalls, often seen at night near railway stations, is safe to eat.

Medical
The standards of health care in Japan are good, as reflected in the life expectancy of the average Japanese, which is the highest in the world – about 73 years for men and 78 for women (1972 figures). Medical personnel are generally trained to high standards and many Japanese doctors would rate highly in any country. Likewise, there are many good hospitals with up-to-date equipment and facilities.

The other side of the coin is that Japan has its full share of quacks and unqualified practitioners who, if they got through medical school at all, it was more through money and influence than by merit. So if any serious procedure, like an operation, is suggested be sure to get a second opinion even if the first doctor complains about losing face. Better his face than your health and wealth.

Hospital charges tend to be very high and there is the occasional tendency to keep patients longer than necessary in order to increase the income, especially at hospitals that are privately owned by doctors.

There are several hospitals in the large cities that were founded by various Christian groups; their approach to medical care would be more familiar to westerners, so anyone needing hospital care should try to contact them. Also in the larger cities there are several western doctors with whom foreigners will be able to talk more easily. The Tokyo TIC can give more information on these doctors and hospitals.

The common types of shots normally required for overseas travel can be obtained conveniently at the Kotsu Kaikan ('Travel Building') not far from the Tokyo TIC in Yurakucho. Slotted into this building along with travel agents, minshuku and ryokan booking offices and other travel-related businesses, is an office where qualified personnel spend every working day jabbing or zapping (pressure spray injections). Costs are reasonable and they issue you with a card recording the shots.

A lower-priced but less convenient alternative for shots is the Tokyo Port Authority or the health facility at Narita airport.

Dental
Japanese dentists are equipped with the most modern instruments and facilities in the world, and much dental research is carried out in universities, yet as a nation with a very high standard of living, the Japanese have shockingly bad teeth. This is probably the result of carelessness on the part of the tooth-owners more than a reflection on the standard of dentists. Dental work will not be cheap; the Japanese have national health insurance so they don't mind the cost of a filling.

Costs

It is advisable to have your own medical insurance because costs in Japan are extremely high. Being a doctor or dentist are two of the most lucrative professions in Japan. This is reflected in the fact that prospective students at some medical schools must make a 'gift' to the college of up to Y40 million before they are admitted, and the average total cost for six years of study is Y19 million. This of course means that only the children of wealthy parents will get into these schools, and it's the patients who have to ultimately pay off that scandalous 'bribe' for entry. Being Japan this practice will probably continue ad infinitum; service for the general good is not a generally admired concept in this country.

Foreign residents of Japan may be eligible for Japanese health insurance, but this varies from one locality to another.

Contraceptives etc.

The main methods of contraception in Japan are the condom, pessaries (tablets) that are inserted prior to intercourse (two such brands are CCC and Sampoon), gels and foams and the diaphragm; the latter is the least popular.

The message is that contraception is the responsibility of the male, and few Japanese women will be 'prepared' for spontaneous sexual activity. Abortions are readily available at low cost and with no difficulty for both Japanese and foreign women.

The Pill is not generally available to Japanese women, so foreign women travelling in the country should make sure they have their own supply. Foreign brands are not sold in Japan and prescriptions can be hard to fill.

Familiar brands of sanitary protection will be found only at pharmacies like the American Pharmacy that cater to foreign clientele; Tampax is the only brand distributed nation-wide.

Mental Health

If you get the 'coming unstuck' feeling, need advice or help in personal matters or just need someone to talk to for any reason, there is a small choice of agencies who can help.

Tokyo English Lifeline (TELL) offers confidential and anonymous counselling by telephone; they can also refer callers to other agencies that might be able to help. In Tokyo the number is (03) 264-4347. Another useful organisation is Tokyo Community Counselling Service; it refers callers to professional counsellors in a variety of fields; tel (03) 403-7106.

Tokyo Tapes offers an extremely useful and comprehensive range of tape recorded information. Callers phone and request one or more tapes by number. For a listing of tapes by number, tel (03) 262-0224 and ask for tape 302. The listing is also available from Tokyo Tapes, 610 Homat Commodore, 5-13-28 Roppongi, Minato-ku, Tokyo 106; and from the sponsoring organisations, the Franciscan Chapel Centre, St Alban's, St Paul's Lutheran, Tokyo Baptist or Tokyo Union churches.

Toilets

Most toilets in Japan are the Asian squatting type. These are supposedly physiologically the best kind and are personally hygienic because no part of the body comes in contact with it. Many westerners, however, find them uncomfortable and undignified but unless you continually travel first class it will be necessary to use one at some time. When squatting, be careful not to let money or other things fall out of your pockets; some people completely remove their trousers to avoid such an occurrence.

Most public toilets have no paper, so it is wise to have your own when travelling away from familiar territory. There are often dispensers for tissues at the entrance. Where paper is provided, it is almost uniformly of extremely poor quality.

All western-style hotels, some ryokan and most large and modern office buildings and department stores have clean, western-style facilities. Some westerners make mental notes of their location and plan a daily visit to one.

In private homes, youth hostels, ryokans, minshuku and other residential places, there will be a separate pair of slippers at the entrance to the toilet area. Take off the house slippers and change into the toilet ones. Don't forget to change back again when leaving and never wear the house slippers into the toilet – both are social gaffes without peer. It all becomes instinctive after a while.

Don't be surprised or shocked at the sight of men urinating in public, especially at night after coming out of a bar after an evening of hard drinking. Even in daylight it is not unknown to see one facing a wall.

POSTAL

The Japanese Post Office is generally reliable and efficient, though it is by no means cheap and it has been known to lose letters (as I can certify). Post Offices keep quite generous hours. District post offices are open 8 am to 7 pm on weekdays; from 8 am to 3 pm on Saturdays; and 8 am to noon on Sundays and national holidays. 'District post office' means the main post office of the ward ('ku'). Local post offices keep shorter hours: 9 am to 5 pm on weekdays; 9 am to 1 pm on Saturdays; and closed on Sundays and holidays. Local post offices can accept letters for overseas destinations (air and surface), but registered mail, small packets and parcels can only be sent overseas from the district offices.

The central post offices of Tokyo and Kyoto have some counters open 24 hours a day, so you can send letters and parcels, and collect poste restante and registered mail.

Mail can be addressed into, out of and within Japan in romaji (Roman letters). To avoid letters going astray, write or print clearly, as mail sorters and carriers are not linguists.

In Tokyo there is a special post office

for overseas mail, It is called, naturally enough, Tokyo International Post Office (*Kok'sai Yubin-kyoko*). They know all regulations regarding foreign mail. It is located in Otem-achi and is shown on the TIC's Tokyo guide map. In theory you can obtain information in English by phone; tel 241-4877.

International Postal Reply Coupons (kosai henshin kitteken) can be bought if it is necessary to pre-pay postage from a foreign country. One coupon is adequate for postage for a minimum cost letter by surface mail from nearly every country in the world. The coupons cost Y140 each. This cost is extremely high, several times the actual cost of postage from overseas countries, so it may be cheaper to send a money order for postage.

For wrapping parcels most post offices supply free twine. If you need cardboard boxes, grocery stores and many other shops discard them every day.

Airmail envelopes should not be used for domestic mail. There may be a surcharge for coloured envelopes as they require special handling. Stickers may be attached to postcards as long as they don't appreciably add to the weight or thickness.

Philatelists may be interested to know that Japan, like every other country, regularly issues commemorative stamps (kinen kitte). These are sold at every post office in the country on the day of issue but usually they disappear quickly the same day. After that they can be purchased (until sold out) at Tokyo CPO, near Tokyo station, Marunouchi side. The philatelic counter is at the end of the building nearest the station and is open until 4 pm. Stamps available are displayed on a board.

Receiving Mail

Mail can be sent c/o Poste Restante (General Delivery) to any post office in Japan, but preferably to the Central Post Office, which is usually very close to the main railway station of each city. Things to note are: 1. letters are usually only held for 30 days before being returned to the sender; and 2. the Japanese seldom use the service and most people don't know that it exists. Postal clerks in smaller post offices may even be unsure where to put such letters, so there is a risk they will go astray.

At the post office, ask for either tome oki or kyoku dome and have your passport or other identification ready.

American Express offices hold mail for customers. They can ask for proof that you are a customer, but this can simply mean someone who has bought their travellers' cheques. Mail is normally held for 30 days, but they will hold it longer if it is marked "Please hold for arrival'.

The addresses of branches that hold mail are:

Tokyo
  c/o American Express, Halifax Building, 16-26 Roppongi 3-chome, Minato-ku, Tokyo 106.
Osaka
  c/o American Express, Kita Hankyu Bldg 3rd floor, 1-4-8 Shibata, Kita-ku, Osaka.
Okinawa
  c/o American Express, Awase Shopping Centre, 241 Aza Yamazoto, Okinawa-shi 904.

To reach the Tokyo office take the subway to Roppongi and leave the platform at the end nearest the rear of the train (if coming from Ginza). Turn left from the platform and then right at street level when you leave the station. Walk past the 'Almond' coffee shop (a well-known rendezvous), across the little street that goes downhill and turn right at the main thoroughfare. After a 5-10 minute walk, the large American Express sign will be visible on the left side of the street.

In Osaka, the office is near Osaka station.

Embassies Some embassies will hold mail for their passport holders, but they may normally return it after 30 days, unless it is marked 'Please hold for arrival'

The embassies of Australia, Canada, South Africa, New Zealand and USA will hold mail; but the UK embassy will not.

Banks Some banks will hold mail for their customers. For example the Royal Bank of Canada will, but First National City Bank would not.

Hotels and Youth Hostels will hold mail for their guests. Hotels are usually quite safe places to have mail sent but the hostels vary. In my own experience I had mail arrive safely, but a friend had her mail sent to one YH and when her letters were finally turned over to her, every one had been opened. This is not typical however.

TELEPHONES

Japanese phone numbers have nine or ten

digits, usually in three groups. The first group is the area code and is only used when dialling from another zone. For some peculiar reason brackets are often written around the second group, not around the area code as is commonly done in other countries. The latter method is sometimes used in Japan and is used in this book.

Local calls in Japan cost Y10 for three minutes. There are several kinds of public (pay) phones. The most common type is red, sometimes with a gold band. It can hold six Y10 coins, uses them one at a time, returns unused coins and can be used for local or inter-city calls. These are found in many shops, stations, etc. There is a smaller sort of red phone, only for local calls, which takes one coin and cuts off after three minutes.

Pink pay phones are found in private homes and operate exactly the same as large red ones.

Yellow phones are the same as large red ones, except they can hold up to ten Y10 coins and nine Y100 coins; they are the most useful for inter-city direct-dialled calls.

Blue phones are also identical to large red phones in function but rarely take Y100 coins.

Olive green phones are of two types; some accept Y10 and Y100 coins plus 'phone cards', while others accept only 'phone cards'. The phone card is a type of credit card for a fixed amount (Y500, Y1000, etc) purchased at tobacco and other shops. The card is put into a slot and the cost is deducted during the call from the credit value contained in a microchip on the card. The amount of credit remaining is shown by an indicator on the phone and the card is returned to be used for subsequent calls till its initial value is used up. New in 1984 these phones are being installed all around the country.

Emergency numbers for use anywhere in Japan are: Police 110; Ambulance 119. However the person answering will probably only speak Japanese. Yellow and blue phones can be used for making emergency calls without coins.

International

In theory calls can be made to any country although it's doubtful that a call would actually be completed to North Korea or Albania. Calls can be made through an operator or by dialling directly. To call the overseas operator, dial 0051 from anywhere in Japan. For information about overseas calls, ring (03) 270-5111.

Collect calls can be made to Canada, USA, South Korea, Hong Kong, Taiwan, Australia and western Europe.

ISD (International Subscriber Dialling) calls can be made from any private telephone not specifically disabled, from hotels and from some pay phones, and are billed in units of six seconds.

TELEGRAMS

Until 1985, domestic and overseas telephone and telegraph services were under the control of one body, KDD. The government decided, however, to change it to a private system (much the same as in the UK) and at the time of revising this book the system for sending telegrams had not been announced. Previously the telephone information number, (03) 270-5111, was also used for telegraph inquiries; they should be able to provide the correct new number.

Within Japan, telegrams can be sent in roman letters from major post offices and offices of the telegraph company, NTT.

Overseas telegrams can be sent to most countries of the world and are accepted in roman letters at telegraph, telephone or post offices. Hotels catering to foreign customers can also help.

Any group of 10 letters is accepted as one word so words may be run together to economise, if the recipient can successfully separate them; but remember that letters can get mistransmitted.

ADDRESSES

Visitors to Japan should know from the

outset that it is almost impossible to find a place just from the address. Even Japanese find it very difficult.

Addresses are not by street. In fact, most streets have no name at all; only the most major avenues have names, and even then, some Japanese may not be familiar with these. Addresses are by district, not by street. The smallest district is the *chome*, usually only a few blocks in area. Within the chome, each building has a one-digit or hyphenated two-digit number, eg 4-4. What makes the system interesting is that until 1955, the numbers were assigned by chronological order of construction, not by location!

The next larger unit may have one of several names: *cho, machi* or no name at all. Next comes *ku* which is the equivalent of a ward. In Tokyo, well known ward names are Chiyoda-ku, Chuo-ku (Central Ward), Minato-ku (Harbour Ward) and Shinjuku-ku. For example an address of the form '1-2-3 Nishi Meguro' means the same as '2-3 Nishi Meguro 1-chome'; the '2-3' refers to the building number.

Published maps are available that show the breakdown of every chome, building by building, but few foreigners bother with them. It is common, however, for any business, store, etc, to print a small map on its business card (*meishi*) or advertisements, showing the location relative to the nearest railway or subway station.

There was an effort during the Occupation to assign numbers and letters to the major thoroughfares of Tokyo. But this attempt to rationalise a non-system was definitely not appreciated and was dropped when the Japanese were given full control of their own affairs.

The names of cities are properly followed by the suffix *shi*, as in 'Yokohamashi'. The word means city and is tagged on to distinguish between cities and prefectures (*ken*) of the same name; there is an Okayama-shi and Okayama-ken, for example. The cities of Kyoto and Osaka, by the way, are special administrative districts known as *fu*; they are not

properly *shi*. In the countryside there are many *mura* or villages. Another word found often in addresses in the countryside is 'gun', which corresponds to 'county', one step smaller than *ken*.

Japanese addresses sometimes have commas in the middle of a line. When the whole address is printed on a single line, this can be confusing to a reader who is unfamiliar with the system.

ELECTRICITY

Electricity service everywhere in Japan is 100 volts AC, an odd voltage used nowhere else in the world except Korea (and they're changing to 220 V). Northeast of an imaginary east-west line just south-west Tokyo, the frequency is 50 Hz (cycles); south-west of the line it is 60 Hz. Most 117-volt equipment such as shavers and hair dryers, designed for use in North America, will work satisfactorily, if a little slowly or with reduced heat output. The plug has two flat pins.

LAUNDRY

Anyone staying at hotels or ryokan can have their laundry done by the hotel. Dry cleaning shops and depots are common in every suburban area. Travellers using youth hostels, etc, will have to do their own washing, in many cases in a wash basin or sink using cold water (not very pleasant in unheated washrooms in midwinter!). A manicure brush is useful for scrubbing.

The coin-operated washing machine reached Japan a few years ago and is very popular. Many are operated in conjunction with 'sento' (neighbourhood public baths). Many youth hostels have washing machines for the use of their guests.

MEDIA
Radio
The only regular broadcasts in English are those of the Far East Network (FEN) or the American armed forces. While they are slanted towards the interests and tastes of people in the services (very heavy

on pop music and sport), they also have hourly news broadcasts and an hour-long news, sports and commentary segment between 6 pm and 7 pm on weeknights. Those who missed out on, or who want to relive, the golden days of radio can hear rebroadcasts of 1940s and '50s programs such as *The Whistler* and *Amos 'n' Andy*. Listening areas and frequencies (kHz) are: Tokyo (810); Sasebo, Kyushu (1566); Iwakuni, near Hiroshima (1575); Misawa, Northern Honshu (1575); and Okinawa (650). Tokyo area programs are listed daily in the *Japan Times*.

There are a few minutes of news in English each day on NHK, the government broadcasting organisation.

The Japanese AM stations are heavily biased toward pop music, Japanese style, although there is a substantial amount of the western variety as well. Program notes are published in the English-language dailies.

FM fans will find a very limited number of stations in large cities like Tokyo and Osaka – only two stations each. They broadcast several hours of classical, pop, jazz and 'easy listening' music each day. The FM frequencies used in Japan are 76-90 MHz, below the international standard FM band 88-108 MHz found on most radios, so a special radio tuned to the local bands, or a converter, is necessary to pick up the broadcasts. If you want to buy good Japanese hi fi gear to take home, buy the foreign frequency model and use a converter while in Japan.

TV

Most programming in Japan is in Japanese only. Imported programs and films are dubbed. However, there are some programs which can be picked up on cable TV (to some apartment buildings and most hotels catering to foreigners) and heard with their original soundtrack. A new development in the electronics field is multiplex broadcasting of TV soundtracks. With an adaptor, it is often possible to receive the original soundtrack of the film or program instead of the dubbed version, though there may be some lack of continuity if segments have been cut.

Watching the Japanese programs, even if you can't understand a word of the dialogue, can give many insights into modern Japanese life. The role of women is clearly seen on one program after another – they are usually there only to provide a little scenery and to say *hai* (yes!) in obsequious agreement with every statement of the male who is, by definition, the most important and intelligent person on the screen.

SPORTS
Sumo

Not well known to foreigners except for its 'fat wrestlers', Sumo is a very Japanese sport and interesting to watch. Two men face each other in an earth circle and grapple when they both feel ready. The loser is the first one pushed or thrown out of the circle or who touches the ground with any part of his body other than his feet. The action lasts from a second to a couple of minutes.

There are six basho (tournaments) per year according to the following schedule: early January (Tokyo); mid-March (Osaka); early May (Tokyo); early July (Nagoya); mid-September (Tokyo); mid-November (Fukuoka).

Seats cost from mid-hundreds to mid-thousands, but the best view is that on TV, broadcast live from 4-6 pm, with a summary of all 15 bouts late in the evening.

Baseball

The Japanese are as baseball-mad as the Americans and fans of the sport might enjoy seeing a game while in Japan. The players are good although it is admitted that the US leagues are at a higher level.

Skiing

Japan offers good skiing if you live here but it would not be worth making a special trip. Information on ski areas and resorts

is available from the Tourist Information Centre. Some are mentioned in general descriptions of the areas, later in the book.

FILM

Japan is the land of photographers. Whatever the occasion, the Japanese take a photograph of it, with themselves or family or friends in it – front and centre. Taking photos is part of the social process, as the participants in the occasion almost invariably get together a few weeks later to show and exchange photos. If they then photograph the reunion as avidly, they have the makings of an infinitely long chain of social gatherings.

The implication of this is that film is consumed in huge amounts and is available everywhere in the country. Prices are reasonable, probably comparable with those in the USA, a bit higher than Hong Kong and Singapore and lower than in many other countries.

The three major film companies are the great yellow father, Kodak, and the two Japanese companies, Fuji and Sakura (Konica). Polaroid film for recent model cameras is also available.

The vast majority of film sold for the amateur market is for colour prints. Colour slides are not popular (no prints to share with others!), and represent only about 10 per cent of film sales. This means that slide film can be difficult to find outside the big cities.

Kodak films are a known quantity around the world, with a well-deserved reputation for quality products. Colour print films of both Fuji and Sakura are both well regarded, giving good colour and grain in all speed types.

Colour slide films from Fuji have been building up a good reputation overseas but Sakura colour slide films have not yet established themselves as being in the same league as the other two.

Processing

Prints Because of the vast number of colour prints made every year, processing is available 'everywhere' and at reasonable cost; colour prints cost as little as Y25. Films left at local camera shops will usually be processed and returned in one to two days. There are depots around the larger cities where film may be left in the morning and picked up late in the afternoon. There is one such seven-hour service depot in the Mitsu-koshi department store facing the Ginza and others around the city, some near the major hotels frequented by overseas visitors. Some depots offer one-hour processing.

Slides All slide films can be sent for processing by any camera shop in the country. The seven-hour developing depots can get Ektachrome and the Japanese slide films developed in three to four days. For faster service of Kodak slide films (than the usual six to eight days) take your film to the Kodak depot in the Ginza and ask for fast processing. They can have the films back in two days.

Kodachrome, with prepaid processing, is not available in Japan. If you can obtain prepaid mailers for Kodak processing (sold In USA, Hong Kong and other countries), you can probably save money. These mailers and developing of Kodachrome with development included in the price, are honoured in Japan and should be sent to: Far East Laboratories, Ltd., 14-1 Higashi-Gotanda 2-chome, Shinagawa-ku, Tokyo. They could also be left at the Kodak depots in the Ginza or Aoyama.

If you are carrying undeveloped film on an overseas flight, you should carry it by hand and request a hand inspection of films and cameras. Signs on X-ray machines saying they don't affect film cannot be trusted. ISO 100 film can be exposed up to four times before the effect is noticeable, but high speed films in the ISO 800-1600 range will show random colouration or streaks after a single exposure.

THINGS TO BUY

Even back in the good old days when a US dollar was worth more yen and price tags were lower, there were relatively few bargains in Japan. The only good buys (price wise) were in cameras and other optical goods, electronic products (radios, hi fi gear, etc), watches, motorcycles, cars and oil tankers.

Well you can forget about the oil tankers now – the Koreans are building them cheaper.

As for the other goods, prices have gone up with inflation, as they have everywhere and the value of the yen has skyrocketed so that there are even fewer 'bargains' today, if the word only means low prices. However the quality of manufactured goods has continued to improve, with features undreamed-of only a few years ago so you're paying more but getting value for money.

It comes as a surprise to most westerners to find that many Japanese-made goods cost more in Japan than they do at home. The main reason is that the distribution system in Japan is notoriously long and complex, with many links in the chain, each of which tacks on its mark-up. Foreign importers can usually buy in huge volume and distribute the goods more efficiently and therefore more cheaply. Even where import duty is applied prices can be lower than in Japan.

Japan's distribution system is actually a form of social welfare. Many of the people employed in sales and distribution have relatively few skills, do not work for companies that can pay large retirement pensions and are actually surplus to the task of distributing the goods, but are supported by the system as a type of tax.

A large number of Japanese goods sold overseas are made for export only and are never seen on the domestic market. An example is the miniature cast-iron grill called a 'hibachi'; this has never been used in Japan and can only be found in stores selling to US service people. So if a friend at home asks you to buy a particular product, in most cases you would be advised to refuse politely because unless it's a common and competitive product (like a camera) it will probably be cheaper at home.

One of the big surprises about Japan is that much of its industry is small and inefficient which also ultimately adds to the price of the end product. The large car assemblers of components, like the car manufacturers, buy many of their parts from very small companies that may only have a few pieces of machinery and depend on long working hours by family firms to survive financially.

There are many hand-made artistic and decorative items still being made with the exquisite attention to detail for which Japan has long been famous. They exhibit the best workmanship imaginable – flawless lacquerware, hand-forged swords and knives, incredibly beautiful hand-woven fabrics and textiles – the list goes on and on. Naturally the time-consuming hand labour involved makes these items costly, but the quality of the work justifies the price. The coexistence of the finest centuries-old artistry with some of the world's most modern mass-produced goods is one of the fascinations of Japan.

While Japanese stores are usually very competitive with each other, especially for items like cameras and electronic goods, there is very little bargaining and certainly none of the camel-market haggling of some countries. The Japanese regard this with contempt, as bad manners. However it is possible that a store clerk, after quoting a price, might add an accessory to sweeten the deal.

When shopping for a camera, or other expensive item, it is generally not a good idea to go with a Japanese friend. Because the Japanese have little tradition of bargaining they tend to pay the first price asked. If you are with a Japanese friend and the price you are offered with him is not as good as you've seen elsewhere, just politely postpone the purchase. Don't bluntly say you can get it cheaper somewhere else, as things aren't done that way in Japan; say you'd like to think it over.

Customs Inspection at Home

Travellers should determine what they are allowed to take back to their home country without incurring duties. Check with your embassy if you're in doubt.

Americans should take note of US trade mark regulations. In addition to the dollar limit on what can be brought back duty-free (now $300), many goods of foreign origin are registered with the US Customs service by trademark. These companies have the right to limit the volume of private imports of goods bearing that trademark; some companies totally ban private imports, while others place no restrictions on such activities. Items made in Japan that fall into this category include cameras, binoculars, lenses and hi fi gear. The booklet *Trademark Information* can be picked up at the US embassy in Tokyo, or ordered by mail from: Department of the Treasury, US Customs Service, Washington DC 20229, or the US Government Printing Office, Washington DC 20402.

Tax-free Buying

Most goods sold in Japan have a national sales tax of 10-35% imposed on them; list prices and price tags in most shops include this tax. Foreign tourists can purchase many types of goods free of this tax. A card is stapled into your passport at the time of purchase and is removed by Customs at the port of departure. You may be asked to prove that you have the item in your possession to ensure that the goods are actually being taken out of the country.

Only some stores, generally located in popular tourist areas, offer goods on a tax-free basis; many of these, such as camera shops, will have a prominent 'Tax Free' sign. An individual item must have been registered for sale tax-free to allow its sale on that basis. Thus, a shop selling to the domestic market would not stock tax-free items.

The tax-free price is not the lowest possible price; it is only the starting point for negotiations. For items such as cameras it's possible to obtain a further discount of 5-25% depending on the brand and the store.

Some 'sharper' operators trade on the gullability of tourists and sell 'tax-free' but with no discount from list prices (shops at Narita Airport tend to operate on this system). Most shops though, in a competitive environment, will give good discounts, especially in Shinjuku where competition is cutthroat.

Remember too, that the discount available from some shops selling at domestic, with-tax (*kazei*) prices, can be much greater than the saving at tax-free stores, (especially for cameras), as the sales tax is on the manufacturers price not the selling price.

Although tax-free (*menzei*) purchasing is intended for tourists and other short-term visitors, those on working visas may be able to buy tax-free during the first six months or when planning to leave Japan.

Cameras

Cameras and lenses are among Japan's best-known products, with a reputation for quality at reasonable prices. Despite increases in the value of the yen, the industry has almost eliminated all international competition in 35 mm cameras, and it dominates most of the other camera markets.

Japanese-made cameras are often slightly cheaper in Hong Kong and Singapore, but the difference in price is not enough to lose sleep over.

The lowest prices in Japan can be found in Tokyo, especially in Shinjuku, a sub-city with many large stores of all kinds. Some shops in the Ginza area sell at very reasonable prices but others are fully aware that many well-heeled foreign

tourists pass by their doors, so they feel no need to reduce their prices excessively.

The Yodobashi and Sakuraya stores in Shinjuku are close to the Takano Building and are easy to find from the station once you are above ground on the east side. Both are brightly lit and the store jingles are repetitious, incessant and loud.

There are other branches of these two stores, plus those of Doi Camera on both the east and west side of Shinjuku station.

As with most purchases, you should compare prices carefully if you want a bargain. Make sure you are comparing identical equipment.

Many brands of Japanese-made photographic equipment are not available in Japan. For example, one company may make the lenses sold under several different names overseas; the only private brand lenses normally available in Japan are Komura, Sigma, Tamron and Tokina. Some companies put different name plates on the same model of camera in different markets, and some models are never sold in Japan.

If you buy a camera it is wise to check immediately that it is giving correct exposure and is functioning properly. Servicing is faster and much easier in Japan than elsewhere.

The best way to check it (other than the simple check of operating the shutter on all speeds at the store) is to run a roll of colour slide film (Kodachrome 25 or 64 films can be recommended; don't use print film) through the camera and check if the pictures are satisfactorily exposed. Test pictures should be taken of normal subjects that are evenly lighted and don't contain large areas that are very bright or very dark. If the camera has shutter speeds that can be varied manually, use the full range of them and make a record of the setting for each shot to match them later. If only the aperture can be varied, use the full range available. If you buy extra lenses, test them all, using the full method just described.

Electronics & Hi Fi

Hi fi stores in Japan, especially in Tokyo, are a gadget-lover's paradise. But before rushing in with a bulging wallet, be warned of all these pitfalls.

First, electronic products, like many other Japanese goods, are often cheaper in other countries, whether it's US discount stores, duty-free stores, Hong Kong or Singapore. In other words know your prices. Admittedly, the very latest models may not be available elsewhere.

Next, remember that most electronic goodies are heavy, bulky or both. This makes them prohibitive as checked air luggage. The weight limit for parcel post is only 10 kg and sea freight or express charges are not cheap. (Sea freight charges just for crating something, hauling it to the docks, and customs inspection amount to about Y20,000; then there are the actual shipping costs, documentation charges and customs duties at the other end. The cheapest way to send an item is by air freight.)

If you still want to buy you'll find that many items on display are made for Japan only. Japan's power supply is 100 volts at a frequency of 50 or 60 Hz depending on the region. Low-power equipment may work satisfactorily on 117 V (as in North America) but with no guarantee against damage. The frequency affects motor speeds. (In Australia, UK, Europe and most other countries, supplies are 230-240 V at 50 Hz.)

Japanese TV channels and some other specifications are different from most other countries as is their FM radio band. Because the local models are not usually exported getting service and parts could be a problem. Many Japan-only models have export equivalents with adjustable settings.

If you are buying FM stereo equipment, note there is a specification called the 'stereo de-emphasis time constant'. In Australia, UK and Europe it is 50 microseconds; in North America it's 75. The modification is simple, but would cost a serviceman's time to change. It would be simpler to buy the right model in the first place; some have a switch at the back that allows selection between the two.

Some 'Tax Free' shops specialise in selling the export models. Several shops in the Ginza area stock a few types of electronic equipment, especially portable items like tape recorders and radios, along with camera gear, but the range is usually limited and the higher quality models may be a little rare. Prices tend to be higher than in the 'discount' areas because Ginza real estate is the most expensive in the world.

The best place in Tokyo to buy domestic models of electronic equipment is Akihabara (the name means 'Autumn Leaf Field'). You can get there by JNR Yamanote line; Akihabara station of the Hibiya subway line exits onto a street parallel to and one block away from the electrical area so it is necessary to walk under the JNR tracks to get there. In this district there are dozens, if not hundreds, of shops of all sizes selling everything electrical that is made in Japan. Several have departments specialising in tax-free export models.

Records

The music of a country you visit is always a good souvenir. Some Japanese music is very much an acquired taste, particularly the screechy *gagaku* but other types can be appreciated by almost any western ear for its often haunting beauty. Most pleasing is the music of the *koto*, a long, thin, stringed instrument played while seated on the floor; and the *shakuhachi*, or Japanese flute. The koto and shakuhachi are often combined and complement each other.

One of the most beautiful, and famous, of all Japanese compositions is *Ko jo no tsuki* – 'Moon Over Castle Ruins'; another is *Sakura Sakura*. Both should be enjoyable for any listener and are included on almost every recording of traditional Japanese music.

Clothes

Japan is not a place where you would normally look for clothes, although residents can find some good buys when they become familiar with the market. The main problem is that most visitors would have trouble finding off-the-rack clothes to fit because the physique of the average Japanese is quite different from that of most westerners. The good news is, though, that if you do manage to find something you like, that fits, it is bound to be of good quality and well made.

Finding shoes to fit the average large western foot is also a problem in Japan. If you do need to buy shoes while in Japan you could try Big Shoes Akasaka, 3-21-18 Akasaka, near Akasaka-Mitsuke subway station; Ginza Washington Shoe Store, Ginza 5-chome, diagonally opposite Matsuzakaya department store in Ginza; branches of the Isetan department store; and Ten Shoe Store, Shinjuku west side, north of the big intersection.

If you're coming through Korea, or planning a trip there from Japan, you will find that you can have clothes and shoes custom-made there cheaper than most off-the-rack clothing in Japan.

Antiques

The post-war days when Japanese antiques were sold for a song are long gone. The song has become an operatic chorus with full orchestral backing, and prices for almost anything really good will be from high to astronomical. They are high enough that Japanese buyers have been going overseas for a number of years and buying back Japanese items at foreign auctions. If you don't know your Japanese antiques, it is best to avoid spending large sums. If you see something that you really like, then buy it, but remember Japanese dealers know the value of their merchandise. Prices can vary, depending on how the dealer sizes up the customer.

There are regular flea markets in Tokyo and Kyoto where stallholders set up business. The chances of finding a treasure

are quite remote as these people are not as naive as they might let on.

One warning: if you wish to examine a piece of pottery or glassware, ask the stallholder to hand it to you. The occasional unscrupulous one carefully assembles the pieces of a broken item so that it collapses as soon as anyone touches it, so the customer then has to pay for it.

Eyeglasses

Glasses are expensive in Japan. It is better to get them in Hong Kong, Singapore or Korea, but if this is not possible, lower than usual prices are available at a type of 'self-service glasses supermarket'. The company, Mega ne no Drug, has several branches in Tokyo (and perhaps elsewhere); tel (03) 735-0022 for information.

Calculators and computers

For years there were no inexpensive calculators on sale in Japan such as could be found in Hong Kong and Singapore. Since about 1980, however, a large variety of down-market models have become available, priced from about Y1000. There is a limited variety of multi-function scientific models but most are fairly basic four-function types, many in garish pink cases with cutsie-poo animals for children.

The computer and microchip revolution has spawned a great variety of pocketable machines and whatever I write here will be obsolete before this book is even published!

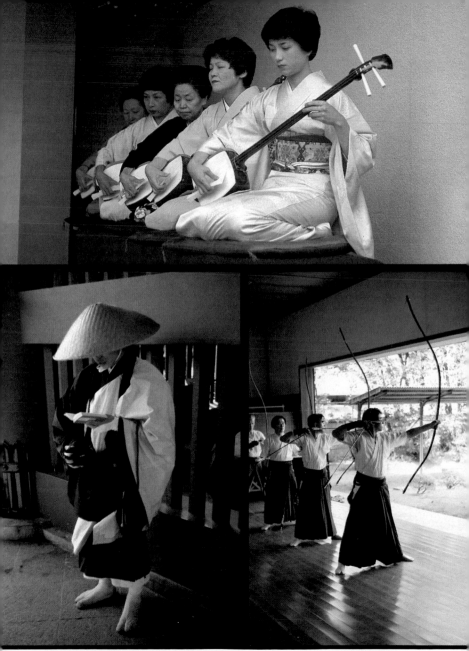

Top: Shamisen players at Takanawa Prince Hotel's annual cherry blossom festival, Tokyo
Left: A pilgrim at Asakusa Kannon temple, Tokyo
Right: Traditional Japanese archery at Ueno, Tokyo

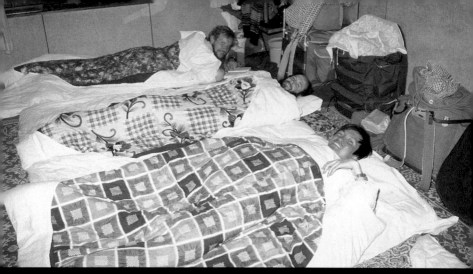

Top: Typical scene in a youth hostel: sleeping on *futons* on the tatami mats
Left: Evening scene in a minshuku, this one in an old thatched farmhouse at Shirakawa-go (Gifu-ken)
Right: A comment on driving conditions in Japan

It is safe to say, however, that already there are pocket size machines that can be programmed to perform quite complex calculations, and the capabilities of these machines will only increase with time. Such pocket computers are available in shops selling electronic goods, computers and cameras. In Tokyo, the Shinjuku and Akihabara districts would have the greatest variety with the best prices.

Watches

The electronics revolution has struck the timekeeping industry as well. There is an amazing variety of electronic watches and they're on sale 'everywhere'. The lowest priced models are sold in simple and inexpensive blister-pack packaging hung on display racks. Cheapie types sell at back street discount shops for as little as Y500; while the advertised brand models begin in the Y1800 range; and stopwatch-option models start from around Y2500. More expensive digital and analog style watches are also available as well as watches from the well-known makers like Seiko, Citizen, Alba, etc.

Conventional mechanical watches are also manufactured in large numbers and varieties of design and price – few are cheap. The best single area for watch shopping is Shinjuku, though good selections at reasonable prices may also be found in the Akihabara area and even the up-market Ginza area.

Books

The Japanese printing industry produces some of the finest quality colour printing in the world. Many books are published in English every year, including books of photographs of Japan and works on other subjects related to the country which make excellent souvenirs. Maruzen and Kinokuniya sell English language books in a number of cities. In Tokyo there are also Jena, Kitazawa and Yaesu stores, the Tuttle shop (which displays titles of that publishing company), plus stores in the arcades of most of the large international hotels; the arcade in the Imperial Hotel probably offers the greatest selection.

Lacquer (makie)

Japanese lacquerware is one of the most beautiful things you could buy in Japan. Every region produces many different objects – bowls, vases, plates, wall plaques, trays – so the variety is enormous. Some cities known for lacquerware are Kyoto, Kanazawa, Wajima and Kamakura. Quality objects can be found in most large department stores as well as specialty shops. Prices for the finest pieces, with gold designs, intricate detailing and flawlessly smooth finish, can run into hundreds of thousands of yen. But smaller, less pretentious pieces can be bought for a couple of thousand.

Cloisonne

This is produced by soldering fine wire to a metal base to trace the outline of a pattern, then filling in the spaces with material that fires to a glassy finish. Cloisonne is a popular purchase in Japan.

Damascene

A steel base is criss-crossed with fine lines, then pre-cut patterns of gold and silver foil are beaten onto the base. The base is corroded with nitric acid, lacquer is baked onto the entire surface, then the pattern is polished out. The revealed gold and silver may then be engraved further.

Dolls

Delicate Japanese dolls make a beautiful decoration in any home. There are several styles of doll made in Japan, such as Hakata clay figurines and the more familiar kimono-clad women with fine porcelain faces and hands. The latter vary in fineness of sculpturing, so it is wise to compare. Department, specialty and tourist shops sell them.

Pearls

The process for culturing pearls was

developed by a Japanese (Mikimoto) and they remain one of the favourite purchases in Japan. Mikimoto is still the world leader in fine pearls, but many other companies also produce good quality pearls.

In the Ise area (not far from Kyoto/Nara) you can see how the oysters are induced to produce pearls, as well as seeing the largest number of the gems that you're ever likely to encounter in your life. It is a good opportunity to get an idea of the range of colours available before buying: gold, silver, grey, black and white. It wouldn't hurt to check prices in Tokyo in advance to see if they are better at the source, but be sure you have exactly the same specifications of size, number, colour, etc, so the comparison is valid. The value of the pearls varies with rarity, of course, so large pearls and some colours are worth more. Because of increasing pollution off the coast of Japan, producers are now harvesting the pearls earlier, so more small pearls are being produced than before. Whether new growing areas in other parts of the world will maintain the supply of large pearls, or whether the larger ones would be a good investment is hard to say.

Americans buying pearls should note a quirk in the law that sets a 2½ per cent duty rate on unknotted strings of pearls, but 27½ per cent for knotted strings.

Cars, Motorcycles & Bicycles

Information regarding the purchase of vehicles is given in the 'Getting Around' chapter.

Swords (katana)

Japanese swords are the finest weapons of their kind ever made anywhere in the world. Because of the great skill and workmanship involved in making these 'jewels of steel', good swords have very high prices, often millions of yen. Few foreigners can appreciate the fine details of a good sword, such as the pattern in the grain of the steel of the blade. Consequently they do not attach the mystique to a sword that the Japanese do and would not wish to pay the high prices demanded. 'Swords' selling for Y10,000 or so are nothing but toys, pieces of ordinary steel shaped like a sword and chrome-plated to give the outward appearance of the mirror-like side of a real sword – made for yokels!

Though not quite the same in purpose or construction, a Japanese knife employs some of the features of sword-making in its manufacture and can be an interesting, functional and cheaper souvenir. The most useful type is intended for cutting sushi and has a blade 250-300 mm long. The better ones are made of two pieces of steel forged together, one hard but somewhat brittle, the other softer and more flexible – in the manner of a sword blade. The knives cost from about Y4500 and up, and with care should last a lifetime.

Kimono

Although the kimono (pronounced ki-mo-no, with equal stress on all syllables) looks beautiful on Japanese women, it does not adapt well to being worn by taller western women. Even Japanese women must take many hours of lessons to learn how to put on and wear a kimono correctly. So-called kimono sold in tourist shops have only a passing resemblance to the real thing. If it is emblazoned with images of Mt Fuji, shrines, temples, cherry blossoms and Tokyo Tower, you can be sure it is not authentic.

Unfortunately, the beautiful cloth for kimono is too narrow to make into western style clothing but can usefully be employed for wall hangings or the like, where it would probably get more exposure than if worn anyway. Good kimono cloth is extremely expensive. It may be seen in any large department store; and some smaller shops sell nothing but cloth and accessories.

Another material to consider for wall hangings is the sash (obi); some of them are also very attractive and costly.

Incidentally, although the style of all kimono looks the same to untrained eyes, there are several styles for various occasions. The length of the sleeves is one style difference; formal kimono have very long sleeves.

Used kimono, often of very beautiful cloth and patterns, may be bought in stores in Tokyo and Kyoto at very reasonable prices; ask at the TIC offices for information.

Model Equipment

For the model 'toy' enthusiast there is a great variety of Japanese-made equipment including engines, radio control equipment, kits etc. Most popular in recent years have been the 1/12th and 1/10th scale electric-powered car and buggy kits, as they are quiet and clean and can be run almost anywhere. Engine-powered vehicles are also popular but are more of a specialty item because of the greater skill required to operate them. The more advanced models of these vehicles are far past the 'toy' stage, being well engineered miniatures with tiny ball bearings, die-cast aluminium all-independent suspension systems with mini shock absorbers, etc. There is also a huge variety of aircraft and model boat kits available, far more than any one shop would have in stock. A catalog is printed every year illustrating every kit and much of the equipment available; it should be available at most shops.

Once again most of the radios sold are for the Japanese frequencies, but most shops can normally obtain the export models.

Be sure that the model you choose can be used legally in your country (some models sold in Japan don't meet certain requirements of countries like the USA), and check the prices against those at home to make sure you're not paying the same or more.

Japanese engines have built up a reputation for quality around the world. The best known brands, with models of almost every size, are Enya and O.S.; for smaller sports-type engines Fuji and G-Mark are recommended; and Saito makes a small range of 4-stroke engines.

Three of the many hobby shops in the Tokyo area are 'Aile Ken 4' across from the Sweden Centre, near Roppongi station; 'Futaba Sangyo' in Akihabara (in the building just before Mansei-bashi bridge, across Chuo dori from the police station); and 'Asami', also in Akihabara but difficult to find on the third floor of a building a few blocks north of Futaba.

Exquisitely detailed miniature railroad equipment is also sold in Japan, particularly HO and N scale. Some locomotives sell for as much as Y150,000 each and are miniature masterpieces of the model maker's art. More reasonably priced model equipment is also available. Two places to look are the Tenshodo and Itoya, both in the Ginza area.

DANGERS & ANNOYANCES

Japan is one of the safest countries in the world for foreigners and locals alike. It is safe to walk on the streets of almost any section of any city or town in Japan at any time of the day or night without risk of assault, mugging or worse. There are a few areas that might be risky, populated by derelicts, and the rougher of the day-labourers (jikatabi, so named for their split-toe shoes), but these areas are far from the usual tourist beat. At one time gangs of youths were robbing intoxicated celebrants in the very expensive Ginza entertainment area, but the police soon put a stop to them. They were more of a threat to locals than foreigners anyway because the Japanese generally carry more cash for entertainment than westerners do. Attacks on foreigners are rare in any case, partly due to general respect for (white) foreigners (often unwarranted!).

For theft of personal belongings, such as cameras, Japan is one of the lowest-risk countries in the world. Probably the riskiest places are those with large numbers of tourists, such as the airports.

Generally though, throughout Japan, particularly away from the large cities, you could leave a suitcase unattended for hours and find it still there and untampered with when you return. There are even tales of absent-minded people leaving cameras on park benches and returning hours later to find them still there, but this isn't recommended. The average Japanese is just very honest. Lost goods will more than likely be turned into the police or transport authority, so if you leave something valuable behind on a train don't give up, as there is a good chance it has been handed in.

The remarks on theft and honesty do not apply to umbrellas; these will disappear without a trace if left in an unlocked drip tray on a rainy day. Also bicycles and motorcycles should be locked. My Honda 550 was wheeled away from the front of my house one night; though it was found later, minus some rather costly parts.

Even if you're sharing a room at a youth hostel, it is usually safe to leave your belongings unattended. Japanese hostellers regularly leave their cameras or other valuables lying on their beds. It is more necessary to be wary of foreigners than of Japanese.

Burglaries are quite common in the big cities, although they are rarely reported in the English-language papers, so take all the usual precautions applicable in any city. In small towns you may find that the locals don't bother locking their doors very much, but don't be insulted if they start locking up when they hear that a foreigner has moved into the neighbourhood!

Violent crime is very rare in Japan and one of the main lessons the rest of the world could learn from the Japanese is how to get along with other people in crowded surroundings. But most of the misunderstandings, by foreigners, of the ways of the Japanese people, stem from a western inability to comprehend the attitude of a society greatly influenced by its accommodation environment. What may seem to foreigners to be insincerity on the part of a Japanese could simply be cross-cultural misunderstanding. Japanese have a trait of talking and acting in such a way as to maintain the greatest degree of harmony, even if it means not telling the truth. In the case of two Japanese, they both know it is not the truth, but they see it as a way to avoid saying something unpleasant to each other, and both try to maintain the required harmony. (This has been called 'mutually comprehensible deception'.) In other words no Japanese who is functioning within the constraints of his society will look for trouble, especially with foreigners.

Very occasionally, after an over-indulgence in alcohol and xenophobia, a Japanese may verbally attack a foreigner, but it's usually when the booze has diminished his ability to function effectively, so such a man is likely to be nothing more than an annoyance.

If, by the way, things ever get to the physical stage, there are two things to remember. First, usually no one will come to your aid. In Japan one just doesn't get involved in the affairs of anyone other than family or acquaintances. Secondly, if the police are involved, any foreigner present is automatically suspected of being the culprit, and is likely to be arrested even if he is an innocent bystander.

Many of the misunderstandings between Japanese and foreigners is a result of misinformation. Many books and movies present a very distorted view of westerners, especially their sexual habits, so sometimes women travellers get openly propositioned. Usually, ignoring the advance or walking away will be sufficient to discourage the man. Conversely, many western men have an equally distorted view of Asian women and their habits.

Natural Hazards

Japan has many popular swimming beaches and many with dangerous undertows. There are drownings every summer weekend so don't take chances. There are few trained lifeguards so always try to swim with a friend.

Like most countries of the world, Japan has mosquitoes. Not in huge swarms but enough to make it advisable to use insect repellent. Their bites are relatively innocuous but the mosquito season lasts from summer to late November.

There are two kinds of poisonous snakes in Japan, both deadly. All the main islands are the habitat of the mamushi; while the habu is found only on the islands south of Kyushu, between Kagoshima and Okinawa. Like most snakes, they will usually try to escape from people if they are not cornered or startled. Snakes are deaf and although they can feel vibrations in the ground, they cannot hear people's approach in advance, so it's quite easy to be upon one before it has a chance to hide.

The mamushi usually grows to a length of 70 cm or so and has a diamond-shaped head with a moderately thick body covered with a pattern of dark circles with lighter centres. The habu is larger, up to two metres long, and has the stronger venom of the two. It is found in both trees and grass, has a diamond-shaped head and a pattern of diamonds on its body.

Earthquakes

Earthquakes are common throughout Japan. Most quakes are very mild, a mere tremble, and not enough to cause any damage.

The most famous disaster was the Kanto earthquake of 1923 when about 40,000 people were killed in the Tokyo and Kanto area. Buildings of that day were mostly flimsy wooden structures and many of the deaths were the result of fires that followed the quake. All buildings in the Tokyo area must now be built to resist earthquake damage, so an equally strong quake today would probably have a lower death toll despite the vast increase in population.

If you are caught in a strong quake, the best actions to take are: 1 – Do not use elevators. 2 – Stand near a supporting pillar or in a doorway, and far from the centre of the room; the former will be the strongest part of the structure, and the centre of a room is the part most likely to collapse. Ducking under a desk or table is a good second-best, and better than no protection at all from falling debris. 3 – Get outdoors if possible and move as far as possible away from buildings.

Doors

Paling into insignificance as a hazard is the warning that anyone taller than 175 cm must be on constant guard for low doorways. Until recently the Japanese were a very short people and doorways were made to suit. Sliding doors (shoji) seem to have a uniform height of 180 cm and train entrances are also low.

FOOD

Travellers in Japan will encounter few difficulties in finding palatable food at reasonable cost. Western food is available at the large tourist hotels and restaurants in the larger cities, but it will be very expensive and cannot be considered when travelling on a budget. If you want to eat at moderate cost you must eat as the locals do.

Japanese food is not spicy so there is no problem for delicate tongues or stomachs. The weird foods that you may have read about, such as grasshoppers or chocolate-covered ants, are just as strange to the average Japanese as they are to foreigners. Yes, the Japanese do eat raw fish (sashimi), but it must be fresh to be eaten this way. If it seems a strange practice just remember how westerners eat oysters. Sashimi has a weak flavour with no 'fishy' taste or smell. Sushi (raw fish or other ingredient with rice), on the other hand, is very tasty. The only other common food that foreigners may find the thought of repulsive is natto: fermented soybeans that look, smell, taste and feel like something moist that was forgotten on a back shelf for too long.

Some typical Japanese dishes are:
Sashimi: slices of raw fish of various kinds.
Sushi: raw or cooked fish, vegetables, egg, etc, on or in rice.
Tempura: batter-dipped and deep-fried fish and vegetables; of Portuguese origin. (The accent is on the first syllable.)
Sukiyaki: vegetables, meat, shirataki (like vermacelli), soya sauce, sake, sugar, water, tofu (soy bean curd), all cooked together at the table.
Jingis Khan: similar to sukiyaki, but the pot has a dome in the centre surrounded by a trough; the vegetables are cooked in the broth while the meat, which is mutton, is cooking on the dome.
Domburi: a bowl of rice with added chicken, egg, meat, etc.
Okonomiyaki: a type of pancake usually cooked on a griddle at the table by the diners themselves; various ingredients are mixed into the batter, eg shrimp, squid, beef.
Fish is the major source of protein. Beef is outrageously expensive, the result of deliberate and scandalous government policy to protect small and inefficient domestic producers who raise only one or two animals on miniscule plots of land. (This also protects the farmers' votes.) Imported beef is sold and resold among dealers (often without leaving the freezer) until it sells in the shops for the going rate, which is approximately ten times the original purchase price. Similarly, the price of rice is much above the world level because the government buys everything produced at a fixed and high price.

Beef is not a traditional item of the Japanese diet. Until the country was opened to the western barbarians in the 1860s the Buddhist Japanese would have been horrified at the thought of killing an animal so that it could be eaten. The famous Kobe and Matsuzaka beef are a relatively recent innovation in the diet. The meat is tasty and tender (and very,very expensive) but to the eyes of a lean meat eater it is very fatty (marbled).

Unless cooking facilities are limited, Japanese food is served all at once so that you have a full choice at any one time; it doesn't normally arrive in dribs and drabs as in 'western' Japanese restaurants. And those who have sampled Japanese cooking from restaurants in the west will know that the cuisine at such places owes as much to showmanship as to Japanese origins. Food served at an expensive restaurant will be as much a treat for the eye as the tongue. Vegetables are sliced in intricate shapes and everything is decoratively arranged. Of course less pretentious restaurants for budget eaters are much more basic and utilitarian.

Western cutlery is available at most restaurants but it is advisable to know how to use chopsticks. Japanese chopsticks (hashi) are shorter than the Chinese variety. In less expensive restaurants they are usually disposable types, joined together and must be broken apart. (About 350 million pairs of chopsticks are used in Japan each month!)

Using chopsticks

Place first chopstick between base of thumb and top of ring finger. (Bend fingers slightly.)

Hold second chopstick between top of the thumb and tops of middle and index fingers.

Keeping the first chopstick and thumb still, move the other one up and down by middle and index fingers.

Some restaurants in metropolitan areas have menus in English but the majority have listings only in Japanese. Choosing a meal is no great problem however, even though staff rarely understand English. Most restaurants have very realistic wax replicas of various dishes on display, so you can always summon a waitress and point to what looks good.

Typical Japanese cooking centres on a bowl of *gohan* (rice), usually has a bowl of *miso shiru* soup (based on soybeans and a good source of protein), and features one or more kinds of vegetable plus a portion (generally small) of fish or meat. More economical dishes are based on noodles, either *soba* (greyish buckwheat), *ramen* (yellow), or *udon* (white wheat). Semi-western food may be found in many towns. Typical offerings are hamburger steak, macaroni and spaghetti dishes, pilaffs, dorias and gratins, usually with a choice of bread or rice. Interestingly, rice served with such dishes comes on a flat plate and is called *raisu* not gohan.

There are many kinds of specialty restaurants in Japan. Typical is a robata-yaki. Generally rustic in decor, they display the raw materials that are available, like whole fish, potatoes, etc; customers pick out the one they want and it is cooked for them. If you want to visit such a restaurant, it is invaluable to have a Japanese companion.

For simple meals and lunches while on the move, some suggestions include *tempura* and *onigiri*. In most towns there will be a *tempuraya* (tempura shop) with freshly cooked pieces of fish, vegetables, meat (called 'katsu', a corruption of the word 'cutlet') and croquets (potato cakes) on display on trays in the window. They are tasty and filling (if a bit calorie-laden because of the deep-fat frying), and not expensive.

A very traditional food for lunches is onigiri, basically a ball of rice with a piece of fish or vegetable in the centre; the outside is wrapped in a sheet of crisp seaweed. The tastiest is sake salmon.

Japanese pastries rate very well by international standards, according to a pastry lover. But beware of the object that

has every appearance of a jelly donut. It has the same shape, the same colour, the same texture. Many an innocent has bitten into one and been shocked by . . . . . .curry! An only-in-Japan invention. (To ask, the word 'curry' is also used in Japanese.)

Etiquette

It is polite to slurp noodles; it makes them taste better. Otherwise Japanese table manners are not so different from those in the west. Observe other diners and follow their lead, especially when drinking (see below). Sake or beer are often drunk with meals but wine is a comparative newcomer and is not common.

Economy Eating

Nearly all department stores and office buildings have restaurants in the basement and offer reasonable cost meals, especially at lunchtime. You can order individual items, but the cheapest way is to order *teishoku*, the day's set lunch; it will usually be on display. A typical teishoku will have a bowl of rice, miso shiru soup, a plate of vegetables, and meat or fish, salad and dessert.

Near most railway and subway stations, there are usually restaurants of many types such as simple noodle shops where everyone stands, Korean barbecues, semi-western style restaurants, sushi shops, coffee shops (kisaten) and others. Simple meals begin around Y500-600. Places catering mainly to drinkers often prove more costly because each item ordered, such as a skewer of meat, is served and charged for separately, and is regarded more as a snack to accompany drinks than as a meal in itself.

The pizza chains Shakey's and Pizza Hut, as well as Trecca in Kyoto, offer a real bargain between 11 am and 2 pm every day except Sundays and holidays – all the pizza you can eat for a fixed price (about Y500). The nutritional value is suspect, but it's certainly very filling and there's lots of cheese.

For breakfast, most coffee shops offer 'morning service', which includes toast and sometimes an egg for the usual price of a cup of coffee alone. Visitors are always shocked at the price of a cup of coffee at coffee shops, usually Y250-350. The usual excuse for the high cost is that you are paying for the space and the congenial surroundings. You can stay all day for the price of a single cup, and young people often have coffee-shop dates. For just a coffee without the luxurious surroundings, chains like Lotteria can be suggested. Their offering, however. will probably not be as tasty as the selection in the good dedicated coffee shops.

If you have cooking facilities where you're staying, you can economise. Residential neighbourhoods have vegetable, fruit and meat shops, and supermarkets have spread widely since their introduction in the late 1960s. As well as eggs, meat, fish, chicken, vegetables, cheese and milk, etc, you can get a large variety of instant ramen (dried bundles of noodles) that cook in a few minutes. After cooking add the provided seasonings to make a broth. Supermarkets also usually offer a good selection of prepared food such as sushi, tempura (meat, fish, squid, vegetables, etc) and croquets (potato with or without corn, curry, etc).

For those on a super tight budget, bakeries slice the heels off loaves of bread and you can get a bag of them at little or no cost. Peanut butter and jam are available. Jam from Soviet satellite countries is good; probably that from Bulgaria is the best. Much of the domestic product lacks fruit.

For more detailed information, a good inexpensive book is *Eating Cheap in Japan*.

ALCOHOL

Alcoholic beverages of all kinds are expensive in Japan compared with most western countries. At neighbourhood shops beer costs Y215 for a 633 ml bottle, while a 500 ml can from a vending machine costs Y200 or more. Alcoholic drinks of all kinds are sold in local shops without restrictions, and beer, sake and whisky are usually available at almost any eating establishment. Beer is the favourite alcoholic drink in Japan. Japanese beers are well regarded by beer connoisseurs, and are generally brewed in a German or Czech style. Well-known brands are Kirin, Sapporo, Suntory and Asahi.

Imported whiskies and wines are available, especially in larger cities, but there are few bargains. Johnnie Walker Black Label sells for Y5800 and up, nearly always more (760 ml bottle); Red Label costs Y2900 or more. The locally-made Suntory Black Label is said to compare well with imported Scotch and costs less. Brandy and cognac are incredibly expensive in Japan. If you like them or have a Japanese friend who does, be sure to bring it in duty free.

Japanese wines have not reached very high levels of quality and most of the best-known widely advertised brands are very ordinary. It is only in recent years that the Japanese have developed much appreciation of wine and there is no tradition of making or drinking it, so the efforts that have produced high quality beer, sake and whisky haven't yet reached the wine industry. Because of costs in Japan it is said that there is no incentive to make the necessary investments for improved processing facilities and that wines can be imported cheaper. There is a limited selection of wines from many countries on sale in the metropolitan areas; prices are seldom below Y900. The Australian wines selling in this range have been the standard lines of good and reliable quality, but not outstanding, and sell for about double their home price – for Japan that is a remarkably small ratio.

Sake

This is pronounced 'sah-kay', not 'sah-key'. It is the traditional Japanese drink and is very pleasant with Japanese food and on its own. Sake is served hot in small

180 ml flask from which it is poured into tiny cups. The flask, or *tokkuri*, is usually a decorative item made of pottery; it makes a good memento of Japan, along with a set of *sakazuki* – sake cups.

Sake is brewed from a mash of rice that has been cooked with water and fermented, so it is more like beer than wine, except that the alcohol content can be as high as 17% which is more than most wines. It is certainly possible to get drunk on it, but it is not as potent as much folklore would lead one to believe.

There are several grades and types of sake. The highest grade is tokkyu (shu). Next comes ikkyu (shu), then nikyu (shu). Sake from different regions of Japan has different characteristics and tastes, so these designations do not indicate the flavour, only the quality. In addition to the standard types of sake, other types are made like amazake (sweet sake) and otoso (sake with suspended rice solids). They are worth trying; some may be seasonal.

In shops, sake is sold in large 1800 ml bottles, as well as in smaller sizes. The size is a traditional measure called *issho*. At festivals a common sight is a large wooden keg of sake, opened by simply smashing in the lid; the contents are handed out freely in a square wooden box with neatly dovetailed leakproof joints. These boxes are of 180 ml capacity and were the traditional way of measuring granulated solids, like rice, as well as liquids. These boxes (masu) make good souvenirs of Japan; the 180 ml size is called *ichi-go*.

Other drinks

Another alcoholic drink popular these days is *shochu*. It is a distilled liquor made from rice, wheat, sweet potatoes, sugar cane – anything containing sugar that can be fermented.

The Kagoshima area of Kyushu is the shochu capital of Japan, though it is made in many areas. The distillation process is a copy of brandy-making that was introduced by foreign missionaries in the late 1500s,

and shochu was once the beverage of feudal lords and the upper classes.

Earlier this century, shochu was popular throughout Japan, but at the end of the war materials for high quality shochu were not available and bootleggers blended it with anything on hand, including highly poisonous methyl alcohol. From then on it gained a bad reputation as a low-class drink associated with jikitabi (manual labourers nick-named for their split-toed boots) who get blotto on it regularly.

In recent years new processing methods have been introduced so that most of the impurities that cause bad hangovers have been eliminated. Good shochu is little more than alcohol and water, about 25-35% (50-70 proof); the strength will be marked somewhere on the label. The leading brand is Jun ('purity'). It is very low in price, Y590 for a 720 ml bottle, a fraction the cost of whisky.

A popular home-made drink, based on shochu, is *umeshu*, which translates as 'plum wine'. It is made by soaking green, sour plums in shochu to which has been added lots of rock crystal sugar. The process is started in late June or early July and lasts at least three months. The result is delicious but very sweet and potent.

Drinking Customs

When drinking beer, sake, etc, with a Japanese person, the proper etiquette is to fill his glass or cup after he has filled yours. While he is pouring, hold your cup or glass up so that he can fill it more easily. If you don't want anymore, put your hand over the glass. If you are new at the game, a Japanese may think you're unfamiliar with the 'rules' and may fill his own glass. This is normally considered bad manners and the Japanese say te jyaku which means 'who fills his glass with one hand, drains it with the other'; in other words an alcoholic. Before he can pour anything into his glass, take the bottle from him and fill his glass. This may result in a mock fight, but the gesture will be appreciated.

When drinking in company, it is an

honour for the senior person to offer his cup to a guest, then fill it. The guest then rinses the cup and returns it to its owner, and fills it for him. Actually, among the Japanese it is the inferior who offers the cup to his superior, but in the case of visiting foreigners the normal practice may be reversed – or the host may be implying that the guest is the honoured superior.

When drinking with Japanese people, particularly those who are making a good salary, it will be difficult to pay any share of the bill. Customarily one person, often the most senior, will pick up the tab and pay everything. It is necessary to think up some way to repay the favour at a later date.

With students and other people who are not very wealthy, the bill is usually split up according to who had what. As a foreigner you may sometimes have trouble paying for your share, but if you are drinking among friends they will not put up a fuss – it is only strangers who want to give the foreigner a good impression who will insist on paying the whole shot.

Getting drunk is one of the few safety valves open to Japanese to escape the manifold duties and obligations they must continually observe. Because of this, almost any behaviour while drunk is excused. Consequently, hordes of faceless salary men, who show little individuality or personality during working hours, get quite thoroughly smashed quite frequently, sometimes nightly. They sing loudly, sometimes perform dances that can only be described as bawdy, and carry on in a manner quite 'un-Japanese'. Getting drunk is a very popular activity in Japan, and doing it with a group is almost a ritual, helping to cement interpersonal relations with co-workers, etc. Records in China mention that the Japanese were much given to drink at festivals 2000 years ago, so the process has a long history.

Virtually the only (though common) ill-effect of this excess drinking is that many drinkers don't know their limit and cannot hold their liquor (literally). The results of their overindulgence maybe seen on streets, railway platforms and even inside railway cars, especially on Friday and Saturday nights. If you see people avoiding one end of a train car, you can suspect that that is the reason.

Drinking Places

There are two main types of drinking establishments in Japan, those strictly for drinking (usually with music and comfortable surroundings), and those for drinking with pleasant female companionship, ie hostesses.

Bars, pubs and other drinking places range in price from reasonable to astronomical. The appearance of the place does not necessarily give an accurate indication of the prices to be paid. A place that looks expensive probably will be; nightclubs and similar places are guaranteed to take a huge bite out of a wallet. However, looking modest or even rundown is no guarantee that it will be cheap; some simple looking places are extremely expensive, either because of special service, atmosphere, or whatever that appeals to Japanese on huge expense accounts. There are stories of innocent *gaijin* walking into such joints, ordering a single beer and being presented with a bill for Y18,000!

To avoid such over-charging, stand bars are the answer. Many are operated by large companies in the liquor business, like Suntory and Nikka. Otherwise the safest course as soon as you enter an unknown bar is to ask the price of a drink and check if there is a cover charge; some places charge a couple of thousand yen as soon as a customer sits down. A favourite lurk of even better quality places is a dish of peanuts or other nibbles (called a 'charm' in Japanese) that the customer is obliged to pay for at a price equal to a couple of drinks. Foreigners can sometimes get away from this racket by politely indicating that they don't want it and feigning lack of understanding.

Places with hostesses are always going to be much more expensive than those for drinking only. Customers are charged for the time that girls sit with them. Anyone going in only to drink, without benefit of hostess, would probably be unwelcome. Hostesses are part of the Japanese system of male ego-boosting; they flatter and flirt and act as a listening post for the man's frustrations in life. Often these women are available for other outside activities, usually on a paid basis, but sometimes on a purely friendly basis, if she likes the customer. Boye de Mente's book *Bachelor's Japan* gives some specific advice on this topic.

The services offered by hostesses range from sitting opposite the customer and simply pouring his drinks, to sitting on the customer's lap without benefit of undergarments and doing everything. The latter type of place is usually garishly decorated with bright lights (often pink) and are further identified by touts outside who try to entice customers in. Such places are never cheap.

Beer halls are popular and relatively inexpensive places for a drink. They can be recognised partly by the prominent jugs and bottles of beer in the window, although many restaurants also offer beer and have similar window displays; there is often a rather thin line between a restaurant and a beer hall, as both serve food as well as drinks.

Almost any restaurant of any size will offer alcoholic drinks with the meal, particularly beer and sake.

The words for large, medium and small mugs of beer are: *dai, chu* and *sho*.

During the warm months many department stores open beer gardens on the roof, often with live entertainment. Prices are reasonable, the height of the buildings gives relief from the hot air at ground level, and it's a good place to see Japanese having a good time.

For economical drinking, with a simple list of drinks such as sake and beer, and simple decor (sometimes scruffy), invest-igate the 'workingman's nightclub' or *aka chochin*. These are found in many places and almost invariably near stations. The name literally means 'red lantern' which is what will be found outside the establishment to identify it.

PLACES TO STAY

The travel industry is well established in Japan and there is accommodation of almost every type throughout the country. In the big cities, like Tokyo, there are hotels that match the world's best plus a variety of places to stay that range down the price scale. In provincial cities there are usually some facilities with a claim to being comfortable and familiar to westerners; and virtually everywhere there is accommodation of some sort.

For budget travellers the word is that there is absolutely no dirt-cheap accommodation of the kind found in most of the rest of Asia, such as the Chinese hotels, losmen, etc. The cheapest room anywhere will be from about Y1500 per person, per night.

Visitors staying at the luxury-style hotels will no doubt have made reservations before leaving for Japan, so information on them is not really relevant here. Most of the info on the following pages deals with accommodation more in the range of budget travellers.

For the most part there is no listing, in this book, of places to stay in the sections dealing with individual cities because of the sheer bulk of time and work required to obtain and update such listings. An exception is that many youth hostels have been mentioned under their appropriate locations; and there are occasional special listings, such as the historic thatched-roof farmhouses in Shirakawago, that function as minshuku and take guests. After a traveller has been in Japan for a few days, the system of finding a place to stay becomes more familiar.

The Japan National Tourist Organisation (JNTO) has prepared several booklets and brochures on accommodation, which are available from the TICs. One JNTO publication worth mentioning is *Reasonable Accommodations in Japan*, which lists economical places to stay in 26 cities around Japan. 'Reasonable' in this case means Y3500 and up per person. Accommodation charges quoted in Japan nearly always mean 'per person'.

If you arrive in a fair-sized city without having booked accommodation the local railway station usually has an office that can help you find a place to stay, although their listings may not include the least-expensive places available. Some hints are given in the section on ryokan for finding these.

Hotels

Hotels as they are known in the west, with beds, familiar furniture and amenities, can be found in the major cities (especially ones frequented by foreign business people), as well as in popular resort and tourist areas. In smaller centres a 'hotel' is likely to have a mixture of western and Japanese style rooms, with an equal confusion about what is expected in service. The quality of facilities and service in Japan can vary from internationally accepted levels in the major centres to something much less pretentious (but nearly as expensive) in more remote areas.

A good listing of over 250 hotels of international standard, along with nearly 160 ryokan, is contained in the JNTO publication *Hotels and Ryokan in Japan*. The places listed usually have air conditioning or central heating and other modern facilities. Prices for rooms of various sizes are listed along with the contact address and the means of getting there.

Business Hotels

This type of accommodation has appeared in Japan in recent years. It is intended primarily for travelling businessmen who want respectable and clean accommodation without the high cost of luxury hotels. It achieves economy by eliminating frills like room service – each floor has vending machines for drinks, etc. The rooms vary widely in size, but generally tend to be on the small side, with the worst ones being ridiculously cramped. It is worth asking to have a look at the room in advance if you suffer from claustrophobia. Costs vary from Y2000 to Y5000 for a single; doubles cost somewhat more.

At least two books that list business hotels around Japan are available at bookshops. The larger is called *Zenkoku Business Hotel* and the smaller *Mini-mini Zenkoku Business Hotel*. The former lists 1600 BH's around Japan, the latter nearly 620, with 68 in the Tokyo area alone. Both are written only in Japanese so a little work is involved in using it, but it is not difficult to match the kanji of place names on a map with those in the books. Organisation is by ken (prefecture).

Ryokan

To sample the best of Japanese life try to spend at least one night at a ryokan. At its best, the ryokan embodies the finest Japanese hospitality and elegance, providing a simple but flawless traditional Japanese style room with high quality furnishings and the best in food and service. The senses should be pleased or soothed in all ways including visually, so a good ryokan should have a beautiful garden, not necessarily large, but definitely elegant. Unfortunately, there are many places called ryokan that do not live up to such expectations, but if the facilities are of high standard then the time spent there can provide some of the best memories of Japan.

There are 80,000 or so ryokan scattered around Japan. However there are many where foreigners would not particularly want to stay, and others where a foreigner would not be allowed to stay. There are a few reasons why a good ryokan might refuse to accept a foreigner. Some will not let you stay, not because of racism, but because they are very exclusive – even Japanese cannot book into them unless introduced by someone of high enough position who ensures that the visitor is worthy enough of being allowed to stay there. Other ryokan do not want foreigners to stay because of bad experiences in the past with foreigners who didn't know how to behave, didn't understand the system or made demands that the staff were not able to meet. In general Japanese are convinced that their way of life is completely beyond the understanding of foreigners, and that foreigners of any kind will just not fit in. If you can make yourself understood in Japanese many more ryokan will be open to you.

The JNTO has prepared two booklets containing listings of ryokan that are accustomed to or prepared to accept foreign visitors. Titled *Japan Ryokan Guide* (303-E), and *Hotels and Ryokan in Japan* (305-E), they are available from JNTO offices and the TICs in Tokyo and Kyoto. Each booklet has a section giving further details on what a ryokan is like and explaining how a guest should behave. Another booklet *Enjoy Japanese Life at Ryokan* is published by the Japan Ryokan Association, and also describes the features of the ryokan and how to enjoy them. It is available at the Tokyo TIC.

Bookings can be made in every part of the country at any travel agent, especially JTB. Also every railway station of any size has an information office, *ryoko an nai jo*, that has listings of all accommodation in the surrounding vicinity. They can make reservations on the spot, but it is rare to find anyone who can speak English at these offices and remember they don't always list the lowest-priced places. There are usually many ryokan in the vicinity of any major station so if you want to find your own try walking around the area. Look for large numbers of shoes at the entranceway, or entrances that are wide and open, as distinct from the rather secluded entrances to the average private house. People at small tobacco shops or other local businesses can often help in finding a ryokan.

There are combined train and accommodation 'specials' for travel to Kyoto from the Tokyo area, in which the costs of the train and ryokan/hotel are combined into a reduced-price package. The combined cost of Tokyo-Kyoto Shinkansen fare plus one night in an economy ryokan of reasonable quality on a trip that I made, was less than the cost of the normal return Shinkansen fare. Individual travel agents make their own arrangements; the best known to contact for such packages is JTB (Japan Travel Bureau).

Minshuku

Short-time visitors to Japan usually have little opportunity to see the inside of a Japanese house. Even fewer stay overnight. However it is a simple matter to arrange to stay at a minshuku, a family home that takes guests. There are minshuku (pronounced minsh'ku) in every area with tourist attractions, such as historic towns, coastal villages, hot spring resorts, ski areas, etc, operated by local people such as fishermen, farmers and townspeople.

Some minshuku are interesting in themselves and are an actual attraction for visitors. At Shirakawa (Gifu-ken) there are many huge old thatched-roof houses in an isolated valley. Many of them are minshuku and afford the opportunity to spend the night in a very unusual farmhouse, even by Japanese standards, one that may even be a couple of hundred years old.

For travellers not on an absolutely bare-bones budget, minshuku are the best places to stay to gain an impression of what the real Japan is like.

In a minshuku a guest is made to feel like part of the family and it's a unique way to experience the warmth of ordinary Japanese. Foreigners are rare, and you may be the first ever to stay at a particular home. The hosts may have a few misgivings at first because many Japanese have never met or seen a foreigner, but if you can reassure them that you won't use soap in the bathtub then they will relax and there will be no problems. The big problem may be that they are too kind – there are many stories of hosts pouring drinks all evening (at no charge) because of the honour of the visit!

Minshuku are not hotels so there is minimum 'maid service'. Guests may have to make their own beds at night, put the bedding away in the morning and provide their own towels etc.

Charges are relatively uniform throughout Japan, about Y3500 per person, per night including supper and breakfast. It is possible to negotiate a reduction if meals are not required, but they are often local delicacies and it may be one of the few opportunities to sample typical Japanese home cooking.

If you have no knowledge of Japanese but would like to stay at a minshuku you could contact Tescort and ask if any members would be interested in accompanying you on such a trip – at their own expense.

Travellers on their own, however, can easily find a minshuku from a railway station of any size. There is usually an information office, *an nai jo*, with listings of minshuku in the surrounding area. They will phone ahead and make bookings, also giving warning that a foreigner is on the way.

Travellers who begin their excursion from Tokyo can make reservations by computer. There are several offices in Tokyo that can do this, but the most convenient is Travel Nippon, on the 5th floor of the Yurakucho Bldg (near the

TIC), because they speak English. The address is: Travel Nippon, 2-2-1 Yurakucho, Chiyoda-ku, Tokyo. Tel (03) 572-1461; open Monday to Saturday from 9 am to 5 pm.

A very good leaflet in English describing minshuku and how to behave at one (folding bedding, eating, etc) is available from: Japan Minshuku Association, New Pearl Bldg Rm 201, 10-8 Hyakunincho 2-chome, Shinjuku. Tel 371-8120. Accompanying it is a listing of a large number of minshuku in nearly all regions of the country that are better prepared than the average minshuku to take foreign guests; a map shows their general location.

Youth Hostels

Budget-watching travellers in Japan usually stay in Youth Hostels. There are about 520 of them scattered nearly everywhere in Japan that people normally want to go. They are clean and respectable and reasonably priced – by Japanese standards anyway. There is usually no other accommodation at prices as low, although some ryokan and minshuku may be in a similar price range.

To stay at most youth hostels in Japan you need a valid membership card issued by a Youth Hostel association belong to the International Youth Hostel Federation (IYHF). It is best to buy a membership card in your home country, but if this isn't possible, then an International Guest Card (IGC) can be purchased from national headquarters in Tokyo or from the prefectural head office. The price is approximately US$9. Some hostels, detailed below, do not require a YH membership card; a foreign passport is adequate.

The International Guest Card is also available as a replacement in case a card is lost. The purchase price (less Y100) will be refunded, within Japan, after a replacement card has been received from the original issuing office and shown at the Tokyo head office.

Despite the name, there is no age limit on who may use the hostels. There are, however, more regulations than at other types of accommodation. Until recently these regulations included curfew at 9 pm; hostels were closed between 10 am and 3 pm and hostellers were segregated by sex. Some of these restrictions have now been eased. A regulation sleeping sheet is required at nearly every hostel (these can be rented but the cost soon mounts up, so its better to have your own) and only a few hostels permit a sleeping bag to be used.

The best listing of hostels by far is the *(Japan) Youth Hostel Handbook*. Anyone planning to stay at more than a couple of hostels would be well advised to buy it, either by mail or on arrival in the country. It costs Y350 and is written mostly in Japanese, but there is adequate explanation in English and profuse use of symbols so that foreigners can use it easily. It lists every hostel in Japan by district (with maps to show general locations) with a code number and the address in both Japanese and romaji. There is also a detailed map and access information for each hostel, the telephone number (for booking or assistance in finding the hostel), the number of beds, costs of meals and heating, dates when open and the type of hostel.

The YH Handbook is sold by many

hostels around the country and at the national headquarters in Tokyo, a 10 minute walk from Ichigaya (described in the Tokyo section). Hours are 9 am to 5.30 pm on weekdays; and 9 am to 4 pm on Saturdays. It can also be ordered and sent by mail within Japan or overseas.

The national HQ also has a free booklet *Hostelling Way in Japan*. It has much more info on hostel rules, rail fares, a list of hostels with bicycle rentals, distances between cities and much more, but its prices might be out of date.

There is also a free JNTO booklet *Youth Hostels in Japan*. It lists every hostel in the country by region, but it lacks maps for locating them. Only the name is written in Japanese, not the address, which could make it difficult if you need assistance in finding the hostel.

The third and least satisfactory listing of hostels is the *IYHF Handbook Vol II* which lists hostels in Africa, America, Asia and Australasia. This booklet, Y600 in Japan, lists less than half the hostels in Japan, gives no instructions in Japanese, and is not detailed in its description of locations. For travel in Japan it is a waste of money but it might be useful in the other countries it covers.

There are eight types of hostel in Japan: built and managed by the JYHA (51); built privately (107); built with government subsidy – municipal (75); managed by other youth organisations (55); private houses (61); temples (76); shrines (7); and ryokan (144).

As a general rule it is best to avoid JYHA hostels. While they may have the best facilities, too often the staff tend to be unfriendly, officious or even rude. No doubt there are good JYHA hostels and perhaps it's unfair to judge them by a few but given the opportunity it is preferable to stay at other types, especially the temples, shrines, private homes and ryokan. Staff there are usually friendly and the atmosphere relaxed.

Hostellers staying at Buddhist temple hostels may be wakened abruptly at 6.30

am by drumming. This happens at Jofuku-ji, a Zen temple in a particularly beautiful valley on Shikoku island. The priest there speaks English and invites visitors to join in zazen meditation.

As a general rule visitors may use the 75 municipal hostels without having a YH card – a passport is adequate. Useful ones to know about are Hinoyama YH at Shimonoseki (the port for the ferry from Pusan, Korea); and both Nagai YH and Hatttori-Ryokuchi YH at Osaka.

Generally very little English is spoken at any of the hostels or at the head office. If corresponding with the head office, always send International Postage Reply Coupons for the return postage. YH associations everywhere operate on tight budgets and cannot afford to pay return postage.

During the busy seasons (New Year holidays, March, late April to mid-May, July and August) it is advisable to make advance bookings. This is most easily done by computer in Tokyo and Osaka. In Tokyo, booking offices are located at: Keio Dept Store (6th floor), Shinjuku; and Sogo Dept Store-2 basement (near the TIC), Yurakucho. In Osaka you can book at the Sogo Dept Store near Osaka station.

It is necessary to pay a Y200 deposit (credited to the cost of the room) per person, per night, plus a booking fee of Y50. The offices in Tokyo are open daily, except Thursday, from 10 am to 6 pm.

An alternative to computer booking is the use of return postage paid postcards. Blank ones are available from post offices but it's much simpler to use pre-printed ones that have spaces for all the required information. These cost Y80 for ten from the head office. Postage in Japan is Y140.

If you cannot book ahead it will usually be possible to get a bed at most hostels throughout the year with the possible exception of the most popular areas during the school holidays. These areas are around Kyoto/Nara and the resorts, especially those in the mountains. To check on vacancies the simplest way is to telephone a day or two in advance and make a booking. Japanese hostellers usually don't mind making the call for foreigners. Another reason for planning ahead is that some hostels inconveniently take holidays that are not listed in the Handbook.

If you're planning to eat the hostel supper on the first night it is essential to phone ahead, or arrive early enough to permit the cook to prepare the extra food. Hostel meals are nutritionally adequate but very few are gastronomic delights. A typical meal consists of: 1 breaded pork cutlet (fatty); a portion of shredded cabbage; a piece of fish sausage; miso soup; 3 slices of cucumber; 1/8 of a tomato; 8 french fries; 1/3 of a banana; 1 mandarin; 14 pieces of cold macaroni with mayonaise; and as much rice as you can eat.

Many hostels have *jisui* (members cooking), which means that hostellers can have the use of a gas cooker and pots and pans. The gas is usually metered so it can be a contest to try to finish cooking the meal with one 10 yen coin. There is a small charge, Y20-30, for the use of the kitchen.

Staying at youth hostels offers other advantages in addition to the relatively low cost; in particular the opportunity to observe what Japanese homes and people are like. Although the hostels are institutional in nature, and many buildings are modern structures with not a hint of Japanese tradition in them, many others are like enlargements of the traditional Japanese house. They may have the soft tatami mat floors, sliding shoji doors and many typical architectural details. The bath will be like than of an average home (though probably larger) and hostellers sleep on mats laid out on the tatami. The modern buildings usually have furniture to match and western-style bunk beds.

Staying at hostels also provides the chance to meet a number of young Japanese and find out what makes them tick. While few can converse in depth in foreign languages, it is usually possible to carry on simple conversations with them. One feature immediately noticeable to westerners is the general lack of social mingling of the sexes. To overcome this shyness there may be a 'meeting', the Japanese word used to describe an hour-long get together in the evening. This can include a talk about the attractions of the nearby area, transport facilities, etc, followed by party games which serve the purpose of breaking down the barriers of shyness. Most westerners opt out, unless dragged into attending, as it is all in Japanese and often childish. During the summer there are often unscheduled and informal activities like bonfires, fireworks, playing traditional games, or dancing to the music of a portable cassette player.

Most hostels are goldmines of information on attractions in the surrounding area. There are usually bulletin boards covered with train, bus and boat schedules and other useful info. Usually it's all in Japanese but you should be able to get some help in deciphering it.

Virtually all hostels have posted rules and hours for eating, bathing, lights out and getting up. At busy hostels these are usually rigidly adhered to, but during the off-season or when there are few people staying there, the rules may be greatly relaxed especially for foreigners, who often receive deferential treatment everywhere in Japan.

In recent years several rules have been relaxed at the 75 or so municipal hostels: curfew has been extended from 9 pm to 10.30 pm, with lights out at 11 pm. A radical departure from the past is that alcohol is allowed in some hostels as long as the drinkers don't disturb other guests. Whenever possible, married couples will be given rooms together in these hostels. The curfew is no hardship, by the way, except in large metropolitan areas, as Japanese towns go to sleep early.

Bathing usually has its rules too. At some hostels you can take a bath at any time during the evening, while at others you may not use the bath outside the prescribed hours even though the tub is sitting unused and full of water that will go to waste. It is almost impossible to take a bath or shower in the morning. To do so would run counter to centuries of tradition.

Being public institutions, municipally-owned hostels often have magnificent locations on prime real estate. Hinoyama YH at Shimonoseki commands a superb view of the Kanmon Strait, which separates Honshu from Kyushu, and the graceful suspension bridge which spans the gap. And Ura-Bandai YH (1606-Tohoku) is only a short distance from an emerald-green lake and numerous other smaller ponds of similar intense colour. It also features a good view of the jagged top of Mt Bandai. There are many other hostels around the country with equally fine settings.

If you stay in a hostel where you must share a room with Japanese hostellers you may find you have to fight a guerilla action to get a window open for fresh air during the night, even in mid-summer. There seems to be a perpetuation of the idea held in medieval Europe that night air is somehow dangerous and must be shut out at all costs, even on a hot night in a small eight-bunk room. The modern hostels with solid concrete walls and close-fitting doors and windows are the worst in this respect. The older, more traditional buildings are sufficiently draughty so that this is not so much of a problem (though they're also cooler in winter!).

Another possible inconvenience is the noise of other hostellers which may keep you awake at night or wake you very early in the morning. The polite way to ask them to be quiet is to say: *Shizuka-ni sh'te kudasai*; or for a much stronger effect just say: *shizuka-ni shiro!* in a firm tone.

Pensions

The word 'pension' has been borrowed from the French and in Japan refers to accommodation in a somewhat rustic lodge-type building. There is a strong association with sports and they are usually located in fairly remote country areas. Many are situated near ski slopes and may have other sporting facilities like boating, swimming, tennis, walking trails, table tennis, cycling and so on.

Pensions are generally operated by younger people so the spirit is more open and unrestricted than youth hostels, while the facilities are more elaborate and luxurious than those of a minshuku and more homey than a hotel. Prices are higher than those of a minshuku: the cheapest are about Y3400/5400/7900 for single/double/triple plus Y1500 for dinner; while more expensive ones run up to Y5200/7200/9700.

The pension idea has only been operating in Japan since about 1973, but there are already more than 200 around the country, from southern Kyushu to Tohoku. The pensions are not especially set up for foreign guests, but anyone with a sense of fun and adaptability will be able to get by and enjoy the features offered.

Pensions are listed, often with photos or sketches, in a book called *Japan Pension Guide* (revised annually), which is available at bookshops for about Y700. It is written only in Japanese but you should be able to understand the important features – like price. In addition the TICs in Tokyo and Kyoto can give further information and assistance. Bookings can be made by calling the following offices, (the help of a Japanese-speaking friend will probably be needed): Tokyo (03) 295-6333; Osaka (06) 448-2641; Sendai (0222) 65-0534; Fukuoka (092) 471-7555.

Temples

Many Buddhist temples can accommodate visitors overnight and at some of these you may participate in prayer and religious observations such as zazen meditation. At others the accommodation can be regarded just as a room – usually traditional tatami style – that happens to be on temple grounds. Most temples are very graceful structures, representative of what foreigners think of as the traditional Japan, so it is a good idea to stay at a temple at least once during a visit to Japan.

It is easy to find a temple that accepts guests; at least 75 function as youth hostels (along with their religious purposes of course) and they're all listed in the YH Handbook with a symbol. A few temples are modern concrete structures that lack the grace of the traditional wooden temple buildings which embody the finest skills in Japanese woodworking. In the following, the temples with numbers in brackets are those in the YH Handbook.

Many temples are quite historic. *Zuiryuji* (3207, Takaoka) is about 350 years old and has several large buildings. Other temples are set in beautiful surroundings, such as *Jofukuji* on Shikoku (7404) which is on a hillside overlooking a valley. Jofukuji is a Zen temple and one of the young priests speaks good English and invites his guests to join in zazen meditation. Because it is a 'family' temple it is small, and no advance arrangements need to be made to stay overnight, though a phone call in advance would be prudent, as with any hostel.

There are five temples in the Kyoto area that accept lodgers. They are: *Enryaku-ji* on Mt Hei – the number one temple of the Tendai sect, with a history of 1200 years; *Myoren-ji* – noted for its beautiful garden; *Komyo-ji Shukubo, Daishin-in* – a former detached palace of the emperor Hanazono that was later rebuilt as a Zen temple; and *Inari Taisha Sanshuden*. The last named is actually a shrine, not a temple, and is the most important of the many Inari shrines in Japan. It is noted for its more than 1400 torii gates that have been placed along paths that wind up the mountain.

The prices (accommodation only) range from Y1500 to Y3500. Some offer meals as well. To stay at any of these temples, it is best to make arrangements through the TIC in Kyoto. They will also give any information that may be necessary.

In the area around Koya-san (reasonably close to Nara) there are more than 50 temple lodgings available, virtually covering the mountain. Koya-san is very important in the Buddhist history of Japan and is very popular with pilgrims so accommodation may be hard to obtain. Costs are Y4500 and up, with two meals. Reservations can be made through the JTB, or through the Koyasan Tourist Association, Koyasan, Koya-machi, Into-gun, Wakayama-ken. Tel (07365) 6-2616.

Cycling Inns

There is a small network of cycling inns which have been set up specifically for bicycle travellers, both those on their own bikes and those who rent bikes at the inns. The facilities and costs are similar to those at the youth hostels, except there is usually a workshop for bike repairs as well. The buildings are all new within the last few years and the aim is to eventually have one every 100 km or so; at the moment there is about 20 of them.

The inns have been built in regions of natural beauty that invite exploration by bike; often there are specially constructed cycle paths that are separate from regular highways. In many cases it would be worth a trip to the area for sightseeing. Rental charges are reasonable, from as low as Y200 for four hours plus Y50 per additional hour, to a maximum of Y250 per hour.

Information about locations and bike rentals can be obtained from a booklet issued by the Japan Cycling Association called *sai-ku-ring-gu te-mi-na-ru* ('cycling terminal'). Although it is in Japanese only, approximate locations are shown on a sketch map at the front. Detailed addresses and specific information on how to get there from the nearest railway station is given with the description of each inn and its facilities. Copies can be obtained from the JCA. It may be easier to contact the Japan Bicycle Promotion Institute first as they have English-speaking staff who can give info and assistance. Write to: Mr H. Konno or Mr H. Ise, Japan Bicycle Promotion Institute, Nihon Jitensha Kaikan Bldg, 9-3 Akasaka 1-chome, Minato-ku, Tokyo. Tel 583-5444.

Kokumin Shukusha (People's Lodgings)

People's Lodgings are accommodation and recreation facilities in a number of popular resort and natural park areas throughout Japan. They have been built by local authorities under the guidance of the Ministry of Health and Welfare as a means of bringing a vacation in attractive surroundings within the reach of most Japanese. The room charge of about Y3400 a night with two meals is lower than that of most ryokan.

The Lodgings are open to anyone, Japanese or foreigners, and no membership in any organisation is required. During the summer and busy travel seasons, they tend to be fully booked, or it may be necessary to share a room. Otherwise, anyone showing up at the door will be given a room and couples will be put together if possible.

Bookings are most easily made through JTB which issues vouchers for reserved rooms, but this system is in effect for only about 70 per cent of the Lodgings and it takes about a week. Bookings can also be made privately by mail or phone, provided you can speak or write Japanese. The TICs have a complete listing of all Lodgings in Japan; it runs to several pages and is not a published booklet, so it is necessary to inquire in person.

Kokumin Kyukamura

These 'Vacation Villages' are intended mainly for stays of several days for workers who want a quiet, relaxing rest. They are primarily in quiet locations, sometimes near famous resort or sight-seeing areas, sometimes in rather remote regions. There are 27 throughout Japan; 19 have camping grounds with good facilities and about half have sporting facilities. Rates run from Y1500 per person for room only. Usually two or more different menus are available at different prices.

The Villages haven't been used much by foreigners and there is no quick booking system available. There is an office in Tokyo, but the simplest way is to go to the Tokyo TIC, explain your travel plans, and ask their advice.

Seishonen Ryokamura

This 'Youth Village' program, which began in the late 1960s, would provide a good way to see Japanese life in the more remote areas as all 50 or so villages are located in fairly isolated parts of the country. They are situated in actual villages or towns (or nearby) that have been losing population and are in danger of becoming ghost towns.

Often there is a central lodge plus a very simple camping ground. Rates are similar to those of minshuku, Y3500-400 with two meals.

As with Vacation Villages it would be best for any foreigner who is interested in staying at a Youth Village to contact the TIC in Tokyo and discuss travel plans. They can make suitable recommendations and suggestions. Staff at the TIC warn that hosts at the Youth Villages are not familiar with foreigners, so a little knowledge of Japanese would be useful.

Camping

Camping has not caught on in Japan to the same extent that it has in western countries, because there isn't the same reliance on car transport, but the number of camping grounds is increasing yearly. The JNTO publication *Camping in Japan* is an excellent list of camping grounds and is available from the TICs in Tokyo and Kyoto.

Camping facilities vary from spartan to ultra-elaborate, with prices to match. Some have only tent sites and a source of fresh water, while others have bungalows and cottages as well. Most grounds are open only in July and August. In Japan summer is, by definition, only those two months, even though the weather is warm through June, all through September and often well into October.

Many young Japanese set up their tents in almost any open space in the country. This is forbidden in national parks and the intensive cultivation of land makes it difficult to find open and flat space in many areas, but tents in vacant fields are a common sight. Probably the campers ask permission before setting up camp; this could be a problem for someone not able to speak Japanese.

Love Hotels

There is one other type of public accommodation available throughout Japan, but due to its very nature it gets much less promotion as a 'place to stay' than the more socially acceptable ryokan and minshuku etc. This is the Love Hotel. The Japanese usually refer to it as 'Abec Hoteru', 'abec' being the closest pronunciation possible to 'avec' the French word for 'with'. These places rent rooms for short periods but they may be used purely as overnight accommodation, as long as you are aware of their peculiarities.

The busy period is during the day and the early evening; business generally begins to slacken off in the later evening, and they will usually rent rooms for the night for little more than the short-term charge of earlier in the day. So if you can wait until quite late in the evening you can obtain quarters that are usually comfortable and clean (though perhaps a trifle over-decorated) at a cost of about Y5000-5500 a single. You will probably have to vacate the room quite early in the morning though or it may be necessary to pay the hourly rate for every hour of extra sleep-in.

Many love hotels have facilities rather out of the ordinary, such as floor-to-ceiling mirrors, often with a mirrored ceiling too, for good measure. The decor may resemble the harem of a sultan or other equally lush and plush places. A common feature is a colour videotape recorder for instant replay of the action.

Once you learn to recognise the word 'hoteru' in Japanese you will find them everywhere. Outside a sign usually shows two prices – one for a 'rest' (gokyukei), about one hour; the other for a 'stay' (goshukuhaku), which normally means overnight. The price is quoted for one room, not per person as is the case at most other types of accommodation.

Entry to the 'hoteru' is the ultimate in discretion. After passing through a narrow entrance, the customers can no longer be seen from the street and usually the person admitting them is out of sight behind a curtain. After the use of the room, the fee is paid to an anonymous hand. One never sees the staff and supposedly vice-versa. Customers never see each other either by the way, as each room has a separate entrance for maximum privacy. Outside the cities there are also 'moteru' for the motorised trade. While Japan does have motels of the kind found in western countries, the majority are of the variety just described. There is usually no mistaking one type from the other, as the exteriors of love hotels and

motels are often the ultimate in bad taste, with garish pink neon signs bordering the roof, flashing signs and outlandish architecture. There is one the shape of a ship, while another in the Gotanda section of Tokyo is known throughout the country for its pseudo-feudal castle architecture, complete with turrets and other gewgaws.

Servas

Travellers who are sincerely interested in meeting Japanese families and interacting with them have the opportunity to stay in Japanese homes free of charge, through the international organisation Servas. As described earlier in this book, the program should not be looked on as a cheap way to travel, as people who stay with families are expected to participate in some aspects of daily life.

Communes

There are several communes scattered around Japan, some of which welcome guests. These are described under the section on Meeting the Japanese.

House Hunting

For those who plan to remain in Japan for a considerable period of time and who wish to have their own accommodation, here are some tips and general information on house hunting in Japan.

Costs

Housing in Tokyo and other metropolitan areas is very expensive; in smaller places prices are considerably lower. In the metropolitan areas, a single room about three metres square, may be found for less than Y20,000 a month, but any reasonable accommodation (solo) with a minimum of facilities (kitchen with sink, gas outlet, bath/shower, toilet) and close to central Tokyo, will usually cost at least Y40,000 or more like Y50,000-60,000. Places with a shared toilet and bath are less expensive and there are some bargains to be found if you can spend a long time looking. These prices refer to normal 'everyday Japanese' accommodation; for apartments and houses comparable in size and facilities to those found in the USA, Canada or Australia, the rents are astronomical – from Y250,000 up to Y2 million a month.

Room sizes are measured by the number of tatami mats that do or could fit. There are actually at least three 'standard' sizes of tatami in use in Japan but one mat is roughly a metre wide and two metres long. A small room is three mats (san-jo); a medium one is 4½ mats (yo-ji han); and a large one is six mats (roku-jo). Larger rooms do exist but are not common. Room types are listed as either Japanese-style (wa), with tatami; or western-style (yo), with a concrete or wooden floor, probably carpeted. In Japanese language listings, it is common to see abbreviations such as 2LD, 3LDK, etc. the digit is the number of rooms, 'L' is living room, 'D' is dining room, and 'K' is kitchen.

Apartment buildings and concrete houses have higher rentals than wooden buildings because of the greater comfort, strength and earthquake resistance.

It is usually necessary to have a bundle of money on hand before moving into your own accommodation. First, there is one (or more) months' rent in advance; second, there is a deposit (Shikikin) of one to four months' rent, refundable when leaving – minus the cost of any repairs; and third, there is 'key money' (rekin), which is nothing but a bribe to get the place. Rekin is commonly two months' rent, occasionally one, and rarely none. This money is not returned. Fourth, there is frequently a maintenance fee, which may vary from a reasonable Y1000-3000 per month to Y10,000 at the more ritzy addresses. Finally there are separate charges for gas, water, electricity and telephone – all of which are expensive. Telephone installation charges are high compared with North American rates.

Location

Tokyo is a huge city and, despite quick train service, commuting long distances

can waste a lot of time. Remember though, that express service can make a place further out of the city a better choice than one closer to the centre of town. After settling into a job or routine and stabilizing your activities, ask others about the best or preferable residential areas so as to make the most of your position. In Tokyo for example, everyone wants to live in Roppongi/Azabu because they are close to downtown and the area has the brightest of night lights. The Hiroo and Shibuya areas are well-regarded, while Ebisu, Gotanda and other areas can be equally convenient and less expensive, even if they're not quite as fashionable. Check access to subways, JNR lines or bus lines (but remember that buses don't run after 9 pm).

Finding Accommodation

After deciding on one or two areas of interest, the next step is to find listings of places available. The most common ways are agencies, newspaper ads, bulletin boards and word of mouth.

Near almost every railway station, and elsewhere in most districts, are rental agencies (fudosanya) with listings of apartments, houses and rooms for rent in that district. The agent (fudosanya-san) will ask about the type of accommodation required, number and sizes of rooms and any other feature desired, then will prepare a list of places that might be suitable, taking clients to see them until one is found that is satisfactory. His charge for each placement is usually one months' rent. Add this to all the other charges listed earlier and you may have to lay out seven months' rent before moving in. Fudosanya-san rarely speak much English except for the ones who look like used car salesmen and specialise in the horrendously expensive rental market catering to foreign executives on large living allowances.

Newspaper advertisements for accommodation are usually for high-priced executive-style places, but occasionally there are reasonably priced ones. Newspaper ads appear daily but the *Japan Times* on Friday has the most comprehensive Tokyo listings.

Bulletin boards may have ads for apartments, houses, rooms, sub-lets, 'house-sitting' arrangements or shared accommodation. Look for them at supermarkets in areas with a large foreign population, or at the Tokyo TIC, Com'inn and International 3F Club.

In large cities there are usually regular English-language news-sheets that may have listings of apartments, etc. The *Tokyo Weekender* and *Tokyo Journal* have sizeable sections of classified ads including accommodation. Occasionally there are some moderately-priced apartments listed by their owners (so there is no agent's fee).

Getting There

BY AIR

There are eight international ports of entry by air into Japan: Tokyo, Niigata, Nagoya, Osaka, Fukuoka, Kumamoto, Kagoshima and Naha. The first four are on Honshu, the main island, the last is on Okinawa, far to the south of the main islands, and the rest are on Kyushu, the southernmost of the four major islands.

Tokyo

Tokyo has the largest number of international flights but nearly all go to Narita airport, nearly 60 km out in the country. Getting into central Tokyo from there takes an absolute minimum of 1½ hours. (Further details are given in the Tokyo chapter.) The only international airline to fly into convenient Haneda airport is China Airlines; most domestic flights use Haneda.

Niigata

Niigata, on the north coast almost due north of Tokyo, is the port of entry from Khabarovsk (USSR) for travellers using the Trans-Siberian railway or Aeroflot route from Europe. Only about a third of the passengers from Europe are able to get bookings on the ship from Nakhodka to Yokohama, and the rest must fly into Niigata. The city is easily reached by bus from the airport. Niigata is linked to Tokyo by JNR train in about 4½ hours (by the fastest express).

Nagoya

Nagoya, near the middle of the country, is connected with Hong Kong, Seoul and Manila. The airport is about half an hour away from Nagoya station by regular airport bus. The station is a stop for all Shinkansen (bullet) trains and there are bus services east to Tokyo and west to Kyoto and Osaka. Nagoya itself is a commercial city with little of interest to tourists, but there are many attractions within easy reach, so it is a starting point worth considering.

Osaka

Osaka is a good starting point for travel in Japan, as it is close to Kyoto, the premier tourist attraction city in the country; and the trip from the airport is short and simple. Buses from the airport go to various destinations, including Kyoto and the Osaka station area; from Osaka station it is a short trip to Shin-Osaka station, one of the major stations of the Shinkansen which offers rapid connections well to the north of Tokyo and as far west as Fukuoka, in northern Kyushu.

There are flights to Osaka from Los Angeles, Hong Kong, Singapore, Bangkok, Seoul, Manila, Kuala Lumpur and Taipei.

Fukuoka

Travellers from Antwerp, Brussels, Hong Kong, Seoul, Pusan and Taipei can use Fukuoka (in Kyushu) as a convenient entry point. From there it is easy to circle around Kyushu, then carry on through western Japan to Kyoto, Tokyo, etc. Fukuoka is the western terminus of the Shinkansen. There is a frequent bus service between the airport and Hakata station. (The station is named Hakata after the city where it is located, across a river from Fukuoka.)

Kumamoto

The rather provincial city of Kumamoto is linked to points in Korea. It is a gateway to the volcano Mt Aso, and Nagasaki is not far away in the opposite direction. A circle around the rest of Kyushu can easily be arranged.

Kagoshima

This is the southernmost city in the main islands and has several places of interest in and around the city. There is regular bus service between the airport and Nishi-Kagoshima, the main station of the city. From here you can travel up through Kyushu, seeing virtually everything of interest without backtracking. Flights link Kagoshima with Hong Kong, Nauru, Ponape, Seoul and Singapore.

Naha

The major city of Okinawa, Naha is a good starting point for exploring the numerous islands to the south of Kyushu. There are many flights from Naha to a number of cities on the main islands, as well as boat connections to several cities, like Tokyo, Osaka, Kobe, Kagoshima and Hakata.

AIR FARES

Fares change every day, but the following are an indication of what was available at the time of writing. The cheapest fares are always those offered by cut-price agents, not the 'official' fares which the airlines themselves will quote.

From Europe

Among the larger London discounters, such as Trailfinders, there are fares from around £350 one-way to Tokyo. If you want to go via Hong Kong, you can get there for around £250 in the low season and fly Hong Kong to Tokyo for around £150, possibly less if you buy the ticket in Hong Kong.

From other parts of Europe there are the usual Apex (advance purchase) tickets, with prices varying with the season. There are also a lot of cheaper deals to be had if you shop around in person, especially in Amsterdam (try the area around the Dam Square), Brussels and Zurich. London is still, however, the European centre for cheap tickets.

From Australia & New Zealand

There are no great bargains here, even Apex tickets are relatively costly. An Apex return costs about A$998 (or A$670 o/w) from Melbourne or Sydney; and NZ$1844 return (NZ$943 o/w) from Auckland.

Open tickets that offer Tokyo as a stop-over seem to be the better deal. The open one-way ticket Melbourne-Singapore-Bangkok-Hong Kong-Taipei-Tokyo-Seattle costs A$980 – or an extra A$75 to fly on to Dallas. JAL offer a Melbourne-Tokyo-London return for about A$1530 (low season).

From Asia

Discounting is alive and well in Hong Kong and Singapore, but Bangkok, once the discount capital, has become less attractive for bargain hunters. From Hong Kong you can fly to Tokyo for around HK$1000 (about US$130). There are also cheap deals available from Singapore and Penang in Malaysia.

From the USA

Cheap fares to Asia are now fairly readily available from the US, check the travel supplements in Sunday papers for adverts. Typical fares to Tokyo from Los Angeles are around US£330 one-way; or US$275 from Honolulu. If you are going on to other parts of Asia you may get the best deal with a ticket to say Hong Kong or Bangkok via Japan. Cheap deals are also available from New York.

Round-the-World Tickets

Special fares which may be worth considering are round-the-world (RTW) tickets, many of which go via Hong Kong, Tokyo or other points in the region. These tickets are generally offered by two airlines who combine their routes to offer a complete circuit of the globe. The deal varies from airline to airline but usually the ticket permits you to fly anywhere along the two airlines routes so long as you keep moving in the same direction. Usually there are restrictions as to the life of the ticket (you must complete your travel in a year, for example) and the number of stopovers you are permitted. Sometimes the first flight has to be firmly booked in advance but usually you can make other flight plans as you go along. These tickets offer many of the advantages of a multi-stop full fare ticket but at a much lower price.

Curiously RTW tickets are not widely marketed or available in the US, although a number of US airlines play a role in them. There are so many different tickets and so many variations that it's wise to consult a travel agent. Round-the-world tickets typically cost about US$2000 if travel is all in the northern hemisphere. Tickets that dip down into the southern hemisphere (ie include Australia on their routing) typically cost about US$500 more.

An alternative to these airline administered RTW ticket is one simply fixed up by a travel agent specialising in discount tickets. A London agent, for example, could combine a cheap fare from London to the US West Coast with a second fare from there to Tokyo and a third from Tokyo back to the UK. This could easily undercut the cost of an airline RTW ticket.

BY SEA

There are no longer any regular passenger liner services between Japan and countries of Europe, North America, etc. Cruise ships stop occasionally, but even these have been coming less frequently in recent years. The main ports for them are Yokohama and Kobe, and visitors on ships that stop at both can leave the ship at one and rejoin it at the other.

For cruise passengers with one or two nights in the Yokohama-Tokyo area, suggested places to visit are Nikko,

Kamakura and Tokyo. If your ship calls at Kobe next, you can travel from Tokyo to Kyoto by Shinkansen train, catch a glimpse of Mt Fuji, tour Kyoto for a while, then go on to Kobe to rejoin your ship.

Apart from cruise ships there are a few cargo ships sailing the Pacific that take passengers. Most prefer to take passengers for the entire trip, to the final destination, so it may be harder to get a booking to Japan on a ship going to other ports. The best advice is to find a capable travel agent who can find a freighter that will be going to Japan. Fares vary enormously but usually even the cheapest will be considerably more expensive than flying.

Nakhodka & the Trans-Siberian

The only regular passenger service to Japan (apart from the ferry service to/ from Korea) is operated by the Soviet-owned Far East Shipping Line, between Nakhodka (east coast of the USSR) and Yokohama (near Tokyo). The frequency of service has decreased considerably over the past few years, and a single ship is now used for virtually all sailings. The 1985 schedule is probably typical of sailings for the next few years: two sailings per month in March, April and October; three in September; four from May through August; and an extra sailing by a second ship in July over the route Nakhodka-Yokohama-Hong Kong-Yokohama-Nakhodka. The ships take 51 hours from Nakhodka to Yokohama, 54 hours the other way. The bad news is that less than a third of the passengers reaching Nakhodka by rail or air are able to obtain bookings on the ship; the rest must fly to Niigata. The Trans-Siberian sector is typically nine days travelling between Moscow and Nakhodka with a break at Khabarovsk and Irkutsk.

Almost all travellers have had good comments on the ship service and most have been satisfied by the Trans-Siberian rail trip.

The representatives of the company are United Orient Shipping and Agency Co. in

Tokyo (tel 475-2841/3). Information is also available from the Japan-Soviet Tourist Bureau in Tokyo (tel 432-6161), Osaka (tel 531-7416), and Nagoya (tel 263-4990). The Tokyo TIC usually has a leaflet giving more details and directions for getting to the Tokyo representative office.

Korea

There is a thrice-weekly (each direction) ferry service between Shimonoseki (at the far west of Honshu) and Pusan in Korea. The Kampu ferry is the least expensive way of getting from Korea to Japan, the lowest fare is Y8000. Further details of the ferry are given in the section on Shimonoseki and the TIC in Tokyo has a handout information sheet with complete details.

Many people want to go between Tokyo and Seoul to renew visas. The cheapest way to do this is by a lengthy trip by train or train and boat to Shimonoseki, ferry to Pusan, and train or bus from there to Seoul and back. Unless you are desperate to save every last yen, you should consider flying directly between Tokyo and Seoul; the three-day excursion fare is only about Y10,000 more than the combined surface fares, and is one heck of a lot more convenient. In addition, the horror stories of Immigration officials in Shimonoseki (well-founded) make it advisable to bypass that as a point of entry unless the traveller has lots of money on hand when entering Japan.

Taiwan

There is a weekly boat service from Keelung, in northern Taiwan, to Naha on Okinawa, departing Keelung at the beginning of the week. There is also a boat every two weeks from Takao (Taiwan) to Naha, leaving Takao near the middle of the week. The latter boat continues to Osaka. Services from Naha to Taiwan are detailed in the section covering Okinawa.

Getting Around

Japan has an excellent public transport system in most areas. This chapter summarises what is available but cannot give complete details of every train as there are more than 28,000 a day throughout the country. Sources of further information for the traveller are mentioned where appropriate.

JIKOKUHYO

The single most useful book for travel in Japan by public transport is the *Jikokuhyo* – or 'book of timetables'. This invaluable publication runs to well over 700 pages with timetables for every form of scheduled transport in Japan – trains, buses, planes, ferries, even cable cars. If there were scheduled stage coaches, they'd be listed too.

There are several editions on sale, some large, some small. The recommended one is the large size ('oki-jikokuhyo') because its maps are more detailed and it has information on bus lines and ferries, which the small ones do not. It is issued monthly, costs about Y700, and is available from any news stand or bookstore. The entire book is written only in Japanese, but even if you can't read a single Japanese character you can still use it quite easily.

There is a version with some English, identified on the cover as *JTB'S Mini-Timetable* but, while its publication is a

kind and appreciated gesture, the book only lists long-distance ferries (and no local services between adjacent islands); the few expressway buses (but none of the large number of services found through so much of the country); express train services (but no local trains); and airlines. The English extends basically to the romanisation of the names of major places on the maps and the major cities in the actual timetables. For short or simple journeys it should be adequate, but for extensive independent travels you should learn how to use the large Japanese version.

The secret to using the all-Japanese version lies in the maps at the front of the book, which show the entire country region by region. Note that the maps are distorted to fit the pages and that north is somewhere off to the right. All but the last map show surface transportation; the last shows air connections. JNR Shinkansen (super express) trains are shown by a red line of alternating solid and hollow sections while main JNR lines are shown in solid black, and JNR local lines are solid light blue. Private railway lines are shown by a narrow black line with crossbars. Expressway buses are shown by a hollow red line; JNR bus routes on ordinary roads are shown as hollow blue lines; and private bus services are represented by a narrow blue line. A cable car or funicular railway looks like a stretched coil spring; and a ferry is indicated by a thin red line, except for the Hakodate-Aomori run (operated by JNR) which is a broken black line. The availability of rental cars near a station is shown by a red car symbol. A cable car system, with gondolas suspended from cables, is known as a 'ropeway'; and a funicular railway is a 'keburu' (cable).

Areas of touristic interest are shaded green and have a number in green that corresponds to a brief description (in

Japanese) at the top and bottom of the page.

The key to using these maps is the number (sometimes with a letter) written in red beside the transportation line. The number refers to the page which has the timetable for that service; the letter, if any, refers to the section of the page. It's that simple.

Although all place names are written only in kanji (Japanese characters), it is easy to match the names of large cities with the names printed in romaji on other maps. There is a commercial railway map available with the name of every major station printed in romaji.

Following the maps of various sections of the country are maps detailing the transport facilities in and around Osaka, Nagoya and Tokyo. The final map represents all air services within Japan; the name of the major cities is in a circle and air connections are shown by a straight line drawn to the name of the other city. The colour of the line corresponds to the airline, the names of which are all in Roman letters (eg JAL, ANA, etc). Beside the name of the linked city is a number that corresponds to the sub-section of the airlines section of the book (located at the very end of the final section). City names are in kanji only.

The book is broken up into about 20 sections, with bits of information and advertisements scattered among them. In a typical issue (they don't change much in format), the first section gives schedules for Shinkansen, 'L' Limited Express (tokkyu) and sleeper services. The second section shows the most convenient connections for the fastest service over long distances, eg Tokyo-Nagasaki, or Sapporo-Tokyo. Sections 3-18 give the schedule of all intercity services, line by line. Section 19 gives the schedule of all JNR lines operating in the Tokyo-Kawasaki-Yokohama and Osaka-Kyoto-Kobe metropolitan areas. Section 20 is a great catch-all of everything else: JNR fare information; JNR highway (express) buses; private trans-

portation of all types (railways, buses, ferries, cable cars), region by region; boat services to and around Okinawa and other southern islands and bus services on the islands; long distance ferry connections; excursion and sightseeing bus tours; and airlines (domestic).

INTER-CITY PUBLIC TRANSPORT TRAINS

The railway network in Japan is by far the best in Asia and can be ranked among the most comprehensive in the world. Trains in Japan are punctual, range in frequency from adequate to amazing, and in speed from pokey to phenomenal. They include the famed Shinkansen super-expresses (bullet trains), among the fastest scheduled trains in the world. Fares are not cheap, but not exorbitant.

There are both government-operated (JNR) and privately-owned railways that carry passengers in Japan. The government system provides long distance service throughout the country, as well as services around the cities of Tokyo and Osaka. The private lines usually run only comparatively short distances – up to 100 km or so – and are usually regarded as commuter lines. Some private lines run to nearby resort areas. An exception are the private lines in the Kinki district which provide the fastest, cheapest and most convenient services. The private lines are discussed in more detail in the section covering intra-city transport.

Stations are usually close to the centre of a city, except in Tokyo where stations of private lines are spread around the periphery of the city and are linked by the Yamanote loop line.

Japanese National Railways (JNR)

The government-operated railway is called JNR in English, but most Japanese know it only as *kokutetsu; koku* means 'country' or 'national' and *tetsu* means 'line'.

Fares are calculated by distance and the class of service. There is a base fare from point A to point B, to which are added surcharges for the various types of expresses, seat reservation charge, 'Greensha' (first class) and sleeper/roomette.

The JNTO booklet *The Tourist's Handbook* can be useful for buying tickets as it has English and Japanese phrases written in the format of an order form.

There are more than 28,000 trains every day throughout Japan, and in *Jikokuhyo*, JNR train schedules fill more than 320 pages! There is a summary of services printed in English, and given out free by the JNTO, called *Condensed Railway Timetable* (407-E). It gives the schedule of all Shinkansen services as well as tokkyu and kyuko (express) trains and explains the various discounts and surcharges.

The TICs in Tokyo and Kyoto give out photocopied sheets of the schedule (and required changes of train) for travelling between Tokyo and Kyoto/Osaka by Tokaido line (non-Shinkansen trains). These trains take about 10 hours compared with less than four by Shinkansen but the fare is less than half. Other sheets from the TIC cover JNR services to and from northern Honshu, including the ferry service (JNR) between Hakodate on Hokkaido and Aomori on Honshu. The TIC offices are the best sources of information for most travel inquiries, but they do not sell tickets.

There are travel information centres at all major JNR stations. At Tokyo station (Yaesu side), the Travel Information Service is clearly labelled in English and some staff members speak adequate English to be helpful (if you speak slowly and clearly). Travel agencies like those listed for reserved ticket sales, can also supply information, though they may not have anyone who can speak English.

If you are travelling in the spring, be warned that for many years there has been a nationwide strike of JNR services during this busy time. It has usually lasted only a few days but can be a great interruption. Private railways and subways may be struck at the same time.

JNR Services

The basic level is called *futsu* (also 'kaku eki teisha' or 'kakutei') and these trains stop at every station. It is the slowest service and is usually limited to relatively short runs of about 100 km. Around major cities the quality of coaches on such service is good; on country lines the standard may not be so high – there the local trains are called *donko*, a folksy word with a descriptive sound, but a foreigner who uses it will find that the Japanese are amused.

Kyuko means 'ordinary express' and refers to trains that make only a limited number of stops, skipping a number of stations en route. With the exception of a very small number of *kaisoku* services (translated as 'rapid' on timetables and notices), there is a surcharge for kyuko trains. The surcharges are:

Up to (km)	Yen
50	500
100	700
150	900
200	1000
200 plus	1200

Reserved seats are available for a further Y500 surcharge.

The kaisoku services most likely to be encountered by foreign visitors are the Tokaido and Yokosuka-sen lines between Tokyo and Yokohama; the Chuo-Honsen line from Tokyo and Shinjuku, west to Takao and Tachikawa; and the Shin-Kaisoku service on the Tokaido Honsen line from Kyoto to Osaka, Kobe and Himeji. Kyuko trains are normally used for moderate distances.

Tokkyu means 'limited express' and such trains stop only at major cities. They are the fastest trains (other than the Shinkansen) and are used for long distance travel. Surcharges for tokkyu trains are:

Up to (km)	Yen
50	700
100	1000
150	1500
200	1800

300	2000
400	2200
600	2600
600 plus	3000

Reserved seats are an extra Y500.

Shinkansen

The fastest trains in Japan (and the fastest in the world until the advent of the French TGV service) are the three Shinkansen lines. They are known to foreigners as 'bullet trains' but the name actually means 'new trunk line'. These lines run from Tokyo to the west (Nagoya, Kyoto, Osaka, Hiroshima and Hakata); northeast (Sendai and Morioka); and north (Niigata). They are detailed in the Tokyo section.

The trains run at a maximum speed of 240 km/hr, and a ride on one is something that should be experienced at least once. The trains run on a continuous-welded track on a concrete roadbed, so there is no sway and no clickety-clack. It is necessary to look at the speedometer in the buffet car to believe the speed at which it is travelling. With more than two billion passengers carried without a single fatality, it has an incredible safety record.

As with ordinary JNR trains, there are both regular and Green Car (first class) coaches. The surcharge for a Green Car is:

Up to (km)	Yen
100	1300
200	2800
400	4200
600	5400
800	6600
800 plus	7800

Only the first coach of a train is a non-smoker. The Japanese have not yet heard of the practice of dividing coaches into smoking and non-smoking sections. The smoking cars will be very easy to identify because of the thick atmosphere.

Don't look for gourmet meals and high-class dining facilities that should complement such fast, high class trains. One Japanese newspaper columnist has complained of 'awful' coffee, 'the world's worst sandwiches', and dining facilities that are 'a step below most lower class slum eateries'. This exaggeration is a warning not to expect too much.

Overnight sleepers

For long distance travel an alternative to the Shinkansen train is one of the overnight sleeper trains. These leave in the evening, travel through the night, and reach their destination early the next morning. The main services are from Tokyo and Osaka, with stops at stations near the starting point to pick up more passengers and at several stations prior to the terminus. The most important of these services are:

Tokyo	– Hamada (San-in coast)
Ueno (Tokyo)	– Kanazawa (Hokuriku)
	– Aomori
Tokyo	– Nagasaki (Kyushu)
	– Kagoshima (Kyushu)
	– Kumamoto (Kyushu)
	– Miyazaki (Kyushu)
	– Hakata (Kyushu)
	– Shimonoseki (W. Honshu)
Osaka	– Nagasaki
	– Kagoshima
	– Miyazaki

The list of surcharges for the sleeping car is quite long because of the several types of accommodation (private compartments, upper/lower bed etc); plus the distance, plus whether it's a local, kyuko, or tokkyu train. For the maximum charges, for a trip over 600 km by limited express, the surcharges range from Y7500 to Y16500. These surcharges must be paid by the holders of a Japan Rail Pass.

Buying tickets

Tickets to any station in Japan can be bought at any JNR station. For short distances, there are usually ticket vending machines and for longer distances they can be bought at the ticket window.

There are no reserved seats on futsu trains. There are both reserved and unreserved seats on kyuko, tokkyu and Shinkansen trains; and reserved tickets can be bought a month in advance or a few minutes before departure. Seats on any of these trains can be reserved at any station with a Green Window (midori-no-madoguchi), which means all major stations in the country including most stations in Tokyo. (The name refers to the green over the window or the green band around glassed-in offices.) Reserved seat tickets may also be bought at offices of Japan Travel Bureau (JTB), Kinki Nippon Tourist Corp., and Nippon Travel Agency.

Seats on the Shinkansen can be reserved in Canada and the USA through JAL offices by passengers who will be flying by JAL to Japan.

JNR Fares

As noted earlier, train fares are calculated from a base fare plus added surcharges, and these rise with monotonous regularity; increases are virtually an annual occurrence. Shinkansen fares are now almost as high as air fares. For complete up-to-date fares, refer to the JNTO publication *Condensed Railway Timetable*. Some sample fares are listed below. For journeys over 100 km, student fares are available which give a 20 per cent discount off the regular fares. For a return JNR train/ferry trip, exceeding 600 km one-way there is a 20% discount on the return section.

From Tokyo to:	Regular	Shinkansen
Shizuoka	2,800	5,300
Fukushima	3,900	7,200
Niigata	4,700	8,700
Sendai	4,900	8,900
Nagoya	5,200	9,200
Kyoto	6,800	11,800
Morioka	7,000	11,700
Osaka	7,200	12,200
Hiroshima	9,700	16,100
Shimonoseki	11,00	17,400
Hakata	11,500	19,400

Japan Rail Pass

A definite travel bargain in this country largely bereft of bargains, is the Japan Rail Pass, which is exactly the same in concept as the Eurail pass. A JRP entitles the holder to use all JNR train, bus and ferry services (including kyuko, tokkyu and the Shinkansen) without surcharge, for a period of seven, 14 or 21 days for Y25,000, Y41,000 and Y53,000 respectively. There is a 50% reduction for children under-12 and a 45% surcharge for first class 'Green Car' service. Since the Shinkansen return-fare between Tokyo and Kyoto is Y23,600, the bargain of the JRP is obvious. The JNR network covers most parts of the country that visitors would want to see. Note however, that the pass is not valid on private railway lines so there may be occasions when a pass holder may have to pay separate fares.

A JRP cannot be purchased in Japan. It must be bought in a foreign country through an office or agent of Japan Air Lines, the Japan Travel Bureau or Nippon Travel Agency – almost any travel agent should be able to arrange this. The pass is open dated, so you can postpone validating it until the day you wish to begin your travels. The pass can be validated at a major station, such as Tokyo, or at the JNR counter at Narita Airport.

Technically, foreign residents of Japan are not permitted to use the JRP even if a friend has purchased the pass for them before entering the country themselves. The validation procedure is supposed to require checking the passport of the pass holder for the date of entry and the status of residence, to prevent residents from using the pass. The office at Narita follows the procedure scrupulously; other offices might be less diligent so it is the purchaser's gamble. If contemplating this it would be wise to inquire of the travel agent when purchasing the pass if it is refundable if unused.

Excursion Tickets

JNR also has excursion tickets (*shuyuken*). There are four different types: ippan shuyuken, route shuyuken, mini shuyuken and wide shuyuken.

Top: Western fast food has arrived in Japan
Right: Signs in Tokyo's Akihabara area
Left: Commuting in Tokyo's rush hour; note the gloves

Top: Many businesses use 'English' words in signs with no rhyme or reason
Left: The ubiquitous game of pachinko
Right: Typical Tokyo sidestreet

Wide shuyuken This is an all-inclusive ticket for direct travel (no stopover en route) from any place to a distant point, unlimited travel on JNR train and bus services within the designated area and direct travel back to the starting point. In the north of Japan there are two 20-day schemes for travel in Hokkaido (one for all points on Hokkaido, one for the southern part only, and a variation of the first that includes an air flight in one direction); and another route in Tohoku (northern Honshu) for 10 days. In the south of Japan there is a 'wide shuyuken' for travel anywhere in Kyushu for 20 days by JNR train and bus, with the option of a boat trip in one direction from Beppu (Kyushu) to Kobe/Osaka, or from Beppu to Takamatsu (Shikoku). Others offer unlimited travel within Shikoku for 20 days, or unlimited travel in the San-in area (the north coast of western Honshu).

Mini shuyuken This is similar to the wide shuyuken but covers a smaller area and has a shorter period of validity.

Route shuyuken This is for travel along certain designated routes that take in a number of places considered worth seeing. It is valid for 30 days and gives a 10% discount over regular fares.

Ippan shuyuken This is an excursion ticket over a route chosen by the traveller. It must take in two or more designated areas with travel of more than 201 km (train, bus, boat) before returning to the starting point. It is good for 30 days and gives a 10 per cent discount.

There are a number of options resulting from the number of schemes. It is advisable to obtain copies of the photocopied info sheets from the TICs in Tokyo or Kyoto. The same information is available at any JNR or JTB office or travel agents but few of the staff at these places speak English as they do in the TICs.

Excursion tickets can be purchased at any JNR station in Japan with a Green Window office, or from any travel agency.

Groups of 15 or more receive a discount of about 10%.

Economy Coupons are available for JNR trains plus hotels and sightseeing on approved JNR routes.

Special Trains
Steam locomotives ('SL' in Japanese!) can be seen at two places in Japan. JNR phased out its last SL in December 1975, but the clamour of Japanese steam fanatics led them to revive some services

on the Yamaguchi line in southern Honshu, the only line where the water towers, etc still remained.

The service commences in late July and runs daily except Tuesday and Friday; and from September through November it runs on weekends and national holidays. Trains make one daily round trip, leaving Ogori (one stop on the Shinkansen from Shin-Shimonoseki) at 10 am and arriving at Tsuwano (65 km inland toward Masuda on the north coast) at 12.10 pm, travelling at speeds of up to 65 km/h and stopping at eight stations on the way. The return trip leaves Tsuwano at 2.20 pm. Trains have five coaches with a seating capacity of 400 but it is advisable to book as the trip is very popular. The one-way fare is Y950; a reserved seat is an extra Y500; and tickets can be bought at any JNR station's Green Window.

The only line in Japan where steam locomotives were never completely phased out, is the short Oikawa line in Shizuoka-ken. It runs from Kanaya (about 190 km south-west of Tokyo and 12 km west of Shizuoka city) to Senzu.

The basic SL service is an almost daily run of the 'Kawaneji' train, leaving Kanaya at 11.35 am, reaching Senzu at 12.54 pm and returning at 2.30 pm. During the off season it only runs on weekends but is operated regularly during the week through July and August. The schedule is printed in *Jikokuhyo*; and the Tokyo TIC or any travel agent can give more info. For the 40 km trip trip, either by steam or diesel, the fare is Y1270.

In 1979 a C-56 type locomotive, built in Japan between 1935 and 1939 was brought back from Thailand where it had been used during WW II to haul war supplies on the infamous Thailand-Burma railway. It will be used on the Oikawa line.

Anyone interested in mobile antiques should take a ride on the two surviving cars on a one-km branch line of the Tsurumi electric line between Musashi, Shiraishi and Okawa; the Tsurumi line originates at Tsurumi station of the Keihin-Tohoku line (JNR) in Yokohama. The two coaches which are over 50 years old are irreplaceable because they are the only ones in Japan that can be operated singly. They are three metres shorter than standard 20-metre coaches so they are the only ones that can negotiate the sharp bends and use the short station platforms of this line. The ride lasts two minutes.

AIR

There are five airlines operating on domestic routes in Japan. JAL (Japan Air Lines – *Nippon Koku*) operates only among Tokyo, Osaka, Sapporo, Okayama and Okinawa. ANA (All Nippon Airways – *Zen Nippon Koku*) and TDA (Toa Domestic Airlines – *Toa Koku Nai Koku*) link a large number of smaller centres with the largest cities. ANA also serves the same trunk routes as JAL; and TDA serves a couple of them. SWAL (Southwest Air Lines – *Nansei Koku*) is a regional carrier serving a number of small islands around Okinawa. NKA (*Nippon Kinkyo-ri Koku*) serves some areas of Hokkaido.

Domestic air services radiate from large cities, eg Tokyo, Osaka, Sapporo, Nagoya, Okayama and Naha (Okinawa). Thus travel between regional cities is not possible without passing through one of the large airports.

At Tokyo, Haneda airport is used for all domestic flights, except for about 10 a day which link Narita airport with Sapporo, Osaka, Fukuoka and Nagoya.

Listed below are sample fares (one way); return fares are 10% cheaper than two one-way fares.

TOKYO TO:

Chitose/Sapporo	Y25,500
Sendai	Y12,200
Nagoya	Y12,400
Osaka	Y15,600
Hiroshima	Y23,100
Fukuoka	Y27,100
Kagoshima	Y31,500
Naha	Y37,300
Nagasaki	Y31,100

SENDAI TO:	
Chitose	Y18,700

NAGOYA TO:	
Chitose	Y33,200
Sendai	Y20,600
Nagasaki	Y23,000
Kagoshima	Y23,100
Naha	Y35,000

OSAKA TO:	
Sendai	Y25,000
Nagasaki	Y19,000
Kagoshima	Y19,700

HIROSHIMA TO:	
Kagoshima	Y18,500

KAGOSHIMA TO:	
Naha	Y22,500

BUS

Japan does not have intercity bus services on the scale of most other countries. Most long-distance travel is by train (especially the super-fast Shinkansen), or by air. The reason for this is that highways are narrow and crowded, cities and towns are incessant and the speed limit is a maximum of 60 km/h. The only high-speed roads are the expressways linking major cities.

Highway buses operate on some of these expressways. The main run is Tokyo – Nagoya – Kyoto – Osaka. From early morning buses run to/from Tokyo along the Tomei kosokudoro (expressway); and to/from Nagoya and Osaka/Kyoto along the Meishin kosokudoro. To get from Tokyo to Kyoto/Osaka, it is necessary to change at Nagoya. Transfers are not particularly well co-ordinated, with buses leaving Nagoya just before the arrival of most buses from Tokyo, but the next one is usually less than 30 minutes later. The last bus from Tokyo to connect for the trip to Kyoto or Osaka (separate buses) leaves Tokyo station at 11 am; although buses continue to depart from Tokyo until 3.30 pm for Nagoya, and later for closer terminal cities like Shizuoka. Fares are Y4500 for Tokyo-Nagoya; and Y1800/ 2200 for Kyoto/Osaka.

The only direct buses between Tokyo and Kyoto/Osaka (no change at Nagoya) run at night, leaving late in the evening and arriving early next morning. There is only a single departure time for the night bus on each route, although several buses may leave at once. The night bus is popular so it is advisable to make a booking as far in advance as possible. They can be made up to eight days in advance at any JTB office or at the Green Window of large JNR stations.

The buses are quite comfortable, with reclining seats, so sleeping on them is not too difficult and they are definitely more comfortable than sitting up on a night train over the same distance. The cost, including reservation charge is a bit over half the one-way Shinkansen fare, and it saves a night's accommodation cost.

Another highway bus service runs west from Osaka station along the Chugoku kosokudoro to Tsuyama (roughly north of Okayama). These run only during the day.

A third service runs northeast from Tokyo to Sendai and Yamagata. These run only at night, leaving late in the evening and arriving early the next morning. Further details are given in the Sendai and Yamagata sections.

It is possible to use the highway buses (particularly those running in daylight) to reach intermediate points along the expressways. The buses don't go into the cities along the route, but stop at lay-bys just off the expressway, and from there passengers can walk to a nearby local road to catch a local bus to the station.

There are countless bus routes linking country areas with the nearest JNR station, as well as quite long bus routes in areas that are too mountainous or too sparsely populated for railways.

All long-distance, highway, and scheduled country buses are listed in *Jikokuhyo*. Information in English for Tokyo-Nagoya-Osaka/Kyoto services is available from the Tokyo and Kyoto TICs.

The system of fare collection on

scheduled country runs (mostly from railway stations) is the same as is used in some cities. The passenger takes a ticket from a machine at the back entrance; the ticket shows the zone where the passenger boarded. A mechanical sign at the front of the bus shows the fare payable at that point by passengers getting off, zone by zone.

FERRIES

There are many ferries linking up wide-spread parts of Japan. The word may conjure up the image of a short trip on a small boat across placid and sheltered waters, but in actual fact many Japanese ferries are large ocean-going ships of 10,000 tonnes or so, and voyages may last up to 30 hours. Such ships are equipped with restaurant and bar facilities and usually have baths as well.

The cost for the lowest priced class is usually lower than competing land transport and is often more enjoyable, with the bonus of an economical 'sea cruise'. The cheapest fare is for an open room with tatami floors that are shared by all passengers. During the busy summer season these may be crowded and smokey, while at other times they may be nearly empty. There are other classes including private cabins.

The only 'hazard' of the tatami class is that there may very well be several parties of noisy sake and shochu-tippling merry-makers nearby, particularly after harvest season when farmers who have brought in their crops set off for their annual vacation. These groups of people are the 'real' Japanese, rustic and simple, quite bawdy and an eye-opener for the person who knows only the prim and proper Japanese businessmen. The drunker they get, the happier they get and the louder they sing. They usually know many folk songs (which all tend to sound alike), and when truly in their cups, their dances become extremely earthy with blatant sexual themes. Even though it may be at the cost of a few hours sleep, this is a good way to get to know another side of the complex personality of Japan and to meet the most genuine people in the country. Any gregarious traveller is sure to be invited to join them.

Many ferries leave at night so you can save the cost of accommodation, but it can mean that the ship passes through well-known scenic waters, such as the Inland Sea, at night. In the summer however, the sky becomes light as early as 4 am and much of the best part of the Inland Sea can be seen from at least one ferry.

Many ferries carry motor vehicles – cars and motorcycles. The charge for a motorcycle is about 1½ times the 'tatami' class passenger fare. Anyone travelling by bicycle, especially if it's a collapsible model, would have no trouble taking the bike along on any boat.

In addition to long-distance ferries, there are many boats operating in the Inland Sea between Shikoku and Honshu, and between Kyushu and Shikoku. There are also many ships that operate between the main islands and small islands offshore, and sightseeing excursion boats that cruise for relatively short distances along the coast or loop back to the point of origin. There are also several ships that operate among the chain of islands that extends south from Kagoshima to Okinawa.

Following is a list of the main long-distance ferries, with the cheapest 'tatami' class fares.

OTARU (Hokkaido) TO:

Niigata	Y5,000
Tsuruga	Y6,400
Maizuru	Y6,400

SENDAI (N.Honshu) TO:

Tomakomai	Y8,600

OARAI (N.Honshu) TO:

Muroran (Hokkaido)	Y4,200

TOKYO TO:

Tomakomai	Y11,500
Kushiro	Y14,000

Nachi-Katsuura	Y8,800
Kochi	Y13,500
Kokura	Y12,000
Naha	Y19,100
Tokushima	Y8,200

KAWASAKI TO:

| Hyuga (Kyushu) | Y17,200 |

NAGOYA TO:

| Sendai | Y9,300 |
| Tomakomai | Y15,000 |

OSAKA TO:

Takamatsu	Y2,300
Matsuyama	Y4,300
Beppu	Y5,700
Kochi	Y4,400
Shin-Moji	Y4,700
Hyuga	Y7,400
Kagoshima	Y10,000
Naha	Y15,000
Imabari	Y3,700
Sakate	Y1,900

KOBE TO:

Oita	Y4,900
Kokura	Y4,700
Hyuga	Y7,400
Matsuyama	Y3,400
Naha	Y1,500

HIROSHIMA TO:

| Beppu | Y3,500 |

NAHA (Okinawa) TO:

| Hakata | Y12,600 |
| Kagoshima | Y11,500 |

KOKURA TO:

| Matsuyama | Y3,400 |
| Sakai-Izumi | Y4,700 |

For further up-to-date information on scheduled passenger shipping, there are other useful sources.

Jikokuhyo, the bible of all scheduled transport in Japan, shows ferry routes on maps at the front of the book. Ferries are shown as thin red lines each with a number and a letter which refer to the page and section in which the schedule and fare are printed.

The TICs have free info sheets listing a number of boat services, along with fares, schedules and dock locations. The lists are not complete, however.

The sheet *Ferry Services in Northern Japan* has details on the following ferry routes: Sendai-Tomakomai; Tomakomai-Hachinohe; Hakodate-Oma; Hakodate-Aomori; and Hakodate-Noheji. This sheet does not list services between Aomori and Hakodate and Aomori-Muroran. The former are listed on the TIC sheet *Transportation for Northern Japan*; the latter are listed in the Hokkaido section of this book.

The TIC info sheet *Coastal Shipping Services* lists mostly ships from Tokyo and Kawasaki. They are: Kawasaki-Hyuga; Tokyo-Kushiro; Tokyo-Tomakomai. It also details services from Osaka/Kobe to Matsuyama and Beppu.

INTRA-CITY PUBLIC TRANSPORT
TRAINS – URBAN & SUBURBAN

In the Tokyo and Osaka area, JNR trains operate as part of the city mass transit system, where they are called *kokuden* trains. Loop lines circle the central district of both cities, while other JNR lines and private railway lines act as feeder systems from the outlying areas into the central districts. In Tokyo the loop line is called the Yamanote line; in Osaka it is the Kanjo line. Several other cities are also served by JNR and private railways in a similar manner.

The private railway lines usually run for comparatively short distances, less than 100 km, and link the major cities with surrounding suburban areas or nearby resorts. In the Tokyo area, for example, 11 private railways connect directly to the Yamanote loop line – some even act as continuations of subway lines.

In the early days of railway building, the founders discovered that it was good business to build department stores over the large stations, hence many lines bear the name of well-known stores, such as Keio, Odakyu or Hankyu, and many lines start from store basements.

In many cases, private railways run virtually parallel to JNR lines and serve the same destinations. The private lines are usually less expensive, sometimes as low as half the JNR fare, and also have a reputation for better service, cleaner equipment and more polite personnel, though this may not always be true.

Details of the rail services in each city or region are given in the appropriate chapter.

SUBWAYS

There are subway systems in Toyko, Kyoto, Osaka, Nagoya, Yokohama and Sapporo. They offer a convenient and quick means of getting around these cities because they run free of traffic congestion.

In each city the stations are well marked above ground and can usually be used by foreigners without difficulty because there is adequate information in English. Published maps show the locations of stations. In Tokyo, Yokohama, Osaka and Nagoya, the subways are augmented to a greater or lesser extent by private and JNR railway lines. Subway maps, sometimes with romanised names, are usually available free at stations, and tourist literature (particularly for Tokyo) often has maps.

In Tokyo there are 10 separate lines operated by two independent authorities, so there are complications that can arise when using them. There is an extensive description of the system in the chapter dealing with Tokyo.

Commuter Passes

Passes valid for one, three or six months are available for all forms of public transport in Tokyo and other major cities. A single pass valid for travel on two separate systems (JNR plus subway, for example), can be purchased at the office of either of the destination stations (except for small stations).

BUS

Every Japanese city of any size has extensive bus services. Unfortunately it is difficult to use them because their destinations are written only in Japanese and the drivers don't usually speak English. An exception is that buses in Nikko have signs in English because so many foreign tourists use them. It is necessary to know bus routes in advance before they can be useful, which means that only long-term residents will get much out of them. Buses are also subject to traffic delays, so they are often slower than trains and subways.

Two systems of fare collection are used. In Tokyo and some other cities, the fare is a flat sum paid on entering. The fare is normally clearly marked on the cash box beside the driver and there is usually a slot at the right side of the box that gives Y10 coins in change from a Y100 coin. There may be two slots on top of the cash box – the left one is for tickets, the right for coins.

In many other cities and country runs the fare depends on the distance travelled. Passengers enter by the rear door and take a ticket from a dispenser at the right of the steps. On the ticket is a number indicating the fare zone at the place of boarding. At the front of the bus is an illuminated mechanical sign that shows the fare to be paid if you leave the bus. The fares advance as the bus moves along. Pay at the front when you leave.

Most buses in Japan have recorded messages identifying the next stop, which is very helpful if you speak Japanese. A separate fare must be paid for each bus boarded; except in Nagasaki which is the only city that has adopted a system of transfers.

TAXIS

Taxis used to be a bargain in Japan but now their prices match the high prices for everything else. Prices are almost uniform throughout the country.

The flagfall is Y470 for the first two km, then Y80 for each additional 395 metres (in Tokyo, slightly further in other cities), plus a time charge when the taxi is moving at less than 10 km/h. The flagfall cost is displayed prominently in both windows on the left side of the vehicle and sometimes in the rear window.

From 11 pm to 5 am there is a surcharge of 20%. That, at least, is the official rate. Because the subways and trains stop running soon after midnight drivers have a sellers market and it is difficult to get a taxi after 10 pm, especially on rainy nights. Drivers expect two to four times the meter fare, and some customers hold up two or more fingers to show the bribe rate being offered. (Many company employees have taxi coupons that they use for this purpose.) A red light sign in the left front window indicates an available taxi; green means that a night surcharge is in effect; and yellow indicates that it is answering a radio call.

Taxis can be flagged down on the street. It is sufficient to stand at the edge of the road with an outstretched arm, fingers bent slightly downward; never whistle for a taxi. In most cases taxi drivers are polite and patient but it is not unknown for some of them to pass by foreigners and pick up nearby Japanese. Taxis can be summoned by phone in cities; there is a 20 per cent surcharge for this service.

There are taxi stands near most stations and drivers are reluctant (or prohibited) to stop on the street nearby. At night, in busy areas like Ginza, Roppongi, etc, a taxi stop is often the only place you can get a taxi.

Japanese taxi drivers are not linguists and only very rarely will they understand English. Say your destination in Japanese, if possible, otherwise have it written in Japanese. It is also useful to have the address where you are staying written in Japanese; hotels have cards which are prepared for this purpose. Sometimes the hotel name is different in English and Japanese – eg the Imperial (in Tokyo) is 'Teikoku hoteru' to the Japanese. Addresses are notoriously difficult to find in Japan, so don't get upset and berate the driver if he takes a long time and has to stop at one or more police boxes to get you to your destination. This is simply standard operating procedure.

Tipping is not the practice in Japan unless the driver has performed some unusual service, like helping with heavy baggage, or has spent a long time finding a difficult address. A driver might even refuse to accept the money, although reports of this happening are not so frequent these days. Don't try to open or close the passenger side (left) door. It is operated by the driver in almost all taxis and they get quite angry if customers close the door because it damages the mechanism.

RICKSHAWS

There are a few rickshaws in use in Japan. They can be seen every day in the back streets around the Ginza. When traffic is clear, the vehicle moves along surprisingly fast and smoothly. These rickshaws are not for rent by the general public – they carry geisha to teahouses and restaurants where they will entertain in traditional style with songs, dances and stories.

At various places around Japan a few rickshaws have been dusted off and revived as tourist attractions, but they are as much a novelty to the modern Japanese as they are to westerners. They have been

seen at the charming old town of Kurashiki (near Okayama), at Furukawa (near Takayama) and at Nagasaki but reports are that tourists don't use them enough for the operators to make a living.

The rickshaw has its origin in Japan (not China), and the name is a corruption of the Japanese 'jin riki sha' meaning 'man powered carriage'. However, Neil Pedlar, a writer for the *Japan Times*, wrote that the rickshaw was probably invented by an American, Jonathon Goble, who came to Yokohama as a missionary and wanted a carriage for his wife. Further, the rickshaw is a copy of a vehicle called a 'brouette' first used in Paris in 1669! Goble copied the design from an encyclopedia.

PRIVATE TRANSPORT
MOTOR VEHICLES

For the person with the yen and the Yen, plus lots of time, there is no better way to see Japan completely and thoroughly than by private car or motorcycle. A car can be purchased or rented, with or without a driver. A motorcycle will be an expensive proposition, but some readers may wish to use one. Because of the time involved in buying (and selling) a vehicle, this will usually only suit people who are staying for several months or more.

Driving Licences

A domestic licence of most countries or an International Driving Permit can be used for a limited period in Japan. If you are staying in the country for a considerable length of time, however, it will be necessary to obtain a Japanese driving licence, which is a fairly simple procedure. Arm yourself with a couple of 25 x 30 mm photos, your Alien Registration Card (or Certificate of Residence), a few thousand yen and your valid foreign licence and go to the Sameizu Shikenjo (licence office). A sign at the entrance will direct you to the counter where an English speaking person will explain the rest of the procedure, which is all routine and involves nothing more difficult than a simple eye test

(glasses are allowed). An International Driving Permit can be obtained easily after you have been issued your Japanese licence.

Long-term residents should note that the licence runs approximately two years, to your birthdate. No renewal notice is sent out, so you must keep track yourself.

The Sameizu Shikenjo licence office can be reached by bus or train. Bus 98 from Oimachi station (JNR Tokaido line or Tokyu Oimachi line), or 93 from Meguro station (JNR Yamanote line) run in front of the office; the stop is Tokyo-to Rikuun Jimusho-mae and the office is about two minutes walk on your left.

By train, the line is the Keihin-kyuko out of Shinagawa (reached by JNR or by transfer from the Mita subway line at Sengakuji station) to Sameizu station. From the station turn right, then left and continue down the narrow street towards the main (multi-lane) road. Turn right and cross at the crossing further down; the licence office faces the crossing.

Make sure you obtained your driving licence before coming to Japan as getting one in the country is a long drawn-out and expensive affair.

Travellers who are passing through Singapore and who will be away from their own countries for several years may find it useful to obtain a Singapore driving licence (very simple on presentation of your valid licence). The Singapore licence can be renewed easily by mail, something that might be difficult in your own country if you have no permanent address. And with the Singapore licence it's possible to obtain a Japanese or other licence as required. If the licence from home is valid for motorcycles it should be endorsed for the same in Singapore as should an International Driving Permit from there. Obtaining a licence for a motorcycle over 400cc is difficult in Japan.

Driving Conditions

Roads in Japan are generally as good as they need be. This means that all roads are hard surfaced except for the rarely travelled ones high in the mountains. With the exception of expressways, all roads are narrow relative to the heavy traffic that they carry and minor country roads are so narrow that one car may have to pull off the road to let another pass. The result is that it's impossible to make good time over long distances. A typical good day's driving will cover 200-250 km and this will require eight to 10 hours. The main roads are so built-up that they seem to be part of one continuous town. Traffic lights are frequent along these highways and seem to be always red. They also continue to operate through the night even when there is negligible traffic from side roads.

Passing slow vehicles is a near impossibility. Apart from the almost inevitable endless line of vehicles ahead and heavy oncoming traffic, there are few passing zones. Where there are straight and flat stretches, especially in Hokkaido and Tohoku, there will normally be a solid line on the road indicating no overtaking. Conversely and idiotically when these roads get into the mountains and visibility is poor, dotted lines commonly extend around blind corners.

Despite the problems and frustrations, the rewards in the 'good parts' can make driving all worthwhile.

For less exasperating driving conditions and the chance to see a more 'typical' Japan, it is preferable to use the less travelled highways (generally inland). Often they are little slower than the main roads and vastly more enjoyable.

For drivers in a hurry to get from point A to point B, there is no substitute for the expressways. There is quite a large network of these already built and construction is progressing on others throughout the country. (One pessimist predicts, however, that the huge building program will be completed just in time for them to become the most magnificent bicycle paths in the world when the oil supply runs out.)

Expressways run nearly the full length of Honshu and through much of Kyushu. There are some feeder expressways from country areas and in metropolitan areas there are several, often parallel to each other though separated by a few km. They are the only way to get through major cities quickly.

Tolls are incredibly high. For a car, from Tokyo to Nagoya (360 km) it costs Y4,800; Tokyo to Kyoto (510 km) it's Y6,700. This is substantially higher than the bus fare and a good fraction of the cost by Shinkansen. It is less for a motor cycle, but not much. Speed limits on expressways are 100 km/h; they are the only roads in Japan with such 'high' limits.

Interchanges ('inta' in Japanese) are well marked in both romaji and kanji, but it's advisable to know the name of the desired exit in advance. For example, on the Meishin expressway (Nagoya-Kobe) the exit for Osaka is not named Osaka, but Toyonaka (which I found out by overshooting and exiting at Amagasaki, a good distance further on). Road maps show the name of each interchange, but usually only in kanji. Expressway signs in cities are almost exclusively in kanji, so it is essential to know the kanji for your destination before starting out. Signs along city streets are also usually only in kanji.

Fuel is readily available almost everywhere in Japan, the only exception being in remote areas with little traffic. Fuel has always been expensive in Japan. The cost of regular has been in the range of Y140-160 per litre; and motor oil is incredibly expensive, from Y1000-1500 per litre.

The single greatest frustration when driving in Japan – even a danger to one's mental health – is the speed limit. Incredible as it may sound the maximum on highways in open area is only 60 km/h. This limit, laughably low by international standards, is the maximum allowable, but it's often felt by the authorities that this heady speed is rather risky so it is common to find limits as low as 50 or even 40 km/h in open areas in the countryside. Even more ridiculous – going up mountain roads, there are often signs calling for a reduction in speed!

The sad thing about these limits is that they are strictly, if unpredictably enforced. A speed trap will always be located in the only straight and level section of an otherwise twisty and hilly road, where the temptation is greatest to ease the frustration of being held back by long hills and other lengthy and slow stretches of road.

Offenders are flagged down by a red and white banded pole held touching the road. There is usually an 'office' complete with table and chairs set up in the wilderness to mass-process the victims, with 10 or more police sitting there writing out tickets. This is why you will only see patrols on main highways and why driving habits on mountain and winding roads are so bad.

Right of way at an intersection of equal size roads that have no markings goes to the vehicle on the left. Where a small road enters a larger road, all vehicles on the larger road have priority. That, at least, is the law, and it's useful to know in theory but many Japanese are unsure whether right of way is to the left or right and in practice there seems to be no clear rule. An objective evaluation is that the right of way lies with the bigger vehicle. Not for nothing has the *nihonglish* word 'dampu' evolved – it means a belligerent and reckless driver, and is a corruption of the English 'dump truck'. This gives a good indication of who are the most dangerous drivers in Japan.

The penalties for driving after drinking are very severe and can result in on-the-spot licence cancellation for a year.

The Japan Automobile Federation (JAF) has a booklet which details the traffic laws. It is available by mail (within Japan) for Y1120 (including postage) from: JAF, 3-5-8 Shiba Koen. Minato-ku, Tokyo 105. Or from JAF headquarters (opposite the entrance to Tokyo Tower) for Y1000.

Motorists may wish to consider member-

ship in the JAF. It offers the same sort of road service as similar associations in other countries. Reciprocal benefits are given to members of the automobile associations of Australia, Canada, Germany, Great Britain, Holland, Hong Kong, New Zealand, Singapore and the USA. Membership also gives a discount when buying JAF publications, and members can have strip maps made up for their journeys around Japan. Membership costs Y4000 per year plus a joining fee of Y2000.

Navigation

Finding your way around Japan, especially outside the cities, is not too difficult. International road signs, as found in Europe, are used for information, warning and prohibitions so there is no need to be able to read Japanese. Where words are used on the sign there are also numbers in many cases indicating times, dates or speeds, so they can be frequently understood.

In the past most directional signs were printed both in kanji and romaji, but in recent years these have been replaced by new ones with kanji only. (Considering the Japanese are making so much fuss and noise about becoming an 'international nation' this practice has been attracting deserved criticism.) If a sign in both scripts appears and has your destination written on it, memorise the kanji! You can be sure that at a major intersection the signs will be written only in kanji and if you don't know the characters you are in trouble.

When driving in large cities on ordinary streets, never try to take short cuts. Except in Kyoto and Sapporo, there are scarcely any two streets that run parallel for more than a few hundred metres, and you can get so completely lost in such a short time that it exceeds belief. If you do get lost, swallow your pride and go back the way you came, hoping not to encounter any one-way streets. On several occasions I've had to navigate with a compass!

Road maps are given out free by some service stations but generally they have to be purchased at appreciable cost. There are no maps that are labelled extensively in romaji; the best you can look for is maps with key cities and perhaps large towns, marked in both scripts. A further complication is that the city names are printed in kanji (characters) while railway stations are shown in hiragana (phonetic symbols representing syllables), so that one cannot be used to locate the name of a place written in the other script.

Maps are available from several sources. The JAF sells a book of maps which cover the entire country. The maps are to a suitably large scale and have many places identified in romaji as well as kanji. Being a single book and relatively small, the maps are convenient to use. The books cost Y2000, less 10% for members of JAF or any of the nine affiliated foreign associations). JAF also sells a series of individual regional maps at Y450 each.

I used the *Hi-Power Map* series for my travels. These have enough names in both scripts to be useful and are printed on paper-like plastic that was not affected by periodic soakings. They are larger and less convenient than the JAF book of maps, and 10 maps at Y600 each are needed to cover the entire country but it's easier to plan a long journey with them because each map covers a larger area. There are two series of Hi-Power maps – one by region (useful), one by prefecture (requires many).

A hint on map reading: the legend that explains the meanings of the symbols is in Japanese only. Roads marked in pale pink or pale green are unpaved roads, usually high in the mountains and their surface is usually rough and treacherous for motorcyclists.

Driving Habits

The average Japanese driver is reasonably competent though there isn't the long history of mass motoring in Japan that there is in Europe and elsewhere. In fact prior to the mid-1960s very few people owned cars and the Japanese car industry was virtually non-existent.

As a result of the late start, Japanese driving for a while was abysmal, but the gross stupidity that seemed prevalent in the early 1970s has almost completely disappeared as a result of improved driver education and police law enforcement – or perhaps all the idiots just wiped themselves out.

One major exception occurs on mountain roads where every Japanese male driver seems to go silly, thinking himself highly skilled with the trained reflexes of a racing driver. The fact is that the low speed limits prevent them from gaining any experience at high speeds on any kind of road, let alone twisty mountain ones. Almost every driver cuts straight through curves so it's advisable to sound your horn at every blind corner. Evidence of the bad driving is that there is scarcely a metre of guard rail in all Japan that isn't scraped or bent. Bottles of flowers by the roadside, often with a wooden stake or some personal possession, are mute testimony to a fatal accident, and are a common sight.

The other bad drivers are found in the cities and are usually young people who race, recklessly on city streets, often in large numbers. In a typical operation, Tokyo police once rounded up 258 people late one Saturday evening, along with 257 of the 863 vehicles that were travelling in 13 groups. Police mobilised 230 patrol cars for the operation. The 'hot rodders' themselves are not dangerous but their driving can be a hazard to anyone else on the roads.

Another dangerous spinoff from the low speed limits is that drivers generally have little appreciation of the increased distance required to stop from a high speed. Many will drive so they are almost touching the vehicle ahead, depending on their reflexes alone to save them if a sudden stop is called for. In many cases it appears they don't think ahead to logical developments resulting from their driving, or even the obvious consequence of events that they can see. Thus too many don't predict the need to slow down or stop, and charge along at full speed till they have to slam on the brakes to avoid what could be seen to be developing for the previous several seconds.

Truck drivers are the worst on the roads. While many are sane and safe, too many drive in an irresponsibly 'playful' manner, indulging in games of chase, and drive almost touching the vehicle ahead. I have seen a multi-tonne concrete mixer being driven through manouvres I would not want to perform in a sports car. One of the worst smashups in Japanese road history is believed to have been caused by the driver of a large truck loaded with chemicals playing 'tag' with other drivers. The rear-end collision in a tunnel of the Tomei Expressway (Toyko-Nagoya) killed seven people and destroyed 173 cars in the pile-up and ensuing fire.

Again most drivers in Japan are okay, but watch out for the crazies.

Importing Vehicles

Motor vehicles (cars and motorcycles) can be imported into Japan for periods of one year on a carnet (explained later), or on permanent basis if for more than a year. However, it is not a good idea to import a vehicle into Japan. Shipping rates are high, customs clearance, port clearance and other charges will add substantially to the cost and tax (though not duty) will have to be paid, this being computed on the cost of the vehicle plus shipping charges. In addition to these and other likely charges, many mechanical modifications will have to be made to bring the vehicle into conformity with Japanese safety and anti-pollution requirements. Since Japan has the strictest anti-pollution regulations in the world, this is likely to be expensive. Unless the car can be bought overseas to Japanese specifications it is better not to bother importing a foreign car. If you must have a foreign car it is no more expensive in the long run to pay the

Japanese price for it, incredibly high as it may be (roughly three to four times the domestic price for a USA-made car for example). The required modifications will bring it into this range anyway. In general it is better to buy a Japanese-made car and leave the overpriced foreign imports to the ostentatious local residents who have more money than sense.

Anyone wishing to import a vehicle into Japan should contact a Japanese government representative overseas for up-to-date information on regulations as they seem to change constantly.

Buying

Buying a new vehicle is much less difficult than a second-hand purchase because the price and conditions are more or less fixed, and finding a dealer is easy.

When buying a second-hand car or motorcycle, language may be the main problem because it's necessary to look around, use Japanese newspaper listings, and negotiate with someone who probably doesn't speak English. For help with this language barrier contact Tescort in Tokyo and other cities. They can arrange for a Japanese person who wishes to practice his English to accompany you.

Shaken

For second-hand cars and motorcycles a big consideration is *shaken*. This dreaded word in the motoring world of Japan is a combined road tax, registration fee, insurance premium and vehicle inspection. It is an expense every two years and comes due on the same date whether ownership changes or not, so the time remaining is an important factor in the cost when buying a used vehicle. The worst aspect of the shaken system is that it is government-sanctioned extortion that benefits the great number of service centres that make the inspections. Even if no work is needed on the car and the check takes only a short time, the motorist is liable for the full charge just to have the papers filled out. For my 550cc motorcycle it cost Y50,000;

for a car it can be double this or more depending on the size of the vehicle. Motorcycles under 250cc are exempt from the inspection but insurance is still compulsory.

Exporting a Vehicle

If you buy a car or motorcycle in Japan and wish to take it to another country for a period of less than a year, you can obtain a carnet from the JAF that lets you do so without the problem of paying the duties in cash and trying to get them back when leaving. The carnet is a book of several pages, each of which guarantees that the JAF will pay the duties owed if the vehicle is sold in the other country. The JAF does not do this out of the kindness of its heart of course – you must leave a cash deposit equal to the highest amount of duty that would be charged in any of the countries to which you tell them you plan to take the vehicle. For countries like Indonesia the duty rate may be as high as 160 per cent of the purchase price of the vehicle. There is nothing in the carnet which tells you for which countries it is valid nor the amount of deposit made to the JAF. When you finish your travels in foreign countries, you send the carnet back to the JAF and obtain a refund on your deposit. It is not necessary to belong to the JAF to arrange a carnet.

Worth noting, is that a carnet bought in Japan is extremely expensive – the administrative charges are possibly the highest in the world. For five pages (one page per entry into a country) the charge is Y9000; for 10 pages, Y15,000; for 25 pages, 20,000. Also some countries near Japan, like Taiwan, Hong Kong, Singapore and Malaysia have, in the past, allowed a Japan-registered motorcycle to enter without a carnet or other formalities. Check with the diplomatic missions of those countries if you plan to go there. Since shipping costs are appreciable, it would be cheaper for anyone planning to travel in the Singapore-Malaysia-Thailand area to buy a bike in Singapore and

arrange a carnet there. Not only are the administration charges lower but they will probably accept a guarantee letter from your bank in lieu of a cash deposit. A carnet can be arranged through the Automobile Association of Singapore (336 River Valley Rd, Singapore 9) for a bike bought in Japan, possibly by mail. The only drawback with purchasing in Singapore is that large model bikes are not regular stock items and they have to be ordered long in advance from Japan.

CARS

Generally the only foreigners in Japan who buy new cars are those who will be staying for a year or more. Before buying ask friends if a car is really useful; they may feel, through experience, that a car is often more bother than it's worth in the city, and getting into the country takes considerable time. Within cities it is often more convenient to use public transport and taxis. Parking places are difficult to find, on-street parking is being actively discouraged by the authorities and commercial parking garages are expensive. It may even be preferable and cheaper to use public transport to reach a vacation area and then rent a car there.

With the advent of the strict anti-pollution laws, domestic models of Japanese cars are generally less desirable than the export models because of the way the added equipment affects the performance. Thus there is now little incentive to buy in Japan and ship home; though this is possible on a commodity-tax-free basis. Prices in Japan are not much lower than they are in many foreign countries and with the cost of shipping it might be cheaper to buy in your home country.

Buying a second-hand car can be a money saver for the long term resident, and there are some good buys for someone who wants a car for only a few months of travel in Japan. Buying second-hand involves the same worries as in any country – Japanese used car salesmen enjoy the same reputation for high business principles as do their brethren around the world. However a used car in Japan is likely to be safer than one bought in the USA or other countries where there is no system of compulsory vehicle inspection. As mentioned earlier, *shaken* is very expensive – about Y100,000 for a typical car, and an important factor to consider when buying a car.

If buying from the owner, have him drive the car for a few minutes to see if he lugs the car into too high a gear. This is a common habit in Japan – how they can ignore the protesting knocking sounds emanating from the engine is beyond comprehension – but this is bad for the bearings and may have caused damage.

Used cars for sale by foreigners are advertised in *Tokyo Weekender*. Such advertisers would be easiest to deal with because they will more than likely speak English, but it is still necessary to negotiate the hurdle of change of registration. Servicemen at American bases often have used cars for sale.

MOTORCYCLES

A person who likes motorcycles can have a very enjoyable time touring Japan by bike. There is the individual freedom afforded by any motor vehicle plus the added advantage of being able to get through spaces that can stall a car for long periods when traffic gets snarled. I once got my bike across construction scaffolding where a road in the mountains had completely slipped away and down the side of a hill. Another advantage of bikes in Japan is that they can be parked almost anywhere – even on the sidewalk.

Anyone planning to tour Japan by bike should already have learned to ride one and have at least a year's experience elsewhere before even considering riding around Japan. You should also have a licence specifically validated for motorcycles. Obtaining a driving licence in Japan is a lengthy and expensive process and should be avoided if possible; if starting from scratch you must put in time

on smaller bikes before being allowed to progress to larger ones.

Most bikes in Japan are used for utilitarian purposes, like deliveries and except in metropolitan areas, large bikes (over 250cc) are quite rare. Although many fire-breathing super bikes are built in Japan, most are exported. There are no Japanese-made bikes for sale in Japan (new) that are bigger than 750cc.

An interesting sight near Tokyo on weekends are Japanese men, dressed immaculately in costly leathers, riding very expensive foreign bikes. It's quite impressive seeing so many top class machines all in one cluster despite the fact they're all held back by the 60 km/h speed limit and very heavy traffic. Highly visible, but not usually seen travelling with other groups, are Harley-Davidsons; the H-D phenomenon is actually worth a trip to Japan just to observe. Some men buy the largest H-D touring machines, load them with every available accessory, then outfit themselves so they resemble American highway patrol police, right down to shoulder patches and badges on their tailor-made uniforms. (The badges are on sale in Ueno with a choice of cities and states.) The owners then parade their machines through the streets of Tokyo and elsewhere. They can't help but make an impression – of some kind.

The optimum size of a bike for touring Japan is 250cc. This is the smallest size allowed on expressways and the largest allowed on the major streets of Tokyo between 11 pm and 6 am (a crude way to try to eliminate the problem of bike gangs that race around the city at night). Best of all, a 250cc bike is the largest size that is not subject to *shaken*; and because of the low speed limits there is little sense buying anything bigger anyway.

Many years ago there was no problem with buying a bike in Japan, riding it while there, then taking it home. However, there are now so many different regulations in various countries regarding lighting, switch operation patterns, reflectors and other things that a domestic model bike cannot be registered in the USA (for example), while the USA export model cannot be ridden on Japanese highways. Export models that are manufactured in Japan can be bought in Japan and delivered to a shipping company. Some bikes are being made in the USA and may not be available in Japan at all. The domestic models could, of course, be modified to meet foreign regulations, but the cost of this together with all the shipping expenses, could easily bring the total price up to about the same as you would pay at home.

Bikes imported into Japan may have engines larger than 750cc but because the maximum size of Japanese-made made bikes sold in Japan is only 750cc some Japanese bikes are exported and then re-imported!

If you want a new bike and are travelling through Singapore it would almost certainly be cheaper to buy one there. There is no duty payable if the bike is exported within a certain period of time and it couldn't be as expensive to ship from there as it is from Japan.

If you wish to buy a large (over 250cc) bike new, the best dealers will be in the large cities – Tokyo, Osaka, etc. Large dealers are better able to give discounts or may include accessories instead of a price reduction. The dealer can take care of the paperwork for registration, insurance, etc.

Honda has the largest dealer network in the country, followed by Yamaha, then Suzuki. Kawasaki dealers seem comparatively rare. Remember that dealers in smaller centres don't normally work on large bikes so they may not carry spare parts.

After considering the cost of a new bike you may decide to buy a second-hand one and sell it later, though even used bikes are rather expensive in Japan. This may seem surprising because Japan must be the ultimate throw-away society; things are usually discarded at the first sign of

trouble. Bikes however seem to be the exception and used bikes are more expensive than they are in Australia, for example, and almost certainly the USA as well. My three-year-old Honda 550 with 4000 km on the clock cost Y270,000: the bike was Y220,000 and *shaken* added Y50,000.

Prices for used bikes have strange patterns. For example a used 400cc bike won't be much cheaper than a used 750cc (because the demand for the latter is less), and the price of bikes up to 250cc are also not low because they escape the very high recurring cost of *shaken*.

My most earnest advice is to avoid even considering the purchase of one of the countless models of cute little mini-motorscooters that have multiplied like rabbits in the past few years. Though their prices are attractive they are hazardous to drive as about 60 per cent of them are assembled with the rear wheel out of line with the frame. The result is that the back end continually tries to go off to one side, and riding one requires constant leaning, to balance the machine. Looking at scooter riders in Japan might lead you to believe that every one of them suffers from curvature of the spine!

When buying a used bike in Tokyo first check the *Tokyo Weekender*. Since advertisers are usually other foreigners there should be no language problem in negotiating. You could even run an advertisement yourself, saying what size bike you want (and the date of your arrival in Japan if you're doing it from another country). Write to: *Tokyo Weekender*, 55-11 Yayoi-cho-1-chome, Nakano-ku, Tokyo 164. The Tokyo TIC sometimes has used motorcycles advertised on its bulletin board so you could check there or place your own ad. Service men at US bases around Japan – there are several within an hour or so of Tokyo – sometimes have bikes for sale.

The largest concentration of used bike shops is in the Ueno area of Tokyo, along the streets parallel to Showa-dori; this runs north-south past Ueno station (JNR); and near Ueno subway station (Hibiya and Ginza lines). The dealers are to the north of the station.

The Japanese newspapers also have bikes advertised and there are many motorcycle magazines with pages of bikes for sale. As with buying a car you can get help over the language barrier with the aid of someone from Tescort.

Be sure to test ride any bike. There is a 50-50 chance it will pull to one side – don't reject it immediately as roughly half the bikes in Japan suffer from this malady. The most likely cause is simply that the rear wheel has been cocked sideways when adjusting the chain tension – one side has been tightened more than the other. This is easy to check by looking at the index marks on the arm.

If you're touring Japan by bike it is useful to carry a tyre repair kit and pump. There is nothing worse that getting a flat tyre high up on a mountain road; this recommendation is based on personal experience.

When having a bike serviced in a small town keep an eye on what's going on. I once had an oil change performed in a town on Hokkaido. When I wasn't watching the 'mechanic' tightened the drain plug with an immense wrench. At the next oil change, the plug didn't come out – the entire bottom of the oil tank broke free!

Elastic luggage straps, preferably about 60 cm long are very useful and are available from motorcycle accessory shops. Worth looking for in small local bike shops are 'cottage industry' straps cut from old inner tubes as they are long and very strong.

Another tip is to put your clothing in individual plastic bags and wrap them with elastic bands when you put them in your pack, to keep them dry if you get rained on (not uncommon!). Rain gear is useful to carry with you but it might be cheaper in other countries; a vinyl jacket and pants costs about Y1500. Helmets are required by law on all but small bikes; even if not required they should be worn at all times. An HA RS-Z helmet with chin guard costs about Y9000 after discount.

Japan is no more dangerous than other countries for motorcyclists – possibly less so because the speed limits are so low – but you must be aware of a few idiocies that persist. Car and truck drivers in Japan have no appreciation of the space needs of bikes (or any other vehicles) and

will drive close behind, unable to tolerate the sight of a clear space ahead of the vehicle in front. They will also go to ridiculous extremes to squeeze past a motorcycle, even if there is no space in front of it, passing within inches and totally oblivious of the danger to the rider who might have to make a sudden swerve to avoid something.

Many car drivers simply don't know the law regarding motorcycles. Small bikes are required to hug the edge of the road and not exceed 50 km/h. Ignorant motorists – found in large numbers in small towns and remote areas – rarely see a bike bigger than 125cc and they just don't know that larger bikes have the same right to travel down the middle of the lane as a car does.

Riders must always beware of taxis – they will cut into the curb without warning to pick up a fare, so you must be on the watch for prospective passengers by the roadside as much as the taxi drivers.

Motorcycles are not available for rental for long-distance touring though occasionally they may be obtained for local sightseeing.

It seems that this section does little but paint pictures of gloom and doom. But anyone who is objective knows that motorcycling can be dangerous so it is foolish to hide the hazards. Despite all this, however, touring by motorcycle is one of the most enjoyable ways to see Japan.

RENTAL CARS

For those not travelling on the tightest of budgets a rental car can be a viable way of travelling in Japan without having to depend on the vagaries of public transport. Costs are not unreasonable, especially if shared with two or three others, and cars are available at stations (and elsewhere) throughout the country. As it can take hours to get out of the big cities, and there are usually long dull stretches before reaching 'the good bits', and because cars can be reserved in one city from another, it is perfectly feasible to take a train over the long and uninteresting distances, then rent a car for local sightseeing. Because of the low speed limits on ordinary roads and the extortionate tolls on the few expressways, a rental car is not recommended for covering long distances.

Two of the main companies are Nippon Rent-a-Car (associated with Hertz, which allows world-wide reservations) and Toyota. Both have brochures in English, available at their desks at Narita airport, and at the TICs. Cars of several sizes and most cost ranges are available.

The following rates for Nippon (Hertz) are representative and of course are subject to change. These rates are for unlimited distance (no per-km charge), although the car must be returned with a full tank. Different companies have different policies regarding distance charges; unlimited travel is generally cheaper in practice. Vehicles can be rented for six hour, 12 hour or multiples of 24 hour periods. The first price in the following rates is for the first 24 hours, the second price is for each additional day.

1200cc	Charade	Y6,000	Y4,000
1300	Civic	Y7,500	Y5,000
1500	Mirage	Y11,000	Y6,500
1500	Corolla	Y12,200	Y7,500
1600	Corona	Y15,000	Y8,600
1800	Galant	Y17,000	Y10,700
2000	Crown	Y21,500	Y12,800

A discount is often available for many of the Nippon rates, and Toyota may well have a similar system. At the time of filling out the rental forms it is possible to join the 'No. 1 Club', which gives you a membership card and entitles you to discounts. Brochures give full details.

It is generally possible to rent a car in one city and leave it in another, but a rather stiff charge is added. Insurance is covered in the rental charge.

Cars can be reserved for pick-up almost anywhere in Japan through both companies by contacting the following offices:

		Nippon	Toyota
Tokyo	(03)	496-0919	264-2834
Osaka	(06)	344-0919	344-6831
Nagoya	(052)	203-0919	882-1310
Fukuoka	(092)	472-0919	441-1651
Sapporo	(011)	758-0919	
Sendai	(0222)	63-0919	
Yokohama	(045)	251-0919	
Kyoto	(075)	671-0919	
Hiroshima	(082)	245-0919	
Takamatsu	(0878)	61-0919	
Miyazaki	(0985)	51-0919	
Okinawa	(0988)	63-0919	

Other car rental companies are:

	Tokyo:	Osaka
Japaren	352-7635	632-4881
Mitsubishi Rent-a-Car	294-4871	345-6188
Nissan Rent-a-Car	584-2341	458-7391
ACU Rent-a-Car	364-2211	

If you really want to impress someone you can rent a Rolls Royce in Tokyo. The rates are very reasonable – Y49,500 for six hours; Y59,500 for 12 hours and Y89,500 for 24 hours. If you're interested phone Mr Hayashida on (03) 485-6064; ask if the price includes a full tank of petrol.

There are also car rental offices at some railway stations; these are indicated in *Jikokuhyo*.

HIRE CARS

Hire cars with drivers can be arranged through travel agencies or the larger hotels that cater to foreign tourists. They can also be contacted directly in the following cities: *In Tokyo:* Imperial Hire-Car Service, tel (03) 264-7441; Kokusai Hire-Car Service, 242-5931; and Nihon Hire-Car Service, 213-6741.

In Kyoto: Kyoto Hotel Hire-Car Service, (075) 211-1818.

In Osaka: Nihon Kotsu Hire-Car Service, (06) 532-5671.

English-speaking drivers are available. The cost of a hire car is about double that of a taxi.

BICYCLES

Anyone in good health with the time and desire to see Japan in depth and at low cost could consider the bicycle. It offers the maximum interaction with nature and people in the countryside, and the greatest convenience in seeing many cities like Kyoto.

A bicycle is a practical proposition because it can be dismantled and packed into a special carrying bag that may be taken into the passenger compartment of a train or put in a car, to bypass boring stretches of countryside or to get out of the major cities more easily.

If you already own a good touring bike, you can transport it to Japan by air freight, by mail (if the frame isn't too big), or as part of your checked luggage, either dismantled and packed, or assembled (some airlines).

Japan is one of the world's major bicycle producers so it could be worthwhile buying a bike in Japan, either ready-made or made-to-order. Unfortunately export models are not sold in Japan and most domestic models might be on the small side for tall foreigners, though anyone under 175 cm (5'9") tall would have a huge number to choose from.

Although sales brochures indicate many bikes as being suitable for people up to 182 cm, keep in mind that this means 182cm-tall Japanese – which means that westerners of the same height would find that the frame of such bikes was too short and they could never straighten their legs.

Bags for carrying dismantled bicycles on trains are available from Marty Davidson in Tokyo, tel 405-5680. A bike enthusiast, he might be able to give advice on finding large bikes.

For those who can comfortably use a domestic model, the bikes made by Bridgestone, Fuji, Maruishi, Miyata, Nishiki, Sekine, Silk, Tsunoda and many others are worth considering.

Brochures of these manufacturers can be obtained by writing to: Japan Bicycle Promotion Institute, (Att: Mr H Kono or Mr H Ise), Nihon Jitensha Kaikan Bldg, 9-

3 Akasaka 1-chome, Minato-ku, Tokyo. Tel, 583-53444; both men speak good English.

There are four main types of bike sold in Japan: Camping, Touring (or Randonneur), Sportif and Racing.

Camping bikes are very strong, but heavy and slow and are built to carry large loads of camping gear over bad roads. They are a common sight in warm weather with loads of everything imaginable slung on everywhere, including bags hung from the axles. It is not a recommended type for overseas visitors.

Racing bikes are also unsuitable for touring, being uncomfortable, twitchy in handling, lacking in comforts like mud-guards, fragile (especially the tyres) and expensive. Road Racer bikes are between Sportif and Racing machines and can only be recommended for one-day runs.

The Touring and Sportif models are both quite light, typically 11-12 and 12-14 kg respectively. The major difference between them is the gearing. Touring bikes have a wider spread between the two front sprockets and may also have lower low ratios in the rear cluster. The end effect is that Touring bikes are a little stronger and are able to carry more on rougher roads, while the Sportif types are intended for higher speeds with less luggage.

Many bikes of all the main types are designed for quick disassembly, a definite plus feature. Such bikes are called 'rinko' (short for rinkosha); in catalogues they are usually indicated by a wrench symbol.

There is a possible Y150 surcharge each time a bike is taken on a train. If desired, membership in the Japan Cycling Association, may be bought by mail by writing to Japan Cycling Association, (Att: Mr Sakon), Tokyo Cycling Assoc-iation, c/o Maeda Industry Co Ltd, 3-8-1 Ueno, Taito-ku, Tokyo. Tel 833-3967/8/ 9.

If there are difficulties communicating with the JCA, call Mr Kono or Mr Ise at the Japan Bicycle Promotion Institute (tel 583-5444). The JCA has functions and activities like weekend rides.

If you wish to try out a variety of bikes before buying one, there are two complexes, near Tokyo (Izu-hanto peninsula) and Osaka, with a vast number of rental bikes of different types plus a variety of tracks on which to try them out. The name in Japanese: *Cycling Sports Centre*! There is also overnight accommodation (advance reservation recommended), and there are other sports and recreation facilities.

Second-hand bikes are available in Japan, but as with buying anything else, the language problem has to be overcome. Several bicycle magazines have ads. A Japanese friend or someone from Tescort might be willing to assist. Other sources are police-recovered bicycle sales and suburban 'junk yards' that sell a great variety of second-hand merchandise.

Bikes are available for rent by the day at a number of places in Japan. All the Cycling Inns (described in the section on Places to Stay) have bikes for rent at reasonable rates; so do several youth hostels. The *Youth Hostel Handbook* indicates these with a symbol but does not have a central listing of such hostels, although another of their publications *Hostelling Way in Japan* does; the booklet is free on request from the national HQ in Tokyo.

The general road maps suggested earlier for motor vehicles are equally useful for cyclists. In addition there are three maps that have been made up specifically with the cyclist in mind. They show the location of every youth hostel, places that rent bicycles (shown by a red bicycle symbol, with telephone number), special bicycle roads and touring routes, 'Koku minshukusha' (accommodation), road gradients – even a star rating system for the difficulty of the touring courses. Of all the maps available for touring by road in Japan, these have by far the largest number of places identified in romaji as well as in kanji. The disappointing thing is that they only cover the central third of

Honshu. Further maps in the series are intended to cover all Japan, eventually.

The maps are printed by the Bridgestone company and are called *sai-ku-rin-gu ma-pu* (cycling map); English is written on the back of the folder, but the front is only in Japanese. They cost Y650 each and should be available at bookstores. If you have trouble obtaining copies, contact the Japan Bicycle Promotion Institute.

HITCHING

For saving money and getting to know Japanese people, there is no better way of getting around Japan than by hitching. The Japanese must be the kindest people in the world to thumbing foreigners and the main difficulty is to avoid taking unfair advantage of them. Tales abound of drivers going hours – even days – out of their way to take travellers to their destinations, all the while buying their meals and sometimes even taking them home overnight.

The Japanese themselves rarely hitch-hike and many drivers are not familiar with the meaning of an outstretched thumb. Many a foreigner has found himself taken to the next town and dropped off at the railway station!

It is useful to make up a large sign in kanji showing your destination, with the addition of the characters for *homen* which means 'area', or a literal-minded driver may go past believing that only that destination will do, when he is going a slightly shorter distance. So carry stiff paper or cardboard and a felt tip pen. Another tip is to stand at traffic lights in towns (there are many) and ask drivers if they are going your way. Neighbourhood children may be willing to help. In country areas hitching is no problem because it's easy to reach the highway and vehicles have space to stop.

For straight-through long drives it is hard to beat trucks. They are often going long distances, and drivers frequently try to arrange another lift with a truck going beyond their stopping point. Though they never speak more than a few words of English, they are invariably good natured and interested in their passenger. Often this is their first meeting with a foreigner. It gives them added prestige to be able to show off a *gaijin* in the cab of their truck.

They are usually quite earthy and the closest inheritors of the ancient Japanese spirit. They will most likely know and sing traditional folk songs and be familiar with other elements of folk tradition – a contrast to the court culture that produced the refined tea ceremony and kota playing. etc.

Any women hitching alone or in pairs, who may have some doubts about the whole business, would be well advised to stick to trucks with green number plates – they are company owned and the drivers are much more likely to behave themselves.

Another potential risk for western women is the young Japanese male in his jazzed up car who wishes to impress her with his highly developed driving skills and finely honed reflexes (although these 'petrol-heads' can be found in any country!). The fact is (in Japan at least) because of the low speed limits he will have had very little experience with fast driving of any kind, especially on twisty roads. And in the presence of a western woman he is likely to get a bit reckless, especially on mountain roads where young Japanese male drivers go silly anyway.

For rapid travel between cities, the expressways are by far the fastest way to go. The points to remember are, firstly, that the long-distance trucks are like nocturnal animals, so the expressways are choked with them at night. Secondly it is not permitted to hitch at the edge of the road on an expressway.

The best way to get started is to stand before or at the entrance toll gate. Attendants have been known to help by asking drivers if they can give you a lift to your destination.

Once you have a ride ask where the

driver is going. If he plans to exit before your destination, ask him to let you off at the next *tsugi no kyukeijo* (or 'rest area') *de orosh te kudasai.* You can then ask around other truck drivers (they usually stand around in groups talking), or you can stand with your sign near the exit from the parking lot where it leads back to the road. Often your driver will ask for you so you'll be passed from truck to truck across the country.

You will probably be treated with such kindness that you are sure to want to return the favour in some way. This will be difficult, as they usually refuse to take money and will not let you pay for their meals; usually they will want to treat you! Before setting out, stock up on fruit, candy or *sembe* (rice crackers) and feed them to your driver as you go along; you can leave the rest of the box or package when you get out. Foreign cigarettes are also very popular (the Japanese smoke like chimneys) – bring them as your duty free allowance.

Be sure to try to talk to your driver; he will appreciate some attempt at communication even if he speaks no English. If two people are hitching together it is all too tempting to talk to each other all the time, and if the driver is alone he may get annoyed at being ignored after his kindness in stopping.

Please don't ask the TIC for advice on hitching; it is not legal, they say, and they don't wish to get involved.

The following directions explain how to get to the entrances of the main expressways from the major cities of Japan.

Tokyo (northbound): The Tohoku Expressway (Tohoku Kosoku doro) begins at the city of Iwatsuki, more than 30 km north of Tokyo.

Take the JNR Keihin-Tohoku line from any station between Shinagawa and Tabata to Omiya. Exit from the platform at the end closest to the front of the train; immediately to the left will be stairs down to the Tobu-sen line. Take it to Iwatsuki,

the fifth stop; the train fares will total around Y500.

Exiting from the front of the station, walk down the main street until you reach the second large street on the right; ignore the side alleys. Walking for 10-15 minutes will take you under the overhead roadway, to the expressway entrance.

Maps show the expressway as being planned to begin closer to Tokyo, so check with the TIC to find out if you can reach the entrance more easily.

Tokyo (southbound): Take the Shin-Tamagawa line to Yoga, the fifth station after Shibuya. Shin-Tamagawa line is a continuation of the Hanzomon subway line and may be entered by continuing along that line, or at Shibuya, where the entrance is close to the statue of Hachiko, the famous dog. At Yoga, the overhead roadway of the Tomei Expressway (Tomei Kosokudoro) is about half a km to the south of the station; there is a police box near the station if directions are needed. Ask: *kosoku doro wa, dochira?*.

When you reach the roadway, pass under it and turn to the right. A few hundred metres alongside the roadway, a ramp rises to the right up to the entrance; a service road continues straight. You can stand in the vee between the roads (but be ready to run quickly if a car stops because the ramp is narrow and there is a risk of causing an accident); or you can take the safer course and stand further back on the service road before the ramp splits off. It might also be possible to enlist the help of toll gate operators.

Nagoya: Take the subway bound for Hoshigaoka or Fujigaoka; the destination is Hongo station but many trains terminate before there at Hoshigaoka. In such a case, change to a later train that goes all the way. The entrance ramps for both northbound and southbound traffic are near Hongo station.

Kyoto: From the front of Kyoto station take bus No 19 or 20 and watch for signs by the roadside for the Meishin Expressway. Get off and select the correct ramp for the desired destinations – Osaka, Kobe and points south, or Nagoya/Tokyo and points north.

Note that it is not worthwhile trying to hitch within the area bounded by Kyoto-Osaka-Kobe; they form one vast conur-

bation and trying to find your way by road is more bother than it's worth. Trains are much quicker and more convenient, even if you have your own vehicle.

Because of the great build-up of towns around Kyoto, when heading toward the north coast, it is simplest to take the JNR train to Kamioka and start hitching from there.

Tokyo

Tokyo is one of the most populous cities on earth, the centre of government and commerce in Japan and a major industrial city. It is difficult to put an exact number on the actual population because in the central part it varies by nearly two million between day and night. The actual Tokyo administrative area is 2031 sq km and includes many sub-cities. Adjacent Kawasaki and Yokohama form one vast conurbation with Tokyo itself. Therefore, while the population of Tokyo is quoted at around 12 million, it totals 15 million or more when these areas are included.

Tokyo can be enjoyed for shopping and entertainment, but it has relatively little of historic sightseeing interest; what did exist was largely destroyed by the 1923 Kanto earthquake or wartime bombing. It is better to go to Kyoto, Nara, Kamakura, Nikko, etc, for sightseeing. On the other hand Tokyo is a very interesting place to live and explore slowly and in depth.

Information
Tourist Information Center (TIC)

The single best source of information for travel in Japan, and a surprisingly large range of other types of info to interest overseas visitors, is any of the three information offices operated by the Japan National Tourist Organisation (JNTO). The offices are located at Narita Airport, in downtown Tokyo and in Kyoto.

Tokyo TIC is located near the Ginza area of Tokyo on Harumi-dori, about 200 metres from Mitsukoshi Department Store on the way to Hibiya-koen (park). From Mitsukoshi you can see the railroad bridge (used by Shinkansen and local trains) down Harumi-dori; the TIC is just beyond the bridge, on the left. It is clearly marked with a large illuminated sign with yellow letters 'TIC' on a black background.

Access from JNR trains: If travelling on the Yamanote or Keihin-Tohoku lines, get off at Yurakucho station. Walk to the end of the platform in the direction of Shimbashi station and look for the sign 'For Hibiya Area'. Note the Sogo Department Store on the right (it has a Youth Hostel booking office in the basement) and exit from the station on that side. Then turn left and walk along the street, keeping to the right of the elevated railway tracks. At the major road (Harumi-dori), the TIC office will be clearly visible across the street.

Hibiya line: Get off at Hibiya station and leave the platform at the end closest to Ginza station (next stop). Walk up to the exit and double back between the exits (there's one on each side of the passageway). Take Exit A4, walk up the steps and the TIC sign will be visible about 50 metres ahead.

Chiyoda and Mita lines: Get off at Hibiya station on either line. Both stations are located some distance from the Hibiya line's Hibiya station, but they are all connected by underground passages. After exiting from the platform, follow signs for the Hibiya line. This will lead to a long passage that has an entrance to the Hibiya line at the near end. Walk past this, along the passage as indicated by signs 'Passage for Ginza'. Exit A4 will be to the right.

The following are some of the publications available from the TIC.

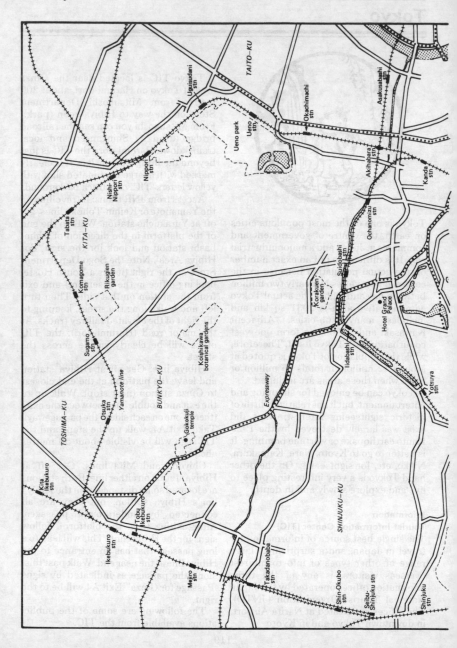

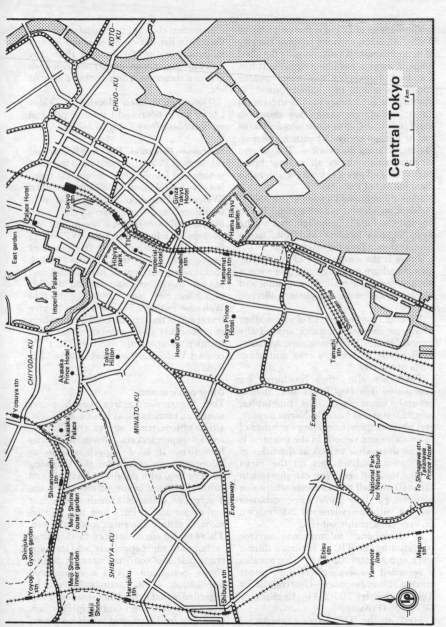

Central Tokyo

0   1 km

Tourist Map of Tokyo is the best map of Tokyo available, showing parts of the city of most interest to visitors, plus detailed maps of some areas like Shinjuku. It has the best subway/railway map, colour coded to match the colours used to identify the actual cars (or the individual lines); and station names are shown in kanji and romaji, so destinations and fares can be figured easily. A bonus is the map 'Transportation Network – Tokyo and vicinity' which shows all railway lines, both JNR and private, for a considerable distance out of the city.

Map of Tokyo and Vicinity, also a JNTO publication, shows the area around Tokyo beyond the Fuji/Hakone/Izu area to the west; Nikko to the north; and Chiba to the east. It is excellent for orientation.

Tokyo is the simple title of an information brochure on the city. It gives some history, general and sightseeing info, and has listings of some museums, galleries, etc.

Walking Tour Courses in Tokyo describes what you can see in walks around the Imperial Palace, Ueno-koen park, Asakusa, a bit of the Shitamachi area and other parts of the city.

There are also other brochures for specialised aspects of Tokyo and Japan in general (summarised JNR timetables, info on trains and buses to Narita airport, etc) plus pamphlets on a large number of other cities and regions in the country. It will be worthwhile to look at the titles of the various publications on the racks behind the staff area. You can also talk to the staff and tell them exactly where you plan to go; they have filing cabinets bulging with miscellaneous information on every imaginable subject.

A telephone information service operated by the TIC is available during working hours; tel 502-1461. There is also a recorded message giving info about current cultural events and festivals in the Tokyo area; tel 503-2911 (English) or 503-2926 (French).

Staff at the TIC have a wealth of information about a huge variety of topics; they have listings on economical accommodation in the Tokyo area (but they don't arrange reservations) and can even give assistance on where to find a dentist etc.

The office is open Monday to Friday from 9 am to noon and 1 pm to 5 pm; and on Saturdays from 9 am to noon.

Welcome Furoshiki For newly arrived residents of Tokyo (ie transferred business people and families from overseas) there is a very useful information service called 'Welcome Furoshiki'. A furoshiki is a traditional Japanese square of cloth used to wrap and carry items; it is symbolic of a package of information that 'WF' offers free. A WF member visits the homes of newcomers, gives the 'bundle' (which contains a great deal of useful info) and answers questions about settling into this unfamiliar new land. (Please note that Welcome Furoshiki is not set up to give travel info of the type desired by travellers or anyone just passing through; that job is handled competently by the TIC.) To contact Welcome Furoshiki, phone 352-0765.

Other publications:
Tour Companion, a free weekly paper aimed at tourists, is available at hotels, airline offices, travel agents, the TIC and some supermarkets frequented by foreigners. It is a superb source of information on events for the following week or two, with details of festivals and cultural/entertainment offerings in the Tokyo area. It also lists phone numbers of embassies and airlines and has info on movies, gallery showings, concerts, etc. There is also space devoted to shopping, restaurants, night spots, etc, and its maps show places of touristic interest, banks, shops, restaurants. It is a commercial publication so its listings should be regarded in that light. Single copies (Y150 when ordered) and subscriptions are available in Japan and overseas from:

Tokyo News Service Ltd., Tsukiji Hamar-ikyu Bldg 10Fl, 3-3 Tsukiji 5-chome, Chuo-ku, Tokyo 104.

Tokyo Journal, a monthly publication, covers a lot of ground. Its front pages have short articles on various subjects related to Japan, some of interest mainly to residents and others for anyone interested in the country. The larger part is devoted to information about coming events such as concerts (classical and popular music), dance, kabuki and other traditional Japanese performing arts, films, and exhibitions at museums, galleries and department stores. It also lists pubs and similar places which feature live jazz etc, a large number of restaurants and drinking places, conversational lounges, travel agencies and other services, Japanese language schools, miscellaneous classified ads, and a number of low cost accommodation places. It also has useful maps with banks and important buildings used as landmarks. Cover price is Y300 and it's available at most bookstores (especially in large hotels), the American Pharmacy, many travel agencies, supermarkets and restaurants popular with foreigners. Single copies and subscriptions are available in Japan and overseas from: Cross Culture Jigyodan Cl. Ltd., Magatani Bldg 3Fl, 5-10-13 Toranomon, Minato-ku, Tokyo 105.

Or: US – Japan Cross Culture Centre, Japanese-American Community and Cultural Centre, Suite 305, 244 So. San Pedro St, Los Angeles, CA 90012.

Tokyo Weekender is a weekly free newspaper aimed at foreign residents in Tokyo. The lead article may be on any topic under the sun, but every issue has social, fashion, food and entertainment pages. There is a weekly film review, and a listing of foreign language films at Tokyo theatres. Occasional articles deal with the Japanese and life in Japan, past and present and give some insights rarely seen elsewhere, such as discussions of the plots and often anti western slants of Japanese films and TV shows. It provides good coverage of the six annual sumo wrestling tournaments and has a classified ad section for goods, services and accommodation of interest to foreigners. It is released Fridays and can be picked up at the TIC, most large hotels, the American Pharmacy, many supermarkets and pubs or restaurants catering to foreign clientele (mostly in Roppongi and Akasaka). Single copies and subscriptions are available in Japan and overseas from: Tokyo Weekender, Oriental Bldg, 55-11 Yayoi-cho 1-chome, Nakano-ku, Tokyo 164.

Books

Numerous publications covering specific aspects of Tokyo have come on the market in recent years and are suggested for use if exploring Tokyo in greater detail.

Footloose in Tokyo, by Jan Pearce (Weatherhill; Y1500), is a series of walking tours in the vicinity of the 29 stations of the Yamanote loop line, giving background not only on the specific area, but also on Tokyo and Japan in general.

Around Tokyo, Vol I and II, by John Turrent and Jonathon Lloyd-Owen (Japan Times; Y1200), are compilations of columns from the Japan Times describing a large number of well-known and obscure attractions in Tokyo and vicinity.

Tokyo Now and Then, by Paul Waley (Weatherhill; Y5000), describes Tokyo in great detail as it is now and how it was in the past; with many interesting anecdotes to bring to life the things you can see.

More Footloose in Tokyo, by Jean Pearce (Weatherhill; Y1200), covers the Shitamachi area plus Narita in a manner similar to her earlier book – a walking tour with descriptions of what you're seeing and its significance/history.

Discover Shitamachi, by Enbutsu Sumiko (name written Japanese style, published by The Shitamachi Times; Y1500), deals with Shitamachi in greater detail than Jean Pearce's book, making it somewhat heavier reading but it contains more insights and information.

A Parent's Guide to Tokyo, by Hartzenbusch and Shabecoff (Shufunotomo; Y1500), is a collection of articles originally printed in the Tokyo Weekender with the theme of where to take children (and teens and tourists) for amusement in Tokyo. The articles were originally written in 1973 and generally updated in 1981 so the info is, for the most part, current.

Tokyo City Guide, by Connor and Yoshida, is (if not out of print) a well-regarded and lively aid for seeing and appreciating this giant city.

Things to See

How do you begin to look around a city that is home to 12 or 14 million people? Is it even possible to explore Tokyo? Not really, but there are ways to nibble at parts to get some idea of the whole.

Tokyo was, in the past, described as a collection of villages and except for the fact that many of these 'villages' are now cities in their own right with city-centres of large stores and commercial buildings, the description is still relevant.

In Edo days (to about 1867) there were two major divisions of Tokyo – Shitamachi (pronounced *Sh'ta machi* meaning 'downtown') for the common folk, and Yamanote ('near the mountains') for the wealthy and powerful. (The Yamanote train line largely encircles the Yamanote area, hence its name.)

Although a centre of power since the early 1600s, there is little of historic interest in Tokyo. This is partly because Kyoto continued to be the imperial capital with the figurehead emperor, his court and the elaborate structures (such as temples and palaces) that went with it, while Tokyo was more a military and governing centre that did not attract such grandiose construction. It is also because the great Kanto earthquake and wartime bombing destroyed much of the city.

In the following pages are some general words on modern Tokyo, followed by further detail on a few of the major areas of greater interest to visitors. This will be enough to keep anyone busy for a couple of days. For more detailed explanation it is advisable to obtain one or more of the many guide books to Tokyo that have been published in recent years; they give vastly more detail on the attractions of this city than can possibly be crammed into a general book of this sort.

For a quick introduction to the city, a long-recommended and still valid suggestion is to ride the Yamanote loop for one circuit of the city, a trip of about an hour. This will show how so much of the city is made up of low (one or two-storey) houses interspersed with taller apartment and commercial buildings. Since the line passes through most of the major sub-city areas, it also gives a view of the tremendous amount of development that has taken place in these clusters.

All of Tokyo, with the exception of some small pockets in the Shitamachi area, was quite literally flattened by bombing during the last stages of World War II. Photos from that time show vast expanses where not a building was left standing as far as the eye could see. The contrast with today, only 40 years on, is phenomenal.

The first post-war buildings were tacky, flimsy wooden structures, a few of which still stand here and there through the city. The next generation saw these replaced by generally drab and dreary, but functional, concrete structures. With the incredible increase in public wealth in the past 10 years or so, these are progressively being replaced by architectural showpieces, often of very visible and imaginative, though sometimes non-functional, shape. These are giving an entirely new and stylish look to many parts of the city, initially in the fashionable areas, but also in local neighbourhoods. Walking through some of these nouveau riche areas, like Harajuku, Roppongi, Shinjuku, etc, gives the realisation that Tokyo (parts, anyway) is developing into a city that ranks well in the world for physical attractiveness – something unimaginable 15 years ago. Part of the enjoyment of Tokyo is just looking around at some of the more attractive, or outrageous, of its physical assets.

For a better understanding of the character of the various elements that make up this enormous city, it is worth spending the money on Jean Pearce's book *Footloose in Tokyo*.

In general, to 'attack' Tokyo successfully, read the following pages, pick up a map and literature from the TIC, obtain copies of *Tour Companion*, pick out the places of interest and go!

Ginza, Hibiya and the Imperial Palace

If any part of Tokyo were to be called its 'heart', it would be the Ginza district. In this one area are the country's major department stores, many other high fashion shops and the most expensive restaurants and drinking establishments – for very big spenders only. Close by, is the Marunouchi financial district, and just a short walk away is the reason why this area first came to prominence, the Imperial Palace.

Dating from Edo days this was the area where the higher ranks of society obtained their necessities and fineries, and the tradition has continued. The following is a brief look around.

Imperial Palace Grounds

One might expect a magnificent castle to stand in Tokyo, as they once did in Osaka and Nagoya, but Tokyo never had such huge buildings despite the quite massive walls and embankments that can be seen. It is not possible to enter the actual palace grounds except on 2 January and 23 April – New Year and the emperor's birthday. At other times visitors must be content with a stroll around the moats and a look at the fortifications and the scenic east garden.

If starting from the TIC, just turn left and go a couple of hundred metres to where a moat comes into view to the right then continue along until the first road across the moat. This leads to a large open park area, Kokyo-mae Hiroba (Imperial Palace Plaza), and further on Kokyo Gaien (Imperial Palace Outer Garden). The large, open pedestrian-only area to the left leads to Nijubashi bridge, which gives the only good view into the grounds. With the bridge in the foreground this is a typical Japanese castle 'view' – a fortification wall with a white defensive building atop it.

A few minutes walk north (use the Tokyo map from the TIC for these explorations) brings you to the entrance of Higashi Gyoen (East Garden), which is open most days till 3 pm. Entry is through some of the massive stonework of the original defensive walls, and the garden has many of the attractive features of Japanese gardens. A small zig-zag bridge here is unusual, being of Chinese derivation and seldom seen in Japan. In Chinese mythology evil spirits can only move by hopping and can turn only with great difficulty. By walking in zig-zags, as here, the spirits hop into the water and drown. (The same story explains why there is a high sill to step over when entering the gate of a temple; the evil spirits cannot hop over it.)

The only other sightseeing relative to the palace is to stroll at leisure along the moats around the walls. Except during the cherry blossom season there is little incentive to go beyond the Sakuradamon gate. But when the blossoms are out, the area at the top of the hill and beyond has some of the most magnificent displays of this short-lived spectacle in the country.

The path around the palace is a well-known jogging route, with distance markers. The nearby Imperial Hotel (successor to the one designed by Frank Lloyd Wright) has a jogging map.

The moats by the way, are home to a large number of graceful swans, and in winter attract many migratory birds including some, like the mandarin duck, that are quite exotic for the centre of a huge city.

The Imperial Palace can be reached from Hibiya stations of the Chiyoda, Hibiya and Mita subway lines; Nijubashi-mae station of the Chiyoda line; Otemachi station of the Mita, Marunouchi and Tozai subway lines; Tokyo station of the Marunouchi line; and Tokyo and Yurakucho stations of the JNR Yamanote and Keihin-Tohoku lines.

Ginza Area

If you follow Hibiya-dori, the road that runs along the edge of the southern-most moat (closest to the Ginza area), for about 15 minutes (past the end of Hibiya-koen park) you'll find yourself at *Zojo-ji* temple. The temple itself is unremarkable, being a post-war concrete structure, but one of its entrance gates, dating back to 1605, survived the war and still has its Niosama guardian gods. If you are not going to Kyoto or Nikko, where other such gates and gods may be seen, this is a good chance to see who kept the evil spirits at bay.

Walking along Harumi-dori (the road that passes the TIC) from the palace, soon brings you to the 'bright city lights' with shops of every imaginable kind, selling cameras, pearls, cloisonne ware, etc. The shops are mostly for the Japanese, but there are several which cater to foreign visitors, and the International Arcade is in this area. Continuing on Harumi-dori for a few hundred metres leads to the traditional looking *Kabuki-za* theatre, Tokyo's major kabuki theatre.

The main landmark in this area is the Ginza crossing, identified by the main Mitsukoshi Department Store on one corner and the circular San-ai building diagonally opposite. The cross street at this intersection is Chuo-dori, on which the majority of the Ginza department stores, etc, are located. One of the simple must-do's of a visit to Japan is a walk through a large department store to marvel at the range (and sometimes price!) of goods available. This may give some idea of the type of furniture etc, that finds its way into Japanese homes, although any chairs, high leg tables etc, are for use by 'untypical' families. Furn-

iture intended for tatami living, such as low tables, is often beautifully finished, flawless lacquer that would be a show piece back home if it weren't for the size, weight and cost. Lacquer and ceramic dishes, cups, etc, of high quality (and matching price) may be seen here and give a quick education in Japanese taste – useful when deciding what souvenirs to take home. The Japanese do not eat from utensils decorated with temples, dragons, Mt Fuji, etc.

To the left (north) from Ginza crossing, Chuo-dori leads to Akihabara and Ueno. The few km to Akihabara can be walked in about an hour, and you can get some idea en route of what makes modern Japan tick. What makes the walk interesting is that, in addition to the many modern buildings, banks and other commercial establishments with their modern computer systems etc, there are still some old-fashioned shops selling antiques, kimono, dolls, fans or zori (the dress sandals worn with kimono).

Chuo-dori is blocked to traffic in the Ginza area on Saturday and Sunday afternoons when shoppers stroll at will and tables are set up for eating. Exotic western food is available at McDonalds.

Akihabara, the fantastic 'electronics' district, can also be reached by train (Yurakucho, Tokyo or Kanda stations) or the Hibiya or Ginza subway lines.

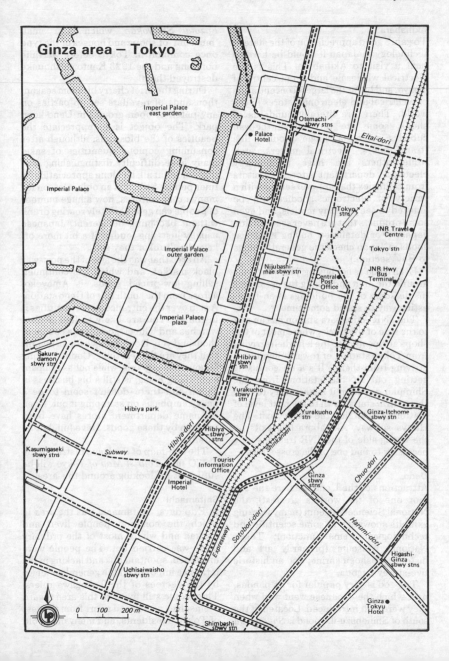

Ginza area – Tokyo

Akihabara

To gain a good appreciation of the state of technology in Japan it would be hard to beat a visit to Akihabara. This is the electrical wholesale and retail centre of Tokyo, and by far the largest concentration of electrical and electronics stores in the world. There are literally hundreds of shops, some are tiny hole-in-the-wall cubicles selling a single product line (transformers, electrical meters, etc), while others are huge multi-storey electrical department stores. Visitors from countries that are well served with a variety of electronic goodies will be amazed to see so many models, and even some products that are never seen outside Japan. (For details on buying electrical goods in Japan check the general 'Things to Buy' section.)

Even if you're not buying, just wandering around the area and taking the escalators inside some of the buildings is an interesting way to spend some time.

The JNR Akihabara station has an exit to the side of the tracks where most of the shops are located (to the left when arriving from Tokyo station, or toward Shinjuku if arriving from there). It's a bit confusing getting out of the station; from the Shinjuku direction it is necessary to take the central stairs down to the next level of platforms, then find the correct exit. The Hibiya subway, Akihabara line exits on the wrong side of the JNR tracks, so it's necessary to find one of the cross streets.

Ueno

Attractions of the Ueno area are the zoo (not one of the world's greatest); the National Science Museum (many working exhibits showing how some scientific and technological items function); Tokyo National Museum (primarily art and history); Toshogu shrine; and an historic five-storey pagoda.

The zoo is very popular for its pandas, over which the Japanese went wild when they were first introduced. Located at the south of Shinobazu-ike pond is *Shitamachi*

Fuzoka Shiryokan, which is a small 'museum' of shops and houses of the type once common in Tokyo before wartime bombing and the 1923 Kanto earthquake destroyed them.

During the brief cherry blossom season, thousands of revellers set up parties on any patch of open ground in Ueno-koen park. The object is to appreciate the beauties of the blossoms, although after consuming copious quantities of sake, many have difficulty distinguishing anything much at all, let alone appreciating its finer points. Still, it is an object lesson for many other cultures, how a huge number of people can get absolutely roaring drunk without becoming belligerent. Japanese usually just sing louder, if a bit more off key, the drunker they get.

An area that was the site of the post-war black market, and which has continued selling low-priced goods, is Ameyoko, across from the south exit of Ueno station. A sign over the entrance street identifies it in romaji. You are likely to find 'Rolex' watches and 'Gucci' goods for a couple of thousand yen. Don't believe for an instant that they are the real thing. Counterfeiting famous-brand goods, while not as rampant as in Hong Kong, is still a big business in Japan and there doesn't seem to be a heavy emphasis on stamping it out. Even big-name department stores have been taken in by these goods. Have fun, but be careful.

The sub-map of the Ueno district in the JNTO map *Tourist Map of Tokyo* will be sufficient for looking around this area.

Shitamachi

In Edo days, Shitamachi was the area in which the common people lived and worked and where most of the ordinary trade was carried out. The people were unrefined, spontaneous and lacking in the reticence imposed on the general populace by the decrees of the Tokugawa rulers. The people still living in this area regard themselves as a breed apart from the rest of Tokyo's residents, and many of the old

Top: View of Mt Fuji
Left: Rice harvesting, Noto peninsula
Right: Daibutsu (the great Buddha) at Kamakura, near Tokyo

Top: Nihon Matsuri festival, Tokyo
Left: Dragon dance at Asakusa temple, very much of Chinese origin
Right: Typical summer festival, in Tokyo — carrying a mikoshi (portable shrine)

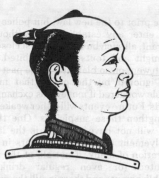

attitudes and ways of life survive, although it, like every other part of Japan, has changed much in the past decades.

There is no place marked 'Shitamachi' on a map; it is an ill-defined area generally to the east of the Yamanote line, from above Ueno to the Tsukiji area. It was an artificial creation of the shogun who wanted to keep all less-desirable elements in one area where they could be watched more easily. The famous Yoshiwara pleasure district was an important part of the scene, taking care of the sexual desires of all men of Edo. Although prostitution was made illegal in 1958, the same sort of activities go on under a different güise, both in the old Yoshiwara district and everywhere else in Japan.

The modern institution was, until recently (early 1985) called a *toruko* or 'turkish bath', but protests by Turks finally brought a change. These establishments are now called *soapland*, from the female attendants' practice of bathing the customers, often using their own bodies to apply the soap.

The heart of Shitamachi is *Asakusa Kannon* temple, properly known as *Senso-ji*. A visit can be combined with a walk through some of the back streets.

The temple is very active with worshippers praying for some sort of assistance, lighting bundles of incense and catching the smoke to rub on afflicted parts of their bodies to relieve an ache or pain, or just plain enjoying themselves.

The approach is lined with shops selling every manner of tourist junk. The shopping street is often described in terms like 'street of gaily decorated souvenir shops'.

As a single place to visit, I am less than enthralled. If you're going to Kyoto you will see much finer and older temples with extraordinary woodwork; Senso-ji and its five-storey pagoda are both post-war concrete reproductions, and thus lack the features of workmanship that make Japanese temples so remarkable. It is worth visiting during its annual festivals in March and October however; times will be given in *Tour Companion* but get there an hour or so before. The festivities feature a Chinese-style dragon; held up by numerous poles, it twists and writhes around the temple courtyard in a most remarkable way.

The books *More Footloose in Tokyo* and *Discover Shitamachi* are invaluable for exploring this area in depth.

Senso-ji can be reached by Ginza or Asakusa subway to Asakusa subway station, or by a special double-decker bus from Ueno station (as well as regular buses but they have no markings in English).

After sightseeing near the temple, an alternative to the usual way back is to take the water taxi down the Sumida-gawa river to Takeshiba pier, beside Shiba Rikyu and Hama Rikyu gardens, close to Hamamatsu-cho JNR station at the edge of the harbour and near Tsukiji fish market.

Shinjuku

Shinjuku is the up-and-coming sub-city of Tokyo. Due to its geological stability, (an important factor in earthquake-prone Japan) it has Tokyo's only collection of high rise buildings. It is also the place to go for the best camera shopping and excellent 'other' shopping, and has a large percentage of the entertainment establishments of the city.

The high-rises are all located on the west, or 'new city', side of Shinjuku station (which is reputed to be the busiest in the world, and a good contender for the title of 'most confusingly laid out'). On this side, down the small side streets, are the main stores of Yodobashi and Doi camera stores as well as any number of other shops specialising in computers and just about anything else you can think of.

The highway bus terminal for buses to the Mt Fuji and Hakone areas is close to the main Yodobashi store, and is clearly shown on the TIC map. This part of Shinjuku has also attracted a number of large hotels; in one small area there is the new Hilton, the Century Hyatt, the Keio Plaza and the Shinjuku Washington plus many others. Adjacent to Shinjuku station are two major department stores, Odakyu and Keio; trains of the same line leave from stations in their basements.

The east side of the station has most of the major department stores and many fashion-oriented shops. The two largest camera stores, Yodobashi and Sakuraya, have their 'showpiece' branches side by side facing the small square overlooked by a giant 'TV screen' (which is made up of thousands of light bulbs). The Nakano building next door, by the way, is the most valuable piece of real estate in Japan. Nearby, the Kinokuniya bookstore has large numbers of foreign-language books (mostly English), and its ground level entrance is a popular meeting place because of the shelter it offers.

Shinjuku has hundreds, possibly thousands, of restaurants and drinking places. Some, like those found in the area just mentioned, could be described as family oriented, while others cater to different tastes and include pink salons, gay bars, no-pants coffee shops, peep shows, etc.

Until a new law came into effect in February 1985, the sex scene was almost wide open, particularly in the area known as Kabukicho on the east side and north of the major shopping streets. Live sex shows and activities that would be surprising even in Bangkok, were commonplace prior to the new law, but police can now enter any establishment without a warrant, all such businesses must close by midnight and touts are prohibited. So much went on so blatantly in the past and was ignored by the police that many people wondered if money was exchanging hands. Future events will either weaken or strengthen these suspicions. One thing that will not have changed is the large involvement of yakuza gangsters in the operation of many, if not all, of the sex-oriented (or even regular drinking) establishments and there is still the risk of being stuck with a horrendous bill for a single drink. If you walk or are enticed into a place with large numbers of hostesses sitting with customers, it is advisable not to sit down unless you have established in advance what it will cost you. The Y18,000 glass of beer was invented in places like these.

It is doubtful that the new law will have more than a temporary effect on 'the business', and the large number of love hotels in the area, which are exempt from the midnight curfew, will doubtless continue to be busy. By the way, if patronising one of these hotels, note the price schedule on the wall; sometimes the first hour is comparatively cheap but the second hour jumps considerably in price.

Meiji-jingu

Meiji-jingu is probably the finest shrine in Japan and well worth a visit. It was built early this century to honour emperor Meiji, who reigned during the eventful period 1867-1912, when Japan changed from a self-isolated feudal country to a world power, largely under the guidance of this emperor. The shrine was destroyed during the war and rebuilt afterwards in the original style.

The shrine grounds are extensive and heavily wooded, offering a respite from the bustle of the city. Its broad paths lead to the main shrine building, a simple structure of traditional style and the finest of materials and craftmanship. Because of its exalted status among the shrines of Japan, it is a popular place for blessings for various events, and you can often see such ceremonies being performed by priests in traditional costumes.

Visiting the shrine is particularly worthwhile on 15 January, 'Coming of Age Day', when countless young women in beautiful kimono attend Meiji-jingu as part of the customary celebrations. It is very crowded but a wonderful opportunity to take many colorful photos. Another good day to visit is *Shi-go-san* festival day on 15 November when young children dressed in very ornate kimono are taken there. New Years Day, although a customary time to visit the shrine, is not recommended as the grounds are incredibly packed.

The entrance to the shrine is close to Harajuku station (Yamanote line) or Meiji-jingu-mae station of the Chiyoda line.

Yoyogi-koen and Harajuku

Close to Meiji-jingu are Yoyogi-koen park and Omote-Sando boulevard, as well as the youth fashion shopping district of Harajuku.

Omote-Sando ('main approach to a shrine') is a high fashion shopping district and being one of Tokyo's few tree-lined streets, (short though it may be), it has some of the flavour of a Paris boulevard.

Any day of the week is a good day for fashion window shopping/buying, and there are some tourist oriented shops with reasonable prices.

On Sundays, Yoyogi park is the setting for the *take-noko-zoku* ('bamboo shoot tribe'), young people who meet here every weekend, share the same outlandish costume that identifies their group and dance to music from portable cassette players. Nearly all favour fifties 'Golden Age' rock 'n' roll classics; an era known to these people only as folklore, as it was an era the rebuilding Japanese nation didn't participate in. Greased-back hairstyles are the norm and the clothes are from around those times. One of the sources of the wild clothes is the back streets of nearby Harajuku, the teen fashion centre.

Harajuku is more than just the crazy youth fashions though, it also has high-fashion and high-price clothing, and some very high-style eating places. Anyone young at heart can enjoy a stroll and will see evidence that Japan has become one of the world's wealthiest nations.

Shibuya

Shibuya, one stop by the Yamanote line south of Harajuku, is another popular shopping and entertainment area. Like Harajuku and Shinjuku the area appeals to a particular age group, in this case those of about senior high school age. For this reason there are plenty of fast food and generally moderately priced restaurants. It is also a high fashion area, with many modern and interesting buildings, imaginative window displays, etc.

The most famous landmark in Tokyo is the statue of the dog Hachiko; just look for a few hundred people standing around in an open area on the north-west corner of the station, and you'll find it. The main area of interest in Shibuya is the mall, where most of the popular restaurants are located; it runs from the very large intersection, diagonally across from Hachiko. The two major roads making up the intersection both lead to major shopping areas. The one to the right leads to the most fashionable street, which features some trees, transplanted British phone booths, many imaginative building fronts and more department stores. The Tokyu Hands is a store out of the ordinary for any country, and can be reached by turning left down the upper side of the Parco department store. It must surely be the ultimate leisure craft emporium in the world. Supplies for nearly every imaginable handicraft are available on its multiple levels. Do you want a traditional Japanese saw or plane, an ultra-accurate micrometer or miniature lathe, a model boat kit, interior decoration supplies, art materials, the makings of metal or lapidary jewellery, electrical-electronic hobby equipment, a computer or you-name-it? It's all here, and more!

Roppongi

Roppongi has become the main playground of the people of the modelling, TV and movie world with numerous discos, bars and restaurants. Despite its trendy reputation it's no less affordable than the entertainment establishments of Shinjuku. There are several restaurants operated by or under the supervision/franchise of westerners, so there are many places offering western food.

Roppongi is most easily reached by Hibiya subway line. The exits at the front of the train, when travelling towards Ginza, lead to Roppongi crossing, the main intersection. On one corner is the best-known landmark, the *Almond coffee shop*, which is a popular rendezvous point. The majority of the favourite entertainment places are on this side of the expressway, on both sides of the major cross road and in the many side streets running off it. It could take a lifetime to explore this territory.

Gardens and Parks

Considering its population and the area it covers Tokyo, by western standards, is a generally parkless city. Basically, cities in

花菖浦

明治神宮御苑拝観券　　大人

Entry ticket to Meiji Jingu Garden

Japan are for commerce and housing, which is obvious to anyone accustomed to large areas of public greenery. Tokyo does however, have a few sizeable parks that make for pleasant strolls but they would be of more interest to foreign residents than those on a short visit looking for a garden with the traditional Japanese characteristics. (The best of these in the Tokyo vicinity is Sankei-en in Yokohama.)

The best parks in Tokyo would be Korakuen garden, Rikugien garden, the National Park for Nature Study and Shinjuku Gyoen park. All are shown on the

TIC map. Others are Hama Rikyu garden and Koishikawa Botanical Garden. The parks are enjoyable in summer when the shrill sound of the *semi* (cicada) may be heard; indeed they are often loud enough to make conversation difficult. Their 'me-me-me-me' or chirring sound is one of the memories of Japan.

Museums and Galleries

Tokyo has a large number of interesting museums and galleries. Visitors to Ueno park can visit both the Tokyo Metropolitan Art Museum and the Tokyo National Museum.

The TIC pamphlet *Tokyo* lists the main museums that would be of interest to visitors. The *Tokyo Journal* lists the major museums, galleries (art and photo), and department store exhibits (a major type of gallery in Japan), and the displays/themes for the coming month, along with the prices and special features. *Tour Companion* has a similar listing, updated weekly; and the weekend issues of the English-language newspapers give details of the displays for the coming week.

Lookouts

Several tall structures around the city offer views of the huge expanse of Tokyo. In the clear weather of winter the view may extend to Mt Fuji. Tokyo Tower, 333 metres tall, is a slightly enlarged copy of the Eiffel Tower and has an observation lounge at the top, along with a wax museum and restaurants. Access to the first level costs Y600 and it's a extra Y400 to get to the 250m level. As Tokyo is a very flat city, built at the edge of the Kanto Plain, it lacks any features of particular note, so one of the less expensive or free viewpoints may be preferable.

The World Trade Centre building has an observatory on its 40th floor; access costs Y400. The bargain, which gives as good a view as any, is the 52-storey Sumitomo Building in Shinjuku (west of the station). The observation level is on the 51st floor; and there are several restaurants of not-unreasonable prices (by Tokyo standards) on the top floors that offer a good view while you dine.

Tokyo Disneyland

In April 1983 Tokyo gained the first Disneyland outside the USA. Built at a cost of hundreds of millions of dollars, to strict Disney standards, it offers the same type of attractions as the US original including the 'lands' theme. There is Westernland, Adventureland, Fantasyland, Tomorrowland and World Bazaar, plus a number of rides, such as a Mississippi paddlewheeler and the Western River Railroad and a variety of other forms of entertainment. The 51 metre Cinderella Castle is the focal point and symbol of the park.

Tokyo Disneyland is open every day during summer (April through August); closed on Tuesdays from September to November; and closed Tuesdays and Wednesdays from December through February (except during holidays). In summer the hours are 9 am to 10 pm; and in winter, 10 am to 6 pm. Admission costs only Y2700 for adults and Y2300/1600 for high school students/children, but there is a separate charge for each attraction. A 'passport', entitling you to enter all attractions as many times as you like, for one day, costs Y4200/3800/2900 (weekdays only); and a 'Big Ten' book of tickets gets you into 10 attractions.

There are two simple ways to get to Disneyland. The first is by Tozai subway to Urayasu station, from where a shuttle bus (from the nearby terminus) runs to the entrance about 20 minutes away. The bus costs Y200 for adults and Y100 for children. The second is by a 35 minute shuttle bus ride from Tokyo station, which costs Y600. The shuttle buses leave from the Yaesu (east) side of the station; on the Yaesu side, take the north exit (kita guchi) and follow the tracks to the left.

Festivals

There are festivals in Tokyo or nearby

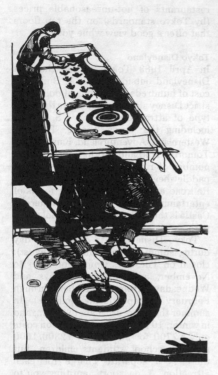

tourist literature and maps, for a fraction of the cost. However, for those who find climbing the seemingly endless stairs of the subway and train stations a bit tiring, or who only have a limited amount of time and no worries about watching their yen, a bus tour certainly offers convenience. There are daily tours of the high spots of Tokyo for Y9,000-10,000; and a tour of the major industrial factories for Y10,000. Night tours take in a glimpse (extremely brief and not really worth the high price) of a stage show, a geisha show, and the kabuki theatre, plus a sukiyaki dinner, for Y12,000-13,000. There are other tours to Kamakura, Hakone, Nikko, etc, but again they are very expensive compared with the ease and cost of using public transport. Information about all available tours is given in *Tour Companion* and in pamphlets given out at all major hotels and the TIC.

Personally guided tours of central Tokyo and Shitamachi, using public transport for economy, are given by Mr Oka. Phone (0422) 51-7673 for details.

Epilog

Tokyo is rather surprising. At first glance it appears to be a rather featureless jumble of uninspiring, often drab, buildings. But after a little looking around you come to appreciate it for what it is, a huge community with many interesting places to see and things to experience; a place that grows in appeal with each day or year. There are many places in Japan with more readily identifiable 'things to see' but none offer the combination of a giant metropolis with 'everything' and the 'local village' atmosphere that exists just under the surface.

Near Tokyo

There are many places of interest within easy travelling distance of Tokyo. They can generally be visited as day trips out of Tokyo, though an overnight away from the city will give a better appreciation of the more distant ones. The following is a

nearly every month. The TIC has free information sheets that list all festivals in Tokyo and all over Japan; and the weekly handout *Tour Companion* is an excellent source of info. The major festival of the week is given front page treatment and others on at the same time are also described. Festivals are least frequent in winter, begin in spring (rice planting time), are very numerous in late summer (Obon season), and climax in autumn with the harvest-related festivals.

Tours

There is a variety of guided tours for seeing Tokyo. They cannot be recommended to the budget traveller as the same attractions can be seen by using public transport, this book and other summary of excursions that would be of major interest to short-term visitors; they are described in detail in the following chapters.

Kamakura is the home of the great Buddha statue, one of the most famous sights of Japan, and has several famous/scenic temples.

Yokohama has Sankei-en garden, one of the best in Japan; and also has the only Chinatown in the country.

Kawasaki has an interesting park that has numerous old thatched-roof farm houses that have been moved here from various parts of Japan. It offers the simplest way to glimpse what life was like a century or two ago.

Hakone This area takes in a scenic mountain and lake; in good weather you can get a magnificent view of Mt Fuji.

Mt Fuji The area around Fuji-san offers many scenic views of the mountain and surrounding lakes.

Kawagoe has a large number of well-preserved century-old shops and houses, and gives some idea of the appearance of a city of those days.

Matsumoto has the only surviving authentic castle in the northern half of Japan.

Nikko has the incomparable splendour of the Toshogu and Daiyuin mausolea, plus lake and waterfall scenery.

Mashiko is the closest town to Tokyo where pottery is made in notable quantities.

Things to Buy

Tokyo is probably the best place in Japan for shopping for Japanese antiques, handicrafts and 'modern' optical and electronic goodies. (It is advisable to refer to the general 'Things to Buy' section earlier in the book, before setting out.)

If buying a camera or lens, first check prices at the discount stores in Shinjuku before laying out any money. Some stores in and near Ginza do give reasonable prices but others count on the fact that

many well-off foreigners are not aware of the lower prices that are available. Three companies in Shinjuku are in intense competition, Sakuraya, Yodobashi (the original camera discounter) and Doi. (There are other camera stores as well, so it might be worth checking out what they're offering.) All three stores have tax-free (*menzei*) departments that should be able to offer the lowest price, but it never hurts to check the with-tax (*kazei*) price, as strange things in the distribution system sometimes allow these to be lower. It's also wise to check prices of camera and lens separately; sometimes it's cheaper to buy each piece at a different shop.

Generally, the lowest prices in the country and the greatest selection of lenses and accessories will be found in Shinjuku. Also, the main offices of the major manufacturers are in Tokyo, and special-order items would be easier to obtain. Never buy a foreign-made camera in Japan as the prices are outrageous.

The Akihabara area is the place for the greatest variety of electrical and electronic goods at their lowest prices. Several stores have departments or floors to display models specially designed for use overseas (correct voltages, specifications, etc). Another source of such models, though their prices may be higher, is the shopping arcades in large hotels and the International Arcade, which is more-or-less under the railway tracks in the Yurakucho area, close to the TIC.

Japanese dolls are available in the department stores as are items used by the Japanese in every day life such as lacquerware, pottery and other ceramic goods. Department stores are generally not the bargain centres they are in western countries, but generally have a name for above-average goods, in both quality and price.

There are several flea markets held in Tokyo on an irregular and regular basis. Because of the changeable nature of the date, time and venue of these it is best to contact the TIC for details.

Entertainment

Visitors to Japan have the chance to see a variety of traditional Japanese performing arts, while foreign residents need not worry about being cut off from western varieties of entertainment.

Kabuki is a very Japanese form of theatre, with spectacular costumes, highly stylised actions and fantastic stage effects. Plots are often thin, or even incomprehensible, but kabuki is worth seeing at least once for the visuals alone. There are several theatres in Tokyo where kabuki is performed: Kabukiza, Shimbashi Embujo, Kokuritsu Gekijo (National Theatre), and Asakusa Kokaido. Kabukiza and Shimbashi Embujo are well set up for English speaking audiences, having radio earphone commentaries on the play as it progresses. The earphone devices rent for Y600 plus a refundable deposit. (These may not be available for use in the lowest price seats.) Program notes in English may also be available at the theatre, giving a detailed description of the action, act by act. Prices are lower for matinees, and there is sometimes a reduction for foreign visitors with their passport. Prices start in the Y1500 range. For listings of presentations playing, with a summary of the stories, check the *Tokyo Journal* and/or *Tour Companion*.

Noh drama, more restrained and refined than kabuki, is another famous performing art. Performances are given at a variety of theatres including Kanze Noh-gakudo, Hosho-Noh-gakudo, Ginza Noh-gakudo, Tessenkai Butai, Kita Noh-gakudo, Umewaka Noh-gakudo, Yarai Noh-gakudo and Kokuritsu Noh-gakudo. Up-to-date listings are given in the *Tokyo Journal* and *Tour Companion* and the TIC would also be able to give info.

Bunraku puppet plays, an equally interesting form of theatre, are occasionally presented in theatres such as Kokuritsu Gekijo. Information is available from the same sources as for Noh and kabuki.

In addition to the traditional Japanese performing arts there is a surprising variety of western-type entertainment. Road shows of western pop and rock performers regularly appear in the larger cities. These cities support several symphony orchestras and smaller chamber groups of high quality and concerts are given regularly. The best listing of these events will be in the *Tokyo Journal* and *Tour Companion*.

Foreign movies are shown with their original soundtracks and Japanese subtitles and are usually screened in Japan soon after their release. Typical admission

price for first run films is Y1500. There are also 'cheap movies', reruns at lower prices; these are listed separately in *Tour Companion*.

Places to Eat

Tokyo has an incredible range of eating places, ranging from modest stand-up soba (noodle) shops to posh restaurants and nightclubs serving international cuisine at international prices. Although out of the price range of the average reader of this book, French cooking, second only to the best offered in France, is available in Tokyo, as is other top-rated international cooking. A guide to the higher-level places and a few moderately priced ones as well, is the book *Good Tokyo Restaurants* by Rick Kennedy. There are extensive listings and advertisements for various kinds of restaurants in the *Tokyo Journal, Tour Companion* and *Tokyo Weekender*; the first two give some indication of prices.

Japanese office workers and students depend on the countless restaurants in the vicinity of the major stations for the majority of their 'bought' meals, so the prices there are about as reasonable as can be expected in Japan. All the popular entertainment areas, like Shinjuku, Harajuku, Shibuya and even Ginza, have many reasonably priced restaurants and beer halls. They usually have wax replicas of the food, with prices, in the window so it's easy to order and there are no surprises when the bill arrives.

There are many Shakey's Pizza and Pizza Hut shops throughout the city, plus other well-known American fast food outlets like Kentucky Fried Chicken, McDonald's, Wendy's, etc. The young Japanese have taken to these with a passion, so there will only be more and more as time goes by. There are also some branches of American restaurant chains like Victoria Station and Red Lobster, though these are not budget eateries. If you look around you'll find there is no problem finding virtually any kind of food in Tokyo.

Meeting the Japanese

Visiting a country without meeting some of the people is wasting half the cost of getting there, especially in Japan where it is so easy to find Japanese people who are interested in getting to know foreign visitors. And Tokyo, being so cosmopolitan, is the best Japanese city to meet the locals, exchange ideas and talk about your respective countries. Of course, not all Japanese have an overwhelming desire to meet foreigners, and some would probably prefer that we all stayed at home, but the following is a guide to meeting the ones that do.

Home Visit

An admirable program organised by various authorities throughout the country is the Home Visit plan. A number of Japanese families have agreed to host foreign visitors in their homes for a couple of hours in the evening. (Further details are given in the section on Meeting the Japanese, earlier in the book.)

The TIC office makes the arrangements for such visits in Tokyo. Although they can possibly arrange things for a same-day visit (if absolutely necessary) they are much more comfortable with a couple of days notice. There are host families who speak English, French, German, Italian and Chinese.

Conversation Lounges

An institution that has popped up in the last few years and seems to be gaining popularity, is the conversation lounge. The basic format is a coffee shop offering various diversions such as magazines, videotapes, games, etc, and the opportunity to chat informally with Japanese customers (usually relatively young). There is no organised program and the type of people there can vary from one day to the next, but visiting one can be a good way to learn a lot about contemporary Japanese in an informal manner. The best listing of such places is in the *Tokyo Journal*.

International 3F Club

One of the most useful organisations in Tokyo to know about, whether you are staying for a few days, or for months, is the International 3F Club, '3F' for short. (The name makes perfectly good sense to the person who thought it up, and it is not for us to pass judgement of the selection of 'Freedom, Friendship and Forward Action' as a theme.)

The club provides the opportunity to meet a large number of English-speaking Japanese in congenial and informal surroundings at the 'Cocktail Party' every Thursday from 6 pm to 9pm. Foreigners are welcome, are admitted free and drinks are reasonably priced, though the selection is limited. The format is open – just find someone to talk to.

It is primarily a Japanese social club, so not all speak English or other languages, and some are not necessarily interested in talking to foreigners. The club has an unofficial purpose of introducing potential marriage partners as the joining fee is very high for Japanese members, which screens out the indigent.

The location of the Cocktail Party, and many other 3F activities that may be of interest to foreigners, is the Japan International Friendship Centre.

From JNR Shinanomachi station (Chuo yellow line, through the middle of Tokyo), turn right along the major road and go a few hundred metres. Cross at the second set of traffic and follow the little lane downhill to the first bend where a lighted sign identifies the building. Walk in, sign the register and meet the people.

The fact that they speak another language and are interested in foreign contact, means the Japanese members are not typical of the general population and they may be more outspoken and candid than average. This makes them more interesting to know, and it's possible to learn a great deal about modern-day Japan and Japanese by talking with them for an evening or more. As with any group of people, not all are conversational wizards and some are complete bores but it's almost impossible to avoid meeting someone interesting and many a romance has blossomed as a result.

Some foreigners however, have gone to the club blatantly 'on the make', and have propositioned girls or shown an excessive degree of personal attention. This kind of behaviour is offensive in Japan and does nothing to enhance western reputation.

The activities of the 3F Club do not end with the Cocktail Party. It also organises a large number of activities for its members, including classes in traditional Japanese crafts, dinner parties, get-togethers of various types and weekend excursions to ski resorts, temples, hot springs, the 3F lodge near Yamanaka-ko lake, etc. These activities are only open to members (unlike the Cocktail Party which is free to foreigners); membership is about Y6000 for an individual, Y10,000 for a family (the cost is much higher for the Japanese). There is a separate charge for each activity.

In recent years 3F has had a sort of 'fellowship' program under which visiting foreigners are given accommodation in return for performing various duties for the club, such as hosting at parties, teaching English etc. Further details can be obtained in Japan by phoning 812770.

Miscellaneous

There are several other organisations that may be of interest to visiting or resident foreigners.

The Society of Writers, Editors and Translators (SWET) has the written English word as the theme. It would be of interest to anyone involved with any aspect of writing English (editing, technical writing, rewriting, translating, advertising etc) and has practical seminars and other get togethers.

The group can be contacted by writing to: SWET, PO Box 8 Komae Yubinkyoku, Komae-shi, Tokyo 201.

The Forum for Corporate Communications is an association of people involved in public relations and related activities. They have luncheons with guest speakers. Notices of forthcoming events are listed on the back page of the *Japan Times*.

The Tokyo Gay Support Group can give information on the gay scene in Tokyo and has a list and map of gay bars etc. The group can be contacted by phone on (03) 453-1618; or by mail: CPO, Box 1901, Tokyo 100-91.

The International Feminists of Japan may be contacted by telephone: (03) 783-9665 (Anne Blassing), or (03) 354-8565 (Tokyo Women's Information Network – TWIN); or by mail: IFJ, CPO Box 1780, Tokyo 100-91. The IFJ Newsletter is published monthly and is available overseas by subscription. Notices of meetings appear in the English-language dailies and in the *Tokyo Journal*.

Religious

Christian There are numerous churches in the greater Tokyo area, representing virtually all the major denominations. For listings, refer to a Saturday issue of the *Japan Times, Tokyo Weekender* or the *Tokyo Journal*.

Jewish The Jewish Community Center (near Hiroo subway station of Hibiya line), has Friday, Saturday and holiday services, Talmud classes and provides other services and support to the Jewish community. Tel: 400-2559.

Moslem The Islamic Center in Setagaya-ku provides a place for prayer and other activities. Tel:460-6169.

Hindu For information regarding Hindu religious activities contact the Indian Merchants Association in Yokohama (tel (045) 662-8685).

Places to Stay

There is a wide variety of accommodation available in the greater Tokyo area, ranging from hotels that match the world's best (with matching prices) to more modest and affordable.

The good news for budget travellers, especially of the backpack type, is that the number of places catering to them has increased greatly in the last few years. So the choice of places to stay is much more varied and the chances of finding a room more likely. However, the number of people travelling in Japan has also gone up, so it may still be necessary to make quite a few phone calls to find a room, especially in popular seasons.

The list in this book, of places to stay is much more extensive for Tokyo than for any other city, because this is where the majority of travellers land and need a roof over their heads for a night or two while getting organised. Listings of alternative sources of accommodation can be found at the TICs at Narita airport and in the city, in *Tour Companion*, in the booklet *Hospitable and Economical* (ryokan accommodation), and in *Tokyo Journal*. The 'top of the line' hotels are not listed here because the people who use them are normally travelling on a pre-arranged itinerary with all accommodation reserved. If you arrive in Tokyo and wish to stay at these places but have no reservation, there is a desk at Narita airport that can make on the spot bookings for more than 25 of Tokyo's top hotels.

The following listings begin with the youth hostels, though there is private accommodation available with fewer restrictions and at no higher cost. However the YH locations are quite central and they can be useful for getting info on the other hostels throughout the country. After the hostels come the reasonably priced private accommodation, then the ryokan and business hotels and other hotels at relatively moderate cost.

Youth Hostels

Tokyo Kok'sai (International) Youth Hostel. The main youth hostel of Tokyo is a bit of a showpiece and one of the best in Japan – as befits the municipally operated hostel in the nation's capital. Located on the 18th and 19th floors of a new high-rise building, it has a good view over the north of the city, enormous baths and comfortable rooms.

Hostel regulations are similar to those that will be encountered throughout Japan, possibly a bit more relaxed; the doors close at 10.30 pm (and don't open until 6.30 am – which is a bit awkward if you need to catch an early flight), and visitors can normally only stay for three days. Being municipally owned, you don't need to be a YH member to stay; a passport for identification is sufficient. The telephone number is (03) 235-1107. Room charge is Y1650 per night plus about Y250 if heating or air conditioning is in use.

The hostel can be reached by JNR and two subway lines, as follows; all stations are named Iidabashi.

The JNR Chuo (yellow) line, running between Akihabara and Shinjuku is the most convenient transport to the hostel. You can transfer to this line from the Yamanote and Keihin-Tohoku lines (through Ueno) at Akihabara; and at Ochanomizu from the Chuo (orange) line. Leave the station at the front of the train (if coming from Akihabara) then turn right at the street and walk downhill about 20m. Turn right into the open plaza area and walk into the arcade covered by the arched glass roof, to the elevators (on the left); the left hand bank of elevators goes to the top floors and the 18th floor reception desk.

The Yurakucho subway line, from Yurakucho (near Ginza) and Ikebukuro brings you closest to the hostel at Iidabashi station, but it has the fewest transfers from other lines. These can only be made on JNR at Yurakucho (walking distance from Ginza and Hibiya subway stations); at Nagatacho on the Hanzomon line (from Shibuya); and from the Shinjuku line. At Iidabashi station, leave the platform at the rear of the train (if coming from Ichigaya), follow signs for exit B2 and finally take exit B2a. At street level, walk uphill the short distance to the JNR station and turn left into the plaza.

The Tozai subway line runs between Otemachi/Nihombashi and Takadanobaba. You can transfer at Otemachi (Marunouchi, Chiyoda and Mita lines), Nihombashi (Ginza line), Kayabacho (Hibiya line), Kudanshita (Shinjuku line) and Takadanobaba (Yamanote line); both the Ginza and Hibiya lines pass through Ueno.

The other hostel is *Yoyoji Youth Hostel*, located in one of the dorms constructed for the Tokyo Olympics. You can get there from Shinjuku station, change to the Odakyu railway and go to Sangubashi, the second stop. The hostel can also be reached via Harajuku JNR station or Meiji-jingu-mae or Yoyoji-koen stations of the Chiyoda subway lines, but these require longer walks. Tel (03) 467-9163.

There are also youth hostels in Yokohama and Kamakura, both within an hour of Tokyo.

Private

Okubo House This place is in a category all its own. Although it is privately owned, it requires guests to leave by 10 am, and has a midnight curfew. However, because of its singular nature and the fact that it has been a fixture for foreign travellers for years, it deserves some extra space. Okubo House was originally a workman's dormitory until it was discovered by foreigners, and it's been a mainstay since then. It has mostly dorm rooms (male only) for Y1400; and some single and double rooms starting at Y2600. (A hint; take your bath early!) Okubo House is near Shin-Okubo station (Yamanote line); turn left from the station exit, then left again at the first side street and walk almost to the T-junction about five minutes away. Tel 361-2348.

In recent years quite a few private homes have opened as communal-type accommodation, with shared cooking facilities, one or more common rooms with TV, etc, and dormitory and individual bedrooms (singles, doubles). There are no curfew regulations as there is with the youth hostels and Okubo House, so guests can come and go at will, and remain during the day. Most offer cheaper weekly and monthly rates and many guests stay on for months because of the community atmosphere that develops. These houses are the closest equivalent to the cheap hotels found on the travellers' route through southeast Asia and India.

Because of the number of places in the following list it is only possible to give their general location, so it will be necessary to phone and ask directions. In many cases one of the guests will answer the phone, so getting instructions in English should be no problem. In some cases there is more than one house, the phone number given is for the 'coordinating' centre. In the case of some of the popular places for which there is a waiting list, like Yoshida House, the owner has alternative accommodation (sometimes dormitory style) where guests can stay while waiting for a private room.

The following list is alphabetical, with the lowest daily single room or dorm charge only (listed to the nearest Y100). Most places have doubles at higher cost.

Ajima House. Tel 366-0484; Y2000; Musashi-Sakai stn. of Chuo line, 20 min. west of Shinjuku.

Apple House. Tel 962-4979; Y1700; Oyama stn. near Ikebukuro stn. by Tobu Tojo line.

English House. Tel 988-1743; Y1700; near Mejiro stn. on Yamanote line.

Foreigners' House Masuoka. Tel 381-7026; Y2000; Nakano (close to Shinjuku by Chuo line); several houses.

Green Peace. Tel 915-2572; Y1500; Ueno area.

International House California. Tel 209-9692 or 376-7605; Y1600; Kami-Kitazawa stn. 12 min. by Keio line ex-Shinjuku.

Japan House. Tel 739-7925; Y1600; 3 stops past Shinagawa toward Kawasaki by JNR.

Let's Go World House. Tel 479-1425/6; different locations out of Shibuya (one stop) and Shinjuku (15 min.).

Magome House. Tel 754-3112; Y1600; near Nishi-Magome stn. of Asakusa subway line.

Mickey House. Tel 936-8889 or 371-2252; two houses; Y1300 – near Kami-Itabashi stn.

(Tobu Tojo line nw from Ikebukuro); Y1600 – near Takadanobaba stn. (Yamanote line).

Tokyo English Center. Tel 0424-88-8762; Y1300; two locations: Chofu and Mitaka by Chuo line west from Shinjuku.

Tokyo English House. Tel 384-0918; Y1600; three locations: Honancho (Marunouchi subway, 4 stops past Shinjuku), Higashi-Ogikubo (10 min. by Chuo line west from Shinjuku), and Toritsu Daigaku (just past Naka-Meguro by Toyoko line).

Tokyo House. Tel 391-5577; Y1400; Ogikubo stn. on Marunouchi subway or JNR Chuo line.

Tokyo English Mansion. Tel 384-0918; perhaps only monthly; two locations.

Tokyo International House. Tel 945-1699; Y1000-2000 (one week min.); several locations in central Tokyo.

Toyama Houses. Tel 948-2383; several locations on the west side of Tokyo.

Yoshida House. Tel 926-4563; Y1300; the original and favourite house near Toshi-mae stn. west from Ikebukuro stn. by the Seibu Ikebukuro line; and others at different locations.

Ryokan and Minshuku

Staying at a ryokan or minshuku is probably the best way to experience what life is like in a Japanese house. Most places have a range of prices (with and without private bath etc.) and rates may be lower by the week. The prices below are for the cheapest category for single/double.

Ryokan Mikawaya Bekkan. Tel 843-2345; Y4500/8600; near Asakusa subway stns. of Ginza and Asakusa lines.

Ryokan Namiju. Tel 841-9126; Y4000/7000; near Asakusa stn. (Ginza and Asakusa subway lines), and Tawaramachi stn. (Ginza line).

Minshuku Chojuso. Tel 378-3810; Y3300; near Shinjuku stn. of JNR and Marunouchi subway.

Inabaso Ryokan. Tel 341-9581; Y3900/7000; near Shinjuku stn. of JNR and Marunouchi subway.

Ryokan Okayasu. Tel 452-5091; Y3500/6000; near Tamachi and Hamamatsu-cho JNR stns.

Sawanoya Ryokan. Tel 822-2251; Y3600/6600; near Nezu stn. of Chiyoda subway line, Ueno area.

Ryokan Sasuiso. Tel 441-7475; Y3600/6600; near Gotanda stns. of Yamanote line and Asakusa subway line.

Suigetsu Hotel (Ohgaiso bldg). Tel 822-4611 or 828-3181; Y3500/6000; near Nezu stn. of Chiyoda subway, Ueno area.

Yashima Ryokan. Tel 364-2534; Y3000/4600; near Okubo stn. of JNR Chuo (non express) line from Shinjuku stn., or Shin-Okubo stn. of Yamanote line.

Ryokan Fuji. tel 657-1062; Y5000; near Koiwatsu stn. of JNR Sobu line from Akihabara stn.

Kimi Ryokan. Tel 971-3766; Y2600/4000; near Ikebukuro stn of JNR Yamanote and Marunouchi subway lines.

GETTING THERE
Narita Airport

Nearly all international flights to Tokyo arrive at Narita airport (Narita Kuko), located 66 km out in the countryside east of Tokyo. It takes at least 1½ hours to get from there to central Tokyo, making it one of the world's most inconveniently located airports.

A high speed rail service was included in the 'planning' stage, but less than 1% of the land required for the rails was ever purchased, and the present 'system' for getting into Tokyo was assembled from existing rail lines plus a new bus service. (The authorities would prefer that the public not know, but there is a blocked off station for the planned rail service beneath the terminal building.) Narita 'errport' (as it has been called) is Japan's contribution to the world's collection of vast projects started on half-vast ideas. It would have been better to enlarge the existing and infinitely more convenient Haneda airport, which would also have avoided the opposition to Narita, (from farmers and student radicals), that still continues, with occasional sabotage and other disruptive tactics. For this reason you may encounter a police check when entering the airport for outbound flights. These security measures account for the high airport departure tax of Y2000.

Faced with the problem of coping with

Narita airport, how do you use it? First, fly China Airlines if possible; their flights land at Haneda airport, so you avoid the problem in the first place. Unfortunately this isn't possible for everyone as CAL is usually heavily booked.

Arrival

If you must use Narita you'll find that the airport has well-signposted routes through quarantine/health, immigration and customs check points.

Before leaving the customs hall you can purchase Japanese currency at a window at the centre of the row of exit doorways. Other money changers are in the arrival lobby and on the Arrivals (4th) level. The rates at these places are the same as the banks in the city. Remember the Yen is the only currency that can be used in Japan; it is illegal and impossible to use anything else, including US greenbacks.

The arrival concourse (ground floor) is the first place where incoming passengers can be met by friends. There are north and south wings of the terminal, so be sure that anyone meeting you knows the flight number and airline so they can be in the right place. It would be more courteous though to arrange to meet them in Tokyo because of the inconvenience and cost involved in getting out to the airport.

Before heading into Tokyo stop at the TIC office which is tucked away, almost

Narita airport

Tourist Information Centre • Japan Travel Bureau • Baggage claim area • Customs arrival area • Information centres • Domestic departure lobby • South Wing • Limousine Bus counter (ticketing office) • North Wing

out of sight, at the junction of the central block and the south wing, on the side nearest the runway; it is sometimes omitted from airport directories. Other 'information centres' in the centre of each wing are generally useless because most of the staff don't speak English. The TIC information that will be of immediate use is *Tourist Map of Tokyo (405-E)*, *Map of Tokyo and Vicinity*, and *Tokyo (222-E)*; the last is available in several languages.

The *Tourist Map of Tokyo* has the best subway map available, with place names in both Japanese and Roman characters (romaji); it's very useful when faced with a fare chart written only in Japanese.

The TIC is open from 9 am to noon, and 1-8 pm on weekdays and on Saturday mornings. Unfortunately the JNTO doesn't recognise that travellers arrive seven days a week at all times of the day and night.

Another counter in the concourse can arrange accommodation in one of more than 25 hotels in Tokyo. These hotels, however, begin in the moderate price range and work up.

The Japanese National Railways (JNR) counter at the centre of the central block, can give info on JNR services, make bookings and sell tickets. There are usually English-speaking personnel on duty. They can exchange a Japanese Rail Pass voucher for a pass. However this operation may be better done in Tokyo after you've had time to settle down and plan your travels; it does not have to be changed immediately. JNR is not a recommended way of getting into Tokyo from the airport.

Next to the JNR counter is an information and ticketing counter for the Keisei rail line, one of the two most convenient ways of getting into Tokyo. Reservations for their Skyliner train can be made here, and they will probably have copies of their timetable in English.

On the other side of the JNR counter are counters for Toyota and Nippon (Hertz) car rental agencies. No one in their right mind would try driving in Japan on first arrival, but brochures could be useful for future reference.

Only two means of getting into Tokyo from Narita airport are practical, Keisei railway and the airport bus. Any others are too expensive or inconvenient. A taxi would cost a small fortune, about Y14,000, and a hire car about double that. JNR

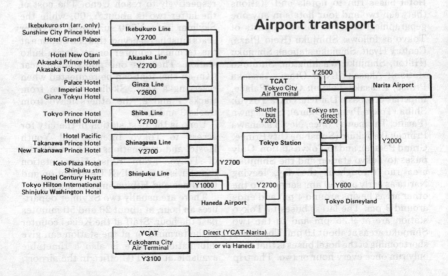

Airport transport

trains are costly, infrequent, slow, and leave only from JNR Narita station, a longish bus trip from the airport. Do not endorse your Japan Rail Pass just so you can use JNR into Tokyo! JNR can be recommended only if you're going to the Chiba and Boso-hanto peninsula area. Buses for the JNR Narita station leave from in front of the central block; more details are available at the JNR info counter.

To Tokyo

For many travellers, the most convenient transport (though not the cheapest) into the Tokyo area is by one of the many buses – misleadingly called 'limousines'. The bus service has the added advantage of not having to carry your baggage any further than the terminal exit. Buses run from the airport terminal to a number of destinations in the city, some to hotels and railway stations and some to the Tokyo City Air Terminal (TCAT). The hotel and station buses are the most convenient way into the city, then the Keisei railway, and thirdly the TCAT buses.

Hotel buses run to hotels and stations (between two and four hotels in any one geographical area), in different parts of Tokyo as follows: Shinjuku (Keio Plaza, Century Hyatt, Shinjuku station); Shinjuku (Hilton, Shinjuku Washington, Shinjuku station); Akasaka (New Otani, Akasaka Prince, Akasaka Tokyu); Ginza (Palace, Imperial, Shinbashi Dai-Ichi, Ginza Tokyu); Shiba (Tokyo Prince, Okura); Shinagawa (Pacific, Takanawa Prince, New Takanawa Prince); Ikebukuro (Sunshine City Prince, Grand Palace); and to Tokyo station. Only buses to Tokyo station and the Shinjuku area run throughout the day, leaving Narita as early as 6.50 am; services to the other areas begins around 4 pm and ends around 9 pm. The latest buses to Tokyo station are at 9.35 pm and to the two Shinjuku areas at about 10 pm. The major shortcoming of the hotel buses is that they only run once every hour or two. The trip

takes from 80 to 120 minutes but these times could be extended by an hour or more during the 'rush' hour when everything slows down. The fare to the hotels and stations is Y2600-2700, half price for children and the handicapped.

Keisei trains The least expensive way into Tokyo is by one of the Keisei line trains, which are more frequent and not much more complicated than the hotel buses. Trains leave from Narita-kuko station, six minutes from the air terminal by frequent shuttle bus (from position 4 in front of each of the wings of the airport terminal). Tickets combining the bus and train fares can be bought at the Keisei counter in the airport terminal, or separately on entering the bus and at the train station. The total price is the same.

There are two types of service on the Keisei line: 'Skyliner' trains which run non-stop to the terminus at Ueno, on the northeast side of Tokyo; and two slightly slower (but cheaper) express runs, tokkyu (special express) and kyuku (express). The Skyliner takes one hour and the tokkyu and kyuku take 73 and 90 minutes respectively to reach Ueno. The cost of the latter two is about Y800, while the Skyliner has a Y700 surcharge. Skyliner seats must be reserved; this can be done at the terminal counter or at Narita-kuko station. There is one non-smoking car (Kin-en-sha) that can be requested when reserving a seat. Skyliners leave from tracks 1 and 2; the others leave from tracks 3 and 4.

Ueno is the best station in the city for access to Tokyo International Youth Hostel and destinations in the northeast of Tokyo. From Keisei-Ueno station transfer is easy to JNR Ueno station and the Ginza and Hibiya subway lines.

There are usually two Skyliner departures an hour, at about 20 and 50 minutes past the hour. Staff at the Keisei counter at the terminal or at the station can give information. There is also a timetable available at the TIC office in the airport, and one posted on a pillar facing the ticket machines at the station. On timetables lacking English, a Skyliner is usually identified by a blue dot, a tokkyu train by a red circle, and a kyuko by a red triangle.

Those travellers who don't wish to go to Ueno or that side of Tokyo may find the following useful. Some tokkyu and kyuko trains (about 15 per day), switch off the Keisei tracks at Aoto and run on the tracks of the Asakusa (pron. *Asak'sa*) subway line, as an Asakusa line train to it s normal destination. The terminus (marked on schedules) is Nishi-Magome, on the southwest side of Tokyo, and the trains pass south of the centre of the city, skirting Ginza. You can transfer easily to JNR lines at Asakusa-bashi, Shimbashi and Gotanda and to other subway lines as follows: Hibiya line at Ningyo-cho and Higashi Ginza; Ginza line at Asakusa; Mita line at Mita. Also at Sengakuji, you can change to a Keihin-kyuku train for Kawasaki, Yokohama and through Yokosuka to the tip of the Miura-hanto peninsula.

The last of the direct Nishi-Magome trains leaves around 5.20 pm, but don't despair if you arrive later. Take any regular (non-Skyliner) train bound for Ueno and get off at Aoto. Board the next train arriving at platform 1. This may go through to Sengakuji or Nishi-Magome, or may stop after six stations at Oshiage. If the latter, take a train from platform 1 at Oshiage for Nishi-Magome, or from platform 3 for one that switches off at Sengakuji for Kawasaki, Yokohama, etc. Staff at the Keisei counter or at the station can help with info.

Buying a ticket at the station is no problem despite the almost incomprehensible markings and fare chart. The simplest course is to buy the lowest price ticket from machines 3-8 and pay the difference at the destination; the cost is the same but make sure you hold on to your ticket.

The first part of the trip in from Narita is

through farming country, with many rice paddies, and even one thatched-roof house visible to the right of the train.

TCAT buses offer a direct service from the airport to the TCAT office at Hakozaki, a rather remote corner of Tokyo away from subway or JNR stations. To proceed from TCAT the choices are a taxi (rather expensive to almost anywhere in the city), the regular shuttle bus the 2½ km to Tokyo station (from where the JNR tracks are about 10 minutes away and the subways even further), or a walk to Ningyo-cho or Kayaba-cho subway stations.

The closer of these is Ningyo-cho, on the Asakusa and Hibiya lines; this is also one of the stations served by the trains from the airport to Nishi-Magome, so if this is where you want to go there's little point taking the bus and then having to walk. To get to Kayaba-cho subway station, turn right when leaving the front entrance of TCAT, cross the street, and walk straight along the broad street (passed Ningyo-cho station on the right), for a few blocks until the first major cross street. Turn left and cross over a bridge and continue on till you reach the station, which is on the Hibiya and Tozai line; the latter is convenient for reaching Tokyo International Youth Hostel.

The cost of the bus is Y2500 (half price for children and the handicapped) and there are departures every five to 30 minutes. The nominal travel time into the city is one hour, though this could be doubled during morning and evening peak traffic. Buses (identified by the word 'limousine') leave from in front of both wings of the airport terminal and tickets can be bought at well-marked counters inside the building.

To Haneda Airport Haneda is used for nearly all domestic flights; there are only about 10 which use Narita. The most convenient way to transfer from Narita to Haneda is by bus ('limousine'). The fare is

Y2,700, departures are every 20 to 50 minutes and the trip is scheduled to take 80 minutes (except during traffic slow-downs). Basically you should allow at least 4-1/2 hours between scheduled arrival at Narita and scheduled take-off at Haneda.

An alternative to the bus – for the adventurous – is to take the Keisei/Asakusa line route to Shimbashi, transfer to the JNR Yamanote or Keihin-Tohoku line as far as Hamamatsucho, then take the monorail from there. This might halve the fare, but at the expense of much more time and effort.

If, when first arriving in Japan, a city other than Tokyo is your first destination, it is best to try and get an international flight to a point closer to it. In most cases, however, Osaka and Nagoya are the only other major airports with large numbers of connections, and there are no major airports north of Tokyo.

To Yokohama Passengers destined for Yokohama will find the bus service (another 'limousine') to Yokohama City Air Terminal (YCAT, not far from Yokohama station) is by far the quickest and most convenient way, taking about 30 minutes (nominal). Buses leave every 20 to 50 minutes.

Haneda Airport

Because of the running contretemps between the governments of Taiwan and (mainland) China, Taiwan's national airline, China Airlines, was denied the dubious privilege of using Narita when Japan recognised the Peking government. China Airlines have been crying all the way to the bank ever since because they have the most convenient service into Japan of any airline. They have several flights a week from Taipei and the US west coast, but advance bookings are required because of the airline's understandable popularity.

Nearly all Japan's domestic flights use Haneda airport and central Tokyo is easily reached from Haneda by the monorail. The way from the terminal to the monorail station is clearly marked and tickets are available from vending machines which give change. The monorail terminus is at Hamamatsucho, on the south side of Tokyo, which is also served by JNR trains of the Yamanote and Keihin-Tohoku line.

Transfer between Haneda and Narita airports can be made most easily by shuttle bus which costs Y2,700. Buses operate between 9.10 am and 8.50 pm. Remember it's wise to allow about 4½ hours for connections between flights at the two airports.

The simplest way from Haneda to Yokohama is by bus (from Haneda Tokyu Hotel) to Yokohama City Air Terminal (YCAT).

Departure

To Narita Sage advice for anyone going from Tokyo to Narita airport is to begin your trip four hours prior to your departure time, to allow for traffic delays and missed connections plus the security check (if using the Keisei route), check-in, Immigration formalities, etc. The most convenient ways to get out to the airport, in order, are hotel bus, Keisei train and TCAT bus.

The earliest buses from the Shinjuku area, which stop at four hotels and

Shinjuku station, leave at 6.24 am and 7.04 am. Buses also leave the other hotels listed in the section on getting from the airport to the city. The Tokyo TIC would have up-to-date information on the exact times throughout the day that these buses depart.

Narita airport can also, of course, be reached using the Keisei railway, starting from either Keisei-Ueno station (in Ueno) or from any station along the Asakusa subway line.

Keisei-Ueno station is close to Ueno stations of JNR and of the Hibiya and Ginza subway lines. The easiest access from the JNR station is to leave the train platform by the overhead passageway located at the north end (away from Tokyo stn.), walk along the passage toward track No 1, exit, cross the road, turn left and walk down the hill; to the right, about 50 metres along is the entrance to the underground Keisei station. The transfer from the subway lines is well marked and should be no problem.

Skyliner tickets can be bought in advance at JTB offices and Keisei-Ueno station as well as the airport terminal and station buildings.

If you're travelling from the central or southwest parts of Tokyo, the service by the Asakusa subway line is the most convenient as it allows easy transfer from other lines, as described in the section covering the trip in from Narita. About 20 trains a day on this line continue past the usual terminus at Oshiage, and go all the way to Narita-Kuko station. The train schedules are quite irregular so it's advisable to plan in advance to be sure of getting the right train. The TIC usually has timetables of Keisei trains.

If there is no Asakusa line train going directly to the airport at the time you want to go (or if you miss the right train), carry on to Aoto and catch one of the expresses coming from Keisei-Ueno bound for Narita (city) or Narita-kuko (airport) station. (Some local trains also pass through Aoto, as do some that stop prior

to Narita. Signs on the station (tracks 3 and 4) identify the terminus of every train, in romaji, so these local ones can be avoided. (Local trains have the destination written in black kanji, expresses in green or red.)

Some trains of the Asakusa line terminate at Oshiage, six stations before Aoto. If you get one of these, simply take the next train on to Aoto and change as just described.

If your train goes only as far as Narita (city) station, walk to platform 5 and catch a train for the airport station, the next stop.

From Narita-kuko station, the terminus, take the shuttle bus for the short trip to the airport. There will be a security check prior to boarding the bus so have your passport ready. They may inspect your baggage, but the officials are usually more thorough with the luggage of Japanese passengers, because of the continuing series of terrorist attacks on the airport by student radicals.

The third recommended way to get to the airport is the 'limousine' bus from TCAT which runs direct to the Departures level at the terminal. Many (but not all) airlines permit complete check-in at TCAT, so you don't have to touch your bags again till your final destination. For these, a bus is assigned to each flight, and the flight is held if the bus is held up. To allow for potential traffic problems, check-in at TCAT is typically three to four hours ahead of departure.

At TCAT, everything is self-explanatory, buses operate throughout the day and the fare is Y2500.

Apart from taxi (not cheap) there are two ways to reach TCAT, subway and shuttle bus. From Ningyo-cho subway station (Hibiya and Asakusa lines), there should be a sign, 'For Tokyo City Air Terminal' on each platform directing passengers. At the street-level exit, turn left and walk 10-15 minutes to the overhead expressway, under which TCAT is located. If you're walking from Kayaba-cho subway station, the TIC Tokyo map should give clear enough directions.

The other way to TCAT is by shuttle bus from Tokyo station which leaves every 10 to 40 minutes; or from various hotels at irregular times. The bus from Tokyo station leaves from in front of the TDA office opposite the front entrance (Yaesu side, the side remote from the Post Office). The shuttle bus costs Y200 and takes 10 minutes.

After check-in at Narita airport, you can shop for duty free items in the terminal buildings; you can also buy after passing through Immigration. Remember airport departure tax is Y2000. Turn in any certificates for tax-free purchases just before the Immigration check. The ground won't open up and swallow you if you fail to do this, it is largely an exercise to keep the bureaucrats employed.

From Yokohama As described in greater detail in the Yokohama section, the simplest way to Narita airport is by bus from Yokohama City Air Terminal. Buses leave every 20 to 50 minutes, take about 1½ hours and the fare is Y3100.

To Haneda From Tokyo to Haneda airport is such a simple process that one sentence of instruction is about all you need. Go to Hamamatsu-cho station (JNR Yamanote or Keihin-Tohoku lines), follow the signs to the monorail, buy a ticket, ride the train, and you're there.

From Yokohama The most convenient way to reach Haneda from Yokohama is by bus from YCAT. They leave every 20 to 60 minutes and take about half an hour.

GETTING AWAY

Japan's well developed and efficient transport system means that you can get to almost any part of the country from any part of the country, with relative ease. And from Tokyo there are a number of options to make further travelling throughout Japan interesting and varied.

Air

With the exception of a very few flights out of Narita, all domestic air transport to/from Tokyo goes through Haneda airport. Haneda is easily reached by monorail from JNR Hamamatsu-cho station. There are direct flights from Tokyo to about 35 different cities, while even more are accessible with a transfer at the other major regional airports of Sapporo, Osaka, Nagoya, Fukuoka and Naha (Okinawa). Sample air fares are given in the general Getting Around section.

Rail – JNR

Shinkansen There are three super-express Shinkansen lines linking Tokyo with the most important regions of the country. The Tokaido Shinkansen line runs through Nagoya and Kyoto to Osaka, at which point the name of the line changes to Sanyo Shinkansen (no change of train needed). The trains continue through Okayama and Hiroshima to the terminus at Hakata, in northern Kyushu. Tokaido Shinkansen trains leave from Tokyo station and do not stop in the metro Tokyo area. The Tohoku Shinkansen runs northeast through Sendai to Morioka; and the Joetsu Shinkansen runs north via Takasaki to Niigata on the north coast; both leave from Ueno station.

These are the most important trunk lines in Japan, linking the majority of the biggest cities. They are explained in more detail in the general Getting Around section.

Tokaido line Trains of this line begin at Tokyo station, offer express service to Kawasaki and Yokohama and continue some distance down the coast, generally as far as Atami, Odawara, Shizuoka or Toyohashi. From these latter stations there are connections on to Nagoya and from there to Kyoto and Osaka. Within the Tokyo area these trains stop only at Shimbashi and Shinagawa. This line, along with the Yokosuka line, is the quickest route to Yokohama. The Tokaido line trains that stop at all stations are regarded as kaisoku service and there is no surcharge for them. Fast expresses (kyuko and tokkyu trains), that bypass nearly all stations are, of course, much faster but there is a surcharge. Only trains leaving late in the day (after about 6 pm) run directly to Nagoya. About three trains leave late at night and reach Osaka early the next morning, but these are uncomfortable as the seats are nearly bolt upright. One night train has sleepers and another has reclining seats available.

Yokosuka line trains begin at Tokyo station, provide express service to Yokohama and continue on through Kamakura and Yokosuka to Kurihama, at the bottom of the Miura-hanto peninsula. All Yokosuka line trains are kaisoku expresses so there is no surcharge. Trains leave Tokyo station every five to 15 minutes. Within metro Tokyo they stop only at Shimbashi and Shinagawa stations. Most begin as Sobu Hon-sen line trains from Chiba; from Tokyo station they continue as Yokosuka line trains (and vice-versa in the opposite direction).

Chuo line There are two 'Chuo' lines. The Chuo Hon-sen ('Main Line') originates at Shinjuku station and gives express service (with surcharge) westward, with Matsumoto as it terminus. Some trains stop at Tachikawa, and all stop at Hachioji, Otsuki (a gateway to the Mt Fuji area), Kofu and a small number of other stations. Chuo-sen commuter lines originate at Tokyo station or come from Chiba, and run as far as Mitaka or Takao, west of Tokyo.

Takasaki line This begins at Ueno station and runs northward through the Kanto plain to Takasaki or beyond. There are connections through the mountains to Niigata by the Joetsu line. Regular Takasaki line trains that stop at all stations are normal fare; the expresses have a surcharge.

Tohoku Honsen (main line) begins at Ueno and overlaps the Takasaki line as far

as Omiya, then turns northeast to run through Sendai and Morioka to Aomori, at the far north of Honshu. Local trains (all stations, no surcharge) run as far as Utsunomiya or Kuroiso, from where you can transfer to another local train to Fukushima; and from there, make another transfer to Sendai. Since the advent of the Tohoku Shinkansen, only one other express goes as far as Fukushima. There are overnight sleeper services to Akita, Yamagata, Morioka and Aomori.

Joban line services run from Ueno through Mito to the east coast and follow the coast northeast to Sendai; most trains run only to Mito or Taira. Only a single express runs direct to Sendai, while two others are expresses as far as Haranomachi, with a transfer to a local express for the rest of the journey.

Sobu line As with the Chuo line, there are two types of Sobu line service, Sobu-sen and Sobu Hon-sen. The Sobu-Honsen (main line) runs between Tokyo station and Chiyoshi (up the coast from the Chiba peninsula) giving express service to Chiba, Narita city and Chiyoshi. Express trains to Narita (terminus) operate as kaisoku trains (no surcharge), but expresses to Chiyoshi have a surcharge. A large number of the Sobu Hon-sen trains into Tokyo, continue past Tokyo station, becoming trains of the Yokosuka line, giving express (kaisoku) service to and beyond Yokohama. The Sobu-sen line gives local service between Chiba and Ochanomizu, at the latter station it changes name to the Chuo line (yellow) and runs through Shinjuku as far as Mitaka, stopping at every station. Coming from Chiba, the point at which the Sobu line and the Sobu Hon-sen lines split is Kinshi-cho.

Private railways

The private railways generally act as commuter feeder lines between Tokyo and smaller communities. Only a few run to areas of any touristic interest or are likely to be used by the average traveller.

The following lines are mentioned at some
point in this book as being of some use to
get to places of interest. Details of these
services are given in the write-up for the
specific attraction.

Line	From	To
Keihin-Kyuko	Shinagawa	Kawasaki, Yokohama, Yokosuka, Miura peninsula
Toyoko	Shibuya	Yokohama
Odakyu	Shinjuku	Odawara, Hakone area, transfer for Mt Fuji area
Tobu Tojo	Ikebukuro	Kawagoe
Keisei	Ueno	Narita, Narita airport, Chiba
Tobu	Asakusa	Nikko

The JNTO's *Tourist Map of Tokyo* has
one map showing the private lines and the
subway lines that run to their starting
stations. The subway lines are not identified by name, but the accompanying
subway map shows the private lines as
black lines, so the two maps can be used in
conjunction to identify the starting points.

Buses

The only major bus connections out of
Tokyo are: the expressway buses to
Nagoya, Kyoto and Osaka; night buses to
Yamagata and Sendai; expressway bus to
the Mt Fuji area; and the expressway bus
to the Hakone area. These are all detailed

in either the general Getting Around
section, or in the the write-ups, in
following chapters, of the actual
destinations.

Ferries

Ferries from Tokyo and vicinity offer
reasonably low cost transportation to a
number of distant parts of Japan, with the
bonus of a 'sea cruise' and the economy of
saving accommodation costs for one or
two nights.

From Tokyo, there are ferries to:
Tomakomai and Kushiro (Hokkaido);
Nachi-Katsuura (Kii peninsula); Kochi
and Tokushima (Shikoku); Kokura
(northern Honshu); and Naha (Okinawa).
There are also ferry services from Kawasaki
to Hyuga (western Honshu); from Oarai
(near Mito) to Tomakomai and Muroran
(Hokkaido); as well as several boats to the
nearby Izu islands.

GETTING AROUND

Tokyo has a comprehensive public transportation system. Although large and
complex, it is easy to use once it is
understood, and it's the cheapest way to
get around the city. Comprising the
system are suburban feeder buses, 11
private railways, 10 subway lines in two
separate (though linked) systems, JNR
train lines and city buses. The major
shortcoming is that there is no system of
free transfers between systems; a separate
fare is required for each. Note that your
ticket must be kept through the ride and
surrendered at the end of the journey
(except on buses).

Try to avoid the peak periods 7.30-9.30
am and 4-6.30 pm; there are millions of
people on the move, and it will seem they
are all in your coach. It is also a time that
will destroy any illusions about the
'exquisitely polite Japanese' as they have
no compunction about squeezing past you
to get ahead in the line or about putting a
hand (or, more politely the back of their
wrist) in your back and pushing as soon as
the doors open.

JNR Trains

The government-operated JNR (kokutetsu in Japanese) runs several lines in the Tokyo area. Most important are the Yamanote loop line that circles the city in both directions, the Chuo line that crosses the city, and the Keihin-Tohoku line. Other lines feed into these. Fares are a minimum Y120, are charged by distance and tickets are sold by vending machines. Fares are given on a large map over the machines but you need to know the name of the station in kanji. This can be obtained from the JNTO's *Tourist Map of Tokyo*. Most stations have maps of the lines but in romaji only; to ask for one say 'Kokuden no chizu-o kudasai'.

One way around the fare problem is to buy a minimum fare ticket and pay the difference at the 'Fare Adjustment' window at the destination. A perplexed look when standing at the ticket machine will probably prompt some assistance.

Ticket machines may sell a single value ticket or have a row of buttons to choose from (two rows actually; the bottom one is for children's tickets). The machines give change so it is safe to insert coins in excess of the fare.

If you put coins into the wrong machine and realise the mistake before pushing a fare button, you can get the coins back by pushing the button marked トリケシ (*torikeshi*). If you buy a ticket for a fare higher than required, take it to the Fare Adjustment window and ask for a refund or push the button marked ヨビダシ (*yobidashi*). This is also the button to push if the machine jams and keeps your money. You cannot get a refund at the end of your journey.

Commuter passes are available and permit an unlimited number of trips between any two stations in the Tokyo area (and all stations in between). They can be issued to include one other transport system, such as a subway line or bus. Passes are available for three or six months, so may be of more interest to residents.

Special day-excursion tickets are available, valid for unlimited travel for one day within the bounds of the Yamanote line. It is called a 'free kipu', (this mixture of English and Japanese is quite common).

Note that it is often quicker to reach a destination by using a combination of JNR and subway than to use one system exclusively, but it will be more costly because separate tickets are required for each.

At any JNR station in Tokyo it is possible to buy a ticket to any station in Japan, except for Shinkansen and reserved seat tickets which must be purchased at a station with a Green window.

Every JNR station in the Tokyo area (and generally throughout the country) is identified by signs over the platform in romaji as well as Japanese, but they are rather high and difficult to see when standing in a train. There aren't many signs so watch carefully when entering a station. On either the overhead sign or on another sign at platform level there is normally the name of the station in large kanji and romaji, and in the lower left and right corners are the names of the next station in either direction. On each platform, hanging overhead near the edge of the platform and at right angles to the tracks will be a small sign giving the names of major stations ahead along that line; there is usually one sign in romaji.

The number of signs in romaji indicating the route to follow to change trains, or for particular platform or station exit, varies widely. Tokyo station is well marked with illuminated and colour-coded signs in English; but busy Shinjuku has the signs but nearly everything is in Japanese.

Several JNR lines run within the Tokyo area and to nearby cities, so the following brief explanation may be useful.

Remember 'kaisoku' trains are semi-expresses, skipping several stations thereby giving faster service, but without the surcharge usually applied to express services.

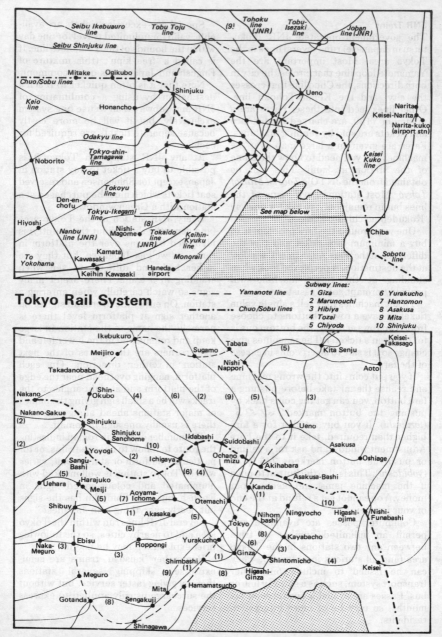

Tokyo Rail System

Subway lines:
1 Giza
2 Marunouchi
3 Hibiya
4 Tozai
5 Chiyoda
6 Yurakucho
7 Hanzomon
8 Asakusa
9 Mita
10 Shinjuku

– – – Yamanote line
–··–··– Chuo/Sobu lines

Tokyo station

Track	Line	Route
1/2	Chuo orange	Express to Shinjuku and beyond.
3	Keihin-Tohoku	Local service north to Tabata, Omiya.
4	Yamanote	Loop line anti-clockwise to Ueno, Shinjuku, etc.
5	Yamanote	Loop line clockwise to Shinagawa, Gotanda, etc.
6	Keihin-Tohoku	Local service to Shinagawa, Yokohama, Ofuna.
7/10/12	Tokaido	Express to Yokohama; local and express beyond Odawara, Atami,Shizuoka, etc, with connections to Kyoto, Nagoya and Osaka.
14/19	Tokaido Shinkansen	Super-express to Nagoya, Kyoto, Osaka and on to Hiroshima and Hakata.

Underground

Track	Line	Route
1/4	a:Yokosuka and b:Sobu Hon-sen	a: Express kaisoku to Yokohama; local service on to Kamakura, Yokosuka and Kurihama. b: express kaisoku to Chiba and Narita; express (surcharge) and local service to both and beyond.

In the following table, abbreviations are used for the names of the lines: To = Tohoku Hon-sen line; Ta = Takasaki line; Jo = Joetsu line; Jb = Joban line; S = Shinetsu (north coast, not detailed here).

Track	Line	Route
1	Keihin-Tohoku	Local service to Tabata, Omiya (terminus).
2	Yamanote	Loop line anti-clockwise to Tabata, Ikebukuro, Shinjuku, etc.
3	Yamanote	Loop line clockwise to Tokyo, Shinagawa, Gotanda, etc.
4	Keihin-Tohoku	Local service to Shinagawa, Kawasaki, Yokohama, Ofuna (terminus).
5	To, Ta, Je, S.	
9	To, Ta, S, Jb.	
10	Jb.	
13	To, Ta, Jo.	
14	To, Ta, S.	
15	Jo, Jb.	
17	To, Ta, Jb.	
18	To, Jb.	
19/20	Joetsu Shinkansen	Super express service through Takasaki to Niigata.
21/22	Tohoku Shinkansen	Super express service through Fukushima and Sendai to Morioka.

Shinjuku station		Route
Track	Line	Expresses (surcharge) west to Otsuki, Kofu
1/2/5	Chuo Hon-sen	and Matsumoto.
		Kaisoku express to Tokyo station
3	Chuo orange	(morning only).
		Kaisoku express to Tokyo station (rest of
4	Chuo orange	day).
		Kaisoku express west as far as Takao.
6	Chuo orange	Local service east through Akihabara to
7	Chuo/Sobu (yellow)	Chiba.
		Loop line anti-clockwise to Shibuya,
8	Yamanote	Gotanda, Shinagawa, etc.
		Loop line clockwise to Ikebukuro,
9	Yamanote	Tabata, Ueno, etc.
		Local service west to Mitaka.
10	Chuo yellow	

Transfers to tracks 13-18 require a little searching as they are not in line with tracks 1-12; they are to the east side of the station and downstairs from the overhead concourse. The way to the Ginza and Hibiya subway lines can be followed easily as can the route to Keisei railway station.

Yamanote (loop) line

Yamanote trains are green.

The Yamanote line circles the central part of Tokyo. Trains run in each direction at very frequent intervals through the day, tapering off later at night. Like all trains in the Tokyo area, service stops soon after midnight, although these trains are usually the last public transport to stop for the night.

There are 29 stations around the loop and a circuit of the line takes about an hour. A trip around the loop gives a good introduction to the city. Three of the stations are the starting points for JNR intercity trains.

Trains from Tokyo station, which is a copy of Amsterdam station, include the super-express Tokaido Shinkansen through Osaka to northern Kyushu, plus ordinary and express services southwest down the coast, and trains east and southeast. Ueno station is the starting point for all trains to the north and northeast. Services include the Tohoku and Joetsu Shinkansen as well as ordinary and express trains. Shinjuku is the start for express trains west towards Kofu and Matsumoto as well as ordinary services some distance westward.

All the private suburban railways begin at their own stations adjacent to stations of the Yamanote line.

Keihin-Tohoku line

Keihin-Tohoku trains are blue.

Trains of this line run from below Yokohama into Tokyo and north to Omiya, stopping at every station. From Shinagawa (SW Tokyo) to Tabata (N Tokyo), they run parallel to the Yamanote line around the east side of the city and either line may be used over this distance.

Chuo line

Chuo trains are yellow or orange.

There are three Chuo lines; the Chuo Hon-sen line originates at Shinjuku station and is a westward express, so not relevant here.

Chuo yellow trains stop at every station across the city from Shinjuku station to Ochanomizu station. From the latter (which means 'Tea Water') they continue east to Akihabara and onward, giving local service as far as Chiba. From Ochanomizu to Chiba the name changes to the Sobu line. Chuo yellow trains also run west beyond Shinjuku station, giving local service as far as Mitaka.

Chuo orange trains begin at Tokyo station and give kaisoku express service to Shinjuku (and vice versa). En route they stop only at Kanda, Ochanomizu, Yotsuya and Yoyogi. Beyond Shinjuku there are two types of service. 'Ordinary' kaisoku trains make the same stops as Chuo yellow trains, as far as Mitaka, but continue west to Takao. Tokubetsu ('special') kaisoku make only one stop between Shinjuku and Mitaka and skip several stations between Mitaka and Takao. There are three tokubetsu kaisoku trains per hour, in addition to more frequent kaisoku. Both types of Chuo kaisoku train use the same platform, so it's necessary to use a timetable to predict which will be the fast service.

Sobu line
Trains of the Sobu line run from Chiba only as far as Ochanomizu, but the same train continues to and beyond Shinjuku as a Chuo yellow train, stopping at stations across the city. Passengers in a hurry to get to one of the intermediate stations take a Chuo orange train to Yoyogi or Ochanomizu, and can change there to a Chuo yellow. Those going from Shinjuku to Akihabara can take the Chuo orange to Ochanomizu and change to the Sobu line just by walking across the platform.

Yokosuka line
Yokosuka trains are cream and blue.

The Yokosuka line starts at Tokyo station and provides express service southwest to Yokohama (28 minutes). Trains of the Yokosuka (pron. 'Yoh-kohs-kah') line stop only at Shimbashi and Shinagawa in the metro Tokyo area. They continue beyond Yokohama and Yokosuka to Kurihama on the Miura peninsula (detailed in the previous Getting Away section).

Tokaido line
Tokaido trains are orange and green.

The Tokaido line starts at Tokyo station and provides express service southwest to Kawasaki and Yokohama. With the Yokosuka line it is the fastest way to Yokohama (28 minutes), is the only JNR express that stops at Kawasaki, and only stops at Shimbashi and Shinagawa in the Tokyo metro area. They continue beyond Yokohama to various destinations, and other trains of the Tokaido line run through to Osaka (detailed in the Getting Away section).

Main JNR stations
The multitude of platforms at some stations in the Tokyo area is confusing even to residents and overwhelming to newcomers. The following information should be useful and, since the renovation work at Tokyo and Ueno stations was almost finished at the time of writing, there is a good chance that the info will remain accurate for quite a while.

Tokyo station Tokyo is the main station for lines southwest, southeast and east, as well as the starting point for some trains running west past Shinjuku.

The table, accompanying the map, on page 153 is useful for orientation but locals and expresses, leave from the same platforms it is necessary to check a timetable to be sure of getting the right type of train.

The last four lines are fairly confusing because trains arrive from both directions at all platforms and depart in both directions from two of them. Consult a timetable to be sure of getting the right one. There is a large timetable (with English) at the foot of at least one of the escalators. Tokyo station has two sides: Yaesu is the major side, Marunouchi the minor. An underground passage links them. It is one of the best signposted station in Japan as regards English, colour coding, illuminated signs, etc.

Tokyo station (Yaesu side) is the point of departure for highway buses to Nagoya and on to Kyoto/Osaka, as well as the night buses to Yamagata and Sendai. The shuttle bus to TCAT is across the road from the Yaesu side exit. Information services are also on the Yaesu side.

The Marunouchi subway line is on the Marunouchi side.

Ueno station Ueno is the station for trains headed north and northeast, and with the advent of the Tohoku and Joetsu Shinkansen lines, it has become Japan's largest station. It is not difficult to get confused but the station is fairly well signposted and with the platform details on page 153 it shouldn't be too hard to transfer trains. For orientation, the important thing to remember is that the main concourse is above the tracks at the north end (the end away from Akihabara and Tokyo stations). The entrance to the Shinkansen lines is past line 12; escalators descend four levels to the tracks. Platforms 1-4 serve trains that circle Tokyo or run to points nearby, while others serve destinations further away. As with Tokyo station, several lines depart at various times from any number of platforms so check a timetable for the right one.

Shinjuku station Shinjuku is claimed to be the busiest station in the world, with two JNR lines, two subway lines, and three private railways delivering passengers to or near it. Only one long-distance JNR line leaves from it, the Chuo Hon-sen. The main problem is that the station is very poorly marked in English and has ticket machines for two private railway lines side by side with those for JNR trains. The information in the previous table, regarding trains and platforms, will therefore be all the more valuable.

An underground passage on the north side of the station links east and west sides. The Marunouchi subway line station is in the passageway; and Keio and Odakyu private railways have their stations on the west side of the JNR station. Tickets for Keio and Odakyu trains can be purchased on the east side and permit passage through the southern tunnel under the platforms of the JNR trains.

Shinjuku station is probably the most bewildering on earth; it's an architectural disaster, with very poor planning of concourses, passages, stairs, etc. And for visitors the negligible signposting in English makes the whole thing even worse.

Subways & Private Railways

Tokyo has a good subway system; trains are frequent and clean and they cover the city intensively within the Yamanote loop line and beyond it some distance, especially to the east. The system is made up of 10 lines: three municipally run *Toei* lines – Asakusa, Mita and Shinjuku (sometimes referred to as Toei 1, 6 and 10 respectively); and seven private *Eidan* lines – Ginza, Marunouchi, Chiyoda, Tozai, Hibiya, Yurakucho and Hanzomon. Passengers can transfer among the Eidan lines and among the Toei lines without extra charge, but a transfer from one system to another requires a new fare to be paid. Special transfer tickets can be bought at the beginning; the cost is the same. Similarly a new fare must be paid when transferring to/from the JNR system, private railways or buses.

Every line connects with the JNR Yamanote loop line somewhere, some also to the Sobu or Chuo line, and at least one subway line joins a JNR line or one of the 11 private railway lines. The transfer in these cases usually involves nothing more difficult than walking to another platform and in some cases you may only have to cross the platform or just wait where you are for a following train on the same platform. On the other hand, changing to a different system may involve a considerable walk and you may even have to leave one station and walk to the connecting station.

It is common for a subway line train to continue some distance beyond its terminus and run along the tracks of a private line. (A new fare is charged as soon as the journey crosses the boundary of the second system.) An example is the Hibiya line, many trains of which continue beyond the subway terminus of Naka-Meguro and continue along the tracks of the Toyoko line (which runs between Shibuya and Yokohama) as far as Hiyoshi. At the other end of the Hibiya line, some trains continue beyond the subway terminus, along the tracks of the Isezaki line through to Kita-Kasukabe.

At stations serving lines of both subway systems there are machines selling tickets for both, as well as ticket machines for transfer to any connecting private railway line. There may be up to a dozen machines, each one with different markings (only in kanji). It's complicated even for the Japanese, so don't be embarrassed to ask for help. The JNTO's *Tourist Map of Tokyo* has two small maps that are invaluable for solving such problems. The map *Communications Network* shows the names of all private railway lines in both romaji and Japanese; as does the map *Subways in Tokyo* which details all the subway lines and shows the connecting railway lines. By referring to the maps (the latter one especially) it is easier to understand the signs on ticket machines and on the fare maps; the lines are color-coded. Following is the colour code of Tokyo subway lines.

Eidan
Ginza	orange
Marunouchi	red
Chiyoda	dark green
Tozai	light blue
Hibiya	grey
Hanzomon	purple
Yurakucho	yellow

Toei
Mita	dark blue
Asakusa	pink
Shinjuku	lime green

Every station in the subway system is clearly identified in romaji on walls and pillars in the station. Signs, also in romaji and colour-coded the same as on fare maps, indicate which direction to walk when transferring from one line to another.

The timetable for the line using each particular platform is posted over the platform. The symmetrical kanji identifies services from Monday to Saturday (*heijitsu*); the other identifies Sundays and holidays (*kyujitsu*). On private railway timetables the red, green or blue numbers represent express services; and the black numbers indicate local trains.

Commuter passes are available for travel between any two specified stations in the Tokyo area; periods are for one, three or six months. Commuter tickets (*kaisuken*) are also available for travel between two specific stations and give 11 rides for the price of 10.

Buses
There is a large network of bus routes throughout the greater Tokyo area. They mostly act as feeders to railway and subway lines, often through incredibly narrow streets. Most routes are laid out between large JNR stations. Buses generally stop running after 9 pm.

The drawback of buses is that the destination is only written in kanji and the drivers rarely speak English. However, since the destination signs are nearly always the name of a station, you can find the kanji for them by checking the names of stations on the JNTO Tokyo map. At every bus stop there is a sign with the names of the destination stations (in Japanese), a route map and the schedule.

Buses are, of course, subject to the delays of Tokyo's heavy traffic, so bus travel is slow in the morning and afternoon peak periods. In Tokyo the fare is paid when entering the bus and the fare is marked on the cash box. Strips of tickets are also available.

Buses are most useful to residents who have the time to establish what lines are most useful to them. At least one map

Great Tokyo Detailed Map (Nippon Kokuseisha; Y680 at bookshops), shows bus routes, but check the date of publication.

Streetcars
There is a single surviving tram line in Tokyo, running from Ikebukuro to Oji (on Keihin-Tohoku line), not a generally useful route.

Near Tokyo

The region around Tokyo offers some of Japan's most interesting attractions, including Kamakura, Mt Fuji and the Hakone area. This chapter follows an arc around Tokyo from the south-west to the south-east.

West from Tokyo

There are several individual attractions and interesting areas to the west of Tokyo. Many can be visited as day trips or weekend outings, or en route to Kyoto and other destinations in western Japan.

Although generally industrial/commercial in nature, Kawasaki and Yokohama have an attraction or two each and the many interesting sights of the historic city of Kamakura are only a short distance beyond Yokohama. South of Kamakura is the Miura-hanto peninsula, and west of the city lies Odawara, gateway to the Izu-hanto peninsula, the Hakone area and Mt Fuji. Going west from the Hakone/Fuji area takes you along the south coast (generally heavily urbanised and uninteresting); going north leads inland via Matsumoto through much more interesting and less-travelled regions. The following section describes each in turn, with optional routes.

KAWASAKI

Kawasaki is a typical Japanese industrial city with virtually nothing of interest to visitors, with one notable exception – a museum of Japanese farmhouses.

Nihon Minka-en

The name means 'Japan Farmhouse'. It is a collection of traditional thatched-roof buildings that have been moved to this peaceful forested site from many places around Japan. The museum offers a very convenient way to get a glimpse of how Japan looked in centuries past; the oldest building dates from 1688. A pamphlet in English, given at the entrance, explains the origin, use and unusual points of each building. Visitors are free to wander through the interiors of many. The second floor of one building is a museum of traditional farming implements, utensils and tools plus some armour and weaponry. It is closed on Mondays; no entry after 4 pm.

Access from Tokyo is by Odakyu line from Shinjuku station to Muko-ga-oka Yuen station; the express from track 5 takes about 30 minutes. From the south exit (minami guchi), look for the monorail and follow along to its right; continue straight on at the main road where the monorail turns left. The museum is a 15 minute walk from the station.

With an early start it should be possible to take in Nihon Minka-en and Yokohama's Sankei-en garden in one day. From Muko-ga-oka Yuen, backtrack one stop to Noborito and change to the JNR Nanbu line going south to Kawasaki, then change to a train to Yokohama. (At Muko-ga-oka Yuen you can get a single ticket that permits the transfer to the JNR line; tickets are issued from the left-most of the vending machines – buy a low-priced ticket and pay the difference later.)

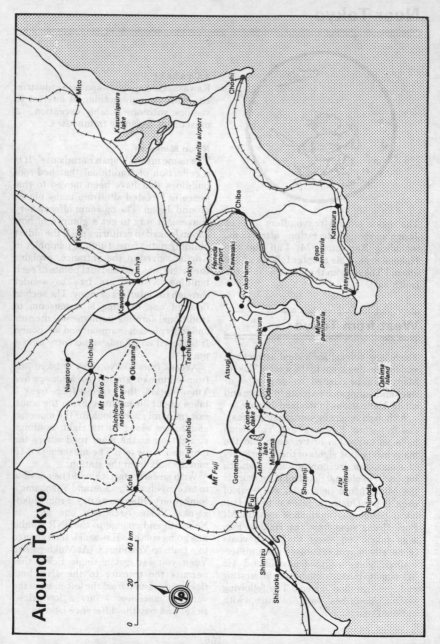

Around Tokyo

0   20   40 km

Mito
Kasumigaura lake
Choshi
Narita airport
Koga
Chiba
Katsuura
Omiya
Tokyo
Haneda airport
Kawasaki
Boso peninsula
Tateyama
Kawagoe
Yokohama
Nagatoro
Chichibu
Okutama
Tachikawa
Kamakura
Mt Buko
Miura peninsula
Chichibu-Tamma national park
Atsugi
Oshima Island
Kome-ga-dake
Odawara
Fuji-Yoshida
Kotu
Mt Fuji
Gotemba
Ashi-no-ko lake
Mishima
Shuzenji
Izu peninsula
Fuji
Shimoda
Shimizu
Shizuoka

Top: Children's kabuki on an ornate mobile stage, Nagahama
Left: Costumed children at Asakusa Kannon temple festival
Right: Typical aproned housewife and child dressed up for a festival

Top: Cherry blossoms at Heian-jingu
Left: Autumn at a Kyoto temple
Right: Pagoda of Sojiji temple near Monzen, Noto-hanto peninsula

Other attractions

Kawasaki is known for its 'toruko' red light district (named Horinouchi), and its many love hotels. It is one of the three or four best-known such places in Japan.

Kawasaki has one other attraction, the interesting annual festival *Jibeta-matsuri*. This festival honours Kanamara-sama – deities of the metal phallus. It is based on a fable of a maiden (beautiful and rich, of course) who had an unusual and terrible affliction. She was 'inhabited' by a sharp-toothed demon which bit off the phallus of two successive grooms who tried to perform their wedding night duty. A divinely inspired blacksmith took the girl with the aid of an iron phallus that de-toothed the demon while de-flowering the maiden. And everyone lived happily ever after, especially the Kawasaki business-men who have revived the festival, which also honours the gods of businesses, growth, prosperity, reproduction etc, all being various forms of fertility. Whatever the motives, everyone has a good time during the festival when phalluses are carried in procession and local smiths re-enact the forging operation. The whole thing is a good humoured celebration of the joys of sex.

The festival is held on 15 April, near Kawasaki Taishi station, beginning with music in the early afternoon, a parade of the sacred palanquin and masked people carrying phallic offerings (4-5 pm), followed by the forging (5-6 pm), then an outdoor banquet.

From Tokyo take the Keihin Kyuko line to Keihin Kawasaki station, then transfer to the Kawasaki Taishi line downstairs. Taishi station is about 10 minutes away. From the station (there is only one exit) cross the street outside, turn right and walk about 50 metres.

Getting There

Kawasaki can be reached by train from Tokyo on the Keihin-Tohoku or Tokaido lines, from Tokyo, Shimbashi or Shinagawa stations. These lines continue to Yoko-hama, the next stop after Kawasaki. You can also use the Keihin Kyuko line from Shinagawa station (or from Sengakuji station on the Asakusa subway line). From Yokohama, the Yokosuka line (with blue and cream cars) goes to Kamakura.

There is a daily ferry service between Kawasaki and Hyuga (Kyushu); and a car and passenger service from Kawasaki across the bay (Tokyo-wan) to Kisarazu on the Boso-hanto peninsula.

Yokohama

Yokohama is a port and business city about 20 km from Tokyo. It has become the second largest city in Japan (nearly three million people), but both Tokyo and Yokohama have expanded towards each other and now form one vast conurbation. Being a commercial city there is little for the sightseer and its large office buildings are much the same as those anywhere.

The city has a short history by Japanese standards. Before 1850 it was only a sleepy fishing village but with the signing of the treaty forcing Japan to open its doors after 250 years of seclusion, Yoko-hama became one of six ports open to the world and was made the port for Tokyo. At the time it was an ugly expanse of mud and was chosen by the Japanese officials to keep unwanted and unclean foreigners as far from the capital as possible, in conditions less than pleasant. It has improved somewhat since then.

Information

Beside the Silk Centre Building (facing the harbour) is the Kanagawa Prefectural Tourist Information Centre. It has a good selection of useful information on Yoko-hama and for travel elsewhere in Japan. Tel (045) 681-0506.

There is usually a free handout map but it is of the all-too-typical Japanese type with distorted scales, wrong locations and 'north' off in a strange direction.

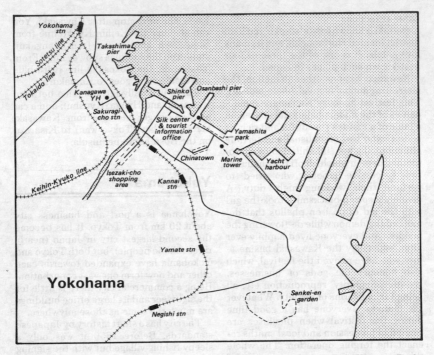

Yokohama

Home Visit

If you wish to visit a Japanese home in Yokohama for a couple of hours in the evening, arrangements can be made at the Tourist Information Centre, at the Yokohama International Welcome Association (ground floor, Silk Centre Building, tel 641-5824), or at the Silk Centre Hotel (tel 641-0961).

Tescort

Visitors who would like an English-speaking Japanese to accompany them around Yokohama, Tokyo, Kamakura, Nikko or other nearby tourist attractions should contact Tescort in Tokyo, tel (03) 478-6577 and ask for Mr Araki.

Things to See

The attractions of Yokohama are limited and most are located quite close to each other: Yamashita Park (along the harbour front), Marine Tower, Port Viewing Park, Chinatown and the Silk Centre Building. The premier destination, Sankei-en Park is a convenient bus ride away.

Silk Centre Building This houses a permanent display of all aspects of the silk industry, from raw cocoon to beautiful fabric. The simplest way to get there from Yokohama station is by bus from the depot beside the Sky Building, opposite the East Exit. Bus 26 passes in front of the Silk Centre; buses 8 and 58 pass nearby (get off at the Post Office).

Marine Tower From the Silk Centre it is a simple walk along Yamashita Park to the very visible Marine Tower. On a clear day it is possible to see distant Mt Fuji; this is more likely in the cooler months or after a day of strong winds. Take bus 8, 26 or 58 from Yokohama station.

Port Viewing Park is an alternative to Marine Tower for viewing the harbour (though not Mt Fuji).The road up to it can be found easily from the vicinity of the Tower. This area is known as the Bluffs and has been the prestige residential area, especially for foreigners, since Yokohama was opened to the outside world.

Chukagai Near the tower is Chinatown (*Chukagai* in Japanese), the only one in Japan. It is known for its restaurants and shops selling Chinese products and curios.

Sankei-en Park After the Tower, catch a No 8 bus to Sankei-en Park. This is one of the most beautiful garden parks in Japan – in my opinion far more attractive than the 'Big Three' at Mito, Kanazawa and Okayama. It dates only from the late 19th century and was built by Tomitaro Hara, a wealthy silk merchant. It is laid out around a large pond, with walking paths circling it and branching off to other places. Wooded hillsides totally obscure the ugly reality of the surrounding 20th century. One of the side paths leads to the Inner Garden which is laid out in the traditional Japanese style and is an excellent example of the landscape gardener's work. Within the Inner Park are several historic buildings, including the traditional-style mansion Rinshun-Kaku; these have been moved here from other parts of Japan.

Elsewhere in the park, on the highest hill, is an old three-storey pagoda in excellent condition. It was built in the 15th century and moved to the park in 1914. A nearby lookout gives a good view of the harbour and on a clear day you can see Mt Fuji, though the view is spoilt by a tall smokestack.

Near the pagoda is another noteworthy building, the **Yonohara farmhouse**, a huge thatched-roof building. It dates from 1750 and is held together only by straw ropes – there are no nails in it whatsoever. This one was moved here in 1960 when the opening of a new dam involved flooding the valley where it was located. The only

other similar buildings are in the Kiso area of Gifu-ken, so take this opportunity if you can.

To return to Yokohama station, or the vicinity of the Tower or Chinatown, take a No 8 bus going in the same direction as the one that took you to the park. Get off anywhere near the Tower. The closest railway station is Ishikawacho on the Negishi (Keihin-Tohoku) line.

Places to Stay
Kanagawa Youth Hostel (tel (045) 241-6503) is about 10 minutes from Sakuragi-cho station. From the station, in the direction of Yokohama station, you can see the 'Golden Centre' Building (that's the name in Japanese if you have to ask someone); there is a wide street on the far side of it. Walk to the right along that street, keeping the elevated railway tracks to the right until you reach a short, steep incline leading up to a steep cobblestoned street to the left and a traffic bridge to the right. Turn left up the hill and the hostel is on the right about 100 metres along.

There are several hotels in Yokohama or if you want to stay overnight in a typical Japanese lodging, eg a ryokan or minshuku, the Tourist Information Centre can help with bookings. There is also an office for minshuku reservations and information located on the balcony beside the Sky Building, at the end of the elevated passageway from Yokohama station to one of the bus stations.

Note that Kamakura is about half an hour away from Yokohama (or an hour from Tokyo) and may be a preferable place to stay. *Nihon Gakusei-kaikan* youth hostel (tel (0467) 25-1234) in Kamakura has 400 beds.

Getting There
Air Most people visit Yokohama from Tokyo but if you are going there direct from Narita or Haneda airports, the most convenient service is by airport bus. It connects with Yokohama City Air Terminal (YCAT), a few minutes from Yokohama

station and costs Y280 (Haneda) or Y2600 (Narita). Travel time from Narita is scheduled at two hours, but extra time should be allowed for traffic tie-ups. There is an average of two buses per hour. When departing, luggage may be checked in at YCAT and not touched again until the destination, and planes are held back for delayed buses if passengers check in at YCAT. (See below for details on how to get to YCAT from the station.)

For connections between Yokohama and Narita airport, it is cheaper but more time-consuming to use trains instead of the airport bus. This involves taking a train from Narita to the Asakusa line (see Tokyo chapter for details), then changing to Keihin-Kyuko line at Sengakuji.

Sea Yokohama is a port of call for cruise ships and is served by regular sailings to and from Nakhodka (USSR) at the eastern extremity of the Trans-Siberian Railway. Passenger ships arrive at the modern Internation Port Terminal located at Osambashi Pier.

To get to Yokohama station from Osambashi Pier you can walk, catch a bus or go by train from the nearer station.

After clearing Immigration and Customs, passengers walk to the mainland. At the entrance to the pier is a small square; on the right side is a map of Yokohama and the first of many indicators pointing the way to Sakuragicho station (from which trains can be caught to Tokyo); on the left is the nine-storey Silk Centre Building. It is a simple 20-30 minute walk to Sakuragicho. If you follow the signs to a tree-lined avenue you can walk along that to Yokohama Park and through there to Kannai station. Both stations are on the Negishi (JNR) line, a local line with trains to Yokohama station.

Buses No 8, 20, 58 and 81 go to Yokohama station via Sakuragi-cho station; buses 11, 21 and 22 terminate at the latter. To get to the bus stop from the pier, walk straight ahead past the Silk Centre Building (on the left) to the first major cross street (the Post Office is to the right). The bus stop is a little further along the street from the far right hand corner.

Train To reach Yokohama from Tokyo or Narita Airport there are five rail services – three JNR and two private lines, Toyoko and Keihin-Kyuko.

From Tokyo station there are two express services, both taking 28 minutes to Yokohama. Both the Yokosuka and Tokaido lines stop only at Shimbashi and Shinagawa in the metro Tokyo area, and each makes one more stop before Yokohama. The Yokosuka line stops at Shin-Kawasaki and the Tokaido line at Kawasaki. Trains of both lines depart at five to 15 minute intervals through the day. Trains on the Keihin-Tohoku line stop at all 12 stations from Tokyo to Yokohama.

From points near Eidan (private) subway lines, the most convenient and cheapest way to go is probably by the Toyoko line which starts from Shibuya. (You can transfer here from Ginza or Hanzomon subway or JNR Yamanote lines, but a separate ticket must be bought.) A direct transfer (without changing platforms) can be made from the Hibiya subway line at Naka-Meguro; a new fare zone begins here because it is the Toyoko line.

From stations on the Toei (Asakusa and Mita) subway lines, go to Sengakuji and transfer there to the Keihin-kyuko line to Yokohama. Many trains leaving Narita Airport station have the marked destination 'Nishi-Magome'. For Yokohama, take one of these trains to Sengakuji and transfer to the Keihin-kyuko line.

Getting Around

Train Yokohama station is a busy communications centre, being served by JNR, three private railway lines, a subway and many buses. The station has undergone extensive remodelling in recent years and there are now relatively good markings in English, sufficient at least to find most connections.

The above-ground facilities over the station include a hotel and a department store and the actual station section is basically a broad underground passageway leading to most of the lines. The main entrance is the west exit (nishi guchi) and is the loading zone for most of the buses. The east exit (higashi guchi) is connected to another bus loading zone by a passage over a major expressway. The train platforms are numbered from the east exit end.

Tracks 1 and 2 are for Keihin-kyuko trains (private line). Track 1 trains go west to Yokosuka and the Miura-hanto peninsula. Expresses are marked with green or red kanji on the front and side of the trains; locals are marked in black.

Trains from track 2 run to Kawasaki and Shinagawa (Tokyo). Some of these continue past Shinagawa to Sengakuji. This station is on the Mita subway line and the train may terminate here or continue some distance along these tracks towards Oshiage. By changing trains when required (as described in the Tokyo section), this route can be used to get to Narita Airport. Red or green markings on the train indicate an express.

Tracks 3 to 10 are JNR services.

Track 3 is Keihin-Tohoku line which becomes the Negishi line after another stop; it provides local service as far as Ofuna, a station on the Yokosuka line.

Track 4 is Keihin-Tohoku line which provides local service to Tokyo and as far north as Omiya. It stops at all 12 stations along the way and costs the same as the much faster Yokosuka and Tokaido lines; in the Tokyo area it runs parallel to the Yamanote line for many stops. This is the line to take for connections with the Shinkansen, which leaves from Shin-Yokohama station. Go one stop to Higashi-Kanagawa station and transfer for a Yokohama-sen line train bound for Hachioji; the third stop is Shin-Yokohama. Keihin-Tohoku trains are blue.

Tracks 5 and 6 are Tokaido line services west to Odawara, Atami and Nagoya.

Tracks 7 and 8 are Tokaido line services to Tokyo, stopping en route only at Kawasaki, Shinagawa and Shimbashi, the latter two being stations in the metro Tokyo area. This is one of the two fastest services to Tokyo. Tokaido line trains are orange and green.

Track 9 is Yokosuka line (pronounced Yo-kos-ka) service west to Kamakura, Zushi, Yokosuka and Kurihama, at the south-east side of the Miura-hanto peninsula.

Track 10 is Yokosuka line express service to Tokyo, stopping only at Shin-Kawasaki, Shinagawa and Shimbashi en route; beyond Tokyo, many of these trains continue to or towards Chiba as the Sobu line. Yokosuka line trains are cream and blue.

Tickets for all JNR as well as Keihin-kyuko trains can be purchased from vending machines in the underground passageway. If you are not sure of the fare to your destination, buy the cheapest ticket and pay the difference at the other end. (Keep your ticket.)

JNR services to Tokyo are more expensive than either the Keihin-kyuko or the Toyoko lines.

The tracks of the second private line are on the west side of the station. The Toyoko line runs from Sakuragicho (two stops beyond Yokohama) to Shibuya on the west side of central Tokyo. It offers convenient transfer to the Hibiya subway line at Naka-Meguro, the JNR Yamanote line and the Ginza and Hanzomon subway lines at Shibuya.

The entrance to the Toyoko line tracks is to the left when entering Yokohama station through the west exit; ticket machines are nearby. (The tracks can also be reached via an entrance directly from JNR tracks.)

Track 1 of the Toyoko line serves trains that only go two stops to Sakuragicho.

Track 2 serves trains bound for Shibuya.

Trains with the destination marked in red are expresses (kyuko) and reach Shibuya 10 minutes faster than those marked in black. These colours are also used on timetables.

To get to the Yokohama subway, follow the passage towards the west exit, climb up the stairs and turn left. Continuing down the passage to the end leads to an open area and exit to the right; the subway entrance is just outside and is identified in English.

Straight ahead at this exit is the entrance to the Sotetsu line that runs west and intersects the Odakyu line to the Odawara area.

Yokohama City Air Terminal (YCAT) is easily reached from the east exit of the station. A shuttle bus runs from stop No 1 about three to five times an hour. Fare is Y110 and the trip takes only a few minutes. Look for dark blue minibuses identified by the letters YCAT on the side. If you don't have to carry luggage it is about a 15 minute walk. Turn left from the front of the station and walk until you see New Japan Motors (a Ford dealer) across the wide road. YCAT is across the road and down the side street.

Beyond Yokohama

KAMAKURA

Now a resort town for day-tripping Tokyoites and residence for many fortunate citizens, Kamakura was effectively the capital of Japan from 1192 to 1333 when the *bakufu* military government of the Minamoto family gained the upper hand in Japan. During that period it became very prosperous but subsequently declined to a regional government centre. It finally lost all special status in 1603 and became a quiet backwater.

Kamakura, the most interesting single place in the Tokyo area to visit for historic remains, should be on everyone's 'must see' list. The best-known attraction is the famous Kamakura Daibutsu – Great Buddha, but there are other sights as well.

Information

Two useful leaflets, *Kamakura* and *Fuji-Hakone-Izu-Kamakura* are available from the Tokyo TIC.

There is a program of volunteer student guides who show visitors around Kamakura at no charge in return for the opportunity to practice English. To fit in with the students' free time, the tours are given only on weekends. The Tokyo TIC has more information and can make arrangements.

Things to See

Kamakura station is a good starting point for sightseeing in the area as it's a terminus for buses as well as the Enoden railway line to Fujiwara and on to the beach resort town of Enoshima. A day pass (*furii kipu*) for unlimited travel on city buses is available for about Y500 but most visitors will not use it enough to make it a bargain. Passes are sold at the ticket office close to the police post, to the left when leaving the bus terminal side of the station.

Finding your way around Kamakura on foot is very simple because of the large number of signposts in English that give the distance to the next attraction (usually a temple or shrine). Every point of interest has a plaque at its entrance giving its history in English. The following route takes in the major places of interest.

Daibutsu

The most famous single sight in Kamakura is the great bronze figure of Buddha (*Amitabha*). It sits in the open, having looked for more than seven centuries with half-closed eyes on the rise and fall of Kamakura as a seat of power. The seated figure is more than 11 metres high, plus pedestal and weighs nearly 100 tonnes. The pose and position of the hands represents the Buddhist symbolism for steadfast faith. The expression on the face is one of great serenity and it is a work of art far superior to the larger Buddha figure at Nara.

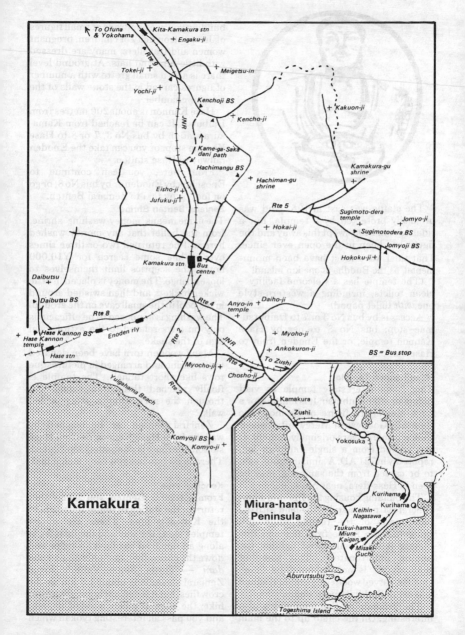

To Ofuna & Yokohama
Kita-Kamakura stn
Engaku-ji
Rte 9
Tokei-ji
Meigetsu-in
Yochi-ji
Kakuon-ji
JNR
Kenchoji BS
Kencho-ji
Kame-ga-Saka
dani path
Kamakura-gu
shrine
Hachimangu BS
Eisho-ji
Hachiman-gu
shrine
Jufuku-ji
Rte 5
Sugimoto-dera
temple
Hokai-ji
Jomyo-ji
Sugimotodera BS
Jomyoji BS
Kamakura stn
Bus
centre
Hokoku-ji
Daibutsu
Daibutsu BS
Daiho-ji
Rte 8
Anyo-in
temple
Daiho-ji
Hase Kannon BS
Rte 4
Myoho-ji
Hase Kannon
temple
Enoden rly
Rte 2
JNR
Ankokuron-ji
Hase stn
Rte 4
To Zushi
BS = Bus stop
Myocho-ji
Rte 4
Yuigahama Beach
Chosho-ji
Rte 2

Kamakura
Zushi

Komyoji BS
Yokosuka
Komyo-ji

Kamakura

**Miura-hanto
Peninsula**

Kurihama
Kurihama
Keihin-
Nagasawa
Tsukui-hama
Miura-
Kaigan
Misaki-
Guchi

Aburatsubo

Togashima Island

The statue was cast in 1252 and was originally protected by a temple, but a tidal wave in 1495 swept this away and the figure has been in the open ever since. That tidal wave must have been monumental, as the Buddha is one km inland! (The temple has a welcome facility – clean toilets, including a western-style one *with* toilet paper!)

Access is by bus No 3 or 7 to Daibutsu-mae stop; bus No 8 to nearby Hase Kannon temple; or the Enoden train to Hase station.

Hase Kannon Temple

This is an interesting temple to visit before or after Daibutsu. It is famous for a huge nine-metre figure of Kannon, the Buddhist Goddess of Mercy (after whom Canon cameras were originally named). It was carved from a single camphor log, reputedly in 721 AD. A similar figure, said to be carved from the same log, may be seen in Hase-dera, near Nara.

The building housing the figure is a new concrete structure styled to blend with the older parts of the temple while still protecting the figure from fire and displaying it with well-placed lighting (no photos, unfortunately). This piece of religious art is accompanied by many smaller, carved wooden figures of Kannon and other Buddhist personages.

The grounds of the temple are also interesting. On the climb up to the main building you see hundreds of small figures of Jizo, patron deity of children, pregnant women and travellers; many are dressed with little bibs and hats. At ground level there is also a small grotto with a number of figures carved in the stone walls of the circular chamber.

Hase Kannon is about 200 metres from Daibutsu. It can be reached from Kamakura station by bus No 3, 7 or 8 to Hase Kannon stop, or you can take the Enoden railway to Hase station.

From here, you can continue to Enoshima by Enoden or by bus No 8; or go on foot or by taxi to Zeniarai Benten.

Zeniarai Benten Shrine

The name means 'money-washing' shrine, from the belief that any money washed here will be returned two or three times over. While some search for Y10,000 notes, the sceptics limit themselves to loose change. The money is placed in little wicker baskets and then swished around in the pool in the small cave on the ground. The washing is supposed to be efficacious only on days related to the astrological sign of the snake.

Many wooden torii have been donated to the shrine and arranged in picturesque rows like short tunnels. The temple is finally reached through a tunnel cut through the rock after a steep uphill walk.

Zeniarai Benten can be reached by walking from Hase Kannon or from Hase station; the route is adequately signposted. There is no bus but you can catch a taxi.

Kenchoji area

From Zeniarai Benten you can either return to the station or follow the roads to the Kenchoji area. There are a few temples along the way and the final leg is along an unpaved road over a ridge and down the curiously-named *Kame-ga-saka dani* – 'Turtle Slope Valley'. From Zeniarai shrine it is about 1.5 km as the crow flies, but it is definitely a much longer hike; the slope is nicely wooded though, and you pass an interesting ryokan which is reached, like Zeniarai shrine, by a tunnel cut through the rock. From the station, the Kencho-ji area is quickly reached by bus No 9 or 10; get off at Kenchoji stop.

Kencho-ji temple

The greatest and most picturesque of the temples of Kamakura, Kenchoji was founded in 1253. The main hall dates from 1646 and has the appearance of well-preserved age. The great sanmon gate and nearby belfry are equally picturesque. Other glimpses of buildings set in pretty gardens or other artistic settings can be found by wandering along the paths of the grounds.

Meigetsu-in

Close to Kencho-ji, this little temple is really only worth visiting in June when the huge number of hydrangea are in bloom.

Engaku-ji

Close to Kita-Kamakura station, this temple dates from 1282 but virtually all the old buildings have been destroyed, many by the 1923 Kanto earthquake. The great sanmon main gate is impressive and one of the buildings is reached through a wooden gate with intricate carvings of lions and dragons. There are glimpses of beauty here and there, but the effect is not maintained, and the main building is made of unromantic concrete. Superficially it resembles Kencho-ji in layout, but has less to offer.

There are other temples nearby that may be explored if time allows but all are low-key. Downhill from Kencho-ji is a side entrance to Tsurugaoka Hachiman-gu shrine.

Hachiman-gu shrine

Occupying the place of honour in Kamakura, the shrine is built on a hillside overlooking the city and a long boulevard that leads to the sea. The boulevard is divided by twin rows of cherry trees that attract throngs of people in spring.

Hachiman is the god of war, so it was natural for the military government (the *bakufu*) to dedicate the shrine to him. The present site was was first used from 1191, the successor to an earlier one founded elsewhere in 1063. The present colourful orange buildings date from 1828. The small museum in the main building houses armour, swords, masks and other historic items.

At the foot of the staircase leading down from the shrine is a Noh stage from which a long stone-paved walkway leads to the front entrance; it is always crowded on weekends and holidays. To the left is the *Kamakura Koku-hokan* (municipal museum) which displays a number of treasures of the Kamakura and Muromachi periods (1192-1573) that belong to various shrines and temples in the area. Near the main entrance to the grounds, to the right, is the Prefectural Modern Art Gallery. Also near the entrance is the steep *taiko bashi* (Drum Bridge) a sort of practical joke in stone as it is so steep that you cannot walk up and over. A running start should be enough to carry you over and crossing it is reputed to grant a wish. The shrine is unbelievably crowded on New Years Day.

Hokoku-ji temple

Access is across Hana-no bashi bridge, an ordinary concrete structure, but look out for the colourful carp in the stream below. The temple is not noted for its buildings, but for the beautiful bamboo grove behind, which is interspersed with numerous historic gravestones. At the teahouse in one corner you can sit and contemplate the small but attractive garden behind the grove.

Hokoku-ji is a zen temple and zazen meditation is held in the garden before 8 am every Sunday; anyone may participate.

Hokoku-ji can be reached from Hachiman shrine or the station by No 5 bus to Jomyoji stop.

There are several other temples and shrines along the same road, including thatched-roof *Sugimoto-dera* which is the oldest temple in Kamakura. Most of these temples however are of historical interest only and have little visual appeal unless you are familiar with Japanese history.

Komyo-ji temple

This temple is usually nearly deserted, yet for visual appeal it is one of the most worthwhile destinations in Kamakura. The temple dates from 1243, although the main building is a modern concrete structure (but of traditional appearance). What sets it apart from other temples in Kamakura is its *karesansui garden* of rock, gravel and greenery, located at one side of the temple; and another garden consisting of a lotus pond (best from late summer) and other picturesque elements, all arranged in front of an attractive building. Unlike most other temples, there is no charge to see either. To get there, take a No 2 bus from the station.

Other attractions of the temple include a large and old-looking sanmon gate, a bell tower with some of the finest wood carvings in Kamakura and a number of interesting tombs.

Although many other temples in the city have extensive burial areas, this is the only one with a memorial for pet animals; look for a large monument on the right with food dishes left out.

Getting There

Kamakura is easily reached in just under an hour by Yokosuka line from Tokyo station (tracks 9 or 10), Shimbashi and Shinagawa stations in metro Tokyo, or from Kawasaki or Yokohama (track 9). From Yokosuka it is the fourth station.

ENOSHIMA

This is a popular beach resort town west of Kamakura. Because it is close to Tokyo it gets extremely crowded on summer weekends.

The main beach is Higashi-hama (higashi = east); on the Katase side of the Katase River is Nishi-hama beach (nishi =

west), accessible by Katase-bashi bridge. Also on the Katase side is an aquarium and Enoshima Marineland.

In the harbour is Enoshima, the island that gives its name to the area. It offers the hillside Enoshima shrine (reached by steps or escalator), various recreation facilities, and scenic views at Chigogafuchi, including two nearby caves.

Enoshima-jinja shrine features a nude statue of Benten, the Indian goddess of beauty, and the only female among the seven Japanese deities of good luck.

There is an observation tower that gives a good view of Mt Fuji in one direction and Oshima Island in the other. The latter (described later in this chapter) can be reached by ferry from Shonan Harbour, on the north side of the island. Enoshima island is easily reached by a footbridge.

Getting There

To get to Enoshima from Kamakura you can go by Enoden train or bus No 8 from Kamakura station. There is also the monorail from Ofuna on the JNR Yokosuka line.

To continue from Enoshima to the Hakone/Izu/Fuji area, take the Enoden line to Fujisawa and transfer to the JNR to go to Odawara or Atami. (This area is described later in this section.)

MIURA-HANTO PENINSULA

This peninsula projects into Sagami-wan Bay between Yokohama and Kamakura. The east side is mainly industrial and commercial and includes Yokosuka Naval Base, the largest US naval base in Japan. The west side and south-east coast is largely beach and resort territory.

A bus from Zushi station runs down the west coast to Misaki station; it passes beaches, the Emperor's walled-in villa at Hayama and several good views of the sea and pleasure craft. During clear weather (late autumn and winter) Mt Fuji is clearly visible.

Aburutsubo

Aburutsubo has a large aquarium – praised by some, a disappointment to others. It is named *Sakana-no-kuni* ('Fish World'). As well as displays of live fish, it has a dome onto which films are projected to give the impression of being underwater.

Buses run between Misaki-guchi station and the aquarium; the trip takes about 15 minutes.

Jogashima Island

Located at the far south-west tip of the peninsula, Jogashima has preserved a picturesque cape as parkland, sparing it from 'development' and the encroachment of urban sprawl. The shore is made of strangely twisted rocks, apparently of volcanic origin. There are several small pools, some with colourful little fish. Anyone wanting a peaceful place for a picnic or just for relaxing by the sea would enjoy it and it's a good destination for a day-trip (or longer if you have the time) to escape Tokyo. It was almost deserted during my late-September visit, but it might be more crowded in summer. There is a youth hostel nearby.

Buses run to Jogashima from Misaki-guchi station; the trip takes about 30 minutes.

Miura-kaigan coast

Above the 'bulge' at the bottom of the peninsula is Miura-kaigan (coast), known for the very long Shonan-hama beach, with good white sand and temperate water.

Access is by Keihin-kyuko railway to any of the three stations: Miura-kaigan, Tsukuri-hama and Keihin-Nagasawa; local buses run along the coast.

There are many minshuku and ryokan along the beach.

From Kurihama, a ferry crosses to Kanaya on the Boso-hanto peninsula (on the opposite side of Tokyo-wan bay); service is approximately every 35 minutes through the daylight hours.

Fuji-Hakone-Izu Area

KOZU

Kozu is the transfer point for JNR train lines between the Tokaido Hon-sen line down the coast and the Gotemba-sen line to Gotemba, a major gateway for the Mt Fuji area.

ODAWARA

Odawara's main attraction is a reconstruction (1960) of Odawara-jo castle. It preserves the outward appearance of the ancient castle but is not 'authentic'. With a genuine 17th century castle at Matsumoto (just north of the Mt Fuji area) there is not much incentive to visit this one.

Odawara can be considered a gateway to the Izu-hanto peninsula to the southwest, and the Hakone area and Mt Fuji to the east and north-east.

Getting There

Odawara can be reached by the JNR Tokaido Hon-sen line. It's an hour from Tokyo by the fastest express; and 1½ hours by local train– Y1240. You can also use the Kodama services of the Tokaido Shinkansen (40 minutes, Y3240); and the Odakyu (Odawara Kyuko express line). Odakyu services are detailed in the section on Hakone because more travellers would use them for that purpose than for getting to Odawara.

Izu-hanto Peninsula

The Izu-hanto peninsula is probably the most popular seaside recreation area for Tokyoites. There are some interesting historical sites and some nice scenery but it is low key and the resorts are crowded during the summer season. It is better regarded as an excursion destination for Tokyo residents and of secondary interest to short-term visitors.

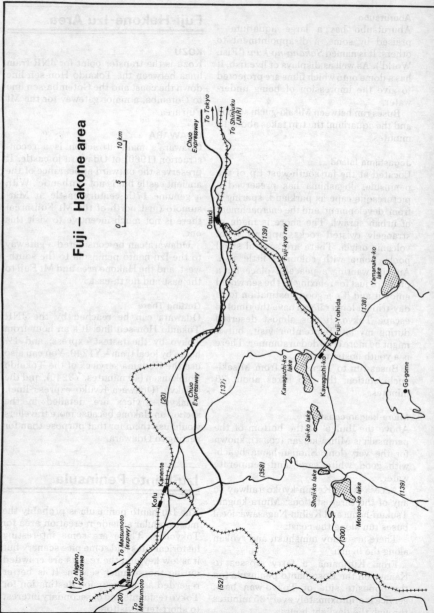

Fuji – Hakone area

To Tokyo

To Shinjuku (JNR)

Chuo Expressway

Otsuki

(139)

Fuji-kyo rwy

Yamanaka-ko lake

(138)

Fuji-Yoshida

Kawaguchi-ko lake

Kawaguchi-ko

Sai-ko lake

Go-gome

(137)

Chuo Expressway

Shojiko lake

(139)

(20)

Kanente

Motoso-ko lake

(358)

Kofu

(300)

To Matsumoto (expwy)

Chuo Expressway

(52)

To Nagano, Karuizawa

(20)

To Matsumoto

Hirasaki

To Matsumoto

0   5   10 km

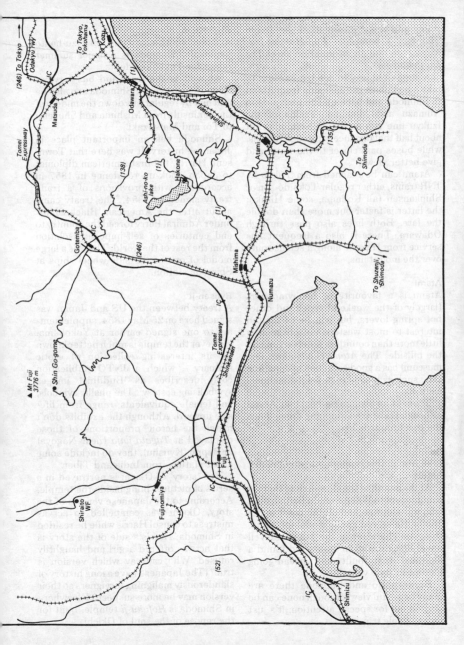

For additional information the Tokyo TIC has a pamphlet *Fuji-Hakone-Izu-Kamakura* and an information sheet *The Izu Peninsula*.

A suggested way to see Izu-hanto is to take a bus down the east side from Atami to Shimoda and back up the west side to Numazu and Mishima. Trains of the Izukyu line run as far as Shimoda, but about half that distance is through tunnels, while buses pass closer to the water and give better views.

Atami can be reached from Tokyo by JNR trains, either regular Tokaido-sen or Shinkansen (all Kodama, some Hiraki); the latter is faster but more than double the fare. Both lines also pass through Odawara. There is also a frequent bus service from Hakone along a scenic route over the mountains.

Atami

Atami is a favourite of honeymooners (largely of the weekend type) and other hot spring lovers, but will be of limited interest to most western visitors as it is little more than countless hotels strung up the hillside. The *Atami Bijutsu-kan* (art museum) has a good collection of Japanese arts, such as wood-block prints, lacquerware etc.

There is no swimming beach at Atami although there are swimming areas down the coast towards Ito.

Ito

Like Atami, this is another town of resort hotels.

At the mouth of the Okawa river there is a monument to Will Adams, a British pilot who was shipwrecked off the coast in the 1600s. He served as the model for Anjin, the main character in the James Clavell novel *Shogun*, and in reality did found a shipyard that built two ocean-going European style vessels.

Between Ito and Shimoda there are many beautiful views, though none can be singled out for special attention; it's just an enjoyable trip.

SHIMODA

At the south-east end of Izu-hanto peninsula, Shimoda is a major summer resort for Tokyo residents.

As well as the train and bus services along the east coast, Shimoda can also be reached by regular bus down the middle of the peninsula from Mishima and Shuzenji to Toi and Matsuzaki.

Shimoda has an important place in Japanese history. It was here that Townsend Harris, the first American diplomat to Japan, took up residence in 1857 in accordance with provisions of a trade treaty signed in 1854. The treaty came about after the American 'Black Ships' under Admiral Perry forced the country to end centuries of self-imposed isolation from the rest of the world. There is a large model of one of the side-wheel ships at Shimoda station.

Ryosen-ji

A treaty between the US and Japan was signed here on 25 May 1854, supplementary to one signed earlier at Yokohama. However the temple is much better known for its interesting collection of erotic statuary – which a JNTO publication coyly describes as 'Buddhist images symbolising ecstasy'. The phallic symbols, and female equivalents, range from life-size upward. Although the exhibits don't match the heroic proportions of those displayed at *Tagata-jinja* (near Nagoya) or Beppu (Kyushu), they do include some erotic statues from India and Tibet.

The 'story' of Okichi is portrayed in a series of pictures hung inside the temple. According to the Japanese version of the story, Okichi was compelled to act as mistress to consul Harris while he resided in Shimoda; Harris's side of the story is that he was offered a girl and haughtily refused. Who can say which version is true? (The Japanese have a long history of slanderously maligning foreigners so their version may be more suspect.) Elsewhere in Shimoda is *Hofuku-ji* temple, built for the repose of the soul of Okichi.

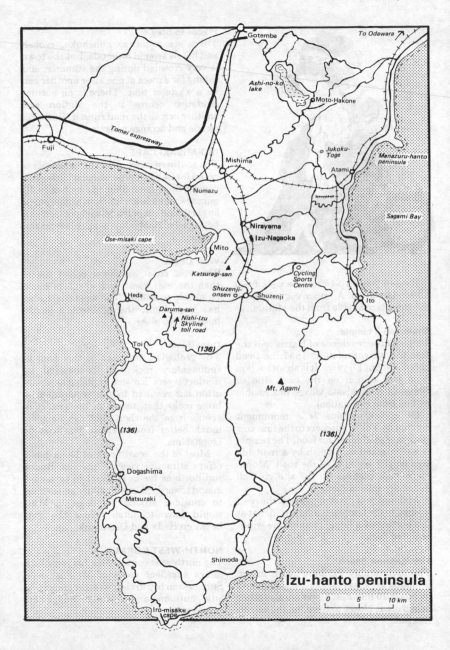

Izu-hanto peninsula

0   5   10 km

Ryosen-ji is a 10-15 minute walk from Shimoda station. A rather vague map of the town is available from the station.

Gyokusen-ji temple
This was the residence of Harris and the first foreign consulate in 1857; he lived here for about 1½ years. It is about two km from the station on the east side of Shimoda at Kakisaki village (accessible by bus from the station).

Of curiosity value is a monument erected by Tokyo butchers to the first cow slaughtered in Japan for food. The temple is well marked in English by a roadside sign on the sea side of the road. Monuments and plaques on the site give all necessary information.

At the edge of the sea, opposite the road leading to the temple, is a tiny shrine set at the bottom of a large, picturesque wind-sculpted rock.

Yumigahama Beach
This is probably the best beach in the Shimoda area, accessible from Shimoda by bus in 20 minutes. There are also other beach areas closer to town, on the way to Kakisaki.

Places to Stay
There are countless minshuku, ryokan and hotels around Shimoda, but the town is very crowded during the summer, and asking for a room at one after another can be a waste of time. There is an accommodation centre at the station and another across the road from it. Both will phone and arrange a room.

IRO-MISAKI CAPE
The southern-most tip of the peninsula is noted for its high perpendicular cliffs. You can get there from Shimoda by bus in 40 minutes, but a boat ride from Shimoda, or an excursion out of Iro-Misaki port, gives a better view. Boat info is available from the station.

West Coast
The west coast has fewer resort towns than the east coast and so offers more enjoyable travelling. The west coast also has Dogashima, the peninsula's single most scenic place.

Dogashima
The geological structure of this area is sedimentary rock that is banded in distinct layers. Erosion or physical separation has resulted in a large number of huge rocks that jut out of the sea. It is scenic from the shore, but can be seen much better from a cruise boat out of Dogashima.

Most of the coast north of Dogashima offers attractive views of the sea. Buses run north as far as Heda, then turn east inland towards Shuzenji, so anyone wishing to continue around the coast to Mito would have to hitch across the gap between Heda and Ose-misaki cape.

NORTH-WEST CORNER
The north-west corner of the Izu peninsula offers excellent views of Mt Fuji over Suruga-wan bay in clear weather (generally late autumn and winter). Suggested places are:

The top of *Katsuragi-san*, easily reached by cable car from Izu-Nagaoka town (accessible from Mishima via Nagaoka station).

The beach at Mitohama (near Mito).

Along the coast between Mitohama and Ose-Misaki cape.

The top of *Daruma-yama*, accessible by Nishi-Izu Skyline toll road.

By hiking from Shuzenji-onsen via Heda-toge pass, one of the best hiking trails on the peninsula.

An unusual sight along the coast between Mito and Ose is the old Swedish luxury passenger ship *Stella Polaris*, now a permanently berthed, floating hotel.

There is a boat service several times a day between Numazu and Matsuzaki, stopping at Heda and Toi.

Mito

Of interest here is a natural aquarium formed by nets stretched between rocks. Dolphins and great turtles may be seen.

NORTH CENTRAL AREA
Shuzenji-Onsen

This town takes its name from Shuzen-ji temple which was founded in the ninth century. It is a typical hot spring resort town with many hotels and ryokan using the hot water.

Unusual is a hot spring, Tokkonoyu, that bubbles forth at the edge of the small river that passes through the town. A roofed, slatted-wall bathhouse has been built around a pool of comfortably warm water. For those not too shy to disrobe and hop in (noone can see in from outside) there is no charge.

There is a youth hostel on the hill behind the town.

Shuzenji-onsen is reached by bus from Shuzenji station, the terminus of Izu-Hakone Tetsudo railway from Mishima. Shuzenji is the transfer point for bus travel though the middle of the peninsula from Mishima to Shimoda. There is also service to Ito and other points on the peninsula from Shuzenji; further inform-ation is available in *Jikokuhyo* or from tourist information sources.

Cycle Sports Centre Less than half an hour from Shuzenji by bus is one of the two cycle centres in Japan. There are several courses and tracks of various types, and hundreds of bicycles for rent. It is well suited for people who want to try a variety of bikes before purchasing, while offering a weekend recreation centre with reason-able cost accommodation.

Nirayama

Egawake, the oldest private house in Japan, is located near this town. The 700-year-old building was the residence of the hereditary administrators of the Izu area, so it is large and has a pretty garden, canopied by a number of tall old trees.

Access is by bus from Nirayama station of the Izu-Hakone railway line between Mishima and Shuzenji.

Mishima

Rakuju-en landscape garden, which dates from late last century, is the main attraction of this town. Mishima is on the Tokaido Hon-sen line, and is the starting point of the Izu railway line to Shuzenji, which runs partway down the middle of the peninsula.

There are many buses through the day (more than 20 in summer) from Mishima to Kawaguchi-ko (north of Mt Fuji), via Gotemba and Fuji-Yoshida. The trip takes 2¼ hours and costs Y1700. There are also up to 10 buses a day to Shin-Gogome, on the south flank of Mt Fuji, probably the most popular starting point for climbing the mountain.

WEST & SOUTH OF IZU/FUJI

West and south from the Izu-hanto/Fuji area the road and train lines run very close to the coast; the inland area is inhospitable mountains with very few settlements. Apart from a couple of attractions around Shizuoka and Shimizu, there is little of interest to anyone except students of

Japanese industrialisation. Unless you want to go directly to Kyoto, there is little incentive to go this way as Route 1 is incredibly busy, and very slow to travel on; a continuous conurbation with countless stop lights. Only trains and vehicles on the Tomei expressway move quickly.

To see some of the 'real' Japan with rural areas and some historic remains, including one of the nation's finest castles, it is better to consider travelling through the Hakone and Fuji areas to Matsumoto (via Kofu).

However for those who wish to take the coastal route, the following describes the few attractions along the way.

Okitsu

This was the 17th stage on the old Tokaido highway from Edo (Tokyo) to Kyoto. There is still a *honjin* (inn) that was designed to accommodate *daimyo* during their periodic travels between Kyoto and Tokyo. The honjin still functions as a ryokan.

Seiken-ji temple has a very pretty landscape garden; it is about one km west of the station.

Fuji

The name of this city sounds inviting, but the place isn't. The only attractions are paper mills and other industries. On a clear day there is a good view of Mt Fuji from trains and motor vehicles passing the city.

Fuji is a junction of the Tokaido Honsen line and the Minobu line to Kofu and on to Matsumoto. For getting around to the scenic areas north of Mt Fuji, however it cannot be recommended as travel time can be as long as five hours. The best way to reach the Kawaguchi-ko area is by bus from Fuji station or Fujinomiya and clockwise around the mountain. In summer, up to three buses a day run out of Fuji along this route; out of season it may be necessary to take a train to Fujinomiya and go from there by bus.

Shizuoka/Shimizu Area

On the south side of Kunozan hill near the coast and between Shimizu and Shizuoka (accessible from both cities by bus) is *Tosho-gu* shrine. Ieyasu Tokugawa was interred here before finally being laid to rest at the magnificent and famous Tosho-gu shrine at Nikko. The shrine, accessible after a climbing more than 1100 steps, is very colourfully decorated.

Nihondaira

This is a plateau atop Udo hill, one valley away from Kunozan hill. You can get to the top by a cable car that begins near Toshogu. Also buses run across it via Nihondaira Parkway between between Shizuoka and Shimizu stations. From the top there is an excellent view of Mt Fuji in one direction (in clear weather) and the bay and Miho-no-matsubara in another.

Rinzai-ji A couple of km to the north of Shimizu station is this temple best known for its beautiful garden. Nearby is *Sengenjinja* shrine. Its festival is 1-5 April.

Toro

In 1943 the remains of a settlement about 1800 years old were discovered in this area (in the vicinity of Rinzai-ji). Excavations have revealed a lot about life in those days including the living places of its people. These so-called 'pit dwellings', while giving the impression of living in squalor, were actually built on ground level but had earth walls about a metre or so high built around the base. The dwellings were round with thatched walls built on a wooden framework. Reproductions of the pit dwellings and some elevated store houses can be seen at the park in Toro; and the museum there has displays of implements excavated from the 16 ha site.

Oikawa Valley

One of the only two steam-powered train lines left in Japan, the Oigawa Hon-sen private line, runs through this valley. (The other steam line, the JNR Yamaguchi-sen in the far west of Honshu reverted to special steam runs after being completely dieselised.) Every day there is one run in each direction between Kanaya and Senzu. The train leaves Kanaya at 11.34 am and Senzu at 2.35 pm and the trip on this ancient steamer takes about 1½ hours.

The journey through the Oi River valley from Kanaya is pretty and at Senzu you can continue on a different line where the cars are pulled by a miniature diesel loco. This one really twists and turns, passing over deep chasms and climbing ever higher. Its terminus, Ikawa, is a popular starting place for climbing in the South Japan Alps.

There is a small youth hostel a short distance from Kanaya.

There is little of interest west of this area until Nagoya.

Hakone area

Hakone, and its nearby attractions, is the closest resort to Tokyo and is therefore very popular with Japanese holiday makers. Because of its popularity with the local population it is also heavily promoted for visiting foreigners – perhaps over-promoted in view of the differences in interests.

The major attractions of the Hakone area are good views of Mt Fuji, Ashi-no-ko lake, some interesting historic remains and other views of the volcanic terrain. Be warned though, that most of the beauty and interest of the area comes from having Mt Fuji as a backdrop, and this mountain is notoriously bashful in spring, summer and early autumn, often totally obscured by cloud even from close up. Because of this, the later in the season (late-autumn and winter) you visit, the better the chance of seeing the undeniably superb form of Mt Fuji. Japanese visitors may not be too concerned with missing the view,

but foreigners who may only have a short time in Japan, should plan their itinerary accordingly.

The following describes a vaguely circular route through the Hakone area which minimises backtracking. The starting point is Odawara/Yumoto-onsen. Access is by JNR and Odakyu train services.

Miyanoshita

The only (low key) attraction here is the Fujiya Hotel, a five minute walk uphill from the station. It was the first western-style building to be constructed in the Hakone district (1878), and has since added wings that are more modern, giving an interesting blend of American colonial and Japanese architecture. The main building has the mustiness of age, rather like a dowager who has known better days. It will appeal mostly to those of a nostalgic frame of mind who wish to see how expatriates once spent their summers. The library and its old books are still there, as is one billiard table.

You can have coffee in the first floor lounge overlooking the pond and garden; prices are reasonable. In the lobby there is a display case with a large number of miniature figures playing 'native' instruments. At basement level there are commercial exhibits of electronic and photographic equipment that have not been changed in 14 years; one of the companies represented even went bankrupt several years ago.

There are several walking trails from Miyanoshita, such as the one to Sengensan.

Chokoku-no-mori

This is the train stop and the Japanese name for 'Hakone Open-air Museum' where sculptures are arranged around a garden. Many people speak highly of it, though the garden and several other attractions are largely aimed at day tripping Japanese who enjoy such 'exotic' western things. Parts of it can be seen from the right side of the train as it passes

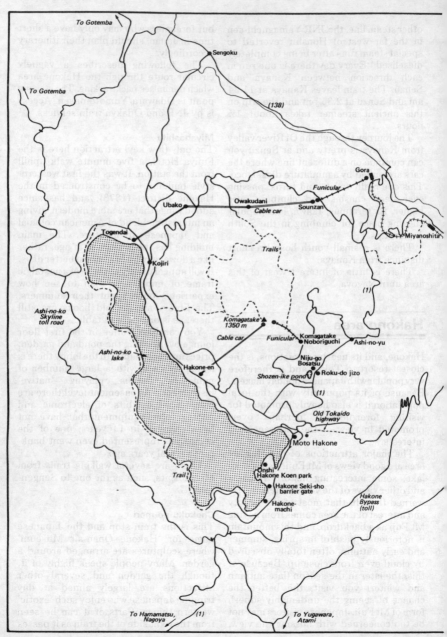

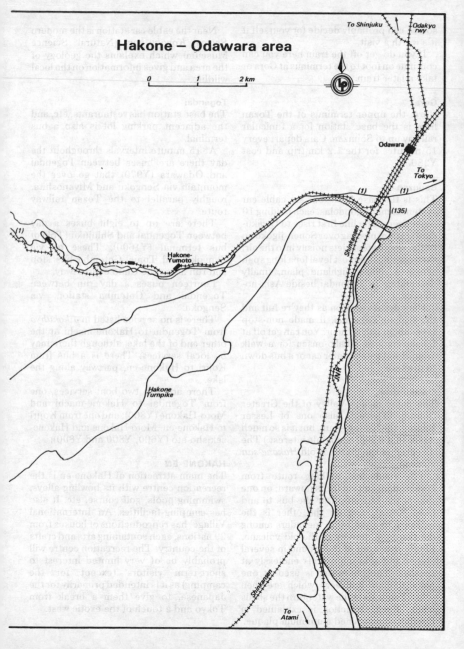

Hakone – Odawara area

0   1   2 km

To Shinjuku

Odakyo rwy

Odawara

To Tokyo

(1)   (1)

(135)

Shinkansen

Hakone-Yumoto

(1)

Hakone Turnpike

JNR

To Atami

Shinkansen

so you can probably decide for yourself if it's worth a visit.

If you do get off the train here you can continue on foot to the terminus at Gora or take a later train.

Gora

Gora, the upper terminus of the Tozan line, is the base station for a funicular railway up to Sounzan. Cars depart every 15 minutes for the 1.2 km trip and cost Y280.

Sounzan

This is the base for a four km cable car system of many gondolas, each holding 10 passengers. The line first rises to Owaku-dani station, passing over Souen-jigoku en route, where steam jets noisily into the air; then continues almost level for a long span across a rolling highland plain, finally descending to Togendai beside Ashi-no-ko lake.

Cars depart as soon as they're full and the trip to Togendai, if made non-stop takes about half an hour. You can get off at Owaku-dani or Ubako-onsen for a walk around and catch a later car or a bus down to the lake.

Owaku-dani

The name means Valley of the Greater Boiling. (There is also one of Lesser Boiling, the Kowaki-dani, but it is so much lesser that it is of negligible interest.) The 'Greater' is the crater of old *Hakone-san* volcano.

The road and walking route from Owaku-dani station leads upward; on one side is the bus stop (for the bus to and from Kojiri), and on the other is the entrance to a path that meanders among the traces of activity of the old volcano. Steam pours out of the ground in several places and grey mud boils endlessly at another. The hot water is used at one place to hard-boil eggs which are then sold; chemicals in the water turn the shells black. Each attraction is explained in English on an etched aluminium plaque.

Near the cable car station is the modern *Shizen Kogaku-kan* (Natural Science Museum) which explains the geology of the area and gives information on the local wildlife.

Togendai

The base station has restaurants, etc, and the adjacent parking lot is also a bus terminal.

At 15 minute intervals throughout the day there are buses between Togendai and Odawara (Y970) that go over the mountain via Sengoku and Miyanoshita, roughly parallel to the Tozan railway route.

There are up to eight buses a day between Togendai and Shinjuku (Tokyo) bus terminal (Y1600). These go via Sengoku and Tomei-Gotemba bus stop and run along the Chuo expressway.

Fourteen buses a day run between Togendai and Gotemba station, via Sengoku.

There is no service listed in *Jikokuhyo* from Togendai to Hakone-machi at the other end of the lake, although there may be local services. There is a bus from Kojiri to Hakone-en, partway along the lake.

There are also two boat services, one from Togendai to Hakone-machi and Moto-Hakone (Y800); and one from Kojiri to Hakone-en, Moto-Hakone and Hakone-sekisho-ato (Y600, Y800 and Y800).

HAKONE-EN

The main attraction of Hakone-en is the recreation centre with its bowling alleys, swimming pools, golf course, etc. It also has camping facilities. An 'International Village' has reproductions of houses from 29 nations, each containing arts and crafts of the country. The recreation centre will probably be of very limited interest to short-term visitors (except for the camping) as it is intended primarily for the Japanese, to give them a break from Tokyo and a touch of the exotic west.

Koma-ga-take Hakone-en is the base station of a cable car (Y550/900 one way/return) to the top of Koma-ga-take mountain (1327 metres).

If the weather is clear, the summit offers a superb view of Mt Fuji and Ashi-no-ko lake.

From the top of Koma-ga-take you can take the funicular railway down to Komagatake-nobori-guchi (Y300/500 one way/return).

Shojin-ike lake is almost directly below the base station. You can take a bus from nearby Ashinoyu to the lake and the historic stone carvings of the Buddhist deity *Jizo*. Get off the bus when several carved stone monuments, about the height of a person, come into view; Shoji-ike lake is just around the corner.

Rock carvings At the end of the lake closer to Ashinoyu, where the road bends, a path leads down a few metres to a large rock covered with 25 carvings of Buddha; this is called *Niju-go Bosatsu*. Some are very artistically executed and all are in remarkably fine condition considering their exposure to the elements from the time of the Kamakura era (1192-1333).

About 100 metres along the road (toward Moto-Hakone) is a large and benevolent figure of *Jizo*, the Buddha of compassion and the patron of travellers, children and pregnant women. The figure is about two metres tall and was carved primarily for the benefit of foot travellers in this very difficult mountain terrain. There are several smaller and less interesting figures nearby; together they are known as *Roku-do Jizo*.

From here, take a bus (or hitch or walk) from the stop on the side nearer Jizo-sama, down to lake level; get off at Seki-sho bus stop at the entrance to Hakone-machi town (at the top of a downgrade) and walk along the short street running off the main road toward the lake. This leads to Seki-sho barrier gate.

HAKONE-MACHI

Seki-sho Barrier Gate During the Edo era under the rule of the Tokugawa military government (1600-1868), travel was tightly controlled to prevent the movement of arms and men. Local *daimyo* were compelled to spend part of each year in Edo (Tokyo), effectively as hostages, so there was frequent movement of *daimyo* and their retainers along this road.

The main checkpoint on the Tokaido highway between Edo and Kyoto was *Hakone Seki-sho*, built in 1619; all travellers had to produce 'passports' at this point. The barrier stood until 1869. An exact reproduction was built in 1965 across the road from the original site and wax figures dressed in period costume show how things looked at the time.

Nearby is the dock for the regular cruise boats to Kojiri and Hakone-en.

Hakone Shiryo-kan A short distance up the road (or along the lake shore) is this small museum, housing materials related to the gate. Most are unintelligible to foreigners and of little interest, but there are some firearms and armour etc. The same ticket allows admission to both the museum and the barrier display.

Onshi-Hakone-koen This is a park next to the museum with peaceful walking paths through a small forest. During clear weather this area offers a good view of the upper part of Mt Fuji complete with reflection in the lake.

During my last visit there I was amused to see, on the easels of a school class, some beautiful paintings of the lake, the opposite shore and Mt Fuji. The children had obviously been well prepared for their trip and were determined to portray the beauty of the area, despite the fact that they actually couldn't see more than 50 metres in front of them due to fog over the lake.

Suginami-ki Just a short distance beyond the garden is the entrance to a section of the old Tokaido highway that runs parallel to the modern road for half a km between Hakone-machi and Moto-Hakone. It is lined with majestic cryptomeria (cedar) trees that were planted in 1618 to provide shade for travellers. The trees make the walk to Moto-Hakone town most enjoyable. From the shore at Moto-Hakone, near the bus station, you get the best shoreside view of Mt Fuji in the area.

MOTO-HAKONE

Hakone-jinja shrine A short walk from Moto-Hakone (and about two km from Hakone-en and the Koma-ga-take base station) is Hakone-jinja. The present main building dates from 1667, though the shrine is believed to date from the eighth century. The buildings are not particularly noteworthy as shrines go but the mysterious atmosphere of the place is. The path is lined with venerable cedars and the shrine is set among equally huge trees, dating from the 17th century.

There is a picturesque torii gate in the lake just offshore. Be satisfied looking at it from a distance as it is made of practical but unromantic concrete.

The shrine festival takes place on 31 August when lanterns are set adrift on the lake as part of the *Obon* ceremonies.

Old Tokaido Highway A short distance up the hillside road from the lakeside bus terminal (by the large torii) is the beginning of a stretch of the original Tokaido road. A pedestrian overpass leads up to it. Because of the hill, the road was paved with stones for a considerable distance to make walking easier and to prevent rain from destroying the path.

Most people will be content with a look and a photo at the beginning but a walk of about 20 minutes takes you to a coffee shop and restaurant in a traditional-style building that also houses Edo era exhibits. Buses return to Moto-Hakone and also go to Odawara (opposite direction), but service is not frequent, about two an hour until mid-afternoon.

Places to Stay

There are many hotels, ryokan and minshuku of all price ranges in the many hotspring resort towns and other centres in the area. The most famous is the *Fujiya* at Miyanoshita, the oldest hotel in the area, while the most luxurious might be the *Prince* beside the lake. As for all accommodation in Japan, reservations may be made in advance through any travel agent in the country.

There is a youth hostel at Sounzan, very close to the base station of the cable car to Owaku-dani, tel (0460) 2-3827.

Getting There & Getting Around

JNR services to Odawara were described in the Odawara section. At Odawara station take platform 11 or 12 for the Tozan railway up the mountain. This train stops at Yumoto-onsen, the terminus for Odakyu Romance Car trains.

Odakyu The Odakyu (Odawara-kyuku) line, running from Shinjuku (Tokyo) Odakyu station is the most convenient way to start a Hakone trip.

The Romance Car train makes the trip to Odawara in 70 minutes (Y1050) while the local and express Odakyu trains (both Y550) take 112 and 92 minutes. The Romance Car trains are much more luxurious and this is perhaps one case when it is worth spending the extra money for first class. Passengers in the first car can look out through the panorama window at the front of the car. However Odawara is not the place to stop as these trains continue several km more to the terminus at Yumoto-onsen (Y1280). The Tozan railway (see below) passes through here at Hakone-Yumoto station, and transfer is easier than at Odawara.

A good buy for economy and convenience (no need to stand in line for tickets during busy times) is a 'Hakone Free Pass'. Sold by Odakyu railway, the pass covers the standard Odakyu rail fare (Romance Car or express is extra), plus cable cars, boats etc, in the area for four days.

An alternative starting point for sightseeing in this region is Togendai, accessible by bus from Shinjuku, Gotemba and Odawara.

Tozan railway This one or two-car train, which resembles a municipal tram, is well-known for its folksy character. The 'little train that could' begins at Odawara and, once into the mountains, struggles valiantly groaning all the while against the steep gradient making stops at Hakone-Yumoto and Miyanoshita (among others) on its way to the terminus at Gora. There are three switchbacks along the way. Trains depart Odawara every 20-40 minutes.

From the Hakone-machi/Moto-Hakone area there is a variety of ways to continue.

Boats Across Ashi-no-ko lake there are regular boats along the route Hakone-machi – Moto-Hakone – Togendai; and Moto-Hakone – Hakone-en – Kojiri.

Bus Every 10-30 minutes through the day there is a service from the bus station in Hakone-machi to Odawara via Ashinoyu, Kowakidani, Miyanoshita and Yumoto-onsen (one hour, Y920).

From Hakone-en there is a regular bus service to Odawara via Kojiri, Kowakidani,

Miyanoshita and Yumoto-onsen (one hour, Y1000).

Buses also go from the Ashi-no-ko area south to Atami via two routes. From Moto-Hakone/Seki-sho there are regular buses south via a route over the mountains, passing through Jukoku-toge pass with its good views of Mt Fuji (in clear weather). One of the stops is Jukoku-toge nobori guchi, the base station for a funicular railway up to a scenic viewpoint. The bus trip takes an hour and costs Y900.

The alternative route is the bus from Moto-Hakone/Hakone-machi via Yugawara (one hour, Y1000) to Atami (80 minutes, Y1150).

About 10 buses a day run from Moto-Hakone/Hakone-machi to Mishima (50 minutes, Y820) and Numazu (70 minutes, Y990).

Mt Fuji area

Every visitor to Japan wants to see Mt Fuji, or Fuji-san as the Japanese call it (*never* Fuji-yama!). It is the symbol of Japan recognised universally and is truly one of the world's most beautiful mountains. It was revered, understandably, for centuries as a sacred peak and is a spectacular sight no matter how many times you see it.

Almost the visual ideal of what a volcano should look like, the now dormant Fuji-san last erupted in 1707 covering the streets of Tokyo 100 km away with a thick layer of black volcanic soot. Its symmetrical, snow capped cone rises 3776 metres from an almost perfectly round base.

Visitors should be forewarned however, that the famous volcano is very bashful for most of the year. In spring, summer and early autumn Fuji-san is usually partly or even totally obscured by clouds, even from close up.

There are several places that offer superb views of the mountain (some of which have already been described): from the Shinkansen as it passes near Fuji city; from the Tomei expressway; from Nihondaira, near Shizuoka; from several places in the north-west corner of the Izu-hanto peninsula; from several places in the Hakone area; and from Nanao-toge pass, between Hakone and Gotemba.

There are also clear views from many points along the roads that nearly encircle the mountain, chiefly between Yamanaka-ko and Sai-ko. West of Sai-ko the view is not as good because of a 'shoulder' at the base of the cone which diminishes the symmetry of Fuji-san as seen from other directions.

From the Tokyo area, the two major access routes to the Mt Fuji area are Fuji-Yoshida/Kawaguchi-ko and Gotemba. The former can be considered the main one of the two for sightseeing if you don't plan to climb Mt Fuji.

GOTEMBA

Gotemba is a typical, rather nondescript Japanese city, with no particular attraction apart from providing the best access to Shin Go-gome ('New Fifth Station') which has become the favourite starting point for the ascent of Fuji-san. (Bus services to Shin Go-gome and Go-gome are detailed in the section on climbing the volcano.)

Views of Mt Fuji are negligible or unexciting almost anywhere in the Gotemba area. After leaving the city the road climbs for several km to the table-land that surrounds much of the mountain, which finally comes into clear view near Yamanaka-ko lake.

To see Mt Fuji from many of its best angles, with the option of climbing from one of the two main base stations, neighbouring Fuji-Yoshida and Kawaguchi-ko are the best starting points.

There are about 24 buses a day between Gotemba and Fuji-Yoshida; most of these go further in each direction – to/from Mishima (1½ hours south of Gotemba) and to/from Kawaguchi-ko (10 minutes west of Fuji-Yoshida).

Yamanaka-ko is a popular recreation area, offering swimming, boating, coffee shops and other kinds of entertainment as well as accommodation.

Fuji-Yoshida

This city, apart from being a transportation centre, has no attraction other than its annual festival on 31 August.

Fujikyu Highland amusement park This

park is mostly of interest to residents rather than visitors (except perhaps visitors with children). It is close to Fujikyu Highland station of the train line between Otsuki and Kawaguchi-ko. The bus station for travel around the north side of Mt Fuji is nearby.

Kawaguchi-ko lake is the second largest of

Fuji Go-ko – the Fuji five lakes, and is a popular resort with Tokyo residents. The largest town on the lake is Kawaguchiko and there is a superb view of Mt Fuji and the lake from atop nearby Tenjo-san mountain.

Kawaguchiko-machi town

Just near Kawaguchiko station, the terminus of the Fuji-kyuko railway line, is a cable car which provides access to Tenjo-san.

Also of interest in the town are two museums. Fuji-hakubutsukan, in front of Fuji Lake Hotel, has exhibitions related to the people, geology, etc, of the area and is noted for the Amano collection of erotic items from bygone days. This is a good opportunity to see some aspects of the large role that fertility symbols played in the lives of the Japanese not so long ago. This very earthy element within Japanese society is not as apparent these days as it once was. The museum is a 10 minute walk from the station.

Yamanashi-ken Visitors' Centre is a museum of material relating to the natural history of Mt Fuji. It is about 15 minutes walk from Kawaguchiko station.

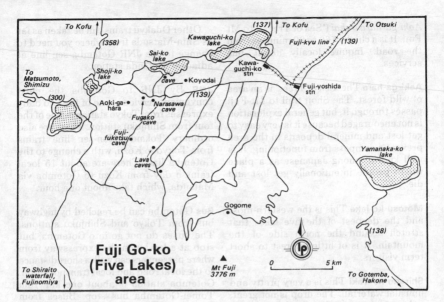

**Fuji Go-ko
(Five Lakes)
area**

NORTH OF MT FUJI

The next attractions lie along the road west of Kawaguchi-ko. The scheduled transport along the route is the bus service between Fuji-Yoshida station and Fujinomiya which passes within walking distance of the places mentioned. There are up to 13 buses a day as far as Motosuko lake; most go to Shiraito falls and Fujinomiya. There are many sightseers so hitching should be no problem.

Sai-ko lake

This picturesque lake is less developed than Kawaguchi-ko and Yamanaka-ko and still preserves much of the wilderness area. There is an excellent view of Mt Fuji from the west end.

A vantage point near the lake is *Koyodai* (Maple Hill), along one of the roads from the main highway.

Saiko Youth Hostel is close by and offers a good view in picturesque surroundings. It is about two km off the main road so you may have to hitch or walk to it.

Narusawa Ice Cave & Fugaku Wind Cave

The former, *Narusawa Huoketsu* is not made of ice, nor is the latter, *Fugaku Fuketsu*, made of wind. Both are lava tubes (or caves), formed when lava from a prehistoric eruption of Mt Fuji cooled on the surface and still-molten material flowed out from below, leaving the rough and jagged inner surfaces. Both are cold, even in mid-summer so a sweater is recommended.

The entrances to the caves are quite close to the main road (Route 139), and each has a bus stop; they are about 20 minutes apart on foot.

There are several other such caves in the area, including *Fuji Fuketsu* on the Shoji trail which has a floor of solid ice.

Shoji-ko lake The smallest of the five lakes of Fuji Go-ko is regarded as the prettiest.

Eboshi-san If you have the time you could climb Eboshi-san to take in the view from Shoji Panorama, the scenic lookout at the summit. There is a superb view over the

Aoki-ga-hara Jukai ('Sea of Trees') to Mt Fuji. It is a climb of 60 to 90 minutes from the road. Inquire locally about bus services.

Aoki-ga-hara The 'Sea of Trees' is an area of wild forest. The Shoji trail to Mt Fuji passes through it, but general exploration is not encouraged because it is very easy to get lost and mineral deposits in the area prevent a compass from functioning. It is well known among Japanese as a place where people intentionally get lost and die.

Motosu-ko lake This is the western-most and the deepest of the five lakes that stretch around the north side of the mountain. It is of little interest to short term visitors.

Shiraito-no-Taki This is a very pretty and unusual waterfall. The drop is not great, only a few metres, but the falls make a semicircle of considerable length. The name translates as 'White Threads' which is an apt description of the countless rivulets of water. It is accessible by bus from Motosu-ko lake. Nearby is another waterfall, Otodome-no-take.

Fujinomiya
This city is of no inherent interest other than as a transportation centre. From here buses leave for Shin Go-gome.

Getting There & Getting Around
Gotemba and Fuji-Yoshida/Kawaguchi-ko can be reached by both train and bus from Tokyo.

Gotemba
Odakyu trains Though few in number, the most convenient services to Gotemba are the four daily expresses from Shinjuku (Tokyo) which, instead of veering south to Odawara at Shin-Matsuda, switch to the JNR tracks at Matsuda and run directly to Gotemba. These take about 1½ hours and cost Y1770.

Other Odakyu trains can be taken as far as Shin-Matsuda from where you need to change to the JNR Gotemba-sen line at adjacent Matsuda station.

JNR By JNR to Gotemba the most convenient service is one of the two daily expresses from Tokyo station or one of the four from Shinjuku station. There are also ordinary Tokaido Hon-sen line trains from Tokyo to Kozu, with a change to the Gotemba line. There are about 15 local trains a day from Kozu to Gotemba via Matsuda, which take about one hour.

Bus Gotemba can be reached by highway bus from Tokyo and Shinjuku stations. The buses do not go into Gotemba, but stop at a lay-by on the expressway from where passengers can walk a short distance to the local road and local transportation. Gotemba station is about one km from Tomei-Gotemba bus stop. Buses from Shinjuku (about eight a day) take 1¾ hour and costs Y1300 to Tomei-Gotemba.

Fuji-Yoshida and Kawaguchi-ko
Train The simplest way of reaching the area is by one of the four direct JNR expresses from Shinjuku (Tokyo). If you take one of these trains note that the train is separated into two parts at Otsuki, so be sure that you are in the correct end.

There is also the JNR Chuo Hon-sen line to Otsuki where you change to the Fuji-kyuko (Fujikyu) line for the rest of the way.

Bus From Shinjuku bus terminal about 10 buses a day run to Fujikyu Highland and Kawaguchi-ko; some of them continue on to Yamanaka-ko; and one goes to 'old' Go-gome on the north side of Mt Fuji. The fare is Y1400 to Kawaguchi-ko; Y1750 to Yamanaka-ko; and Y2000 to Go-gome.

Between Kofu (to the north of Kawaguchi-ko) and Fuji-Yoshida/Kawaguchi-ko there is about 17 buses a day (90 minutes, Y1200). Kofu is a major stop on the way to Matsumoto.

Climbing Mt Fuji

The Japanese have a saying to the effect 'He who climbs Mt Fuji once is a wise man; He who climbs it more than once is a fool'. Those foreigners who believe they are wise will be pleased to know the ascent of Fuji-san is not too difficult.

There are two major starting points, (old) *Go-gome* ('fifth station') on the north flank and *Shin Go-gome* ('new fifth station') on the south flank. From these places the climb is little more than five km and takes just over five hours.

The 'official' climbing season is through July and August when the weather is predictable and the conditions not hazardous to climbers wearing normal cool weather clothes. There are no restrictions on climbers and people do climb throughout the year, but because of the high altitude the weather can change rapidly out of season and the temperatures can plunge with the risk of strong snowfall. If you do decide to climb in winter make sure you take all the necessary precautions; every year climbers die on the mountain because of insufficient preparation.

Anyone in reasonably good health can make the climb and there is no danger of getting lost as there is a continual stream of climbers.

Formerly people climbed during the day, but now increasing numbers of people begin climbing well after dark and continue through the night, watching the sunrise from the top or flank of the mountain. There are huts at various places along the upper reaches of the major trails, but they are crowded and do not have a good reputation for cleanliness. By starting around midnight or a bit earlier, you may avoid the need to stop for a sleep.

The major aim of climbing Fuji-san is to witness the amazing experience of *goraiko*, the sunrise. But although the sunrise is so often spoken of, the fact is that in early morning the top is often enshrouded in mist and visibility is not good until later in the morning. One guide who has made the climb several times (from the north side) recommends watching the sunrise from Hachigome, the eighth station.

The descent can be made more quickly on the north side than the south because a large patch of the mountain side is covered with volcanic sand and you can slide down it very quickly. This is called *sunabashiri* ('sliding on sand').

In olden times before buses went to points high up on the sides, it was customary to walk the distance from the railway stations and then climb to the top. Several trails still exist, but these days they would be better regarded as hiking paths for a day's outing (without climbing). The best known such trails are the Yoshida trail from Fuji-Yoshida station; the Kawaguchi trail from the town of that name (it joins the Yoshida trail at the sixth station); the Shoji trail from the Shoji-ko lake area (which passes Fuji-fuketsu cave along the way); and Gotemba trail from Gotemba. There is also a circular trail around the mountain about half way up.

The following description of climbing Mt Fuji is reprinted with the permission of Jean Pearce who writes a regular column in the *Japan Times* and well-regarded guides for exploring Tokyo on foot.

I know what I should have been doing a year ago. I should have been jogging every morning, doing deep knee bends and running up the subway steps in preparation for what everyone should do once but never twice – climb Mt Fuji. But I know now how to answer this question: What should I take along on the climb?

You don't need much of anything, but you must be a stoic if that is your choice. We climbed in the heat of late July but it was freezing after the sun went down. You can have a year's variety of weather – it rains, the sun beats down, you'll be groping in the mists. Be sure to have a cover-all plastic raincoat. After the storm, you can put it between the layers of your clothing when you get cold to seal in your body warmth, if you have any. And **beware of the sun**. Have a hat to shade your face and wear long sleeves. Even on a hazy day, Fuji-san's sun can inflict a painful burn.

You can buy lemons, hard boiled eggs, soft drinks, beer and sake, and such standard foods as soba and oden. Prices are high but remember, you didn't have to carry them. Take along foods that don't spoil easily such as cheese, cucumbers, nuts, chocolate and sliced meat, and a bottle of water. Toilet facilities are adequate, but don't expect them to be clean or to flush.

Take gloves. Climbing Fuji is not a stroll; you'll be pulling yourself along with a chain over some rocky areas. You'll want them if you come down by way of the lava slide in case you fall. Cinders can leave scars with the persistence of a tattoo. Have a backpack so your hands will be free, and outer clothing with plenty of pockets for immediate necessities like tissue and money. For your feet, sturdy hiking boots and two or three pairs of wool sox.

Accommodations are cozy, your own futon on your own tatami mat in friendly proximity with a hundred or so other hikers. If you don't have reservations at the top, stop early to be sure of space, and don't necessarily believe the resthouse keeper who tells you there is room at the next station. He does not know. Some like to sleep a few hours along the way and finish the climb the next morning before dawn. Since dawn usually arrives about 4.30 am, it seems easier to me to do it all in one piece.

Be prepared for an early morning at the

summit as well. Someone will likely be pulling off your covers at, say 3 am (that's morning?) and if you don't get up then, attendants will be back for your futon some 10 minutes later. The room must be readied for breakfast service for the morning climbers who are just arriving.

There are 10 stations but don't be lulled by that statistic as you look up and count. You can't see the top from the bottom, and there are a number of resthouses between each official station that can delude the unwary.

Climbing the mountain on the same day I did – I climbed with a group from the Press Club and recommend that you find companions – were four blind men, two boys with their bicycles (later I saw them riding around the summit), a one-legged man, an 88-year-old lady and a gentleman of 93. Not everyone gets to the top, but it is worth all the exertion you can extend to make it.

I don't believe there is a mirror on all of Fuji-san, except perhaps a sacred one in the shrine at the top. But it doesn't matter. You won't care after a while. At one stop I saw a woman powdering her nose. It looked pretty silly.

The best season to climb Mt Fuji? There isn't one. Climb it early in the official season (it begins on 1 July and ends on 31 August) and it's bitterly cold; later you'll likely have rain, perhaps a typhoon and pathways lined with discards of earlier climbers, though it wasn't the huge garbage heap that I expected, thanks in part to the tractors that, unseen, ply the back slopes carrying up supplies and returning at least some of the empty bottles. You will still marvel at the old men who jog up the mountains with three cases of beer and a dozen litre-bottles of sake on their backs for their resthouse concession; their sons, if they stay on the mountain, hire the tractor.

Oh yes, on the way back, it took us 4½ hours by bus from the fifth station to the highway at the foot of the mountain, normally a 20 minute drive. Sturdy climbers make the summit in less. When you climb Mt Fuji be prepared for anything. Ganbatte!

Getting There

There is direct access to Mt Fuji's base stations from Tokyo and regular bus services from the nearby towns.

To Go-gome (north side) From Kawaguchiko station there are up to 16 buses a day (Y1350). The latest of these arrives shortly after midnight obviating the need to sleep at any of the huts.

From Shinjuku (Tokyo) a single bus goes directly to Go-gome arriving in the late morning (Y2000) and making the trip in just under three hours. It stops at Fujikyu Highland en route.

To Shin Go-gome From Gotemba station there are up to six buses a day to Shin Go-gome (eastern entrance), the last one arriving in the late afternoon (45 minutes, Y860).

From Mishima station there are up to 10 buses a day, the last one arriving at about 10.30 pm (two hours, Y2100).

From Fujinomiya station there are nine buses a day to Shin Go-gome (western entrance) the last arriving at about 11 pm (75 minutes, Y1800).

Note: These bus frequencies are representative of mid-summer schedules and buses are likely to be much less frequent at other times of the year so be sure to check with *Jikokuhyo* or a source of travel information.

NORTH-WEST OF MT FUJI

From the Mt Fuji area there are many further destinations. Those to the east, south and south-west have been described. It is easy to continue north-west through Kofu to Matsumoto and the many other interesting places described later in the Central Honshu chapter.

Kofu

Near Kofu is a scenic gorge, Shosen-kyo. The most scenic part begins at Sen-ga-taki waterfall and continues for four km through the rocky gorge. Access to the entrance is by bus from Kofu station.

Saitama-ken

This section covers the Chichibu-tama National Park, Kawagoe and Sakitama

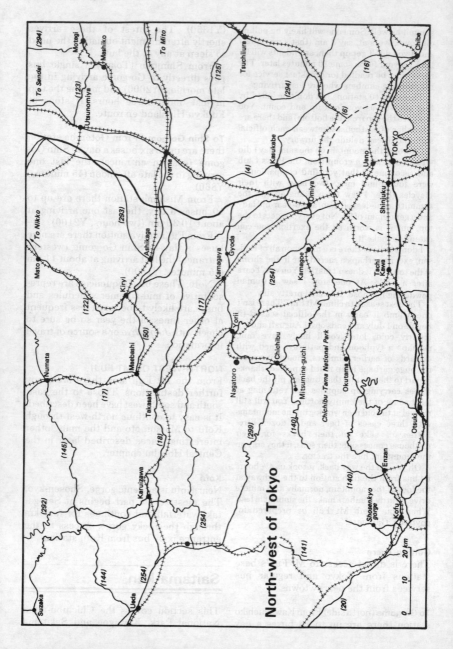

North-west of Tokyo

kofun-koen. Other attractions of Saitama-ken are included in descriptions of the Nagano-ken and Tochigi-ken (Nikko) areas in later chapters.

CHICHIBU-TAMA NATIONAL PARK

This large national park is located northeast of Kofu and Yamanashi. It is divided into two sections, *Chichibu* and *Okutama*, in parallel valleys. Both offer enjoyable nature walks and are especially popular with day-tripping Tokyo residents. A hiking trail extends between the two sections of the park.

OKUTAMA

This section of the park is easily reached by JNR Ome line which begins at Tachikawa (on the Chuo line).

Ome

The attraction here is the JNR Railway Museum, *Ome Tetsu-do koen*. Around the main building are several steam locos formerly in service with JNR. The museum has moving displays of model trains. Meals are available in an elegant old dining car. The museum is in Hikawa-koen to the north of the city, a 15 minute walk from Ome station.

Hinatawada

The general appearance of the town is scenic, with a low mountain looming over it. The town is famed for its plum blossoms which attract many visitors in late February and early March. An interesting festival is held at this time. The best known groves are Yoshino Baien, less than a km from the station.

A walking trail extends beyond the Yoshino area via several low mountains (Sampo, Hinode and Mitake). The trail passes close to Mitake-jinja shrine.

Mitake

Mitake keikoku (gorge) is visible from the train before you reach Mitake station; it can also be seen on foot from the path along either side of the river. The best way to see the gorge is to get off the train at Sawai station (one before Mitake) and walk to Mitake.

Mitake-san mountain (930 metres) is well forested with tall cedars and other trees. A cable car runs close to the top; the base station can be reached by bus or on foot.

The cable car gives easy access to Mitake-jinja shrine and intersects the Yoshino-Hatonosu trail.

The main building of *Mitake-jinja* is about a century old, but the shrine has a history of about 1200 years. The shrine festival, *Hinode-matsuri*, takes place on 8 May and has a procession of mikoshi and people dressed in samurai armour.

Hatonosu The gorge here, Hatonosu-keikoku, can be seen from the train or on foot.

Okutama

The terminus of the railway, this is the point of departure by bus for Nippara cave and Okutama-ko lake.

Nippara shoyudo is the largest cave in the Kanto area and is lit for about 280 metres to allow exploration.

The whole area is pretty in late October when the leaves change colour. It is about 40 minutes from Okutama by bus.

The southern shore of Okutama-ko, created when the Tama river was dammed to provide water for Tokyo, still has natural terrain; the north shore has typical Japanese tourist facilities and about 6000 cherry trees that are usually at their best around mid-April. The lake can be reached in 20 minutes by bus from Okutama station.

Further information on the area may be found in the JNTO publication *Okutama*, available at the Tokyo TIC.

CHICHIBU

The Chichibu part of the park has beautiful scenery and plenty of hiking trails.

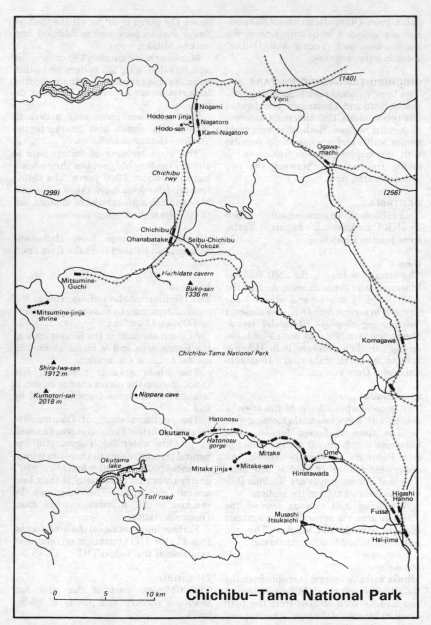

Chichibu–Tama National Park

0   5   10 km

(140)
Yorii
Nogami
Hodo-san jinja
Nagatoro
Hodo-san
Kami-Nagatoro
Ogawa-machi
Chichibu rwy
(299)
(256)
Chichibu
Ohanabatake
Seibu-Chichibu
Yokoze
Hashidate cavern
Buko-san 1336 m
Mitsumine-Guchi
Komagawa
Mitsumine-jinja shrine
Chichibu-Tama National Park
▲ *Shira-Iwa-san 1912 m*
▲ *Kumotori-san 2018 m*
Nippara cave
Hatonosu
Okutama
Hatonosu gorge
Ome
Okutama lake
Mitake
Mitake jinja
Mitake-san
Hinatawada
Toll road
Higashi Hanno
Fussa
Musashi Itsukaichi
Hai-jima

There are two approaches into the park area: Chichibu-tetsudo railway and the Seibu railway. The former passes along the river valley and is intersected by the Seibu line near Ohanabatake station. The Chichibu line can be reached by changing at Yorii from the Tobu line (from Ikebukuro station, Tokyo), or at Kumagaya from the JNR Takasaki line (from Ueno station, Tokyo).

By Seibu line from Shinjuku station (Tokyo) the trip takes 1½ hours by limited express, longer by local train. By JNR it takes about two hours, and slightly less by the Tobu line.

The Chichibu line route (described below) takes in more and is the only way to reach Mitsumine-guchi, the inner-most station.

Nagatoro area

Several attractions are accessible from stations near Nagatoro. Near Nogami station is *Nagatoro Sogo hakubutsukan*, a small museum of rocks and fossils. A similar museum is *Chichibu Shizen kagaku-kan* (Natural History Museum), five minutes from Kami-Nagatoro station.

Nagatoro is well-known for its nearby scenery, which features sheer rock faces and interestingly-shaped rocks, including a 'rock garden' – a famous rock formation near the river. It is about five minutes from Nagatoro station.

The area is beautiful in spring when blossoms deck a line of cherry trees that stretch 1½ km from Nagatoro to Kami-Nagatoro; in summer when the azaleas are in full bloom; and in autumn when the leaves turn amazing colours.

An excellent view of the area may be had from *Hodo-san*. A cable car goes to the top of the mountain; its base station is easily reached by bus from Nagatoro station. *Hodo-jinja* shrine is close to the upper station.

Kami-Nagatoro A boat ride through the rapids of the Arakawa river is available from either end of the Oyabana-bashi

bridge, taking 25-30 minutes. The terminus is Takasago-bashi bridge.

Chichibu area

The main attraction of the city is *Chichibu-jinja*, 200 metres west of the station, one of the three most famous shrines of the area (along with Hodo-jinja at Nagatoro and Mitsumine-jinja). It is noted for large buildings and its tall, old trees. Its night festival of 3 December is well-known throughout Japan for the procession of lantern-lit *dashii*, ornate historic festival wagons.

Chichibu Shiyaku-sho Minzoku hakubut-sukan, the Municipal Folk Museum, has good displays of articles traditionally used by people of the area in their daily life. It can be reached quickly by taxi or on foot in 40 minutes.

There are two good hiking trails, a relatively short one near Buko-san and another that joins the Chichibu and Okutama areas.

The starting point of the shorter trail is Yokoze station of the Seibu line. It climbs to the top of *Buko-san* (1336 metres), passes *Mitake-jinja* and the entrance to Hashidate stalactite cavern, then descends to Urayama-guchi station (Seibu line). In addition to picturesque mountain scenery, the area around the cavern has a Karst-type topography with large outcroppings of limestone that resemble sheep or tombstones when seen from a distance. (Similar terrain can be found in west Honshu and northern Kyushu.) The cavern may be explored.

The hiking trail to Okutama, called Oku-Chichibu Ginza, stretches between the two sections of the park. From the Chichibu end it begins at Mitsumine-guchi station (the terminus of the Chichibu line). You can climb to *Mitsumine-san* on foot or take the cable car. *Mitsumine-jinja* can be visited along the way; it has a history of about 2000 years. When Buddhism and Shinto were inter-twined, it was the centre for ascetic yamabushi pilgrims and priests of the

Tendai sect of Buddhism; some may be seen today, and halls on the grounds serve priests and pilgrims as well as climbers and hikers.

The trail is about 10 km long, and passes along the ridges that stretch between mountains. The trail splits between Shira-iwa-san and Kumotori-san, one fork going to Nippara, the other toward Okutama-ko lake. The trail is well signposted and there are several lodges and huts along the way.

Points along the route are listed in detail in the JNTO publication *Chichibu*, available at the Tokyo TIC. Many areas like this that offer good hiking are covered by detailed maps that may be purchased at map specialists in large cities. They are often only in Japanese, but the general features can be readily understood.

KAWAGOE

Of all the cities and towns in Japan, Kawagoe possibly has the largest number of old buildings still in use. The main street has many shops in heavily-walled, tiled-roof structures more than a century old. For a glimpse of 'old Japan' a visit to Kawagoe is recommended.

In addition to walking around the town looking at the charming old buildings, *Kita-in* temple is worth a visit to see its attractive main building and garden, visible from an elevated corridor. Nearby is the garden of *Go-hyaku rakan* with 500 statues of Buddhist characters, about 40 cm tall, in a variety of poses. They are a little unusual and of moderate interest.

Kawagoe has an interesting annual festival on 15 and 16 November. On display around the city on those days are 23 or so *dashii* – incredibly ornate festival wagons, some of which are prefectural treasures about 200 years old. On the second night of the festival the wagons are pulled through the streets, some in each direction of the route so that they pass each other. At every encounter, the costumed dancer on each wagon tries to out-perform the other. Each wagon carries

its own musicians and supply of sake, so these performances become increasingly enthusiastic as the night wears on.

The festival dates back to 1648 and is typical of several that used to be held in the area, including in Tokyo. The *dashii* in Tokyo were destroyed during the war, however, so the Kawagoe festival is the only survivor.

Getting There

From Tokyo, the most convenient way to get to Kawagoe is by the Seibu line from Shinjuku, as its terminus (Hon-Kawagoe) is closest to the centre of the city. Alternatives are the Tobu railway (Tojo line) from Ikebukuro (Tokyo) to Kawagoe station; or by JNR from Ueno station (Tokyo) to Omiya, with a change of train to the Kawagoe line, to Kawagoe or Kawagoe-machi stations.

SAKITAMA KOFUN-KOEN

The Kanto plain has been settled for more than 2000 years, as shown by excavations of ancient relics throughout the region. One of the three largest clusters of ancient tomb mounds in Japan can be found near Gyoda, consisting of eight burial mounds plus a museum of artefacts dug up in the area.

Getting There

Sakitama kofun-koen (Sakitama Tomb Park) is reached by taking a JNR train (Takasaki-sen line) from Ueno station to Fukiage station, then changing to a bus bound for Gyoda via Sama. The stop is Sangyo-doro; from there the park is a 15 minute walk.

Chiba-ken

East and curving around the south of Tokyo is Chiba-ken. The areas adjacent to Tokyo (Chiba-shi city and beyond) are largely residential suburbs and much of the rest of the peninsula is used for market

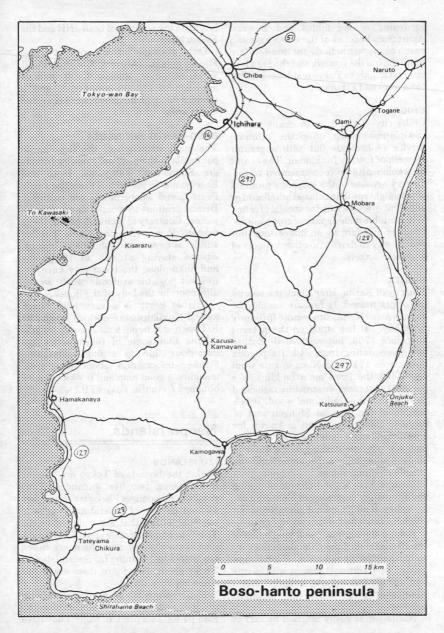

Boso-hanto peninsula

Tokyo-wan Bay

Chiba

Naruto

Togane

Oami

Ichihara

To Kawasaki

Mobara

Kisarazu

Kazusa-
Kamayama

Onjuku
Beach

Hamakanaya

Katsuura

Kamogawa

Tateyama
Chikura

Shirahama Beach

0   5   10   15 km

gardening of vegetables and flowers. Apart from beaches of the south-east and east coasts, attractions for tourists are quite thin on the ground, and the area is of interest mainly to Tokyo residents looking for a weekend excursion.

CHIBA

Chiba city is noted for its many toruko (Soaplands) which offer the ultimate service of brothels but with a greater element of fantasy fulfillment. They can't be wholeheartedly recommended to foreigners because of the language problem which might result in refused admission or apparent overcharging for special favours. With suitable male Japanese companions, however, it might be an interesting (but pricey) way to delve into other aspects of Japanese society.

NARITA

The city of Narita, after which the nearby airport is named, is famous among the Japanese for *Narita-san* temple (properly *Shinsho-ji*). It has stood on the present site since 1705, but succeeded another elsewhere dating from 940. Its pagoda dates from 1711 and Niomon gate from 1838, but the large main building is a recent (1968) concrete structure fashioned to resemble the traditional wood. It is a temple of the unusual Shingon sect of esoteric Buddhism which is known for ascetic practices. It is possible that you may see pilgrims bathing in icy water in winter, or walking endlessly around the temple chanting sutras.

Visitors have a good chance of seeing the interesting ceremony of blessing a car for safety. Results are not guaranteed but any help is useful for driving in Japan.

Behind the temple, occupying much of the 20 hectares of the grounds, is the very attractive Narita-san-koen, a landscape garden of traditional design with ponds and artfully formed and arranged 'hills'. Also nearby is Narita-san historical museum.

Narita-san is easily reached by taxi or bus from the stations of both JNR and the Keisei line.

Only a couple of km away is *Boso Fudoki-no-oka* (Ancient Cultural Park) which comprises ancient tomb mounds approximately 1500 years old, and a modern museum housing relics excavated in the area.

BOSO-HANTO PENINSULA

The main attraction of the Boso-hanto peninsula is the seaside. Popular resorts are Shirahama, Tateyama, Hoto and Katsuyama. In the area of the latter two is Pearl Island where pearls are cultured. Demonstrations by women divers may be put on. Contrary to common belief, these women do not dive for pearls but for edible seaweed and shellfish. Indeed, anyone staying at one of the many minshuku along the coast may have the freshest possible seafood, caught in the afternoon by the lady of the house.

Further north is a very long beach named Kujukurihama – which means 99 Ri Beach, a *ri* being a measure of length.

Note that some of the beaches are hazardous due to strong undertows. Further information about this area, including a good map and booklet can be obtained from the Tokyo TIC.

Nanpo Islands

IZU ISLANDS

Within the bounds of Tokyo are, among other things, two live volcanoes. They present no danger because they are located on two of several small islands south of Tokyo that are included in the Tokyo-to administrative area. The islands, part of the Fuji volcanic chain, are called Izu Shichi-to, meaning Izu Seven Islands. There are in fact more than seven but some are very small.

Until recently the islands were relatively isolated and some were used during the Edo period as a place of exile. They have

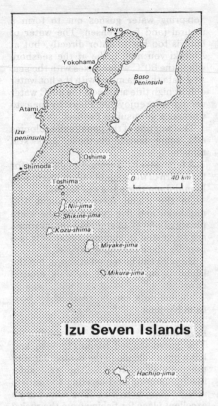

Izu Seven Islands

or Motomachi) and visiting the 'Hawaiian' Botanical Garden of tropical and subtropical plants which grow in the mild climate.

The town of Saki-ichi and the nearby area are known for old houses and customs which differ from those on the mainland. There is a distinct dialect on Oshima and the other islands in the group. The dark costume with a white pattern is unlike a kimono; an 'apron' substitutes for the obi (sash) and the headdress indicates if a woman is single or married.

For places to stay there are about 120 minshuku, 70 ryokan, two youth hostels and five campsites to choose from but advance reservations are suggested.

Bus service makes travel simple. There are two tour buses each day at 7 am and 9 am from both Okada and Motomachi.

It is crowded during summer because it is close to Tokyo and easily accessible by boat from Tokyo, Atami, Ito and Inatori (near Shimoda) and perhaps Shimoda in season and by air from Tokyo.

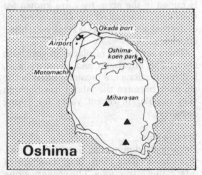

Oshima

now become popular as a holiday resort, especially among young Japanese. The islands can be reached by boat and by air. Schedules change by season so it is best to get up-to-date information on reaching any of the islands from the TIC in Tokyo.

Oshima

This is the largest of the islands (91 sq km); the name means 'Big Island'. Its high point, literally and figuratively, is *Mihara-yama* (758 metres) which last erupted in 1957 and is still smoking.

Activities on the island include swimming at several beautiful beaches, climbing the volcano (on foot or by bus from Okada

Toshima

This tiny island (4.2 sq km) is the smallest of the group. It is round and of volcanic origin but the fires have gone out. There is almost no flat land on the entire island, 60 per cent of which is given over to growing camellias from which fragrant oil is extracted. They bloom in late February and early March. There is one concentration of people in the north, a few hundred people who make their living from the camellia oil business. Accommodation is limited, four minshuku and one ryokan. Access is by boat from Oshima.

Nii-jima

This island (23.4 sq km) is rather elongated with a volcanic peak at each end and long beaches on each side. Swimming is excellent at several places. Maehama (on the west) offers the best swimming and white sand, but is very crowded in season. There is a campsite to the north. In the area is a museum, hotspring, temple and a cemetery from the days of the exiles. Habushi-ura beach has very high cliffs (up to 250 metres); but it is better for surfing than swimming. Another beach is Awai-ura.

The main town, Honmura, is reached by boat from Oshima and Tokyo.

The houses on the south of the island are interesting because they are constructed of lightweight volcanic rock that is mined in the area; they are known for their unusual architecture. Objects carved of the rock are on sale as is locally-distilled shochu.

There are plenty of places to stay with about 235 minshuku and seven ryokan, but reservations are recommended in the summer because the island has become very popular in recent years for young Japanese.

Shikine-jima

Despite its diminutive size (3.8 sq km), this island offers more than its share of interesting attractions. The scenery along the rugged shore is spectacular with 10-30 metre cliffs encircling the island; inland it is mostly flat. Most of the population is found in fishing communities to the northeast, like Nobushi and Kohama.

Shikine-jima and Nii-jima were once the same landmass, but tidal waves in 1688 and 1704 separated them.

There are several beaches around the island, with a variety of surfaces, from rock to sand. There are two beaches where

hotspring water gushes out to form a natural (and free) onsen. The water of both is too hot to enter directly, but at Ahizaki you may bathe at the seashore where the 60°C water mixes with the sea. At Jinata the sea mixes with the hot water only at high tide and cools the 80°C water enough to be enjoyable. Play it by ear as to whether a swimsuit is needed.

This was one of the penal/exile colonies and some traces of those days still remain.

A festival is held around 24 January for the return of the souls of sailors lost at sea. In mid-June there is a sea festival.

On the island there are about 100 minshuku and five ryokan, so there are plenty of places to stay, but reservations are suggested in summer because it is a popular place for young people.

Bicycles can be rented at shops, but the island is small enough to walk around easily.

Shikine-jima can be reached by boat from Nii-jima.

Kozu-shima

This gourd-shaped island (18.5 sq km) has a dead volcano in the centre. Most of the population lives on the west side; fishing, farming and catering to tourists are the main activities. The island is an excellent place for fishing from the rocks; swimming is good at Tako-wan, a white sand beach; and you can also climb the central peak.

There is a boat festival on 5 January; 'Juria' matsuri on the third Sunday in May; Bon odori from 13-16 July; and a shrine festival on 1-2 August.

There are about 200 minshuku and five ryokan.

Bus transport is good in summer and bicycles can be rented.

Access to Kozu-shima is by boat from Oshima and other islands and in summer from Tokyo as well.

Miyake-jima

A round island with a live volcano, this is

the third largest (55.1 sq km) of the group. The most prominent feature is Oyama volcano (815 metres) which last erupted in 1962, leaving a stark black area resembling a collapsed sand castle. Much of the island is surrounded by cliffs 20-30 metres high. Activities include swimming and inland hikes through the forests.

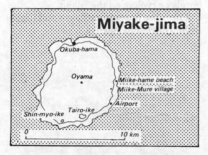

The main beach is Miike-hama; it is unusual for its black sand and is the centre of seaweed harvesting. There is camping nearby but it tends to be crowded and littered in season. Less crowded is Okubo-hama where swimming is good and there is a nearby camping ground.

There are two small lakes, an unusual feature on such an island. Shin-Myo-ike dates only from 1763 following an eruption. It is less than one sq km in area (the Japanese name means 'pond'), and is largely surrounded by cliffs 70-80 metres high. The water is salty and mysteriously takes on seven different colours through the day. You can climb to the rim and look down on the water. The other lake, Tairo-ike, is only a smidgen bigger (1.2 sq km) but much older, 2000 years or so. It contains fresh water and is used as a water supply reservoir, so swimming and camping etc are banned. Although the island has a nearly tropical climate the lake has many qualities of a mountain lake, an interesting contrast on such a small island.

There is a boat festival on 2 January; a shrine festival on 8 January; and ajiisai (a type of blue flower) festival in mid-June.

There are plenty of places to stay, as on the other islands: 130 minshuku, 12 ryokan and a youth hostel.

Access is by boat from Oshima or Hachijo-jima, or by air from Tokyo.

Mikura-jima

Although this smallish (20 sq km) circular island is only 20 km from Miyake-jima (an hour by boat) there is only infrequent service, six or seven times a month. It is rugged, with cliffs 100-300 metres high round the periphery, a 100-metre waterfall on the west side and a dead volcano in the middle. There is not a single stretch of level road on the island, there is no public transport and the entire population lives on the north side.

There are 12 ryokan, adequate for the few who can wait out the period between boats; camping is not allowed.

Hachijo-jima

The most southerly of the Izu group, this is the second largest (71 sq km). It is characterised by two volcanic peaks, *Higashi-yama* (Mihara-sen) in the southeast and *Nishi-yama* in the north-west, and cliffs along most of the rugged coast. It has a mild and wet climate yearround.

Hachijo-jima was the outermost of the islands used for exile and some relics may be seen, such as the ruins of mansions. Tourism is a relative newcomer to the

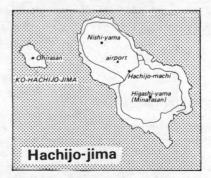

island and some old customs may still be found. A local type of cloth, *ki-hachijo*, is still woven and coloured with vegetable dyes from local sources. It is one of the souvenirs of the island; others are sake, and shell and coral products.

The scenery can be seen by bus tour beginning at Hachijo shi-yaku-sho (city hall) daily at 9.30 am or by rented bicycle. Another attraction is Jiyugaoka-yuen park where bullfights are held twice daily. Like those on Shikoku, Okinawa and some other islands of Japan, and as far away as Indonesia, the fights are not between man and beast but are a test of strength between two bulls; the winner pushes the other out of the ring.

The exiles festival is held on 28 August.

There are nearly 100 minshuku and 22 hotels or ryokan on the island.

There are boats from Tokyo and flights from Tokyo and Nagoya.

Northern Honshu

North of Tokyo are some of Japan's best attractions. A few are man-made relics, but most are natural scenic beauties or curiosities. Perhaps most interesting, especially for the traveller with time to spare and an interest in the 'real Japan', is the legacy of folkways. The northern part of Honshu, called Tohoku ('north-east'), was late in being developed, and in this respect it still lags behind other parts of the country. This is to the disadvantage of the people who live there (though conditions are improving) but to the distinct advantage of foreign visitors who want to see at least some aspects of Japan as it used to be. (There are of course modern amenities, so there is no hardship involved when travelling in the area.) I would rank the Tohoku area with the Noto-hanto (Ishikawa-ken), northern Gifu-ken and Nagano-ken areas as the best in Japan for independent exploration. More folklore, dances and tradition survive, concentrated in these areas than in most other parts of the country.

This chapter describes a route northward along the east coast and through some of the centre, and a southbound route along the west coast and other parts of the centre. This covers the maximum of territory with a minimum of backtracking and also allows description prefecture by prefecture, as their boundaries follow the same geographical features used for

laying out this itinerary. You can also go to Hokkaido and then resume the route without missing anything.

Travellers starting from Tokyo should visit the TIC and obtain information sheets on the areas they plan to travel. Tell them of your proposed itinerary and request their suggestions. Several information sheets are now available and others are added yearly. Sample titles are: *Towada-Hachimantai National Park* (MG-31), *Morioka and Rikuchu Kaigan (coast) National Park* (MG-38), and *Sendai, Matsushima and Hiraizumi* (MG-023). These sheets have up-to-date transportation schedules and fares and list several hotels, as well as giving sketchy sightseeing information of the 'official' variety.

A very detailed guide book covering only Tohoku appeared in 1982 and has become very popular with travellers. *Exploring Tohoku* by Jan Brown (Weatherhill) is almost of the 'telling too much' type, but its plenitude of information has something for everyone and will certainly be invaluable for foreign residents in the area.

Ibaraki-ken

Tokyo is on the edge of the Kanto plain, one of the largest areas of flat terrain in Japan, which is why it was one of the most prized fiefs in feudal times. The plain is intensively populated in all directions outside Tokyo.

TSUCHIURA
An interesting festival, *Hanabi Matsuri*, is held here the first Saturday in October each year. Hanabi means 'flowers of fire' and this is, in effect, a trade show of fireworks manufacturers, who show off their best products in one of the most

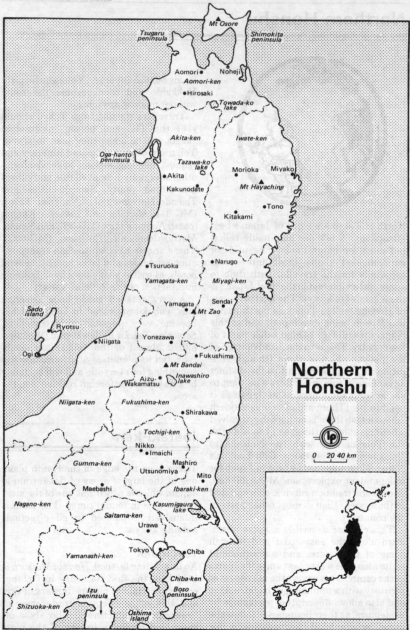

Northern Honshu

0   20 40 km

colourful fireworks displays of the year. Tsuchiura is on the Joban line, which runs to Mito.

MITO

The main drawcard of this city is Kairakuen, a garden traditionally rated by the Japanese as one of the three finest in Japan. I have visited it on two occasions and had the same reaction both times – a feeling of acute disappointment. The garden is, for the most part, little more than open lawn, with clusters of trees or bushes. It seems ironic that two of the most celebrated gardens in Japan (the other is Korakuen in Okayama) are noteworthy primarily for their vast expanses of lawn; perhaps it is this novelty that reaps such a rating. There are many other gardens in the country that would be better examples of what foreign visitors are looking for in Japanese gardens – those at Yokohama, Hikone and Kagoshima, to name just three.

The Kairakuen garden was completed in 1843. Of interest within its grounds is *Kobuntei*, a building (reproduction) where Nariaki – one of the lords of Mito – used to meet learned men, relax and compose poetry. (The town was formerly the home of an important branch of the Tokugawa family.) The building is well made of fine materials and is a good example of the simplicity and refined restraint of Japanese architecture. It is surrounded by tall trees and the atmosphere is very peaceful. Even the shrilling of *semi* (cicadas) in summer adds a note of ruralness, in contrast with the commercial appearance of the surrounding city. The garden is close to Kairakuen station, one stop from Mito station.

Tochigi-ken

The main attractions of Tochigi-ken are the pottery town of Mashiko, ancient Buddha statues at Oya, the incomparably beautiful and ornate Toshogu shine at Nikko, mountain scenery and the start of the valley which has the most thatched-roof houses in Japan.

MASHIKO

Of the several historic pottery centres of Japan, the most accessible from Tokyo is Mashiko, a couple of hours to the north-east. A visit to Mashiko can also be conveniently combined with a trip to Nikko, as they are in the same general area.

The pottery of Mashiko is made entirely from local materials – from clays to glazes. They do not lend themselves to elaborate techniques, so the results are rather simple and seem to me (who professes neither deep knowledge nor interest in pottery) a trifle crude. However to ceramic freaks this equals native charm and the sometimes rough surfaces, simple designs and frequent asymmetry are all to be treasured. The properties of the clay could be improved with additives, but the potters prefer to use only natural materials. If you like pottery you will enjoy a visit to Mashiko. It is also interesting for those who would like to learn something about traditional Japanese methods of making and firing pottery, as there are a large number of 'climbing kilns' and a visit to one is easy to arrange.

The town of Mashiko owes its fame to Shoji Hamada, who found here a town of potters who had been turning out service-able but simple and repetitive designs since 1852. He settled in the town, absorbed their traditions and then built on them, establishing his own kiln in 1930. As his fame spread, it reflected back to the town which had nurtured him. Adding to the fame of the town and the name of Shoji Hamada was the English potter, Bernard Leach, who lived and studied here for several years before returning to his homeland to spread the Mashiko influence.

Things to See

The town is filled with shops selling the

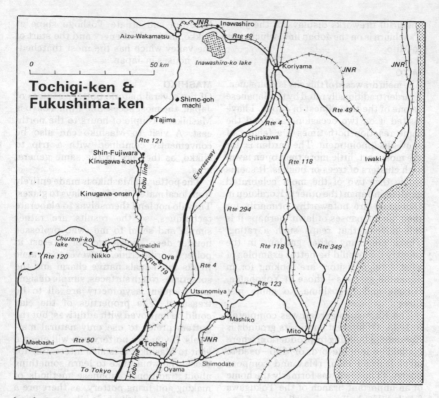

Tochigi-ken &
Fukushima-ken

local wares, so it could take a week to explore it thoroughly. There is a free handout map available at most shops in town. A good starting place is the Hamada 'home', which houses a small museum and other attractions.

The Hamada Home
This is made up of thatched-roof houses moved from elsewhere in the area plus two stone gura (storehouses) of the type found throughout the region. The gura houses the Mashiko San-kokan (Reference Collection Museum), a collection of odds and ends that Shoji Hamada gathered during his travels outside Japan. There are few treasures, and little of his own work. I found the place more interesting for the old farmhouses that Hamada had

brought to this place in 1943. The largest one was built in 1850 and contains furniture and other things that Hamada brought back from abroad. Although visitors are not allowed to enter the house, you can look in through the doors and windows and admire the massive pillars and crossbeams of the building itself, which is a fine example of a traditional house of this era.

There are no nails used in the construction of these houses so they can be easily dismantled and moved. The roof is unusual because bamboo poles are used at the peak to anchor it in place (again typical of the region). There are other buildings of the same type elsewhere in the grounds, one lived in by Hamada's widow.

Shimaoka Pottery

Adjacent to the Hamada grounds is the Shimaoka pottery, also well worth visiting. While many of the kilns used here are small oil or gas fired units, the famous kilns of Mashiko are the traditional nobori-gama wood-fired climbing kilns, two of which are in the grounds of the Shimaoka pottery. There are always some foreign students working in the village and they are often willing to give a guided tour or direct you to other kilns. The kilns have several chambers arranged up a hillside. Firing begins in the lowest chamber, with the gases climbing and pre-heating the other chambers. When the first chamber is thoroughly fired, fuel is then added to the second chamber and the first allowed to burn out. This sequence is repeated until all chambers have been fired. Because of the size of the kilns and the fuel consumption, many of the large kilns are fired only three or four times a year. It is an awesome sight as the flames and sparks shoot high over the stacks at the top of the hill.

There are many of these kilns scattered around the hillsides and they can be found easily enough, but the distances become appreciable. A look at the Shimaoka kilns will probably be adequate

If you are able to arrange a visit, try to look at the carpentry of the new Shimaoka building as well, as it is a fine example of the best traditional Japanese woodworking skill. A crossbeam of untrimmed tree trunk is supported on two poles, each of which has its end shaped to match the shape of the crossbeam, and vertical supports for shelves are keystoned into notches so that they support without nails. The new house took more than a year to build, all the work being done by one family of carpenters.

As for finding pottery to buy, there is no problem whatsoever. There must be few towns in the world with so many shops selling the stuff – some by recognised potters (at high prices) and much at very reasonable prices, turned out by the large number of anonymous workers who make the bulk of the output. Everything, however is hand-made. Those interested in weaving should look for the Higeta Workshop.

Getting There

There are two ways to get to Mashiko. The most convenient is by bus from Utsunomiya station, which is on the Tohoku Shinkansen line; and the other is by the ordinary Tohoku-honsen line, both of which depart from Ueno station in Tokyo. The bus trip takes one hour and costs Y940. There are up to 26 buses a day in each direction, which is more frequent than the train service.

Those who wish to go entirely by JNR train should go from Ueno to Oyama, transfer to the Mito-sen line (24 a day) and go as far as Shimodate (the fifth station, or fourth by express), then change to the Moka-sen line (eight per day), which goes through Mashiko (seventh station)

OYA

At Oya, near the city of Utsunomiya, there are 10 Buddha images carved in relief in the rock wall of the protective overhang. The temple building of *Oya-ji* extends back into the shallow cavern, protecting the images. It is believed that they date from the early Heian period (794-897 AD) and are the oldest stone statues of Buddha in Japan. Nearby is an unmissable, 27-metre concrete statue of Kannon, the goddess of mercy, finished in 1954.

Visible in the surrounding countryside are the quarries and nibbled-away hills that are the source of the soft stone (tuff) used in structures such as the granaries (gura) throughout the region and beyond Nikko. Many small workshops can be seen where the stone is cut into building blocks.

Getting There

The easiest way to reach Oya is by bus from Utsunomiya station; the trip takes about 25 minutes.

Nikko

Nikko is one of the 'must-sees' of Japan, to be included in even the shortest visit. Adjacent to the town are some of the most beautiful buildings in the world, ornately coloured and covered with gold leaf. The surrounding area is also famed for its natural scenery – waterfalls, a lake resort, forests and volcanic mountain peaks.

Information

The trip to Nikko is so popular that the Tokyo TIC has prepared free notes that give useful and up-to-date information on trains, accommodation and sightseeing. Be sure to get them before leaving Tokyo.

Things to See

The term 'sensory overload' must have been invented just for Nikko – particularly when referring to the sheer magnificence of the Toshogu and Daiyuin shrines. Superlatives becoming exhausted long before the sightseeing does.

You should allow at least a full day to absorb it all, though the best way, if time permits, is to spend a night in Nikko and stretch your sightseeing over two days.

Keep in mind that during the summer it usually rains heavily for an hour or two from about midday, so try to get an early start.

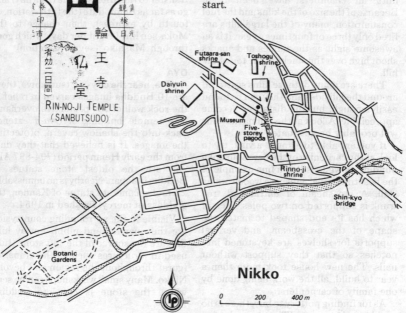

Rinno-ji temple

At the top of the hilly main street stands *Shin-kyo*, the Sacred Bridge, an orange structure blocked to traffic. Follow the road around to the left of the hill, to the footpath up the hill. This leads to one corner of the compound of Rinno-ji temple.

The major point of interest of this temple is *Sanbutsudo*, Temple of the Three Buddhas, the largest in the Nikko mountains. It houses three gilded wooden statues (five metres tall) of *Kannon* a Buddhist goddess with 11 faces and 1000 arms; *Amida-Nyorai*; and the *Bato-Kannon*, believed to be the incarnation of animal spirits.

The large avenue at the left side of Rinno-ji is named Omote-sando ('main approach') and it leads to Toshogu shrine, the most important single attraction in Nikko. To the left of the path is a five-storey pagoda, 32 metres tall, built in 1818. At the entrance to the shrine is a tall granite torii gate.

There is a basic fee of Y230 for admission to the Toshogu shrine, Rinno-ji temple and Futaara-san shrine.

Toshogu shrine

Entry to this shrine is through Otemon, also called Nio-mon gate, with its statues of the guardian *Nio-sama* – Deva kings. The decorations are but a hint of what is to come. From the gate, the path bends to the left. The decorated buildings encountered on the right are the lower, middle and upper storehouses. On the upper storehouse are noted relief carvings of elephants, created by a sculptor who had only ever seen drawings of elephants.

To the left of the path, opposite the middle storehouse, is the sacred stable, the only unlacquered building in the compound. Overhead are various carvings of monkeys; second from the left is a famous panel featuring the three monkeys in the 'see, speak, hear no evil' poses. Carvings of monkeys are reputed to fend of diseases in horses. Visitors can feed the sacred horse, which obviously relishes the tid-bits, by purchasing a small dish of carrot slices.

Facing the upper storehouse, and to the left of the bronze torii, is the *Kyozo* (Sutra Library), which houses nearly 7000 volumes of Buddhist sutras (sacred writings). Beside it is the sacred fountain where Japanese visitors rinse out their mouths to purify themselves before proceeding further. The water is safe to drink.

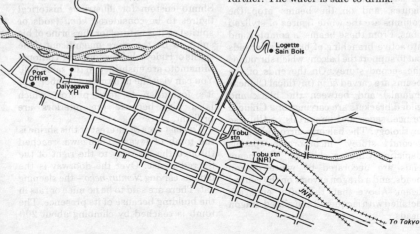

Yakushido temple The next flight of stairs leads to the middle court. The similar buildings on each side are the belfry and the drum tower. Beyond the drum tower is Yakushido, the only Buddhist-style structure in the shrine. Yakushido is famous for its Crying Dragon, *Naki-ryu*, a ceiling painting in an inner chamber. Admission to this inner shrine requires a separate ticket, which may be paid for when first entering Toshogu. Visitors stand on a marked spot, clap their hands together and the echo sounds like the reverberating roar of a dragon. The roof was destroyed in a fire in 1961, along with a very famous painting by Yasunobu Kano (1607-85), so this painting is quite new.

Gate of Sunlight (Yomeimon) Returning to the courtyard and climbing the next set of steps, you come to the most beautiful gate in Japan and one of the most elaborately decorated structures on earth. Yomeimon contains a wealth of intricate carvings, gilt and lacquer work, the details of which would be worthy of display in isolation. The Japanese nickname is *Higurashi-mon* (Twilight Gate), the implication being that you could admire it until overtaken by night. You'll understand the sentiment when you have seen the gate. Among the 12 supporting columns are two seated figures, and on the beams atop the columns are the white figures of stylized lions. From these beams, a complex and attractive branching of brackets spreads out to support the balcony which surrounds the second storey. On the ends of the beams are carved *kirin* (mythical Chinese animals) and between the black and gilded brackets are carvings of a Chinese prince, sages and immortals of Chinese mythology. The balcony surrounding the second storey incorporates panels depicting Chinese children. The beam ends are decorated by white dragon heads, and a dragon cavorts on the central beam. Above that, the rafter ends are detailed with lacquered and gilded dragon heads.

A low fence, also decorated, runs from either side of the gate and surrounds the courtyard. On the inside of the gate, back to back with the seated figures, are colourful *koma-inu* (guardian lions or dogs). Through the gate and to the left is the *mikoshi-gura*, where the mikoshi (portable shrines) are stored. These shrines are carried in the two annual festivals (17-18 May and 17 October). *Kaguraden*, in the courtyard, is the stage used for performances of kagura (sacred shrine dances).

The closed gate facing the courtyard is *Karamon* (Chinese gate). It is predominately white in contrast with the fantastically brilliant colours and gold leaf of the other buildings and structures. The door panels are decorated with carvings of various flowers and bamboo, and the pillars with dragons. The figures around the support beams depict Chinese celebrities.

Karamon gate and the Sacred Fence (Tamagaki) surround the Haiden (oratory) and Honden (main hall), the central buildings of the shrine. The innermost chamber of the Honden (the Gokuden), with its splendid interior (the supply of superlatives is becoming exhausted!) is where the spirit of Ieyasu Tokugawa is enshrined. His body is buried in a simple tomb on the hill behind the shrine. It is a Shinto custom for illustrious historical figures to be considered *kami* (gods or spirits) so it is natural for the shrine of his spirit to be the more magnificent. The spirits of Hideyoshi Toyotomi and Yoritomo Minamoto are enshrined in the same hall. You can visit the innermost chamber, but it's forbidden to take photos, which is a pity because the interiors are brilliant.

The last area of interest at this shrine is the tomb of Ieyasu Tokugawa, reached through the doorway to the right of the Sacred Fence. Over the doorway is the famous carving *Nemuri-neko* – the sleeping cat. There are said to be no mice or rats in the building because of its presence. The tomb is reached by climbing about 200 steps, among immense cedar trees. The tomb itself is severely simple, and resembles a small bronze pagoda.

Back on Omote-sando, around the corner from the pagoda, there is an avenue through the trees. On the left, close to the pagoda, is the shrine museum which houses a good collection of armour and other relics, and has exhibits showing how the buildings are constructed, how the wooden beams are protected by multiple layers of lacquered cloth, and so on.

Futaara-san shrine Further along the path, away from Omote-sando, is Futaara-san shrine. It is of lesser interest, and is best left to see at the end (if you have any energy or interest left).

Daiyuin-byo
This is the shrine to Iemitsu (1604-51) who constructed Toshogu in honour of his father, Ieyasu. It is somewhat smaller than Toshogu, but almost up to its standards in beauty. (I think that the Haiden and Honden are even more beautiful than the equivalent buildings of Toshogu.) In addition, it is possible to stand back some distance to take in their beauty and gain some perspective, as well as to photograph them. (The buildings of Toshogu are closely surrounded by a wall and photography is prohibited.)

Approaching Daiyuin-byo, you first walk through *Nio-mon* (Deva king gate) with its guardian statues. You then pass a small garden and can see the sacred fountain ahead and to the right. Turning left, you climb the stairs to *Niten-mon* (Two Heavens Gate), named for the two Buddhist deities *Komokuten* and *Jikokuten*. On the other side of the gate are the Gods of Wind and Thunder; the former is holding shut the opening of the bag of winds.

After climbing more stairs, you pass through *Yashamon* (named for its four figures of Yasha, a Buddhist deity), and arrive at the middle court with its belfry and drum tower. Between the middle

court and the inner shrine is a Chinese gate, beautifully decorated and flanked by the sacred fence. Time and weather – it snows profusely in Nikko – take their toll of the decorations, and they must be continually repaired or repainted. The intricate carvings of birds were retouched in 1978, so should stay colourful for several years.

Inside the inner shrine is the oratory (Haiden), from which a passageway leads to the inner main hall (Honden), both interiors being richly decorated with carvings and gold leaf. To the right of, and behind, the main buildings is a walkway that leads to the tomb itself, a simple structure by comparison.

The aesthetes look down their noses at Nikko because it is not 'typically Japanese', claiming it is too gaudy etc. It is atypical (though representative Momoyama style) but still not to be missed for the tremendous amount of work that has gone into it – not to mention the sheer visual splendour.

Nikko Museum and Botanical Garden
Beside Hanaishi bus stop (en route from Nikko station to Chuzenji), is Nikko Botanical Garden. A short distance back toward town is Tamozawa villa, a former imperial residence, which is now a museum. Set in a quiet garden, the building is constructed of the finest materials and is a good example of good Japanese architecture, though it is larger than most wooden buildings in Japan.

Festivals
Nikko is noted for several annual festivals. On 17 October and 18 May, there is a great procession of hundreds of people dressed in samurai armour and other costumes of the Tokugawa era. *Mikoshi* (portable shrines) carry the enshrined spirits of Ieyasu, Hideyoshi and Yoritomo. This is a big event and always crowded, but worth seeing for both the glimpse of pageantry and the feel of bygone days. On 17 May, the *Ennen-no-mai* (Longevity

Dance) is also held in front of Sanbutsudo, with two priests in elaborate costume performing ancient dances.

On 5-6 August there are very popular *Waruku-Odori* folk dances during the *Obon* season which honours the souls of ancestors. Similar dances are held in communities throughout Japan at this time, but the Nikko dance is particularly famous.

Other days with festivals are 17 May (at Sanbutsudo); and 14 and 17 April at Futaara-san jinja shrine.

Places to Stay

As befits one of the most popular tourist destinations in Japan, there is no shortage of places to stay in Nikko but it is wise to book ahead through a travel agent (eg JTB or the minshuku association) to be sure of a room. Much available accommodation is of the high-quality, high-cost type, however there are two youth hostels. *Nikko Youth Hostel*, once infamous for its surly,

officious staff, has been transformed by new management into one of the best in Japan, with a relaxed, open house atmosphere.

Getting There

From Tokyo there are two train lines, JNR and Tobu. The latter is the more convenient, as there are many more trains each day, they are quicker and the fare is lower. Tobu trains leave from Tobu station in Matsuya department store in Asakusa, not far from Asakusa station of the Ginza subway line. There are more than 35 trains per day: kaisoku (Y1000, rapid – about two hours); kyuko (Y1500 express – just under two hours); tokkyu (Y2000; special express – 1¾ hours).

NIKKO TO CHUZENJI

A few km beyond Nikko, the road twists upward to Chuzenji-ko lake, a popular summer resort. On the way the bus stops at Akechi-daira, a lookout and the base

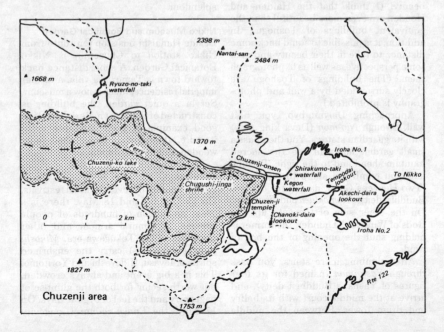

Chuzenji area

station for a 300 m cable car that leads up to a higher lookout (tempodai; three minutes, Y600 round trip). This lookout has a much better view (in clear weather), taking in Kegon-no-taki waterfall. The source of the water is Chuzenji-ko lake, which can be clearly seen, backdropped by the conical peak of *Nantai-san* (2844 metres). From the tempodai there is a trail (for those who wish to take the cable car only one way) that leads to a ridge surrounding the lake (possibly the rim of an old volcano). A 30-minute walk leads to Chanoki-daira, the top station for a one km cable car that leads down to a point close to Kegon falls (Y320/600 one-way/return). A handout map/brochure of the area is available from the Nikko Youth Hostel (and possibly elsewhere in town). On the many walks in this area you will find enough points of interest to last for several days.

Chuzenji-onsen

This is an extremely popular and very crowded town, especially in summer, when the weather is pleasantly cool, and in autumn when the leaves are beautiful. Although the time for the bus trip up from the station is nominally 50 minutes, this can be doubled or tripled on busy weekends and holidays due to the bumper-to-bumper traffic. The lake can be toured by regular excursion boat from various points; either by circling the lake (55 minutes, Y700), or crossing it from the town to Shobugahama (20 minutes, Y400). South from the town, on the shore of the lake, is *Chuzen-ji* temple, which is worth a visit. The principal attraction is a 1000-year-old, tall wooden statue of *Kannon-bosatsu*. The carving, made from a single tree, has far fewer than 1000 arms, and the 11 faces are worked into a crown on a single benevolent visage. The present temple dates only from 1902, when it was moved from a point west of *Chugu-shi* shrine when the buildings were washed away. A booklet in good English explains other details of the temple.

Chugushi-jinja shrine This is the middle shrine of the three that make up Futaara-san. (The first is at Toshogu.) A museum here has a reasonably good collection of armour and swords, as well as portable shrines. The collection is similar to those of many Japanese museums. A trail begins in the shrine grounds and leads to the peak of Nantai-san, a four-hour climb.

Kegon-no-taki Kegon waterfall drops 100 metres from an escarpment into a wide basin below. The falls are not visible from the surrounding cliffs; the best view is from tempodai (as described earlier). A lift takes you to the foot of the falls where the full power of the plummeting torrent can best be appreciated.

Shirakumo-taki ('white cloud') falls This waterfall, one of the many in the area, is located a short distance from Kegon falls. The best vantage point is Kasasagi-bashi bridge, which crosses the ravine near the mid-point of the plunge.

IMAICHI

Travellers going to Nikko from the Utsunomiya or Tokyo direction by train might wish to consider getting off at Imaichi first, then taking a bus to Nikko (13 km) instead of going all the way by train. The reason is that the road is lined for much of the distance with thousands of tall, straight cedar trees. They were planted by a feudal lord over a period of years. He lacked the money to contribute a sumptuous structure when the shrine was being built so he had the trees planted instead. About 13,000 trees still stand, and although the narrow avenue is crowded with traffic during the summer season (especially on weekends) it still retains its stately dignity.

Check with the TIC in Tokyo about schedules and bus connections to make sure you don't have a long wait in Imaichi. Remember that midday rain!

Thatched-roof houses

Route 121 runs north from Imaichi to Aizu-Wakamatsu (in Fukushima-ken). Along this road is the largest concentration of thatched-roof houses I encountered during 30,000 km of road travel around Japan. The road follows a river valley for much of the journey; the scenery is nearly always beautiful and often rustic, with many old houses. Many changes have taken place in the last 10 years though and it is much a part of modern Japan.

There is a bus service the full length of the valley from Imaichi through Kinugawa-koen and Tajima to Aizu-Wakamatsu. There are enough buses to guarantee connections but there may be waits of an hour or more. It is also possible to make the first leg to Kinugawa-onsen or Kinugawa-koen by Tobu line train and the last leg from Tajima to Aizu-Wakamatsu by JNR. But as the houses of interest are along the road the bus will be more interesting, until it reaches the start of the flat and open country around Kami-Miyori (and that place is so close to Aizu-Wakamatsu that there is no reason to change to a train).

OZENUMA

A little further into the hinterland beyond Nikko (westward) is the very popular swamp of Ozenuma. Swamps don't usually sound exciting but this one is a bit special. It is set on a plateau 1400 metres high, with a generous amount of pretty scenery, wildflowers and unspoiled nature, including a lake that reflects nearby low mountains that have patches of snow into late spring.

Trails of logs are laid out as hiking tracks through the swamp but they're usually wet and slippery so take appropriate footwear.

The entry road branches from Route 120 at Kamata, about 50 km from Nikko, and from there it is another 25 km or so. The Ozenuma area can be reached by public transportation. There are up to nine buses a day from Tobu-Nikko station

to Yumoto-onsen (about 1½ hours), where you change to one of the three daily buses as far as Kamata (about 1½ hours). From Kamata, nine buses a day go to Oshimizu (40 minutes) and another 10 run between Numata and Kamata.

Ozenuma can also be approached from the north. Up to three buses a day (2½ hours) run from Aizu-Tajima station, in the thatched-roof valley. There is a youth hostel at Tokura and other accommodation facilities in the area.

Gumma-ken

From Nikko you can travel on through Gumma-ken to Numata. (Gumma-ken is described in the chapter on Central Honshu.)

NUMATA

One route through this part of Japan is between Nikko and Nagano via Numata and Kusatsu. Numata, in addition to being the gateway for visits to Ozenuma, also has one historic relic that might be worth a look. It is the house of a wealthy merchant, built two and a half centuries ago, and believed to be the oldest in eastern Japan. It is located in Numata-koen (park).

Fukushima-ken

Tajima

A little more than halfway up the valley lies the town of Tajima. It has a museum of folk craft, housing items that were used in daily life. One traveller rated it better than the similar but more famous museum at Kurashiki in Okayama-ken. Ask for the *Mingei Hakubutsukan*.

Shimo-goh machi In this region of thatched-roof houses, this small town is noteworthy for a street with more than a dozen such houses, side by side. The appearance of

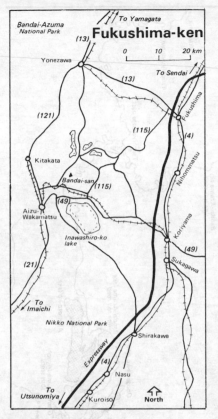

Fukushima-ken

Bandai-Azuma National Park
(13)
To Yamagata
0   10   20 km
Yonezawa
(13)
To Sendai
(121)
(115)
Fukushima
(4)
Kitakata
Bandai-san (115)
Nihommatsu
(49)
Aizu-Wakamatsu
Inawashiro-ko lake
Koriyama
(49)
(21)
Sukagawa
To Imaichi
Nikko National Park
Shirakawa
Expressway
(4)
Nasu
To Utsunomiya
Kuroiso
North

Aizu buke-yashiki This is a reconstruction of samurai housing as it looked at the time of the civil war (most of the city was destroyed by fire in 1868). Museums on the grounds show various aspects of Aizu culture and history.

Iimori-yama During the civil war fighting of 1868, between the forces of the Tokugawa shogunate and those seeking to restore the emperor Meiji, a detachment of teenage army cadets was facing defeat on this hill. Rather than surrender, they ritually killed themselves. The hill, with its graves and monuments, can be climbed on foot or by long mobile sidewalks. A museum, *Byakkotai kinnenkan*, has exhibits from this time.

The most interesting and unusual structure is the strange *Sazaedo*, a sort of Buddhist shrine that is probably unique in Japan. Although the roof over the entrance is of the traditional shape found at many temples and shrines, the main building is a tall, octagonal wooden structure. Inside, ramps spiral upward both clockwise and anti-clockwise, meeting at the top after two complete revolutions. The 'bridge' at the top, joining the two ramps passes over 33 figures of *Kannon*.

INAWASHIRO-KO LAKE

The lake area is a popular resort destination in summer and winter, for swimming and skiing so there are many minshuku and ryokan in the vicinity. The land around the lake is flat and there are few vantage points for a good view. Probably the best point is at Okinashima (take a bus from Inawashiro station). The popular *Okinashima-so kokuminshukusha* (people's lodge) is on a hill above the road; it's a good place to stay but advance booking is usually necessary. There's an excellent view over the lake and, when the atmospheric conditions are right, a superb view of the volcanic peaks of *Bandai-san*.

Next door to Okinashima-so is a bit of a curiosity. It is a very large house of turn-of-the-century western style, named

this area must be almost as it was one or two centuries ago.

AIZU-WAKAMATSU

This city was the site of the strongest castle in Tohoku (north-east Japan) at the end of the feudal era. At the time of the Meiji restoration, the local lord resisted in favour of the Tokugawa who had ruled Japan for about three centuries. Imperial troops battled the garrison for a month and the castle was destroyed. There is a realistic replica of the castle but as there are still authentic castles extant elsewhere, this one is not of great interest. There are, however, attractions nearby.

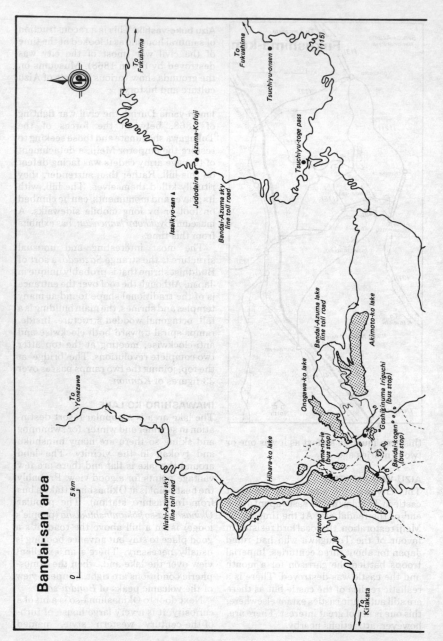

Bandai-san area

0 5 km

To Fukushima

To Fukushima

(115)

Tsuchiyu-onsen

Tsuchiyu-toge pass

Azuma-Kofuji

Jododaira

Issaikyo-san

Bandai-Azuma sky line toll road

To Yonezawa

Nishi-Azuma sky line toll road

Bandai-Azuma lake line toll road

Akimoto-ko lake

Onogawa-ko lake

Goshikinuma (iriguchi) (bus stop)

Bandai-kogen (bus stop)

Urabandai-ie (bus stop)

Hibara-ko lake

Hosono

To Kitakata

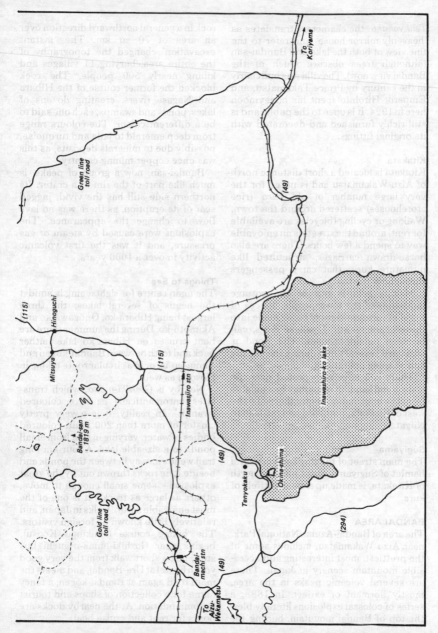

Tenkyokaku. the characters translates as 'heavenly mirror house' and refer to the fine view of both the lake and Bandai-san (although trees obscure much of the Bandai view now). The villa was built early in the century by Prince Takamatsu, and Emperor Hirohito spent his honeymoon here in 1924. It is open to the public and is still richly furnished and decorated with its original fittings.

Kitakata

Kitakata is located a short distance north of Aizu-Wakamatsu and is noted for the very large number of old *kura* (rice storehouses) scattered around the town. Walking or cycling (bicycles are available for rent) around the streets is an enjoyable way to spend a few hours. There are also horse-drawn carriages, structured like miniature kura, that carry passengers throughout the town.

Making *geta* is one of the cottage industries of the townspeople. Pieces of wood in various stages of being made into these characteristic Japanese clogs, can be seen outside houses. The wood is seasoned several times during the cutting and shaping operations.

There is a large map posted near the station and handout maps may be available from the information centre there. To the west of Kitakata, both road and rail lead to Niigata.

Sugiyama

The main street of the tiny and very rural hamlet of Sugiyama, about nine km north of Kitakata, is made up almost entirely of kura.

BANDAI AREA

The area of Bandai-Azuma National Park, near. Aizu Wakamatsu, includes some of the prettiest, most interesting and accessible mountain scenery in Japan. There are several volcanic peaks in the area, mostly dormant or extinct. In 1888, a series of colossal explosions literally blew the top of Bandai mountain, hurling the rock in a general northward direction over an area of 70 sq km. The 'instant excavation' changed the topography of the entire area, burying 11 villages and killing nearly 500 people. The rock blocked the former course of the Hibara and Nagase rivers, creating dozens of lakes, ponds and swamps, each one said to be a different colour. The colours range from deep emerald to jade and turquoise, possibly due to minerals deposits, as this was once copper mining country.

Bandai-san, now a group of peaks, is much like part of the rim of a crater. Its northern side still has the vivid, jagged scar of its eruption, as there was no lava flow to change the appearance. The explosions were caused by steam or gas pressure, and it was the first volcanic activity in over a 1000 years.

Things to See

The main centre for sightseeing is amidst the heads of several lakes; the three largest being Hibara-ko, Onogawa-ko and Akimoto-ko. During the summer there are boat cruises on Hibara-ko lake, either back and forth between Bandai-kogen and Yama-no-ie, or in a circular route taking in Hosono as well.

Nearby is *Goshiki-numa*, which translates unromantically as 'five coloured swamps'. In reality, it is a very pretty cluster of more than 200 multi-coloured bodies of water, varying in size from small ponds to a sizeable lake. A four km long trail wends its way between the ponds and beside it lie rocks thrown out by the great explosion – some small enough to move, others as large as trucks. It is one of the most enjoyable nature walks in Japan, and relatively little known by foreign visitors. The hiking course (Haikingu Koosu), begins near Goshiki-numa-iriguchi bus stop, just a short walk from the very good youth hostel at Ura-Bandai, and meets the main road again at Bandai-kogen, a fancy name for a collection of shops and tourist accommodation. At the nearby docks are boats for rent and cruise boats.

Very close to *Ura-Bandai Youth Hostel* is Bishamon-ike, the largest pond (actually a lake) where rowboats can be rented. The water is so clear that the boats appear to be floating on green air. In the background, glimpsed through breaks in the thick forest, is the stump of Mt Bandai.

A little beyond the end of the trail at Bandai-kogen, there is a road that runs a short distance toward Bandai-san, and a network of trails covering the mountain, some leading around the rim and others extending to the southern foot of the peak near Inawashiro-ko lake. This is certainly one of the most enjoyable walking and hiking areas in Japan.

Towards Yonezawa , the route includes the Nishi-Azuma 'Sky Valley' toll road; and towards Fukushima there are two toll roads, the 13 km-long Bandai-Azuma ('lake') Rine ('line') and Bandai-Azuma Skyline, definitely worth travelling on. The Bandai-Azuma Rine begins near Ura-Bandai Youth Hostel and passes between the lakes Onogawa-ko and Akimoto-ko, providing views of Bandai-san and Hibara-ko lake. It intersects route 115, which goes from Ura-Bandai to Fukushima, either directly or via the Bandai-Azuma Skyline. The skyline road, nearly 30 km long, runs mostly along ridges and the crests of the mountain range, passing through the collection of peaks known as Azuma. The most interesting of these are Azuma-Kofuji (Azuma-Little Fuji), and Issaikyo-san, its neighbour. Both are moderately high (1705 and 1949 metres), but the space between them has filled in considerably so that the road passes very close to the northern rim of Azuma-Kofuji. You can climb up in less than 10 minutes and look or climb down into its crater – probably the most accessible one in Japan.

On the other side of the road is *Isaikyo-san*, an active volcano that jets steam with a continuous roar. Anyone who is the least bit energetic can scramble to the top in 30 minutes or so, and be rewarded by a superb view over the conical-cratered top

of Azuma-Kofuji, the rapid drop to the valley floor and Fukushima city.

Getting There & Getting Around

Jododaira bus stop is located between the two mountains and buses between the Bandai area and Fukushima can be used to get there. A stop-over is possible, continuing on or returning by a later bus. The area is very popular with sightseers, so hitching should be good.

The two main bus stops in the Bandai area are Goshiki-numa Iriguchi (entrance) and Yama-no-ie, the latter located at the edge of Hibara-ko lake. Buses connect these places (and other bus stops in the area of course) with Aizu-Wakamatsu, Inawashiro and Fukushima. There is also a daily round trip out of Fukushima to Jododaira (a 50 minute stop), which circles back via Tsuchiyu-toge pass and Tsuchiyu-onsen. The trip takes 3¾ hours and leaves at 1 pm.

Miyagi-ken

SENDAI

The largest city in northern Honshu, Sendai was flattened during the war and has been rebuilt like any typical commercial city, with many large buildings and straight streets in the central area. One of the main streets, Aoba dori (Green Leaf Avenue), is very attractive in the stretch where the trees are growing. It is rather high fashion, with many shops and good hotels and the feeling of a European city street. The rest of Sendai is unexceptional however, though foreigners there say it's a good place to live as the mountains are an hour in one direction and the sea an hour in the other.

Short-term visitors will only find a small number of attractions, namely *Osaki-Hachiman* shrine, *Rinno-ji* garden, *Zuihoden* mausoleum and possibly the grounds of the former castle *Aoba-jo*.

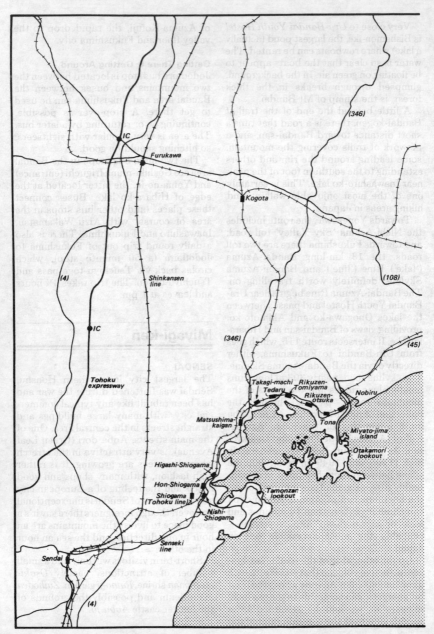

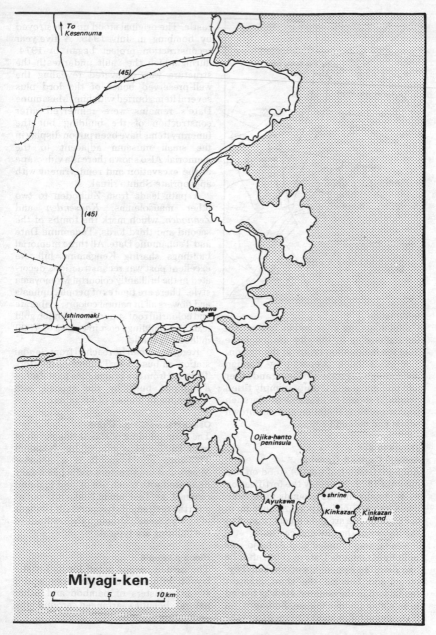

To
Kesennuma

(45)

(45)

Ishinomaki

Onagawa

Ojika-hanto
peninsula

Ayukawa

shrine

Kinkazan

Kinkazan
island

Miyagi-ken

0   5   10 km

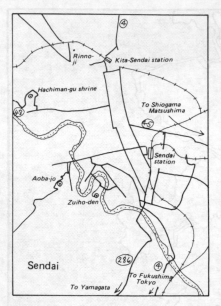

Sendai

Information
Useful maps and information, in English, for sightseeing in the city are available from the information centre in the station.

A guide book prepared by foreign residents gives good sightseeing and other info on Sendai and vicinity. Simply titled *Sendai*, it should be available at Maruzen bookstore, Sendai station and downtown hotels and costs Y1300.

Things to See
Aoba-jo Castle & Grounds
Aoba-jo (Green-leaf Castle) stood on this hill until 1872. Now only the fortification walls remain and the grounds have been made into a municipal park. A museum in the grounds has art and objects related to the history of the city and castle.

Sendai was founded and Aoba-jo was built by Masamune Date in 1600, after he had defeated opponents of Shogun Toyotomi and become the third greatest feudal lord in the country. He was buried in an elaborate mausoleum, *Zuihoden*, on Kengamine hill, a short distance from the castle. The original stood until destroyed by bombing in July 1945. A five-year reconstruction project began in 1974, during which the vault underneath the structure was excavated revealing the well-preserved bones of the lord plus several items buried with him. Masamune Date's remains were reinterred after construction of the building but the funerary items have been put on display in the small museum adjacent to the memorial. Also shown there is a videotape of the excavation and reinterrment with appropriate Shinto ritual.

A path leads from Zuihoden to two other mausoleums, *Kansenden* and *Zennoden*, which mark the tombs of the second and third lords, Tadamune Date and Tsunamune Date. All three memorial buildings sharing Kengamine hill are excellent post war reconstructions decorated in the brilliantly colourful Momoyama style. There are figures of people, animals and flowers all in natural colours, elaborate and colourful roof supports and much gold leaf. The buildings cost in excess of Y800 million to rebuild.

Kengamine can be reached from Sendai station on bus 25 to Tamaya-bashi stop. The road from the bridge goes past *Zuiho-ji* temple, built by the second lord Tadamune in honour of his father.

Osaki-Hachiman-gu shrine
The main building of this shrine survives from 1607 and is one of the National Treasures of Japan. It is a genuine Momoyama-era structure and is beautifully decorated with much use of gold leaf and colour. Like Toshogu in Nikko it is not at all in the restrained style normally thought of as 'Japanese', although the outlines of the building are typical.

Rinno-ji temple
The garden here is noted for its artistic layout, with a pond as the focus, and a stream, clusters of bamboo and other natural beauties arranged around the undulating grounds.

Saito Ho-onkai Museum of Natural History

Featured here are geological and palaeontological specimens of the area, including some dinosaur skeletons. However, the museum is rather small, as is the number of exhibits in relation to the Y300 admission charge.

Festival

To the Japanese, one of the most famous and favourite festivals in the country is *Tanabata* (Star Festival) on 6-8 August. It is based on an old Chinese story of the princess and the peasant shepherd who could only meet once a year. During the festival the city is hung with elaborate paper decorations, but there is almost no action worthy of note and the average westerner would find it about as exciting as a submarine race.

Places to Stay

There are many hotels and ryokan in Sendai, as well as four youth hostels.

Getting There

From Sendai, long-distance ferries ply daily to and from Tomakomai (Hokkaido) and Nagoya. The terminal can be reached by train or bus from Sendai station.

SAKUNAMI-ONSEN

This resort town, 28 km from Sendai, grew up around a hot spring occurring at the edge of a small river. The spring, at the bottom of the gorge which runs parallel to the road, can be reached via the lobby of the Iwamatsu Hotel. The baths, or rotemburo, are five small pools sheltered from rain and snow by a simple wooden roof. The only 'wall' is the gorge face; the other three sides are open to nature and a favourite winter pastime is to sit in the hot water and drink sake while admiring the snow.

Getting There

Access is by JNR Senzan line to Sakunami station; the line runs between Sendai and Yamagata. There is also a regular bus

service from Sendai which runs directly to Sakunami-onsen.

SHIOGAMA

This is the port for Sendai, and of limited interest. The main feature is *Shiogama-jinja* (shrine) a large structure, mostly painted orange and white, although inner buildings are built in a traditional manner with very simple lines and natural wood. In the grounds is a museum of historic relics and exhibits related to whaling, which used to be carried out here. The shrine is on a wooded hill near Shiogama station.

Getting There

Boats run regularly between Shiogama and both Matsushima-kaigan and Otakamori, passing by many of the little islands for which Matsushima Bay is famous. Details on boat schedules is given in the following section on Matsushima.

TAMONZAN

One of the best places to view Matsushima Bay is Tamonzan hill. To get there, take a bus from Shiogama station to Tamonzan stop (the road continues on to a couple of inviting ocean beaches) and walk along the little road to the left of the electric power station (you can't miss it). After a couple of hundred metres there is a concrete staircase which leads up Tamonzan to a little shrine and a good view over the water to the white-shored, tree-covered islands and the small boats passing through the narrow channels between them. Around the shrine, which is likely to be totally deserted, are many figurines of foxes, the messengers of Inari shrines, plus little shrine-shaped 'houses' about 40 cm tall, to shelter them.

MATSUSHIMA

About 40 minutes by train from Sendai lies famed Matsushima Bay which is dotted with more than 250 small islands of strange shapes, covered with twisted pine trees. Some of the islands are inhabited, while others are little more than dots in the water. (Matsushima means 'pine islands'.) The area is regarded as one of the traditional 'big three' of Japanese natural scenery (along with Amanohashidate, north of Kyoto, and Itsukushima, near Hiroshima). It is certainly pretty and worth seeing both by regular cruise boat from Matsushima or Shiogama and on foot around Matsushima.

Oshima Island

The red-lacquered Togetsukyo bridge connects the mainland (just near Matsushima-kaigan station) with this small scenic island. In former times Oshima was the site of ascetic practices by the Buddhist faithful. The only evidence of those days are the many interesting niches and small caves cut in the rocks, and many carved stone memorials and Buddhist figures. The island offers good views over Matsushima Bay.

Kanrantei

The 'Wave Viewing Pavilion', or Kanrantei, is one of the best places for viewing the bay and is just a short walk from the station passed the large park. Kanrantei is a teahouse dating from the early 1600s and was originally part of Momoyama-jo castle in Kyoto. It was 'given' to Masamune Date and moved here when the castle was demolished and its major buildings scattered around Japan.

Matsushima hakubutsukan

This museum, located next to Kanrantei, has an excellent collection of Japanese suits of armour, swords, pikes (used by foot soldiers to fight cavalrymen) and a number of pieces of high quality lacquerware, all of the Date clan.

Zuigan-ji temple

This Zen temple was established more than 700 years ago although the present buildings date 'only' from 1609. They were built under the direction of Masamune Date and are of Momoyama style. The

paintwork is faded and peeled but you can still admire the myriad of ornately carved wooden panels and the decorated sliding doors. The temple is a National Treasure. The grounds are very restful; tall trees shade the large area and you can see the rooms carved out of solid rock that were once the quarters of monks.

Zuigan-ji is across the road from the dock area, down a sidestreet signposted in English.

Godaido

At the left extremity of the dock area are two short red bridges that lead to Godaido on the tiny island of Godaido-jima. Godaido, which could be described as a worship hall, is part of Zuigan-ji and houses five statues of Buddhist figures. The colour that might once have existed on the building has weathered away, but the wood has survived the centuries well and the carved animals under the eaves, the complex supports of the roof and other details are worthy of note. The interior is said to be beautifully decorated, but the building is only opened once every 33 years.

Fukura-jima

The entrance to Fukura-jima is easily identified because the long red bridge out to the island is visible from anywhere near the harbour. There is no historic significance to the island but it is sort of a natural botanical garden.

Saigyo Modoshi no Matsu-koen park

The best, all-encompassing view of Matsushima Bay is from this park on the hill behind the town. The view is good at any time of the day but the best way to enjoy it is to spend the late afternoon on the verandah of the Panorama restaurant with a coffee or a beer and watch the last rays of the sun on the bay. There are also two lookouts which take in different parts of the bay. The simplest way to get to the park is by taxi; or you can go on foot if you feel like a two km climb.

Festivals

On 15 August the Matsushima-Toro-Nagashi festival is held at Matsushima-kaigan. Thousands of tiny lanterns are set adrift from the beach (at about 7 pm) after which there is a fireworks display. The festival is part of the Buddhist observances of *Obon*, the Festival of the Dead, which is held throughout Japan. There is also a lesser festival the following day.

Places to Stay

There are more than 40 ryokan around Matsushima-kaigan and the Matsushima youth hostel on Miyato Island can be reached from Nobiru station, or by boat to Otakamori and then bus (or on foot). It's three km to the hostel. From the dock go left past Otakamori-kanko Hotel and take the left fork in the road further along.

Getting Around

There are both scheduled public boats and charter cruises available around the islands that dot Matsushima Bay and this is perhaps the best way to make the most of this beautiful area.

Scheduled one hour cruises leave hourly between 10 am and 4 pm and take in a major part of the bay's scenic areas. Seats cost Y1800; standing – Y1200 for adults, Y600 for children, with a discount for groups of 15 or more.

Charter boats also cruise the bay at a fixed price (regardless of the number of passengers) determined by the route taken. This can be Y3000, Y4000, Y6000, or Y15000.

In addition to round trip cruises, ships also run regularly between Matsushima-kaigan and Shiogama; two boat lines with a total of 20 sailings a day in each direction. The fare is Y1200 and the trip takes one hour. Between Shiogama and Otakamori (Miyato-jima island) there are three boats daily in each direction; and between Matsushima-kaigan and Otaka-mori there are two boats daily in each direction, the trip takes one hour and costs Y800.

At Matsushima-kaigan the boats dock at the central pier and can be easily located. At Shiogama, boats leave from Shiogama-ko port, a five minute walk from Hon-Shiogama station (Senseki line).

Above Matsushima, you have the choice of continuing on Route 45 along the coast, with the option of a sidetrip down the scenic Ojika peninsula; or following Route 346 and 108 to Route 4 inland.

OJIKA-HANTO

A trip down the beautiful south coast of this peninsula can be recommended, especially if you have your own transport and can stop at the many lookouts. The coastal views include a succession of bays, interesting rock formations, little fishing villages, many fishing boats and of course the ocean itself. This is not good territory for cyclists as there are many steep hills.

There are seven buses a day (1¾ hours, Y1350) from Ishinomaki to Ayukawa near the southern tip; and a daily boat (in each direction) which leaves Ishinomaki at 9.40 am and Ayukawa at 7.30 am.

Beyond Ayukawa (no public transport listed) the road leads around the top of the peninsula to a fine view of Kinkazan Island, just a short distance off the coast. You can sit and admire the view from the restaurant close to the entrance to the toll road.

Ayukawa is a whaling port and the museum (near the dock for the Kinkazan boat) has an exhibit about whales and the industry.

KINKAZAN

A 'mysterious' atmosphere seems to surround this island which is just off the coast of Ojika peninsula. Various visitors have mentioned the peace at night, especially when staying at the youth hostel which is located at *Koganeyama-jinja* (shrine). The name Kinkazan means 'Gold Flower Mountain', which seems to be in reference to the sparkle of mica in rocks on the island.

Koganeyama-jinja is one of the main attractions of the island and is surprisingly large for such a remote place. There may be an early morning (at about 6.30) service, featuring sacred dances by shrine maidens, with traditional music and chanting by priests. The island is covered with dense bamboo groves and forests, and monkeys and deer roam free. Behind the shrine a two km path leads to the top of the mountain where there is another shrine. The walk to the top takes an hour or so.

Getting There
Up to 10 ferries a day run between Ayukawa-ko port and Kinkazan (Y650); the single boat between Ishinomaki and Ayukawa is one of these. In addition there are up to five ferries a day between Kinkazan and Onagawa, which is the terminus of a JNR line.

Routes northward Above the Matsushima-Ojika Peninsula area you can go inland along Route 4 to the attractions in Miyagi-ken and beyond in Iwate-ken or along the east coast. There are several roads and railway lines linking Route 4 with the coast, so it is possible to criss-cross to take in nearly all the attractions without backtracking.

Inland route Route 4 is slow, crowded and not very interesting but *shi kata ga nai* – it can't be helped. To get to Narugo and its nearby geyser turn off onto Route 47 at Furukawa, or take the train.

NARUGO
This town, actually the collective name for a series of hot-spring resorts, has numerous ryokan and hotels catering to the hot-spring crowd, as well as an unmemorable (but adequate) youth hostel. The town is not particularly noteworthy – basically a string of buildings up the sides of a hill – but some very attractive lacquerware is produced here and the town is famous for its *Narugo-kokeshi*

dolls. Kokeshi are very simple, with a cylindrical (lathe-turned) body, round head and simple, painted features. The Narugo dolls 'cry' when the head is turned; one explanation (veracity not guaranteed) being that families made them years ago to honour the souls of girl babies that had been abandoned because there was not enough food to support them (being less-useful females). Many dolls are made in shops along the main street and you can watch the process.

Onikobe-onsen
One of Japan's few geysers, and probably the highest spurting, is located at Onikobe-onsen (a collective name for several onsen, meaning 'ogre's head'). About 14 km above Narugo, the geyser can be reached by bus from Narugo station; just ask to be let off at Onikobe kanketsu-sen-onsen. From the stop, the small park surrounding the geyser is down a side road.

The geyser is 'artificial' to the extent that a hole was bored to tap the underground pool, but the eruption, every 30 minutes or so, is entirely natural. Water shoots at least 15 metres into the air for several minutes. Close by is a warm water swimming-pool that can be used by those who have already paid to see the geyser.

Narugo-kyo gorge

About three km outside Narugo, near Nakayama-daira-guchi, this gorge is an enjoyable place to walk. It follows a small river for about four km. To get there take a bus from Narugo station.

The Tsuruoka area of the west coast is easily reached from this point.

Iwate-ken

HIRAIZUMI

Taking the inland route you come to this ordinary looking town, once the cultural centre of the area, which contains the most historic temple in northern Japan. Nearby are two interesting gorges and beautiful views of typical farmland with some of the largest and finest farmhouses in the country.

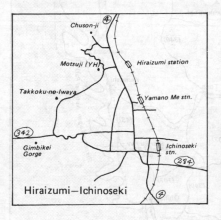

Hiraizumi—Ichinoseki

Things to See
Chuson-ji

This temple was founded in 1105 to accompany a fortress in Hiraizumi built by the Fujiwara family. Of the more than 40 buildings then standing, only two have survived. One, *Kyozo*, is not particularly noteworthy, but the other, *Kon-jiki-do*, is a marvel of finely executed, ornate

decoration. Kon-jiki-do ('golden hall') was originally protected by an outer structure, but recently a new concrete building was put up around it to provide a climate-controlled environment. At the same time, it was restored to its original splendour, using authentic materials from the same sources as the ones used initially. The exterior is lacquered black, and there are large panels of mother-of-pearl and gold leaf. Inside are three altars, each with 11 Buddhist deities (three Amida, six of Jizo and two of Ten). The building is small (only 5.5 metres square) but you can stand for a long time admiring it through the protective plate glass. The remains of three of the Fujiwara rulers lie under the central altar.

The grounds of the temple are very restful, set at the top of a large hill that overlooks fertile farming country. An avenue of tall trees lines the stone-paved road up from the entrance. The entry fee also covers the nearby Sankozo museum.

There are many buses to the temple throughout the day and the entrance is a drop-off point for the bus that runs between Hiraizumi station and Ichinoseki station (the next large town).

Motsu-ji

During the era of the Fujiwara, this was the largest and greatest temple in northern Honshu. All the buildings from that time have been destroyed over the years and nothing but foundation stones and Oizumi-ga-ike pond and garden remain, although there are some picturesque buildings of more recent vintage around the grounds.

The temple grounds would be very peaceful if it wasn't for several PA systems with recorded messages, two of which can be heard at any one time.

The *youth hostel* is in the temple grounds and guests are allowed to walk around without paying the admission charge.

The temple is about half a km from Hiraizumi station. You can get there by bus or by walking out of the station and

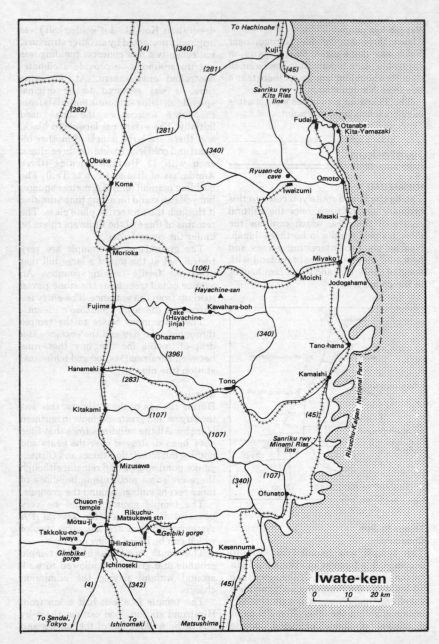

Iwate-ken

0   10   20 km

across the main road (Route 4), then continuing along the road on the other side of Route 4.

Takkoku-no-Iwayu

A few km further along the road that curves past Motsu-ji, is a small interesting temple in the mouth of a cave. It is built on pillars, like a small scale Kiyomizu-dera (Kyoto). The temple is a 1946 reproduction of a much more ancient structure. Faintly visible in the large rock near the temple is an image of Dainichi-Nyorai, believed to date from the late 11th century.

Gimbikei gorge

This gorge is only about one km long and never more than a few metres deep but the river has carved the solid rock into a most picturesque and intricate natural sculpture. You can walk its full length along the banks where there are many Jacob's wells (circular holes bored into the rock by the action of rock-bearing water). It is a very pretty place and well worth a visit.

The gorge, which is past Motsu-ji and Takkoku-no-Iwayu, is easily accessible by bus from Hiraizumi station and the trip there passes through pretty countryside and by large prosperous-looking farmhouses.

Geibikei gorge

Near Hiraizumi is another gorge, but this one is of heroic proportions and is one of the great bargains of Japan. For Y900 you can take a truly memorable 90 minute boat trip up the river and back. The flat-bottomed boat is poled by two boatmen up the slow moving Satetsu-gawa river between grey and blue streaked cliffs and large rocks. On the way upstream the only sounds are the splash of the boatmen's poles, the ever-present cicadas, plus wheeling, raucous crows (which by the way, have a Japanese accent, and say 'haw' instead of 'caw'!). The ride ends at Daigeibiga, a cliff that rises straight and flat for about 100 metres. It is a fitting climax to the ascent.

On the way down, the boatmen serenade their 50 or so passengers with plaintive, traditional songs that echo off the rock walls. This was one of the most beautiful, peaceful, relaxing, 'Japanese' moments of my travels in Japan.

MIZUSAWA

Anyone interested in an unusual souvenir of Japan should look for a little shop in the main street of this town that sells fish traps. These are the simple type, centuries old in design, that funnel water through the trap so the fish is caught in an inner chamber.

KITAKAMI

Though it is not one of the famous Tohoku festivals, Kitakami's annual extravaganza is quite interesting. Its history only goes back 30 years but the format varies from year to year as dancers, floats, etc, from other festivals in Japan are invited to participate. There are usually lion dances, kagura dance displays, sword dances, drumming and fireworks. The festival is held from 7 to 9 August and it's best to inquire locally to determine the best day to visit.

TONO

Tono is a large town situated in a long agricultural valley east of Kitakami on the road towards Kamaishi and the coast. Its relative isolation until the turn of the century has meant that many of the old legends and folk tales have remained more a part of people's lives here than in any other part of Japan. And that's the way the people of Tono want to keep it. They have rejected industrialisation and are endeavoring to retain as much of the atmosphere of the past as is practicable. The town itself is unremarkable, like almost any other in the country but there are still several *magariya* (thatched-roof houses) in the valley, either lived in or used for storage or animals, and some of the old waterwheels are still in use.

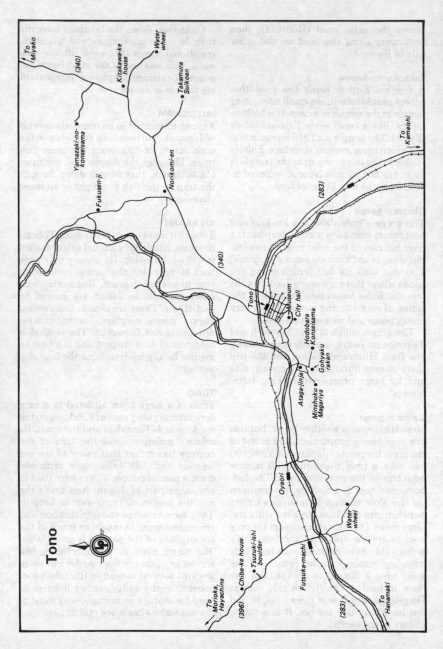

Information

To the right when leaving Tono station is the combined information and accommodation booking office. They have two maps of Tono: one is an all-too-typical Japanese colour pamphlet with cute little pictorial representations of the local sights which give absolutely no indication of where they really are; the other is a 'proper' map. When the two are used together, the first is handy for finding the kanji name for the attraction while the second can be used for actually getting there.

The various attractions around Tono and the roads to them are conveniently signposted.

Things to See

Chiba-ke

This imposing structure, sited on a hill about nine km from Tono (along Route 396), was the home of the Chiba family, very wealthy farmers. It dates back about two centuries and was restored recently because it is regarded as one of the ten most important historic farmhouses in Japan.

Waterwheel

One of the few functioning waterwheels (not decorative) in the area can be found along the road that runs south from Iwate-Futsukamachi station (the second east of Tono station). The word for waterwheel is 'suisha'.

Gohyaku-rakan

Carved in relief on boulders in a shallow ravine and on the hillside are several hundred images of faces, the 500 *rakan* (disciples) of Buddha. They were carved in the mid 1700s by a priest to console the spirits of the hundreds who died of starvation following two years of crop failures. A few of the images can be easily found; the rest of the nearly 400 known to survive could take quite a while to locate.

The gohyaku-rakan can be found by first locating *Atago-jinja* shrine, which is near Route 283, across from a major bridge west of the bus terminal. The stone carvings are about 300 metres up the hill in a peaceful wooded area behind the shrine.

Fukusen-ji

There are several shrines and temples in Tono itself but perhaps the most interesting to visit is Fukusen-ji about six km from the station. There is a large Ming-style gate at the entrance but the feature is a very tall statue of *Kannon*, the goddess of mercy. It is, it must be said, more impressive for its 17 metre height than for the artistry of the woodcarving, even though it was carved from a single piece of 1200 year old wood.

Norikomi-en

The main attraction here is an old magariya house with authentic furnishings to give an idea of what life was like in days gone by. Both in the house and in an adjacent building there are demonstrations of old crafts, such as weaving and straw sandal making. Another building houses hundreds of *Oshira-sama* dolls – simple figures that are little more than a 30 cm stick with a crude face, dressed in a square of brightly coloured cloth. There are also other displays and an old steam locomotive in the grounds of Norikomi-en which is located just past the turn-off for Fukusen-ji

Places to Stay

Near Gohyaku-rakan is *Minshuku Magariya*, a typical L-shaped thatched-roof house, about 80 years old, that offers accommodation. The owner is friendly and this is a good way to get the feel for old Japan. To make a reservation you can ring 01986-2-4564. There are other minshuku and ryokan in Tono and bookings can be made at the office near the station.

Getting There

The train line serving Tono (JNR) runs

between Kitakami (on the Tohoku Shinkansen) and Kamaishi, a nondescript industrial city of the east coast, from where a JNR line runs north to Miyako and beyond. The Sanriku railway Minami Rias sen line runs south from Kamaishi to Ofunato, where JNR services resume.

HAYACHINE-SAN

The mountain, Hayachine-san, has been regarded as a sacred place for centuries. These days it has become a popular destination for walkers and on 31 July and 1 August every year, a very interesting festival is held in the little village of Take on the flank of the mountain.

TAKE

The festival of *Hayachine-jinja* shrine in Take (pronounced Tah-kay) begins on the night of 31 July with performances of a very rare type of theatre unique to this part of Japan. *Yamabushi-kagura* is a collection of stories acted out in dance. Prior to the war, farmers in Tohoku used to regularly act out these very energetic masked dance-dramas in their farmhouses during the winter nights, a tradition hundreds of years old. Since the arrival of television however the performances are limited to this annual festival and others on 3 January, 17 December and the second Sunday of June.

Performances are given on the stage in the courtyard of Hayachine-jinja (Take is tiny so it's not hard to locate the shrine). The music, drumming and cymbals are quite primitive, somewhat reminiscent of Balinese music. At the same time Sumo wrestlers perform in a ring in a nearby field.

The next morning (try to get there by 9 am), there is a procession from the main shrine to a smaller shrine nearby. The preliminaries include the blessing of *mikoshi* (portable shrines), a time-honoured Shinto ritual. Then out comes the most fascinating attraction of the festival, the *shishi*. Twenty or more shishi – townspeople dressed in lion costumes

that are topped with very large wooden masks of lion heads – parade along the road, the heads held high overhead so that the 'animals' are much taller than a man. The masks have glossy black lacquered faces, fiery eyes and gold teeth outlined in red. The mane is made of white tassles of paper and the lower jaw is hinged so it can open and shut.

The procession, which includes many children dressed in white is led by long-nosed, red-faced *Tengu* and the *shishi* stop periodically to give dance demonstrations, accompanied by musicians on drums, flutes and gongs. The jaws of the lions clack resonantly in unison with the music and the whole effect is truly eerie and except for the onlookers you feel as if you've been dropped into a surreal world.

There are further performances of yamabushi-kagura at the shrine following the procession.

Places to Stay

Because Take is a base camp for walking in the mountains, there are several places in the town which offer accommodation, nearly all in the form of very large open rooms with one or more tatami mat per person, depending on the number of guests. There is an information service for the festival (tel 0198-48-5864); they may also be able to help with reservations for accommodation.

Getting There

Take is part of the town of Osama from which there are up to eight buses a day; three of these originate at Hanimake station and a fourth at Kitakami station. Two buses continue on through Take to Kawahara-no-boh, a high point along the road used as a starting point for walking on Hayachine-san.

MORIOKA

The centre-piece of Morioka is Iwate-koen park, formerly the site of Morioka-jo castle, but now just a respite from the crowds. It can be reached from Morioka station via Saien-dori, one of the two main shopping streets (the other is Odori). Across the river and to the left is the Gozaku area, a series of old shops looking much as they did a hundred years ago.

The attractions of the Tazawa-ko lake area are a relatively short distance to the west of Morioka, easily accessible by train and bus as are Akita and the Oga peninsula also to the west and Miyako, Kuji, Hachinohe and Towada-ko lake to the east and north.

COASTAL ROUTE

Northward from the Matsushima area you can continue along Route 45. The road runs close to the sea for much of the way, but except for near Ofunato there is little in the way of coastal sights until Miyako. At Kesennuma you reach the beginning of Rikuchu-Kaigan National Park.

OFUNATO AREA

Scarcely worth the name 'peninsula', the little extension of land below Hosoura has enough natural attractions, to interest the traveller who is not in a hurry. The first place of interest, almost at the tip, is *Goishi-hama*, which means 'Go stone beach'. Go is a popular board game played with black and white stones; the stones found on the beach here are round and black, and in the past provided many 'pieces' of the right size for the game.

The beach is less than a km before the Goishi-kaigan bus terminus, where there is a booking office for the many minshuku in the area, a restaurant and a delightful wooded park.

Back towards town is another attraction definitely worth seeing if you're into seascapes. Anadoshi is a triple arch of rock formed from centuries of erosion.

Getting There

There are regular buses from Ofunato bus terminal or station, via Hosoura to Goishi-kaigan, some of which go on to Anadoshi. From Kamaishi, Route 283 leads inland to

Tono, Hayachine and the attractions along Route 4.

MIYAKO

The city of Miyako is a major gateway for travel up the Sanriku-kaigan coast and with the opening of the Sanriku railway Kita Rias line, travel in the region is now faster and more reliable than on the local buses. The main problem with the line however is that more than half its length is though tunnels, somewhat minimising the sightseeing en route.

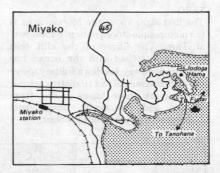

There are two youth hostels in Miyako, both near the station, and there is an accommodation office at the station that can help you find a ryokan, though you might have to persist a little if they say they have no rooms.

The coastal attraction nearest to Miyako is Jodogahama – 'Paradise Beach'. A finger of the cliff reaches out and descends into the water, forming a sheltered cove for swimmers. Walking trails stretch along the coast north of Jodogahama and are marked on the handout map given out at Miyako station.

SANRIKU-KAIGAN

In summer there is a daily cruise boat that goes from Jodogahama to Otanabe leaving at 8.30 am and arriving at 11.15 am. There are also six other boats in each direction that go to Taro and Masaki which are much closer to Miyako.

From the boat you can see the cliffs for which this coast is famous, and the boat goes close enough to shore to see the specific points of interest clearly.

The most spectacular sights are Kitayamazaki and Shimanokoshi, where the cliffs are well over 100 metres high. Once the boat has docked it's possible to go back by bus to an excellent viewpoint built specifically to overlook Kitayamazaki; then continue on by another bus to the next train station and use it either to return to Miyako or continue on to Kuji.

TARO

The first sight above the Miyako area is the picturesque stone column 'Sanno-iwa' at Taro. The finger of the cliff that formerly stretched into the ocean has been eroded away, leaving a solitary tower about 50 metres tall and 10 metres across.

There are three buses a day from Miyako and the cruise boats from Jodogahama go into Taro harbour.

The rest of the coast north to Fudai is a succession of spectacular headlands, wave-washed rocks, eroded arches, sheer cliffs, interesting rock formations and of course the blue ocean itself.

Ryusendo cave

This is one of the three major caves in Japan. Visitors are permitted 300 metres into it, passing stalagmites and stalactites. Ryusendo can be reached by bus from Iwaizumi (which is served by JNR via Moichi). Buses also run directly from Morioka and from Komoto, on the coast. There are ryokan and minshuku at Iwaizumi and at other tourist spots in the area.

Aomori-ken

This is the northernmost part of Honshu and is of interest mainly for access to

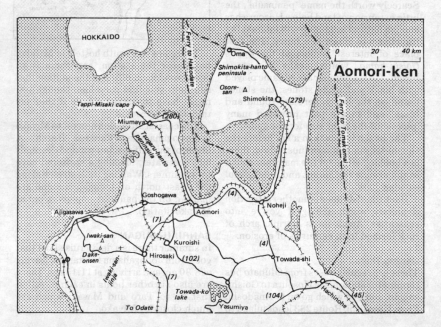

Hokkaido. If you are travelling up the east coast, Hachinohe is the first ferry port; others are Aomori, Noheji and Oma.

HACHINOHE

This coastal city is most noteworthy as the port for regular daily boats to Tomakomai, on Hokkaido. By using this route to Hokkaido it allows you to bypass the relatively uninteresting northern tip of Honshu.

Those interested in archaeology can visit *Kokokan*, a small museum in Hachinohe, which houses several thousand Jomon era relics dug up in the area.

Another attraction of Hachinohe is the city's annual festival (one of many in the region during the first week of August). The festival is a lengthy procession of floats depicting a theme from Japanese or Chinese history or mythology – castles, lucky gods, demons, warriors, dragons and, of course, beautiful maidens – and each float is accompanied by a large *taiko* (drum) beaten tirelessly by a relay of young men. Each float is a group effort of a neighbourhood of the city. It seems that foreigners are still a rarity here even during the festival; I saw no others and was kindly invited to stay in the home of a local family.

MISAWA

Travellers through Misawa, with time to kill while waiting for a train etc, could venture into the amazingly kitsch Komaki-onsen. This large Japanese-style resort complex, includes a large bath of several pools, a park area with reconstructions of famous historic structures, and a lake for boating.

Komaki-onsen is about five minutes walk from Misawa station and admission is Y800.

Shimokita-hanto Peninsula

The eastern horn of northern Honshu is quite flat and rather bland. There are beaches all along the inner coast but they collect all the floating debris so are not good for swimming. With the exception of festival time at Osore-san, most visitors only come here to take the ferry from Oma to Hokkaido.

Osore-san

This mountain has been regarded as sacred since at least the 9th century. *Enstu-ji* temple was built on its flank on the north shore of the small lake Osoresan. The landscape around the lake is desolate, stark and white, the result of underground minerals deposited on the surface by hot springs. The temple is associated with *itako* or mediums, who attempt to contact the dead. This is the main purpose of the annual festival (20-24 July), when blind women (the mediums), go into trances and attempt to contact the souls of departed members of the worshipping families. These activities take place in tents set up on the temple grounds, and are the only remnant in Japan of minkan shinko shamanist rites, once practiced all over the country till they were absorbed and changed by Shinto.

AOMORI

Aomori is famous for its Nebuta festival (3-7 August), when very large floats move through the streets at night. The floats are unusual, huge three-dimensional represent-ations of men and animals that are illuminated from the inside. The sight is memorable. An explanation of the origin

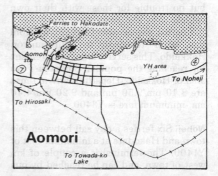

of the festival is given in the section on Hirosaki, which has a similar festival called Neputa.

Places to Stay

The youth hostel can be reached from Aomori station by bus No 1; get off at Sakaimachi-ichome. It is associated with a temple, and a faint drumming may be heard in the morning.

FERRIES TO HOKKAIDO

Hachinohe Two ferry lines run boats between Hachinohe and Tomakomai, Hokkaido, one leaving Hachinohe at 8.45 am and 9.30 pm, two sailing at 1 pm and all taking about nine hours. The 9.30 pm sailing saves a night's accommodation cost, arriving early the next morning. From Tomakomai, sailings are at 9 am, 9.15 pm and midnight. The boat dock can be reached by city bus from Hachinohe station; get off at Shin-sankaikan-mae stop. Minimum fare is Y3900.

Aomori This is the most convenient port for getting to and from Hakodate. In both cities the ferry terminal is close to the station. Signs in Aomori station are in English, so it is not hard to find your way. There are 13 JNR ferries per day and the minimum fare is Y1800.

Ferries also leave from another terminal west of the city and dock at a terminal some distance from the centre of Hakodate. This is inconvenient for foot passengers but no trouble for those with their own vehicle.

There is also another ferry service from this latter terminal, to Muroran on Hokkaido. This service is very convenient for reaching the popular Shikotsu-Toya area of Hokkaido. Departure/arrival times are 3.10 pm/9.50 pm and 9.20 pm/4.40 am; minimum fare is Y3400.

Noheji Six ferries a day sail between this town and Hakodate at a minimum cost of Y1400. The terminal is a couple of km west of town, and can be reached by bus

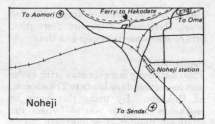

Noheji

from Noheji station. At the Hokkaido side, the ferries dock some distance from the centre of Hakodate, which makes it preferable for foot travellers to go via Aomori.

Oma Ferries cross each way between Oma and Hakodate, three times a day (Y1000). However, the boat docks at the same previously mentioned awkward-to-reach terminal, which again makes it easier for foot passengers to use the JNR service from Aomori which lands in the heart of Hakodate.

TSUGARU PENINSULA

The western pincer of Mutsu Bay at the top of Honshu, is the Tsugaru-hanto peninsula. A spine of low mountains up the middle and a west coast of small lakes and marshes limits the habitability. Only the east coast is very populated and is in fact one endless fishing village squeezed between the water and the hills behind, with nets drying everywhere. By road it is slow going; the JNR line runs along this coast and would probably be faster and more relaxing.

The most notable scenic view is from the northern tip, Tappi-misaki cape, with its semi-circular bay, rocky shoreline and green-covered cliffs that slope into the sea.

Few visitors come here, as the previous major attraction of a ferry connection between Miumaya and Hokkaido has been suspended. To reach the cape, take one of the six daily trains (95 minutes) from Aomori to Miumaya, then a bus from the station to the Tappi-misaki lookout.

The Seikan tunnel under the strait to Hokkaido plunges underground near here. Originally touted as the means of bringing Shinkansen train services to Sapporo, the tunnel was finally completed in early 1985 but its actual future use is still a matter of debate.

NORTHWEST COAST

A train trip down the west coast from the base of the Tsugaru peninsula is an enjoyable way to see this section of Honshu. The JNR line (five per day) between Hirosaki and Higashi-Noshiro (between Akita and Odate) runs as close to the water as practicable and offers excellent vistas over the ocean and rocky coastline for nearly its full length.

JUNIKO

One place to consider a stop is Mutsu-Iwasaki for a bus trip to Juniko. Juniko means 'Twelve Lakes' and takes its name from the many bodies of water dammed by a landslide caused by an earthquake. All are quite small, some big enough for an enjoyable row around, others almost small enough to jump over. An engraved wooden sign at the bus terminal shows the walking trails and the larger ponds; a circuit takes a couple of hours.

Buses are scheduled to meet all five trains from Noshiro (to the south) and three of the five from the Hirosaki direction; and they remain at Juniko for 50 to 100 minutes before returning to the station. Four of the five make good connections with trains bound for Hirosaki, and three with trains for Noshiro.

AOMORI TO TOWADA-KO

The shortest route to the area around Lake Towada, recommended if you're in a hurry, is the direct road south through scenic woodland areas. An enjoyable stop en route is Suiren-numa, a small pond backdropped by four mountain peaks, still snow patched in late July. The area is at its best in autumn. There are at least 11 buses a day.

For those in less of a hurry, the route south via Hirosaki is more interesting.

HIROSAKI
Information
The information office at Hirosaki station may have a copy of the city-produced brochure *Hirosaki* showing a couple of temples that might be of interest – *Chosho-ji* and *Seigan-ji*.

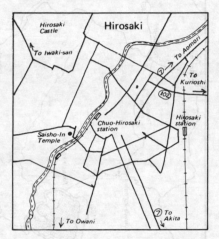

Things to See
Hirosaki-jo castle
This lovely original castle (not a replica) dates from 1610. The moat and walls are also intact, the gates are original (or authentically restored) and the grounds are covered with cherry trees. In any season it is pretty; during the cherry blossom season (late April-early May) and from mid-October when the maples are at their autumn-best it is a truly beautiful place to visit.

Saishoin temple
Standing in the temple grounds is a five-storey pagoda dating from 1672. Although many people believe that Japan is full of such pagodas, they are in fact relatively rare and therefore worth a visit.

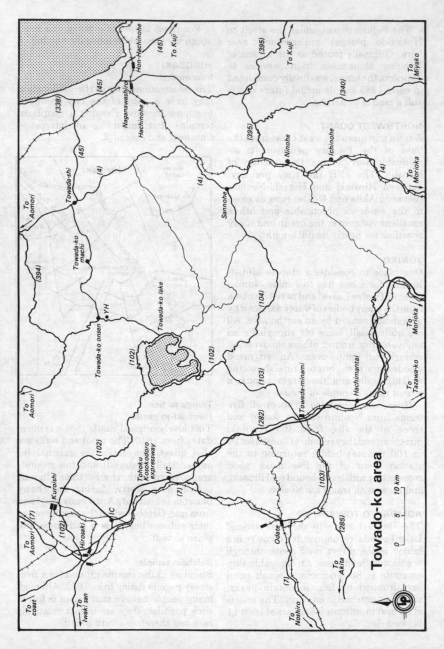

Towado-ko area

0   5   10 km

Festivals

Hirosaki is famous throughout Japan for its *Neputa* festival, 1-7 August, which is very similar to the Nebuta festival of Aomori.

The floats of the festival are smaller than those of Aomori and of a different format – rather like a three-dimensional fan with scenes from Japanese or Chinese mythology painted on the two faces and the edges. Lights inside them, either candles or electric, illuminate the scenes beautifully.

The numerous *dashi* (carts carrying the floats) parade through the streets on a different route each night accompanied by drummers and other musicians. A map showing the route-of-the-day is available from the information office at the station.

The origin of the Neputa (and Nebuta) festival is unknown. One version is that a Japanese military commander used giant figures similar to those carved in the floats to terrify the Ainu (whom he was fighting at Hirosaki), and that he celebrated his victory on reaching Aomori. The *Official Guide* indicates that a military commander, Sakanoue, used such figures in the late 9th century to subjugate rebels (who might well have been Ainu or other tribesmen fighting against the southern Japanese who were advancing into their territory).

These two festivals, along with ones at Hayachine-san (31 July – 1 August), Yamagata (6-8 August) and Akita (5-7 August), make early August an excellent time to visit this part of Japan, especially as its climate is cooler and less humid than that of the southern regions.

Buses are available from Hirosaki or Kuroishi to Nenokuchi and Yasumiya on Towada-ko lake (described later).

IWAKI-SAN

The cone of this 1625-metre dormant volcano dominates the flat countryside west of Hirosaki. In can be climbed in about four hours (7.3 km) from Hyakuzawa-onsen, or can be approached the easy way

by bus and chairlift. Five buses a day go from Hirosaki station to the top of the mountain (*sancho*) from where the chairlift begins. On the mountain, you may see white-garbed pilgrims wending their way up the paths. They are members of the *yamabushi* sect, an offshoot of Buddhism that includes many elements of Shinto. If considering a trip to the top, observe the weather carefully; if clouds can be seen near the summit the view from there may be totally obscured by fog.

Iwaki-san-jinja shrine

Situated on the south-east flank of Iwaki-san, this shrine is surrounded by a large grove of tall, ancient trees. The buildings are painted a reddish-brown, and some doorways and other details have elaborate carvings overhead. According to the *Official Guide*, the shrine is often called 'Nikko shrine of north-west Honshu'. Well, the shrine is pleasing in appearance but bears no resemblance to *Toshogu* (Nikko) and is not worth a special trip for its beauties. It is popular with pilgrims, and busloads of them may be seen being guided through the rites of the shrine by the priests, to the sound of drumming.

Similarly, Iwaki-san's description in the *Official Guide* is: 'The mountain is often called Tsugaru-Fuji because of its remarkable resemblance to Mt Fuji'. Most mountains will resemble Fuji if they are volcanic cones and Iwaki-san is one of at least 12 in Japan so-described!

Akita-ken

TOWADA-KO LAKE

One of the most popular destinations in northern Honshu is the Towada-ko area. The main attraction is natural scenery and an escape from the built-up city areas. The lake is the third deepest in Japan, 334 metres, and is located in an old volcanic crater. The sides of the crater rise sharply as you'll see if you arrive by bus from

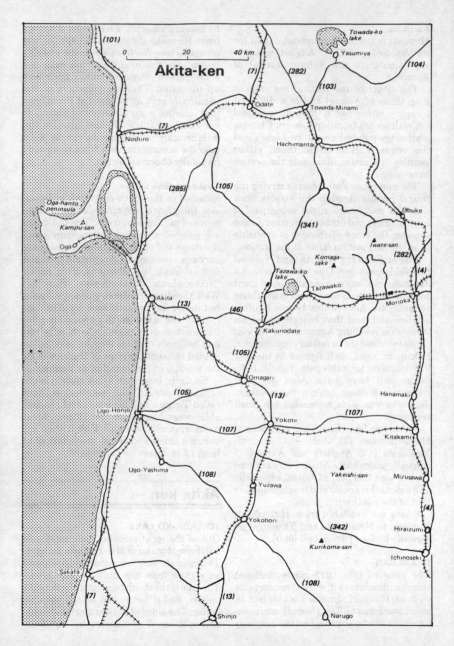

Akita-ken

0   20   40 km

(101)

(104)

Towada-ko lake

Yasumiya

(7)

(282)

(103)

Odate

Towada-Minami

Noshiro

(7)

Hachimantai

Oga-hanto peninsula

(285)

(105)

Obuke

Kampu-san

(341)

Iwate-san

Oga

Komaga-take

(282)

Tazawa-ko lake

(4)

Akita

Tazawako

Morioka

(13)

(46)

Kakunodate

(105)

Omagari

(13)

Hanamaki

Ugo-Honjo

(105)

Yokote

(107)

(107)

Kitakami

(107)

Ugo-Yashima

(108)

Yakeishi-san

Mizusawa

Yuzawa

(4)

Yokobori

(342)

Hiraizumi

Kurikoma-san

Ichinoseki

Sakata

(7)

(13)

(108)

Shinjo

Narugo

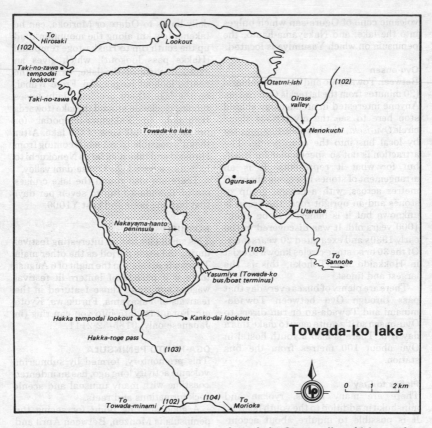

Towada-ko lake

Tawada-minami; the road in snakes down round countless twists and switchbacks to water level.

The area invites exploration on foot but there is a road road the entire circumference of the lake and buses pass over all parts of it at some time during the day.

The main centres of population around the lake (all small) are Yasumiya, Utarube and Nenokuchi. Most of the shore has been left in its natural state, without the rows of souvenir shops etc, that characterise too many resorts.

Oirase valley

The most popular walk in the area is through the Oirase valley which stretches 14 km north-east from Nenokuchi. The Oirase-kawa river originates at the lake and flows through the only break in the crater wall. Along the way its character varies from shallow and placid to a narrow torrent rushing around rocks and plunging over falls. A tree-canopied path follows the river and in October the leaves are amazingly colourful.

From Nenokuchi you have the option of returning to Yasumiya by bus or boat. Boats run every 30 minutes between Nenokuchi and Towada-ko. The trip takes one hour, costs Y1000 and passes by the most scenic parts of the lake, including the volcanic cone of Ogura-san which bulges into the lake, and Nakayama-hanto, the peninsula on which Yasumiya is located.

Oyu-onsen

Between Towada-ko and Towada-minami (20 minutes from the latter) is Oyu-onsen. Anyone interested in archaeology should stop here to see the mysterious stone circle *Oyu-iseki*, which is about 20 minutes by local bus into the countryside. The attraction is not so spectacular for itself, but for what it represents. It is an arrangement of stones in a circle about 46 metres across, with a central group of stones and an upright rock; the origin is unknown but it is believed to be about 4000 years old. It was discovered in the early 1930s and excavated 20 years later. Of the 30 or so stone circles known to exist in Hokkaido and Tohoku, this is the largest and finest.

There are plenty of buses every day that pass through Oyu between Towada-minami and Towada-ko or run direct to Oyu-onsen so it's quite easy to make this a day trip. There is also a youth hostel in Oyu about 100 metres from the bus station.

Places to Stay

There are many hotels, ryokan and minshuku in addition to the youth hostels. It is possible to inquire about accommodation in Yasumiya, but because of the popularity of the area it is risky to turn up without a reservation (particularly during the October school excursion season). Yasumiya, on the south shore, is the transportation centre of the lake area; the name of the bus stop is 'Towada-ko'. *Hakubutsukan Youth Hostel* (Museum YH) is quite close; Towada YH is between Yasumiya and Wainai, on the lake near Hotel Hakka. The other nearby hostels are at Towada-ko machi, Nishi-Towada and Oyu.

Getting Around

Starting from Yasumiya, any of the 17 daily buses to Odate or Morioka, can be taken a few km along the mountain road up the south rim to Hakka-toge tempodai (Hakka pass lookout), which gives an excellent view of the lake; as does the nearby lookout Kogakudai. From Wanai, on the lake, there are four daily buses running clockwise around the lake (towards Hirosaki), to Takizawa-tempodai for probably the best view of the lake. After that it's possible to get a bus coming from Hirosaki and take it as far as Nenokuchi to have a look round the Oirase-dani valley.

There are also round the lake cruises out of Towada-ko (up to seven per day) that last one hour and cost Y1000.

NOSHIRO

This small city has an interesting festival during the same period as the other main Tohoku festivals. On the night of 6 August there is a parade of lantern-lit festival wagons similar to those featured in the festivals of Takayama, Furukawa, Kyoto etc. For up to date info you can ring (in Japanese only) 0185-52-2111.

OGA-HANTO PENINSULA

This promontory, formed by submarine volcanic activity long ago, has an indented coastline with many unusual and scenic rock formations and reefs.

A good starting point for seeing the peninsula is Monzen. Between April and the end of October, boats cruise along the coast from Monzen to Oga-Suizokukan aquarium. A toll road runs along the top of these cliffs so it should be easy to hitch back if desired but no buses are scheduled for this route. The boat schedule is posted at the Monzen bus terminal and is also printed in *Jikokuhyo*.

Oga-suizokukan

This aquarium is definitely worth visiting. In addition to commonplace ocean fish it has some truly weird and wonderful creations of nature that outdo anything that a Walt Disney cartoonist could dream up – some incredibly beautiful, others

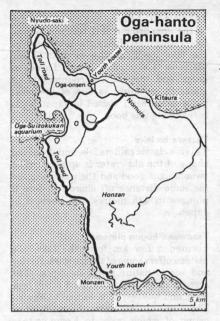

Oga-hanto peninsula

Nyudo-saki
Toll road
Oga-onsen
Youth hostel
Kitaura
Nomura
Oga-Suizokukan aquarium
Honzan
Toll road
Youth hostel
Monzen
0   5 km

equally ugly. There are also several alligators, crocodiles and large turtles.

A very unusual sight here, and at Monzen, are dugout boats still in everyday use (with outboard motors!) The availability of large trees in the area make them very practical.

Nyudo-saki cape

From Oga-suizokukan, you can continue by bus to Nyudo-saki cape via Oga-onsen. From the cape a toll road runs along another stretch of cliff and between two small green lakes, ending at Nomura. At the cape, and elsewhere, you can see masks and costumes of *namahage* (ogres). On New Year's Eve, groups of young men in similar costumes visit homes where they are formally received by the master of the house, pause to honour the family shrine and then walk around the house shouting 'Any good-for-nothing loafers here?'

Places to Stay

There is accommodation available at several centres on the coast, including Oga city and Monzen. *Oga Choraku-ji youth hostel* at Monzen is better than usual. It is part of a 1200 year old temple; an alarm clock is unnecessary because drumming, which is part of the religious ceremony, begins at 6.30 am.

At Oga-onsen there is quite a few ryokan and minshuku, plus another youth hostel.

AKITA

This city is noteworthy only for its famed annual *Kanto* festival (5-7 August) when young men balance tall bamboo poles that support as many as 50 lighted paper lanterns on cross-bars.

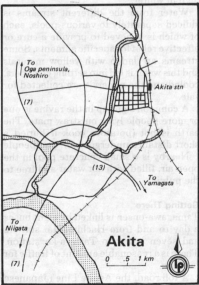

To Oga peninsula, Noshiro
(7)
Akita stn
(13)
To Yamagata
To Niigata
(7)
Akita
0   .5   1 km

TAMAGAWA-ONSEN

South of Towada-ko and below Kazuno, the road splits into Route 282 (which goes to Morioka) and Route 341, which passes through the Hachimantai plateau (Towada-Hachimantai National Park). There are several hot-spring resort towns in the area. Just a little off Route 341 lies Tamagawa-onsen, one of the most typical of these traditional resorts. Nearly all the buildings are old and simple wooden structures built close to the springs. Typical is the large old bathhouse which you pass to reach the ravine that is the source of the hot water. It has several pools and mixed bathing is still the practice but the resort is, like many such hot-spring towns, more of a health clinic and the bathers are mostly geriatrics. In the ravine, there is one stream which has some of the most unusual water you're likely to see – it is brilliant orange. Further upstream, a violent bubbling and boiling marks the emergence of many gushers of hot water, one of which boils two metres high in winter.

Water from the different streams is sluiced separately to various pools, each of which is believed to provide a cure or effective relief for specific ailments. Some streams are laden with yellow minerals and this water is led into settling chambers, cooled and the minerals are collected for sale.

A common sight up in the ravine is one or more people lying on straw mats. The earth is hot (potatoes cook if buried a short distance underground), and people

Nearby is a small concrete pool in the open air, filled with hot water and free to the public.

Getting There

Tamagawa-onsen is linked by eight buses a day to and from Hachimantai station, and seven a day to Tazawa-ko station. There is a reasonable amount of traffic for hitching.

A toll road, the Aspite Line (Japanese name) leads across the mountain range from Route 341 towards Routes 282 and 284, past several peaks. It's enjoyable if you happen to be going that way but not worth a special trip.

TAZAWA-KO AREA

In the area around this lake are several interesting individual attractions, such as the lake itself, nearby mountains and plateaus, Kakunodate town, Dakikaeri gorge and the general countryside. It sticks in my mind as one of the most enjoyable areas I visited in Japan while researching this book.

Tazawa-ko lake

This is a classic caldera lake and the round shape of the old crater is apparent. The swimming is good and the water shallow for some distance off shore – before it plunges to 425 metres, the deepest in Japan.

Tazawako-kogen plateau

Located a few km from the lake, the plateau offers some of the most interesting and scenic nature walks in Japan. The scenery ranges from highland scrub (low trees and bushes) to a dormant volcano. There are several trails, the most interesting of which takes in *Koma-ga-take* mountain and vicinity. The scenery is quite outstanding (if the highland area is not fog-bound) and the walking and climbing are within the range of anyone except cardiac patients.

Koma-ga-take erupted in October 1970 – a fascinating event I was lucky enough to see. Following an explosion, gases shrieked from the earth like the exhaust of a hundred jet engines, then molten rock from underground slowly clogged the entrance, finally sealing the tube. For many minutes the air was silent until, as amazed onlookers watched, a dome began to form and smoke rose over it. Finally, when it had reached a height of about four metres and a diameter of perhaps 10, the pressure became too much and the dome shattered, hurling fragments high into the air. Towards dusk, the red glow of rock chunks could be seen as they traced arcs in the air. The cycle repeated itself again and again.

The tens of thousands of tons of rock

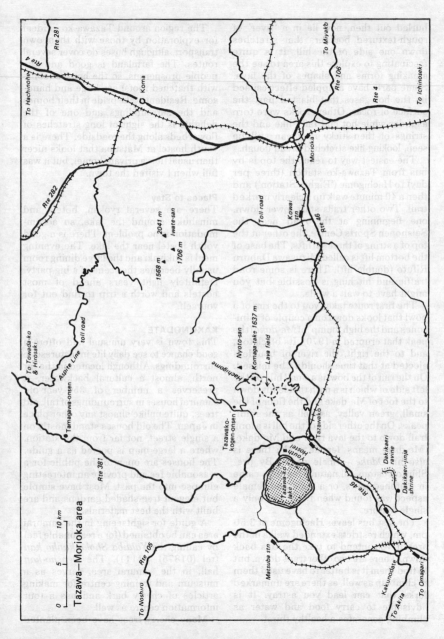

Tazawa–Morioka area

hurled out then, now lie in a 'river' of rough-textured boulders that stretches down one side of the hill. It is quite fascinating to explore this area to see the amazing forms and shapes of the lava. Some parts have a rippled effect caused by the hot gases that blasted past the surface of rocks. Others rocks were torn asunder while hot and taffy-like and the strings of then-sticky rock can still be seen, looking like stretched bread dough.

The easiest way to reach the top is by bus from Tazawa-ko station (three per day) to Hachigome ('Eighth Station') and then a 40 minute walk up a clearly marked trail. Two other trails start lower down, one beginning at the road near the Seishonen Sports Centre, the other at the top of a string of three ski lifts. The base of the bottom lift is called Mizusawa Daburu Rifuto (double lift). There is some road traffic and hitching is possible but you might have to wait a while.

The first route takes you to the rim of a bowl that looks down on a couple of mini-cones and the high 'bump' of *Me-dake* (the peak that erupted in 1970). Its black top, and to the right, the river of boulders ejected at that time shouldn't be missed. On the rim of the bowl is a small hill, on the left side of which is a path that leads down to the foot of Me-dake and the floor of the small, green valley, as well as the mini-peaks. On the other side of the hill is a long trail down to the lava river and Me-dake. (Me-dake means 'female peak'; there is also an *Odake* – 'male peak'. By pre-Shinto custom, all natural features came in matched pairs, or a male and female aspect was found when there was only a single feature.

The last bus leaves Hachigome at 3.50 pm, which restricts extended walks in the area if you intend to take the bus back down. There are two other trails down, but to find them it is better to have used them to climb up as well, as there are unmarked forks that can lead you astray. It is advisable to carry food and water as climbing generates a healthy thirst.

The region around Tazawa-ko is ideal for exploration by those with their own transport, although buses do cover several routes. The farmland is good and the people prosperous, so the houses (some with thatched roofs) are large and handsome. Residents take pride in their homes and the surroundings and one of the delights is the sight of long stretches of flowerbeds along the roadside. There is a youth hostel at Matsuba that looks nicer than usual (it is a private home), but it was full when I visited the town.

Places to Stay

There are several ryokan, hotels and minshuku around the lake, so accommodation is no problem. There is a good youth hostel near the lake. The evening meal is sukiyaki and the large dining room usually becomes the scene of a big party. Definitely light years ahead of most hostels and worth a trip to find out for yourself.

KAKUNODATE

This town is very unusual and offers a good chance to see daily life in picturesque surroundings. Although located in the far north, almost a cultural backwater, it preserves a number of 350-year-old samurai houses in surroundings of tall, old trees, quite unlike almost any other place in Japan. The old houses stand mostly on a single street, not far from the station, where a large map is posted as a guide. The houses are open to the public for a reasonable fee and provide an interesting glimpse into the past. Most have simple but elegant tree-shaded gardens and are built with the best materials.

A guide for sightseeing in the samurai area can be obtained (for a reasonable fee) by calling the *Yakuba Shoko-kanko kan* (tel (01875) 4-1111). The *Densho-kan* hall, in the samurai area, serves as a museum and training centre for making articles of cherry bark and has a tour information centre as well.

Many cherry trees have been planted

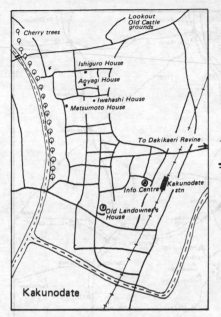

Kakunodate

Map labels:
Lookout Old Castle grounds
Cherry trees
Ishiguro House
Aoyagi House
Iwahashi House
Matsumoto House
To Dakikaeri Ravine
Info Centre
Kakunodate stn
Old Landowner's House

YOKOTE

On 15-16 February each year, this town is the scene of an interesting festival that emphasises the snowy nature of this part of Japan. The people build *kamakura*, igloo-like snow houses, in which the local children play games and serve tea, etc. The station has information on their locations.

Yamagata-ken

The Mogami-gawa river flows through the valley between Shinjo and Tsuruoka. From May to November, boat rides are available to shoot the rapids. The trip takes an hour, costs Y1500, starts at Furukuchi and finishes at Kusanagi-onsen. The former is 20 minutes by train from Shinjo; the latter 10 minutes by bus from Kiyokawa. The boat trip takes in the most scenic part of the river.

TSURUOKA

This out-of-the-way small city plays host to some of the most unusual religious activity in Japan. It is a major centre for *Shugendo* which combines Buddhist and Shinto beliefs. In the city itself is the famous temple *Zenpo-ji*, which has a picturesque pagoda and a building with hundreds of images in every imaginable pose lining its walls. It can be reached by bus from the station. The friendly people at the station information centre can put you on the right bus and are well prepared with any other info or assistance you might need.

HAGURO-SAN

Of the three mountains of Dewa (*Dewa-sanzan*), Haguro-san is the closest to Tsuruoka, the most accessible, and the most interesting to most people. At the top is *Haguro-san-jinja*, a large thatched-roof structure looking like a combination of a shrine and temple. The summit can be reached by bus from Tsuruoka station via

along the Hinokinai-gawa river which flows through the town, so the area is especially beautiful in spring.

Dakikaeri-keikoku ravine

A few km outside Kakunodate is this small gorge, near Jindai station, accessible by train or bus. While offering no spectacular vistas, it provides an enjoyable hour's walk through relaxing surrounds to the upper reaches. The most memorable impression is the intense turquoise colour of the water. The swimming is good in several places.

IWATE-SAN

This mountain (1706 metres), which dominates the area north-west of Morioka, is conical when viewed from the east, but in fact has two peaks. (Naturally it is called 'Iwate-Fuji'.) It is quite easily climbed and two popular starting points are Yanagisawa and Amihari-onsen, both accessible by bus from Morioka.

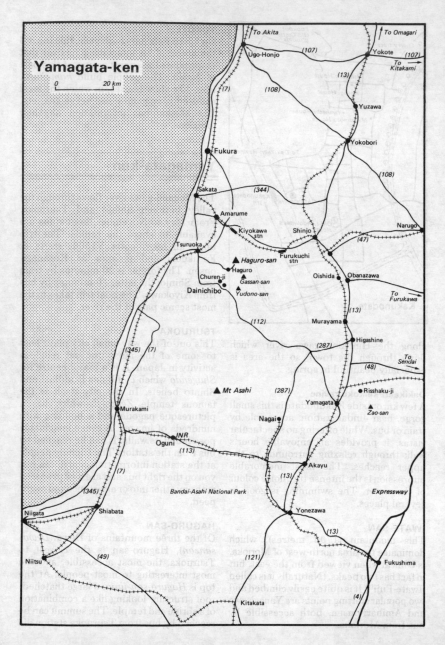

Yamagata-ken

0 _____ 20 km

To Akita
Ugo-Honjo
(107)
To Omagari
Yokote
(107)
To Kitakami
(13)
Yuzawa
(7)
(108)
Fukura
Yokobori
Sakata
(344)
(108)
Amarume
Kiyokawa stn
Shinjo
Narugo
Tsuruoka
▲ Haguro-san
Furukuchi stn
(47)
Haguro
▲
Oishida
Obanazawa
Churen-ji
Gassan-san
●
Dainichibo
Yudono-san
To Furukawa
(112)
Murayama
(13)
(345) (7)
(287)
Higashine
To Sendai
(48)
▲ Mt Asahi
(287)
● Risshaku-ji
Murakami
Yamagata
▲ Zao-san
JNR
Nagai
Oguni
(113)
(7)
Akayu
(13)
(345)
Bandai-Asahi National Park
Expressway
Niigata
Shiabata
Yonezawa
(49)
(13)
Niitsu
(121)
Fukushima
Kitakata
(4)

a toll road. On the mountain you can still see the tiny huts used by pilgrims when they visited for prayer, fasting and other forms of religious penance.

The more interesting and enjoyable way to reach the summit is the traditional way, climbing the long stairway, on foot, through a continuous grove of huge and ancient trees. From the village of Haguro, near the bus station, there is a gateway that leads to steps down to the valley below. This is one of the most beautiful forest glades in Japan. Tall trees line the walking paths and there are several small shrines, a waterfall and a picturesque bridge. Only the ever-present *semi* (cicadas) can be heard. The path leads to a five-storey pagoda, then to the base of the very long staircase that leads to the top. There are more than 1000 steps (I tried counting them!) and at one time this was the only way to go; for anyone with the time and health, it still is. Anywhere on the mountain there is a good chance of seeing *yamabushi*, pilgrims dressed in white and carrying rosaries and bells. During the day you can sometimes hear the sound of a conch-shell being blown by priests as part of their religious observances.

Places to Stay

Many temples and homes at Haguro offer accommodation. Help can be obtained at the Haguro (bus) or Tsuruoka (train) stations if you wish to stay pilgrim-style. The youth hostel is several km down the coast from Tsuruoka and can be reached by train. The information centre at the station can help with other minshuku, ryokan or hotel accommodation.

GASSAN & YUDONO-SAN

Together with Haguro-san, these form the three sacred mountains of the Shugendo sect. Gassan is the main peak, and Yudono is an outcropping on one flank. At the top of Gassan is *Gassan-jinja*, to which pilgrims and others climb in summer. Climbers are advised to take warm clothing as it gets cold even in mid-

summer. A toll road runs to the top of Yudono-san. Probably the most fascinating sights are the mummies of two ascetic priests who were voluntarily buried alive in chambers on the mountain. Both are on display, one at *Dainichibo*, the other at *Churen-ji*. Both temples can be reached by bus from Tsuruoka station to Oami, from where you walk inland for about one km. (You may need to ask for directions.)

Dainichibo The mummy here is always on display in a passageway that encircles the temple. Photos are permitted and some light enters by windows. The *mirabutsu* (mummy) is that of a man who ate no meat or grain, living (if that is the word) on nuts, grass-roots and seeds. His purpose was to remove from his body all substances (like fats) that could rot and when he reached the age of 96 (in 1783) he was buried by his disciples. They dug him up after three years and three months, dried his body and put him on display. His wish was for people to look on his body and be inspired to understand Buddhist ideas.

Churen-ji Only a kilometre or so away from Dainichibo, at Churen-ji, is the second mummy. However, this one is kept in a glass case in the main hall and special arrangements must be made to have the drape removed. This man was an itinerant preacher who travelled round Tohoku and Kanto. In 1821, during an epidemic in Tokyo that was causing blindness, he went there, prayed and as an act of atonement, tore out one eye and threw it into the Sumida river. He was known as the 'priest of the eye'. In 1829, at the age of 62, he was buried at Churen-ji, and dug up after his death.

YAMAGATA

Anyone interested in studying traditional Japanese society would find this town a good place to visit or live for a while. Each section of the town has its own traditional industry or craft and many crafts are still performed as daily work. The father of one of my friends makes his living by hand-forging and polishing agricultural shears. He makes one or two pairs a day and sells them for Y20,000 each.

Festivals

The city's main festival is *Hanagasa-matsuri* (Floral Sedge Hat Festival), on 6-8 August, when thousands of townspeople in costume dance through the streets at night.

ZAO-SAN

This mountain is best known for its winter skiing and Zao is famous for its *juhyo*, or tree monsters. The monsters are not demons that live in trees but actually the trees themselves that in winter get coated so thickly with ice and snow that they become cylinders of white creating a weird and wondrous scene.

The tree monsters can be seen (even if you don't ski) by taking the 'ropeway', a cable car which starts at Zao-sanroku base station. The 1734 metre climb takes 15 minutes and costs Y500/1000 (one-way/return), and goes up to Juhyo-kogen, the lower extremity of the juhyo. A second 'ropeway' rises a further 1839 metres through the juhyo zone to the top, Zao-Jizo-sancho. The combined cost of the two cable cars to the top is Y1000 one way, Y1700 return.

The Zao area has a large number of ski trails for varying levels of skill, and plenty of ski lifts. The 'ropeway' to the summit can also be used repeatedly for skiing through the juhyo zone and costs Y500 per trip.

A year-round attraction of the Zao area is Zao Okama, a caldera lake about 300 metres across. The scenery here is desolate and interesting for the shapes and colours of the rocks.

Places to Stay

There are many hotels, ryokan and minshuku scattered around the mountain, many at onsen (hot spring sites). The largest concentration is along the Zao Echo Line toll road that passes along the southern flank. There are also some lodges on the upper levels, including *Juhyogen Lodge* at the peak. Almost any travel agent can provide information and make reservations.

Getting There

The simplest access to the Zao area is from Yamagata station by the hourly bus to Zao-onsen (45 minutes). An alternative is to take the less frequent bus from Kaminoyama station to Zao-bo-daira and Karita-chushajo; or from Yamagata station to the same two places via Zao-onsen. As with other popular ski areas, there are direct bus services in winter from locations in Tokyo; buses for Zao leave from Ueno station.

YAMADERA

The main attraction of the Yamagata area lies several km out of town. Yamadera ('mountain temple') is properly known as *Risshaku-ji*. The buildings are scattered around the heavily wooded mountainside. Some are perched at the edge of precipices and look as if they will topple at any time. It takes two to three hours of climbing to visit the various temples. The place is best visited with a friend as the exploration can become a bit boring on your own. Access is from Yamadera station, which is reached by bus or train from Yamagata or Sendai.

YONEZAWA

Formerly a castle town of the Uesugi family, the small town is now noted for the tombs of 12 generations of the family. They resemble 12 small wooden shrines laid out in a row beneath tall trees. A bus runs from Yonezawa station.

From Yonezawa, a local road connects with Nishi-Azuma Skyline toll road, which leads to the Bandai-san area (described in the northward section). Route 121 which goes over a mountain range from Yonezawa to Kitakata and Aizu-Wakamatsu is a twisty gravel road in parts, with no buses listed and little traffic. The west coast is also easily accessible from the Yonezawa area; and from Kitakata and Aizu-Wakamatsu Route 49 takes you the 120 km westward to Niigata, a gateway to Sado Island.

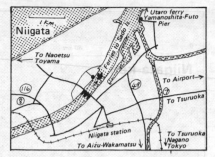

Niigata-ken

NIIGATA

Located on the Japan Sea almost due north of Tokyo, Niigata is an international port of entry and one of the ports for sailing to nearby Sado-ga-shima island.

Tsuruoka (Yamagata-ken) is straight up the coast, but the terrain is not terribly interesting along the way as Niigata lies on a large flat plain in an area which produces more rice than any other prefecture in Japan. The trip south-west is also unexciting. Travellers planning a journey in that direction can make a trip to Sado Island, then return to Honshu at Naoetsu, from where road and rail lead south to Nagano and Matsumoto (Nagano-ken); or west to the Northern Japan Alps/Noto Peninsula areas and inland to Gifu-ken.

Information

There is little to see in Niigata. If you have a few hours to kill, pick up a copy of the glossy brochure *Sight Seeing Niigata* (trilingual – in Russian even!) and see if there's anything that interests you. Copies are available at the information office at the station.

Festivals

12-18 April: *Hakusan-jinja matsuri.* One feature is masked dances by shrine maidens.

20-23 August: *Niigata-matsuri* On the last day of the festival there is a spectacular display of fireworks near Bandai-bashi bridge.

Places to Stay

There are hotels and other accom-modation in Niigata. Assistance may be obtained at the information office in the station. There is a youth hostel on the outskirts of town (tel 0252 29-0935).

Getting There

Niigata is about four hours from Tokyo by express train and is the main port for ferry and hydrofoil services to Sado Island (there is also an air service). Further details are given in the section on Sado Island. The dock can be reached from the station in about 20 minutes on foot, or by bus 14.

The ferry from Niigata to Otaru (Hokkaido) is the most economical way to reach Hokkaido from the north coast. Ferries leave from Yamanoshita-futo (pier), which can be reached by bus 7 from the station.

Niigata airport receives international flights from Khabarovsk (USSR). Many passengers on the Trans-Siberian Railway use this service as there are not enough ferries to Yokohama. The airport is a few km north-east of the city centre; buses connect with Niigata station.

NAOETSU

Situated on the coast south-west of Niigata, Naoetu's main attraction is the ferry service from Naoetsu-wan (bay) to Ogi on Sado Island. If you're travelling south by road (along Route 18) through Naoetsu towards Nagano keep your eyes open for the many old-fashioned pre-war wooden buildings. These old wooden

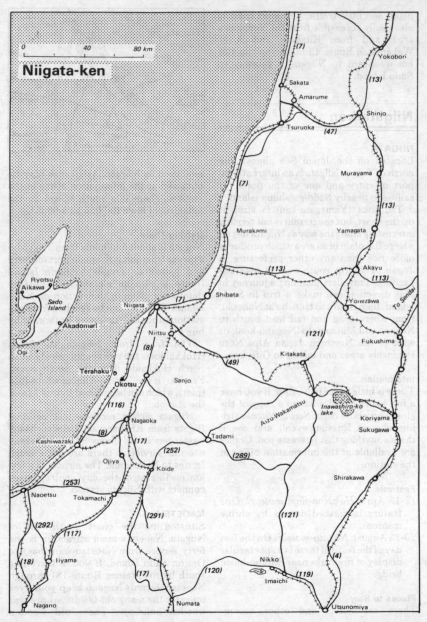

Niigata-ken

0   40   80 km

houses and shops have sliding wood and glass front doors, and canopies that extend over the sidewalk from the buildings. They aren't worth a special trip but do provide a glimpse of something that has vanished almost everywhere else in the country in the rush to plate glass and brick.

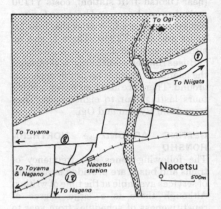

SADO ISLAND

Sado-ga-shima is the fifth largest of the islands of Japan. The main attraction here is the remoteness. Despite the large number of sightseers annually (about one million), the people of Sado continue much as they have done for decades or even centuries. It is like most island communities – the people are more friendly and the pace of life is slower. These, of course, are not things a visitor can actually see but if you have a feeling or atmosphere you should enjoy a visit.

The island is made up of two long, oval-shaped mountain ranges with a fertile valley sandwiched between them.

Ryotsu

The main town on Sado is Ryotsu, a small-townish port city at the north-east end of the valley. Starting from here, one route (along the south side of the valley) first passes *Honma-ke Noh* theatre, where performances of local dances and folk

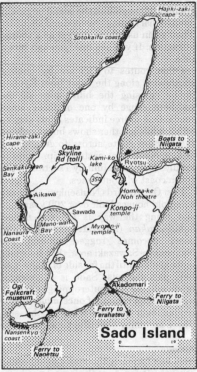

theatre are given during the summer. Check locally for times.

Konpo-ji temple

This is located in a forest setting, 30 minutes from Ryotsu by bus.

Myosen-ji temple

Set in a forest this temple has a 21-metre tall pagoda.

Ogi

This city lies near the south-west corner of the island. It is the other major port for boats to Honshu.

In Ogi harbour there is a chance of seeing 'washtub' boats – perfectly circular, flat-bottomed boats made in the manner of staved barrels. They were once a common sight around the island originally used for harvesting seaweed and shellfish. Their main use these days is as a tourist attraction. If you see one, you can hire a ride.

Other routes to Ogi are by circling south-west along the coast from Ryotsu, or by crossing the hilly spine of the southern range by one of three small roads. One source indicates a bus service on all, while another shows buses only on the western route across to Akadomari and around the eastern tip. Inquire locally. There is definitely a section of the south coast without buses.

Past Ogi, towards Nansenkyo, there are many old houses built over 200 years ago and along the way is the *Ogi mingei hakubutsukan* (folkcraft museum). The coast becomes rugged around the Nansenkyo-Sawazaki area, then becomes quite gentle until the far side of Mano-wan bay, past Sawada. Sado is of volcanic origin and the rock outcroppings have the weird shapes typical of once-molten lava, eroded over the centuries by the sea. There are many beautiful views.

Aikawa

This was formerly the major gold mining centre of Japan, once the largest producer in the Orient. Its miners were often prisoners, many of whom died here. The gold is nearly gone now but visitors can tour one of the mines, Sodayu-ko, which started about 360 years ago. Most of its passages are low and narrow. Mechanised displays (robots) show how the mining was done by hand.

Continuing up the coast, you pass more pretty coastal scenery and indented bays with the Sotokaifu-kaigan coast the most attractive.

Getting There & Getting Around

The main port for boats to the mainland is Ryotsu. During the peak season there are up to seven hydrofoils a day to and from Niigata. The trip takes one hour and costs Y5300. There are also up to nine ordinary

boats per day that take about 2½ hours and cost a minimum of Y1730. There is one boat a day between Niigata and Akadomari; it costs Y1550 and takes 3½ hours, leaving Niigata in the afternoon and Akadomari in the late morning.

Another boat service runs once a day each way between Akadomari and Terahaku (near Okotsu JNR station), costs Y1190 and takes two hours; and between Ogi and Naoetsu there are four a day that take 2½ hours and cost Y1910. There is also an airport near Ryotsu.

Buses run between the major centres on the island, so there is no problem getting around. There are also tour buses offering tours lasting four to eight hours. They leave from Ryotsu and Ogi.

GETTING AROUND – NORTHERN HONSHU

The following times and frequency of trains and buses are provided as samples of services available at the time of writing. Although there is a large degree of repetitiveness of schedules from year to year, there is no guarantee that any particular service will be as listed. Be sure always to check travel plans with an up-to-date *Jikokuhyo* (book of timetables). Because of lack of demand or roads impassible due to snow, many of the services described are suspended from early November to late April.

Trains

There is a good network of JNR lines in northern Japan: a line along both east and west coasts; two roughly parallel lines up through most of the middle; and several crosswise linking lines.

In addition there is a Shinkansen super express line (up to 240 km/hr) linking the region with Tokyo. This line was originally intended to go through Aomori on its way, via a tunnel under the Tsugaru strait to Hokkaido. However, economic reality struck hard and the line was terminated about 80 per cent of the way to Aomori, at Morioka, a considerable distance above

Sendai. Via the quickest express the time from Tokyo to Sendai, the largest city in the region, will be one hour 53 minutes; and to Morioka, 2¾ hours.

Buses

Long distance bus services are not highly developed in Japan. However, there is a convenient overnight bus service in each direction – Tokyo to Sendai and Tokyo to Yamagata. They leave Tokyo at 10 pm and 10.30 pm respectively and reach Sendai/Yamagata at 6 am/6.40 am the next morning. In the opposite direction times are: 10 pm/6 am and 9.30 pm/5.40 am for Sendai and Yamagata respectively.

The fare for both is Y4800, almost exactly the coach railway fare (Y4100 cheaper than the Shinkansen to Sendai) and they save the cost of a night's accommodation. The seats recline, so they're reasonably comfortable, especially the seats at the back where there is more leg room. The buses depart from the bus terminal on the Yaesu (east) side of Tokyo station.

In addition to these long-distance buses, there are many other bus routes within the region to places not served by railways, or between large centres via mountainous routes where railways would be difficult to build. These are shown in *Jikokuhyo* as blue lines, a double line representing JNR bus services on which a Japanrail pass may be used.

Hokkaido

Hokkaido is the northernmost major island of Japan. Although it was settled quite late in Japanese history and, visibly at least, has little of historic interest, it is the home of an aboriginal people who are not related to the Yamato Japanese (who comprise almost the entire population of Japan). And there is evidence that the island has been occupied for about 23,000 years.

Hokkaido's strong suit is natural beauty and outdoor activities and there is a definite flavour of eastern North America. In the river valleys, where most of the population has settled, the terrain features broad, rolling valleys flanked by low wooded hills. Because the climate of Hokkaido is colder than that of the south islands, traditional farming methods and crops did not succeed, so foreign experts (mostly American) were brought in as advisors. With them came large farms, dry-land crops, barns, silos and cows (a rarity elsewhere). These are very exotic to the Japanese but of limited interest to foreign visitors. Most travellers will prefer the coastal, mountain and lake regions where the characteristic Hokkaido scenery, mostly of volcanic origin, can be enjoyed.

History and People

Hokkaido was long a frontier region of little interest to the central governments in the south of Japan. The major groups of inhabitants were native peoples of various origins (mostly unknown), including the Ainu, Gilyak and Oroke.

Not much is known about the Ainu, who also live on Sakhalin Island. Until recently it was thought they were a Caucasian race but now no one is sure. It seems their languages have no known relatives elsewhere in the world, although there are tribes in Siberia with similar shamanist forms of worship based on a cult of the bear and it's been observed that Ainu and Navajo music is similar.

It has also become known that they are recent arrivals on Hokkaido, having settled only about 800 years ago, displacing an even more mysterious people who seem to have occupied the island for much longer. Ainu used to live on Honshu as well and possibly as far south as Kyushu but they were a peaceful people and no match for the more aggressive Yamato Japanese, so they were slowly pushed back into the remoteness of Hokkaido.

Ainu men are very hirsute and the large number of Japanese men (compared to Chinese and Korean) with a heavy beard is probably a legacy of intermarriage early in Japanese history.

Up to the end of the last century, the Ainu lived a life of hunting and fishing and engaged in small-scale agriculture of dry-field crops (no rice). By the last decade of the century the encroaching settlements of the southern Japanese had almost destroyed the Ainus' way of life, and they were a dispirited people seemingly on the way to extinction. Whether in their true interests or as a means of eliminating those who were different the central government adopted a policy to assimilate the Ainu into the mainstream of Japanese life. As a result they have adopted Japanese names, language and customs and would be difficult to identify by sight.

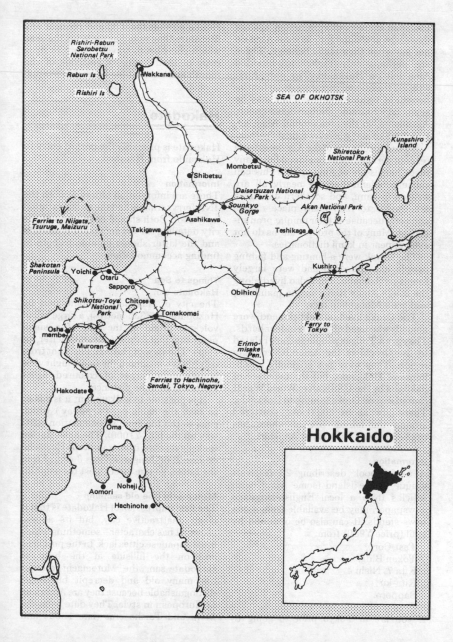

In Japan there is discrimination against those who are 'different', so most Ainu do not advertise their racial heritage. There are perhaps only 15,000 full-blooded Ainu left on Hokkaido. The only Ainu wearing traditional garments do so for the benefit of visiting tourists. They may be seen at Shiraoi, Noboribetsu-onsen, Asahikawa, in the area around Akan-ko, Kutcharo-ko and wherever tourists gather.

No one speaks any of the Ainu languages (except perhaps for a few elders) but many place names are of Ainu origin. This can cause problems because nearly all are written in kanji, and southern Japanese are unable to read many place names correctly because of their unique pronunciation. Many of the pronunciatons do not even appear in kanji dictionaries.

The Gilyak were a hunting and fishing people like the Ainu and were largely found on Sakhalin. They also lived along the lower Amur River on the mainland, and are a Mongolian race.

The Oroke lived on Sakhalin and were nomads who lived off their reindeer herds. They are a Tungas people and are related to the Orochi of the Amur River delta region. They were not originally inhabitants of Hokkaido, but the takeover of Sakhalin by the USSR after World War II caused several Oroke to move to Hokkaido. There are about 30 Oroke scattered around the island, one of whom has opened a small museum at Abashiri.

Information

A useful book describing 23 festivals unique to the island (some Ainu), with articles from a local English-language newspaper, may be available from some news-stands. It can also be obtained by mail (price Y980) from:

Tast Corp.
Tokan Bldg.
Kita 7, Nishi 4
Kita-ku
Sapporo.

If you are in Tokyo prior to going to Hokkaido visit the TIC and request any literature they would suggest for the area which you plan to travel. Also pick up a copy of their listing of festivals of the month and check it for Hokkaido events.

Hakodate

Hakodate is primarily the port of entry to Hokkaido from Honshu.

Information

There are information offices at both the JNR ferry terminal and the railway station next door. Both should have maps of the city detailing the old section of Hakodate and the latter should be able to help in finding accommodation.

Things to See
Hakodate-san

The city of Hakodate is dominated by Hakodate-san (335 metres), a large hill of volcanic origin at the end of a small peninsula that forms a natural shelter for ships. The view of Hakodate at night from this hill is considered the finest night view in Japan; a carpet of coloured lights stretches into the distance.

It is possible to walk up, but it is easier to take the cable car ('ropeway') which runs to the top from a base station partway up the hill (Y1000). The base station is easily reached from tram stops Horaicho on line 2; or Jujigai on lines 3 or 5. From the latter, go one street west then uphill.

Motomachi (the old section)

The first impression of Hakodate is that it is an unattractive city, but its appeal grows. It has character – something which most Japanese cities lack. In the port area and on the hillside at the base of Hakodate-san, the Motomachi district has many old and decrepit buildings, distinguishable because they are American or European in style. They date from the Meiji and Taisho eras (late 1800s and

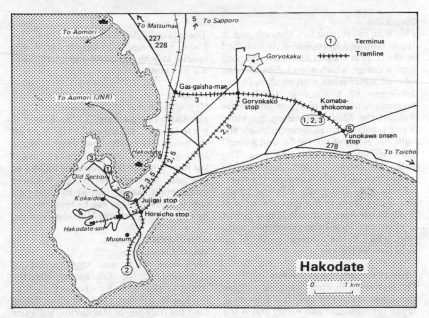

To Matsumae
To Sapporo
5
To Aomori
227
228
Goryokaku
① Terminus
Tramline
Gas-gaisha-mae
3
Goryokako
stop
Komaba-
shokomae
(1, 2, 3)
To Aomori (JNR)
Yunokawa onsen
stop
278
⑤
To Toicho
Hakodate
Old Section
Kokaido
⑤
Jujigai stop
Horaicho stop
Hakodate-san
Museum
②

Hakodate

0   1 km

early 1900s) and have been recognised by the authorities as comprising an area of historic architecture. The area is charmingly seedy for the most part, but it seems the buildings will be preserved and maintained, and probably restored in part.

There is no particular street to see, each one has its quota, but it is interesting just to wander around. Tram 3 passes by a number of such buildings near the harbour terminus, and the streets of nearby hillsides are a good area to explore. One place to look for is an old public hall, *Kokaido*, a large, ageing and sagging wooden building that resembles a Civil War era mansion from the American south.

In the same area is the Japan Orthodox Hakodate Resurrection Church, a Byzantine-style building dating from 1916 and starting to show its age. It's especially pretty at night when lit up. Nearby is the Hakodate branch of the *Higashi Honganji* temple. An amusing

sign post, one of many directing the on-foot explorer to places of interest in the area, shows a sweating priest frantically beating a *mokugyo* (wooden gong), a feature of prayers of that sect.

Like some of the old buildings, the trams in Hakodate are also a trifle decrepit and all the more charming for the nostalgia they engender. Only wooden cars (dating from 1949) are in use – the modern metal ones rusted away in the salt air.

Hakodate Museum

On the other side of the hill is Hakodate-koen (park), an attractive wooded area noted for its cherry blossoms in late April. In the park is *Hakodate Hakubutsukan* (museum) which has a good collection and a modern display of artefacts of the aboriginal races that inhabit(ed) Hokkaido. If you have time to see only one museum in Hokkaido this would be the best choice. It is close to the last two stops on tram line 2, and not too far from the Horaicho stop.

Goryokaku

This is an interesting fort, the only one in Japan built in a European style (finished in 1864). It is shaped like a five-pointed star, a design which allows defenders to rake all approaches with gunfire. It was the scene of a siege in 1868 when supporters of the Tokugawa shogunate resisted the Meiji restoration for more than a month. A small museum inside the walls has relics of the battle, and a small tower allows a view over the area. The walls themselves are low, perhaps five metres high, and there is no superstructure, only the walls and moats. It is now a park and cherry trees in the grounds make it pretty in late April and early May. The fort is close to Goryokaku-gyoen-mae tram stop, which is the common point for all tram lines in the city.

Trappist convent and monastery

The convent is located five minutes from Yunokawa station by bus. It is famous in Japan for its butter and candy and is the only Trappist convent in Japan. The Trappist monastery is located at Oshima-Tobetsu, 26 km from Hakodate.

Places to Stay

There is one youth hostel in Hakodate; it is several kilometres from the station in the hot-spring town of Yunokawa ('hot water river'), a suburb of Hakodate. From the station take a tram 5 and get off at Yunokawa-onsen (the second-last stop on the line). Be sure to get a 5 going the right way. (Trams 1, 2 and 3 go as far as the car barn, one stop before Yunokawa-onsen, which would add over half a km to the distance to the hostel.)

The hostel is located amidst resort hotels and its bath is fed with the same naturally hot (and *very* hard) water, so you can enjoy the privilege without the cost of a resort hotel. The hostel tends to be quite full on weekends. If you arrive early in the day, consider staying in the scenic Onuma area, about 25 km away.

Getting Around

There is an all day tram-and-bus ticket for about Y600 and a 10-tickets for Y1000 special at both the ferry/train station and the bus station.

Hitching

If you wish to hitch to Sapporo and elsewhere immediately, it is necessary to get to Route 5. If arriving by HNF, get off the bus at Gas-gaisha-mae, which is near a large gas holder. Just before reaching it the road from the ferry terminal follows an overpass that curves to the left and intersects a major road at right angles; that is Route 5. Gas-gaisha-mae can also be reached by bus from Hakodate station.

AROUND HAKODATE

West of Hakodate

Matsumae This was the capital of Hokkaido from the 16th century, when the island was known as Ezo. It was the site of the last feudal castle to be built in Japan (and the only one in Hokkaido), but a fire destroyed the original buildings. A concrete reproduction shows the former appearance and about 5000 cherry trees make the place one of beauty from late April.

East of Hakodate

Mt Esan This is an active volcano (618 metres) with steaming vents at the summit and an oval crater. It can be climbed in about an hour and access to the base takes about 2¼ hours by bus from Hakodate.

North from Hakodate

The view from either the train or the road (Route 5) leaving Hakodate is typical of the valley scenery anywhere in Hokkaido – broad rolling farm land interspersed with numerous towns. After 25 km or so, road and rail pass through a tunnel and the scenery changes abruptly. You are suddenly confronted with the very scenic Lake Konuma, which reflects the squat volcano Komagatake. This is the entrance to Onuma Kokuritsukoen (National Park), a very enjoyable place to spend a day or two. Travellers arriving at Hakodate might consider making their way here for the first night in Hokkaido instead of Hakodate.

Koma Visible for the next 20 km or so, Koma consists of three peaks – *Sawara, Kengamine* and *Sumidamori*. It is an ugly brown ulcer on the green countryside, but is nevertheless very scenic. Originally conical, explosions have blasted the top off, leaving an elongated flat and sloping top.

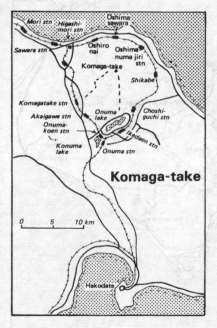

Komaga-take

Mt Higure As well as the view over Lake Konuma, the best outlook is considered to be Konuma Hill and another is the top of Mt Higure (313 metres). It is an easy walk to the top where there are three smaller craters within the large horseshoe-shaped outer rim, which is two km east-west and 1.5 km north-south, sloping towards the sea. Any of the three youth hostels in the

area will have information on the best routes. It is also possible to circle the mountain by train. From the sea side you can see distant Mt Yotei across the bay (weather permitting).

HAKODATE TO OSHAMAMBE
As Komagatake falls behind, the road and railway run parallel to the shore of Uchiura Bay for the next 70 km or so, to a point slightly beyond Oshamambe. They are seldom far from the water and travellers with the time to stop will find beachcombing in this area probably the best in Japan because the bay seems to act as a collection point for anything floating in the area. Stop anywhere distant from habitation and the beach is almost sure to be littered with hand-blown glass fishing floats that have been washed ashore. I stopped at random three times and each time found more than 20 floats within half a kilometre of where I started; carrying them all became a problem! It appears they are replenished regularly because one beach I picked over on the way north had another 25 or so by the time I returned just a month later.

The road passes through many fishing villages; draped everywhere are fishing nets with fishermen making repairs. On flat areas you can often see large pieces of *kombu*, an edible seaweed, laid out to dry.

OSHAMAMBE TO SAPPORO
There are two suggested routes between these cities. One follows the railway and Route 5 inland in a northward loop; while the other continues around the bay, then cuts inland and touches on the Lake Toyako area before continuing through mountainous terrain to Sapporo. The first passes mostly through river valleys and, near Sapporo, a dismal succession of unappealing towns, but it offers the option of a looping sidetrip through Shakotan Hanto (peninsula). The second route passes through much more attractive scenery for most of its length.

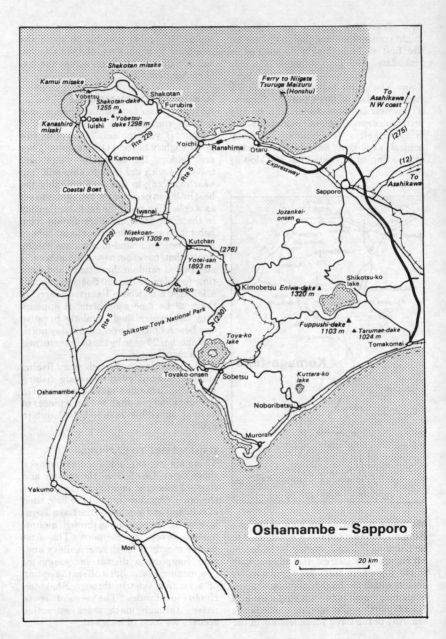

Oshamambe – Sapporo

0   20 km

The traveller who has adequate time and who plans to circle back to the Toyako area, can combine the best of both these routes by taking the first to Yoichi, circling the Shakotan Peninsula to Iwanai, then cutting over to Kutchan and Kimobetsu, and carrying on from there by the second route to Sapporo.

Oshamambe to Kutchan

Both road and rail run parallel through this region of river-valley farmland. Between Niseko and Kutchan it skirts *Mt Yotei* (1893 metres), now extinct. The top is mostly lava-covered, but the lower sections are wooded. Climbing Mt Yotei is popular with the Japanese and is not particularly difficult. (Most 'mountain climbing' in Japan is simply a matter of putting one foot in front of the other for a long enough period.) One popular route is via Hirafu station by bus to Lake Nangetsu-ko from where you begin the climb. The walk up takes about four hours, plus an hour at the top to walk around the three cauldrons. For up-to-date information try the Niseko Youth Hostel in Kutchan.

Mt Nisekoan-Nupuri (1309 metres), also near Kutchan, is rated as one of the four best ski areas in Hokkaido. There are nearby onsen for relaxing in afterward. Kombu-onsen is noted for its autumn leaves.

Kutchan to Yoichi

Yoichi is best regarded as the gateway to the Shakotan Peninsula. The town has an aquarium, and offers tours of the Nikka Distillery, near Yoichi station (Monday to Saturday).

Shakotan Peninsula

The Shakotan Peninsula is noted for its rugged scenery – cliffs rising out of the sea as high as 250 metres and the peaks of two mountains, *Yobetsu* (1298 metres) and *Shakotan* (1255 metres). Two capes mark the tip of the peninsula, Kamui and Shakotan; the former has a huge rock rising abruptly about 40 metres from the

sea. Buses run from Yoichi as far as Yobestu; from there a boat goes around to Kamoenai and Iwanai. A bus also runs between Kamoenai and Iwanai. From Iwanai you can return to Yoichi, thus completing a circle; or go to Kutchan, Kimobetsu and other destinations.

Yoichi to Sapporo

The short distance between these two cities includes the best sand beach on Hokkaido (at Ranshima), as well as shorter stretches of beach at irregular intervals. There are several prehistoric relics in the area. *Oshoro Stone Circle* is a rough circle of large stones about one metre tall, located by Ranshima-kawa river, south-east of Ranshima station. Other indications of early settlement have been found in the area, such as traces of a dwelling, pottery, tools, Oyachi Shell Mound, a fort and a cave with more than 200 pictographs on the walls (both in the Fugoppe area, estimated to be about 1500 years old).

Mt Tengu, three km south-west of Otaru station offers good skiing.

As noted earlier, Otaru is a ferry port with services to and from Niigata, Tsuruga and Maizuru. There is also an overnight boat from Otaru to Rishiri Island off the far north coast of Hokkaido. More details on that are given later.

To Sapporo via Lake Toya-ko

This route continues around the shores of Uchiura Bay, then turns inland to Lake Toya-ko and continues through highland scenery to Sapporo. It is by far the more scenic route and is recommended for travellers in a hurry or for those who will be going in this direction only once. From Toya station (on the bay) there is a regular bus service to Toya-ko onsen on Lake Toya-ko. (The many attractions of the Toya-ko area are described in detail in the section on Shikotsu-Toya National Park).

From Toya-ko, Route 230 climbs to a plateau, passing areas of forest land with broken-top trees, smashed by rock ejected

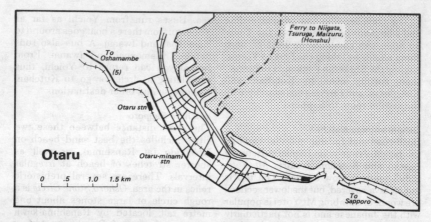

in the 1977 eruption of *Usu-san*. As the road climbs beside the lake, you get a superb view of Nakajima, a cluster of small volcanic islands poking up in the middle of Shikotsuko (Nakajima means middle island.) Other points of interest are Usu-san, probably steaming profusely, and Showa Shinzan. Once on the plateau, the road leaves the lake and the view of *Yotei-san* begins to dominate the landscape. The route from there to Sapporo passes through a very pretty mountain and farming region with few built-up areas.

The road goes via Jozankei-onsen, which is one of the best known spas in Japan. Previous notes on Japanese onsen apply equally here and mixed bathing, formerly the custom here, has gone the way of the auk. At best it is worth a walk around the town; autumn is the best time for such a tour as the leaves are beautiful.

Sapporo

A rarity among Japanese cities, Sapporo is laid out with streets at right angles and has an address system that makes sense to foreigners. (This is true for many other cities on Hokkaido). The reason for this is that Sapporo was only founded in 1869

when the *Kaitakushi* (Commissioner of Colonisation) was stationed here to establish the city as the capital of Hokkaido. Like other 'instant cities' it lacks the soul and the element of disorder that gives older cities their character. The somewhat sterile atmosphere is, however, offset partly by many parks and gardens. Foreigners find it a pleasant place to live, but as a tourist goal it is rather low-ranking. It is at its best when the bright lights of the Susukino district give it a magical touch. Those with a larger budget will find it has the best night life north of Tokyo with more than 3500 bars and cabarets.

The main street, O-dori is famed for its great width (105 metres), but this is a deceptive statistic because most of the space is occupied by a park-like boulevard. This is a popular place in summer when visitors sit around, usually huddled under the inadequate number of trees. (Why do city planners seem to love huge open spaces which become intolerably hot under the summer sun?) At the east end of the boulevard is the TV tower (147 metres) which gives a good view over the entire city.

Information

The first move is to pick up a map from the tourist information centre in the station.

They have a good one showing the points of interest and subway lines and the text gives enough information for most travellers. The JNTO map of Japan also has an adequate Sapporo map on the back.

Things to See

The Botanical Garden The Botanical Garden has about 5000 species of plants from Hokkaido and the rest of the world. It is an attractive setting for a stroll or picnic.

Museums

A number of museums are located in the gardens, the best-known being the Batchelor Museum of Ainu artefacts – named after an English minister who lived in Sapporo for 40 years. The house was moved to its present location after his death and displays his collection of items of daily use. The style of the display is very old and obviously hasn't been touched in years, but the collection is good and worth seeing, although most labels are in Japanese only. To get to the museums you first have to pay an admission fee for the gardens and then extra for each building. One of the other buildings only has a tatty collection of stuffed animals and birds of Hokkaido, including the collection of Blakiston, another Englishman who noted the difference in distribution of animal and plant life between Honshu and Hokkaido. To be sure of seeing the Ainu

museum section, ask: *Kore wa Batchelor no Ainu hakubutsukan des'ka?* Recent information suggests the museum has been closed, so check on the current situation before going.

The Clock Tower Building This is the only Russian-style structure left on Hokkaido, the clock of which has been a Sapporo landmark since 1881.

Maruyama Park and Maruyama Natural Forest Remnants of natural forest that provide recreation grounds and ski slopes in winter.

Mt Moiwa This provides a lookout over the city. It is accessible by cable car from near Ropeway Iriguchi Mae subway station.

Festivals

Sapporo is best known for its Snow Festival, the first weekend of February, when O-dori boulevard is built up with huge snow and ice sculptures of people, famous buildings and mythological figures. These sculptures are probably the most impressive of any winter carnival in the world.

Shopping

The main shopping area is Tanuki-koji (Badger Alley), an eight-block long arcade. Also well known is the underground shopping arcade that stretches from the TV tower under the boulevard and then turns to run to Susukino. It reflects the cold winter climate.

Places to Stay

There are three youth hostels in the Sapporo area. By far the most convenient to reach is the one near the station.

Getting There

In addition to the JNR and road connections, Sapporo is easily reached by air from other parts of Japan. The actual airport is at Chitose, about an hour away by bus. (The JNR bus terminal is beside the station.) The city of Tomakomai is only a short distance beyond Chitose and is the port of entry for ferries connecting with Tokyo, Sendai and Hachinohe.

Getting Around
Sapporo has the nicest subway in Japan. Like those in Montreal and Paris, it runs on rubber tyres and is therefore very quiet. Stations are marked in romaji at the station, but next and previous stations are labelled only only in Japanese, as are trains, maps, etc.

ASAHIKAWA
In the Chikabumi district of Asahikawa, the *Ainu Kinenkan* (memorial hall), combines a reasonably good museum with a large number of souvenir stands that sell Ainu handcrafts – mostly identical wooden bears and statuettes of Ainu people. Many

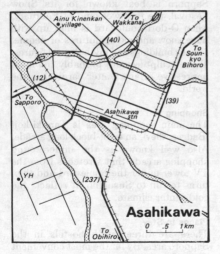

Asahikawa

Ainu live in the area. One or two (usually elderly) people may be dressed in traditional costume and delegated to satisfy tourists' cameras. Dances are performed – when a tour bus turns up. If you are going to Noboribetsu, Akan or Shiraoi, it is not worth seeking out Chikabumi.

From Asahikawa you can make a sidetrip north to Wakkanai or proceed east to the major attractions of that area.

Places to Stay
The youth hostel is quite good, has a ski tow in the back yard and you can get information on buses to Wakkanai or elsewhere. But if you arrive early in the day and are not going to Wakkanai, consider pressing on to Sounkyo, where two youth hostels sit in the midst of beautiful gorge scenery, near good hiking territory.

Rishiri-Rebun-Sarobetsu National Park

The islands of Rebun and Rishiri are combined with part of the mainland on the north-west coast to form the Rishiri-Rebun-Sarobetsu National Park.

WAKKANAI
Wakkanai is as far north in Japan as it is possible to go. It is 250 km from Asahikawa and the road passes mostly through flat land where the scenery consists of spreading farms, barns and silos. Modern farming machinery is the rule here so if you see a farmer on horseback, he will be riding for pleasure.

Wakkanai is reminiscent of Reykjavik in Iceland. The houses are low, with brightly coloured roofs in red, green and blue. The landscape around Wakkanai is quite different from that of most of Japan – it is windswept, with low scrub and few trees along the coast. In late summer the grass is a picturesque golden colour and there is a feeling of splendid isolation, obtainable in so few places in Japan. Those who like the romance of the Hebrides will enjoy the atmosphere of the coast near Wakkanai, especially to the north and west around Cape Noshappu-

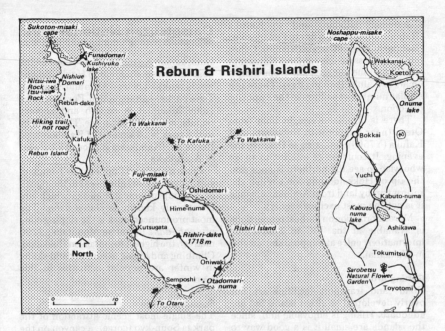

misaki. In late summer the light has a particular 'northern' quality, giving a characteristic mood and atmosphere. The main industry of the district is fishing which also adds to the local colour.

RISHIRI & REBUN ISLANDS

A very popular excursion with the Japanese is the boat trip from Wakkanai to the islands of Rishiri and Rebun. Although close together, the two islands have a totally different history. Rebun has been there for millions of years and was formed by an upthrust of the earth's crust. Rishiri, on the other hand, is a comparative 'youngster', only a few hundred-thousand years old, formed when a submarine volcano built itself above the ocean surface. The picturesque cone of *Rishiri-san* (1719 metres), now gullied by eons of rain, remains as a reminder of the eruption. The magnificent isolation, unspoiled environment, beautiful scenery, seabirds, wildflowers in profusion and

little fishing villages, are the main drawcards to these islands.

An almost circular road runs around Rishiri and bus transport is available (six per day, each way). Hiking courses are set out and connect the major points of interest around the island. Scenic spots include the view of Rishiri-san over the small lakes Hime-numa and Otadomarinuma, and many seascapes and capes that jut into the sea.

Rebun is very low, but nonetheless offers scenic views near Nishi-Uedomani, the view of Tadoshima Island from Cape Sukoton-misaki and the towering rock Jizo-iwa.

Places to Stay
There are three youth hostels on Rebun and one on Rishiri.

Getting There
Access from Wakkanai is by Higashi Nihonkai ferry; two boats a day go to

Oshidomari (Rishiri) and to Kafuka (Rebun); there is one a day to Funadomari (Rebun) and to Kutsugata (Rishiri). Other ferries of the same line run from Katsugata to Kafuka (one per day) and from Oshidomari to Kafuka (two per day). There is a similar number of sailings in the opposite direction.

There is also an overnight boat from Otaru (near Sapporo) to Kutsugata and Kafuka (Y7500), returning to Otaru in the evening. It could be of interest to those who wish to see the northern islands and the tip of Hokkaido but don't relish the return trip by land from Asahikawa, since it is not the most exciting scenery.

More information on the boat connections is available at the TIC in Tokyo, the information centre at Sapporo station and in Wakkanai.

Getting Around

Roads and transport facilities are not overly developed on either island but are adequate. Hiking is enjoyable and, since the islands are small it is a good way to look around.

On Rebun you can take the bus one way and hike back in one day. There is sure to be young Japanese people doing this and they're usually happy to have an extra person tag along. Many will be camping.

SAROBETSU

Sarobetsu is an area of swampy coastline and sand dunes known for the beauty of its wildflowers. It can be reached by bus from Wakkanai to Bokkai; or by train to Bokkai (the northern most point of entry); or to Toyotomi, from where a bus is available (through the middle of the park) to Wakasakanai.

The most important part is *Sarobetsu Gensai-kaen* (Natural Flower Garden); it is about 15 minutes from Toyotomi station. Forget it in the spring, the area floods annually.

Daisetsuzan National Park

Daisetsuzan Kokuritsu-koen is one of the best-known scenic areas in Hokkaido and would rank just behind Akan and Shikotsu-Toya parks as an attraction. For those who enjoy hiking it is superb and is very popular among the Japanese. The entrance to the park is 16 km east of Kamikawa on Route 39. (Kamikawa is about 45 km east of Asahikawa.)

From Kamikawa ('upper river') onward, you get occasional glimpses (to the right), of a group of volcanic peaks which are collectively known as *Daisetsuzan*. The most pronounced peak is the sloping cone of *Asahi-dake* ('Sunrise Mountain', 2290 metres), the highest mountain on Hokkaido. Climbing and hiking in summer and skiing in winter are popular activities in this area.

Soun-kyo gorge

The single most scenic attraction of the park is Soun-kyo (gorge), a canyon on the Ishikari river extending 24 km from the entrance to the park. Rock walls rise sharply on both sides of the road and outcroppings of jagged rock jut from cliff faces. In the middle of the gorge is the hot-spring resort town of Soun-kyo-onsen, with a number of resort hotels and two youth hostels. It is a base for climbing and hiking through Daisetsuzan.

About three km further along the gorge are two picturesque waterfalls, Ryusei-no-taki and Ginga-no-taki, which are close to each other but separated by huge Tensho-iwa ('Heavenly Castle Rock').

Near the end of the gorge are Kobako and Obako ('small box' and 'large box'), closely enclosed sections of the gorge. The walls of the 'boxes' and much of the gorge are columnar basalt, lava that cooled into large crystals. Australians from Victoria will find the gorge like a hundred Hanging Rocks laid side by side. The way in which both were formed is similar.

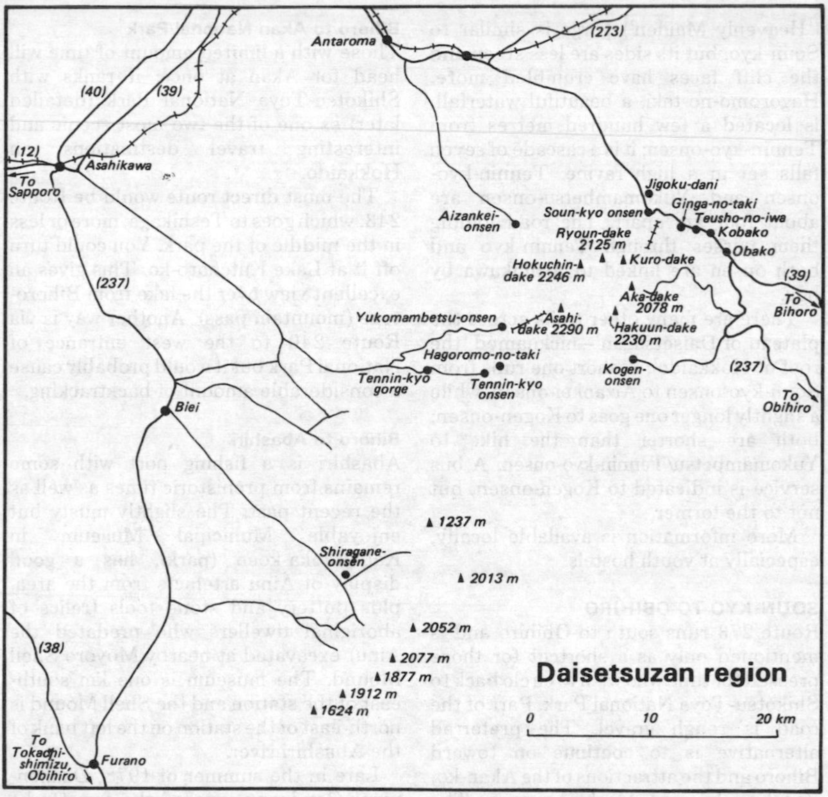
Antaroma
(273)
(40)
(39)
(12)
Asahikawa
To Sapporo
Jigoku-dani
Ginga-no-taki
Soun-kyo onsen
Aizankei-onsen
Teusho-no-iwa
Kobako
Ryoun-dake 2125 m
Kuro-dake
Obako
Hokuchin-dake 2246 m
(39)
(237)
Aka-dake 2078 m
To Bihoro
Yukomambetsu-onsen
Asahi-dake 2290 m
Hakuun-dake 2230 m
Hagoromo-no-taki
Kogen-onsen
(237)
Tennin-kyo gorge
Tennin-kyo onsen
To Obihiro
Biei
1237 m
Shiragane-onsen
2013 m
2052 m
(38)
2077 m
1877 m
1912 m
1624 m
Daisetsuzan region
0
10
20 km
To Tokachi-shimizu, Obihiro
Furano

Exploring Daisetsuzan

The area known as Daisetsuzan (Great Snow Mountain) consists of a number of volcanic peaks, all about 2000 metres high. They do not require scaling gear or great skill but do invite exploration as the terrain is easy to walk through. It is basically an undulating plateau that fills in the area between the various peaks that make up the mountain. The view is one of small craters (some steaming), wildflowers, the crater of Daisetsuzan and open spaces with no signs of civilisation. A network of trails makes walking easy.

The best-known trail runs from Soun-kyo-onsen to Yukomambetsu-onsen; it can be walked in a day with little effort. From Soun-kyo-onsen, a cable car runs a good part of the way up the side of *Kuro-dake* ('Black Mountain', 1984 metres). From there the path is easy to follow past *Ryoun-dake* (2125 metres), *Hokuchin-dake* (2246 metres) and *Asahi-dake* (2290), to the upper station of the 'Daisetsuzan Asahi-dake ropeway' that leads down to Yukomambetsu-onsen. This resort has a good youth hostel, with a view of Asahi-dake, as well as other accommodation.

Continuing along the path you come to Hagoromo waterfall, Tennin-kyo-onsen and Tennin-kyo gorge. Tennin-kyo

('Heavenly Maiden') gorge is similar to Soun-kyo, but its sides are less steep and the cliff faces have crumbled more. Hagoromo-no-taki, a beautiful waterfall, is located a few hundred metres from Tennin-kyo-onsen; it is a cascade of seven falls set in a high ravine. Tennin-kyo-onsen and Yukomambetsu-onsen are about four km apart. The road joining them passes through Tennin-kyo and both onsen are linked to Asahikawa by bus.

There are many other trails across the plateau of Daisetsuzan – nicknamed 'the roof of Hokkaido'. A short one runs from Soun-kyo-onsen to Aizankei-onsen, while a slightly longer one goes to Kogen-onsen; both are shorter than the hike to Yukomambetsu/Tennin-kyo-onsen. A bus service is indicated to Kogen-onsen, but not to the former.

More information is available locally, especially at youth hostels.

SOUN-KYO TO OBIHIRO

Route 273 runs south to Obihiro and is mentioned only as a shortcut for those pressed for time who wish to circle back to Shikotsu-Toya National Park. Part of the road is rough gravel. The preferred alternative is to continue on toward Bihoro and the attractions of the Akan-ko, Kutcharo-ko and Mashu-ko area. The following section deals only with the route to that and other nearby areas.

SOUN-KYO TO SHIRETOKO PENINSULA

After leaving Soun-kyo, Route 39 continues eastward through Onneyu-onsen, Rubeshibe, Kitami and Bihoro. The fields around Kitami are planted with peppermint (claimed to be the world's best), and at Rubeshibe Youth Hostel there is a well-preserved steam engine of the type used in Hokkaido up till the early 1970's. Otherwise there is little of interest along the way. Like many roads that pass through the valleys of Hokkaido, this one is simply a means of getting from place to place and just has to be endured.

Bihoro to Akan National Park

Those with a limited amount of time will head for Akan at once; it ranks with Shikotsu-Toya National Park (detailed later) as one of the two most scenic and interesting travel destinations on Hokkaido.

The most direct route would be Route 243, which goes to Teshikaga, more or less in the middle of the park. You could turn off it at Lake Kutcharo-ko. This gives an excellent view over the lake from Bihoro-toge (mountain pass). Another way is via Route 240 to the west entrance of National Park but it would probably cause a considerable amount of backtracking.

Bihoro to Abashiri

Abashiri is a fishing port with some remains from prehistoric times as well as the recent past. The slightly musty but enjoyable Municipal Museum in Katsuraoka-koen (park), has a good display of Ainu artefacts from the area, plus pottery and stone tools (relics of aboriginal dwellers who predated the Ainu) excavated at nearby Moyoro Shell Mound. The museum is one km south-east of the station and the Shell Mound is north-east of the station on the left bank of the Abashiri river.

Late in the summer of 1978, Daahennieni Gendaanu, one of the few Oroke people who moved to Hokkaido from Sakhalin Island, opened a museum to keep alive the memory of his people, nomads who lived by herding reindeer. (There are still Oroke living on Sakhalin Island.) The Oroke word for the museum is *Jakkadohuni*; it may be known in Japanese as *Oroke Kinenkan*.

North of Abashiri are two lagoons, Notoro and Saroma. In this area and noted on the map in the TIC brochure on Northern Japan is the intriguing 'Coral Grass Gregarious Spot' but, alas!, there is no further explanation. It might refer to an unusual red plant that grows on swampy ground; in September the fields are bright red.

The nearest youth hostel is at Gensei-kaen (next section) or go slightly further north or south to one of the others.

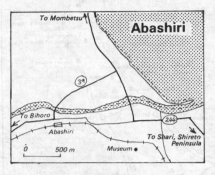

Abashiri to Akan National Park

There are two suggested routes to follow: one is direct, while the other circles around the Shiretoko Peninsula. Both offer better scenery than the route back through Bihoro.

East of Abashiri along Route 244, the first attraction is Gensei-kaen (Natural Flower Garden). This is a strip of coastal sand dune that is heavily overgrown by wildflowers (the result of a dune stabilisation program) which bloom in late June and early July. It begins at Kitahama, continues along the road for about 30 km to Shari and is the target for swarms of Japanese photographers.

Before Shari, about 25 km out of Abashiri, at Hokuto, the road turns off to Koshimizu and then on to Kawayu and Teshikaga. Kawayu is the centre of many of the attractions of Akan National Park.

Instead of turning off for Koshimizu, you can continue along Route 244 to Shari and beyond (on Route 334) to Utoro on the untamed Shiretoko Peninsula. Beyond Shari, you can look inland and see the jagged cone of *Shari-dake* (1545 metres), and later, the rounded outline of *Kaibetsu-dake* (1419 metres). Shari-dake is also visible along much of the length of the direct route.

SHIRETOKO PENINSULA

Shiretoko is an Ainu word meaning 'end of the Earth', and it lives up to its name. The end of the peninsula is a national park, the most 'primitive' in Japan. There is a small number of hiking trails; and roads go along both the north-west and south-east coasts, but not to the tip. A single road crosses it, from Utoro to Rausu.

From the middle to the tip there are three major mountains, *Rausu-dake* (1661 metres), *Io-san* (1563 metres) and *Shiretoko-dake* (1254 metres). At the base of the peninsula is *Kaibetsu-dake* and between it and Rausu-dake is a smaller peak.

Io-san is one of the most unusual volcanoes on earth – when it erupts, it emits pure sulphur. During its most recent eruption, in 1936, more than 15,000 tons of sulphur poured out. The volcanoes (all but Io-san are extinct) are a continuation of the chain that extends through the Kuril chain to Alaska; on Hokkaido, this is the Chishima volcanic zone.

It is almost impossible, however, to see the mountains while travelling along the road, which passes so close to the base of the hills that it has often been hacked out of the rock. The best way to see the beauty and splendour of the peninsula is by boat (detailed later).

The cape is famous for its rugged cliffs that rise as much as 200 metres from the sea and stretch up to 10 km without a break. The cliffs are noted for their black-and-white stripes, layers of volcanic rock alternating with sedimentary rock. Time, wind and water have sculpted them into many fanciful shapes which resemble real objects and beings.

Hot springs There are several places along the shores where hot-spring waters collect in pools near the water's edge, making natural *rotemburo* (open-air pools). One is located near Kamuiwakka-no-taki waterfall. These are popular, especially with young vacationers. There's no charge; just take your clothes off and hop in.

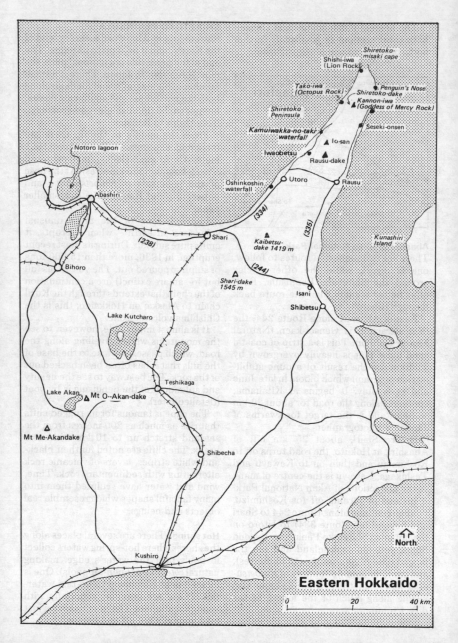

Eastern Hokkaido

Walks One place that rewards hiking is the Shiretoko-Go-ko (five lakes) area near Iwaobetsu. Another destination is Io-san and its two large craters and fuming vents. The four-hour hike begins near Kamuiwakka waterfall. Visible on the seabottom near here is yellow sulphur from the 1936 eruption. Information on other trails can be obtained locally; youth hostels are usually invaluable for such help.

Places to Stay

There are five hostels on the peninsula, three near Utoro (Utoro, Utoro-onsen and Iwaobetsu), and two near Rausu. There is also one each near the north and south bases of the peninsula, Shibetsu and Shari. The former has a Genghis Khan supper similar to that described later for the Shikotsu-ko hostel.

Getting There

In past years there were boats around the tip of the peninsula between Utoro and Rausu but as of 1984 there are only excursions out of Utoro to the tip, Shiretoko-misaki cape, in summer only. There is a 3¾ hour trip (once a day) that costs Y4770; and a 90 minute trip (five per day) that costs Y1850.

Kunashiri Island

This, along with the islands of Etorofu, Shikotan and the Habomai group, was seized by the USSR two weeks after the end of World War II. This was contrary to the Yalta Agreement and there is no legal basis for the occupation because the islands had always been indisputably part of Japanese territory. The issue is very much alive in Hokkaido and you can see numerous signs that show the map of Hokkaido and the occupied islands, a reminder of the Soviet action. Residents of the peninsula would like to have access to the rich fishing grounds around the islands but this is not likely to eventuate because the Soviets have been increasing their presence there in recent years.

Kunashiri can be seen from a boat or from parts of the south-east coast of the peninsula.

Akan National Park

This is one of the two major scenic regions of Hokkaido. The attractions can be divided into two areas, those centred around Kutcharo-ko (lake) and those around Akan-kohan.

KUTCHARO-KO AREA

The main attraction of this area is the remnant of a gigantic volcanic crater, the bounds of which are now difficult to discern. The present body of water is only a small part of the former huge lake. Over time the level of land has changed and new smaller volcanoes have popped up. A good landmark for sightseeing in the area is Kawayu railway station.

Kawayu-onsen

About three km from Kawayu station, Kawayu-onsen is a typical hot-spring resort, full of hotels (most rather costly) and streets lined with souvenir shops – most of which have captive bear cubs or Ainu wood carvers as the attraction. There is a youth hostel in the town.

Kutcharo-ko

This is a caldera lake, but its circular shape has been changed beyond recognition by the intrusion of later volcanoes. Due to the high mineral content the water is a very unusual green, but the nearby terrain is the same level so vantage points high enough to see the colour of the lake are not conveniently located. The best view can be obtained from high ground like Bihoro-toge (pass) on the road from Bihoro. The lake is an enjoyable place to relax and the hostel on its shore uses the baths of the neighbouring hotel, so you have the advantage of a visit to a resort without the painful cost. The bath is quite

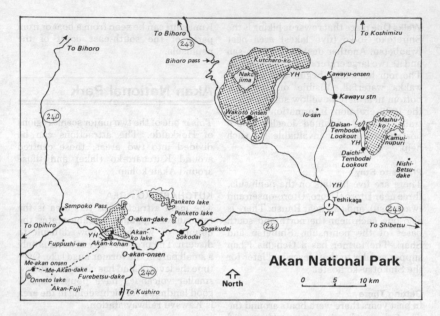

Akan National Park

memorable, with continually overflowing hot water in a pool four metres square and about knee-deep; smooth flat pebbles on the bottom give an unusual feeling underfoot. Large windows give a view out over the lake towards *Mokoto-san* (1000 metres). On my first visit to this hostel (in 1970) hostellers were accommodated in the resort itself, but I'm not sure if travellers late in the season still get this treatment.

Wakoto-hanto
A small bump on the map at the south end of the lake indicates this mini-peninsula, little higher than water level. Hot-spring water rises from below and feeds two open-air baths at Wakoto-onsen, (both are free and mixed); and at Sunayu it warms the sand of the beach (Sunayu means 'hot sand'). There is a camping ground on the peninsula as well as others along the shore. There may be performances of Ainu dances at Sunayu during the summer.

Mashu-ko
Nearby is the remarkable and beautiful lake Mashu-ko. Situated partway up the side of a sprawling mountain, its water is claimed to be the clearest in the world. In 1978 it was clear to a depth of 34.8 metres (41.6 metres in 1911). It is, however, extremely difficult and dangerous to try to reach the water's edge. Like many other calderas, the walls of the old volcano that encloses it rise very steeply, giving negligible foothold. It is better to be content admiring the incredible blue of the water from the two observatories or walk around the rim. Dai-ichi-Tempodai, the look-out spot nearer the town of Teshikaga, gives the better view, showing part of the crater in the peak of Kamui-nupuri, on the far side of the lake. Both observatories (the other is called Dai-san Tempodai) give a good view of the entire lake, which appears to fill two separate craters that have linked. On a sunny day when the colour of the water is the most intense, the view is quite unforgettable.

Dai-san Tempodai is 14 km from Kawayu station; the other is a little further on. There is a regular bus service in the area linking Kawayu station to Teshikaga station via Mashu-ko. Depending on the month there are five to eight buses a day. Hitching should be easy and would get around the problem of inflexible bus schedules.

Io-san

This active volcano emits volumes of steam that can be seen 10 km away on the road from Koshimizu. From two ravines in the side of the earth-brown mountain, sulphurous (smelly!) steam issues forth, gently wafting from some vents, violently jetting with a great roar from others. Around these holes, vivid yellow needles of sulphur have crystallised out of the steam. Io-san means 'sulphur mountain'.

For the ultimate in natural foods, you can buy eggs cooked by the heat of the earth in one of the little saucepan-size pools that boil endlessly. Look for the old woman near the base of the ravines.

AKAN-KO AREA

The area around Lake Akan (Akan-ko) is noted for scenic beauties, mountains, Ainu people, and a weed that behaves like a submarine. Like Kutcharo, Akan-ko is located in the remnants of a huge volcanic crater, the shape of which has also been changed beyond recognition by subsidence and the incursion of the smaller volcanic peaks, *O-Akan-dake* and *Me-Akan-dake*. The size of Akan-ko was originally much greater but the intrusion of O-Akan-dake broke it into the present Akan-ko and two smaller lakes, Panketo and Penketo. On the east shore is an area of bubbling mud called Bokke – which describes the plurp sound of the bursting bubbles (to Japanese ears, at least).

Akan-kohan

The focal point of the lake is the hot-spring resort town of Akan-kohan. Within the town is an Ainu *kotan* (village) where

Ainu people can be seen living their 'ordinary daily life' – amidst the countless souvenir shops. As mentioned earlier the Ainu have been completely absorbed culturally by the ethnic Japanese, and almost no one knows more than a few words of the original Ainu languages. However this is at least a chance to obtain a small idea of the old ways. They may also be seen at shops in town, carving an endless succession of wooden bears.

Marimo weed

Another attraction is this curious weed. Not just any old garden-variety weed, mind you, but one that acts like a submarine, with the ability to rise and sink in the water. Marimo is actually an intertwined mass of hair-like green algae that has formed into spongy spheres up to 15 cm in diameter. Other species live in Lake Sakyo (in Aomori-ken), Lake Yamanaka near Mt Fuji , and in some lakes in Siberia, Switzerland and North America, but it is quite rare elsewhere. The Akan variety is the largest and is considered the most attractive. In the past so many people were taking marimo home as a souvenir that there was a danger they would be wiped out but they are now under government protection.

All excursion boats on the lake stop at a small island on which a marimo 'sanctuary' has been built, and visitors can seen them lying on the bottom of concrete tanks, doing their thing. There is also a glass tank containing many marimo at the Akan-kohan town information office located beside the police station on the short street across the road from the Akan Kanko Hotel.

On 10 October each year there is a 'traditional' Ainu festival in honour of the marimo. It supposedly celebrates Ainu legends about the marimo, but publicity photos show Ainu elders carrying a type of tray used only in Shinto observations. Since Shinto is foreign to the original Ainu culture and worship, one may question the genuineness of the festival.

O-Akan & Me-Akan

The most prominent peaks in the vicinity
of the lake are easily climbed and offer
beautiful views as a reward. Closer to the
town is O-Akan-dake, the trail to which
begins at O-Akan-onsen; ask for the 'O-
Akan Hiking Course'. The summit is 10.7
km from the onsen. Me-Akan-dake probably offers the more beautiful and unusual
scenery from its summit – a weird view of
extinct and active volcanic cones, steam
jets, and the overall impression of being
on the moon. It can be climbed from either
Akan-kohan-onsen or from Me-Akan-
onsen, which is 20 km west of Akan-
kohan. From the former the summit is
10.7 km, but from the latter it is only 2.2
km.

Lookouts

There are two well-known scenic lookouts
on the road (Route 241) between Teshikaga and Akan-kohan. Sogakudai ('Two
Mountains Lookout') gives a good view of
Me-Akan-dake and O-Akan-dake; while
Sokadai ('Two Lakes Outlook') overlooks
(need it be said?) two pretty lakes,
Penketo and Panketo. The whole area is at
its finest in autumn when the leaves turn
into masses of reds, oranges and yellows.

Places to Stay

There are three youth hostels near the
lake, as well as others in the general area,
plus many hotels of varying prices (tending
toward the high, this being a resort
town).

Getting There

Akan National Park is readily accessible
from Kushiro, due south on the coast.
Routes 38 and 240 lead to Akan-kohan
and the JNR line leads to Teshikaga and
Kawayu. Kushiro is of little touristic
interest but is connected with Tokyo by
regular ferry service. (For more details
refer to the general Getting Around
section.)

The attractions of the largely industrial
city include the sanctuary for rare red-

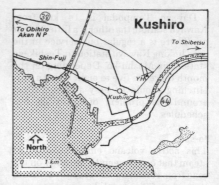

crested white cranes at Tsuruoka (20 km
west of Kushiro station). The number of
resident cranes is small but several
hundred come to feed in the winter. The
other attraction that the local authorities
promote is Harutori-koen (park) with its
lake and an Ainu 'village'. These would be
best regarded as something to see while
waiting for a train or boat connection.

Getting Around

The area is very popular with Japanese
tourists, so there will be no trouble
arranging transport to the various
attractions.

WEST FROM AKAN NATIONAL PARK

This route includes some of the prettiest
countryside in Hokkaido and leads to
Tomakomai, a port for ferries to Honshu
and gateway to Lake Shikotsu and Shikotsu-
Toya National Park.

Akan to Tomakomai

The first destination along Route 241 is
Obihiro, an unexceptional town with a
nice youth hostel very close to the station;
the staff rush out with banners to greet
and send off hostellers. Beyond Obihiro,
Route 38 leads to Tokachi-Shimizu; from
there you branch onto Route 274 as far as
Hidaka and then to Route 237 to Tomikawa
on the coast. From Hidaka you have the
option of the JNR line to Tomakomai.

The road from Tokachi-Shimizu to

Hidaka (Nissho Highway) passes through almost total wilderness and offers many lovely views of the Hidaka mountains as the road snakes up and down over crests; as well as glimpses of the green Saru river as you near the coast. It is a contrast to most roads on Hokkaido, which follow valley floors. About 15 km before Tomikawa is the town of Biratori, known for its large Ainu population, but similar in appearance to any other Hokkaido town. From Tomikawa, it is another 45 km to Tomakomai.

TOMAKOMAI

This port and industrial city is the gateway to the attractions of nearby Shikotsu-Toya National Park. It is close to Chitose airport (which also serves Sapporo, 65 km away), and is connected to Hachinohe, Sendai, Tokyo and Nagoya by regular ferry service. (For more information refer to the general Getting Around section.)

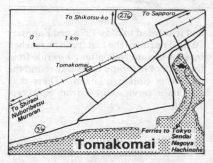
Tomakomai

From Tomakomai ferry terminal, bus 41 runs to the station from where you can make bus and train connections to other parts of Hokkaido. The same bus goes to the ferry terminal, but service is infrequent so a taxi may be necessary if you are rushing to catch a boat.

Side trip down the coast

At the bottom of the peninsula is Cape Erimo and Erimo Prefectural Park. The tip of the cape is noted for 60-metre cliffs that become a line of rocks and reef protruding several km out into the ocean like a line of sentinels. The cape is desolate, swept clear of vegetation by winds, and is usually blanketed by thick fog in summer.

Shikotsu-Toya National Park

If a visitor to Hokkaido could go to only one part of the island, the area of Shikotsu-Toya should be it. The major attractions are around the lakes Shikotsu and Toya, plus the town of Noboribetsu. Some might want to add the town of Shiraoi. Attractions are both natural and human.

SHIKOTSU-KO

Shikotsu-ko is the deepest lake on Hokkaido (363 metres) and the second-deepest in Japan, after Tazawa-ko on Honshu. The classic round shape of a caldera lake has been intruded on by the cones of *Eniwa-dake* (1320 metres) on one side and *Fuppushi-dake* (1103 metres) on the opposite shore. The altitude of the lake itself is 248 metres. Boat cruises are available on the lake from a point near the bus terminal. Swimmers should take note that the bottom slopes gently for the first 10 or so metres from the shore then plummets sharply.

Shikotsu-ko lake

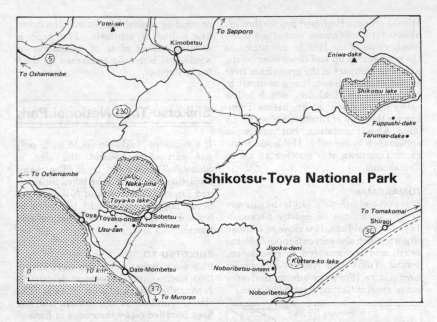

Eniwa-dake The low cone of this volcano is the most prominent feature of the lake-shore. It is steep but can be climbed easily and makes a good day's excursion. The starting point is Poropinai, accessible by a toll road along the lake (beginning near the bus terminal) or by boat from the same place in Shikotsu-kohan. The climb to the crater top takes about three hours and on a clear day you can see as far as Sapporo, as well as Lake Okotampeko on the far side and the other mountains around the lake.

Fuppushi-dake The outline of this low mountain is visible across the lake from Shikotsu-kohan.

Tarumae-dake Behind Fuppushi is this unusual volcano. During its 1909 eruption a dome of lava 450 metres across and 100 metres high formed in the central crater. It varies in its activities these days: some-times it shows few signs of life; most of the time it sends plumes of steam into the sky;

and it erupted in May 1978 and February 1979. The rim of the crater can be reached by a 40-minute walk after a bus ride from the town of Morrapu (part-way round the lake from Shikotsu-kohan). There may also be a service direct from Shikotsu-kohan.

Places to Stay
The *Shikotsu-ko youth hostel* is very close to the bus terminal, as are quite a few more expensive resort hotels. The hostel is noted for its evening meal which is vastly superior to the usual hostel fare . It is a *Genghis Khan*, a filling and tasty Hokkaido specialty of mutton and vegetables cooked at the table on special domed burners. This is a very inexpensive way to try the dish; in summer it is prepared on tables outdoors under a row of tall pines, and the mood is one of a giant party. The hostel is famous throughout Japan for this and for its later entertainment when the dynamic house-mother leads everyone in dancing.

Getting There

Shikotsu-ko is easily accessible from Tomakomai and Chitose; in both cases buses run from the railway station. The trip takes less than an hour.

NOBORIBETSU-ONSEN

If a foreign visitor was to sample only one hot-spring resort in Japan, this would be a good choice. It is one of the few that a foreigner can enjoy fully as onsen are usually sampled only by staying at an expensive resort hotel. In Noboribetsu, however, the famous baths are open to the public and are among the most magnificent and largest in Japan. There are also other attractions in and around the town to add to its interest.

The town is a few km inland from the coastal town (and railway station) of Noboribetsu-shi. It is built on the slope of a hill, with the bus stations part-way up. *Akashiya-so Youth Hostel* is a short distance down the hill from them; other youth hostels are located in the town.

Going up the hill you pass numerous hotels and streets lined with souvenir stalls patronised by large numbers of Japanese tourists, many dressed in the yukata of their hotels. The souvenir stalls

all sell wood carvings of bears and representations of Ainu people (some of fancifully beautiful maidens). The only glimpses of originality are a few anomalies like a Vishnu-on-Garuda, as seen everywhere in Bali, or a large and incongruous Polynesian-like figure – both carved by a Japanese who read many books on folkart. Some of the carvings are well done and would be classed as sculpture if they were not all so nearly identical.

The Baths

Continuing up the hill, the road levels off, and where it branches to the left there is a large brown hotel. This is the Dai-ichi Takimoto hotel, famous for its enormous bath room – and one experience a visitor should not miss.

The entrance for non-guests of the hotel, is to the left of the building. After undressing, (take your own towel), you enter the bath room and the first surprise is the immense size of the cavernous room, at least 100 metres long and half that in width. There are nearly 20 large pools, plus a small number in the women-only section, all of differing size and shape, with water of varying mineral content and temperature. At the far end is a shallow wading pool that has the only cool water in the place – which is worth remembering!

There are numerous fonts where you can sit and wash before taking the waters. The little squirrels gush drinking water; drink frequently to avoid exhaustion from dehydration.

The second big surprise is that there are people of both sexes in the pools. This is one of the relatively few places left in Japan where the custom of *konyoku* (mixed bathing) still prevails.

The correct decorum is to hold your towel in front to cover the 'nether regions'. It is not polite to stare, although some Japanese men were sitting around the women-only section peering intently; that is definitely 'not good form'. It also shows the development of the peeping tom in

Japan – something quite unknown when the human body was no mystery, as in the last century and earlier when all baths were mixed.

It is advisable to go with a friend, because despite the sheer physical pleasure of the baths, it becomes quite boring after a while with no one to talk to. Western women would be well advised to go in with a western man to establish 'ownership'. In that way no peepers will cluster around their pool as *might* happen to women alone. A recent visitor there told me a Japanese man was repeatedly 'looking for his friend' in the women's section and that most women are now wearing bathing suits in the mixed section.

The bath closes to non-guests at 5pm though you may be able to stay on after that time; and it seems possible to go in the evening if you get permission from the front desk.

Jigokudani

Beyond the baths, a further 150 metres or so up the hill, is the unusual and beautiful Jigokudani (Valley of Hell), so named for the evil smell and noise of steam and boiling water that pours forth from the earth. The colourful valley is a ravine with small hills and gullies where the yellow earth has been stained in bands and patches by the minerals deposited by the water over the centuries. The valley is the source of the hot water used in the baths of the town and different pools have different kinds of water. At maximum flow, it can exceed 75,000 litres per minute – a householder's dream.

The path through the valley (the dangerous areas are roped off) begins above the car park at the end of the main street through the town and there is no admission charge. The sense of 'hell' is very appropriate – if you broke through the crust, you could be scalded to death before being rescued. Pleasant thought! Down in the valley is a Buddhist shrine to ward off evil.

Oyunuma

The path through Jigokudani hooks sharply left, at which point there is a small gravel path, labelled in Japanese only as going to Oyunuma. It leads up to a gravel road, across which is the observation point which overlooks the boiling pond. Oyunuma ('hot water pond') is an intriguing large pool of muddy water that boils continuously. It sits in what is believed to be the crater of an extinct volcano and is simultaneously scenic and ugly.

Beside the path are some small stone statues with cloth bibs and a sad story. These are figures of *Jizo*, the protector of children (as well as travellers and pregnant women). One of his responsibilities is the souls of dead children and sewn to each bib is the name of the dead child whose soul is to be helped into the underworld. Areas of subterranean activity like Jigokudani are obviously entrances to hell.

The road crossed while walking to the lookout, leads to Lake Kuttara (to the right); to the left it leads back down to the car park at Jigokudani.

Kuttara-ko

This is a classic caldera lake – almost perfectly round with the surrounding shore rising steeply to an almost level rim. On a crystal-clear sunny day, the water is an intense sapphire blue, said to be even deeper in colour that that of famed Mashu-ko. On a hazy day (judge from conditions over Noboribetsu) only the outline of the lake will be visible and the water will be a characterless grey, making the trip to the lake a disappointment.

From the lookout over Oyunuma, it is about three km to a lookout over Kuttara-ko. It is a further 2.5 km down to the bus terminus/rowboat rental/restaurant at the edge of the lake. Buses leave Noboribetsu-onsen at 10 and 11.40 am and 1.20pm (check locally) stopping at the lake for five minutes. Taxi, hitching and walking are alternative ways of getting there.

Kumayama

Overlooking Noboribetsu-onsen is the high hill Kumayama ('Bear Mountain'). A trip here is recommended although it is rather pricey (Y1000 return by cable car; 10% discount with a youth hostel card.) The major attraction (for foreigners) is a reproduction of an Ainu settlement, with five or six buildings built in the traditional Ainu style – grass thatch over a wooden framework. The bottom building houses a small museum.

Four times a day a number of elderly Ainu re-enact several of their traditional dances, chants and ceremonies – centred on the bear. According to tradition a bear was raised from a cub, then ceremoniously killed, thus releasing the soul of the dead Ainu believed to be trapped within. Nowadays a bewildered bear cub is 'shot' with a blunt arrow that does it no harm. Yes, the whole thing is for the tourists, but it is the only way to get a first hand idea of their former customs. The participants in the ceremonies are mostly in their 70s so even this remnant of Ainu culture may not be around for long.

The performances, at 10.30 am and 3.30, 7.30 and 8.10 pm, are held in the second building from the bottom of the slope. No photos may be taken during the ceremonies and it is unlikely that anyone will pose afterward. To guarantee a good seat, be at the base station of the cable car more than half an hour before a performance (especially in the busy summer season) to be sure of getting a car up the mountain in time.

Another attraction of the mountain is a large enclosure full of very large and dangerous Hokkaido bears. They are obviously bored by a life of sitting around on unyielding concrete and have devised many tricks to cadge biscuits from visitors. Although these bears lead a much better life than those in cages at Shiraoi, both places exemplify a definite shortcoming of the Japanese – a total disregard for animals and their basic welfare. Another building houses a Bear Museum that shows and tells you everything you ever wanted to know about bears – but the text is in Japanese.

Minor entertainment at the top of the mountain includes goose races. The view from the top over the sea, neighbouring mountains and Kuttaro-ko is very good on a clear day.

The base station of the cable car is reached by walking up a short sidestreet off the main street in Noboribetsu and either walking up a flight of steep steps (past a number of souvenir shops) and following the path; or taking a chair lift that runs parallel to it. (The distance is so short that the latter is only for the very tired.) The base station is a just a short distance away in the large building.

Noboribetsu to Toya-ko

During the summer months there are six buses a day over the mountains from Noboribetsu-onsen to Toya-ko-onsen. The trip takes 1¾ hours (Y1300) and is much quicker and more scenic than by train around the bottom of the peninsula.

SHIRAOI

About 3000 Ainu have settled in this town which is about 20 km from Noboribetsu on the way to Tomakomai. It was originally known for its reproduction of a small Ainu *kotan* (village) but is now more famous for its commercialism. To get in to see five or so Ainu-style buildings; the bored, frustrated and pitiable bears in tiny cages; and a five-minute performance of chants and dances by a few Ainu women who look as if they'd rather be elsewhere, you first have to pass through a very large and modern building full of stall after stall of Ainu souvenirs – all staffed by ethnic Japanese.

The redeeming features of the place are a well-presented modern museum of Ainu artefacts and life-size reproductions of daily activities in traditional times, plus an excellent booklet, *Shiraoi & Ainu*. This gives a great deal of information about the traditional way of life, far more than is available from sources other than scholarly journals, and is presented from the Ainu point of view – which is often quite different from that appearing in official Japanese publications.

Compared with this village, however, the 'settlement' on Kumayama is *much* less commercialised, gives a better view of Ainu customs and, comparing costs, is not much more expensive to visit. Kumayama would normally get the nod as the better place to visit but for Shiraoi's good, modern museum and the excellent publication already mentioned.

Shiraoi can be reached easily from Tomakomai or Noboribetsu by train or bus. The bus stop (Shiraoi-kotan) is right in front of the village; from the train station, you walk along the road for about 20 minutes until you see a large archway over a side road.

MURORAN

At the tip of the peninsula is the city of Muroran. Apart from the annual festival (28-30 July), and the cliffs of Chikyu-misaki, the sole attraction of this dark steel-producing city is that it is the

terminus for ferries to Aomori and Hachinohe (northern Honshu). These give the option of skipping Hakodate and the not-so-interesting 150 km to Shikotsu-Toya National Park. From Muroran to Toya-ko-

onsen (Toya station) it is no more than 50 km by bus (eight per day) or train; and Noboribetsu-onsen (Noboribetsu station) is only about 25 km away by bus (eight per day) or train. The train goes to Noboribetsu town on the coast, (from where buses go the short distance up to Noboribetsu-onsen) and on to Tomakomai and Sapporo. All trains for Toya, and about half of those for Noboribetsu/Tomakomai/Sapporo leave from Higashi-Muroran station, three stops from Muroran station.

TOYA-KO AREA

The remaining area of interest in the Shikotsu-Toya National Park is found around Lake Toya. In addition to the beauty of the lake and its central islands, there is much evidence of past and ongoing volcanic activity. Toya-ko lake is another circular caldera, much larger than Kuttaro-ko. In its centre are the islets that collectively comprise Nakajima (middle island); they are the remains of the volcano whose crater forms the basin of the lake.

Lookouts

An excellent view of the lake, Toya-ko-onsen and *Usu-san* can be had from the lookout beside the road to the coast (Abuta). From the T-junction near the bus station and police station, it is 1.6 km up the hill.

Other good views can be found by following the road clockwise around the lake (Route 230 to Kimobetsu). From the same T-junction, the road goes at lake-level for a short distance before beginning to climb to a broad plateau. Just over six km up the hill (one km above the entrance to the Toya Country Club) there is an excellent view over the lake. On the plateau there are other good views of the lake and its islands, and visible inland is the tall cone of *Mt Yotei*. Beyond the red barn-like restaurant/bus stop, the road goes inland and the lake is lost to sight.

There is a road down to Toya-machi (the town of Toya), at lake level, and from

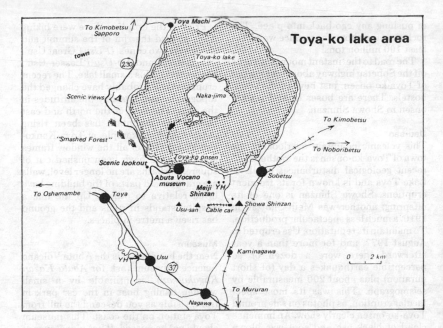

Toya-ko lake area

To Kimobetsu
Sapporo

Toya Machi

town

(230)

Toya-ko lake

Naka-jima

Scenic views

To Kimobetsu

To Noboribetsu

"Smashed Forest"

Scenic lookout

Toya-ko onsen

Sobetsu

Abuta Vocano museum

Meiji Shinzan   YH

To Oshamambe

Toya

Usu-san   Cable car

Showa Shinzan

Kaminagawa

0   2 km

YH

Usu

(37)

To Mururan

Nagawa

there a road circles the lake, back to the youth hostels and hotels. However, the road down is loose gravel and risky on a bike and the view from the lower road only so-so.

Showa Shinzan

'New Mountain of the Showa Era' is one of the most remarkable pieces of rock on Earth. On 28 December 1943, earthquakes hit the area around Toya-ko. Near Sobetsu, to the south-east of the lake, the formerly flat farmland began to rise and during the next two months formed a hill nearly 25 metres high. Between late June and late October, many volcanic eruptions took place and the hill continued to grow. By November it had reached a diameter of 800 metres. The climax came when a tower of hardened lava started to rise through the crust of the earth. By September 1945 it had reached an altitude of 408 metres above sea level, a respectable 150 to 200 metres above the

surrounding terrain. There it sits today, a chunk of colourful yellows and browns, bare of vegetation and issuing steam from many crevices.

At the base of Showa Shinzan is a museum relating to the volcano (nothing special; about Y500), and the *Ainu Kinen-kan* (Ainu Memorial Hall), which contains some memorabilia of the native peoples. Also here is the base station of the cable car to the top of neighbouring *Usu-san* (Y1200). On the road that leads to Showa Shinzan from the lake, where it skirts the east side of Usu-san, the surface has subsided in some places while the edge has been raised more than half a metre in others. It seems that Usu-san is rising at a rate of 15-30 cm each year.

A friend once said that he feels a sort of affection for sharks, tidal waves and volcanoes, for they remind man just how powerless he is against nature. A realisation of the immense forces at work lifting this huge chunk of rock should do the job of pushing any ego back into place. The rock showing above the surface weighs at least 100 million tons!

The road to the 'instant mountain' turns off the Sobetsu highway about four km out of Toya-ko-onsen, just beyond the youth hostels. There are buses from Toya-ko-onsen to Showa Shinzan.

Usu-san

This volcanic mountain overlooking the town of Toya-ko-onsen is the mother of all recent geological disturbances south of Lake Toya and is known for its frequent eruptions. Showa Shinzan is one of its offspring; another was Meiji Shinzan in 1910, a much less spectacular production. To maintain its reputation, Usa erupted in August 1977, and for more than a year afterward there were a dozen or so perceptible earthquakes a day (of short duration) plus about 200 measurable by seismograph. This was its most spectacular eruption, as photos on sale around Toya-ko-onsen clearly show. An immense cloud of black ash and soot was blown about 10,000 metres skyward and 30 cm of fine ash fell on Toya-ko-onsen, causing some buildings to collapse, burying crops, forcing the evacuation of the populace and causing a giant headache for those who had to clean up the mess. Chunks of rock hurled out during the eruption damaged much of the forest land near the town and broken tree tops and stripped branches along the roadside remain as silent witnesses to the event.

Usu-san's activity since then has been confined mainly to blowing out great volumes of steam and gas. Although, in July 1978 Usu again erupted, sending another cloud of ash and dust high into the air, to the delight of visitors (including myself), and the annoyance of the townspeople who had to clean up the thick layer of fine dust that settled on Toya-ko-onsen. At that time, supposedly more than 80% of the volcanic energy had been dissipated, so it's unlikely that any future activities will be so spectacular.

Prior to the eruption there were hiking trails around the rim of the summit and there were two cones, O-Usu ('Great Usu', 725 metres) and Ko-Usu ('Lesser Usu', 611 metres), plus a small lake. The recent eruptions will probably have changed the topography and possibly the altitudes in the area. The land at the north and east feet of the mountain has been rising noticeably. For example, at Toya-Kankokan Youth Hostel all the window frames and doorways have been pushed out of square, the baths are no longer level, walls are cracked and parts of the building have lifted relative to others. Up the hill, a hospital stands in ruins and the ground has risen a metre in places.

Museum

Near the bus station is the Abuta Volcano Science Museum (ask for *Abuta Kazan Kagaku-kan*), identifiable by a small wooden fishing boat in the car park in front, visible as you descend the hill from Toya station on the coast. This museum should not be missed. It has videotapes of the 1977 eruption and the aftermath; a car damaged by ejected rock; a seismograph recording earth tremors as they happen; and most interesting of all a projection room with a model of the volcano complete with 'pillar of smoke'. To the accompaniment of actual recordings of the eruption, 'lightning' flashes through the plume and the floor shakes with terrifying realism, simulating the earth tremors and explosions that actually took place. The museum also has an excellent display of relics from the area and an exhibit of items used until recent times by people in their daily work. The museum is open late April to mid-November.

Places to Stay

The shore of the lake has been heavily built up with tourist hotels and is a popular summer retreat from the heat of Honshu. Swimming and boating (commercial cruises available) are popular activities. The town of Toya-ko-onsen is the largest centre on the lake, and has several deluxe resort hotels. The two youth hostels are about four km out of town on the road to Sobetsu.

Getting There

Toya-ko-onsen is linked eight times a day by bus with Muroran and Noboribetsu-onsen, the latter by a scenic mountain pass. The JNR station on the coast is called Toya, but Toya-machi is on the lake, several km inland and you have to take a bus from the station. (Toya-machi and Toya-ko-onsen are on opposite sides of the lake.)

Getting Around

There is a regular bus service around the lake and surrounding area. Bicycles can be rented near the bus station and are a very convenient means of getting around.

Toya-ko to Noboribetsu

Refer to the Noboribetsu-onsen write-up for information on the bus service between the two places.

GETTING THERE

At the moment Hokkaido is accessible only by plane or ship. To show the risks involved in taking official pronouncements to heart when writing a book like this, I wrote in the first edition: 'Work is under way to build the Sei Kan tunnel under the Tsugara Strait for a Shinkansen-type super-express train from Tokyo to Sapporo, but because the tunnel will be 54 km long, it is not scheduled for completion until 1982. Travel time between the cities will be about five hours and 40 minutes.' In reality as of mid 1984 the Shinkansen line which was being built to northern Honshu, supposed to go to Aomori, into the tunnel and the rest of the way above ground to Sapporo, had not been and will not be built beyond Morioka; and nothing has been built in Hokkaido. The tunnel itself was completed in early 1985 but after 20 years work and the countless billions of yen that have been spent

building it, the authorities are not sure if the tunnel should be used for road vehicles, trains only, or a system of railroad-conveyed road vehicles plus normal railway services. Stand by for future announcements!

Air

The main airport is at Chitose, serving Sapporo. There are also local airports around the island fed via Chitose.

Ferries

There are several ferry lines. Listed below are the main ferry ports in Hokkaido and the cities in Honshu with which they connect.

Visitors with only a few days for Hokkaido should note that a ferry runs from Aomori (northern Honshu) to Muroran, which is very close to the Toya-ko Shikotsu-ko area, one of the two most popular and interesting regions for travellers in Hokkaido.

Hakodate – Aomori, Noheji and Oma. Of these lines, detailed below, by far the most convenient is the JNR ferry from Aomori.

Aomori Two ferry lines, JNR and Higashi Nihon Ferry (HNF), connect Hakodate with Aomori; sailing time is about four hours. The JNR terminal in both cities is close to the station and JNR has at least 10 sailings through the day in each direction. HNF also has 10 sailings in both directions, virtually around the clock, (Y1400). At Hakodate and Aomori, the HNF terminal is some distance to the west of the city and is inconvenient to reach. If you arrive by HNF at Hakodate, you can reach the JNR station by taking the road from the terminal, turning right at the first T-junction, left at the next corner and continuing till you come to the intersection of a major road. The bus stop is across the road and to the right. The name of the stop (written only in Japanese) is Hokudai (Hokkaido University). Take bus 1 to the station.

Noheji HNF has at least six sailings a

day in each direction, around the clock to this small city on Honshu. Sailing time is 4¾ hours. The terminus is a few km to the west of the JNR station; a bus service makes the connection. The cheapest fare is Y1400.

Oma HNF has at least three sailings daily in each direction to this small town at the north of the Shimokita Peninsula. The sea distance is shorter (sailing time is two hours) and the fare slightly less than from Aomori (Y1000) but is balanced out by the longer land distance to reach Oma.

Muroran – Aomori. There are two ferries a day (sailing time about 7½ hours) in each direction and the fare is Y3400. They leave from Muroran at 8 am and 11.55 pm; and from Aomori at 3.10 pm and 9.20 pm. The ferry terminus ('Ferry Noriba') at Muroran is easy to find and is one km from the JNR station. Buses leave from the station as well.

Tomakomai – Hachinohe, Sendai, Tokyo and Nagoya.

Hachinohe Boats of two lines sail three times a day; the trip takes nine hours and costs Y3900.

Sendai There are daily services (by different lines; sailing time 14½ to 17 hours) to/from Sendai. One of these runs between Nagoya and Tomakomai, stopping at Sendai in each direction. The minimum Sendai-Tomakomai fare is Y8600.

Tokyo There is a daily service in each

direction. The trip takes 31 hours and costs a minimum of Y11500.

For further information, refer to the general Getting Around section earlier in the book.

Kushiro – Tokyo. This port gives easy access to Akan National Park. There is a ferry every one to two days in each direction, operated by Kinkai Yusen Ferry. The trip takes 33 hours; cheapest fare is Y14,000. For more details refer to the general Getting Around section.

Otaru – Niigata, Tsuruga, Maizuru (west coast of Honshu). These services are run by Shin Nihonkai Ferry. Tsuruga and Maizuru are quite close to Kyoto, and from both there are four sailings a week in each direction (32 hours from both ports). From Niigata there are three sailings a week in each direction; duration is about 20½ hours. The cheapest fare from Niigata is Y5400 and from the other two ports is Y6400.

Getting Around
There are JNR lines around nearly all parts of the island with bus routes through the more mountainous or unpopulated regions. A peculiarity of the bus services here (and in other similarly isolated parts of the country) is that the summer is considered to end on August 15 – after which services may be reduced or even non-existent.

Central Honshu

This section covers much of what is traditionally regarded as Chubu, or central Japan. For the traveller who wants a feel for the 'real' Japan, this is one of the two or three best regions of the country to visit. Much of the area was, until only a few years ago, quite isolated, and except for boats on narrow rivers some places were completely cut off during winter. As a result, many folk traditions that have disappeared elsewhere still survive quite strongly here. The region also offers much natural beauty, historic remains, and some of the most interesting festivals in Japan.

The areas covered here are Nagano-ken, Gifu-ken, parts of northern Aichi-ken, Fukui-ken, Ishikawa-ken and Toyama-ken. The route followed begins in the north, as a continuation of the description of the Northern Honshu section. It starts with the alps area of Toyama-ken and Nagano-ken, then across Gifu-ken to Fukui-ken and Ishikawa-ken, then circles back near the starting point.

Northern Japan Alps

This region has the highest mountains in Japan, several over 3000 metres. (Keep in mind that 85 per cent of Japan is considered mountainous.) The mountains are widespread and Nagano-ken is known as the 'roof' of Japan. There is also, of course, a southern alpine region but description has been omitted because it is not as accessible as that in the north.

The alps overlap Toyama and Nagano prefectures and some areas are accessible from both directions though many peaks require mountaineering skills. For further information consult *The National Parks of Japan* by Sutherland and Britton, and the JNTO *Official Guide*.

There are, however, three routes into the mountains that can be followed by anyone. One is most easily reached from Toyama (or via the north coast from Niigata/Naoetsu), one runs between Toyama and Shinano-Omachi (Nagano-ken), and one lies between Matsumoto and Takayama.

FROM KUROBE & TOYAMA
The least complicated trip into the alps is a train ride through *Kurobe-kyokoku*, the Kurobe Gorge, on the Kurobe-kyokoku railway. The starting point for the 20-km run to Keyaki-daira is Unazuki-onsen. The train passes through gorges as deep as 2000 metres and is specially designed for sightseeing, with open-sided car carriages consisting of little more than seats and a roof. The trip takes 40 minutes each way, and there are 12 trips daily in season (1 May – 30 November). The fare is Y1550 return. It is not possible to go on past the end of the gorge, you must return to Uozu on the coast, or Toyama. There are several stations along the way so it would be possible to walk through some of the gorge. It would be best to ride in and get an idea of the practicality of walking back through particular sections. Unazuki-onsen is easily reached from Kurobe (on the coast), or Toyama (same railway line); it can also be reached by road.

Although the above trip is easily made,

Central Honshu

0 20 40 60 80 100 km

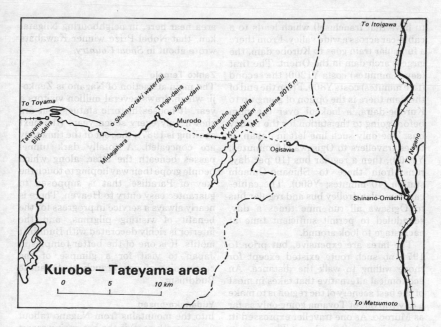

Kurobe – Tateyama area

0   5   10 km

To Toyama

To Itoigawa

To Nagano

To Matsumoto

Tateyama
Bijo-daira

Shomyo-taki waterfall

Tengu-daira

Jigoku-dani

Murodo

Midagahara

Daikanho

Kurobe-daira

Kurobe Dam

Mt Tateyama 3015 m

Ogisawa

Shinano-Omachi

probably the most popular journey in the alps passes through territory that was the province only of alpinists until recent times. The Tateyama-Kurobe Alpine Route takes in the peaks of the Tateyama group, centred around *Tateyama* itself (3015 metres). The route runs between a point near Toyama (Toyama-ken) and Shinano-Omachi (Nagano-ken), and is enjoyed by many partly for its variety of transport (including train, bus, cable-car and trolley bus). The drawback is cost; transport alone comes to more than Y8000 and you may have to rush through to avoid an overnight stay at Y4000-and-up prices.

Toyama to Omachi
From Toyama, the Toyama Dentetsu line runs frequently, via the Tateyama – Kurobe Alpine Route, to Tateyama town (Y840; Y990 express), where a cable-car runs up to Bijo-daira (Y600). From there an hour's bus ride leads to Murodo

(Y1600). En route it passes scenic but rather distant Shomyo-taki waterfall (Japan's longest, including a drop down a sheer 126 metre cliff face), plus the vista offered at Midagahara over the surrounding area. The route is open from 15 May to 5 November and if you travel soon after it opens, you may find yourself in a canyon cut through snow up to 10 metres deep.

Murodo is a base for walking to Mikuraga-ike lake or Jigoku-dani ('Hell Valley') – an area of steaming solfataras (volcanic vents); or for climbing *Tateyama* (Oyama) or *Tsurigi-dake*. The climb from Murodo to Oyama is steep and is nearly five km long. The view from the top takes in a number of surrounding peaks and valleys. The road is usable by private vehicles as far as Murodo. Beyond that you must continue by public transport or on foot.

The route continues from Murodo by a 10-minute LPG bus ride (nine per day) through a tunnel to Daikanho (Y2000; oh, to have that franchise!) which leads to a cable-car across a wide valley. From there a funicular train goes to Kurobe dam, the largest arch dam in the Orient. The first (seven minutes) costs Y1200; the second (five minutes) costs Y800. From the end of the dam there is the option of going up to Kurobe-daira, a lookout over the dam before going to the station for the trolley bus. The only such line left in Japan, it takes travellers to Ogisawa (16 minutes; Y1000), then a regular bus (10 per day) runs from there to Shinano-Omachi station (40 minutes; Y600). The cable-car, funicular, trolley bus and regular bus to Ogisawa all run nine times a day, scheduled to permit sufficient time at each stage to look around.

The fares are expensive, but prior to 1971 no such route existed except for those willing to walk the distance. An economical alternative that takes in most of the best scenery of the region is to make a day trip out of Toyama going only as far as Murodo. As one traveller expressed it: 'A dam is a dam anywhere'. The scenery eastward from the dam to Omachi is not particularly noteworthy. The Tokyo TIC has an information sheet with up-to-date prices and times.

Nagano-ken

Omachi is located on Route 148 which runs north to Itoigawa and south to Matsumoto through a river valley. Nagano and its nearby attractions are situated in another parallel valley separated by a chain of mountains. There are two small local roads across to Nagano.

NAGANO

The city of Nagano lies in a valley hemmed in by mountain ridges on two sides. Nearby are the best skiing areas in the Tokyo vicinity, such as Shiga Heights; snowfalls in the mountains can reach as much as 15 metres over a winter. It was an area near here, in neighbouring Niigata-ken, that Nobel Prize winner Kawabata wrote about in *Snow Country*.

Zenko Temple

The main attraction of Nagano is Zenko-ji, which draws several million visitors a year. It houses historic statues that are shown only every seven years (the next showing is 1987); the rest of the time they are concealed. A totally dark tunnel passes beneath the altar, along which people grope their way hoping to touch the 'key of Paradise' that is supposed to guarantee easy entry to Heaven. There is nearly always a service in progress for the benefit of visiting pilgrims, and the interior is richly decorated with Buddhist motifs. It is one of the better temples in Japan to visit for a glimpse of the ceremonies of one branch of Japanese Buddhism.

Yudanaka-onsen

Into the mountains from Nagano (about 25 km north-east) is the hot-spring resort town of Yudanaka. It has open-air pools which are famous from the photographs of snow-covered monkeys sitting in them keeping warm in winter.

Beyond Yudanaka, you can continue by the Shiga-Kusatsu Kogen toll road to Kusatsu, then cross to Nikko and Oze-numa via Numata. Since there are so few individual attractions in Gumma-ken, this route description is split between this section (as far as Numata) and that on Tochigi-ken (Numata to Nikko).

KUSATSU (GUMMA-KEN)

This is one of the best-known hot-spring towns in Japan, with more than 130 ryokan in the central part of town. Yuba (Hot Water Field), the origin of the hot water, gushes, boiling from the ground. Sulphur residue, left behind as the water cools, is collected and sold as *yunohana* (hot spring flowers), a home remedy.

Netsunoyu, (Heat Bath), is the main public bath and is famous for its exceed-

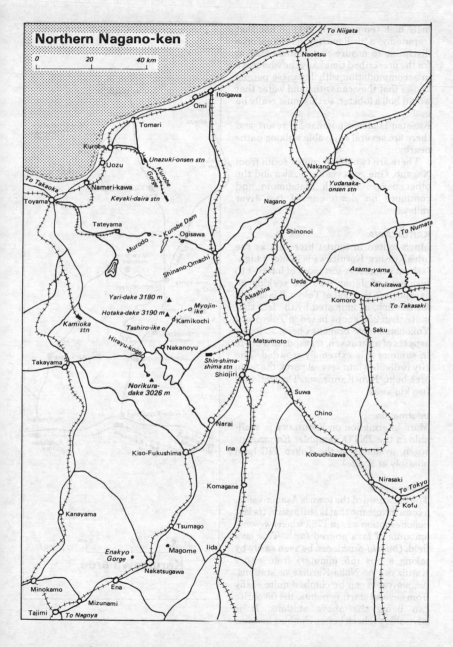

Northern Nagano-ken

0   20   40 km

To Niigata

Naoetsu

Itoigawa

Omi

Tomari

Kurobe

Uozu

Unazuki-onsen stn

Nameri-kawa

Kurobe Gorge

Keyaki-daira stn

Toyama

To Takaoka

Tateyama

Kurobe Dam

Murodo

Ogisawa

Shinano-Omachi

Nakano

Yudanaka-onsen stn

Nagano

To Numata

Shinonoi

To Takaoka

Yari-dake 3180 m

Hotaka-dake 3190 m

Kamioka stn

Tashiro-ike

Myojin-ike

Kamikochi

Ueda

Akashina

Asama-yama

Karuizawa

Komoro

To Takasaki

Saku

Hirayu-koge

Nakanoyu

Matsumoto

Shin-shima-shima stn

Takayama

Norikura-dake 3026 m

Shiojiri

Suwa

Chino

Narai

Ina

Kobuchizawa

Komagane

Nirasaki

Kiso-Fukushima

To Tokyo

Kanayama

Tsumago

Magome

Iida

Kofu

Enakyo Gorge

Nakatsugawa

Minokamo

Ena

Mizunami

Tajimi   To Nagoya

ingly high temperature. It is so hot that (reputedly) a 'drill master' has to enforce discipline to ensure that bathers stay in for the prescribed time. Anyone who stays in accommodation with Japanese people knows that they can withstand water that would boil a lobster, so this must really be hot!

Kusatsu is also a popular ski resort and there are several enjoyable walking paths nearby.

There are two major routes south from Nagano. One goes via Karuizawa and the other passes through Matsumoto and continues on down one of two river valleys.

KARUIZAWA

Much touted in tourist literature as the 'ideal' resort, Karuizawa is in fact a high-fashion summer resort more of interest to residents of Japan who are seeking an escape from the heat of Tokyo. It is largely for the rich, as indicated by the fact that more than 250 shops based in Tokyo and Yokohama have branches here, so it has aspects of a shrunken, transposed Tokyo. In summer it is extremely crowded. The city is divided into several parts, the main area being Kyu-Karuizawa. The station is two km away.

Information

More information on Karuizawa is available in the JNTO pamphlet *Karuizawa-kogen*, available at the Tokyo TIC (and possibly at Kyoto).

Asama-yama

The backdrop of the town is Asama-yama, a conical volcano that is still active. Its last major eruption was in 1783 when awesome amounts of lava poured forth. This lava field, *Onioshi-dashi*, can be seen easily by taking a bus (55 minutes) from either Karuizawa or Naka-Karuizawa stations. Asama-yama can be climbed quite easily from several starting points, the favourite two being the above stations. It is advisable to check before climbing because

Karuizawa area

the volcano still erupts from time to time and climbing is banned when it is active.

There is a good view of Asama-yama as well as the surrounding countryside from Usui-toge (pass), which can be reached on foot in 30 minutes. *Kumano-jinja* shrine is nearby. The pass itself was part of the old Nakasendo highway between Kyoto and Tokyo. Some old towns along this route that still retain much of their original appearance are described in the section of Nagano-ken covering the Kiso River valley, following.

A 30-minute walk from Karuizawa station leads to Shiraito falls, three metres high and spread along a width of 70 metres.

About 300 species of wild birds inhabit the sanctuary near Hoshino-onsen. They can be watched from two observation huts or from the 2.4 km walking path.

Places to Stay

There are many hotels, ryokan, minshuku, villas, camping grounds and two youth hostels around Karuizawa.

MATSUMOTO

Matsumoto is a city situated in the basin of mountain ranges. It posseses one of the finest castles in Japan and this alone makes it worth visiting. Streets nearby are narrow and winding, typical of castle towns.

Matsumoto Castle

Matsumoto-jo is the most easily reached feudal castle in the region around Tokyo. The trip can be made in four hours from Shinjuku station (Tokyo). The castle stands an imposing six storeys above its surrounding moat, and is unusual among Japanese castles because it is black, rather than the usual white. The original castle on this site was built in 1504, but the present structure is from a somewhat later date. However it is important enough to rate as a National Treasure. Swans swimming in the moat add a note of grace to its beauty. In the compound of the

castle is the *Minzoku-kan* (folklore museum) which houses an exhibit of 60,000 items of history, archaeology, folklore and geography.

The castle is a little over one km northeast of Matsumoto station and even closer to Kita-Matsumoto station. The TIC in Tokyo has an information sheet that gives more details on transport, sightseeing and accommodation in Matsumoto.

Getting There

From Tokyo the easiest and quickest way to get to Matsumoto is by JNR train from Shinjuku station (track 1). There are local trains plus expresses and limited expresses, a total of 19 per day. The local is slow but there is little difference in speed between the other two. The express (which costs Y4600) is only 15 minutes faster than the limited express which takes four hours and costs Y3500. The TIC information sheet has updated fare and schedule information.

Other train lines run from Nagano/Naoetsu and from the north coast (Itoigawa). From mid-May to mid-October there is a service by train and two buses through the mountains to Takayama which passes through scenic country.

MATSUMOTO TO TAKAYAMA

The trip from Matsumoto to Takayama via Kamikochi can be recommended as a chance to see an area of relatively unspoiled rural Japan. The route is definitely off the beaten track for most foreign tourists but uses well-established scheduled transportation and takes you through a scenic region of mountains, beautiful valleys and picturesque little farms.

The first leg of the trip is by Matsumoto denki tetsudo private railway from Matsumoto to Shin Shima-Shima (22 minutes; Y560; about 25 trains per day with the first at 3.52 am – for the early birds). Do not mistake this stop with Shimojima which is three stops before Shin Shima-Shima. The next leg is by bus from the terminus across the road from the railway station either to Nakanoyu, which is the transfer point for direct onward travel, (55 minutes, Y1300 15 per day); or on to the scenic delights of Kamikochi (another 20 minutes, Y1650).

From Kamikochi and Nakanoyu there are up to nine buses a day to Hirayu-onsen (55 minutes from Nakanoyu, 70 from Kamikochi; Y1150 from both). Six of these continue to Norikura which is 1¾ hours from Nakanoyu.

To Takayama there are up to three buses a day from Norikura (1½ hours; Y2150), and up to four a day from Hirayu-onsen – and vice versa. The phrase 'up to' indicates that services are more frequent in summer and on weekends.

Schedules are such that you can begin at Kamikochi/Nakanoyu, go to Norikura and spend a couple of hours walking around, then continue on to Takayama the same day. (The same type of connections are, of course, available in the opposite direction.) On the other hand if Norikura does not appeal to you, a Takayama-bound bus leaves within 10 minutes of the arrival of a bus from Nakanoyu. The climb

to Norikura and approach to it across the highland plateau in the bus is probably the most scenic part of the trip.

If you don't want to go all the way to Takayama an alternative is to travel to Norikura from Matsumoto (as described) then return to Shin Shima-Shima directly by bus (Y2550; up to four a day). The schedules for all these trains and buses are given in *Jikokuhyo*, so it is possible to schedule your travels through the region with military precision.

KAMIKOCHI

Some people believe that this highland basin west of Matsumoto is the most beautiful area in the northern alps. The most impressive single view is the one seen during the last few minutes of the trip in from Nakanoyu, just before reaching the cluster of lodges and inns and the parking area. The valley opens up on to a broad flood plain with the wall of mountains behind forming an impressive backdrop. This view alone justifies the trip though there are some very pleasant walks through wooded paths beside the river. There is no lack of company and it is interesting to observe how the normally reserved Japanese greet each other while enjoying the natural surroundings. The number of previous hikers can be judged by the height of the cairns – piles of stones built up one at a time by people leaving a marker of their passing.

Several trails begin at Kamikochi. The main trail from the car park leads to Kappabashi, a famed suspension bridge across the Azusa-gawa river. From the bridge there is a beautiful view of Mt Hotaka, and nearby is a rock sculpture of Walter Weston, a Briton who was the first alpinist to explore the Japan alps in the last century. Prior to this the alps were regarded as sacred or inhabited by evil spirits, and were avoided. Other attractions, apart from the general pleasant mood, fresh air and scenic views, are Tashiro-ike and Taisho-ike ponds and Myojin lake. A three-hour walk from Kamikochi passes

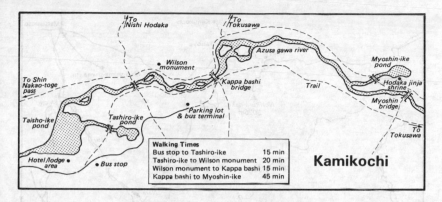

Walking Times

Bus stop to Tashiro-ike	15 min
Tashiro-ike to Wilson monument	20 min
Wilson monument to Kappa bashi	15 min
Kappa bashi to Myoshin-ike	45 min

Kamikochi

Myojin lake, Tokusawa and Yokowao. Trails continue beyond here to nearby high peaks, such as *Yari-dake* (Spear Mountain – the 'Matterhorn' of Japan), but scaling them is for the experienced only. Every year dozens of Japanese are killed in falls from slopes.

Mt Norikura
This is the most accessible peak in these alps, despite its 3026 metre height, as a toll road runs most of the way to the top, crossing an alpine plateau en route. Buses via the Norikura Skyline go as far as Tatami-daira (2½ hours from Kamikochi; less from Nakanoyu or Hirayu-koge), from where a three km hike (90 minutes) leads to the top. It is high enough that a few patches of snow can be found as late as August.

Information
The TIC in Tokyo has an information sheet on this area.

Kiso Region

Along with very enjoyable scenery, the Kiso river valley (south-west of Matsumoto) is worth visiting to see three villages that have remained relatively unchanged for nearly two centuries. Narai, Tsumago and Magome were located along the old Nakasendo highway between Kyoto and Edo (Tokyo). Every year there were grand processions of *daimyo* along this road between the two cities. Their retinue often numbered in the thousands (at least one of 30,000 was recorded), a measure of the power and wealth of the baron. Because the distance between the cities was great there were post stations where travellers could rest overnight. To meet the exalted demands of their guests, the ryokan had to be of high standard. Some of these fine buildings are still standing and a visit to one or all of these towns is highly recommended. Apart from a few collections of old buildings that have been gathered from other parts of the country there are relatively few places in Japan where you can see more than one or two old buildings in any one place. In these three towns however you can see a large number side by side, with only a few newer buildings interspersed. The towns retain their old appearance mainly because they were bypassed when the railways were built late in the last century. Their future is assured because of the interest (rather belated) by the Japanese in their past, and they are popular destinations for Japanese sightseers.

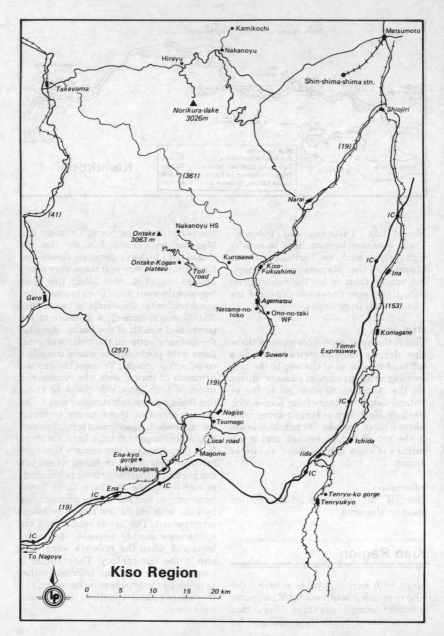

Kamikochi

• Kamikochi

• Nakanoyu

Hirayu

Takeyama

▲ Norikura-dake
3026m

Matsumoto

Shin-shima-shima stn.

Shiojiri

(19)

(361)

(41)

Ontake ▲
3063 m

Nakanoyu HS

Ontake-Kogan
plateau

Gero

Kurosawa

Kiso-
Fukushima

Toll
road

Nezame-no-
toko

Agematsu

Ono-no-taki
WF

(257)

Narai

IC

IC

Ina

(153)

Komagane

Tomei
Expressway

Suwara

(19)

IC

Nagiso

Tsumago

Local road

Ena-kyo
gorge

Magome

Nakatsugawa

IC

Ena

(19)

IC

To Nagoya

Ichida

Iida

IC

Tenryu-ko gorge

Tenryukyo

Kiso Region

0   5   10   15   20 km

LP

KISO-HIRASAWA

If you travel south from Matsumoto and Shiojiri, this is the first town of interest along the valley. It is noted for the production of lacquerware and there is a lacquer museum near the station.

NARAI

One station (JNR) away from Kiso-Hirasawa is one of the 62 post towns used by travellers along the Nakasendo highway. The old buildings are easy to find as they line the main street and are located only a few minutes on foot from Narai station (turn left when leaving the station). The majority of the buildings fronting the street are old, although there is a larger proportion of newer structures than in the other two towns. However, Narai is less accessible, so there are fewer fellow sightseers to contend with and you can enjoy the atmosphere a little better.

There are several buildings open to the public and money would be well spent visiting a few.

KISO FUKUSHIMA

During the Tokugawa era this was the most important barrier gate of the Nakasendo (Middle Way) road. Here the documents of travellers were inspected to verify that they had permission to travel. Life was very strictly regulated in those days (down to such details as to what kind of clothes you might wear and even the position in which you had to sleep!), and most people were not allowed to leave their appointed work or home village. Some mementoes of those days survive in the form of old buildings and exhibits in museums.

Yamamura Daikan Yashiki This was formerly the residence of the Yamamura family, high officials in the Kiso region; it is 15 minutes on foot from Kiso-Fukushima station.

Kiso-Fukushima Kyodo-kan This is a museum of historic artefacts and materials

related to the Nakasendo road and the barrier gates; it is five minutes by bus or 25 minutes on foot from Kiso-Fukushima station.

Kozen-ji temple One of the three largest temples in the Kiso region, the temple is known for its Kanuntei garden. It is close to both of the attractions listed above.

Festivals
21 July – 16 August: *Kiso Odori* – folk dances of the Kiso region.
22-23 July: *Mikoshi Matsuri* – procession of portable shrines.

ONTAKE

Ontake is a popular destination in summer for both pilgrims and those who enjoy hiking. There are many shrines on the mountain (Ontake ranks second only to Mt Fuji in sacredness), so man's presence cannot be forgotten but it is the natural environment that is the main attraction.

One popular starting point for climbing is Nakanoyu from where a climb of about 1½ hours through forest (mostly uphill) and a further half hour on mainly open ground leads to the plateau. From there you can walk and climb south to *Kengamine-dake* or northward to *Tsugushi-dake* – the two main peaks of this active volcano, collectively known as Ontake. Two trails go to Kengamine-dake and the walk is just under two hours. The main feature of the summit is a roaring fumerole that jets out sulphurous steam. An earthquake in early 1984 killed many people in Ohtaki (at the foot of Ontake) and in Nigori-kawa onsen (on the west flank); the latter no longer exists.

The most convenient access for those using public transport is one of the buses from Kiso Fukushima station to Nakanoyu (three per day, each way); or to one of the higher starting points above Ohtaki, such as Ontake-kogen, Hakkai-zan or Tanohara, the end of the line. You can walk between the two roads, well-known landmarks being Rokugome (sixth station) at

Nakanoyu; and Hachigome (eighth station) on the road leading up from Ohtaki. It takes 45 minutes to get from Fukushima to Otaki and 1¾ hours to Tanohara – Y820 and Y1750 respectively.

NEZAME-NO-TOKO

Some distance below road-level is this small but pretty 'miniature' gorge, an outcropping of large rocks through which the river has carved its way through the ages. There is a large area where buses can park (the place is only five minutes or so from Agematsu station); the entrance is to the north of the parking lot. I inadvertently avoided paying the admission fee by walking down a service stairway between the two large buildings. The name means 'place that opens sleepy eyes', but I suppose we have to allow the namers some poetic licence; it's attractive but not outstanding – worth visiting if you have the time.

ONO-NO-TAKI

About 10 minutes by bus from Agematsu station is this cascade some 10 metres high.

SUWARA

A short walk from Suwara station (two stops from Kiso-Fukushima) is Josho-ji temple. It was founded by the Kiso family in the 14th century, although the present buildings date 'only' from 1598.

TSUMAGO & MAGOME

Both these post towns have preserved much of their original appearance. It would be difficult to choose between them, so why not visit both? The walk between them takes about three hours and passes along the old Nakasendo road, although there is a fair amount of uphill walking in either direction. Tsumago is laid out almost on the level (there is a bit of a gap between two sections of the town), while Magome is strung out down the side of a steep hill. In Magome, the *Wakihontin Okuya*, a building shaped like a castle

(built in 1877) has an exhibition of material regarding the old post towns.

Festival

23 November: *Tsumago-matsuri* takes the form of a procession of townspeople dressed in the style of ancient times re-enacting one of the processions of the daimyo who travelled along the Naka-sendo road in feudal times.

Places to Stay

There are buildings open to the public in both towns and many have been converted to minshuku so travellers can stay overnight. The towns are very popular with tourists and the accommodation is usually fully booked in season so it would be advisable to make reservations if possible. Refer to the section on Minshuku for information on bookings from Tokyo.

Getting There

Both Tsumago and Magome are linked with the city of Nakatsugawa by regular bus service (Meitetsu line). From Nakatsugawa station, it takes about 30 minutes to Magome and a bit over an hour to Tsumago. There is also a direct bus connection to Magome from Nagoya; the trip takes about two hours. If you are coming from Matsumoto or Shiojiri, Nagiso is the closest station to Tsumago. More information can be obtained from the TIC in Tokyo which has a photocopied handout on the Kiso region, including transportation.

TENRYU RIVER VALLEY

Another route from Shiojiri southward is through the Tenryu (Heavenly Dragon) river valley to Iida via Komagome along Route 153, or by the parallel JNR line. The scenery is pleasant enough to make the trip enjoyable, and there are a few points of special note. At Ina, the grounds of the former castle Takata-jo are very pretty in the cherry blossom season (probably a couple of weeks later than in Kyoto and Tokyo, etc).

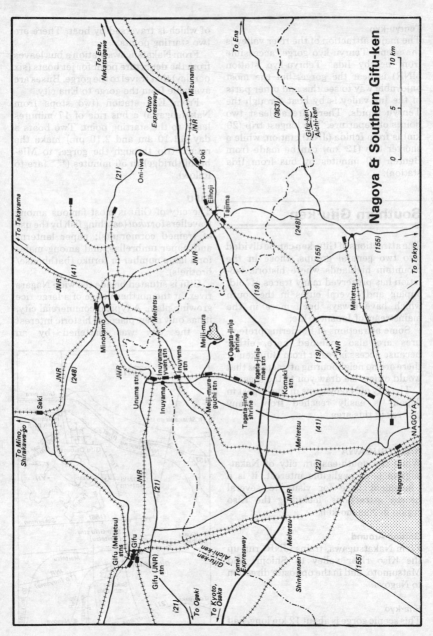

Nagoya & Southern Gifu-ken

Tenryu-kyo

The major attraction of the river valley is the scenic Tenryu-kyo gorge, accessible from nearby Iida. Tenryu-kyo station (JNR) is near the gorge, but the most enjoyable way to see this and other parts of the Ina valley is by boat through the Tenryu rapids. There are at least two points of departure. The longest trip (20 km) is from Ichida (JNR) station, while a shorter trip (12 km) can be made from Benten (10 minutes by bus from Iida station).

Southern Gifu-ken

The attractions of Gifu-ken can be divided into two general groups, those in the mountain highlands where historic isolation has preserved many traces of 'old' Japan; and several cities in the south which have always been more in the mainstream of Japanese life.

Some attractions of bordering prefectures are also included here, either because access is easier from Gifu-ken or there are no neighbouring attractions that would otherwise draw you to the area.

The city of Nagoya, one of the largest in Japan, is easily reached from many centres in this area.

NAKATSUGAWA

While the south-eastern city of Nakatsugawa is of negligible interest, it is a convenient base for visits to several nearby attractions, including the Kiso region in Nagano-ken.

Getting Around

From Nakatsugawa, trains (JNR) run up the Kiso river valley to Shiojiri and Matsumoto, and in the opposite direction to Nagoya.

Ena-kyo

This scenic gorge is about 12 km long, half of which is traversed by boat. There are two starting points.

From Nakatsugawa station a bus leaves from the departure point for jet boats (six per day) that travel to the gorge. Buses are available from the gorge to Ena city.

From Ena station (two stops from Nakatsugawa) a bus ride of 17 minutes leads to the starting point. Two boats a day (11.10 am and 2.10 pm) make the return trip through the gorge, to Miebashi (bridge) in 50 minutes (*** fare to follow).

GIFU

The city of Gifu is most famous among travellers for *ukai* (catching fish by the use of trained cormorants); paper lanterns and paper umbrellas; and among males for a large number of toruko (bathhouse/brothels).

Gifu is situated beside the wide Nagara river, at the northern edge of a large rice growing plain. A typical commercial city, it has only a few places of historic interest as the city was flattened by an

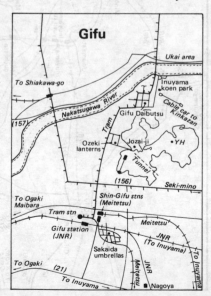

earthquake in 1891 and by bombs during the war. The one major exception is *Shohoji* temple.

Things to See

Shohoji

A very unusual *Daibutsu* (statue of Buddha) is housed in the large orange-and-white building visible from the road. The statue is made of 1000 kg of paper *sutras* (prayers) pasted to a bamboo frame, which was then covered with clay and stucco, lacquered and gilded. The hall is very dim and the artistry not the ultimate, but it is interesting and worth a look if you are in Gifu. The statue is 13.7 metres tall and an ear (elongated very much as a symbol of wisdom) is over two metres long. It was finished in 1747, after 38 years of work, and was constructed to console people who had lost relatives in earthquakes and famines.

Jozai-ji temple

The original temple dates from 1450 but the present one (not far from Gifu Youth Hostel) is quite recent. Visitors should regard the large structure simply as a neighbourhood temple and watch daily life go on around it. It is popular as a playground for toddlers and their ever-watchful mothers.

Kinkazan

The backdrop to Gifu is Kinkazan (Silver Mountain), where you'll find Gifu Youth Hostel and a concrete reproduction of the castle that stood at the peak until the earthquake of 1891. The new castle (1956) houses a small prefectural museum. Exercise freaks can walk up from the city or from the hostel; or the lazy can take the cable-car ('ropeway') from Gifu-koen (park). The castle and mountain, however, are very much 'something else to do' and not attractions of great merit. The castle looks very pretty (and *very* high up) at night when it is floodlit. It can be seen clearly from the *ukai* fishing area.

Ukai

From 11 May to 15 October there are nightly displays on the Nagara river (just above Nagara bridge) of the ancient 'sport' of using trained cormorants to catch fish. The birds are kept on a leash, and a ring around their neck prevents them from swallowing any but the smallest fish. The action takes place at night when the *ayu* (river smelt or sweetfish) can be attracted to the surface by torches blazing over the bow of each boat. One *usho*, (fisherman) in each boat, dressed in mediaeval grass-skirted costume, controls several birds, pulls in each one as it makes a catch, takes the fish, and puts the bird back in the water for another dive.

A large number of people can see the spectacle at one time as there are more than 130 covered boats of different sizes (capacity of 10 to 30 people). Tourists usually go out an hour or two before the fishing starts and dine (meals by prior arrangement), drink, sing and set off fireworks. It becomes a grand party and probably more than a few revellers are unable to focus by the time the boats and birds appear. The sightseeing boats are usually lined up and a 'showboat' of women dressed as geisha performing traditional songs and dances moves up and down past them. After a suitable period of time the fishing boats make their passes up and down.

People wishing to take pictures should keep a few things in mind. The fishing performance lasts only 20-30 minutes and the boats pass by quite quickly. A powerful flash is needed because the distance to the boats will be at least three or four metres, often considerably more.

The cost per person is around Y2000 and bookings can be made at any hotel, tourist agency or at the boat office downstream of Nagara-bashi bridge. The phone number is 0582 62-0104, but it will be necessary to call in Japanese.

The fishing can be seen almost as well from the east shore of the river (nearest town). In summer the water is low enough for you to walk out over the stone river bottom to the main channel near where the boats pass. The added advantage of this is that you can watch later as the fishermen touch shore, remove the leashes and neck rings, feed the birds with their hard-earned supper, put them back in their basket-cages, load them into trucks and disappear into the night. There is no *ukai* when the river is muddy following heavy rains or during the full moon, because the torches cannot attract the fish.

Crafts

Gifu is the best-known centre in Japan for both *chochin*, paper lanterns and *kasa*, paper umbrellas. Paper lanterns were made here as early as 1597. One of the best-known lantern factories is Ozeki; it is located in the Oguma-cho area of the city near the main shopping street, on the road leading up to the tunnel through Kinkazan.

Visitors are allowed to walk through and watch the interesting process. The lanterns are made by winding bamboo or wire around a form made up of several pieces of wood that lock together to give the shape. Paper is pasted to the bamboo strips, and after the paste has dried, the form is dismantled and removed through one end of the lantern. Sometimes the paper is pre-stencilled with a design, while other lanterns are hand-painted at the end of the process. The factory can be recognised by the symbol of a flattened 'O' superimposed on a 'Z' on the building.

There are no large umbrella manufacturers, just small shops (eg Kaida Kasaten) and home workshops, so it is more difficult to see them being made.

Festivals

On 5 April is *Inaba jinja festival* and on 11 May is the opening of cormorant fishing (fireworks at night). On the last Saturday of July and the first Saturday of August is the All-Japan Fireworks contest, held on the Nagara river just above Nagara-bashi bridge.

Places to Stay

There are two Youth Hostels in Gifu. The only one I know first hand is *Gifu Youth Hostel*, perched high on Kinkazan mountain, which is a good location though difficult to reach. The simplest way to get to it is by chairlift, which takes you within a couple of hundred metres of the hostel. However I have been in Gifu several times and have never seen the lift actually moving. (Note: It's only a chairlift so travel lightly.) Near the base of the lift is the start of a path leading up to the same place.

An alternative is to take a picturesque 'Toonerville' trolley in the direction of Nagara-bashi bridge, get off at Shiyakusho-mae stop and follow the road uphill to the tunnel; there is a path to the right that leads up to the hostel. At the stop beyond Shiyakusho-mae, after a sharp right-hand turn, there is another path which also leads up the hill. This stop is close to both the Daibutsu and the base station for the cable-car to the top of the mountain. Any of the walks will take 20-30 minutes. Orienteering fans will find a kindred spirit in the hostel manager, Mr Nomura.

At the other end of the cost scale there are many resort hotels bordering the far side of the river, upstream from Nagara-bashi bridge. They tend to be expensive (Y10,000 and up) which is not uncommon for hot-spring resorts. Gifu is rated as one of Japan's 'sex hotspots', which may also affect room rates. There are also several business hotels in Gifu.

Getting There

Gifu is linked to Nagoya by JNR (Gifu station) and Meitetsu line (Shin-Gifu station) as well as to Gifu-Hashima by bus. (Both Nagoya and Gifu-Hashima are on the Shinkansen). Gifu is linked to Ogaki and Maibara by JNR; and to Inuyama by both JNR and the Meitetsu line (which originates at Shin-Nagoya station). A railway that begins as a tram service on the major cross-road in the city (Route 156) leads to Seki and Mino.

YORO-NO-TAKI

Yoro waterfall is a 32-metre high cascade located in a scenic little tree-lined ravine. The nearby area has been made into a nature park with picnic facilities. The water plummets into a natural pool and visitors may, it is said, take a natural shower. (Take your own soap.)

The name Yoro translates as 'filial piety', and has an interesting history. It is said that Shonai Minamoto was extremely faithful to his aged father and spent his hard-earned money from wood-cutting on sake to keep the old man happy. On one occasion the water near the waterfall is said to have come out tasting like sake, a reward for his filial piety, so that he would not have to spend all his money on the bottled type. The story dates from the 700s so the supply ran out long ago. Access is from Ogaki via the Kinki Nippon railway (25 minutes from Ogaki station) to Yoro station from where a bus (seven minutes) leads to the park.

West of Ogaki is Maibara, a major railway junction for trains to Kyoto/Osaka, and north to Fukui/Kanazawa/Noto-hanto (described later), and the nearby centres of Hikone and Nagahama in neighbouring Shiga-ken.

Inuyama

Inuyama (Dog Mountain) on the Kiso River, is known for its castle, river scenery, shooting the rapids and cormorant fishing.

Things to See
Inuyama Castle

Inuyama-jo is the oldest castle in Japan, dating from 1440. It is a pretty white structure, scenically located on top of a cliff overlooking the Kiso river. It is open to the public, and close to the entrance is a small *Haritsuna* shrine where worshippers (usually older people) come, clap their hands to get the attention of the gods,

make their prayer and leave.

The castle and shrine are a short walk downstream from Inuyama-yuen station of the Meitetsu line

Jo-an

One of the three finest teahouses in Japan, Jo-an is located in Inuyama close to Inuyama-jo. A teahouse is supposed to be the ultimate in restrained refinement, so you may concentrate on the elegant simplicity of the utensils used and the grace of the person preparing and serving the tea. Jo-an is a rather austere, low-key building set in pleasant surroundings. With this background information, it can be appreciated for its inherent worth and purpose, but as a sightseeing attraction it is not everyone's cup of tea (so to speak).

Kiso River

Kiso-gawa has several scenic spots along its banks in the Inuyama area, especially where the castle overlooks the river and where a mysterious rock looms out of the water just upstream of Inuyama-bashi and Inuyama-yuen station. This area of the Kiso River has been dubbed 'Nihon Rhine' (the Rhine of Japan), but only the strange rock fulfills this impression as it would be a perfect home for water nymphs or Lorelei. It's a pity the effect has been spoilt by some garish buildings that have been stuck on its flank but such is the way things are done here. Nevertheless, the general area is very attractive as the banks have been preserved as a nature park, thus being spared the 'benefit' of development with hotels, restaurants, etc. Rocks along the shoreline make a walk upstream from Inuyama-yuen station an enjoyable excursion – forested hill on one side and the river on the other.

Shooting the Rapids

A popular activity in this area is shooting rapids on the Kiso river for about 13 km down to Inuyama. It is a perfectly safe, enjoyable and year-round sport (weather

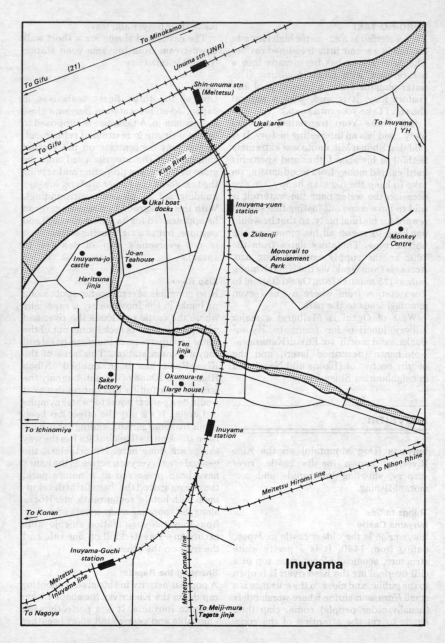

To Minokamo

(21)

To Gifu

Unuma stn (JNR)

Shin-unuma stn (Meitetsu)

To Gifu

Ukai area

To Inuyama YH

Kiso River

Ukai boat docks

Inuyama-yuen station

Zuisenji

Monkey Centre

Inuyama-jo castle

Jo-an Teahouse

Monorail to Amusement Park

Haritsuna jinja

Ten jinja

Sake factory

Okumura-te (large house)

Inuyama station

To Ichinomiya

To Nihon Rhine

Meitetsu Hiromi line

To Konan

Meitetsu Komaki line

Inuyama-Guchi station

Inuyama

Meitetsu Inuyama line

To Meiji-mura Tagata jinja

To Nagoya

permitting) and this is probably the best place in Japan to try it out. Long, flat-bottomed *Kiso-kudari* boats, guided by two or more boatmen with poles, make the descent in about two hours. Recently engine-powered boats have made an appearance; they take half the time.

There are two starting points in the vicinity of Mino-Kamo city, one on each side of the river. One is at Mino-Ota city (part of Mino-Kamo) on the north bank, accessible from Gifu by JNR. On the south bank the starting point is Imawatari, accessible by Meitetsu Hirome line from Inuyama station (to both north and south docks), while buses from Nagoya go only to the south docks (five minutes). A bridge joins the two sides.

There are several companies offering tours, so check to be sure of getting the type of boat you want; more of the traditional boats leave from the south docks. The cost will be somewhat over Y2000 (children about half).

Highpoints of the trip are at Kaniai, the rocks at Sekiheki, Rhine-yuen and the park area along the shore at Inuyama. Rhine-yuen is another starting point for boat rides and is reached from Sakahogi station on the Meitetsu line from Gifu. (The starting points near Mino-Kamo however are probably better.)

Ukai

Inuyama is another of the several places in this region that features cormorant fishing (described in detail under Gifu). At Inuyama, boats carrying spectators to the fishing area leave from the bank of the river downstream from Inuyama-yuen station, at the row of hotels. Most boats leave an hour or two before the fishing begins (soon after dark), which is rarely later than 7 pm, even in mid-summer (just about the only benefit of the refusal of authorities to introduce Daylight Saving Time).

The overall scene can be viewed quite well from the shore on the Unuma side upstream of the bridge, but the boats anchor off-shore and the row of spectator boats is between the shore and the fishing boats. (You can get a better view from the shore at Gifu, and probably at Uji, near Kyoto.)

The cost for boat rental will be about Y1800. Reservations can be made by phone (0568 61-0057) or through hotels and travel agencies in the area.

Meiji-mura

Within the boundaries of Inuyama is an open-air museum of more than 50 buildings and other memorabilia of the era of Emperor Meiji (1868-1910), who regained the position (and power) of emperor from the Tokugawa who had ruled for about 300 years. He pushed Japan into the modern age after three centuries of almost total isolation from the rest of the world. The innovations of his rule ran the gamut of every aspect of Japanese life and within 10 years of his taking power there was a railroad operating in Japan – quite an advance on horses and hand-carried palanquins. This period is called the 'Meiji Restoration' though 'Meiji Revolution' would be more accurate, both for the many changes in Japanese life and the many military battles required to secure his rule.

To most westerners, the items in the museum have symbolic rather than inherent interest. Most of the buildings for example are of 19th century western style and rather common-place in appearance – though to the Japanese they are somewhat exotic. Of world renown is the lobby of the old Imperial Hotel (Tokyo), a famed design of Frank Lloyd Wright.

Meiji Village is most easily reached by taking the Meitetsu-Komaki line from Nagoya or Inuyama to Meiji-mura-guchi station, from where it is a 12-minute bus ride or four km walk. There is also a direct bus service from Nagoya (one hour) from Meitetsu bus centre near Nagoya station.

Places to Stay

There are many hotels and ryokan in

Inuyama, including a number just downstream of Inuyama-yuen station. The youth hostel is about 800 metres upstream of this station and a further 400 metres uphill. It is quite pleasant (bar the noisy PA system) and a bargain – at Y600 it's one of the cheapest youth hostels in Japan.

Getting There

Meitetsu line trains, from Nagoya to Gifu, stop at Inuyama-yuen station (near Inuyama-jo castle). Inuyama station is some distance away. From Gifu by JNR, the terminal is Unuma at the other end of Inuyama-bashi (bridge). The bridge is the only place where I have seen a train caught in a traffic jam; both cars and trains use the same bridge.

FERTILITY SHRINES

The next two stations along the Komaki line from Meiji-mura-guchi are located near two shrines devoted to fertility, both for crops in this rich rice growing valley and for humans. There are shrines of this sort scattered around Japan, but these are among the best-known and the most accessible in the country.

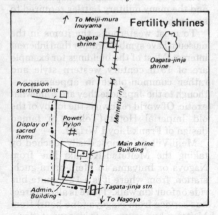

Oagata-jinja This is the female shrine, and houses several natural phenomena, like a cleft rock that resembles the female genitalia. It is a popular place of veneration for women about to marry and those who want children. The shrine is reached from Gakudan station (after Meiji-mura-guchi), by turning right when leaving the station and walking across the tracks and up the road for about 15 minutes towards the forested hills.

Tagata-jinja This is the male shrine. In the small building to the left of the main building is a quite amazing collection of phallus carvings ranging in size from a few centimetres to about two metres – all donated by grateful parents. The shrine is close to Tagata-jinja-mae station, the next after Gaku-den. Souvenirs are on sale at both shrines.

Shrine festivals

Tagata-jinja has a very interesting festival each year on 15 March. A carved wooden phallus, about three metres long, is carried in happy procession from another shrine about one km away accompanied by *Tengu* (a Shinto deity with a very long nose) and several women carrying smaller carvings similar to the main attraction. The procession moves slowly along the small road behind Tagata-jinja, starting early in the afternoon. In the morning, sake casks are broken open and the contents distributed. The people carrying the *mikoshi* (portable shrine) make frequent stops during the procession to partake of the sake. The owners of every field they pass also give them libations, so by the time they reach the shrine (about 3 pm or later) and carry the mikoshi into the main building, the bearers are thoroughly sloshed and have to be guided in the right direction.

There is usually a sign at the shrine indicating the parade route. The procession used to pass along the main road but has now been relegated to the back road, so its format will likely remain unchanged unless the puritanism of the police increases.

Oagata-jinja also has a festival but its format has been changing. Up to 1978 it took place on the morning of 15 March but it has since been changed to the following weekend. In 1978 the procession featured a number of pretty young women (brides-to-be?) on decorated floats as well as the shrine's *mikoshi*, a discreetly covered tree-root that serves as a female symbol. If you are interested in this festival it might be possible to get more information from the TIC in Tokyo.

MIZUNAMI
Palaeontologists passing through this town might find the Fossils Museum of interest.

TAJIMI
About 80 per cent of the porcelain for the Japanese market and more than half of the porcelain exports, are produced in Tajimi's pottery plants. Those interested in pottery could probably arrange to visit one of the 1300 or so plants.

ONI-IWA (Ogre Rock)
Travellers between Toki and Mino-Kamo might wish to stop to look at this interesting gigantic granite formation rising from the edge of the river near Oni-iwa onsen (hot spring resort).

SEKI
The small city of Seki has been known for centuries as the centre of production for many of the finest swords in Japan. To this day there are still many people in the city who make their living soley from this craft, including 12 swordsmiths, plus polishers and other assistants. There is little if any other points of interest in Seki besides the swordsmiths, so it is worth taking a little space to describe the fascinating process by which the swords are made.

Seki swordsmiths
The Japanese sword is the finest weapon of its kind ever created anywhere in the world; it is the ultimate expression of the swordsmith's art. It is unfortunate that their only *raison d'etre* is killing, as they could truly be described as jewels in steel.

When making a sword, a balance must be struck between hardness (for cutting) and resiliency (so that it doesn't snap in service). To accomplish these conflicting goals, Japanese swordsmiths use two processes together; they combine hard high carbon steel and soft low carbon steel in the same blade, and the tempering (heating and cooling the steel quickly to bring it to the correct degree of hardness) is varied over the width of the blade so that the back remains soft while the cutting edge is hard. This process takes a long time.

A swordsmith is permitted, by law, to make only two swords per month, though it is not likely he could make more swords of quality in much less time than this anyway.

It is generally very difficult to see the process of making swords as the smiths are busy and do not relish a continual stream of sightseers. Fortunately however demonstrations (open to the public) are given six times a year at Seki city, on the first Saturday of each of the odd-numbered months. They are given in a corner of the grounds of *Kasuga-jinja* (shrine), where a workshop has been set up duplicating the equipment found in a traditional smithy. Kasuga shrine is straight down the street leading from the town hall. If you are seriously interested in sword making and are not in Seki at demonstration time, there is a city official (Mr Shigeru Matsui) who speaks a little English and *might* be able to arrange an introduction to a practising swordsmith. (Modern smithies, however, are equipped with power-operated machinery, unlike the demonstration smithy.)

Mr Matui's telephone number is 05752 2-3131; it might be advisable to have a Japanese-speaking friend make the call for you.

At the Kasuga-jinja demonstration, a master dressed in traditional costume is accompanied by several apprentices (also in costume). The first striking is the most spectacular. The spongy mass of steel, after being heated in the fire by the master smith, is mashed into a cohesive blob by the hammer blows of the apprentices, a process which sends out a spray of sparks in all directions. The process of heating and beating is repeated a couple of times until the metal has become a small bar about 60 x 200 mm and 20 mm thick. Water is poured onto the anvil, and the red-hot bar is struck on top of it which prevents the metal from oxidising. This slab is scored with a chisel and then folded back on itself.

Now follows the most important stage. The smith rolls the glowing metal block in a small pile of black carbonised rice husks. When the metal is completely smothered in black, he pours a brown liquid over both sides and returns the metal to the fire. The liquid is a type of clay which protects the carbon from burning in the fire. When the metal reaches red-hot temperatures again the carbon is actually absorbed into the surface of the metal.

The rest of the process is a repetition of the above. The number of times this is repeated determines the carbon content of the finished steel and thus its potential hardness. For the hardest steel, to be used for the edge of the blade, the metal is folded 20 to 25 times. The result of this folding is an incredible number of layers of alternating carbonised (hard) and pure (soft) steel. After 20 folds there will be more than a million layers; after 25, more than 33 million layers! Softer steel for the inner structure of the blade may have only 10 to 12 doublings and steel for the side plates (and back, if one is used) might have 12 to 15 foldings. The layered structure imparts a measure of resilience and flexibility that a solid blade would not have.

During the demonstration (from 10 am to 4 pm) there is time to make only a couple of the required pieces of steel. When all the pieces are available they are forged together in a single mass which is then beaten out into the rough shape of the finished sword. The individual pieces made for the edge, core, sides, etc, keep their relative positions through the beating stage and the boundaries can be seen when the sword is polished. The final stage (shaping and straightening a previously made sword) are usually shown during the demonstration.

After the sword has the proper shape, two stages remain – tempering and polishing. To enable the edge to be tempered to a high degree of hardness while keeping the back relatively soft, the blade is covered with clay so that only the edge is exposed. The clay is often made wavy so that the varying widths of the edge are exposed. After heating, plunging the blade into water and polishing, this pattern appears and is one of the signs of beauty looked for in a sword. (The parts of the sword protected by the clay do not cool so abruptly, so they can revert to softer forms of steel, to some extent.)

An interesting finale to the demonstration is a display of the use of some of the finished swords. Bamboo poles are set up and swordsmen, dressed in traditional costume, show how effortlessly the swords can cut through pieces of bamboo. In olden times it was customary to demonstrate the sharpness of a new sword by testing how many condemned criminals it could cut.

Other craftsmen in Seki make the elaborately decorated handles, hand guards, etc, while most factories in the city make knives and other cutting utensils.

If you're thinking of picking up a sword while in town you may want to know the price so you can save up – a sword of the type being made and demonstrated would sell for about Y6,000,000.

Ukai

During the season mid-May to mid-October there is cormorant fishing at Seki as well as the better-known centres of Gifu and Inuyama.

Places to Stay

There are several ryokan and minshuku around the city, including at least two that are operated by cormorant fishermen. It is therefore possible to stay at one of the houses and have dinner on a boat for an all-inclusive price of Y7000 to Y8000 (which is rather high by minshuku standards, even including Y1800 or so for the performance). Two such fishermen are Mr Adachi (tel 05752 2-0799) and Mr Iwasa (tel 05752 2-1862).

Getting There

Seki is easily reached from Gifu by the train that begins service in Gifu as a tram but continues far into the country parallel to the road to Seki and Mino. By JNR, you could go from Nagoya, Inuyama, Mino-Kamo or Takayama.

Northern Gifu-ken

Because of the isolation of this highland area until very recently, many customs and other historical remnants have survived which makes it one of the most interesting areas of Japan to visit. There are two major river valleys and both have many places of interest. One extends northward from Seki along Route 156 to the isolated Shirakawa/Gokayama area, famous for large thatched-roof houses. The other runs north from Mino-Kamo along Route 41 (or from Nakatsugawa along Route 257) to Takayama. There are sufficient road links in the northern region to allow you to travel across from one valley to the next, through pretty mountain scenery.

SEKI TO THE SHOKAWA VALLEY

The scenery along this road is pleasant for most of the journey, with typical small farms and farmhouses, few towns and few signs of rampant modernisation. The only town of note is Gujo-Hachiman.

Gujo-Hachiman

There isn't much to see here but the town is renowned for its celebrations of Obon, when large numbers of townspeople dance in the streets every night throughout August. This 'madness' is known as *Gujo Odori* and is famous throughout Japan. The peak nights are around 13-16 August but any night from late July to early September would be equally good for a visit.

SHOKAWA VALLEY AREA

There is a very interesting region along the Shokawa river valley, south of Takaoka (Ishikawa-ken) which includes Shirakawa-go, Gokayama and other villages.

The area was settled in the 12th century by survivors of the Keike (Taira) clan who were defeated by the Genji (Minamoto) clan in the great battle for Dan-no-Ura, near Shimonoseki, for control of Japan. The Taira fled to this remote area to escape slaughter by their foes.

The area was still considered remote as late as 1961 when construction of the Miboro dam brought it to greater attention. Even until 1978 the only communication during winter was by boat along the river. Nowadays there is a year-round bus service. The description of this region overlaps Gifu and Toyama prefectures, which has made it difficult to obtain information on the area as a coordinated attraction, because prefecturally-prepared travel literature tends to studiously ignore things even a kilometre outside its own boundaries.

Gassho-zukuri (thatched-roof houses)

The outstanding feature of the region is its characteristic large three or four-storey thatched-roof gassho-zukuri houses. These are the largest traditional farmhouses in Japan and many are 200-300 years old. Surrounded as they are by hills and mountains and remote from most influences of the late 20th century, they make the region one of the most charming and traditional in Japan. A visit to such an

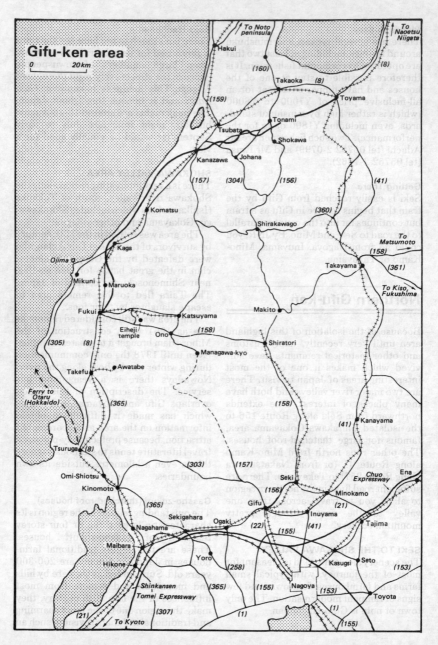

Gifu-ken area

0   20km

To Noto peninsula

To Naoetsu Niigata

Hakui

(160)

(8)

Takaoka   (8)

(159)

Toyama

Tsubata   Tonami

Shokawa

Kanazawa   Johana

(157)   (304)   (156)   (360)

Shirakawago

To Matsumoto

Komatsu

(158)

Kaga   Takayama

Ojima   (361)

Mikuni   To Kiso, Fukushima

Maruoka

Makito

Fukui   Katsuyama

(305)   (8)   Eiheji   Ono   (158)

temple   Shiratori

Managawa-kyo

Takefu   Awatabe   (158)

(365)   Kanayama

(41)

Ferry to
Otaru
(Hokkaido)

Tsuruga   (8)

(303)   (157)   Seki   Chuo   Ena

Expressway

Omi-Shiotsu

Kinomoto   (156)   Minokamo

(365)   Gifu   (21)

Sekigahara   Inuyama   Tajima

Nagahama   Ogaki   (155)   (41)

Maibara   (22)

Yoro   (258)   Kasugsi   Seto

Hikone   (365)   (155)   (153)

Shinkansen   Nagoya   Toyota

Tomei Expressway

(21)   (307)   (1)   (153)

To Kyoto   (1)   (155)

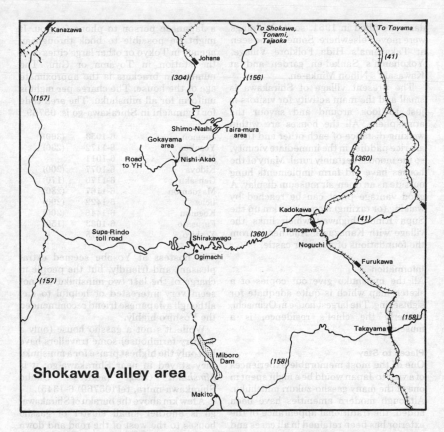

Shokawa Valley area

area (there are relatively few left) should be on the itinerary of any visitor who wishes to get a feel for 'old' Japan.

Gassho-zukuri means 'hands held in prayer' (ie Buddhist-style, with palms together and fingers stretched straight up). In former times, a single house accommodated 30 to 100 people on the ground floor; upper storeys were used for the production of handicrafts (utilitarian in those days, not for sale to tourists) or for raising silkworms; and the attic was used as a storehouse.

The area is increasingly popular with Japanese tourists seeking what remains of

the traditional Japan. As a result, a large number of the houses function as minshuku and take in guests, thus producing an income and ensuring their survival.

SHIRAKAWA-GO

This village is made up of several *buraku* (hamlets) each containing some of the thatched houses. Ogimachi is by far the most interesting as it has the lion's share of gassho-zukuri clustered together (11 of which are now minshuku). Other nearby buraku are Hatogoya and Iijima; which have only a few. The original village of Shirakawa was inundated when the Miboro dam was filled in 1961, so its buildings were moved elsewhere. Some can be seen at Takayama's Hida Folklore Village, Yokohama's Sankei-en garden and at Kawasaki's Nihon Minka-en.

The present village of Shirakawa is small and the main activity for visitors is just to look around and savour the atmosphere. All the houses are within walking distance of each other and there are rice paddies in the immediate vicinity, so the mood is certainly rural. Many of the houses have old farm implements hung outside as an open-air museum display. A good vantage point can be reached by walking (or taxiing) a couple of km up the Supa Rindo highway which links the village with Kanazawa. Another is from the foundations of a former castle.

Information

All the minshuku give out copies of a sketch map which is quite adequate for sightseeing. The largest house in Ogimachi, formerly the chief's residence, is a museum.

Places to Stay

One of the most memorable experiences of a visit to Japan would be a night spent in one of the many gassho-zukuri minshuku. Although modern amenities have been added, the traditional appearance of the exterior has been retained in all cases and the common-rooms often have the original hearth over which is suspended a pot-hook. All guests eat together and, if my experience at the *Juemon* was typical, the lady of the house keeps everyone company, pours beers and sake for them (ordered separately) and even sings folksongs of the region and performs local folk dances.

Departing from the usual practice of this book I have listed below the names and phone numbers of almost all the minshuku in Ogimachi. In the July-August season this area is very popular and it is advisable to phone ahead to be sure of having a place to stay. None of the proprietors speak English so you will need a Japanese person to phone for you. It might be possible to book through an agency in Tokyo or other large cities or at the station in Toyama or Gifu. The number in brackets is the approximate age of the house. The charge per night is uniform for all minshuku. The area code for Ogimachi in Shirakawa-go is: 05769.

Juemon	6-1053	(300)
Yosobe	6-1172	(230)
Nodaniya	6-1011	
Kidoya	6-1077	(200)
Gensaku	6-1176	(170)
Magoemon	6-1167	(280)
Iicha	6-1422	(200)
Koemon	6-1446	(200)
Furusato	6-1033	(150)
Yoshiro	6-1175	

The hostess at Yosobe seemed extra-pleasant and friendly, but the people in charge of the last two minshuku did not seem very interested or helpful to me, although a Japanese friend recommended the Yoshiro highly.

While it's not a gassho house (only a country farmhouse) some travellers have had only the highest praise for a minshuku they stayed in near Shirakawa-go; it is *Minshuku Osugi* (address: Okubo Shirakawa-mura, tel (05769) 6-1345).

A few km above the buraku of Shirakawa-go is another small cluster of gassho houses to the west of the road and down near the valley floor. There is a minshuku advertised on a sign at road level (Toichin-sa: tel (07637) 3632), but the surroundings are not as picturesque as at Shirakawa-go.

Getting There

The Shirakawa-go area can be reached by public transport from Nagoya, to the south, from Takaoka to the north and from Takayama to the east. From Nagoya, a simple way is by JNR train to Mino-Ota (nine per day; one hour); and from there by JNR to Mino-Shirotori (also nine per day but generally not connecting; two hours). From Shirotori there are five buses a day (two hours) to Onimachi (via Makito); they terminate at Hatogaya, a short distance beyond Onimachi. There is also a single bus from Nagoya station to Onimachi (5¼ hours) and Hatogaya. From Gifu, not far from Nagoya, there are many JNR trains to Mino-Ota (40 minutes); plus many buses through the day from Shin-Gifu station through to Shirotori (just over two hours). From Takaoka JNR runs as far south as Johana (20 per day) from where two buses a day run south to Hatogaya (one hour). Two buses a day also go from Takaoka station to Shimonashi (bypassing Johana; 1½ hours) where you can transfer to a Johana-Hatogaya bus. From Takayama, you can go by bus to Makito (six per day; 1½ hours) and then change to a Shirotori-Onimachi bus.

There are two routes to and from Kanazawa. The old one is via Route 304 to Taira-mura, where it meets Route 156; buses run on this route. The new Supa Rindo ('Hakusan Super Forest Pathway') toll road runs much more directly through the mountains and links Shirakawa-go with Route 157 straight to Kanazawa, but there is no bus service. Two-wheeled vehicles are not, unfortunately, allowed on this road.

Gokayama

A little further north, across the boundary into Toyama-ken, are the gassho houses of Gokayama (which is technically part of Kami-taira, or 'upper Taira' village), beginning at Nishi-Akao. There are so few that they can be identified by name. First comes the Iwase family; a little further on, at Suganuma (Kami-Taira) you find the houses that make up the *Gokayama Seishonen Ryoko Mura* (Youth Tourist Village) which offers accommodation. Near the Tourist Village is a road that turns off and runs inland to the west. This leads to *Etchu Gokayama Youth Hostel*, itself a gassho house (tel 07636 7-3331). Another house (Murakami family) can be found at Kami-Nashi (Upper Nashi), a hot spring town. At Shimo-Nashi (Lower

Nashi) you can see traditional Japanese paper (washi) being made at *Goka-shi Kyodo Kumiai* (Goka-city Paper Producers' Cooperative).

Toga

You can also find gassho-zukuri in the Kami-Momose section of Toga village. I haven't been there but believe there are five thatched houses close to each other. Being not so well-known and more remote it may be less touristy. There should be at least one minshuku in the area.

Getting there may not be too easy; one map indicates a good road direct to the village from just above Furukawa/ Takayama, with a minor road linking that road to Inokuchi, a little above Taira. But another major map gives no hint of such a road.

MINO-KAMO TO TAKAYAMA

North from Shirakawa-go along Route 156 and branching to Kanazawa on Route 304, you pass through some very pretty countryside. Continuing along 156 towards Takaoka, after the fork to 304, is less memorable but still enjoyable. Route 41 north from Mino-Kamo and Route 257 north from Nakatsugawa – both major routes to the Hida region and Takayama – meet just below Gero.

Gero

This is a typical hot-spring resort, basically a collection of concrete hotels that feature the mineral-laden water, mostly for therapeutic benefits. There are no attractions for the casual visitor, except that travellers with time to spare could check out one travel publication's mention of a village of gassho-zukuri houses transplanted here from Shirakawa-go when it was flooded by the waters of the Miboro dam. (I cannot guarantee its existence.) Those in a hurry can rely on the existence of houses still at Shirakawa-go, and a 'village' of houses transported to Takayama.

Another attraction of Gero is the *Chubu*

Sangaku Kohkogaku Hakubutsukan (Archaeological Museum).

Zenshoji

One stop above Gero is Zenshoji station; nearby is Zenshoji temple, the largest in the Hida region. Hida is the name given to the region generally above Gero to beyond Takayama.

Takayama

The city of Takayama ('High Mountain'), often called Hida-Takayama, has been a prosperous area for several centuries, and there is a tradition of cultured living here that you would not expect to find in such an isolated river valley.

Several fine old houses and other buildings survive in the city; these and other attractions make wandering around Takayama interesting, pleasurable and one of the most worthwhile places in Japan to visit.

Information

Your first stop should be at the information booth in front of Takayama station to pick up a copy of their English-language booklet *Hida-Takayama*. It lists all the places of interest to visitors, with a brief description of each, and locates them on a map. Ignore the reference to the 'pubic gym'; despite the well developed sex industry in Japan this is sure to be a disappointment.

If you are starting from Tokyo you should also obtain from the TIC a copy of the information sheet on Takayama; it has more details on train connections and accommodation.

Things to See

Hida Kokubunji temple This is the oldest temple in the Hida region, originally founded in 746. The main hall is about 500 years old.

Kusakabe Folkcraft Museum (Kusakabe Mingei-kan)

The house itself, dating from 1880, is a fine example of the residence of a wealthy merchant (Kusakabe family) of that era. The interior features heavy beams of polished wood which enhances the overall elegance of the rest of the building. There is also a collection of folkcraft items from the region. It is closed Wednesdays from December to February.

Yoshijima House

A neighbour of the Kusakabe house, this building was the residence of the Yoshijima ('Old Island') family, also wealthy merchants. The two are among the finest houses in Takayama. Yoshijima House is closed on Tuesdays from November to February.

Shishi Kaikan

This is an exhibition of the elaborately carved and ornately lacquered wooden lion-heads used for dances during processions.

Hachiman Shrine

The shrine is the site of the annual autumn festival. In the grounds is *Takayama Yatai Kaikan*, an exhibition hall containing four of the 23 *yatai*, elaborately decorated festival wagons, arranged as you would see them in an autumn or spring procession. This at least gives an impression of the magnificence of the festival for those who are unable to see the real thing.

Higashiyama Teramachi

Teramachi means 'temple town' and comes from the row of 10 temples at the foot of *Higashiyama* (East Mountain). (The youth hostel, at *Tenshoji* temple, is in this area.)

Hida Fubutsu-kan

This is a museum showing artefacts related to the way of life in the Hida region.

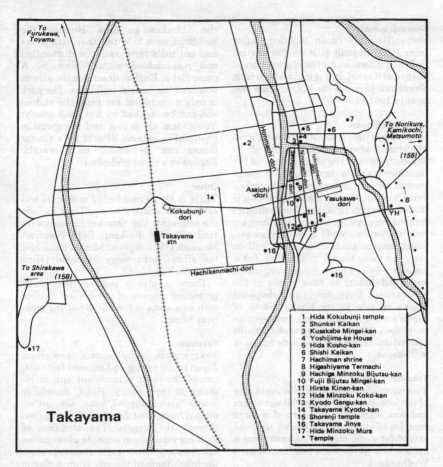

Takayama

To Furukawa, Toyama

To Norikura, Kamikochi, Matsumoto

(158)

To Shirakawa area (158)

Honmachi-dori

Ninomachi-dori

Sannomachi-dori

Ichinomachi-dori

Asaichi-dori

Yasukawa-dori

Kokubunji-dori

Takayama stn

Hachikenmachi-dori

YH

1 Hida Kokubunji temple
2 Shunkei Kaikan
3 Kusakabe Mingei-kan
4 Yoshijima-ke House
5 Hida Kosho-kan
6 Shishi Kaikan
7 Hachiman shrine
8 Higashiyama Teramachi
9 Hachiga Minzoku Bijutsu-kan
10 Fujii Bijutsu Mingei-kan
11 Hirata Kinen-kan
12 Hida Minzoku Koko-kan
13 Kyodo Gangu-kan
14 Takayama Kyodo-kan
15 Shorenji temple
16 Takayama Jinya
17 Hida Minzoku Mura
• Temple

Hachiga Folk Art Gallery (Hachiga Minyoku Bijutsu-kan)

The folk-art collection of the Hachiga family is housed in this building.

Hirata Memorial Hall (Hirata Kinen-kan)

Art objects belonging to the Hirata family, descendants of a wealthy merchant, are displayed in this museum.

Kyodo Gangu-kan

This museum houses about 2000 trad-itional toys from different regions of Japan.

Municipal History Museum (Takayama Kyodo-kan)

Built in 1876 and formerly a storehouse, this building belonged to the Nagata family and now houses many items of local history as well as a famous Enku statue. The latter is one of many well-known statues roughly sculpted with a hatchet by the itinerant priest Enku.

Shorenji temple

Shorenji temple (main building dating from 1504) is built in a unique ancient style and is famous for the elegant curved shaped of its roof. It was moved here from Shirakawa-go when the Miboro dam was built in 1961.

Furui-Machinami

Step back in time with a stroll down Furui-Machinami where old houses and shops line both sides of the street. Many of the buildings are restaurants, coffee shops or souvenir shops (the owners have to make a living too), but the overall impression is that of a century or so ago. The buildings with the large spongy-looking 'ball' hanging from the eaves are old sake warehouses, where various kinds of sake are still on sale. For more than a millennium Takayama has been known for its carpenters and woodworkers so have a look at the small chests, trays, bowls and chopping blocks on sale in the shops. Some of Japan's most tasteful souvenirs, such as woodblock prints, papier mache figures and special sake flasks are made and sold in Takayama.

Takayama Jinya

This imposing building was the residence of the local governor in the Tokugawa era and was originally the heart of a large complex of buildings. Now most are gone except for eight samurai barracks and a garden behind the main building. Closed Wednesdays.

Hida Folklore Village (Hida Minzoku Mura)

With the mountains that surround Takayama as a backdrop and the interesting setting of the park itself the first impression here is that of a functioning ancient village. It is probably the best park of its kind in Japan, with many traditional farmhouses (mostly thatched) and other buildings up to 500 years-old set up around a pond. The reservation includes houses from a number of districts in the mountains around Takayama, including

the Shirakawa-go area. Because the buildings were held together with ropes and not nails they could be dismantled and reassembled without damage. A pamphlet in English describes the salient points of the various buildings. The park is only a couple of km from the station and can be reached by bus (half hourly; Y200), taxi or on foot and is especially beautiful in autumn. (Parks on a similar theme can be found in Kawasaki, Kanazawa and on Shikoku.)

Other

There is also a number of museums and exhibitions worth visiting. They include the following: the Shunkei Lacquerware Hall (Shunkei Kaikan); Fujii Folkcraft Museum (Fujii Bijutsu Mingei-kan); and the Hida Archaeology Museum (Hida Minzoku Koko-kan).

There is also a pair of delightfully grotesque statues of pot-bellied goblins with long arms in the middle of the main river bridge.

Festivals

Takayama is justly famous throughout Japan for its spring and autumn festivals, two of the most magnificent and interesting in the country. Huge, incredibly ornate festive wagons, *yatai*, are put on display for most of the day and later pulled through the streets. The tradition of building yatai began a couple of centuries ago as a supplication to the gods to protect the inhabitants of the city from a plague that was ravaging the country. Their prayers seemed to be successful so the custom continued (a sort of preventative medicine) and the carts became more magnificent each time as a spirit of competition developed among wealthy merchants. As Takayama was a wealthy town the best materials and construction could be afforded. To duplicate one today would cost about half a million dollars! A booklet is available which gives the history of each yatai – some are nearly 300 years old. During the rest of the year the wagons are stored in yatai-gura, tall concrete storehouses with no windows and very tall doors. As mentioned earlier there is a permanent display of four yatai during the rest of the year at *Yatai-kaikan*, in the grounds of Hachiman shrine.

The wagons (which are hard to describe as they resemble nothing known in western countries) include intricate wood carvings that form panels and pillars of the structure, antique tapestries of European origin, and other embellishments. In addition there is a small number of mechanical 'dolls' that perform amazing movements and tricks, all controlled by wires and push-rods; the ingenuity of their designers deserves greater recognition. A typical doll 'walks' out along a beam, rotates and bows to the audience, pivots around completely a couple of times, then releases a shower of flower petals. One yatai even has a couple of acrobats that swing from perch to perch.

The performance times of the dolls during the display of the yatai is indicated on a board near the wagons. It pays to arrive early for a performance to get a good place, as the crowds are very heavy.

The spring *Sanno-matsuri* is held on 14-15 April near Hie-jinja (shrine); and the autumn *Yahata-matsuri* on 9-10 October in the grounds of Hachiman-jingu. There is a total of 23 yatai, 12 are shown at the spring festival and the other 11 in the autumn. There are also parades of people in various feudal costumes. An interesting feature is one of the musical instruments, a circular metal pan that is struck with a wooden mallet to produce a peculiar 'ging' sound; it seems to be found only in this district.

Places to Stay

There is a youth hostel in Takayama at *Tenshoji* temple (tel (0577) 32-6345), however it was not the most pleasant I encountered. The house-mother had a love affair with the PA which, like most PA systems, had only one setting – full blast.

At 10 pm (lights-out) she continued for 15 minutes to tell her charges to go to sleep while they were all lying in the darkness waiting for her to keep quiet!

As might be expected in a town that is very popular with Japanese sightseers, Takayama has plenty of minshuku and ryokan. Reservations may be made at offices set up for the purpose, located near the station. One is at the information booth in front of the station; another is down the street to the left; and a third at the far side of the department store opposite and to the right. They are signposted only in Japanese, but the Kanji for 'minshuku' are prominent and can be recognised easily.

The phone number of the Takayama Minshuku Association is (0577) 33-8501/2; the Takayama Ryokan Association is (0577) 33-1181. Have someone call in Japanese, as it is unlikely that anyone will understand English. There is also a Kokumin-shukusha (Peoples' Lodge), tel (0577) 32-2400. The cheapest hotel is the *Meiboku* (tel (0577) 33-5510) which has double rooms for Y8000. The *Hida* and *Green* hotels are more expensive, tel (0577) 33-4600 and 33-5500 respectively.

Getting There

From the south, Takayama is easily reached by JNR train from Nagoya etc, via Gifu. There is also a year-round bus service to and from Gifu; and from mid-May to mid-October from Matsumoto, by a combination of two buses and a train via Shin-Shima-Shima (as described earlier in this chapter). From the north there is JNR service to and from Toyama and possibly a bus service. Highway 41 is a major road linking Nagoya with Toyama and there is quite heavy traffic, so hitching should be no problem.

Getting Around

Since the city is laid out with streets at right-angles (a rarity in Japan) it is easy to find your way around Takayama and it is small enough that the energetic can see it on foot or by bicycle. The latter can be rented from at least two shops on the main street (to the left when leaving the station, on the opposite side of the street) and rental is Y1500 per day.

There is a regular bus service that goes to or near most of the attractions of the city and circles back to the station. A 'free pass' (the 'Japlish' term) costing Y770 is available; it gives unlimited travel for two days and can be bought at the station. Buses run every 20 minutes between 9 am and 4.40 pm.

FURUKAWA

About 15 km above Takayama is the small city of Furukawa ('Old River'). It has a number of old houses and the appearance of some of its streets is, overall, perhaps more traditional than that of Takayama. It is a pleasant place to walk around and there is a chance that a rickshaw will be available for short rides.

Festival

Furukawa is probably best-known for its annual festival, which is well worth trying to see. *Furukawa-matsuri* is held on 19-20 April. The feature is a night procession of a huge drum on which two men sit back-to-back and swing their hammers down to strike both ends in unison. The festival dates back 1500 years, so I was told, to the time when drums were used to scare boars away from the crops.

The festival lasts two days and it is advisable to see all of it. During the day there are processions of the nine *yatai* (festive wagons similar to those at Takayama and Kyoto). The wagons are elaborately decorated, though they are not as large or imposing as those in the other two cities. Two of them also have ingenious mechanical dolls which are on display on the second day of the festival. Times for their performances are posted beside the *yatai-gura* (the concrete buildings where they are stored the rest of the year). Unless there have been any changes, the times for the *kirintai yatai* (a kirin is a

mythical dragon) are 1.30 and 3.30 pm; while the *seyutai yatai* can be seen at 10 am and 3 pm. The dolls are at least 150 years-old (ca 1820) and are marvels of design skill, similar to those described for the Takayama festivals. These dolls can also be seen at one of Nagoya's festivals.

During the processions of the first day many townspeople in old costumes accompany the wagons. Children are dressed at their best (as they are for the more crowded Takayama-matsuri) and it is a splendid chance to photograph them dressed in very beautiful kimono. Many boys play the unusual 'ging' instrument described in the section on the Takayama festival.

Throughout the festival young men go from door to door performing a *shishi-mai* (lion dance). The *shishi* has a magnificently carved wooden head with jaws that clack shut in a most amusing way. If there are children nearby, the dancer operating the head may get right down to the ground to try to scare the child – usually he or she laughs with delight. Two assistants manipulate the lion's body and the dancers are accompanied by a small troupe of flute players and a drummer who keeps rhythm with healthy wallops on a wheeled drum.

After dark on the first night bonfires are lit at several intersections of the town and at about 10 pm the lids of the sake casks are broken open and the contents liberally distributed to the young men carrying the drum, as well as to any passers-by who wish to indulge. Any foreigners present (usually few) receive special attention and it becomes a problem keeping sober enough to see the rest of the festivities, let alone take pictures.

The fires and sake help to keep the young men warm, as the nights are very cold (nearby ski-fields still have large patches of snow on them) and they wear nothing but haramaki around their middles and a loincloth. After they have become sufficiently soused, one after another demonstrates his balancing skills by scaling a bamboo pole and lying

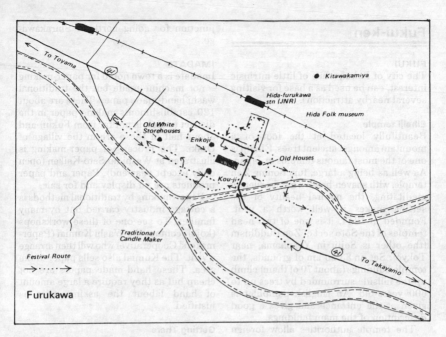

To Toyama

Kitawakamiya

Hida-furukawa
stn (JNR)

Hida Folk museum

Old White
Storehouses

Enkoji

Old Houses

Kou-ji

Traditional
Candle Maker

Festival Route

To Takayamo

Furukawa

on it, all his weight held by the small circle of the pole pressing into his belly.

Not long afterward, the procession with the large drum begins. The drum (about 1.5 metres in diameter), the two drummers and at least 10 other people carrying lanterns, are supported on a large structure of bamboo poles and beams that is carried through the streets on the strong shoulders of many (usually inebriated) young men. The drum is preceded by a large number of people in costume who carry lighted paper lanterns; the effect is beautiful. Most houses, ryokan and minshuku along the parade route (it circles through the town several times through the night) have upper-storey windows that can be removed completely to give a good view of the parade – by far the best vantage point to watch it. The celebration and inebriation are, by the way, historically part of Japanese festivals and have been for the last 2000 years. During the festival there

is a special table set up at the station to help people find rooms. However many of the rooms are at ski lodges many kilometres out of town, accessible only by taxi, so it would be worth trying to arrange accommodation in advance. There is a youth hostel at Takayama, but the drum procession takes place too late at night to allow time to see it and get back in time for lights-out.

48 Waterfalls

Between Takayama and Furukawa there is a turn-off (signposted in Japanese) pointing the way to 48 Waterfalls (Yonju-hachi taki), about eight km off the main road.

They are a pleasant low-key bit of scenery – the water flow and the drops are moderate – but they provide a peaceful walk relatively remote from humanity – well most of it anyway.

Fukui-ken

FUKUI

The city of Fukui, while of little intrinsic interest, can be used as a base for visiting several nearby attractions.

Eiheiji temple

Beautifully located at the foot of a mountain amongst ancient trees, Eiheiji is one of the most famous temples in Japan. As well as being a large, functioning Zen temple, with shaven-headed monks silently meditating, the natural beauty of the setting makes it well worth a visit. Founded in 1244, it is one of two head temples of the Soto sect of Zen Buddhism (the other is Sojiji in Yokohama, near Tokyo). Set on 33 sq km of grounds, the temple buildings (about 70 of them) climb up the hillside surrounded by trees up to 600 years-old. An English pamphlet is given at the entrance and gives a good description of the main buildings.

The temple authorities allow foreign visitors to stay at the temple and participate in Zen meditation. (Refer to the notes on Zen meditation earlier in the book.) At Eiheiji visitors are expected to follow the same discipline as Japanese participants, starting with meditation at 3.30 am. Arrangements should be made in advance by writing to: Sanzenkei, Eiheiji, Eiheiji-cho, Yoshida-gun, Fukui-ken.

The temple (less than 20 km south-east of Fukui) is easily reached by Keifuku Dentetsu railway or by bus. The train is most easily caught from the east side of Fukui station (behind the building). A bike path between Fukui and Eiheiji runs mostly along scenic river banks.

Kuzuryu gorge/Managawa gorge

Both of these gorges, noted for their scenery, are in the vicinity of Ono. The former is close to Echizen-Shimoyama station (JNR), and it is likely that buses run to the latter from Ono station (JNR). Ono is on the road to Shirotori, the junction for going north to Shirakawa-go.

IMADATE

Imadate is a town noted for paper-making – not machine-made but the traditional washi hand-made paper. There are about 120 establishments making paper in the district (which is not far from Fukui) and about half of these are in the village of Otaki. The process of paper-making is illustrated at Washi-no-Sato-Kaikan (open daily except year-end). Paper and paper products are.on display and for sale.

Paper-making by traditional methods is a cottage industry carried out by many families. To see one of these workshops (kojo), contact the Washi Kumiai (Paper-makers' Cooperative) who will then arrange a visit. The Kumiai also sells paper of the area. These hand-made papers are not cheap but as they require a large amount of hand labour the asking price is justified.

Getting There

Access is from Takefu (18 km south of Fukui by JNR) by a local line, the Nanetsu-sen. The destination is the final station, Awatabe, which is in Imadate.

ECHIZEN TOGEI MURA

Echizen Pottery Village was set up to preserve and continue the tradition of ceramics that has existed here for centuries. Echizen is one of the 'Six Ancient Kilns' and has been a pottery making centre since the Kamakura Era (1192-1333).

Many potters of note have workshops and showrooms in Togei Mura and most have no objection to visitors. Other pottery, both modern and historic, is on display at Fukui-ken Ceramics Museum (Fukui-ken Togeikan) nearby. It is open daily except Mondays, the third Wednesday of the month, national holidays and the New Year period. Local kilns can be tracked down using a booklet (in Japanese) available at the museum.

Amateur potters can take single lessons

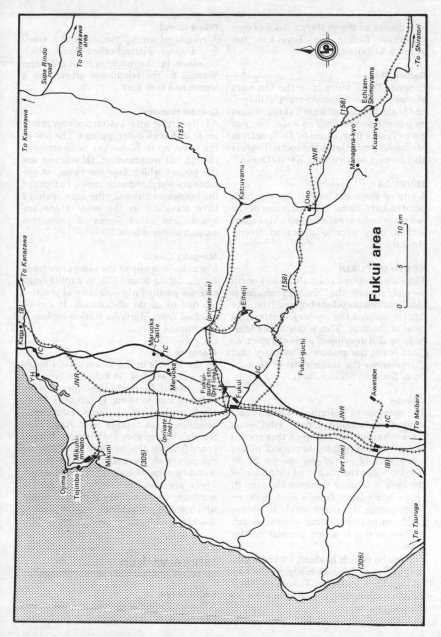

Fukui area

or a course at the pottery school (Togei kyoshitsu) beside the Togei-kan (tel 07783 2-2174).

Getting There

Echizen Togei Mura is in the Ozowara section of the Miyazaki-mura (village), and is easily reached from Takefu station by bus in less than half an hour. You can get to Takefu from Fukui by JNR, or from Maibara, 55 minutes to the south. There is also a direct service from Kyoto/Osaka.

TSURUGA

A city on the coast nearest the northern point of Lake Biwa, Tsuruga is one of the two ports in the area (along with Mai-zuru) with a ferry service direct to Otaru, Hokkaido.

NORTH OF FUKUI

The entire Echizen coast all the way north to and around the Noto Peninsula is ideally suited to cyclists because it is quite flat terrain and the scenery is attractive most of the time. This is one of the least built-up and developed parts of Japan, so there is not the amount of industry that characterises the south coast of Honshu from Tokyo to Shimonoseki.

Tojimbo

The coastline of Tojimbo is a small-scale version of Britain's Land's End – an outcropping of volcanic rock that cooled in a pattern of roughly hexagonal pillars rising sharply out of the sea for 25-30 metres. Since the rock is an extension of the land it is easy to scramble over it; cruise boats leave from a cove between outcroppings. It is impossible to photograph without including several dozen tourists as this is a very popular destination.

Tojimbo (which is about 30 km northeast of Fukui) is most easily reached by taking a tram-train from Fukui to Mikuniminato station, then changing to a bus for the last two km.

Ojima Island

A couple of km up the coast is a small forest-covered island called Ojima, which is joined to the mainland by a bridge. Visitors to the island are greeted by a shrine and torii gate.

Coastal scenery

A little further up is a stretch of very pretty coast with rock outcroppings. The rest of the coast up to Kanazawa is interesting, though not outstanding. Of interest are the houses which face the coast, as the roofs are weighted with rocks. In front of the houses in autumn (the only season I have travelled in the area) there are boards and other forms of protection against winter winds.

Maruoka Castle

Maruoka-jo is one of the oldest castles in Japan, dating from 1575. It is quite small and not particularly notable – of greatest interest to castle aficionados. It can be reached from Maruoka station by bus in 15 minutes.

Places to Stay

Of the hostels in the Fukui area, I found *Youth Hostel 3404* (in Fukui) to be rather institutional. More pleasant, though some distance out of town, is *Gankeiji Youth Hostel*, which is a large functioning neighbourhood temple near Kaga. The temple's history goes back several hundred years (though the present buildings are comparatively recent), and the housemother is exceptionally kind and pleasant. There are some minshuku right on the northern coast overlooking the water, which would probably be a good place to spend the night.

Ishikawa-ken

KANAZAWA

A favourite of Japanese tourists, Kanazawa has much to recommend it to foreign

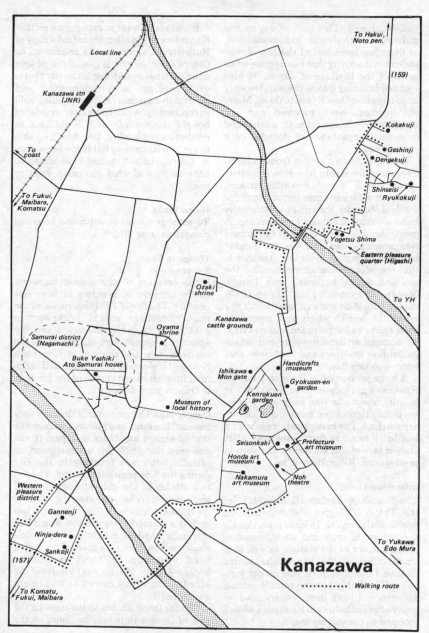

To Hakui,
Noto pen.

(159)

Local line

Kanazawa stn
(JNR)

To coast

To Fukui,
Maibara,
Komatsu

Kokakuji

Geshinji
Dengakuji

Shinseisi
Ryukokuji

Yogetsu Shima

Eastern pleasure
quarter (Higashi)

To YH

Ozaki
shrine

Kanazawa
castle grounds

Oyama
shrine

Samurai district
(Nagamachi)

Buke Yashiki
Ato Samurai house

Handicrafts
museum

Museum of
local history

Ishikawa
Mon gate

Gyokusen-en
garden

Kenroku-en
garden

Seisonkaki

Prefecture
art museum

Honda art
museum

Western
pleasure
district

Gannenji

Ninja-dera

Sankoji

(157)

Nakamura
art museum

Noh
theatre

To Yukawa
Edo Mura

Kanazawa

To Komatu,
Fukui, Maibara

Walking route

visitors as well. This part of Japan has undergone relatively little industrialisation, so there has been less of the tear-down-and-rebuild activity that has destroyed so much of the heritage of Japan. It also escaped bombing during the war, the only large city other than Kyoto to do so. Many old buildings have survived and old neighbourhoods are almost unchanged from their appearance of decades or a century ago.

Strangely, being so far from cultural influences like Kyoto (the area is heavily covered with snow in winter making transport in former times very difficult for much of the year), the city has historically been a centre of culture and learning. A major factor is that it is one of the richest rice-growing areas and was the largest feudal land tenure in Japan. Another is that the Maeda clan who controlled the city and region, beginning with Toshiie Maeda (who captured the city in 1583) valued education and a cultured life. They spent the wealth wisely and promoted such crafts as lacquerware and weaving, encouraged artisans to settle and established fine buildings and traditions that survive to this day.

A large proportion of the attractions of Kanazawa are located near Kanazawa-jo (castle), mostly around an irregular loop encircling Kenrokuen garden, and can be seen on foot. The castle can be reached by bus in 15 minutes from Kanazawa JNR station (about 2.5 km away); the stop is pronounced 'Kenrokuen-sh'ta'.

Information

The photocopied information sheets from the Tokyo TIC give useful details on accommodation etc. In Kanazawa there's a large guide map and an information office in front of the station, as well as a small office at the handicrafts centre (*Kanko Bussan-kan*). If you do get lost, you will probably have no trouble getting assistance; I have never experienced so many offers of help as in Kanazawa when I stopped to consult my maps.

If you really want to experience all that Kanazawa has to offer, try to find a copy of Ruth Steven's guide book *Kanazawa: The Other Side of Japan*. It is a labour of love and describes everything in the city that is worth seeing, in a lighthearted and informative manner. Its first printing sold exceptionally well (Kanazawa residents bought thousands!) so it is difficult to predict its availability. You should be able to get it in Kanazawa but if you see a copy in Tokyo, snap it up and read ahead to have an idea of what you really want to see.

Home Visits

To arrange a visit to a private house in Kanazawa, ring 20-2075.

Things to See
Kanazawa-jo

Little remains of the former imposing castle because of a series of fires last century. The fire of 1881 destroyed all the major buildings except Ishikawa-mon gate, parts of the walls, moats and the armoury *sanjuken nagaya*. The site of the castle is now the campus of Kanazawa National University (to be relocated in the near future). In one corner of the grounds is Oyama-jinja shrine.

Oyama-jinja The gate of this shrine is very unusual in design and history and is unlike that of almost any other in Japan. It was designed in 1870 by a Dutchman, a scientist who was teaching in the city during the westernisation period. The top two stories of the gate strongly suggest two squared arches, one atop the other, of traditional Chinese design. Filling the top arch is a stained glass window which was originally used as a lighthouse to guide ships on the Sea of Japan. The shrine itself dates from 1599 and was built to honour Toshiie Maeda, the founder of the Maeda clan; it was moved to its present site in 1873.

Similar (rare) arches to the ones on the gate of Oyama-jinja may be found on the

Karamon (Chinese gate) of the innermost buildings of Toshogu shrine in Nikko; and another in Nagasaki at Kofukuji (nicknamed the 'Chinese' temple).

Gyokusen-en garden This was the garden of the Nishida family and is laid out in a circular style around a pond.

Ishikawa-ken kanko Bussan-kan
Ishikawa-ken is famous for several handicrafts including some of Japan's finest lacquerware, cloth weaving and dyeing, pottery making, wood carving and others. This museum makes it possible for visitors to see some of the crafts being produced. Master craftsmen give daily demonstrations in lacquerware, carving of wooden heads for *shishi* (lion dolls), gold beating, *kaga yuzen* (fabric dyeing), and *kutani* (pottery-making). An excellent pamphlet in English gives sufficient explanation of the crafts to understand the processes. Demonstrations are given on the third floor. There are restaurants and shops selling a wide variety of handicrafts native to the area. In addition, there is a tourist information office at the entrance but beware of their map of Kanazawa. It is an all-too-typical Japanese handout map, very stylised, not to scale and north is off to the left. (Closed Wednesdays is winter.)

Kenrokuen Garden
Considered by the Japanese to be one of the three finest landscape gardens in the country, Kenrokuen, which dates from 1819, covers 10 hectares. Roku means 'six' and Kenrokuen combines the six features considered essential to fine gardens: vastness, solemnity, careful arrangement, coolness (water), age and pleasing appearance.

The garden is spacious and encloses two ponds. It is, to me, by far the most attractive of the 'Big Three' gardens. However, although Kenrokuen is certainly worth seeing, for some viewers it does not quite live up to its advance billing. The

north entrance to the garden is across the road from Ishikawa-mon gate, but there are also other entrances.

Seisonkaku On the southern edge of Kenrokuen is Seisonkaku, a beautiful two-storey mansion built by one of the *daimyo* for his mother. It is a fine example of Shoin-zukuri architecture. In addition to the design and workmanship of the house and garden there is also an exhibit of many items used by the Maedas. (Closed Wednesdays.)

Ishikawa-ken Bijutsu-kan (Prefecture Art Museum) A very short distance from Seisonkaku, this museum is most worthy of note for its collection of kutani pottery.

Nohgaku Bunka Kaikan (Prefectural Noh Theatre) Noh plays are performed here frequently, mostly by amateur groups, but there is a regular professional performance on the first Sunday of every month. (Some sources claim the third Sunday, so be sure to check!) Performances last from 9 am to 5 pm. The theatre dates from 1972 and includes the stage that was salvaged from the old Noh theatre that stood beside the town hall. The theatre is just a short distance south of Seisonkaku. (Closed Mondays.)

Honda Zohin-kan (Memorial Art Museum) Also located near Seisonkaku, at the top of the hill, this museum houses a collection of items used by the Honda family, the chief retainers under the Maeda.

Nakamura Kinen Bijutsu-kan (Memorial Art Museum)
Close to the Honda Museum, this is a large Japanese-style house that belonged to a wealthy sake dealer named Nakamura. He donated the house and his collection of Oriental art (including fine lacquerware and utensils for the tea ceremony) to the city. (Closed on Tuesdays and the day after national holidays.)

Kyodo Shiryo-kan (Museum of Local History)

This museum has a variety of exhibits of local archaeology, folklore and history, including one relating to the processions required of local daimyo to Edo (Tokyo) in feudal times, which often involved thousands of people. The building looks incongruous, as it is a western-style red-brick structure built as a high school in 1891, at the time when westernisation was in full swing. Note that on the map included with the information sheets available at the Tokyo TIC, this is labelled 'History Museum'. (Closed Mondays.)

Samurai district

Walking through the little lanes of the old samurai town of Nagamachi gives at least an impression of olden times. There are several typical narrow crooked streets lined with packed-earth, tile-topped walls that keep out curious eyes. Most of the houses however are actually from the Meiji era (1868-1910), rather than genuine samurai-built houses. One authentic samurai house which has been restored and is open to the public as a museum is *Buke Yashiki Ato* (closed Wednesdays). Another old house, *Saihitsuan*, is used for demonstrating *yuzen*, the traditional method of hand-painting patterns on silk for kimono (closed Thursdays in winter). For a look over two former samurai gardens, have a coffee at either Kaga-no-niwa or Nokore (both closed Thursdays).

After visiting the samurai area and shopping in the many stores along the nearby main street, you can return full-circle to Oyama shrine or leave it till last along with a more leisurely look at the handicraft-making displays at the handicrafts centre.

Higashi (geisha) district

Higashi is one of Kanazawa's two 'old' districts, most popular with visitors because they preserve much of the atmosphere of former times. According to one story, the Maedas decreed that geisha

areas and temples be placed on the banks of both the Agano and Sai (west) rivers, so that invaders would be distracted by one or the other. More likely it was a way to minimise their effect on daily life, just as Tokyo had the Yoshiwara area set aside for its geisha houses. The main attraction is just wandering along the back streets among the old houses and temples. Visitors are allowed into one of the still functioning geisha houses, the Shima (usually open 9 am to 5 pm; closed Mondays). Another, the Yogetsu, has been turned into a minshuku.

Teramachi

This is the second of the 'old' districts. The geisha houses are no longer mentioned but the temples still remain, including Myoryuji, one of the most unusual in Japan.

Myoryuji

Dubbed *Ninja-dera* (Ninja temple) this is not merely a temple but a type of fortress with labyrinthine secret passages, hidden traps and exits, that would serve to hold off invaders while the *daimyo* escaped. Myoryuji was the Maeda family temple. There are tours lasting 20 minutes, but the temple is so popular that it is generally necessary to make reservations (tel 41-2877, in Japanese); on Sundays and holidays it may be impossible. The best time to go is mid-afternoon. If there are not many people scheduled for a tour, it may be possible to squeeze in without a reservation. Some of the guides may speak English. (Closed first and 13th of each month and New Year.)

Edo-mura

Of interest to many will be Edo-Mura, a 'village' of Edo-era (17-19th century) buildings that were moved here from different parts of Japan. Some of the buildings are luxurious mansions and houses, while others give an idea of the less-exalted conditions of the ordinary people. The village is well done, but the number of buildings is rather small (about 20) in view of the rather high admission charge (Y650).

Included in the price, however, is admission to nearby Danpuen, a small village concentrating on crafts; a minibus goes every 20 minutes between the two villages. The village rather suffers in comparison with the similar park in Takayama but it is worth seeing if you don't have to pinch pennies. Access is by Hokuriku Railway bus 12 from Kanazawa station to Yukawa Onsen; Edo-mura is a short walk uphill.

Festivals

There are many festivals through the year. Most are small neighbourhood affairs but there are some very large and well-known ones as well.

10-16 February: Performances of *dekumawashi* (a kind of puppet theatre unique to the area) at the community centre of Oguchi. Performances are at night, so it is advisable to make prior arrangements for accommodation in the village.

19-20 April: *Gokoku-jinja* Spring Festival featuring dances by shrine maidens.

15 May: Shinji Noh performance, given outdoors at *Ono Minato Jinja* (in Kanaiwa); a 370-year-old ritual.

13-15 June: *Hyaku-man goku matsuri* celebrates the entry into Kanazawa, in 1583, of Toshiie Maeda, first lord of the Maeda clan. (Other sources say 12-14 June, so check in advance.) Features include a procession of people in colourful feudal costumes (on the last day), folk dancing in the evening, geisha show at Kanko Kaikan, tea ceremony at Kenrokuen and Seisonkaku, and martial arts displays.

24-25 July: At Ono, three mountain demons (villagers in bright costume) spend two days going from house to house exorcising demons with flutes and drums. Ono can be reached by bus from Musashi.

1-3 August: *Ono-minato-jinja matsuri*, held in Kanaiwa town, is famous for its carved wooden floats.

15 August: Obon dances at Hatta village (night); its *Sakata Odori* is one of the few in Japan in which old costumes are worn and music is live, not recorded.

October: Through the month there are local shrine festivals.

19-20 October: Dances by shrine maidens at *Gokoku* shrine.

15 November: *Shichi-go-san* (7-5-3) festival, celebrated everywhere in Japan. Go to *Ishiura-jinja* to see children dressed in beautiful kimono.

Places to Stay

There are two youth hostels in Kanazawa, one of which is the cheapest in Japan (Y300), but it is so far out in the country that it is not worth trying to find. It also has a very early (and noisy) reveille. There are many hotels, ryokan and minshuku (especially in Higashi); bookings can be made at the station. There is a very interesting inn/restaurant in a 150-year-old farmhouse, *Zenigame*, a few km out of town toward Edo-mura (tel 35-1426).

Getting There

Kanazawa is easily reached by train from Tokyo, Nagoya, Kyoto, Osaka, etc, via Maibara (on the Shinkansen); or by plane to nearby Komatsu airport.

FROM KANAZAWA TO THE NOTO PENINSULA

Between Kanazawa and Haui are two large and venerable houses, Okabe-ke and Kita-ke, the homes of local governors in the Tokugawa era. In addition to administering the law, these officials collected taxes in the form of rice. Okabe-ke is somewhat larger but both houses (which are about 10 km apart) have collections of relics from that age. Okabe-ke is accessible by bus from Kanazawa station and is close to Menden station (JNR); Kita-ke is near Minami-Hakui station and there may be a bus service as well.

Keta-jinja

There is nothing of interest at Hakui itself, but just a few km north is Keta-jinja (shrine), which faces the sea and is set in a picturesque grove of trees.

Myojiji temple

Only a short distance north and a little inland of Keta shrine is Myojiji one of the great temples of the region. Its five-storey pagoda looks out over the surrounding flat countryside and the view of the temple at the top of a long flight of stone steps is quite beautiful and memorable (except for the inevitable wires draped right across the middle of the scene, which will appear in any photo). The temple was established in the 13th century, although most of the present buildings date 'only' from the 1600s. There is a handout pamphlet, in perfect English, that explains the history of the temple and each of the main buildings.

Noto-hanto

The Noto-hanto peninsula contains some of the most picturesque scenery in Japan. There are still large rice paddies, farmers working diligently and typical rural scenes that have remained almost unchanged for decades. Cyclists will particularly enjoy this area as there are relatively few hills. The outer (soto) coast of the peninsula is much more rugged and scenic than the calm inner (uchi) shore. The finest scenery begins just above Kanazawa and continues around to the eastern tip at Cape Rokugo, while there are beautiful, though less dramatic views past the cape down to Nanao on the east coast.

Information

The information sheets from the TIC in Tokyo are very useful for train, bus and boat schedules and should be picked up for up-to-date information.

Noto Kongo

About 15 minutes above Myojiji, a small roads turns off Route 249 to Fukuura and the shore. Between Fukuura and Togi is a 14 km stretch of coast known as Noto-Kongo, noted for its scenic formations of eroded rock. Most memorable are Gammon, a grotto 54 metres deep and 15 metres wide; and Taka-no-su (Hawk's Nest), a rock that rises 27 metres and projects far over the sea. Buses run along this coast, leaving from Hakui (50 minutes away), or Sammyo (30 minutes). Boat cruises lasting about 20 minutes leave from Fukuura.

Seki-no-hana

Above Togi a small road turns off Route 249 and runs to and along the coast, rejoining the main road further along. The scenery is attractive most of the way especially around Seki-no-hana. This road is part of the regular tourist route between Togi and Monzen.

Monzen

Near Monzen is *Sojiji* temple. Strangely located in this remote area, it was the national headquarters of the Soto sect of Zen Buddhism (founded in 1321) until 1818, when most of the buildings were destroyed in a fire. After that, the headquarters were moved to Sojiji in Yokohama. The present buildings are attractive, especially in summer when the cicadas are chirping loudly. Sojiji and Monzen are accessible by bus from Anamizu (on the uchi coast) as well as being on the regular bus run around the soto coast. The temple is a five-minute walk from Monzen bus station.

Sojiji is a functioning Zen temple, and visitors may obtain accommodation and participate in meditation. It is best to make reservations in advance by writing to: Sojiji, Monzen-machi, Fugeshi-gun, Ishikawa-ken. Tel (07684) 2-0005. It is apparently not possible to obtain accommodation on the spot. Costs range from Y3500 to Y5000.

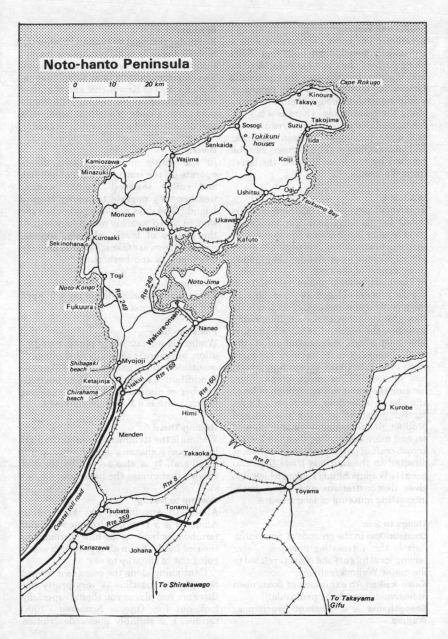

Noto-hanto Peninsula

0   10   20 km

Cape Rokugo

Kinoura
Takaya
Takojima
Suzu
Iida
Sosogi
Tokikuni houses
Senkaida
Wajima
Koiji
Kamiozawa
Minazuki
Ushitsu
Ogi
Tsukumo Bay
Monzen
Ukawa
Anamizu
Kafuto
Kurosaki
Sekinohana
Noto-Jima
Togi
Noto-Kongo
Rte 249
Fukuura
Rte 249
Wakura-onsen
Nanao
Shibagaki beach
Myojoji
Rte 159
Ketajinja
Hakui
Chirahama beach
Himi
Rte 160
Kurobe
Menden
Takaoka
Rte 8
Toyama
Rte 8
Coastal toll road
Tsubata
Tonami
Rte 359
Kanazawa
Johana

To Shirakawago

*To Takayama
Gifu*

Monzen to Wajima

Inveterate sea-coast buffs armed with a sufficiently detailed map can find roads along parts of the coast between Monzen and Wajima, but the area isn't generally famous for scenery. Your own transport would be useful, though there are buses along the main roads. There is a 5.5 km hiking trail along the coast (no road, so it is still quite primitive) between Minazuki and Kami-Ozawa. The former can be reached by bus from Monzen, the latter from Wajima.

WAJIMA

This small city on the northern coast is noted for its large-scale production of good quality lacquerware (on sale everywhere in town). About one person in every four of Wajima's population is engaged in some aspect of the craft.

There are several places were you can see the process of lacquerware making. In the area near the harbour, countless little shops turn out chopsticks with interesting patterns, the result of repeated dipping. The best single demonstration of the whole process can be seen at the main store of Inuchu (daily except Sunday). It can involve 18 or more steps, from forming the wood to the addition of layer after layer of lacquer, interspersed with careful polishing to make the finished product gleaming-smooth; a true work of art and more demanding than the better-known craft of pottery making. Somewhat directed to the tour-bus trade (but also good) is Wajima Shikki Kaikan which also gives demonstrations and has a small, interesting museum of lacquerware.

Things to See

Omatsuri-kan In the grounds of Sumiyoshi-jinja is this interesting museum, , containing local folk art and objects related to the major Wajima festivals.
Kiriko-kaikan An exhibition of floats used in festivals around the peninsula.
Sodegahama is a pleasant beach near Wajima.

Markets

Every day (except the 10th and 25th of the month) there is both a morning market (*asa-ichi*) and an evening market (*yu-ichi*). The former from 8 am to midday at Honcho-dori of Kawai-cho; and the latter on the grounds of Sumiyoshi-jinja from 4 pm to 7pm. Goods sold include handicrafts and other tourist items as well as food.

Divers

In the winter months, women divers operate off the coast looking for shell-fish and edible seaweed. (In the warmer weather they migrate to nearby Hegura Island.) The days are long gone when the women dived wearing only a loincloth so the photos of lovely, shapely, topless, smiling divers are fakes. The true *ama* are older, stocky and bashful.

Festivals

There are annual festivals on 4-5 April and 23-25 August.

Places to Stay

Wajima is an extremely popular destination, but there is generally no shortage of accommodation, except in July-August. In addition to youth hostels there is a large number of minshuku. Near Sodegahama beach, there is a Kokumin-shukusha.

Getting There

Wajima is the terminal station for the JNR line from Kanazawa and further south (Maibara). It is also served by the bus service that circles the peninsula.

Wajima to Sosogi

About 10 km inland on the road to Anamizu is a very picturesque village of farmhouses built on the hills surrounding the rice fields. From all reports it is worth going out of the way to see.

Continuing along the coast east toward Sosogi, the coastline is very pretty but there are two places you should especially look out for. One is *Senkaida* ('1000 terraces'), a suitably poetic description for a broad ravine in which paddies have been built in terraces from sea level high up the side of the tall hill. Just before harvest time (late August-early September) would be the most colourful of all times to see this, as the rice then takes on a rich green-gold hue. (The same is true of all rice fields of course, but few are as beautifully located as Senkaida.)

A little further on is a fine view of the kind that is comparatively rare in Japan these days as modernisation continues to take over. Terraced rice fields drop down to the sea, surrounding a small Shinto shrine. Its torii gate stands before the tiny building and behind the shrine is a small, thick grove of trees. It is the epitome of traditional Japan.

SOSOGI

At this town, a road branches inland from Route 249 toward Ushitsu. About 400 metres from the junction stand two of the largest traditional farmhouses in Japan. They are worth a visit both for their historic value and their aesthetic design. Both are thatched-roof buildings of the highest quality materials and traditional Japanese carpentry. One of the highest ranking court families (the Tokikuni) has lived in this area since the forces of the Taira clan (also called Heike) were defeated by the Genji (Minamoto) in the battle for control of Japan at Dan-no-ura in 1185. The Taira fled to this area and the nearby inland mountain regions of the Shokawa river to escape extermination. Their descendants live in the Shirakawa-go/Gokayama area.

Things to See
Tokikuni Houses

The house closer to Sosogi (they are a five minute walk apart) is Shimo-Tokikuni-ke (lower Tokikuni house) and it is at least 300 years old. Inside its spacious interior are many relics of the past. Foreign visitors are given a recorder with a taped explanation of the house, room by room.

The nearby Kami-Tokikuni-ke (upper Tokikuni house) is newer having been built in the last century to replace the first house that had become unusable. It shows few signs of age, the finest materials and workmanship were employed in its construction and it took 28 years to build. It is intriguing to find such a fine building and garden in such an out of the way place but it was built to suit a person of very high rank, a descendant of the Kyoto nobility.

Visitors are given a notebook with a handwritten explanation of the house's history and a description of the high points and exhibits, room by room. A story in the notes tells how one of the rooms was reserved for receiving guests only of *Daina-gon* rank or higher, which was above that of the local governor and many court officials, so they were not allowed to enter. On one occasion it was necessary to receive a person of lesser rank but before he was allowed in, the golden carving of a swallow-tailed butterfly (symbol of the Heike and indicating the resident's rank) had to be covered.

Buses of Hokuriku Railway run from Wajima station to Kami-Tokikuni-ke bus stop in 45 minutes, and from Suzu station (further east) in one hour.

Museums

There are two other museums in Sosogi. *Wajima Minzoku Shiryokan*, which houses local folk art and items of daily use, is located between the Tokikuni houses. The other is *Noto Shuko-kan* and is a more general art museum with no particular relation to the Noto area. It is south-east of Sosogi and separate from the other attractions.

Places to Stay

There are several minshuku and some hotels near the two old houses. There are, in fact, minshuku in virtually every town and hamlet along the coast.

AROUND THE COAST TO TAKAOKA

The coast east of Sosogi is pleasantly scenic, with outcroppings of eroded rock at intervals. Route 249 doesn't go out to the tip of the peninsula but a good road does lead out to Cape Rokugo (Rokugo Misaki) near the town of Noroshi. An 11 km hiking trail (Misaki Nature Trail) begins at Takaya and continues through Kinoura to Noroshi. At Noroshi, cape Rokugo and its lighthouse can be reached in 10 minutes on foot.

Below Noroshi, the uchi or inner (east) coast becomes much more placid and peaceful. While there are many pretty views, they are not the outstanding scenic areas found along the outer coast.

Suzu

The main attraction of this hot-spring and port town is *Kiheidon*, a large house which serves as a museum for local artefacts. artefacts.

Koiji

There is a nice white beach here, 10 minutes walk from Koiji station or six minutes by bus from Iwatsunami station.

Tsukumo

The name means '99 indentations' and indicates the scenic attraction of this bay. It can be seen from any of the sightseeing boats that leave from Ogi (Noto Ogi station).

Ushitsu

Ushitsu's Toshiyama Park affords an excellent view of the bay. The park, which incorporates two old houses that act as local museums, is 10 minutes by bus from Ushitsu station. The town's annual festival is from 7-8 July.

Noto-Shima

Little fishing villages and outdoor activities (swimming, hiking and camping) are the main attractions of this island.

You can get there by boat from Nanao (five per day) and the trip takes about 30 minutes. There is a festival on the island on 31 July.

Wakura Onsen

This is a typical, rather expensive, hot-spring resort of hotels and ryokan.

Anamizu

This town is also of negligible interest but it has a festival on 22-23 July.

Nanao to Hakui

Along Route 159 between Nanao and Hakui there are many beautiful old wooden houses, particularly between Nanao and Kue.

Places to Stay – Noto-Hanto

There are 12 youth hostels around the peninsula, nine peoples' lodges and probably hundreds of minshuku as well as hotels and ryokan. The hostels are listed in the Youth Hostel handbook, the JNTO booklet on hostels, and on the information sheet *Noto Peninsula* given out by the Tokyo TIC. One hostel I found very pleasant was the *Noto-Katsurazaki Youth Hostel*, right beside the water near Kafuto station.

Getting Around – Noto-Hanto

There is a frequent and convenient bus service to all places of interest around the Noto Peninsula, making it the recommended means of transport. In brief, there are special sightseeing buses around the north-east end of the peninsula between Wajima and Anamizu/Ushitsu, plus regular buses that cover the following steps: Kanazawa-Togi; Togi-Monzen; Monzen-Wajima; Wajima-Ushitsu; and Monzen Anamizu.

Trains run Hakui-Nanao-Wajima, and Nanao-Takojima. There is a JNR service to Wajima and Takoshima (a little east of Suzu), but for the loop around the peninsula there are only buses. Since Wajima is more or less in the middle it is not a useful starting point.

As there are many places to see and visit, and because the land is relatively level all around the peninsula, it is one of the best areas of Japan to explore by bicycle. Cyclists and other independent travellers should have detailed maps to enable them to follow little roads closer to the coast. The preferred direction of travel is clockwise, the Kanazawa area being a good starting point, so the sun will be to your left or behind you through the most scenic parts.

Toyama-ken

TAKAOKA

Near the eastern base of the Noto Peninsula is Takaoka. The city is noted for its lacquerware as well as copper and iron products and is the main source of large cast bells. If you are interested in artistic foundry work, you might be able to arrange a visit to a workshop; try the town hall (*shi-yaku-sho*) for contacts.

Sightseeing potential in the city is limited but it does have the third largest *Daibutsu* (statue of Buddha) in Japan. However, although it is described as being of bronze it looks more like green-painted concrete and cannot be compared with the serene beauty of the famous Daibutsu at Kamakura near Tokyo.

Things to See
Zuiryuji

The best place in Takaoka to visit is in fact the youth hostel (3207) because it is actually a large and venerable temple about 350 years old. Zuiryuji is a Zen temple of the Soto sect. The main building and the ceremonial entry gate are large and the spacious grounds are surrounded by a traditional wall. It is unusual to find such a splendid structure in such a remote area as this and there is a peaceful feeling because there are no hordes of tourists. It is not worth a special trip but for anyone who plans to stay overnight in the area it can be highly recommended. As a bonus the wife of the priest speaks good English and can tell you a bit about the place.

Takaoka

Temples

Other temples in Takaoka are *Kokutaiji* and *Shokoji*. Shrines include *Imisu* and *Keta*. The foundations of the old castle and its moats still stand and are rather pretty during the cherry blossom season. The castle grounds have the buildings of the civic centre, etc, and are not otherwise interesting.

Festivals

There are festivals on 14 January and 2-3 June as well as the following:

1 May: procession of *dashi* (large carved and decorated wagons). The dashi used in this procession are old but not as fantastically elaborate as those of Takayama or Kyoto.

15 May: night processions of at least seven large floats lit by lanterns.

3-7 August: *Tanabata*, with pretty paper decorations on the streets – but not much action.

23 September: *Daibutsu* festival.

Around Takaoka

As well as using Takaoka as the starting point for trips around the Noto peninsula, you can take Route 156 south to the very interesting Shokawa river valley and the old houses of Shirakawa-go area described earlier. There are buses from Takaoka station through the valley. There is also a JNR line as far as Johana, from which another road links up with 156 at Taira-mura, the northern extremity of the area

of old houses mentioned above. The attractions of the Japan alps, south-east of Takaoka, are described in the sections covering Niigata-ken and the northern parts of Nagano-ken and Gumma-ken.

Kinki District

The Kinki district, one of the traditional divisions of Japan, comprises, roughly, the region between Nagoya and Himeji, and from the north of Lake Biwa to the bottom of the Kii Peninsula. This region, together with eastern Kyushu, is the part of Japan longest settled by the present-day Japanese. The original inhabitants of Japan, about whom little is known, were swamped by later arrivals who settled first in Kyushu, then established a series of military outposts along the south coast of Japan up to the Tokyo area.

The origin of the name 'Kinki' is lost but the characters of the name mean 'near the moat', possibly related, in an obscure manner, to the mysterious remains in the mountains of a defensive wall more than 60 km in circumference.

Within the Kinki region are many of the prime attractions of Japan: Kyoto, the imperial capital for nearly 1000 years and a repository of temples, palaces and gardens as well as historic arts and crafts; Nara the capital before Kyoto, with even more ancient temples and other remains from the past; Toba, with its cultured pearl industry and nearby coastal scenery; Himeji and Hikone with historic and picturesque castles and many other historic and natural attractions.

The description moves from east to west, covering in turn, the areas around Nagoya, Lake Biwa, Kyoto, Nara, Osaka, Kobe, Himeji, Ise/Toba and the Kii Peninsula.

For detailed information on travelling in the Kinki District see the Getting Around section at the end of this chapter.

Kyoto

If there is one city in Japan that every foreign visitor should experience, it is Kyoto. As it was the imperial capital for nearly 1000 years it has the finest temples, palaces, villas and gardens in Japan, as well as the most refined culture and lifestyle.

Some over-enthusiastic writers have described Kyoto as one of the most beautiful cities in the world. It isn't. Kyoto is a modern Japanese metropolis with its full share of Japanese urban ugliness. However, dotted through the city and clustered around the edges are oases of tranquility and beauty, exemplifying the best that is/was Japan.

The name is pronounced, by the way, so that the 'y' is a consonant (as in 'yet') not a vowel; the first syllable is 'Kyo', and does not rhyme with 'pie'. The last syllable sounds like the english word 'toe'. Some foreigners in Japan have been heard to garble the name 'Kyota'. The name Kyoto simply means 'capital city'; (Tokyo, the successor capital, means 'east capital').

Information
There is no shortage of information on what to see in Kyoto. It is the only city other than Tokyo with a government-operated tourist information centre (TIC). Staff speak English well (plus other languages) and are absolute goldmines of information about any place, activity, art or craft in the Kyoto area and elsewhere in Japan. For this reason, the section on

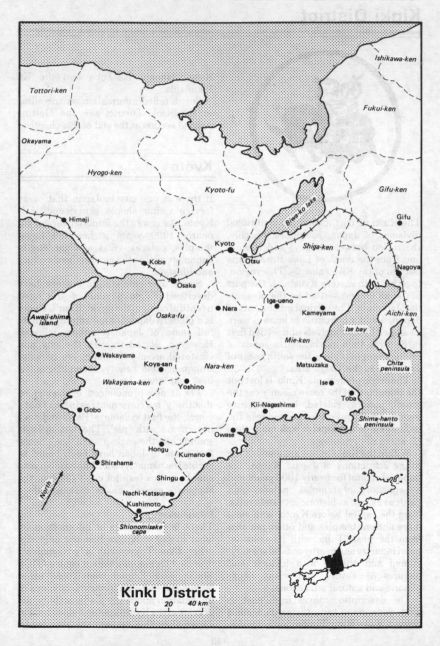

Kinki District

0   20   40 km

Kyoto places more emphasis on how-to-see and what-to-see than on detailed descriptions. Unless you arrive Saturday afternoon or Sunday, your first stop should be the TIC to pick up one of the excellent maps of Kyoto and the booklet *Kyoto Nara* (also available at the Tokyo TIC), and to ask any specific questions you may have about travel-related topics. They have a great deal of other information on photocopied sheets and in printed booklets; particularly useful is *Walking Tours in Kyoto*, and some rail maps.

The bulletin board in the office lists all the cultural and other performances and activities for the following several weeks and is the most up-to-date source of information about such events.

The TIC has information about accommodation in various price ranges, and will call to make reservations (unlike the Tokyo TIC). Low cost places are listed later in this section, mostly for the benefit of those who arrive after 5 pm on weekdays, or on Saturday afternoon or Sunday. The Tokyo TIC has a hand-out list of accommodation that may be useful for making advance reservations, but it has occasionally omitted popular places (like Mrs Uno's house).

A very handy booklet is *Monthly Guide Kyoto*, which lists events of the month in good detail and has descriptions of a large number of temples, shrines and palaces. (Much of the book may be in Japanese but the English section is excellent.) It also lists the better hotels (with prices), tours and other useful information. The booklet is not available at the TIC, but may be obtained at the large hotels that cater to foreign visitors. It is also available in Japan by mail for a total of Y600 from:

Monthly Guide Kyoto
30-5 Chajiri-cho
Arashiyama
Nishikyo
Kyoto-shi

The above should not be confused with another publication, *Kyoto Monthly Guide*, which is produced by the Kyoto city government. This one is much more detailed regarding events for the month. It is available at the TIC or by mail in Japan on receipt of a Y70 stamp, from:

Tourist Section
Dept of Cultural Affairs and Tourism
Kyoto City Government
c/o Kyoto Kaikan
Sakyo-ku
Kyoto.

Both publications are very useful.

The Kyoto City Tourist Association publishes a worthwhile guide book simply called *Kyoto*. It contains useful information such as airline phone numbers etc, and is a steal at Y300. For a very good explanation of many of the attractions of the city and their significance in history, purchase a copy of *Kyoto, A Contemplative Guide*, by Gouverneur Mosher.

A useful publication for residents of and visitors to the Hanshinkei region (Osaka-Kobe-Kyoto) is the several-page 'newspaper' *Kansai Time Out* which is a monthly guide covering social, cultural and other events of interest to foreigners including festivals and films etc. The TIC in Kyoto should be able to tell you where to obtain a copy or it can be ordered by subscription at Y3000 per year (in Japan) from:

Kansai Time Out
Ken-an Bldg. 2F
Kitanagasa-dori 2-chome
Chuo-ku
Kobe 650

It might be possible to arrange single copies by phoning 078-332-4533.

Another publication, more of interest to those staying long-term, is *A Resident's Guide to Kyoto*, a compilation of nearly every bit of information that one needs when arriving to stay in Kyoto for a while. It can be purchased at the YWCA for Y500, by domestic mail for Y1000, or by foreign mail for Y1500, from:

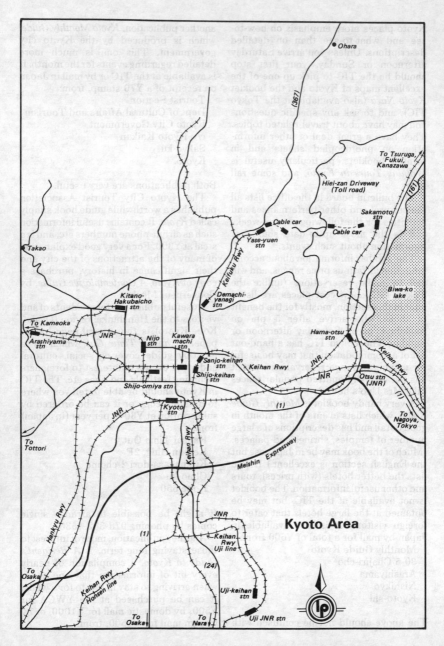

Kyoto Area

YWCA Thrift Shop
Muro machi-dori, Demizu-agaru
Kamikyo-ku
Kyoto-shi 602

There is a thrift sale at the YWCA on the third Saturday of every month, a good place for bargains, exchanging information with other foreign residents and even home-made western-style munchies and crunchies. (The YWCA is shown on the TIC map.)

Tickets and any other travel bookings are available from the JTB offices near the north entrance of Kyoto station and on Sanjo, east of Kawaramachi. There is generally English speaking staff on duty.

Post Office The Post Office offers basic services 24 hours a day, including mail pick-up from Poste Restante. A passport or other identification will be required. Postal rates are conveniently noted in English in the main section.

Home Visit It is possible to visit a private home in Kyoto for a couple of hours in the evening to see what Japanese home life is like. Members of the participating families speak English or other foreign languages. Arrangements should be made as far in advance as possible (usually this can be done in a day, but more time should be allowed). Travel agencies and large hotels can make arrangements; you can also contact the Kyoto City information office at Kyoto station (tel 371-2108). General information on the programme is given in the introductory section of this book.

Things to See
Kyoto Gosho Palace
This is the Imperial Palace in Kyoto and is considered to be the centre of the city, from where you go 'up' or 'down'. The palace itself is of only moderate interest, but the office of the Imperial Household Agency is at the entrance. You apply here for permission to visit some other places associated with the Imperial family.

Kyoto Gosho was the residence of the emperor in the days when he lived in Kyoto. The present building dates from 1855, replacing one destroyed in a fire. Although the capital was Kyoto from 794, this site was not used until 1788 when a palace was built to replace an older one that was also destroyed by fire. The main buildings are replicas of the former structures and are quite simple in design, though made with the finest materials and construction methods. A guide accompanies all visitors so the details are explained.

To enter you must fill in an application and show your passport, so arrive about 20 minutes before the tour at 10 am or 2 pm. (There are no tours on Saturday afternoon or Sunday.)

The palace is one of the most peaceful places in Kyoto because Japanese must wait for months to get permission to enter and few do. Any Japanese accompanying you will have to wait at the entrance. It is a privilege for foreigners to be able to enter so easily.

Before or after the tour, file your application to visit Katsura Imperial Villa and Sento Imperial Palace if desired. Permission will be given for a specific date and hour, usually within a day if requested, but you should apply soon after arriving in Kyoto to allow for delays. A permit is also required to visit Shugakuin Imperial Villa, but read the comments on it before applying.

Go-jinja
This little shrine, across from the west side of the Gosho, is not noteworthy except that instead of the usual *koma-inu* guardian dogs/lions at the entrance, it has two pigs.

Sento Imperial Palace
There is another palace on the south-east side of the same grounds. In addition to the buildings (which have been rebuilt many times) there is a garden completed in 1630 and designed by Kobori Enshu, possibly the most famous of all landscape-

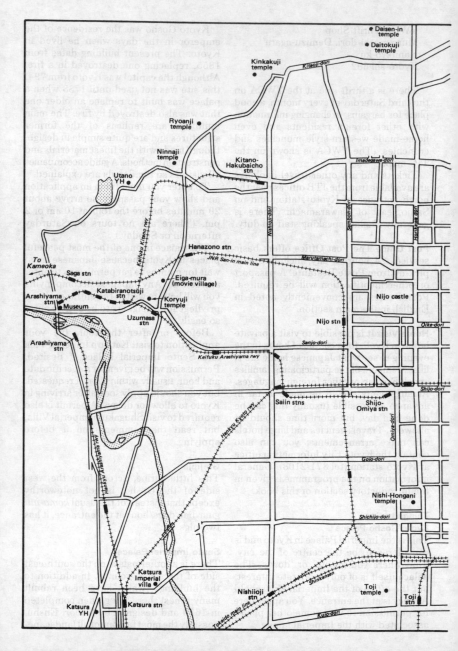

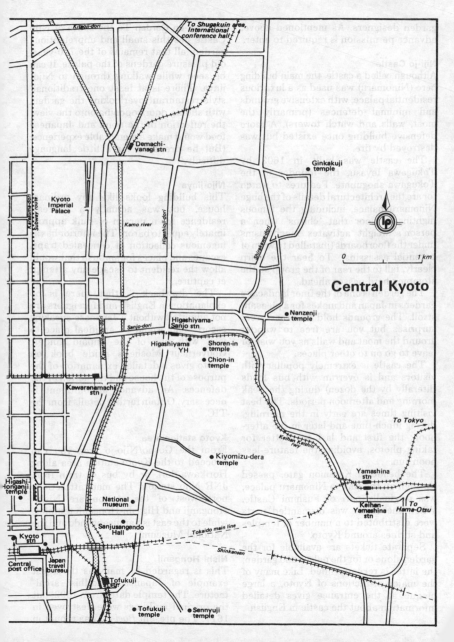

Central Kyoto

0 _____ 1 km

To Shugakuin area,
International conference hall

Kitaoji-dori

Demachi-
yanagi stn

Ginkakuji
● temple

Kyoto
Imperial
Palace

Kamo river

Higashioji-dori

Karasuma-dori
Subway route

Shirakawa-dori

Sanjo-dori

Higashiyama-
Sanjo stn

Higashiyama
YH

● Shoren-in
temple

● Chion-in
temple

● Nanzenji
temple

Kawaranamachi-dori

Kawaranamachi
stn

Keihan Keishin rwy

To Tokyo

Higashi-
honganji
temple

● Kiyomizu-dera
temple

Yamashina
stn

Keihan-
Yamashina stn

To
Hama-Otsu

National
museum ●

Sanjusangendo
Hall

Tokaido main line

Kyoto stn

Central
post office

Japan
travel
bureau

● Tofukuji

Shinkansen

● Tofukuji
temple

● Sennyuji
temple

garden designers. As mentioned above, advance permission is required to enter.

Niji-jo Castle

Although called a castle, the main building here (Ninomaru) was used as a luxurious residential palace, with extensive grounds and minimal defences (primarily the moat, walls and watch towers). A more defensive building once existed but was destroyed by fire.

The castle was built in 1603 by Tokugawa Ieyasu, the founder of the Tokugawa shogunate. Features to watch for are the architectural details of the huge Ninomaru palace, including the famous nightingale floor that 'chirps' when a person's weight activates mechanisms under the floorboards (installed to warn of potential assassins). To hear the chirp clearly, fall to the rear of the group so the stomping herd passes ahead.

The garden is one of the finer landscape gardens in Japan and makes for a pleasant stroll. The grounds hold no other great surprises but you are free to wander around the moat and walls as you wish or leave to go on to other places.

The castle is extremely popular with visitors and is overrun with bus loads (literally by the dozen) during the peak morning and afternoon periods. The best visiting times are early in the morning, during lunch-time and later in the afternoon; the first and last are better for taking photos, avoiding the feature-less noon sun.

The beautiful Karamon gate, passed through on the way to Ninomaru palace, was originally part of Fushimi Castle. When the castle was dismantled parts were distributed to a number of temples and shrines around Kyoto.

Separate tickets are available for the garden alone or for the palace and garden; the latter is recommended. Like many of the major attractions of Kyoto, a large plaque at the entrance gives detailed information about the castle in English.

Shinsen-en Garden To the south of Nijo Castle lies this small and unpretentious garden, all that remains of the 700-year-old pleasure gardens of the palace. It can be seen while walking through to Nijo-jinya. There is at least one traditional-style restaurant overlooking the garden, with sliding doors opening onto the view; the reflection in the pond and Japanese food would make a memorable experience. (But be prepared for a little language difficulty!)

Nijo-jinya

This building looks like any ordinary house, but was actually a fortress-residence for a person of rank approximately equal to baron. The interior has as ingenious collection of concealed traps, escapes and places for ambush that would allow the resident to escape any attempt at capture.

The drawback is that there is no explanation in English and foreigners are not admitted without a Japanese-speaking escort. This would be an ideal place to visit with one of the unpaid guides. Gouverneur Mosher's guide book on Kyoto gives a detailed explanation of the purpose of the house and the action of the defences. An advance appointment is necessary. Obtain further details from the TIC.

Kyoto station area

From the Gosho/Nijo-jo area you can proceed to the Kyoto station area along Horikawa-dori, or by bus or train from JNR Nijo station. The main attractions north-west of the station are Nishi-Honganji and Higashi-Honganji temples, while to the east is Sanjusangendo and the National Museum.

Nishi-Honganji

This is regarded by many as the finest example of Japanese Buddhist architecture. The temple dates from 1592, but the original buildings were destroyed in 1617. The present *Boei-do* was rebuilt in

1636, and the *Amida-do* in 1760; the former is the northernmost of the large main buildings.

The Shoin building was originally part of the old Fushimi Castle and was moved here when the castle was dismantled. Not to be missed is the very colourful Karamon gate in the south wall. Of typically flamboyant Momoyama style, it has much gold inlay on the metal fittings and brightly coloured carved figures of animals and humans, many obviously of Chinese derivation.

There are four tours a day, at 10 and 11 am, 1.30 and 2.30 pm. Though lengthy (if the explanation is being given only to Japanese visitors), this is the only way to see the interior buildings, the two Noh stages, Komei-no-en (a pretty garden of rocks, gravel and greenery), and other glimpses of beauty such as wide verandas made of a single plank of wood. Not open to the public, unfortunately, is the more beautiful Hyakka-en garden.

Costume Museum Close to Nishi-Honganji is an interesting museum with costumes, both original and replicas, worn in Japan over the past 2000 years. It is on the fifth floor of the Izutsu Building. There is an English-language pamphlet and the costumes are also labelled in English.

Higashi-Honganji

This temple has the largest wooden structure in Kyoto. The temple was founded in 1602 but the present buildings date from 1895. It is worth a visit.

Kikokutei Garden

This large strolling-type garden is/was a villa of the abbot of Higashi-Honganji temple. Unfortunately it has been neglected and allowed to run down, but it is little visited and provides a haven of relative peace. An interesting scandal has been hovering around it, as the abbot transferred ownership to a private individual without consulting the 10,000 or so temples affiliated with Higashi-Honganji.

Toji

To the south-west of the station and therefore a little off our track, this temple on extensive park-like grounds has the tallest pagoda in Japan (55 metres). The *kodo* (lecture hall) is a simple building containing only a few large gilded statues. This was the first temple I visited in Kyoto, and in the late afternoon, with the sun shining in the doorway and reflecting off the floor, the effect was quite mysterious. The first Europeans here must have been similarly impressed by the unfamiliar symbolism. The pagoda dates from 1644, the lecture hall from 1598 and the main hall from more recent times.

East of the station
Sanjusangendo

The name means '33 bays' and refers to spaces between the pillars of this long, narrow structure which dates from 1266. The spaces are filled with a huge and intriguing collection of 1001 life-sized statues of Kannon, Goddess of Mercy. (If they look small, remember that the Japanese were once very short; many old people in the countryside are no taller than these figures.) Some of the statues wear 'necklaces'; the face of each statue is different and if a visitor sees one that resembles himself, it is customary to donate such a decoration. The central figure is a seated 3.3 metre statue of 1001-handed Kannon (from 1254) and her 28 helpers. Also take time to look at the large (but dusty) sculpted wooden statues in the back corridor. Signs in English explain all attractions briefly. The temple is famous for its archery festival on 15 January when arrows are shot along the long verandah.

National Museum

The National Museum is just across the road from Sanjusangendo and is worth a visit for its large collection of Japanese artefacts from prehistoric to recent vintage. The pottery from about 2000 BC shows how little this craft has advance since 'primitive' times.

Although the museum is conveniently reached from Sanjusangendo, it might be worth saving (literally) for a rainy day. Admission is free on the 15th of each month (closed Mondays and at year-end).

Kawai Kanjiro Pottery

This is the house and workshop of the late Kawai Kanjiro, a noted potter. Those interested will find displays of his work, the workshop and a climbing kiln. (Closed Mondays, mid-August and year-end.)

Chishaku-in

Of somewhat less interest, but pleasant to visit during a long Kyoto stay, this temple has an attractive garden with an unusual pond that extends under the porch of the main building. A special building is used to exhibit wall and door paintings from the 16th century that survived fires in the main building. They are considered masterpieces of their type, but may not appeal to everyone. An English-language pamphlet gives further details.

Kiyomizu-dera Temple

This temple is very popular with visitors and included on every tour. It is unusual as the *honden* (main hall), is built out on pillars from a hillside. The grounds are especially lovely during the cherry blossom season and autumn. The present buildings date from 1633 and include a picturesque Sanmon gate at the entrance and a three-storey pagoda as well as the famous pillar-supported verandah.

Access from the south is by walking up the long hill from Gojozaka bus stop, either through the cemetery (southern-most road) or up the shop-lined road. These shops and those along the other approaches, have a large variety of pottery and other crafts as well as countless souvenirs and Kyoto-type nibbles.

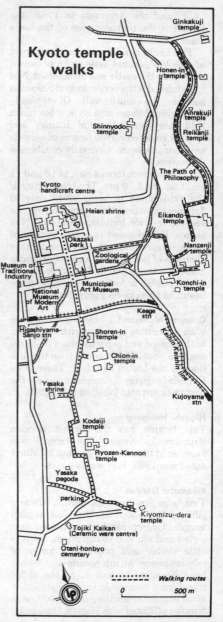

Exploring the Back Streets

Several little streets near Kiyomizu-dera make this possibly the most enjoyable area of Kyoto for strolling. When leaving Kiyomizu-dera, take the right-hand road downhill and note the first street that branches off to the right, down a set of stone steps. This is Sannen-zaka. Explore the main road as desired (also the road off to the left when leaving the temple), but return to Sannen-zaka.

Like the main road, Sannen-zaka has numerous little shops selling a variety of knick-knacks. (If you see something of interest in any of the shops in the area I suggest you buy it there as some shops have goods that can't be found anywhere else.)

A short distance along Sannen-zaka, to the right, you will see the entrance to *Sakaguchi*, a lovely little garden teahouse with a pond. For a few hundred yen one can order soba (noodles) or tea and have them while enjoying the view. Pleasant, tinkly koto music provides the background and guarantees one of the most 'Japanese' experiences available.

A little further along is a coffee shop that I enjoyed, the *Boga tei*. The front and interior are modern and European in appearance but there is a pleasant courtyard at the rear with the incongruous combination of traditional Japanese garden, with stone lanterns, trees etc, and a Mediterranean-style patio; and the adjoining gift shop is in a traditional house. The coffee shop can be easily identified by the decorative little Japanese shelter (to the right) over the pay phone.

A little beyond here Sannen-zaka curves off to the left and Ninen-zaka branches to the right, down another set of steps. There are more knick-knack shops, teahouses and coffee shops along the way, some in garden settings. In the latter case you can look through the entrance gates to see if the attraction is appealing.

Sannen-zaka, by the way, continues on to a pagoda, the five-storey *Yasaka Gojonoto*, all that remains of a once-grand temple. The grounds are closed, however, so it is not worth a walk to see. Photographers will find that the view along the road is ruined by numerous power lines, but the little uphill road to the east shortly before the T-junction, gives a good silhouette of the top four storeys. (A telephoto lens will be needed to cut out foreground clutter.)

The road forming the T-junction at the end of Ninen-zaka leads up to *Ryosen Kannon*, a large concrete seated figure of Kannon. The figure is of no historic importance, but the appearance of the statue is peaceful and reassuring. It is surrounded by a wall, but you can see through the gate without paying the entry fee if you don't want to go in.

Continuing on the road that runs along the foot of the grounds of Ryozen Kannon (reached by zig-zagging left from the end of Ninen-zaka) you pass another couple of tea gardens, temples etc, which can be looked into. The roads ends in a T-junction at *Kodai-ji* temple which can be easily identified by the strange looking spire 'growing' out of the roof.

Just before the end of the road, on the right hand side, is *Rakusho* coffee shop. At first it appears to be like any of the other countless coffee shops in Japan but this one has an interesting attraction of its own – a charming little garden with a long narrow pond. Around the pond are typical Japanese decorative motifs, like a stone slab across the water that serves as a bridge, many colourful flowers, tastefully positioned moss etc. The garden is actually a century old and earlier was the centre-piece of a more classical tea garden, but it has moved with the times. The most interesting feature of the place is the large number of huge decorative carp in the pond. The have won the Kinki district championship for several years and are the pride and joy of the distinguished-looking owner who potters around carrying out maintenance. It is not necessary to buy anything as visitors are allowed to enter just to look, but it is a good place to take a break, prices are typical for Japanese coffee shops and the owner's daughter-in-law speaks English.

This area around Kiyomizu-dera (also described in the pamphlet on walks in Kyoto) is, more than any other area in Kyoto, conducive to a relaxing stroll rather than a rushed attempt to see everything in a day. Not all visitors will have the luxury of time, but those who do are sure to enjoy it, as the area has a mood difficult to find elsewhere in Japan.

Yasaka-jinja

Not far away is Yasaka shrine. It has several photogenic brilliant-orange buildings as well as one of the largest granite torii gates in Japan (on the south side), dating from 1646. It is one of the best places in Japan to see people 'waking the gods'; shaking and whipping a thick rope attached to a rattly gong at the eaves, then putting their hands together in prayer. It is said to be a favourite of geisha from the nearby Gion entertainment area.

Adjacent Karuyama-koen park has a pleasant little pond and Japanese-style garden arranged around it. It is as much of interest to see how Japanese enjoy their leisure as for its own attractions. It provides a path to nearby Chion-in Temple.

Chion-in Temple

The huge Sanmon gate at the south (main) entrance to this hillside temple is the largest in Japan and dates from 1619. It also has the largest bell in the country. The main building is impressively large and is best seen from the large open area in front. The interior is equally large and is an excellent place to examine the great range of Buddhist symbols and other ornate gilded decorations; it is a feast for the eyes. The temple is active and there is a good chance of observing priests chanting prayers for deceased members of visiting families.

The garden and large building behind the main temple are also worth visiting.

Although there are always other visitors around, the temple is rarely overcrowded. An English-language pamphlet gives the history of the temple and serves as a primer on the Jodo sect, of which it is the head temple.

Shoren-in

This is one of my favourite temples. It is off the beaten path enough for it not to be overrun with hordes of sightseers, so you can enjoy its lovely little garden, the peace and the blending of the buildings (and their architectural details) with the setting at the foot of a hill. Birds can be heard in nearby trees. It is delightful in the late afternoon, especially in autumn when the trees are beautiful; 2 – 3.30 pm is good in November, later in summer when the sun is higher. After exploring the buildings and the views from there, return to the entrance, don shoes, and walk around the garden, which is entered by a tunnel under one of the corridors (to the right when leaving the building). An English-language handout gives the history of the temple.

North-east of the Station
Nanzen-ji

Another highly recommended temple to visit, especially when the autumn leaves are at their colourful best is Nanzen-ji which began as a villa for a retired emperor, and was made into a temple in 1291. The present buildings date from post-1600. The grounds have many tall, venerable cedar trees, so the approach to the entrance is canopied by nature. The buildings of the temple feature the finest construction techniques, rooms with exquisite details (some opening onto to lovely little gardens), sliding doors with fine, treasured paintings and several rock-and-sand Zen gardens. Nanzen-ji means 'south Zen temple'. A leisurely walk will be rewarding.

To the right inside the main entrance is a simple room where you can sip tea (ocha) for Y200 extra. It is a good chance to appreciate the beauty of the tea ceremony, sitting in the simple room on tatami mats, looking out at the little waterfall. An English-language pamphlet gives the history of the temple.

Toriyasu
Another peaceful and beautiful place for rest and refreshments is Toriyasu, a teahouse/restaurant/garden just across from the right-hand corner of the grounds of Nanzen-ji. Koto music provides the background and tall trees the shade.

Eikando
The grounds of this temple are gorgeous during autumn and enjoyable at other times. A graceful stone bridge arches over the pond, and the temple buildings enclose small gardens, including one of rocks and sand raked into elaborate patterns. Unfortunately, loudspeakers babble incessantly and destroy any potential for peaceful exploration.

Kyoto Dento Sanyo Kaikan (Centre of Traditional Industry)
This museum is worth visiting for its beautiful lacquerware, masks and robes for bugaku dances. It also has a reproduction of a typical, traditional Kyoto house with its long corridors (nicknamed unagi-no-nedoko, 'bedrooms for eels') as well as exhibitions of hand-forging knives, and other traditional crafts. The museum is located to the right of the National Museum of Modern Art and can be recognised by it unusual architecture, with a curved wall up to the second floor and a traditional square form for the upper storey. The TIC map has only the English name, which no Japanese would understand to give help with directions. The Kyoto Municipal Art Museum and the zoo are nearby.

National Museum of Modern Art
This has many large and attractive works – note that 'modern' refers to the past century or so.

Heian-jingu shrine
A Johnny-come-lately among Kyoto's shrines and temples, Heian-jingu was built in 1895 to mark the 1100th anniversary of the founding of Kyoto as the capital of Japan. It is a three-fifths scale reproduction of the palace built in 794; the present buildings are large, so the imagination runs overtime picturing the originals. Actually the present buildings do not even date to the last century; a mysterious fire in 1976 caused extensive damage, resulting in the reconstruction of the main hall and several other buildings. The shrine has an extensive and pretty garden, known especially for cherry blossoms in the spring. It is a popular place for wedding parties, so keep your eyes open for brides in beautiful wedding kimono. Also, take bread crusts to feed the carp in the pond. The huge torii at the front entrance is the largest in Japan (23 metres high).

Kyoto Handicraft Centre
Although a commercial establishment, this is a good attraction. On its several floors craftsmen may be seen using their traditional skills in damascene, woodblock print-making (carving the plates and actually making the prints), pottery (making and painting), doll making and several other crafts. Work is in progress every day of the week, but some of the people take Sunday off. For a convenient one-stop look at a number of traditional crafts, it can't be beaten. Like Heian-jingu, it is on the route of almost every tour, although a visit on your own would be more enjoyable, allowing you to move at your own pace. The products being made are sold on the premises, along with a large variety of other good-quality souvenirs (plus some tourist rubbish).

Ginkaku-ji
This temple was originally built in 1489 as a hillside retreat of a shogun and converted into a temple after his death. The intention was to cover the walls of the

main building with silver foil; although this was never done, the name *Ginkaku* (Silver Pavilion) was given to it anyway. (In Japan intention counts for a lot, a tradition carried on into many aspects of modern life, for better or worse.)

The effect of the buildings and the rock-and-sand garden (including some unusually shaped piles of gravel), and careful use of greenery is one of restrained elegance. It should perhaps be visited before the more flamboyant and spectacular Kinkaku-ji (Gold Pavilion Temple) for it may seem to suffer by comparison, although it is probably a better expression of Japanese taste and quietude (at least of the educated classes).

It is about two km from Heian-jingu and the others so a bus or taxi will save time. A plaque at the entrance gives the history in English.

North-west of the Station
Daitoku-ji

Daitoku-ji is a functioning Zen temple, made up of 22 separate temples of which eight are open to visitors. Each one is explained on the ticket (payment is separate for each). Three of the best-known are *Daisen-in, Zuiho-in* and *Koto-in*. (It has been criticised for the commercialisation of the temples.)

Kinkaku-ji

This is probably the best-known temple in Kyoto (if not Japan) because its pavilion is covered with gold leaf. The pavilion, set beside a large pond in which it is reflected, is very beautiful and worth a visit. (It is on the itinerary of virtually every full tour of Kyoto.) The present building dates only from 1955, replacing the previous structure (1397) that was destroyed in 1950 when it was set on fire by a student-monk with deranged metaphysical notions. Mishima based his well-known *Kinkaku-ji* on this story.

Even though it is popular with every visitor to Kyoto and therefore crowded, a visit is recommended for the lovely views around the pond, and the wooded grounds. It is especially beautiful when the leaves change colour in November. An English language pamphlet tells the history of the temple and its high points. Access from other parts of Kyoto is convenient by bus or taxi.

Ryoan-ji

This temple houses the most famous rock-and-sand *seki-tei* garden in Japan. It is an enigmatic arrangement of 15 rocks in groups of various sizes in a sea of grey-white gravel that is raked daily into set patterns. A tile-topped earthen wall surrounds it on three sides; the fourth is a verandah of the temple where viewers may sit and admire it. The unknown designer in the 1470s left no explanation of the meaning of the garden (if any), so numerous interpretations have been concocted.

There's more to the temple than just the garden – small groves of trees, a pond, a giant *moku-gyo* (wooden gong that makes a 'tonk' sound when struck), a carved stone well in the shape of a coin (the water is safe to drink), the paintings on the interior sliding doors, and many details of the buildings. Ryoan-ji is in walking distance from Kinkaku-ji. (Pronounce the 'Ryo' of Ryoan-ji as one syllable if you want Japanese to understand you.)

Ninna-ji

The great gate of this temple fronts onto the street, and at each side of the entrance is a huge, fearsome Nio-sama guardian god. One has an open mouth, the other closed, like Koma-inu. These are some of the finer Nio-sama in Japan, and they are better lit than most (good for photos). The grounds are large and at their best when the cherry blossoms are out; at other times the temple is only of moderate interest.

(The area between Kinkaku-ji and Ninna-ji is covered by the TIC publication 'Walking Courses in Kyoto'.)

Kitano-tenmangu Shrine

Quite the opposite of the flamboyant Heian shrine, Kitano is old (1607) and of a restrained Japanese style in natural wood. Its size and the beautifully coloured details and carvings, set this apart from most shrines.

WEST OF KYOTO
ARASHIYAMA

This area is on the western edge of the city, where the Hozu river emerges from a gorge and tree-covered hills spring up. Though it is often promoted as a tourist attraction, most of it will be of limited interest to short-term visitors unless nature walks are of particular appeal. (It *is* of great appeal to the Japanese, who are city-bound much of the time.) Arashiyama-koen (park) is a pleasant area at the end of a picturesque footbridge across the river from Arashiyama station (Keifuku railway); it is at its prettiest in spring because of the many cherry trees on the grounds.

The area north and west of Arashiyama is shown on the TIC's *Walking Tour Courses in Kyoto*, but it does not detail east of the museum, so you will need to rely on the TIC Kyoto-Nara map or the one in this book.

Arashiyama Museum One of the better museums in Japan, this is located at the north end of the bridge near the station. *Kyoto-Arashiyama Hakubutsukan*, to give it is proper name, will be of greatest interest to war buffs, but also has general appeal. It has one of the best collections in Japan of ancient armour, helmets, swords, halberds and other weapons, as well as incredibly ornate and fine lacquerware. What sets the museum apart from others, however, is its display of World War II weapons, including the only Zero fighter left in Japan (all were destroyed by American authorities, but this one was fished out of Lake Biwa in 1978); a midget suicide submarine (raised from off Izu Peninsula); and an enormous gun barrel from the sunken battleship *Mutsu*. This immense piece of steel is 19.3 metres long and about two metres wide at the breech end; it fired a shell weighing over 1000 kg up to 40 km.

Tenryo-ji Temple The landscape garden behind the abbot's quarters is well known, although the buildings are of recent vintage (about 1900).

Nison-in Temple The grounds of this temple, north-west of Tenryu-ji, are planted with maples which are famous for their autumn colour.

Ukai Every night between 1 July and 31 August (except on nights of full moon or after heavy rains when the river is muddy), there is a performance near Arashiyama bridge of fishing using cormorants as the divers. (Details of this activity are given in the Gifu section in the chapter on Central Honshu.) The best view and the most fun is on a boat, but the river is not too wide, so the action can be also be seen from shore or the bridge.

Koryu-ji

One of Kyoto's oldest buildings and a very large number of exceptionally old Buddhist images are found in this out-of-the-way temple.. The original temple was said to have been constructed in 603 AD by prince Shotoku. The Lecture Hall (kodo) was built in 1165 while the *Hakkakudo* building dates from 1251. The new fireproof *Reihohan* (treasure museum) has on display a large number of historic carved wooden statues, including the famous *Miroku-Bosatsu*, which was crafted in the Asuka period (552-645) and which is still in remarkably good condition. There are many other figures nearly as old. Even if you don't understand any of the significance of the figures, you can still appreciate their workmanship and marvel how well these wooden figures have survived the years.

Although the temple is close to Usumasu station of the JNR San-in line, trains are rather infrequent compared with buses. You can take bus 71, 72 or 73 from in front of Wimpy's, to the left of Kyoto station.

Eiga-mura The name means 'Movie Village', and is a studio used for making films that require a traditional Japanese setting. There are streets of buildings of the samurai era, others of later eras. Visitors are welcome to watch 'filming' when a camera, dolly and crew show up at some spot on the set, actors go through their lines with action and the camera rolls. One suspects there is no film in the camera because only a single take is made of each scene, but movies are an illusion anyway aren't they, and it's all good entertainment.

There are also exhibitions explaining some of the special effects used in films. The studio is in walking distance of Koryuji temple so refer to that section for access information. Many people can usually be seen walking to it so there's a good chance you can follow the crowd. If not, ask 'Eiga-mura dochira?' Everyone seems to enjoy it.

Saiho-ji

Formerly very popular with visitors because of the unusual beauty of the 200 or so varieties of moss that have been planted in the garden. But the hordes of sightseers caused neighbours of this temple to protest, with the result the garden has been closed to general admission since July 1977. Entry is still possible, but only to those who write for an appointment and are willing to pay Y3000 as well as fulfill some other obligations. I visited the garden several times before the closure and found it nice but not special, and consider the fee exorbitant. If you wish to check send a reply-paid postcard, giving name, address, age, occupation and desired date of visit to:

Saihoji
56 Kamigatani
Matsuo
Nishi-kyo-ku
Kyoto-shi.

SOUTH-WEST OF KYOTO
Katsura Rikyu Imperial Villa

This villa was built for the brother of an emperor and was finished in 1624. It was painstakingly repaired and restored over several years up to 1982. The buildings are of very simple design, but are made of the finest materials by the best craftsmen available. It is considered the zenith of restrained elegance, the highest point in purely Japanese architecture.

The villa is under the control of the Imperial Household Agency and it is necessary to make an appointment in advance. (Details are given under Kyoto Gosho at the beginning of this section.) Although there may be a wait of two to three days, it is sometimes possible to go the same day. The villa is closed Saturday afternoons, Sundays, national holidays and from 25 December to 5 January.

It can be reached from Arashiyama/ Saihoji, or from central Kyoto (Shijo-dori area) by different branches of the Hankyu railroad.

SOUTH & SOUTH-EAST OF KYOTO

The TIC has a small photocopied map that is useful for general orientation in this area as far south as Nara.

Tofuku-ji

This temple is at its best in November, when the maples in the ravine (crossed by picturesque Tsuten-kyo bridge) are at their best. Some of the architectural details of the buildings are noticeably different from those of most temples, and the karesansui garden of mixed greenery and raked sand has a beauty of its own.

Access is from Tofukuji stations of both JNR Nara line and Keihan hon-sen (main line).

Fushimi-Inari Taisha Shrine

This is the largest of the 32,000 Inari shrines found throughout Japan. They honour the patron deities of agriculture and business, two of the most important activities in the country, which ensures their continued popularity. For this reason, you are likely to come across a family or members of a small business praying for success in a new venture. The fox is the messenger of the shrine deities, which explains the large number of fox statues on the grounds.

The shrine is famous for the huge number of orange-painted torii erected over some of the paths that wind up the mountainside. There are more than 1000 of them, so close together that they form a tunnel. They have been donated by worshippers whose supplications were answered.

At various shrines along the route you may see hundreds of miniature torii (sold at the entrance) that have been left by worshippers – they can be seen stacked like firewood at the end of the season.

Those energetic enough to climb to the top – there are many paths branching off, many leading considerable distances away – may find a stone monument engraved with the profile of Charles Bronson! He is used as the symbol of virility by a line of male cosmetics called 'Mandom'.

There is a good chance of seeing some sort of ceremony at the main building; there may also be performances of the slow and graceful sacred Kagura dances by shrine maidens.

The shrine is reached easily from Inari station of the JNR Nara line, or Fushimi-Inari station of Keihan hon-sen line. It is one of very few in Kyoto with no admission charge.

Daigo-ji

The oldest structure in Kyoto is the five-storey pagoda of this temple at the far south-east of the city; it dates from 951. Nearby Sambon-in has one of the finest landscape gardens in Japan. There is no nearby train station; ask the TIC for access information.

Fushimi-Momoyama Castle

This is marked on the TIC map and you may be tempted to see it. However it is only a modern concrete reconstruction of a castle that stood here centuries ago before it was torn down and many of its parts moved elsewhere. The modern version offers nothing that can't be seen better elsewhere (such as Himeji or Hikone, both relatively close to Kyoto). Some of the parts of the old castle may be seen at Nijo-jo and Nishi-Hongan-ji.

Manpuku-ji

This is the head temple of the Obaku sect of Zen, probably the least-known of the three Zen 'schools' in Japan. It was introduced from China in the mid-17th century and until the mid-1700s was headed by a Chinese monk. Every attempt is still made to preserve Chinese traditions. The buildings are of Chinese architectural style, which makes them unique in Kyoto.

Access is from Obaku stations JNR Nara line or Keihan main line (the former is closer).

UJI

For centuries this has been a resort for the wealthy and powerful of Kyoto. It is best-known for *Byodo-in* temple and *ukai*.

Byodo-in This temple is unusual for its elongated structure which dates from 1053. It is meant to portray a phoenix-like bird of Chinese mythology and is the building seen on the Y10 coin; it is considered the finest structure of the Fujiwara era. However, most of the painted details inside the main building have disappeared with time and you may be somewhat let down by the temple and grounds.

Ukai A suggestion is to see Byodo-in late in the afternoon, have an evening meal or a snack and then watch the cormorant fishing on the river at Tonoshima Island (very close to the temple). Ukai is held every night from 11 June to 31 August, except during full moon of after heavy rains. You can rent a boat only, or arrange for a party/supper with food and drink. (A person who speaks Japanese would be helpful for this; the TIC might be able to offer suggestions.) The actual fishing lasts only 20 to 30 minutes, so the Japanese watchers make a party out of it. The fishing takes place close to shore and can be seen quite well without taking a boat, but the boat can be more fun.

Access to Uji is by the JNR Nara line, or the Keihan line for which Uji is the terminus. Byodo-in is on the same side of the river as the JNR station; from the Keihan station you cross the bridge and turn left.

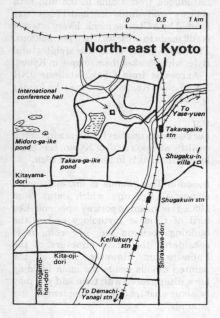

North-east Kyoto

NORTH-EAST OF KYOTO
Shugaku-in Rikyu Imperial Villa
This villa dates from 1629; the upper garden is built around a pond and is considered the most scenic part of the grounds. The landscape is mostly lawn and rolling hills and not worth a special trip to see, at least until after seeing most

of the other places listed here. It is at its best in autumn. Advance permission must be obtained from the Imperial Household Agency. (Refer to the Kyoto Gosho details at the beginning of this section.)

Kyoto International Conference Hall (Kokusai Kaigi-jo)
A source of civic pride, the Conference Hall is a six-storey building constructed in 1966 beside the Takara-ga-ike pond and used for many international gatherings. It can be reached from Kyoto station by bus 5, 36 or 65;·it is about one km from Takaragaike station of the Keifuku line out of Demachi-Yanagi station (to the north-east of the city). The fastest access is by subway north to Karasuma-Shakomae, which is linked to the hall by bus 36. From here it is simple to get into the city for sightseeing. The Ohara area is easily reached because the Conference Hall is close to the bus and rail connections to Yase-yuen and Ohara.

Enryaku-ji
This is a very large temple complex on *Mt Hiei*, the highest point in the ridge that separates Kyoto from Lake Biwa. Temples have stood here since 788, when Emperor Kammi (who founded Kyoto as the capital) ordered its construction to guard against 'evil spirits' from the north-east. One theory suggests that the spirits were Ainu or another race who predated the ethnic Japanese (Yamato).

Enryaku-ji grew to an astounding 3000 temples and its private army of several thousand armed monks was more powerful than any government force. They terrorised other Buddhist sects and often attacked Kyoto itself if their wishes were not met. In 1571 Nobunaga Oda, who began the unification of Japan after the civil war, killed or dispersed the monks and destroyed every temple. After this, Enryaku-ji was limited to one-twentieth of its former size. Today there are still 130 temples on the mountain. The main building is the huge *Kompon-cho-do*.

Top: Interior of an old farmhouse at Nihon-Minka-en, Kawasaki
Bottom: Old lady and one of the characteristic walls of Kurashiki

Top: Interior of Tagata-jinja shrine, typical of any large Shinto shrine
Left: An Ainu elder, Noboribetsu
Right: Shinto priest at Meiji-jingu shrine

There are four possible routes to Enryaku-ji. The first two are either by Keifuku private railway from Demachi-Yanagi station or by bus from Kyoto station to Yase-yuen and then cable railway to the top. The third route is by train to the west shore of Biwa-ko lake, then a cable railway to the top of Hiei-san. There are two stations near the base station: Sakamoto station of the Keihan line (from Sanjo-Keihan station in Kyoto, with a change of trains at Hama-Otsu); and Eizan station (JNR), which is on the Osaka/Kyoto – Nagahara/Omi-Shiotsu line. Fourth, there are also at least 10 buses a day from Kyoto station to the temple. The third is the most scenic route.

OHARA

This small village is well-known for *Jakko-in* and *Sanzen-in* temples. The women of Ohara have long been famous for their characteristic costume and customs. Unusual in Japan, they carry loads on their heads. They may be seen on occasion in Kyoto selling produce from Ohara; in Ohara itself they may be working at souvenir stalls.

Access to Ohara is by bus which originates at Kyoto station and passes by Sanjo-Keihan and Yase-Yuen stations on the way, or by Keifuku railway Eizan-sen line to Yase-Yuen (the base station for the cable railway to Mt Hiei) then by bus to Ohara. During the leaf-viewing season the buses are packed, so a start from Kyoto station is advisable to guarantee a seat (or even getting on a bus).

Sanzen-in This temple has, like most other temples, images of historical interest which become rather repetitive to westerners who know little of Buddhism and its art. However, the main temple has a setting of lush green, and the grounds are extremely beautiful in late October – early November when the leaves change colour. It is naturally very crowded at that time, but still well worth going to see. An English-language pamphlet gives historical information.

Kurama-dera Temple

Accessible by Keifuku railway from Demachi-Yanagi station (continuing from Takaraga-ike station on the Kurama-sen line), is Kurama-dera temple. Although the temple dates from 770, the present main hall is only from 1971 so it is of little architectural interest. However the grounds are very pretty in late October – early November, so this is the best time for a visit. There is also an interesting festival on 20 June.

There is a good hiking trail between Kurama-dera and Kibune-jinja shrine; it also is most recommended during autumn.

NORTH-WEST OF KYOTO

TAKAO

This is possibly the supreme area for maple-viewing, several km into the mountains north west of the city. There are three temples to visit while admiring the foliage, *Jingo-ji* (at Takao), *Saimyo-ji* (at Makino-o), and *Kozan-ji* (at Togano-o); all are within walking distance of each other.

On the approach to Jingo-ji, tables and mat-covered areas are set up on level patches of ground and on platforms so visitors may lunch beneath the canopy of brilliant colours. The view of a Japanese family, with one or two of the women dressed in kimono, eating amidst such beauty is a memorable picture of Japanese civilisation at its best.

Visitors may find a speciality of the season on sale, maple-leaf tempura; the batter tastes good but the leaf is terrible.

Buses run as far as Takao; check with the TIC for schedules.

Shooting the Rapids (Kameoka)

An enjoyable excursion, especially during the heat of the summer, is to shoot the Hozu rapids. The starting point is Kameoka, accessible by JNR Sanin-sen line or bus from Kyoto station. The dock is at Hozu-ohashi bridge. The trip lasts about two hours and is exciting without being dangerous. It finishes at Arashiyama. The 'season' is from 11 March to 30 November.

There are generally six boats a day, so inquire at the TIC to be sure of getting a seat.

ENTERTAINMENT IN KYOTO

If you aren't worn out after a day's sightseeing, or if you want a break during the day from a seemingly endless round of temples and shrines, what else is there to do in Kyoto? There are many events that would fit into the 'cultural' category, performing arts that have been passed down through the centuries and represent some of the highest levels of achievement in these fields in the world. Naturally these are not going to be everyone's cup o-cha, but it would be a pity to ignore this side of Japanese life. Those looking for something less highbrow will discover that Japanese popular taste can be as earthy as that anywhere.

Dance & Theatre

Through the year, at various times and theatres, there are performances of the traditional arts Noh, Kabuki, Bunraku, Kyogen and others. As Osaka is less than an hour away by train, performances of Kabuki and Bunraku (puppet theatre which originated in Osaka) given there are also in easy reach. These performing arts are explained in greater detail elsewhere in the book.

A highly recommended condensed version of all the major Japanese arts – dances by geisha, traditional bugaku dances, koto music, Bunraku, flower arrangement – can be seen between 1 March and 29 November twice daily at Gion Kaburenjo Theatre. The show is called Gion Corner and lasts an hour; performances begin at 8 and 9 pm. Each 'act' is long enough to give a feel for the skill, but short enough not to be dull (most seem too short). Tickets can be bought at the door, but bookings or advance purchase may be advisable during busy seasons.

There are many performances of traditional dances at certain times of the year. Examples are *Miyako-odori* (Cherry Blossom Dance) throughout April, when numbers of beautifully dressed *maiko* (apprentice geisha) perform traditional dances; and *Kamogawa-odori* in May, when geisha of the Ponto-sho area perform.

To check on what is happening, obtain the booklets mentioned earlier and be sure to stop in at the TIC where the bulletin board lists all the events of that month and the staff can give further details of anything of interest.

Coffee Shops

For other innocent entertainment there are many coffee shops. Some are only places to sit and chat; a coffee shop 'date' is a common boy-girl activity, which helps explain the high prices – you're not paying for the coffee, but for the space. Many shops offer music, recorded or live; the latter is jazz, while recorded music may be jazz, classical or in-between. Because such shops come and go it is pointless to list them here; the TIC people can give suggestions. It is possible to meet people at such places, but it's all the luck of the draw.

Bars & Clubs

There is a huge number of places for drinking, as is true of any large city in Japan and some are reasonable in cost and quite enjoyable to visit. But beware of what would be called 'clip joints' in any other country – these are accepted in Japan because of the generous expense accounts. It is not unknown to be billed well over Y10,000 for a beer! There are many little little pubs and 'stand-bars' (Japanese term) many of which are run by companies that make or distribute whisky. These reasonably-priced places can be identified after a little practice. Don't be embarrassed to ask prices – remember the possible consequences! Avoid any place that has touts in front enticing customers in, and places with hostesses, unless you are able to check prices for all services. Hostess charges can skyrocket. The TIC may be able to give suggestions.

Bars in international hotels will be safe from gouging (though not cheap), but will generally have an international atmosphere, not the Japanese one that visitors presumably have paid a lot of money to enjoy.

There are many lower-class clubs where strippers and similar entertainment may be found. Finding them on your own may be difficult, if not impossible, so a Japanese friend would be invaluable in locating one; also a lone foreigner might well be refused entry. The cost of such a place would not be cheap; if a girl can earn Y10,000-30,000 for an 'all-nighter', she's going to expect a fair proportion of this for playing around in a club.

Seasonal Events

There are many seasonal sights and entertainments in Kyoto – some natural, some 'man-made'.

Cherry Blossoms The exact time of the blossoms varies over a range of several weeks from year to year, but is generally around early-mid April. The best places to see blossoms are Kiyomizu-dera, Heian-jingu, Daigo-ji, Maruyama-koen park, Arashiyama-koen park and Nanzen-ji. Yoshino (Nara-ken) is a mountainside planted with thousands of trees and can be seen as a day trip from Kyoto. Also highly recommended is Hikone; its castle grounds are covered with cherry trees and the moats are lined with them.

Maple Leaves The temples of Kyoto are among the most beautiful places in the world in autumn. The temple founders planted the grounds, which are generally located in the hills around the city, with maples. The leaves of these trees change colour in a fiery display of reds and oranges rarely matched anywhere else in the world (a difficult admission for someone who comes from eastern Canada!) and their beauty underscores the fine lines of the walls and roofs of the buildings. The peak period is usually early-mid November. Temples noted for their foliage are Eikan-do, Nanzen-ji, Kiyomizu-dera, Tofuku-ji, Sekiya-Zen-in, Kinkaku-ji, and Ryoan-ji. Areas close to the city include Arashiyama, Sugino, Kiyotani valley, Yase, Ohara (Sanzen-in and Jakko-in), Mt Kurama and Kibune and Takao (Jingo-ji and Kozan-ji).

Markets

There are two monthly flea markets. One is at Kitano-jinja on the 5th of every month, and the other is at Toji on the 21st. For the best selection it is best to arrive early in the morning. Don't expect any valuable antiques, as these people know the worth of their goods. (*Warning*: Don't pick up any antiques; some unscrupulous dealers carefully assemble already broken items so they 'break' when touched, obliging payment.)

Zen

Those interested in Zen will be disappointed to learn that you cannot join meditation on a casual basis in the Kyoto area without an introduction. The reason is that many other foreigners joined in, didn't know what to do, would not conform to the customs and distracted those who wanted to participate properly. Anyone who is seriously interested should contact the TIC or arrange an introduction through a previous teacher elsewhere. Those just becoming interested would be better advised to go to Tokyo, where there are facilities for teaching Zen in English. (This is described earlier in the book.)

Museums

There are many museums other than the few detailed here. If the following sound interesting, inquire at the TIC for more information. Japan Historical Museum

(*Nippon Rekishi-kan*); Kiyotaki Folkcraft Museum (*Kiyotaki Mingei-kan*); Kyoto Ceramic Hall (*Kyoto Tojiki-kaikan*); Kyoto Folkcraft Museum (*Kyoto Minzoku-kan*); Kyoto Municipal Museum of Art; Kyoto National Museum of Modern Art; *Kodai Yuzen* (has old yuzen-dyed items); and the Steam Locomotive Museum (*Umekoji Joki Kikansha-kan*).

Arts & Crafts

Kyoto is famous for a number of handicrafts of the highest quality, a legacy of its past as the capital for nearly 1000 years; a period when there was a continual demand for fine fabrics and lacquerware etc. Many of these goods are still produced by the traditional methods evolved centuries ago and you can see several types of craftsmen at work. As well as the crafts mentioned here, it is possible to arrange an introduction to other specialists through the TIC or City Information Office.

Kyoto Handicraft Centre Described earlier, this is well worth a visit to watch a variety of craftspeople in action. Goods may be purchased on the spot.

Tatsumara Silk Fine silks are on display here and demonstrations are given on fingernail weaving. Inquire at the TIC for more details.

Inaba Cloisonne Demonstrations are given of making cloisonne ware. Inquire at the TIC.

Municipal Museum of Traditional Industry Described earlier, this has displays of many handicrafts of the very highest quality, along with live demonstrations of some crafts.

Yuzen An interesting and quite extensive live display here shows the historic process for producing the incredibly beautiful material used for one kind of (very expensive) kimono. *Yuzen Bunka Kaikan* (Yuzen culture centre) is on the west side of the city near Nishi-Kyogoku station (Hankyu railway Kyoto-sen line). A leaflet and more information are available at the TIC

Pottery There are several potteries in the area, but they do not encourage visitors because of the interruption to their work. An exception is Kotobuki Toshun which has set up special facilities in the Kiyomizu-Yaki Danchi building so that visitors can see how pottery is made and even make some for themselves. This is usually only for group tours, so inquire at the TIC if you are interested.

Things to Buy

Kyoto probably offers the largest variety of traditional Japanese handicrafts of any city in the country. There are many shops near the station and near many of the major temples and other tourist attractions. There are also several department stores and the Kyoto Handicraft centre. A commercial map, 'Shopping Guide Map of Kyoto', is useful for locating specialty shops. It should be available at the TIC and hotels. The TIC staff can also help you find anything out of the ordinary.

I found that the tax-free shops along Kawaramachi-dori gave slightly less discount on photographic equipment than the lowest-priced shops in Tokyo, but the difference wasn't enough to worry about. If Kyoto is your first stop in Japan it is better to spend the extra yen and have it available to photograph the beauties of Kyoto rather than saving a small sum.

Festivals

There are many festivals in Kyoto, but because information is so easy to obtain there is no need to list them all here. The JNTO pamphlet on Kyoto/Nara has a good listing as do the monthly booklets listed earlier.

The most famous festivals, that are worth making a point to see, include the following:

15 May: *Aoi Matsuri* A procession of people in costumes of centuries ago passes through the streets from Kyoto Gosho Palace to Shimogamo and Kamigamo shrines.

16-17 July: *Gion Matsuri* Probably the supreme Japanese festival. Huge festival carts are pulled through streets on the 17th. There are 29 in all, of various sizes, all several tonnes in weight and built like miniature temples, small boats etc, with the finest lacquer covering, gilded ornamentation, and some with European tapestries – they are a fantastic sight. The night before, they are on display in little sidestreets; many may be entered on the payment of a fee. Also open are some of the old nearby houses where families display their treasures, such as suits of armour. The TIC can give information on the route and display sites. Accommodation is hard to find at this time, so it is necessary to book ahead, or to commute from a nearby city or town.

16 August: *Daimonji* Five huge bonfires that trace out one Chinese character each light up five mountains surrounding Kyoto. City lights are doused to add to the effect. It is the culmination of the Obon season when the spirits of the dead are believed to return to earth. During this season you may find neighbourhood dances with hundreds of people in kimono, moving in great circles and performing the slow and graceful movements of the dance. The best vantage points are Shogun-zuka hill (Hagashi-yama) and Yoshida-yama hill, near Kyoto University.

22 October: *Jidai Matsuri* The name means Festival of the Ages, and it is a procession of people in historical costumes of the 13 main periods of Kyoto's history.

Day Trips Kyoto is close to most of the really interesting sightseeing territory in Japan. A number of places can be visited in a day using Kyoto as a base or you can go out on circling routes and return after a few days. Day trips include Nara, Hikone, Himeji, Osaka, Ise and Yoshino (in cherry-blossom time). Extended trips would be the area around Nara and around the Kii-hanto peninsula. (Information on train services in the region is given at the end of this chapter.)

Food
To help with the search for a good restaurant, the Kyoto Restaurant Association has printed a pamphlet, *Kyoto Gourmet Guide*, avaiable at the TIC. Staff at the TIC would also probably be willing to suggest a good restaurant and perhaps even a sample menu if your visit was not at one of their busy times.

For budget diners there are many little restaurants with realistic wax displays which show you the available dishes. A former student of Kyoto University recommended *Nakagima* for economical food (open Monday to Saturday). For a real bargain (of doubtful nutritional value) one can gorge on pizza at *Trecca Pizza*; all you can eat for about Y500. It is open between 11 am and 2 pm, Monday to Saturday. It is located on Kawaramachi-dori near Sanjo-dori on the second floor of the BAL Fashion building. As in other Japanese cities there are McDonalds, Kentucky Fried Chicken and other familiar American fast food shops.

Places to Stay
A large number of places offer reasonably-priced accommodation in Kyoto, along with hotels of the international luxury class plus some ryokan that are even more costly.

For the full listing of cheap places to stay it is best to obtain the photcopied sheets 'Moderately-priced Accommodation in Kyoto' from the TIC in either Kyoto or Tokyo.

There are six youth hostels in and around Kyoto. Those nearest the station are *Higashiyama* (tel 761-8135) and *Matsusan* (221-5160). Because of their proximity to the station they are more likely to be booked. Both *Utano Youth Hostel* (462-2288/9) and *Kitayama* (492-5345) are about 50 minutes by bus to the north of the city (a little less if you take the north-south subway line); the latter is more out of the way. Some distance into the country (more than an hour by bus) are *Ohara Youth Hostel* (744-2721) and *Oharago Youth Hostel* (744-2721).

Favourites with travellers who don't care for the restrictions of youth hostels are two private homes, *Tani House* and *Uno House*.

Tani House (492-5489) is a spacious, traditional-style house with several rooms, one each set aside for males and females, plus several smaller rooms suitable for couples or whoever happens to get there first. The only disadvantage is that it is a considerable distance from Kyoto station. Access is by subway to the north terminus, then a westbound bus 214, 204 or 222 to Funaokakoen stop where a small road can be seen across the main road from a tailor shop. Follow this and turn right at the third little side-street (it faces an earthen wall inset with tiles).

Uno House is conveniently located not far from the south-east corner of the Kyoto Gosho. Access from Kyoto station is by bus 4, 14, 54, 200 or 215 to Kawaramachi-Marutomachi stop. From the large intersection walk west to the second small street on the south side and turn left (there's a bank on the corner). The house is on the east side and a very small sign anounces 'Uno'. Travellers arriving in Kyoto by bus from Osaka airport should get off at Kyoto Hotel (on Kawaramachi-dori), a 20 minute walk to the south of Uno House. The house is something of a wonder and quite untypically Japanese, with so many added-on rooms and wings that it is a bit of a rabbit warren. It is advisable to ensure that the payment of your room is written down at once, as in my experience it has been forgotten and attempts made to collect it again. This slight disadvantage is out-weighed by the convenience of simple cooking facilities and the closeness to the city. Despite her forgetfulness and grumpy appearance, Mrs Uno is good-hearted, and occassionally has a room for long-term occupancy. (It might be a good idea to check with the TIC about Uno House as Mrs Uno is getting on in years.)

One of the benefits of staying at these two places is that the other travellers you meet there often have useful information and interesting stories.

There is another private home run by another family named Tani. It is to the south of the city (681-7437).

A relatively new place that welcomes foreigners is the *English Guest House*. Shared accommodation is Y1300 per night, with slight reductions by the week or month. It is located to the northeast of the city, accessible by subway to Kitaoji station (terminus), then by eastbound bus Kita 6, Kitaoji to Takanoshako-mae stop. Phoning ahead would be advisable on (075) 223-1059 (am); or (075) 722-0495/6 (pm and weekends).

The least expensive ryokan are *Ichiume* (tel 351-9385, Y1500), *Sanyu* (tel 371-1968, Y1500), and *Yuhara* (tel 371-9583).

Others in increasing order of cost are given below. Prices are for the lowest-priced room.

Ryokan: *Rakutuso Bekkan* (tel 761-633, Y3900), and *Rakutuso Honkan* (tel 761-6336, Y8000 for two), both near Heian-jingu.

YWCA: *Kyoto YWCA* (tel 431-0351, Y3500, women only).

Western-style hotels: *Pension Utano* (tel 463-1118, Y3200); *Traveller's Inn Honkan* (tel 771-0225, Y3800), near Heian-jingu; *Traveller's Inn Hotel Sun Shine* (tel 771-0225, Y3800); *Hokke Club* (tel 361-1251, Y4000);*Kyoto Business Hotel* (tel 222-1220, Y4000); *Kyoto Central Inn* (tel 211-1666, Y5080); *New Ginkaku Inn* (tel 341-2884, Y5500); *Tokyu Inn* (tel 593-0109, Y5900); *Pension Shimogamo* (tel 711-0180, Y8200).

Those on large budgets who wish to sample a really fine ryokan in beautiful surroundings should enjoy *Rankyokan*, which is on a hillside overlooking the Hozu river, just above Arashiyama and set among tall trees. The price is over Y10,000 per person.

Temple Accommodation Many people wish to stay in a temple in Kyoto. Unfortunately, as with Zen meditation, previous foreign guests have not conformed with customs and rules of the temples and soured any desire of temple staff to have foreign visitors. Anyone sincerely interested in staying at a temple and able to demonstrate both some genuine interest in the religious aspects and a willingness to conform to custom should contact the TIC for further information.

Getting There
Air

By air you can reach Kyoto easily from many points in Japan as well as overseas, as it uses Osaka International Airport. Buses run every 20 minutes through the day in each direction, making the rounds of several of the better-known hotels (the Miyako, Kyoto, JAL, International and Grand) as well as Kyoto station.

Hitching

To hitch out of Kyoto east to Nagoya or Tokyo or west to Hiroshima and Shimon-oseki, take bus 19 or 20 from the station until signs for the entrance of the Meishin expressway (marked in English) come into view. Find the entrance for the direction you want and hold up a sign (in Japanese) showing your destination. It is not possible to hitch on the freeway except at rest stops, so it is necessary to get a car going in the Hiroshima direction (which means switching freeways at Osaka).

Osaka is so close that it is not worth hitching; take the train.

To hitch toward Tottori (north coast) it is simplest to take the train to Kameoka and start there (according to one source)

but you could also take one of several buses (or Hankyu train) to the Katsura area and hitch on Route 9.

However, it seems the authorities are beginning to discourage hitchhikers out of Kyoto (possibly too many), so ask among other travellers for an update.

Getting Around

Kyoto is covered by an extensive network of bus routes. The major ones are shown on a sub-map on the TIC Kyoto map. A much more detailed map (in Japanese only) is available at the bus centre in front of Kyoto station. If possible, however, it is advisable to chat to the TIC staff because some of the buses are infrequent. In briefest terms there are two loop bus lines, 206 and 214. The former goes along Higashi-oji, Kita-oji and Karasuma streets on the way to and from the station; while the latter uses Kawaramachi, Kita-oji and Nishi-oji streets. The character following the number tells the direction. A one-day pass for unlimited travel on city buses is available but you might not use it enough to justify the cost. There is also an '11 tickets for the price of 10' deal. Both are available at the bus centre and further information can be obtained at the TIC.

Kyoto has a modern subway line running from Kyoto station north along Karasuma-dori (dori = street) to Kita-oji-dori on the northernmost major east-west road. The Hankyu private railway line (Kyoto-Osaka) intersects it at Shijo-Karasuma and provides east-west service via four stations along Shijo-dori. Several JNR and private rail lines can be used for transport within Kyoto. These are shown on the TIC map.

Taxis are plentiful. Don't worry about telling the driver your destination, if he doesn't understand your pronounciation he can read it in Japanese on the TIC map.

Bicycles may be rented at the Bridgestone bike shop on the corner of Muromachi and Shimocho-jamachi streets and from a couple of shops near Sanjo station. Most of Kyoto is flat, so this is a practical means of getting around, though the savings in bus fares might be negligible. The TIC can also give suggestions.

There is no problem whatever in finding your way around Kyoto on your own, even if you do not speak a word of Japanese. Kyoto is one of the few cities in Japan laid out on a rectangular grid (modelled on ancient Chinese capitals), transport facilities are well developed and tourist ionformation is readily available. I recommend that you pick up a TIC map and set out independently, as this will give you a much better feel for this historic city. Even if you do get lost you may well stumble across something more interesting than what you set out to find. One of the few commercial maps which is to the correct scale is the area map of Kyoto published by Shobunsha. The name is printed only in Japanese, so you will need to ask for it. Most streets and places are marked in English.

Bus tours are available, but virtually all go to the same destinations: Nijo-jo, Kyoto Gosho and Kinkakuji temple in the morning; Heian shrine, Sanjusangendo temple and Kiyomizu-dera temple in the afternoon.

As described in the introductory section of the book, the better students of English of the Tesco company are willing to act as unpaid guides for English speaking visitors to Kyoto. Phone 06-311-253 and ask for the Tescort co-ordinator.

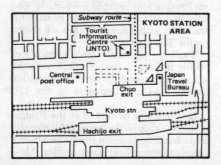

Nara-ken

The city of Nara is a very famous and popular destination for visitors to Japan, as it pre-dates Kyoto as the imperial capital, and some temples from that period still survive. The Nara plain was one of the most important areas in the early history or Japan and many remnants abound. There are also other attractions in the southern parts of the prefecture and the adjoining Kii-hanto Peninsula.

NARA
Usually mentioned in the same breath as Kyoto, Nara is another ancient capital of Japan, only 42 km from Kyoto and usually included in any tour of the country. It was the first permanent capital of Japan, from 710 to 784, previous to which the capital was moved after the death of each emperor. Nara witnessed the introduction of Buddhism into Japan, with the resulting far-reaching effects on culture and the arts. Amazingly, some of the temples and other structures from that period still stand. Although they were then in the city of Nara, the present city is considerably smaller, and many of them are now some distance out in the country.

Information
The TIC in Kyoto has a useful pamphlet *Kyoto Nara* that has some sightseeing information to complement the following pages; and the JNTO Kyoto-Nara map is quite adequate for sightseeing in Nara city. The TIC in Tokyo also has a printed sheet *Walking Tour Courses in Nara*. Finally, the Nara City tourist Information Office is located on the first floor of the Kintetsu-Nara station.

Voluntary Guides
To make your visit more interesting and enjoyable, the Nara YMCA will introduce you to one or more English-speaking Japanese who will act as unpaid guides for sightseeing around Nara. (As in Kyoto, it

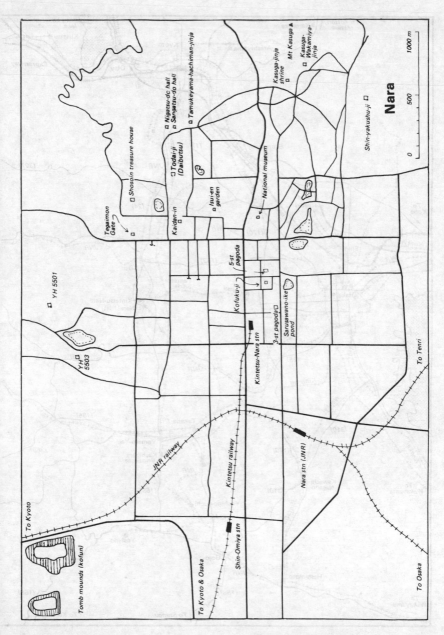

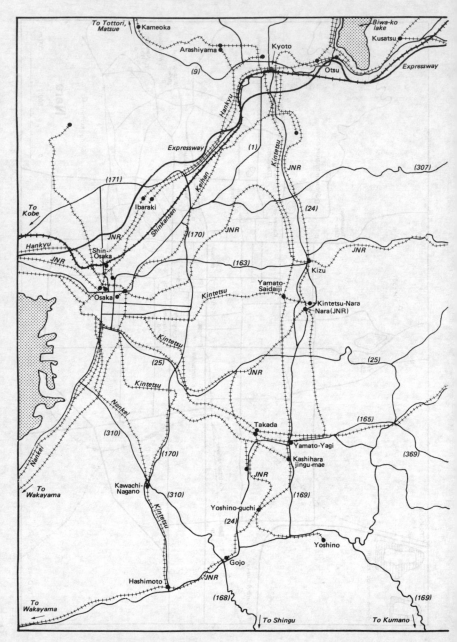

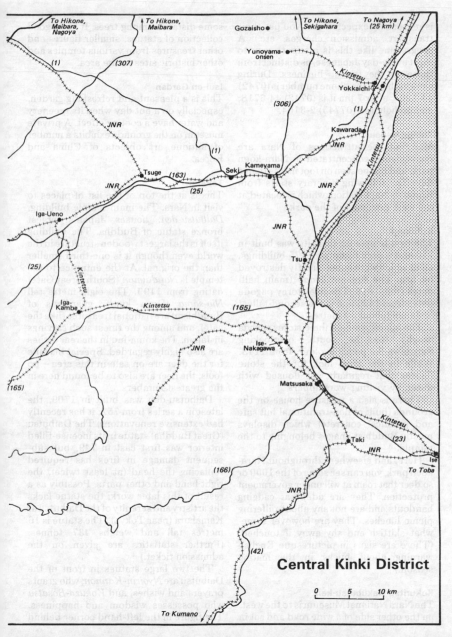

Central Kinki District

0   5   10 km

is reasonably expected that you pay their transport, admission charges, etc.) A programme like this is a superb way to meet every-day Japanese, as distinct from those in the tourist business. During working hours the phone number is (0742) 44-2207; after 7 pm it is (0742) 44-6718; and on holidays (07745) 2-3104.

Things to See
Many of the attractions of Nara are conveniently concentrated in Nara-koen park, and can be seen on foot in less than a day. The following itinerary starts from Kintetsu-Nara station, which is located at the west extremity of the park.

Kofuku-ji
The first temple on this site was built in 710 and it once comprised 175 buildings, all of which were subsequently destroyed by fire. The present *kondo* (main hall) dates from 1819. The five-storey pagoda dates from 1426 and is the second-tallest in Japan (about 50 metres).

The smaller, graceful three-storey pagoda nearby (to the south, overlooking Sarusawa-ike pond) is older, from 1143. While in the area, look for the stone figures that regularly get doused with water by visiting worshippers.

There is also a treasure house on the grounds (built of non-traditional but safe and practical concrete) which displays mostly Buddhist images belonging to the temple.

Here, and elsewhere throughout Nara-koen park, you can see some of the 1000 or so deer that roam at will under government protection. They are adept at cadging handouts and are not shy about pilfering picnic lunches. They are however somewhat skittish and shy away if touched. (There are signs in picturesque English warning about bucks in the mating season.)

Kokuritsu Hakubutsu-ken
The Nara National Museum is to the west, on the other side of a wide road and set in some distance among trees. It has a good collection of statues, smaller figures and other treasures from various temples and other historic sites in the area.

Isui-en Garden
This is a pleasant and refreshing garden, especially on a hot day when its greenery and water have a cooling effect. A private museum on the grounds exhibits a number of antique art objects of China and Korea.

Todai-ji
This is at the top of the list of places to visit in Nara. The main temple building, *Daibutsu-den*, houses Japan's largest bronze statue of Buddha. The building itself is the largest wooden structure in the world even though it is one-third smaller than the original. At the entrance to the temple is *Nandaimon* (South Great Gate) dating from 1199. The eight-metre tall *Nio-sama* (Deva kings, guardians of Buddhism) are national treasures (like the gate), and among the finest such carvings in Japan. The koma-inu in the rear niches are also highly regarded. Special biscuits for the deer are on sale in this area – no fools, the deer are also to be found here in the greatest numbers.

Daibutsu-den was built in 1709, the latest in a series from 752; it has recently had extensive renovations. The Daibutsu (Great Buddha) statue in its incense-filled interior was first cast in 749, but subsequent damage in fires has required replacing the head (at least twice), the right hand and other parts. Possibly as a result of this later work, the statue lacks the artistry and serenity of the Daibutsu at Kamakura (near Tokyo). The statue is 16 metres tall and weighs 437 tonnes. (Further statistics are given on the admission ticket.)

The two large statues in front of the Daibutsu are *Nyoirin-Kannon*, who grants prayers and wishes, and *Kokuzo-Bosatsu* who possesses wisdom and happiness. The figure in the left-hand corner behind the statue is *Komokuten*, one of the four heavenly guardians who destroy all obstacles in the path of Buddhism. Another of the guardians, *Tamonten*, is found in the right-hand corner – he is trampling a demon.

Kaidan-in is a separate temple west of the Daibutsu-den; it contains clay images of the four heavenly guardians (all national treasures).

Sangatsu-do is the oldest structure of Todai-ji, dating from 733. Many statues of national treasure merit are displayed.

Kasuga-taisha Shrine

One of the best-known places in Nara, Kasuga-taisha is famous for its forested setting and lanterns. There are approximately 3000 lanterns, some of stone and standing as tall as a man, others of bronze and hung from the eaves of the various buildings that make up the shrine. Seen against the bright orange and white of the buildings. the effect is very photogenic. Lanterns line nearly all the paths of the shrine grounds, and this is within the area roamed by deer, so one is quite likely to poke its head out between two of them for a very cute picture.

The lanterns are all lit twice a year, on the day of the *Setsubun* festival (variable: 2 or 3 February), and on 15 August. The annual festival of the shrine, *Kasuga-matsuri*, is held on 13 March and features a colourful procession.

In addition to the four shrines (surrounded by a gallery) that make up the main shrine, there is also *Kasuga-Wakamiya-jinja* to the south. Here it may be possible to see *Kagura* (sacred dances) in the *Kagura-den*, the southern-most of the three buildings. The annual festival of this shrine is the greatest in Nara, and is a procession of large numbers of people in costumes and armour of ancient times. It is held on 16-17 December.

Shin-Yakushi-ji

This temple is of modest interest and is known primarily for its central seated image and 12 clay figures of 12 divine generals.

OUTSIDE NARA

The other attractions are somewhat outside today's city, which gives an idea of the size of the old capital.

Horyu-ji

This is one of the most important temples in Japanese history, art and culture. Its construction began in 607 under the direction of Prince Shotoku, the man depicted on the Y10,000 notes and one of the great builders of the Japanese state. Amazingly, some of the original structures still stand; others were added or rebuilt in later eras.

Easiest access is by bus from Kintetsu-Nara station, either directly to Horyuji-mae stop, or after a visit to *Yakushi-ji* and other temples.

The temple is divided into *Sai-in Garan* and *To-in Garan* (west and east minsters). Sai-in is now larger, since more of its structures have survived. A leaflet given on entry has a map that identifies the buildings. The following is a brief description.

Sai-in Garan Entry is via *Nandaimon* (South Great Gate), a national treasure dating from 1438 (rebuilt), a walled avenue, then *Chumon* (Middle Gate), also a national treasure and dating from the year of the temple's construction. The red deva king (guardian of Buddhism) in the gate symbolises light; the black king, darkness. The five-storey pagoda is one of the oldest wooden buildings in the world and reputedly incorporates the same timbers used in its original construction. It was dismantled during World War II for safety.

The open-fronted *kodo* (990) houses several important statues: the gilded main figures are *Yakushi-Nyorai* (2.6 metres) and two attendants (1.7 metres). The *kondo* (main hall, another national treasure) is also one of the oldest wooden

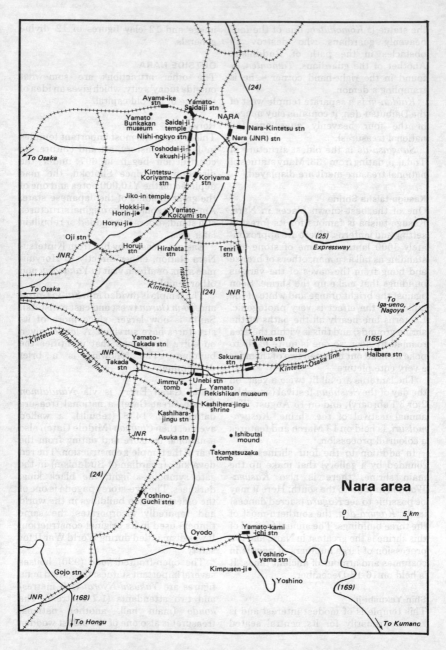

(24)

Ayame-ike stn
Yamato-Saidaiji stn
Yamato Bunkakan museum
Seidai-ji temple
NARA
Nishi-nokyo stn
Nara-Kintetsu stn
Nara (JNR) stn
Toshodai-ji
Yakushi-ji
Kintetsu-Koriyama stn
Koriyama stn
Jiko-in temple
Hokki-ji
Horin-ji
Yamato-Koizumi stn
Horyu-ji
Oji stn
JNR
Horuji stn
Hirahata
Tenri stn
(25)
Expressway
To Osaka

To Osaka
Kintetsu
Kintetsu
(24)
JNR
To Iga-ueno, Nagoya

Kintetsu Minami-Osaka line
Yamato-Takada stn
JNR
Takada stn
Miwa stn
Oniwa shrine
(165)
Sakurai stn
Haibara stn
Kintetsu-Osaka line

Jimmu's tomb
Unebi stn
Yamato Rekishikan museum
Kashihara-jingu shrine
Kashihara-jingu stn
Ishibutai mound
Asuka stn
Takamatsuzaka tomb

Nara area

0   5 km

(24)
Yoshino-Guchi stns
Oyodo
Yamato-kami-ichi stn
Yoshino-yama stn
Kimpusen-ji
Gojo stn
JNR
(168)
Yoshino
(169)
To Hongu
To Kumano

buildings in the world and houses many important images, both sculptures and castings.

Shoryo-in has a statue of Prince Shotoku at age 45 (figure and building are national treasures), while *Daihozo-den* (two concrete buildings) have displays of many treasures of the temple.

To-in Garan Leaving the Sai-in area and passing through *Chumon* and *Todaimon* (Middle and East Great Gates), you come to the To-in Garan precincts. The octagonal building in the central rectangle is *Yumedono* (Hall of Dreams, used by Shotoku for meditation), rated the most beautiful rectangular building in Japan. Dating from 739, it also contains a number of fine images, including several national treasures. There are several other buildings in the grounds, many of which also house historic images. Chugu-ji temple is a former nunnery attached to *To-in Garan.*

Horin & Hokki Temples
In the vicinity of Horyu-ji are two other historic temples, Horin-ji and Hokki-ji. They date from 621 and 638 respectively, and also house several treasured images. The pagoda at Hokki is believed to date from 685.

Nara-ken Minzoku Hakubutsu-kan
The Nara-ken Museum of Ethnology features a number of traditional farmhouses from the early 18th century that have been moved from various places in Nara-ken and re-erected. Inside them, items once used in daily life but obsolete for decades or centuries are displayed with photos or drawings to show how they were used. Exhibits represent the three main geographical/cultural areas of Nara-ken: Nara plain, the Yamato highlands and the mountains of the Yoshino area. Most interesting are the full-size scenes with life-like models of farmers, lumberjacks, teapickers and others, all dressed in authentic garb. Some of the dummies were actually dressed by people who still

make their living in the way portrayed, so even the underwear is correct!

Access is from Kintetsu-Koriyama station, from where you take a bus to Yoda-Higashiyama (15 minutes). It might be possible to go by bus directly from Horyu-ji or Toshidai-ji/Yakushi-ji, so inquire locally.

Yakushi-ji
Constructed on this site in 718 after being moved from elsewhere, this temple has a considerable number of treasured figures, including the first bronze Buddha image made in Japan – the *Yakushi-Nyorai*. The unusual 34-metre pagoda looks like a six-storey structure, but such buildings always have an odd number of levels; this one has a sub-roof between each 'real' roof, and is the only one of its kind in Japan. The pagoda is the only structure of the temple that has survived in its original form; all other buildings are later reconstructions. An excellent English-language booklet is given out on entry and explains the salient points of the temple.

Yakushi-ji may be reached by the bus that goes to Horyu-ji, or from Nishi-Nokyo station of Kintetsu railway (reached with a change at Yamato-Saidai-ji station).

Toshidai-ji
This temple is highly regarded for its architecture and harmonious arrangement of structures. Like the other major temples of Nara, Toshidai also has a number of figures that rate as national treasures. The temple is less than one km north of Yakushi-ji; you can walk or go by bus, but the former is in fact quicker.

Places to Stay
Most foreign visitors to Nara probably make it a day trip out of Kyoto. However, anyone wishing to explore the area in greater detail will find a good range of accommodation available, including hotels and ryokan. Accommodation can be booked in advance through any travel agent in the country (though JTB is the

biggest), and help is available at the railway stations.

There are two youth hostels in Nara. *Nara Youth Hostel* (tel 0742, 22-1334) should be avoided if there is any choice in the matter. The staff, even temporary help, act as if they are doing the hostellers a great favour by letting them stay, insist that both meals be taken there without option (many, including myself, do not care for a Japanese breakfast, and a hostel supper is rarely a gourmet feast), and are generally officious.

The alternative is *Nara-ken Seishonen-Kaikan Youth Hostel* (tel 0742 22-5540 or 26-4305) which is much better. It can be reached by following the main road that passes the Kintetsu station downhill to the north-south road that begins north of where the overpass road ends. Follow it north for a little over a km, turn left and walk uphill for about five minutes; it will probably be necessary to ask along the way, as there are no clear landmarks.

Getting There

Train service is good between Nara and Kyoto, Osaka, Nagoya and the Ise/Toba area. Refer to the Getting Around section at the end of this chapter.

Nara Plain Area

Nara city is located near the northern end of the Nara plain, an area that was settled early in the history of the northward movement of the Yamato people from Kyushu on their way to control of the Japanese islands. One legacy of this period (shared with Osaka, which was also an important city in this era), is a large number of tomb mounds or *tumuli (kufun)*, possibly showing an ancestral link between the Yamato people and Korea, where tumulus-building has long been a tradition.

These mounds are easily seen beside Route 24 out of Nara en route to Kyoto (tombs of Uwanabe and Konabe, as indicated on the JNTO map, plus an unlabelled one). Others at Asuka kofun, believed to date from the 7th century, were only opened in 1972 and have a number of very colourful murals of Korean and Chinese style. At Uneki, near Kashihara, the Archaeology Museum displays many relics of the late Stone Age and other prehistoric items from the area.

Omiwa-Myojin

This is believed to be one of the oldest shrines in Japan. The buildings are scenically located amidst tall trees. It is near Sakurai and accessible from Miwa station.

KOYA-SAN

Koya-san is a mountain famous as the centre of the *Shingon-Mikkyo* (True Word) sect of Buddhism. On its flat top are more than 120 temples carrying on a tradition from 816 AD. It is a place of pilgrimage for the faithful, especially for those with family members buried in the extensive cemetery, which is actually one of the most interesting things to see. Koya-san has also become a mountain resort providing an escape from the heat and humidity of the lower areas.

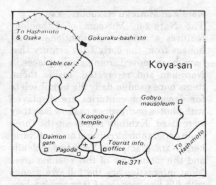

Information

Koya-san is best visited for its symbolic value, being a community of temples. But as an object of architectural study, compared with the beautiful buildings of Kyoto, it is not worth a special trip. The Tokyo TIC distributes a single-page information sheet that gives some more details on Koya-san, although its map is typically not to scale.

Things to See

Buses run from the upper cable-car station into the centre of the small community, or you can take a taxi or walk the three km or so into town. The road is lined with tall cedars and leads to the main temple on the west side of the community.

Gobyo

If a bus is available it is better to go directly to Gobyo. This is the mausoleum of Kobodaishi, the founder of the temples and a great teacher of Shingon, who also devised the hiragana syllabary for writing Japanese in a simpler form than using kanji. From Gobyo there is a very pleasant and peaceful walk through the great cemetery, where tombs and memorials are set amidst a forest of very tall cedar trees. The path leads to Ichinohashi (First Bridge), from where you can walk through the town and visit any of the large number of temples on the way. There is only one main street so it is impossible to get lost. At the intersection with the main road is an information office that can supply a map, some literature and give assistance in finding a room.

Kongobu-ji Temple

Just a short distance beyond the town is Kongobu-ji (Temple of the Diamond Mountain, rebuilt in 1861), the chief temple of the sect and the best one to visit if time is limited.

Other

Nearby (downhill and across the road) is the pagoda *Daito*, located in a large courtyard, and built in a style uncommon in Japan (rebuilt 1937). The interior features brilliantly coloured beams and

houses five sacred images of Buddha in different incarnations. Other buildings are the Golden Hall (for ceremonies) and Miedo. (The pamphlet from the information centre identifies the buildings.)

Further along the road below the latter cluster of buildings is *Daimon* (Great Gate), a large wooden structure from 1705; it is similar to such gates at other old temples. The youth hostel (at Henjosan-ji) is near here.

Places To Stay

There are 53 temples on the mountain that provide accommodation. Most, if not all, have been developed into attractive places to stay, with lovely little gardens. Each of these temples is virtually owned by its abbot, and then inherited by his son (natural or adopted). By charging about double the tariff of most temples elsewhere in Japan (about Y5000 a night), the abbots have turned them into a very lucrative business, and many are reputedly quite weak in the theology of their sect. Since wealth is required to advance in the religious hierarchy of the sect, this operation of the temples as money-making ventures is encouraged. (Remember that these comments apply to the Shingon-Mikkyo sect only, and other sects are still close to the original tenets of their faith.)

Getting There

The direct route is by Nankai private railway from Namba station (Osaka). From other centres (eg Kyoto and Nara) you can go via JNR to Hashimoto station and change there for the final 21 km by the Nankai line to the terminus at Gokuraku-bashi station. From there a cable-car runs to the top of Koya-san.

Getting Around

From Koya-san you can go west to Wakayama and continue around the Kii-hanto Peninsula. From Gojo, Route 168 runs south to Hongu, Shingu and other attractions of the peninsula (described in the Mie-ken section) covering the more interesting parts of the area. Three buses daily make the scenic run between Gojo and Shingu, and another two from Gojo to Hongu.

YOSHINO

The view of the cherry blossoms on the side of Yoshino-yama (north-east of Koya-san) is famous throughout Japan. There are about 100,000 cherry trees and in season the blossoms form a massive blanket of pink, stretching a long distance up the slope. Because of the differences in temperature from the top of the mountain to the bottom the trees mature at different times so *sakura* on Yoshino can last for a couple of weeks.

From Yoshino station of the Kintetsu railway, a nearby cable car rises to the main road through the settled areas of the mountainside. You can then walk or take a taxi to the main temple area.

The mountain has been regarded as sacred for centuries and is a centre of Yamabushi religious activities. The main temple, *Kimpusen-ji*, is of this sect and the old wooden gate, *Kuramon*, encountered during the climb up the road from the cable car belongs to the temple. Kimpusen-ji is a National Treasure, and its age shows in the weathered timbers and inside pillars. It is reputed to be the second largest wooden building in Japan.

Typical of almost any tourist destination in Japan, the main street is lined with souvenir shops and eating and drinking places. Several of the latter have balconies overlooking the trees on the hillside. The little shop with the giant toad sign sells Chinese-type traditional medicines.

Partway along this level stretch, just past the small temple with an unusual low pagoda, stands a stone torii gate. Pass through through it, on the road downhill, and you come to the most historic place on Yoshino. *Sho-in* dates from 1336 and was a resort villa used by a number of emperors through the years. It is very famous in Japanese history although it

would be of more interest to students of traditional architecture than the casual visitor. The small garden is only of passing interest but near the parking lot there is a lookout which offers the best single view over the sea of cherry trees covering the facing mountainside. When the blossoms are at their peak, the sight is magnificent and explains the popularity of Yoshino for successive emperors.

Near the torii gate the road forks; take the road uphill to *Kizo-ji* temple which is now a combination youth hostel and commercial ryokan providing accommodation for travellers and pilgrims.

Nearby is *Chikurin-in*, a villa built by the famous tea master Sen-no-rikyu, who was forced to commit *seppuku* (ritual suicide) for preventing *shogun* Hideyoshi from taking his daughter as a concubine. The present main building is a highly regarded (and priced) ryokan open to the public when not being used by visiting members of the royal family. The beautiful garden behind the ryokan should not be missed.

Numerous roads wind their way up and across the Yoshino mountainside and can be followed into the mass of cherry trees. There are several large maps posted in prominent places in the village.

To the east and south of Yoshino is a heavily-wooded wilderness area that would appeal to hikers. Accessible from the Nara plain side of the mountains, is a point on the flank of *Mt Odaigahara* (1695 metres), which is the starting point for hikes to Owase (on the east coast of Kii-hanto Peninsula) and Doro Gorge to the south. These are both described in the section on Southern Kii-hanto Peninsula along with the rest of the coastal region. (The Odaigahara area is the wettest region of Japan and the mountain top is often fog-bound.)

Getting There

Yoshino station is the terminus of the Kintetsu line from Abeno-bashi station (Osaka); travellers from Kyoto transfer at

Kashiwara-jingu-mae. You can also go most of the way by JNR, changing to the Kintetsu line at Yoshino-guchi.

During many months of the year there are three buses a day to Odaigahara from Nara-Kintetsu station. The bus passes through Yamato-Kami-Ichi (two stops before Yoshinoyama station). There are also two buses a day between Nara and Kumano (on the south-east coast) which passes Wasabi-dani, the point where the toll road to Odaigahara branches off Route 169; it should be possible to get off there and transfer to the other bus (if schedules match) or hitch the rest of the way.

Mie-ken

Mie-ken, east of Nara-ken, is divided by a coastal ridge of mountains. On the Nara side of this ridge is the area around Iga-Ueno. Most of the other attractions of Mie-ken are on the coastal side of the mountains. From there you can conveniently travel in a clockwise route around the Kii-hanto Peninsula and up the west coast to Wakayama and Osaka – as described in the following pages. (The part of Mie-ken adjacent to Nagoya was described immediately after the section on Nagoya.)

IGA-UENO

This small city east of Nara has some unusual history and an attraction almost unique in Japan. (The name simply means 'Ueno of the Iga region' to distinguish it from other places called Ueno which is a common name in Japan.)

Information

A pamphlet on Ueno in quite good English is given out at Ueno castle and may also be available at the TICs in Kyoto and Tokyo. It also contains information on some other places of lesser interest.

Ueno Castle

Ueno has a small but picturesque castle. Although the present building dates from only 1953, it is a reminder of when the rulers of Iga had to defend their fertile lands against neighbouring, powerful Kyoto and Yamato. As part of their defences (beginning around the 1200s) they developed the *Ninjutsu* art of stealthy combat to defeat foreign armies in the mountains. *Ninja*, the practitioners, were trained in invisibility, poisons, sabotage, espionage, assassination and other genteel arts. (Ninja are featured in the James Clavell novel *Shogun*.)

In the grounds of the castle is *Ninja-Yashiki* (Ninja House), an ordinary-looking building that actually has a number of hidden passages, hiding places and weapons caches. These are demonstrated frequently during the day for visitors.

Elsewhere in the grounds is *Ninjutsu Shiryo-kan*, a museum of weapons, clothing, climbing devices and other ingenious items used by ninja in their work – such as an iron claw that would tear a victim as if by the claw of a bear, armour and several kinds of throwing weapons. This is one of very few places in Japan with such a large display of items of this black 'art'. (Another is nearby at Akame 48 Falls.) Ninjutsu is explained well in Stephen Hayes' book *The Ninja and Their Fighting Art* (Tuttle).

Festival

23-25 October: *Tenjin-matsuri* festival is a 400-year-old Demon Procession. It features a procession of more than 100 'demons' in masks and costumes, as well as nine ornate festival wagons, similar to but smaller than those of Kyoto's Gion-matsuri. Masks and other items from the procession are displayed at the museum beside the Ninja-Yashiki.

Getting There

The castle is reached by walking up the hill from Ueno-shi station of the Kintetsu line, which may be reached by transferring from the JNR Kansai hon-sen line at Iga-Ueno station, or by branching off the Kintetsu Osaka line at Iga-Kambe. The Kansai line runs between Osaka and Nagoya via Nara, the latter between Osaka and Matsuzaka. Both are easily reached from Kyoto and Nara.

Akame 48 Falls

Due south of Iga-Ueno is a very pleasant gorge known for its 48 waterfalls. Many are rather small, especially higher up near the source, but the large ones are quite impressive. The riverside walk is a rare way to enjoy nature with no sound but the shrilling cicadas, some birds and the rushing water. There is a good chance you will see some of the large and very colourful butterflies for which Japan is noted. Higher up the gorge there is an inviting pool.

Just inside the entrance to the park is a very non-descript concrete cage containing some equally non-descript animals; they are giant salamanders, found only in this area.

Before the entrance to the park (on the left going in) is a small building that houses a good (if modest) museum of historic articles used in daily life. Possibly of greater interest is a sizeable collection of ninja weapons and devices. If you can't locate the building ask for 'Ninja hakubutsu-kan'.

The entrance to the falls ('Akame Taki') is reached easily by bus (12 per day) from Akame-guchi station of the Kintetsu-Osaka line, three stations west of Iga-Kambe station (the junction for Ueno city.

Osaka

Osaka is one of the most important cities in Japanese history and was a thriving trading centre almost 2000 years ago. It is now a commercial and industrial city, second in importance only to Tokyo, though it has slipped behind Yokohama in population, to third position. Despite its history as a power centre (as narrated in *Shogun*), there is very little of historic interest within the city due to the passage of time and heavy bombing during the war. There are a few attractions north of the city, across the Shin-Yodo river.

Osaka can be recommended as a port of entry, as it is in the centre of the main island of Honshu. It is close to Kyoto, the single most important tourist destination in Japan. (The airport serves Kyoto as well and is actually closer to both cities than Narita is to Tokyo.) Osaka is a hub of train services, so it is easy to travel in many directions; there are also some bus services and long-distance ferries to several cities.

Osaka has air connections with approximately 30 cities in Asia, Europe and the USA. 'Neighbouring' cities include Bangkok, Beijing, Bombay, Calcutta, Cheju (Korea), Guam, Hong Kong, Honolulu, Kaohsiung (Taiwan), Manila, Pusan, San Francisco, Seattle, Seoul, Shanghai, Singapore and Taipei.

Information

At Osaka station there are three places giving information. The one at the rear of the station books business hotels and can give some information and may have a simple map, but basically is not in the information business. The Osaka city information office, just inside the entrance to the right, occasionally has English-speaking personnel on duty, and can give some sightseeing literature and a map. They may be able to help with finding accommodation. In past years the main information office was in the middle of the main concourse and gave information of all kinds in good English as well as arranging accommodation. However, a complete remodelling of the station seems to have had some effect on functions, and I could not find the same service during a visit in early 1984. Perhaps later travellers

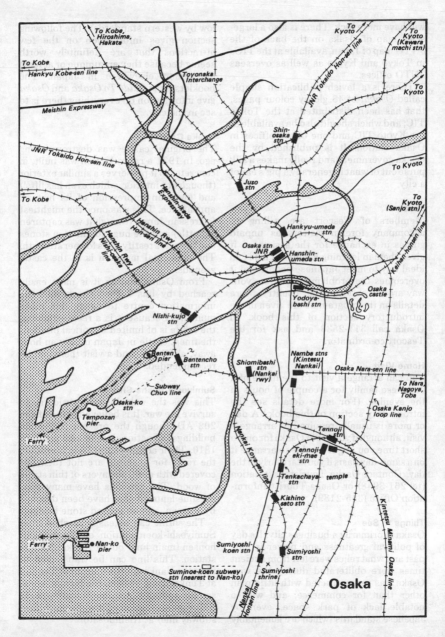

Osaka

will have more luck. There is also a large-scale map of Osaka on the back of the JNTO map of Japan, available at the TICs in Tokyo and Kyoto as well as overseas JNTO offices.

There is a lavish publication simple called *Osaka*, of 48 glossy colour pages, that has been distributed at the Tokyo TIC, and which should also be available at the Kyoto TIC and one of the offices in Osaka station. It is published by the Osaka government and really makes a silk purse out of what is generally a pig's ear of a city.

Tescort
Members of Tescort are willing to accompany foreign visitors as unpaid guides in exchange for the assistance it gives them in learning English. This is an ideal way to meet Japanese people and it overcomes the problems of finding your way around an unfamiliar country. More details on the programme are given in the introductory section of this book. In Osaka call 311-2533 and ask for the Tescort co-ordinator.

Home Visit
You can arrange a visit to the home of a Japanese family for a couple of hours in the evening. (For more details see the introductory section of this book.) A day or more is usually required to arrange a visit, although if you are in Osaka for only a short time you might be able to arrange it on a same-day basis if you start early in the day. Contact Osaka Tourist Association (tel 261-3948) or Osaka Tourist Information Office (345-2189).

Things to See
Osaka is primarily a business city. Its day of political greatness and power is long past and what relics were left from ancient times were obliterated during the war. Osaka was reconstructed with little plan other than for commerce, and with a notable lack of park space, even by Japanese standards (which are lamentably low by western standards). The following section gives information on the few attractions that are definitely worth seeing because they are unique or at least uncommon elsewhere in Japan. The booklets *Your Guide To Osaka* and *Osaka* give information on everything there is to see in the city.

Osaka Castle
The original castle was destroyed long ago. In 1931 a reproduction was built, in concrete, so it preserves a similar exterior (though not interior, which even has lifts!) and gives an impression of its historic appearance. This was once the mightiest fortress in Japan (though it was captured in battle) and the huge foundation stones and the gates testify to its former strength. The municipal museum is in the castle grounds.

From Osaka station it is most easily reached by bus 2 (but check with the information centre to verify this route number). Because it is a reconstruction, the castle is of limited historical interest; the finest castle in Japan is only an hour away, at Himeji, and a visit there can be recommended.

Sumiyoshi-taisha Shrine
This was the only historic structure to survive the war. It is believed to date from 202 AD, though the present four main buildings (all national treasures) are from 1810. Their architectural style is unique; the roofs for example are not tiled but covered with multiple layers of thin strips of wood. The grounds have many picturesque lanterns that have been donated by seamen, and an arched stone bridge.

The shrine can be easily reached from Sumiyoshi-koen station of the Nankai-honsen (main line) out of Nankai-Namba station. This line can be transferred to from the Nanka shuttle line out of Tennoji at Tenkachaya; or from the Nankai-koya-sen line (out of Shiomibashi station, near Sakuragawa station of the Sennichimae subway line) at Kishinosato.

Shitenno-ji

Often mentioned as an attraction of Osaka, this temple was totally destroyed during the war and the main buildings later reconstructed in concrete, a material which cannot begin to reproduce the qualities inherent in Japanese wooden temple design.

Keitaku-en Garden

Located beside the Municipal Art Museum (*Bijutsu-kan*) in Tennoji-koen park, this very pretty garden is considered an excellent example of the Japanese circular garden. It is open without reservation on Tuesdays, Thursdays and Sundays, and with reservation on Wednesday, Fridays and Saturdays. It is easily reached from Tenno-ji stations of JNR or subway.

The Mint

There is a museum of coins from around the world, but the main attraction is the cherry-blossom season when the grounds are open to the public.

Other

There are few sights in Osaka that can't be found elsewhere but if you have time to kill in the area, look through *Your Guide to Osaka* for more ideas.

For combined shopping and sightseeing, the underground shopping centres are worth a visit, as they're usually very attractive. They are generally located at the terminuses of the various private railway lines. The arcade at Hankyu Umeda station is a good starting point; it has one section that resembles the roof of a cathedral, complete with stained glass windows.

Although Osaka is unlovely by day, with lots of large buildings, parts of it are quite pretty at night, particularly the Dotombori area where the lights of large multi-coloured advertising signs are reflected in the water of a canal. Fountain sprays in the canal serve the double duty of adding a note of beauty while helping to purify the water. Many shops and restaurants line the nearby streets.

NORTH OF OSAKA
Expo 70 & its Legacy

Osaka came to international attention by hosting the World Fair, Expo 70. The use of the structures as pavilions ended in September 1970, but some of them have been preserved and converted to other display purposes, and the famed garden has survived.

Japanese Garden A garden incorporating the elements for which Japanese gardens have become famous – the placing of rocks, water, 'hills', trees and other shrubbery – was created for Expo 70 and is one of the most pleasant places to visit in Osaka.

National Museum of Ethnology This is located on the old Expo grounds and has been rated as very worthwhile by all who have visited – some who live in the area have returned several times. Exhibits include items of daily use, plus video tapes of festivals, music, etc , from a large number of countries. Most interesting and exotic to the Japanese is Spanish flamenco. Access to both the garden and museum is by bus from Ibaraki-shi station of the JNR Tokaido line, or Ibaraki-shi station of the Hankyu Kyoto line. These stations are between Osaka and Kyoto (closer to the former) and can very easily be visited from Kyoto as a day trip.

Koriyama Honjin

This is in the same area. During the Edo era (1603-1867), feudal lords were compelled to spend part of their time in Edo (Tokyo) as virtual hostages, so there was much movement of their parties to and from Edo. To provide accommodation fit for people of such exalted rank, inns of the finest construction and facilities were set up along the route. Koriyama Honjin was one; it looks much as it did then, and is open for inspection with many historical items on display. It is accessible from JNR Ibaraki station.

Japanese Farmhouse Museum (Nihon Minka Shuraku Hakubutsu-kan)
This open-air museum is an interesting collection of 12 traditional thatched-roof farmhouses of the type once common in Japan but now quite rare. They were brought to Hattori Ryoichi Park and reassembled in a village-like arrangement. The buildings house exhibits of traditional furniture and items used in daily life. There is an English language pamphlet available. Hattori Ryoichi is accessible from Sone station (before Toyonaka) on the Hankyu Takarazuka-sen line from Hankyu Umeda station, or from Ryokuchi-koen subway station. (It is closed on Mondays.)

SOUTH OF OSAKA
Sakai Nintoku Tomb Mound The greatest tomb mound in Japan, covering a larger area than the Great Pyramid (about 460,000 sq metres), is located a short distance south of Osaka. The keyhole-shaped mound is 478 metres long, 300 metres wide at the flat end and as high as 35 metres. An immense amount of work went into its construction, involving the movement of 1.45 million cubic metres of earth. Three moats surround it.

After this description it is only fair to say that it is not worth the effort (for most people) to see it, as there is no high point from which to view it and from ground level it looks like little more than a broad ditch surrounding a low hill. It's more interesting for what it represents. For several hundred years, from the fifth century onwards, the Osaka area was the residence of the rulers of Japan who had the power and resources to build these tombs. One theory is that this was the eastern tip of a crescent of the same ethnic group that stretched to Kyushu and into part of Korea, and that the labourers who built the tomb were captives from wars on the Korean peninsula. This is only interesting speculation at this point, but would explain how so many people could be assigned to non-productive work. The

practice of building these mounds seems to have died out in the seventh century, possibly indicating a shift of power to a 'native' clan.

Access is from Mozu station of the JNR Hanwa-sen line (from Tenno-ji station), or from Mikuni-oka station of Nankai Koya-sen line (from Shiomibashi station of Nankai line, near Sakuragawa subway station).

Yoshimura-ke House
This is a large farmhouse built in the 17th century and preserved in excellent condition. It is accessible from Takawashi station of Kintetsu Minami Osaka-sen line, which leads to Yoshino.

ENTERTAINMENT IN OSAKA
Food
While Osaka has few 'touristy' attractions, it has a well-deserved reputation for good dining. If you have no friends to act as guides, contact Tescort and inquire whether any Japanese members would be interested in dining out.

Bunraku
Osaka's contribution to the world's performing arts is Bunraku puppet theatre. The puppets are more than a metre tall, have realistic faces and are beautifully costumed. (I say 'faces' rather than 'masks' because the mouths, eyebrows and eyes can move, making life-like expressions.) Each doll is manipulated by one to three people standing behind it, moving the head, arms and legs in such a realistic manner that it seems to take on a life of its own. The master puppeteer is visible and dressed in traditional costume, while his masked assistants are dressed in black. There is a narrator, and musical accompaniment by shamisen.

In early 1984, Bunraku acquired a permanent home in Osaka, the *Kokuritsu Bunraku Gekijo* (National Bunraku Theatre), a five-storey, Y65 billion building in Minami-ku (ward). Inquire locally about performances of this interesting art.

(The TIC in Kyoto should be able to help.)

Kabuki

Performances of Kabuki are also given at various times through the year; the theatre is *Shin-Kabuki-za*, near Namba station of the subway or Nankai line. Information is available from the same sources mentioned for Bunraku.

Takarazuka Girls' Opera

This is an 'institution' in the Kansai area, a music hall in which all performers are young women. Programmes include revues, musicals and adaptions of light operas. The 4000-seat theatre, the largest in the Orient, is part of Takarazuka Family Land, a large recreation centre with cinemas, gardens, etc. Access is by Hankyu-Takarazuka line from Hankyu Umeda station.

Clubs & Bars

Being a large business centre, Osaka has all the nightclubs, cabarets, hostess bars, etc found in any large Japanese city. The same warnings also bear repeating – that many (if not most) are aimed at expense account spenders and can be *very* expensive. If prices aren't posted, ask before ordering anything. A safe and relatively inexpensive way around the problem is to take an evening tour that includes a nightclub and cabarets.

Things to Buy

Because of the relatively small number of foreign visitors to Osaka, there is a correspondingly small number of tax-free shops for cameras etc. Based on a very small sample, I found that discounts were smaller than those available in Tokyo, and about the same as (or a little less than) those in Kyoto, but it might be possible to shop around and do better than this. One place to look for would be Doi Camera, one of a chain of shops across the country; their Tokyo branch in Shinjuku has very favourable prices. Kimura Camera is

another widespread chain but their prices in Tokyo vary from branch to branch, so there is no assurance of matching Tokyo prices.

Festivals

9-11 January: Imamiya Ebisu-jinja (Niniwa-ku).

22 April: Shitennoji temple.

14 June: Sumiyoshi-taisha.

24-5 June: Tenmangu shrine (Tenjin matsuri).

30 July-1 August: Sumiyoshi-taisha.

11-12 August: Ikutama-jinja shrine (Osaka Takigi Noh performances at night).

Places to Stay

Because it is such an important business centre, Osaka has a large number of hotels of various prices, from luxury class to business hotels, ryokan, etc. Help in finding a room is available at Osaka station. Most travel agents can make bookings at the larger hotels if you are arriving from another part of Japan. International hotels are not listed here because any overseas travel agent worth his salt has the same information and can make bookings in advance at little or no extra cost.

There are several youth hostels in and near Osaka. *Osaka-Shiritsu-Nagai Youth Hostel* (tel 06 699-5631/5632) is located in the municipal sports ground. It has 102 beds, is quite pleasant and one of the cheapest hostels in Japan. It is reached from Nagai station of either the JNR Hanwa line (south from Tennoji station) or Midosuji subway line. No card is required, only a passport. *Hattori Ryokuchi Youth Hostel* (tel 06 862-0600) is located north of the city in the same park as the Farmhouse Museum. It has 108 beds and is reached via Ryokuchi-koen station of Midosuji subway line. *Sayama-Yuen Youth Hostel* (tel 0723 65-3091) is small (24 beds) and located to the south of the city. It is reached by Nankai railway Koya-sen line via Sayama-yuen-mae station. Other hostels in the area can be located with the help of the information service at the station. Failing that, a Japanese person could ask for additional phone numbers by telephoning any of the hostels listed. The hostels of Kyoto and Nara are also within range of Osaka, but if Osaka hostels are full the others probably will be too.

Getting There
Osaka airport is close to the city and convenient to reach. Travellers who plan to visit Kyoto should consider landing at Osaka instead of Tokyo and beginning their travels there.

Clearing Immigration and Customs is straight-forward; the immigration officials there have a reputation for being among the most reasonable in Japan and they seem more willing than those at other international ports of entry to give a 90-day entry period if you are entitled to it by bilateral agreement.

Buses that depart from the front of the terminal building are the most economical way to get in from the airport. The most useful destinations for most travellers will be Shin-Osaka station (for Shinkansen trains), Osaka station (for most JNR services; posted as Osaka-Umeda, the name of the district in which it is located), and Namba, another station south of the city. There are also buses direct to Kyoto and Kobe. There are buses every 10 to 20 minutes to most destinations; the trip takes 20 minutes into Osaka and one hour to Kyoto.

Buses to the airport leave from several points in Osaka; one is in front of the Daimaru building, about three minutes walk to the right when leaving the front of Osaka station.

Inter-city trains
Kyoto, Nara and Kobe can be reached in less than an hour by train from Osaka; while Nagoya and a large number of other places in the Kinki district can be reached in a somewhat longer time. For details of services in the Kinki district, refer to the transportation section at the end of this chapter.

For longer distances, the Shinkansen offers very fast service to Tokyo (about three hours) ; and Hakata (Fukuoka, in northern Kyushu) is 3½ hours in the opposite direction. Shinkansen services are detailed in the general Getting Around section (covering all of Japan) early in the book.

The subway stations for inter-city train services are: Shin-Osaka (New Osaka) station for the Shinkansen (it is one stop from Osaka station); and Osaka station, which is the main JNR station, also used by Shin-Kaisoku and other trains of the Tokaido and Sanjo lines. Shin-Osaka station is on the Midosuji subway line, while Osaka station and the Umeda stations of the Hankyu and Hanshin lines are on the Midosuji, Yotsuhashi and Tanimachi lines. The Keihan line intersects the Tanimachi, Sakaisuji and Midosuji lines at the three stations following Kyobashi station (JNR on the Sanjo line) and Kyobashi is also the transfer point from the Katamachi line (to/from Nara) before it terminates at Katamachi.

Tennoji, on the Kanjo, Tanimachi and Midosuji lines, is the starting point for the JNR line to Wakayama; the Kintetsu line to Koyasan; and the Nankai Koya-sen (to Koyasan) and Nankai Hon-sen to Wakayama.

Namba stations of the Kintetsu/Nara line (to Nara) and Nansai Koya line (to Koyasan) are close to stations of the Yotsuhashi, Midosuji and Sennichimae subway lines. (Transfer to the Kintetsu Nara line is also possible where it intersects the Sakaisuji and Tanimachi lines.) The JNR Minato-machi station (for trains to Nara) is close to the Namba stations.

Long-distance Ferries
There are ferry services to Shikoku (Takamatsu, Matsuyama, Kochi, etc) and Kyushu (Beppu, Moji, Kanda, Kokura

and Kagoshima). These generally run daily and sail overnight saving the cost of accommodation. (See the general Getting Around section early in the book for details.)

Getting to the Docks Ferries from Osaka to points on Shikoku and Kyushu leave from three different docks – Benten-futo pier, Tempozan pier and Osaka Nanko pier.

Benten-futo pier: Take the JNR Kanjo-sen (loop line) or the subway Chuo line to Bentensho station. From there it is a five minute bus trip by regular city bus from the station. In addition you can take city bus 53 from Osaka station or bus 60 from Namba station to 'Benten-futo' stop.

Tempozan pier: Tempozan pier is most easily reached by Chuo-sen subway line. The terminus, Osaka-ko station, is a three minute walk from the pier. In addition to the subway, buses 53 and 88 from Osaka station, 60 from Namba station and 107 from Tenmabashi go to Tempozan terminal.

Osaka Nanko pier: Osaka Nanko can be reached easily by taking Yotsuhashi-sen subway line to its terminus, Suminoe-Koen, then taking a bus from there (15 minutes) to Osaka Nanko (the end of the line). There are also buses from Sumiyoshi-koen station of the Nankai-densha private railway line, but it is advisable to check the frequency of these buses in advance.

Subways and City Trains
Osaka has six subway lines: Midosuji, Tanimachi, Yotsuhashi, Chuo, Sennichimae and Sakaisuji. All but the Chuo line run roughly north-south for much of their length, although Midosuji, Sennichimae and Tanimachi lines run east-west for part of their length, and the Chuo line is primarily for east-west service.

While the subway lines criss-cross the central part of the city, the JNR Kanjo-sen loop line circles around the central district. Trains run in both directions and the subway lines intersect at many places, making transfer simple. They also cross

the Kanjo line at several points, but there is not always a station near the intersection where you can transfer between JNR and subway lines.

Separate tickets are required for JNR and subway lines and tickets must be kept and surrendered when leaving the system. A subway map in English is available at the information centre at Osaka station.

Buses
A map of all city bus services in Osaka is available (Japanese only) at the small information office near the bus departure area in front of the station (to the left when leaving the station). Ask for a 'basu (bus) no chizu'.

Hitching
Between Osaka and Kyoto, forget it. It takes too long to try to get a ride and back into the city at the other end. Take the train. For hitching to more distant points, it is necessary to reach the Meishin Kosokudoro freeway (between Kobe and Nagoya) or the Chugoku Kosokudoro freeway from Osaka to the western end of Honshu. There is no simple way to get started, as the interchanges are all to the north of Osaka, and it is necessary to take a train or local road to the entrance; or start at an entrance in Osaka itself and try to get a car that will switch to the exact road you want to take. (The latter requires a sign indicating where you want to go, as hitching is not allowed on the freewways themselves.) One entrance is close to Osaka station and leads onto the Osaka-Ikeda route, which leads to Toyonaka interchange (Meishin), and Ikeda interchange (Chugoku); the latter is near the interchange for Osaka airport. Somewhat to the north-east is another entrance to a local freeway (Kinki Freeway) that becomes Chugoku and intersects the Meishin at Suita. The starting point is the Kadoma interchange, which is about a km from Kadoma station of the Keihan-Kyoto line. (Ibaraki, on the Meishin Freeway, is about two km from the Ibanaki JNR

station and there may be a bus passing close to it.) Alternatively you can use the slower national highways which switch from Route 1 (from Tokyo) to Route 2 (to Shimonoseki at the far west) in front of Osaka station. However, this is in the middle of Osaka, so hitching could be rather poor. If you are near the station, ask at the information office for a map and suggestions for getting a better starting point.

West of Osaka

KOBE
Kobe is an international port of entry to Japan, mostly for passengers of cruise liners, and also an industrial and commercial city. In a reversal of the old saying, it is considered a nice place to live but you wouldn't want to visit there. *Mt Rokko* provides a view over the city, but there is relatively little else for a short-term visitor. (New residents will learn the points of interest from old hands soon after arrival.) For this reason most of the

following information refers to getting to the nearby cities of Kyoto, Nara and Himeji.

Visiting liners dock at Pier 4. From there a wide road (known among foreigners as The Bund) goes straight to Sannomiya station, effectively the main station of Kobe. Bus 92 runs between the station and the port and taxis are also available.

Home Visit
A visit to the home of a Japanese family (afternoon or evening) is an enjoyable experience and can be arranged by contacting the organisers (Sannomiya Kotsu Centre Building, 2F, near Sannomiya station; tel 391-4753), or through your hotel or shipping company.

Food
Kobe is famous for a type of beef that takes the name of the city. It is reputed to be delicious (and is very expensive; even more so than the already outrageous prices charged for beef of any kind in Japan), but it is very fatty and might not appeal if you are accustomed to lean beef.

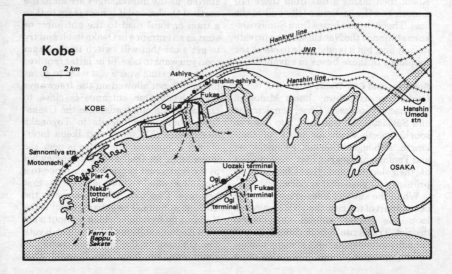

Places to Stay

Kobe has many hotels, business hotels, etc. Feedback regarding the youth hostel has not been favourable – unfriendly staff etc, so it might be preferable to stay in Kyoto or Osaka if space is available.

Getting There

Trains

Kyoto, Osaka and Himeji can all be reached quickly and conveniently from Kobe. Even passengers on cruise liners could reach Kyoto for some sightseeing and be back at the ship on time. (An alternative is to leave the ship at Kobe and rejoin it at Yokohama, if the ship goes there next.) All major train services in the region are detailed in the Kinki district transportation section at the end of this chapter.

Shinkansen super-express trains use Shin-Kobe station which nestles at the foot of the mountain that over-shadows the city. This station can be reached from the main JNR station, Sannomiya, in about 10 minutes by bus 4 or by taxi. (The extra speed of the train may be counter-balanced by the less convenient station (and cost) for going to Osaka or Kyoto.)

Regular JNR services, including the speedy Shin-Kaisoku expresses, use Sannomiya; Kobe station is relatively unimportant.

The main station of the Hankyu line (to Osaka and Kyoto) is Hankyu-Sannomiya. Similarly for the Hanshin line (to Osaka only) the main station is Hanshin-Sannomiya, terminating at Hanshin-Motomachi. All the Sannomiya stations are close to each other.

Ferries

There are ferries between Kobe and Konoura, Tosa-Shimizu, Matsuyama, Imabari, Takamatsu, Tokushima, Niihima and Kawanoe on Shikoku; Oita, Kokura, Hyuga and Beppu on Kyushu; and Okinawa. Details of the sailings to/from the destinations on Kyushu and Okinawa plus Matsuyama, Konoura and Tosa-Shimizu are given in the general Getting Around section early in the book. Services to the relatively close points on Shikoku are detailed in the write-ups on the places on Shikoku.

Naka-Tottei pier is in Kobe harbour, in central Kobe, at the end of the broad avenue known as 'The Bund'. The pier is easily identified by the red Port Tower. Boats to Okinawa leave from near the end of the pier; passenger ferries to Kyushu leave from the end nearer land; and car ferries to Kyushu leave from the middle.

The other ports, Ogi, Uozaki and Fukae, are collectively known as Higashi-Kobe-ko (East Kobe port). The map shows their relative locations.

Ogi and Uozaki are reached most conveniently from Ogi station of the Hanshin line; and Fukae from Fukae station of the same line. At Ogi station the docks are on the track-4 side of the station, on the far side of the expressway (Hwy 43); there is a guide map at the station.

Express trains do not stop at these stations, so it is necessary to take a local train from Kobe/Osaka, or an express from either city to Hanshin-Ashiya and change there to a local train. Trains from Osaka leave Hanshin-Umeda station. From Kobe they leave Hanshin-Sannomiya and Hanshin-Motomachi stations.

The JNR Tokaido-honsen line passes further to the north of the Hanshin line; Setsumotoyama station would be the one for Uosaki and Ogi docks, while Fukae dock seems about equidistant from Setsumotoyama and Ashiya stations. A taxi would be recommended from either JNR station, while the distance is not too great to go on foot from the Hanshin stations.

AKASHI

Apart from the stone walls and two turrets remaining of the old castle, the main interest of Akashi is that it is one port for ferries to Iwaya on nearby Awaji-shima island; the trip takes 25 minutes.

HIMEJI

The city of Himeji is noteworthy for the finest castle in Japan. Begun on a modest scale in the 16th century, it was expanded by later daimyo until it reached its present form in the early 1800s, and was restored to nearly original condition in the 1960s. It is located on a hill not far from Himeji station, and its white form can be seen soon after leaving the station's front exit.

Other, lesser, attractions of Himeji include the unusual cemetery of *Nago-yama* (15 minutes from the station by bus), and *Enkyo Temple* at the top of *Shosha-san* (eight km from the station). Access from Shosha station is by bus then a cable-car.

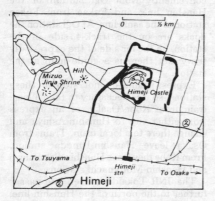

Hakuro-jo Castle

Hakuro-jo (White Egret Castle) is made up of 78 individual buildings, the main one standing five storeys high. It is a defensive castle despite its aesthetic appearance, approached by narrow paths that can be showered with arrows from slits in the walls. In contrast, the upper part (which was unassailable) was designed for the best in gracious living, as defined by the tastes of the day; this can be seen in the delicate wood carving and bronze decorations around the rooms.

A couple of hours can easily be spent exploring the interior and exterior, observing the defensive details, racks for spears, the massive wooden pillars that support the upper storeys, etc.

The castle is easily reached on foot in 15 minutes from the station (less by taxi). The lighting for photos is most dramatic as the sun gets low in the sky. An interesting vantage point for those determined enough and with a telephoto lens, is the top of the hill where *Mizuo-jinja* shrine stands.

Festivals

3 April: Rice Planting Festival at Hiromine-jinja.

17-18 April: Spring Festival at Hiromine-jinja.

14-15 October: Kenka-matsuri is held at Matsubara Hichiman-jinja (near Shirahama-no-miya station),

Places to Stay

There are many hotels, ryokan, etc, because Himeji is a major destination for Japanese sightseers as well. The youth hostel is rather dilapidated and the staff reportedly uncaring, so, given the choice, staying elsewhere might be preferable.

Getting There

Information on trains connecting Himeji with Kyoto, Osaka and Kobe is given in the general Getting Around section at the end of this chapter. Westward you can use regular JNR services (to Hiroshima etc) as well as the super-express Shinkansen trains. It is necessary to consult a time-table because only a limited number of Shinkansen trains stop at Himeji.

Kii Peninsula

The broad peninsula that projects southward between Nagoya and Osaka can be broken into three major areas for sightseeing convenience as well as for 'ranking' them in interest. They are: Nara & Area

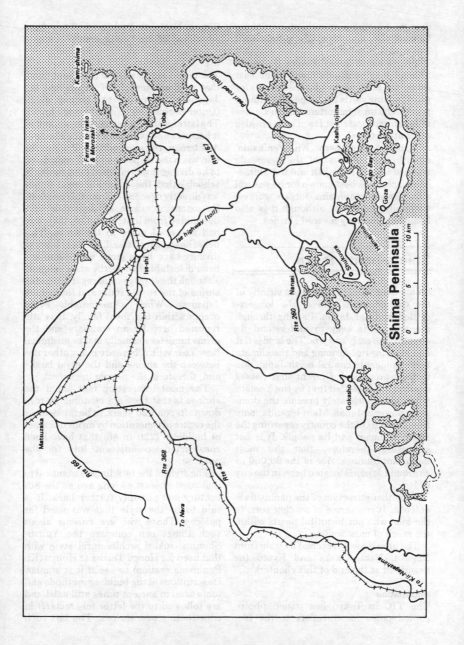

Shima Peninsula

Kami-shima

Toba

Rte 167

Ferries to Irako & Morozaki

Pearl road (toll)

Kashi-kojima

Ago Bay

Goza

Ise highway (toll)

Ise-shi

Kamimura

Shimmura

Nansei

Rte 260

0 5 10 km

Gokasho

Matsuzaka

Rte 165

Rte 368

Rte 42

To Nara

To Kii-Nagashima

described earlier in this chapter), 'Shima-hanto & Ise', and 'Nanki & Southern Kii Peninsula'.

'Shima-hanto & Ise' covers the small Shima-hanto peninsula area on the east side of the main peninsula. It is famous for pearl farming and is the home of Mikimoto pearls. The most important Shinto shrines in Japan are located at Ise. There are also other attractions.

'Nanki & Southern Kii Peninsula' describes all the rest of the peninsula south of Osaka, Nara-ken and the Shima-hanto area. It is best known for its natural attractions of mountains, forests, gorges, waterfalls and rivers, although it is also home to some very revered shrines.

Shima-hanto & Ise

Shima-hanto peninsula and the vicinity of the city of Ise is one of the longest-settled parts of Japan. Passing through the area, it is easy to understand its attraction to early settlers. The land is flat and ideal for rice farming and the climate is the mildest in central-north Japan due to the warm Black Current that passes nearby. It was settled first by the Yamato tribe, which ultimately became the dominant power in Japan. Many legends come from this part of the country regarding the origin of Japan and its people. It is not surprising, therefore, that the most important Shinto shrine of the 80,000 or so around Japan is located here, in the city of Ise.

The other attraction of the peninsula is at Toba. It is a shrine of another sort, to the man who put beautiful pearls within the reach of most wallets.

The area is easily reached by train from Nagoya, Nara, Osaka and Kyoto (as described at the end of this chapter).

Information
The TIC in Tokyo has issued photo-copied notes for travellers to the Ise-Shima National Park area. They have additional information on transportation.

ISE
The grand shrines of Ise represent much that is characteristic of Japan and the Japanese. There are two shrines, *Geku* (Outer Shrine), and *Naiku* (Inner Shrine). The latter is somewhat more important, as it honours and is considered the abode of *Amaterasu*, the sun goddess. Prior to the war, when the emperor was still considered to be divine, it was claimed (and taught in schools) that the Japanese royal family was directly descended from this goddess. By extension, since all Japanese were descended from that family they therefore had a special place in the world. This belief has largely passed, and the claims of divinity have been given up. Shinto has been disestablished as the state religion, although the shrine is still regarded as the shrine of the royal family and thus of the Japanese. When a memorable event occurs within the royal family, it is still reported here by an emissary and the prime minister normally makes an annual New Year visit. There are many other ties between the shrine and the royal family and, therefore, the people in general.

The most interesting fact about the shrines is that they are customarily torn down after only 20 years, to be replaced as the centre of veneration by an identical set of buildings (220 in all) that have been constructed on adjacent lots for the purpose.

The style of the buildings is identical to that used at least as long ago as the 8th century and possibly further back. It is said to be the style that was used for palaces. Those who are curious about such things can compare the Yuitsu-Shimmei-zukuri architectural style with that used for Hongu Taisha at Hongu (Kii Peninsula section) to see if it is similar. Descriptions of the building methods and tools used in ancient times still exist and are followed to the letter (character?) in constructing new shrines. The last such

Top: Rickshaws can still be found, especially at tourist destinations
Bottom: Young women in their best kimono at the Furukawa Matsuri festival

Top: Diving demonstration by ama who collect edible seafish and seaweed
Left: Tagata-jinja fertility festival
Right: Sorting pearls by colour, Mikimoto Pearl Island

reconstruction, the 60th, was completed in 1973 after nine years of work. The cost was more than Y4500 million; one wonders if the practice can continue in the future, because building costs and methods are changing so rapidly and few young carpenters want to bother learning the traditional, specialised skills. All the buildings are assembled using dowels and interlocking joints; there are no nails.

Geku is located in Ise-shi (city) and Naiku is six km away, outside the city.

Geku (Outer Shrine)

Geku shrine is located within 15 minutes walk of the two stations (JNR and Kintetsu lines). It honours *Toyouke-Omikame*, Goddess of agriculture. Like those of Naiku, the buildings of Geku are built in the traditional style dating from the times before Chinese influence swept over the country. The shrine dates from 478 AD. Also, like Naiku, the grounds are covered with magnificent, tall, ancient cedars.

The main entrance is easily seen from the road. You follow the path under two torii (gates) and past the large Magatama-ike pond. To the right of the first torii are the *Anzaisho* and *Sanshido*, a combined building where the emperor and other members of the imperial family rest when visiting. Just past the second torii is the *Kagura-den*, where performances of sacred dances are presented (fairly frequently).

A bridge to the left leads to the shrines *Kaze-no-miya*, *Tsuchi-no-miya* and *Taka-no-miya*. Continuing straight on leads to the main shrine. The architecture of the buildings is severely plain – unpainted, fine, hinoki (cypress) wood, with a thatched roof – but four fences surround the buildings and block much of the view from ordinary eyes; only members of the imperial family and their envoys are permitted beyond the Tonotamagaki gate.

The sightseeing is far from spectacular. You should enjoy/appreciate the mood and atmosphere of the wooded grounds

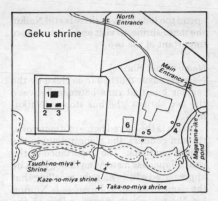

Geku shrine

Legend for both maps

1 Shoden (main hall)
2 Saihoden (west treasure hall)
3 Tohoden (east treasure hall)
4 First torii
5 Second torii
6 Kagura-den (sacred dance hall)

Naiku shrine

and take it for what it is, one of the two most sacred shrines in the country. Don't spend too long here, as there is still Naiku, the inner shrine, to visit and it is the more important of the two.

Naiku (Inner Shrine)

Naiku is easily reached from Geku by the regular bus that runs between between the two shrines. the bus stop is 'Naiku-mae'.

Naiku is the sacred home of *Amaterasu*, the sun goddess, the highest deity in the Shinto pantheon. The importance of the sun in Japanese history/mythology can be appreciated a little more by recalling that the name of Japan in Japanese is Nippon (or Nihon), which means 'origin of the sun'.

The shrine grounds are entered by crossing Isuzu-kawa river by Uji bridge, a picturesque structure. From here the faithful follow one of several paths to the riverside where they wash their hands and rinse their mouths as purification. The many tall cedars on the grounds give a peaceful mood and the size of the grounds (over 66 hectares) swallows up the large number of people who visit.

The usual route takes visitors through the first and second torii, past the Kagura-den (hall of sacred dances) and on to the main shrine *Shoden*. As with Geku, the four rows of fences block a large part of the view of the buildings – after all, a lady (especially a goddess) needs her privacy. Photos are prohibited and it is customary for men to remove hats and overcoats.

Again the style of architecture is ancient and severely simple, with thatched roofs. Beside the shrine is the open space where the previous shrine stood until 1973, when the present buildings were finished and consecrated and the goddess (along with her belongings) moved into her new quarters amidst very solemn ceremony. The accompanying map will be valid until 1993 or so.

On the same compound with the Shoden (main hall) are two treasure houses, *Tohoden* and *Saihoden* (East and West Treasuries) in which are housed

about 2500 treasures of the shrine – fine clothing, lacquerware, swords, etc. These are made anew each time along with the buildings and represent the finest of craftmanship in the best Japanese tradition. In previous times these were destroyed when the new shrines were opened. But today, because of the great value of these objects as representations of the work of perhaps the last generations who were part of the 'old ways', they are preserved and displayed at *Chokokan*, the museum of the history of the shrine.

Included among the treasures in the two treasure buildings (not on display) is the sacred mirror, one of the three sacred treasures of the imperial throne. The others are the sword and jewel. (The sword was lost in the battle of Dan-no-ura in Kanmon Strait (Shimonoseki). The jewel is kept in Tokyo.) A news item stated that some antique rickshaws (*jin-riki-sha*) were being operated at the shrines (entrances). If you wish to try one, keep your eyes open. Proceeds are for charity.

ISE TO TOBA

There are two main routes to Toba, Ise-Shima Skyline and Route 167/railway.

Ise-Shima Skyline

From a point near Naiku, a toll road runs along and over a ridge of the Asama mountains to Toba-shi (city). The scenery is pretty, with distant views of the water and the indented coast (though it is not worth a special trip from elsewhere just to partake of the view). At the top of the ridge is *Kongoshoji* temple. Two buses an hour make the trip from Naiku to Toba station, the last in mid-afternoon.

Route 167/railway

Travellers by Route 167 or JNR from Ise to Toba might want to stop for a look at a sight dear to the hearts of the Japanese, *Futami-ga-ura*. This is a pair of rocks that jut out of the sea close to each other, not far from shore. In keeping with the traditional Japanese view of nature as

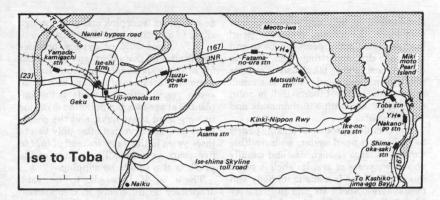

Ise to Toba

representations of *kami* (spirits/gods), or other 'semi-animate' objects, the rocks have been regarded as male and female (exactly in the same manner as assigning gender to most or all mountains in the country). Being male and female what could be more natural than for them to be wed? So, wed they are (their name, *meoto-iwa*, means wedded rocks) with thick ropes of twisted and braided straw of the type used to make the shimenawa rope often found between the uprights of many torii, especially after the harvest season. The ropes are replaced every 5 January in a colourful ceremony.

The rocks are likened to Izanagi and Izanami, the founders of Japan (in mythology at least), who are honoured yearly by National Foundation Day, a national holiday.

Near the rocks is an aquarium, Sea Lion House, and Marine House where women divers give demonstrations.

There is a *Youth Hostel* (4404) that is also a temple, not far from the rocks.

The rocks are about a km from Futami-no-ura station (JNR). Buses from the station, as well as from Toba, Ise-shi, Uji-yamada, Naiku and Geku go close to the stretch of beach (Futami-ga-ura), sea wall and hotels that preceed the short walkway around the base of the cliffs to the lookout near the rocks.

TOBA

Toba is famous as the place where the cultivation of pearls was perfected. The Toba area is still one of the most important pearl farming areas of Japan. Until Kokichi Mikimoto began his research in the late 1800s, the only pearls were accidents of nature. If a grain of sand or other foreign material happened to find its way into the shell and irritate the oyster, the irritant would be covered with layers of nacre, forming a pearl. Mikimoto reasoned that it should be possible to introduce such an irritant artificially, so he began experimenting in 1888. By 1893 he had succeeded in producing a pearl, though it was not spherical, and by 1905 had succeeded completely.

Since then his company continued to grow and his name is now well-known around the world. (He died in 1954.) Always dedicated to top quality, and a bit of a showman, Mikimoto once burned hundreds of kilos of pearls of inferior quality that he had rejected, but which his competitors would have sold. Such pearls are now used to decorate items of lesser value.

Tatoku-shima island, where he performed his experiments, is now the site of a very interesting museum where all stages of producing cultured pearls are shown, both as a static display of photos and materials (with flawless English text), and exhibitions by young women of how they insert the irritant, remove a pearl from an oyster, match pearls by colour and size, then drill and string them. Also on display are some fabulously valuable displays utilising pearls, such as a small scale model of the Liberty Bell in solid silver (16.9 kg), with 336 diamonds and 12,250 pearls.

The complete process of making pearls begins with a pearl oyster, an incredible variety, of large enough size and usually about two years of age. Its shell is pried open, an incision is made in its body and two spheres, about six mm in diameter (the irritant) are introduced into the wound. For collectors of trivia, the irritant is made from the Pig Toe shell, a variety found along the Mississippi River. (After trying thousands of materials, Mikimoto found this to be the best.) Along with the two spheres a small piece of tissue about a mm square, from the body of another oyster, is introduced. This piece is cut from the band of tissue at the juncture between the body of the oyster and its shell; it is the tissue that excretes the nacre that deposits as Mother of Pearl. The oyster 'adopts' this and uses it to coat the irritant with layer after layer of nacre. By this method, one oyster can be used to produce two pearls.

The oysters are suspended in special racks hung below rafts in the sea; these rafts can be seen in Ago Bay and other sheltered bodies of water in the region, where the temperature and other conditions are ideal. The nearby Black Current guarantees a plentiful supply of plankton, the food on which oysters thrive.

The racks are pulled up four to six times a year and the shells are cleaned of marine growths, then they are lowered again. After about three years they are lifted out a last time and the pearls are taken out, sorted to remove imperfections and odd shapes, classified by colour, then drilled and strung. The range of colours is quite amazing to anyone who is not familiar with pearls, going from pink and gold through silver to a distinct blue tint.

Only about 50% of oysters produce pearls after all that effort, and only about 5% of these are suitable as gems. In past years, the lifespan of oysters was six to seven years, with the seeds being implanted at age two, but pollution is raising its ugly head these days, and the pearls must now be harvested after only two to three years in the water instead of four to five years as before. The quality of the pearls is also said to be slipping.

There is, - if it needs to be said, absolutely no difference in composition between cultured and naturally-occurring pearls; the former just increases the harvest and guarantees consistent quality. Where do the oysters come from? They grow on trees. When females are spawning, they release thousands of larvae into the water, to come to rest where they may. Trees are lowered into the water and, with luck, larvae will cling to the branches. After two to three months they are raised and transferred to a better place where they can grow to sufficient maturity to allow the irritant implantation.

Every 40 minutes there is a display of women divers. Similar divers may be seen in action near Toba and in nearby sheltered bays and coves, like Ago Bay. There are still about 3500 of them actively diving, but this is only half the number of a few years ago.

There is so much nonsense written about these white-clothed divers that it is time to put the record straight. They do not dive for pearls. Before Mikimoto's successful experimentation their ancestors did dive for the gems of the sea, but they could not make a living at it today. The whole idea of cultivating pearls is to sidestep the hit-or-miss (mostly miss) business of looking for natural pearls. Also, natural pearls are often misshapen and/or discoloured, while cultivating them gives a good yield of nearly-perfect spherical ones.

What the women do dive for is seafood,

both shellfish, like abalone, and octopus, as well as edible seaweed. Any pearl oysters that they find can be used to grow pearls by implantation of a nucleus. But they do not dive for pearls, and publications and tour pamphlets that repeatedly refer to them as 'women pearl divers' are verging on dishonesty. Their activities are interesting enough, with their peculiar whistling breathing sound, that such publicity is uncalled for.

Other attractions of Toba

The aquarium at Toba is considered one of the best in Japan. Other related attractions are Dolphin Island (*Iruka-jima*) and the marine museum (*Burajiru-maru*).

Getting There

There are regular boat excursions out of Toba to nearby islands, including Kami-shima, scene of Mishima's story *Sound of Waves*.

There is a ferry service across the bay to Irako at the tip of Atsuma-hanto peninsula (at least 13 times daily), as well as to Gamagori on the 'mainland' between the peninsulas (at least six a day); these places are all on the east side of the bay, below Nagoya, and offer a convenient way to bypass that city if you're planning to travel to Tokyo via the south coast. (It should be said that this is the least desirable and interesting way to get to Tokyo; routes via the Kiso region and the Noto peninsula are much more interesting.)

AGO BAY

This bay, sheltered from the ocean tumult and incredibly indented, offers the beauties of nature and the finest scenery of the Shima-hanto peninsula. A common sight is the number of rafts from which pearl oysters are suspended in the water. They should not be mistaken for even rows of poles protruding from the water near the shore; these have nets strung horizontally among them and edible seaweed grows on them. Ago Bay is ideal

for pearl oysters because the water temperature is always between 17 and 22°C and there is plenty of food.

KASHIKOJIMA

This is the main town on Ago Bay. From it, sightseeing boats leave regularly on excursions that circle the bay. It would be a good way for a closer look at the rafts, and there is a good chance of seeing *ama* (women divers) at work. Near Kashikojima station is Shima Marineland which houses an aquarium.

GOZA

This town affords a good view, from *Kompira-san* hill, of both the Pacific Ocean and Ago Bay. It can be reached from Kashikojima by boat or by bus.

Places to Stay

There is a Youth Hostel (4406) not far from Kashikojima, at Isobe. It sits on a hill, giving a good view over a smaller bay. However it is a JYH hostel and has some of the characteristics of one, since the housefather is a regional Youth hostel executive. The biggest drawback of the place is that the rooms are almost hermetically sealed and are very stuffy (the Japanese never open windows at night, even in summer), a shame because it is so close to all that fine sea air.

NANKI & SOUTHERN KII PENINSULA

Most travellers who plan to continue from the Ago Bay area to southern Kii peninsula destinations like Shingu by road (hitching or own transportation) would find it preferable to backtrack to Ise and beyond to connect with Route 42 (or railway) rather than following Route 260 along the coast. Few roads require more time to travel a given distance than this one. It winds in, out, up, down, over and around every combination of cape, ridge, hill and promontory imaginable. The scenery is pleasant, as it passes through fishing villages and coves of pearl rafts or seaweed 'frames', but it tends to quickly

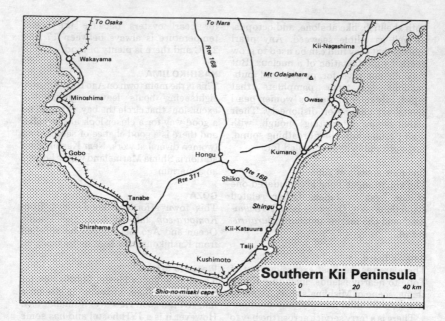

Southern Kii Peninsula

become variations on a theme rather than new melodies. From the youth hostel at Isobe I followed the road by motorcycle for what seemed like hours and only reached Shukuura, at which point I turned back to Ise.

Places to Stay

As in all parts of Japan that are popular with tourists there are accommodation facilities everywhere, including hotels, ryokans, minshuku and youth hostels.

Getting around Southern Kii-hanto

JNR services loop around the entire Kii-hanto peninsula from Nagoya to Osaka, as well as branching off to Toba. The Kintetsu Nippon line runs from Nagoya to Kashikojima in the Shima-hanto peninsula. There are many local bus services. The northern part of the peninsula is intensively served by a number of railway lines as detailed at the end the chapter.

Wakayama-ken

NANKI

The Kii peninsula (Kii-hanto) is still relatively unpopulated due to its mountainous terrain. Two areas have been combined into a national park, the forest lands named for Yoshino, and the sea coast area, named after Kumano. Yoshino itself is in Nara-ken and is covered in the section on that part of the country (earlier in this chapter).

The Japanese way of treating this area for tourist publicity purposes is a little peculiar, and is similar to the practice mentioned elsewhere for southern Toyama-ken. Mie-ken extends almost to Shingu, so literature issued by Mie-ken covers much of the south-east coast, but not Shingu, while Wakayama-ken literature describes the rest of the south-east coast and all the south-west coast. This isn't of much use to travellers who are trying to see the whole region and who might have only one lot of literature. This book covers the Kii peninsula in what seems like a logical manner, beginning from above Owase and continuing around Wakayama, taking in inland areas conveniently reached from the coast.

USUGI-DANI

Inland from a point 10 km or so above Owase (just a short distance below Funa station), a road leads inland to Usugi-dani, considered one of the grandest valleys in Japan. A publicity photo shows a very pretty series of cascades and pools and a rustic suspension bridge.

The valley leads close to Mt Odaigahara, a mountain much more easily reached from Yoshino (and described in more detail in the section on Nara-ken).

There are trails in the area between Odaigahara and Owase (32 km), and to Doro-kyo. Serious hikers can obtain more detailed information on the spot.

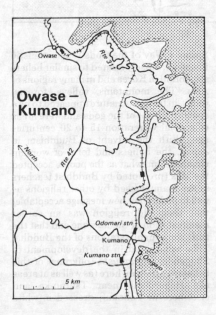

Keep in mind that there is no scheduled transport in to Usugi-dani and that Odaigahara has the greatest rainfall of any area in Japan.

OWASE

The town is an important fishing centre but of limited touristic interest. Along the shore of Owase Bay are rock formations of columnar basalt, similar (though smaller) to those of Land's End in Britain.

KUMANO

The attractions of Kumano ('Bear Field') are the sea and cliffs. Two popular sights are Onigajo ('Ogre's Castle'), a large chamber in the cliffs. Near it the rock has been weathered to an unusual texture, slightly resembling the exterior of the brain. It is about a km east of the station, along the coast.

In the opposite direction, also along the coast, is a rock formation known as Shishi-iwa ('Lion Rock') because of its resemblance to a lion.

Kumano is the starting point for a trip by raft through the rapids of the scenic Doro-kyo gorge. Sightseeing information for the gorge, including this trip from Kumano, is given in the description of the area around Hongu.

SHINGU

The name Shingu ('New Shrine') reveals Shingu's main attraction, *Kumano-Hayatama Taisha* (shrine), one of the three main shrines of the Kii-hanto peninsula. The others are at Hongu and Nachi. Unlike the weathered buildings of Hongu, those of Shingu are of more recent 'tradition' and are brighter and more colourful. Its festival is on 15 October.

INLAND FROM SHINGU

A short distance inland, up the valley of the Kumano River are Hongu and Doro-kyo gorge. Between Shingu and Hongu, the road passes through the Kumano-kawa valley. The pretty, relatively-unspoiled scenery makes the trip enjoyable.

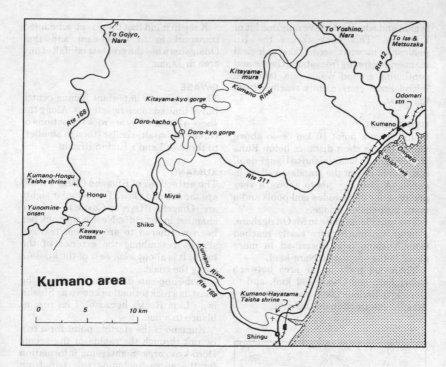

Kumano area

0   5   10 km

Hills rise on both sides of the valley and the water is a beautiful emerald or jade green. In seasons of heavy rainfall, like the September-October typhoon season, several waterfalls thunder close to the road or can be seen clearly nearby.

Buses run from Shingu station to Hongu (70 minutes) and on to Gojo (4¾ hours).

HONGU

Hongu, which means 'Main Shrine', is the most important of the three great shrines of Kii. Nearby are a couple of typical mountain hot spring resorts with *rotemburo* (open-air hot spring baths).

The areas near the Kii peninsula were settled early in Japanese history and the mountains of the peninsula appealed to the religious feelings of the people. The early folk religion, the predecessor of

Shinto ('Way of the Gods') was animistic in nature, closely related to similar beliefs still found in Korea and in many regions of Asia. The mountains, valleys, forests, rocks, in fact all of nature appeared to be a special habitat of the gods and were areas of special veneration 15 to 20 centuries ago. With the advent of Buddhism in Japan, the beliefs and form of worship changed somewhat as the people accepted the idea (promoted by Buddhist teachers in the manner used by other religions as well to make their new message acceptable) that their old religion was an earlier manifestation of the new one and that the gods were manifestations of the Buddha. This culminated in the development of Shugendo. *Yamabushi* (pilgrims) of this belief may be seen here (as well as at areas like Haguro-san near Tsuruo-ka and elsewhere in Tohoku), dressed in white with unusual (and hard to describe) 'ornaments', perhaps ringing bells as they proceed. Such yamabushi indulge in ascetic practices like bathing under icy mountain waterfalls and other forms of corporal mortification. More information is included in the section on Tohoku.

The main shrine is at Hongu and is set in wooded land near the town of the same name. The present buildings are quite large and have a natural weathered colour. Their architectural style is an uncommon form used in the early 10th century for palaces. Its festival is 15 April.

Access is via a long path attractively lined with tall cedars. This is not too far from the wettest place in Japan, so lush greenery can be expected. In other areas of the Kii peninsula there are still virgin forests with some trees 600 to 1000 years old. The name 'Kii' is a contraction of *Ki-no-kuni*, or 'country of trees'.

YUNOMINE

In past days *yamabushi* pilgrims included bathing in the hot springs of Yunomine as part of their devotions. These days it is more like a typical onsen, with visitors who indulge in the hot water for the same reasons as elsewhere, for health and pleasure. Along with hotels (large and small), and their private baths, there is also a rotemburo, a natural hot spring pool in the middle of the stream, surrounded by a simple wooden fence and an equally simple (and quite traditional) bathhouse.

KAWAYU

This is another hot spring resort town. It also has a rotemburo open to all comers. There is a youth hostel (5612) here.

DORO-KYO

This gorge on the Kitayama-kawa river is considered the finest in Japan. Cliffs rise 50 metres vertically from the green water, nature-sculpted rocks decorate the way, and in June azaleas and rhododenrons bloom on the cliff faces. The gorge stretches several km along the river with alternating rapids and wide, calm areas. The three major sections are Oku ('inner') doro, Kami ('upper') doro, and Doro-hatcho. Shimo-Doro ('lower Doro') is the entrance and not so noteworthy. Doro-hatcho means 'eight cho', signifying eight cho of tranquil water, a 'cho' being an old measurement of 109 metres.

There are three ways to see the gorge. First, from Shiko (on the road through the valley), long glass-roofed boats leave from docks behind a building resembling a restaurant (which it is), and go as far upstream as Kami-Doro. The day I went to the area (in mid-September), the river was swollen from heavy rains and boat trips were suspended. There are usually eight trips a day, the first at 8 am, the last at 3.15 pm. The trip up takes 50 minutes, there is a 20 minute rest and the return takes 45 minutes.

Shiko boat terminal can be reached by bus from Shingu station in 30 minutes, or from Kawayu-onsen in 20. The four buses a day from the latter are timed to meet a departure. Further information is available at the youth hostel.

Second, if you don't want to spend the money, and are content with seeing only part of the gorge, you can go by road to Doro-hatcho. Maps indicate future road construction to link this point with Kitayama-mura and an offshoot to join Route 311 to Kumano is also likely, but the completion date is uncertain.

The third way is no longer certain, but could be worth checking up on closer to the spot. In past years there has been a ride through all the rapids on a long, narrow 20-man raft. Rides were exciting, requiring 'wettable' clothing because of frequent spray.

Rides began at Kitayama-mura, a village accessible from Kumano station by a once-a-day bus to Shima-oi plus a minibus ride from there to the starting point. The ride lasted three hours, ending at Miyai, not far from Shiko and cost Y5000. The contact telephone number was (073549) 2331, in Japanese.

ALONG THE COAST

Between Shingu and Nachi-Katsuura, the next major centre along the coast, is the Nachi-Katsuura terminal for regular long distance ferry services to Tokyo and Kochi (on the island of Shikoku).

Schedule information is given in the general Getting Around section earlier in the book.

The terminal ('ferry noriba') is close to

Usui station, above Nachi. There are 12 trains a day between the two places, but note that the ferry leaves for Tokyo hours after the last train.

NACHI-KATSUURA

This is the collective name for the district between Nachi and Kii-Katsuura; both are station names. The several attractions of the area give it the most concentrated sightseeing of the southern part of the peninsula.

Places to Stay

There are Youth Hostels at Nachi, Katsuura and Taiji.

Nachi-taki

The highpoint of the Nachi area is the 130 metre high Nachi-taki waterfall – one of the deepest plunges in Japan. The falls are reached by taking a short bus ride from Nachi station. From the stop there is a brief and enjoyable walk down steps, between rows of tall and very old cedars to the falls.

Nachi-Taisha shrine

Beside the falls and located there from ancient times because of its obvious strong connection with the Shinto spirit world, is Nachi-Taisha, one of the three great shrines of the Kii area. It was founded in the 4th century. Its festivals are 1-7 January and 14 July.

Seiganto-ji

Immediately beside Nachi-Taisha is the temple Seiganto-ji.

Myoho-ji temple

At the top of the twisty toll road is the temple Myoho-ji.

Kii-Katsuura

From a place near Kii-Katsuura station you can take a boat ride around a group of pine-covered islands called Kii-no-Matsushima. The name implies a comparison with the 'real' Matsushima near

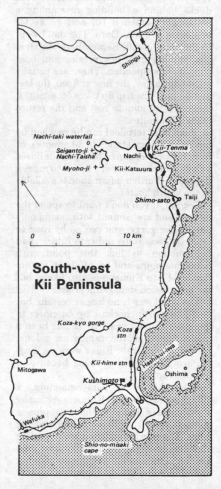

South-west Kii Peninsula

Shingu

Nachi-taki waterfall
Seiganto-ji
Nachi-Taisha
Myoho-ji
Nachi
Kii-Tenma
Kii-Katsuura
Shimo-sato
Taiji

0   5   10 km

Koza-kyo gorge
Koza stn
Mitogawa
Kii-hime stn
Hashikui-iwa
Kushimoto
Oshima
Wafuka
Shio-no-misaki cape

Katsuura area

Sendai, one of the scenic 'big three' that are supposed to send the Japanese into fits of ecstasy. The ones at Kii are scenic, one islet being perforated, another (visible from shore) resembling a camel in silhouette, while others come in a variety of other pine-covered shapes. A good lookout point is from the narrow peninsula on which Katsuura-onsen is located.

TAIJI
Taiji has been the centre of the whaling industry in the Kumano district. On a small peninsula a little more than a km from Taiji station, five minutes by bus, is Kujira-hama-koen (Whale Beach Park). Its main attraction is *Geirui-hakubutsukan* (Whale Museum) – which has displays of articles associated with this now-criticised

industry. As well there are some full-size 'reproductions' of whales to show their immense size. Unfortunately, Japan is one of the few countries still hunting these behemoths of the deep.

KUSHIMOTO
This city is located at the base of the peninsula and is the entrance to the Shio-no-misaki cape. A short distance north-east of the city, and a little closer to Kii-Hime station, is the unusual rock formation Hashi-kui-iwa, a row of about 30 large rocks, spaced quite regularly in a line, stretching into the sea. They do resemble what their name means, 'bridge pillars'. Other writers likened them to a procession of hooded medieval monks.

KOZAKAWA-KYO
Inland a short distance from Kushimoto is a pretty gorge, Kozakawa-kyo. The Koza-kawa river has eroded the rocks of its bed and flanks into interesting shapes and textures. Much of the rock was apparently formed with trapped bubbles; the water has removed the solid surface, leaving a strange perforated appearance.

The road through the gorge turns off Route 42 at Koza, and the gorge begins shortly after, at Taka-ike ('High Pond'). It continues for 15 km to Mito-gawa, from where a local road returns to the coast while the 'main' road continues some distance inland before rejoining Route 42.

North-west from Kushimoto along the south-west coast there are pleasant views from both the road and train, although there are not as many identifiable attractions as there are on the south-east coast.

SHIRAHAMA
Along with Atami and Beppu this is regarded by the Japanese as one of the three best hot spring resorts in Japan. This information, however, is not likely to excite foreigners who do not have such a history of enjoying 'the waters'. As

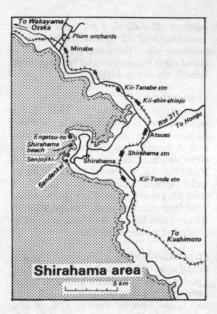

Shirahama area

5 km

consolation, in addition to the delights of the flesh (or at least partial amelioration of the aches, pains and troubles of corporal existence), there are also scenic pleasures at the water's edge and the enjoyment of a very good white sand beach; 'Shirahama' means 'White Beach'.

A short distance to the north of the beach is the islet of Engetsu-to ('Round Moon Island'), known for the hole in its middle. South of the beach are the layers of rock 'plates' of the Senjojiki formation, and just around the promontory are the cliffs of Sandankei. The seascapes are considered among the best on the Kii peninsula and there is a good view from Heisogen hill, behind the town. A cable-car runs to the 130-metre summit from Shirahama. During the summer festival, large sand sculptures are built on the beach

Places to Stay

In addition to more than a hundred hotels of all types, some with floor shows at night,

there is also a Youth Hostel at nearby Tanabe, very close to Kii-Tanabe station (third stop from Shirahama station).

TANABE

There are several good swimming beaches near this port city. The best-known is Ogigahama. The name of the station is Kii-Tanabe.

MINABE

In late January to mid-February Minabe-gawa-mura is a popular destination for tourists who flock to see the huge plum groves, which have about 300,000 trees, on the surrounding hills and valleys. They are a couple of km inland from the station; buses are available from the station.

GOBO

There is a good white sand beach, Enju-ga-hama, about half a km long, near this small city.

ARIDA (ARITA)

On Arita-kawa river, there is nightly *ukai* (cormorant fishing). The usual type of ukai is described in the section on Gifu, but there is a difference here. Usually the fishermen ride in boats which have a blazing fire in an iron grate at the bow. Here, however, the fisherman wade in knee-deep water, holding a torch in one hand and the leashes of the cormorants in the other. Sightseers watch from boats nearby. More information for finding the exact site of the action can be obtained on the spot. Arida Youth hostel would be able to help; it is located near Yuasa railway station. (There is no Arida station.)

WAKAYAMA

This is the city for which the prefecture is named. Historically it was important as a castle town and residence of a very important *daimyo*. It is now a commercial and industrial centre of very limited touristic interest. Its 'trademark' is *Wakayama-jo* (castle) but, like many castles in Japan, it is a reconstruction

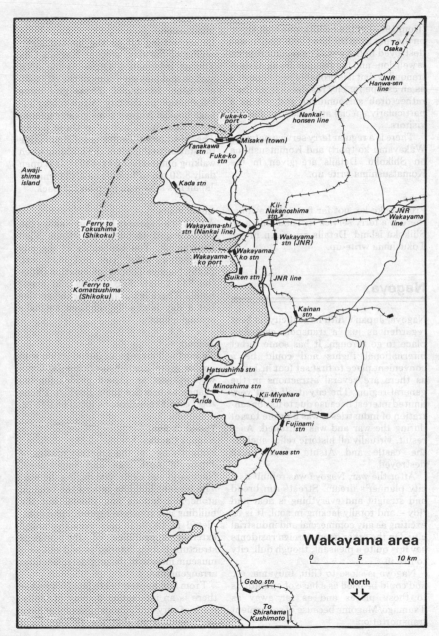

Wakayama area

0   5   10 km

North

(from 1958) of the historic one that stood on the spot from the late 1500s until it was destroyed in the war. The reconstruction is well done and the grounds are an oasis of tranquility, but it is probably best regarded as an escape for city residents from their rather drab surroundings and not as a particularly special attraction for foreign visitors.

There is a regular ferry service between Wakayama-ko (port) and Komatsushima on Shikoku. Details are given in the Komatsushima write-up.

Fuke

From Fuke-ko, not far from Wakayama, there is a ferry service to Toku-shima on Shikoku island. Details are given in the Tokushima write-up.

Nagoya

Nagoya, Japan's fifth largest city, is best regarded as just a transport centre, a place to go through. It has some direct international flights and could be a convenient place to first set foot in Japan as there are several attractions in the general region. The city itself is of very limited interest because due to its concentration of industries it was a prime target during the war and was flattened. As a result, virtually all historic relics such as the castle and Atsuta shrine were destroyed.

After the war, Nagoya was rebuilt as a city planner's dream. Streets run broad and straight and everything is neat and tidy – and totally lacking in soul. It is as exciting as any commercial and industrial city. On the other hand, foreign residents say it is quite a pleasant, though dull, city to live in.

Nagoya is close to Gifu, Inuyama, etc and could be used as a base of operations to those places and as far away as Tsumago/Magome because of convenient transportation.

Information

Before setting off on the limited sightseeing of the city, stop at Nagoya City Tourist Information Office at the JNR station and pick up a copy of the city map and other brochures. These give more information on the city. A full-colour 32-page booklet *Nagoya* gives greater information than space allows in these pages. The information centre is located inside the station to the left of the building when walking out (tel 052 541-4301). It is open daily 8.30 am to 7 pm. The JNTO map of Japan has a Nagoya map on the back.

Home Visits

A visit to a Japanese home in Nagoya can be arranged through the Home Visit Programme. You can apply at the city information office (tel 961-1111 ext. 2245), Nagoya Tourist Information Office (tel 541-4301), JTB offices and major hotels. There is no charge for the service but a day is usually required to make arrangements.

Tescort

Tescort will arrange an introduction with one or more English-speaking Japanese who will act as unpaid guides for the chance to practice their English. Phone the Tescort coordinator – (052) 581-1872.

Things to See
Nagoya Castle

Formerly one of the greatest castles of Japan in both size and importance, Nagoya-jo was destroyed during the war. The present building retains the original stone foundations and moats, but the building is a concrete reproduction completed in 1959. It preserves the grand external appearance of the original structure but its interior is laid out as a museum instead of the original residential arrangement.

From late September to late November there is an interesting display of 'dolls' made of chrysanthemum bushes that have been shaped so that the flowers form

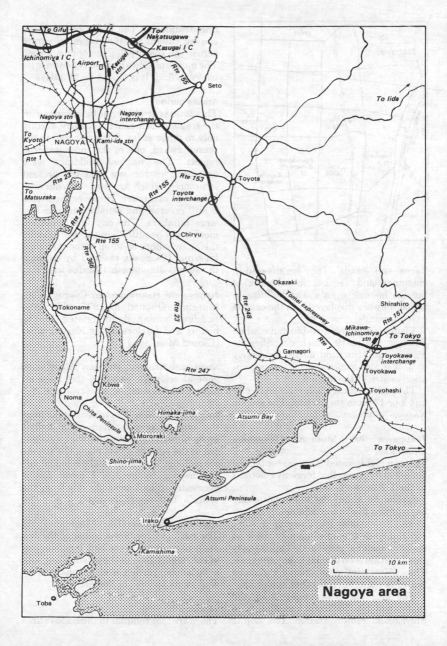

Nagoya area

0   10 km

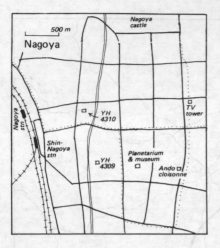

'faces' and 'hands'. They are dressed in costumes and set out in tableaux of famous historic events. The building in which they are displayed is in the central castle grounds.

Visitors are given a brochure when entering the castle which describes its history and structural details extremely well. It is also available from the information centre at the station.

The castle is most easily reached by city bus 5 or 17 from the station. The stop is Nagoya-jo-minami.

Tokugawa Art Museum (Tokugawa Bijutsukan)

This is a highly-rated museum containing historical treasures that formerly belonged to the Tokugawa family.

Literature about the museum usually has wording like 'it contains nearly 10,000 items ... ' like armour, swords, scrolls, etc. But while the museum may house so many treasures only a disappointingly small portion is on display at any one time. The Y500 admission charge could be better spent at several other museums.

The museum is accessible from the castle bus No 16 from bus stop 6 at Shiyakusho subway station. The stop is Shindekimachi. The same bus number can be caught for the return trip from across the street going the opposite way. The museum is on a back street and a little tricky to find. It is closed on Mondays.

Atsuta shrine

This 2000 year-old shrine (site) ranks with the greatest shrines in the country, second only to those at Ise. It is dedicated to the sacred sword, one of the three imperial regalia. The original buildings were destroyed in the war and the present structures, which are made of concrete, are not as attractive. However the shrine is still revered and worshippers come in large numbers. The day that I visited, mothers in beautiful kimono were taking their newly-born children to the shrine for blessing. It's easily reached by subway; the stop is Jingu-nashi ('Shrine west').

Nagoya-shi Hakubutsukan (Nagoya City Museum)

Opened in 1977, this large building houses items related to the history and folklore of the Nagoya area. (Closed Mondays.)

Municipal Science Museum

Along with general scientific exhibits, this museum has a planetarium.

Nagoya TV Tower

The tower not far from the station is promoted as a tourist attraction. Considering that the city is laid out at the edge of a vast plain; the streets are rectangular-regular; and it is industrial/commercial by nature, I never felt it necessary to look over the city from the tower's 180 metre height.

Higashi-yama-koen (East Mountain Park)

The park (84 hectares) is one of the few areas of greenery in the city. It houses one of the largest zoos in the orient along with a botanical garden and a conservatory with many species of flowers.

Temples

There are four temples in the Nagoya area

that might be worth visiting, especially if you don't have the opportunity to go to Kyoto.

Kosho-ji has a five-storey pagoda, built in 1808.

Nittai-ji was built in 1904 to house a relic of the Buddha, a gift of the King of Siam; the name means 'Japan-Thailand temple'. Near the temple is Gohyaku Rakan hall. It takes its name from the 500 statues of Rakan, disciples of Buddha. Each face and pose is said to be different.

Kenchu-ji has an historic two storey gate at the entrance, dating from 1651.

Ryusen-ji also has a large, picturesque gate at its entrance, though it is not historically noted.

Crafts

World famous Noritake china is made in Nagoya and visitors may tour the factory at 10 am and 2 pm daily (except Sundays and holidays). English-speaking guides are provided.

Visitors can watch the process of hand-painting cloisonne ware daily from 10 am to noon and 1 pm to 5 pm (except Sundays and holidays) at Ando Cloisonne. The workshop can be reached by subway to Sakae station. Ando is 10 minutes walk along Otaumachi-dori avenue.

Festivals

There are several festivals in the Nagoya area that would be worth seeing if you are in the area.

1 January: New Year's rites at Atsuta shrine.

13 January: (lunar) Naked Men's festival at Konomiya.

Early April: Cherry Blossom Festival at Nagoya castle.

16-17 April: Toshogu jinja matsuri – this is a small local shrine festival, but interesting nevertheless. On the 16th there are performances of Kagura, ancient sacred masked dances with equally ancient and strange gagaku court music.

18 May: Toyokuni-jinja-matsuri yagumo koto and dances.

1 June: (lunar) Tenno-matsuri of Tsutsui-cho area (but celebrated throughout the city).

5 June: Atsuta shrine festival.

20-21 July: Port festival (fireworks, etc).

26 July: Shimono-ishiki-kawa (river) festival of Sengen-jinja.

late September to late November: Chrysanthemum Doll show (Nagoya castle).

mid-October: Nagoya-matsuri – music, dancing, tea ceremony, folk songs/dances, kagura sacred dances/music are scheduled for the second Saturday and Sunday of the month. The high points are the procession of the Three Feudal Lords (both days), and the parade of eight dashi, elaborate wooden festival wagons of the type seen at the famous festivals at Kyoto, Takayama and Furukawa. A very interesting feature of these dashi is the display of mechanical dolls that are associated with some of the carts. These ingenious dolls, well over a century old, perform an amazing number of tricks and movements, all controlled by wires. Similar ones can be seen at Takayama and Furukawa (Nagano-ken).

Places to Stay

There are three youth hostels and many hotels and business hotels in Nagoya. *Miyoshi Ryokan* (tel 052 583-0758) is a small ryokan about 10 minutes from Nagoya station. It is shown on the map.

Two other hostels in the city area are *Aichi-ken Seinen-Kaiken* (tel 221-6001) and *Nagoya Youth Hostel* (tel 781-9845).

The information office at the station can help find accommodation. It is also possible to stay at nearby places like Inuyama and Gifu.

Getting There – International

Travellers from Hong Kong, Seoul, Guam and Manila can fly direct to Nagoya. As the airport is only 30 minutes away from Nagoya station by bus (every 15 minutes), it is very convenient, especially when compared with the mess at Tokyo. Processing is quick as there are few such international flights.

The airport is not far from Kasugai station of the Meitetsu line that goes to Inuyama/Gifu passing the shrines of Tagata and Oagata on the way. There are several attractions in those areas, all of which are described under Gifu-ken.

Buses to the airport leave from Nagoya Bus Terminal, which is located in the Meitetsu Department Store, to the right when leaving the JNR Nagoya station.

Getting There – Domestic

Nagoya is a stop for all Shinkansen trains and is also served by regular JNR trains and several private lines. All connections to other points in the Kinki district are detailed in the Getting Around section at the end of this chapter; Shinkansen services are given in the general Getting Around section earlier in the book; and private lines to other nearby destinations are outlined below.

There are regular bus services west to Kyoto/Osaka and east to Tokyo; these are also detailed at the end of this chapter.

All JNR lines use Nagoya station. Kintetsu trains leave from Kintetsu-Nagoya station which is attached to Nagoya station. Trains of the Meitetsu line (north to Inuyama, Gifu, etc, and south to the Chita peninsula) leave from Shin-Nagoya station in the basement of the Meitetsu department store, to the right when leaving Nagoya station.

There is a second Meitetsu station at Kamiida, within the city limits but some distance from Nagoya station which can be reached by bus No 1 from the latter. But it is simpler, for passengers who wish to use it (to Meiji-mura or Tagata/Oagata shrines), to go to Inuyama from Shin-Nagoya station, change trains at Inuyama and backtrack slightly along the other line.

Ferries There is a daily ferry in each direction linking Nagoya, with Sendai (Northern Honshu) and Tomakomai (Hokkaido). The boat leaves Nagoya in the early evening, reaches Sendai the next morning and Tomakomai the morning of the third day. More details are given in the general Getting Around section early in the book. Ferries leave from Nagoya Ferry Terminal which can be reached by city bus from the station. It is not too far from Nagoya-ko subway station.

Hitching To hitch out of Nagoya along the Tomei expressway (to Tokyo or Kyoto/Osaka), take the subway from Nagoya station (platform 1) to Hongo. About half the trains terminate before Hongo at Hoshigaoka; if yours does, wait for the next one, which will terminate at Fujigaoka. Trains bound for Fujigaoka are shown in red on the timetable in stations. On ticket machines, the line is shown in yellow.

The entrance to the expressway is close to Hongo station. See the section on Hitching for more information.

Getting Around

Nagoya has a subway system of three lines. It is easy to use and has stations marked in romaji (although the station names on maps are not). The free handout map from the information centre shows the stations.

SOUTH-EAST FROM NAGOYA

To the south-east of Nagoya are the two peninsulas of Chita and Atsumi, looking like pincers poised to close on Mikawa Bay. Their attraction for Nagoya residents is a glimpse of nature, especially wild flowers in season, but they are of limited interest to foreigners.

The Chita Peninsula can be reached by Meitetsu train from Shin-Nagoya station. The line ends at Noma, unless the extension to Minami-China is finished. Noma is a beach resort. Buses run from both places to Morozaki at the tip. The most exciting attraction here is the sight of buildings and other park facilities covered with sea shells.

From Morozaki, ferries cross eight times daily in both directions to Irako: the fare is Y500. Ferries also cross Ise Bay to Toba five times a day and there is a service (14 each day) to Toba from Irako. The fare is the same for both, Y750. There is a service to Toba from Gamagori as well, but at Y3000, it is much more expensive. There are also island-hopping services in the Mikawa Bay area, along the route Kowa (noted for beaches) – Himaka-jima – Shino-jima – (considered the most attractive) – Gamagori. Morozaki is another starting point to Himaka-jima to pick up the route.

At Irako, bicycles can be rented at the service centre of the Toyotetsu railway (near the port) and at Irako Koku-min Kyuku-mura (vacation village). The Toyotetsu line itself does not begin until half-way along the peninsula, so it is just as easy to go by bus from Irago all the way to Toyohashi station.

Those wishing to hitch on the Tomei expressway to Tokyo or Kyoto/Osaka would find it easiest to take JNR from Toyohashi to Mikawa-Ichinomiya and backtrack a couple of km to the Toyohashi interchange ('inta' in Japanese). Route 1 passes through Toyohashi, but this road is very congested, slow to travel on, and the scenery is depressing nearly all the way to the Mt Fuji area.

NORTH FROM NAGOYA

Information on areas immediately to the north is included in the section covering Gifu-ken in the previous chapter.

SOUTH-WEST FROM NAGOYA

To the south-west are the attractions of the Toba area and the Kii-hanto peninsula. Toba and surrounding areas are described after the write-ups on Kyoto and Nara. The following entries are the major places encountered between Nagoya and Toba and are located to the east of the mountain range dividing them from the Nara area.

Transportation between Nagoya and the south-west area is described at the end of this chapter.

YOKKAICHI

There is nothing but industries in the city itself, except for its annual festival on 26-27 September – a procession of a feudal lord and townspeople in costumes of that era. Inland about 20 km is Yunoyama-onsen ('Hot Water Mountain Hotspring'), at the foot of Gozaisho-dake.

Yokkaichi is a transfer point for travellers to the Toba area using JNR trains.

GOZAISHO-DAKE/YUNOYAMA-ONSEN

The main attraction (apart from the hot springs of the town, which are sufficient inducement for Japanese) is the mountain Gozaisho-dake, 1210 metres. Its upper reaches rank among the three most famous among Japanese mountaineers. However, no climbing skills are needed to enjoy the views of the rock faces on the way up, as a cable-car system takes passengers almost to the top in 20 minutes. The very top of the peak is reached by a separate lift.

At the top, you can see Biwa-ko lake (on a clear day) and there is a sanctuary near the top for Japanese serow, a kind of antelope.

There are three waterfalls in the area, Kugurido-no-taki, Ao-taki and Hyakken-taki. Ao-taki is the most easily reached, by hiking from the base station of the cable-car.

Places to Stay

There are about 30 hotels of varying prices in the onsen and a youth hostel near the top.

Getting There

Access is from Yokkaichi Kintetsu station, by Kintetsu Yunoyama-sen (line) to Yunoyama-onsen station and by bus to the hot spring town itself (and the base station).

SUZUKA

The largest motor racing circuit in the world is located near this industrial city.

ISENOUMI PARK

Between Yokkaichi and Tsu stretches the long beach of Ise-no-umi prefectural park. Beaches include Tsutsumi-gaura, Chiyozaki, Akogigaura and Gotemba. Another, nearer Tsu, is Niezaki.

Shiga-ken

The main attraction of Shiga-ken is Lake Biwa, Japan's largest lake, but there are also places of interest in some towns nearby.

Because of good transportation facilities in this area, attractions around Biwa-ko can be visited as a day trip out of Kyoto. Train services are described in detail at the end of this chapter.

Many cruise boats operate on Biwa-ko and are the most enjoyable way of sightseeing as most of the shore and surrounding land is low and flat. The most popular destination on the lake (possibly the only identifiable landmark!) is Chikubu-jima island. Other boats base their itineraries on the Omi-hake, or Eight Views of Omi, the historic name of the area.

The following section gives schedules for boats operating on the lake in the summer of 1984. These probably won't change much in future years but it's always wise to check for up-to-date schedules. These are published in *Jikokuhyo* and are also available at the TIC's in Tokyo and Kyoto and from any travel agent.

Boats to Chikubu-jima with stopover

from Hama-Otsu: 10.30 am (2½ hours); return: 1.50 pm; Y3450 round trip.

from Nagahama: 10.50 am, 1.10 pm (25 minutes); return 12.40 pm, 3 pm; Y3050 round trip.

from Hikone: 12 noon, 2.20 pm (35 minutes);

return 11.20 am, 1.40 pm, 4 pm; Y3350 round trip.

from Imazu: 10.30 am, 11.30 am, 12.30 pm, 1.30 pm, 2.30 pm (20 minutes); return: 10.55 am, 11.55 am, 12.55 pm, 1.55 pm, 3.30 pm; Y2250 round trip.

Although no information is listed, it may be possible to take a boat from one place to the island, and another from the island to a different place, thereby avoiding any backtracking; the fact that there is a boat from Chikubu-jima to Hikone before any boat from Hikone to the island indicates that this is possible.

There are also round-trip cruises around Chikubu-jima without a stopover:

from Hikone: 10.20 am, 11 am, 1 pm (2 hours) Y3350.

from Imazu: hourly from 10 am to 3 pm (1¾ hours) Y2550.

Omi-hake cruises

Ogoto – Hama-Otsu: 9.50 am, 12.15 pm; Y230.

Hama-Otsu round trip: 9.30 am and 12.30 pm daily through most of the year; plus 11 am and 2 pm daily, from July 20 through August 31 and on Saturdays, Sundays and holidays through most of the year.

Cruises on the 'Michigan' (see below for details)

Hama-Otsu round trip: 10 am, 11.50 am, 1.40 pm, 3.30 pm (90 minutes) Y2000.

'Showboat' cruise (round trip from Hama-Otsu: 6.30 pm (2¾ hours) Y4000 and up. Note reservations are essential for the Michigan (tel. 0775-24-5000 in Japanese or use a travel agent.

The Michigan

Totally non-Japanese, but worth considering as an attraction nonetheless, the Michigan is a 900 ton stern-wheeler (paddle-wheel ship), ideal for the shallow lake with its one metre draft. The ship is 59 metres long and 11.7 metres wide and was outfitted virtually on a cost-no-object basis (its Y1.7 billion cost could have purchased a 20,000 ton cargo ship).

There are four decks, the first three with dining facilities of increasingly higher quality (all with a foreign theme). On the third level is a stage where Dixieland music is played during the 'Showboat' evening cruise.

EASTERN SHORE
NAGAHAMA

The name means 'Long Beach'. This is not a very interesting town except during the Nagahama-matsuri festival, 14-15 April, and possibly during another festival in October.

Nagahama-matsuri

This festival is one of the more interesting in Japan and is worth trying to see. The festival features 12 *yatai* (festival wagons) which are used as portable stages on which children in costume present *Hikiyama-kyogen*, (a type of comic drama). The stages are covered with miniature roofs of the same graceful shape and construction as those on temples. The wagons are decorated with elaborate carvings, gilt, and even Gobelin tapestries showing European soldiers, which are believed to have been brought from Belgium in the 16th century.

On the evening of 14 April, the yatai are gathered in lantern-light at *Hachiman* shrine. The next day the yatai are moved from the shrine into positions on the city's streets and performances of the kyogen are given, each one lasting 20-30 minutes. Then the wagons are moved ahead to a new position (replacing the wagon that had been standing there) and another performance begins. The process is repeated throughout the day.

Watching the moving of the wagons is as interesting as the plays themselves, as each yatai weighs many tons and is only a little narrower than the small streets through which they advance. The wheels cannot be steered, so the wagons must be man-handled sideways with the use of long levers. More than one protruding advertising sign gets knocked off each year, even at the second-storey level, as the carts are about six metres tall.

Hachiman-jinja is a 10-15 minute walk from the east exit of the JNR Nagahama station. On festival days it is easy to follow the crowds, but there are also usually signs near the station indicating the location of the shrine and the parade route.

Other festivals

2-5 September: Kehi-jinja, a procession of men dressed as warriors of feudal days.

15 October: Hachiman-jinja (similar to the April festival).

Kanagasakigu-jinja

In cherry-blossom season (early to mid-May), the 2000 trees in the grounds of this shrine are very beautiful.

Daitsuji temple (Nagahama Betsuin)

This temple, about 500 metres east of the station, is designed in the rather flamboyant Momoyama style, and dates from 1586.

Getting There

Nagahama is three stations north of Maibara, a major junction on the Tokaido main line and the Shinkansen.

NORTH OF BIWA-KO

Not too far north of this area are two ports from which the long-distance ferries sail for Otaru on Hokkaido, the northern main island. Tsuruga is described with Fukui-ken (earlier in the book), while Maizuru is described at the end of the write-up on Chugoku (western Honshu).

MAIBARA

Maibara has no notable attractions of its own, but it is an important junction for many JNR services. Travellers going northward to Nagahama, etc, will transfer here from the main Tokaido line or from the Shinkansen.

HIKONE

Little mentioned in tourist literature, this small city can be reached from Kyoto or

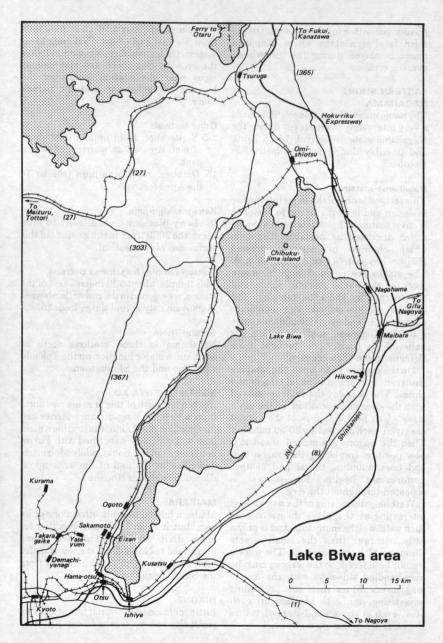

Ferry to
Otaru

To Fukui,
Kanazawa

Tsuruga

(365)

Hoku-riku
Expressway

(27)

Omi-
shiotsu

To
Maizuru,
Tottori   *(27)*

(303)

Chibuku-
jima island

Nagahama

To
Gifu,
Nagoya

Maibara

(367)

Lake Biwa

Hikone

Shinkansen

Kurama

JNR

(8)

Ogoto

Sakamoto

Eizan

Takara-
gaike   Yase-
yuen

Kusatsu

Demachi-
yanagi

Hama-otsu

Kyoto

Otsu

Ishiya

Lake Biwa area

0   5   10   15 km

(1)

To Nagoya

Hikone

1 Rakurakuen Park
  and Ii Museum
2 Genkyuen
  Garden
3 Tower
4 Taiko-mon
  (drum gate)

Gifu in an hour, and is worth a visit to admire its pretty feudal castle overlooking Lake Biwa, and one of the loveliest gardens in Japan. Both can be reached by a 10-minute walk along the road leading from the front of Hikone station.

Hikone-ji

The castle, perched scenically atop the only sizeable hill in the area and close to the waters of Biwa-ko, was finished in 1622 and is one of relatively few original castles remaining in Japan. The main building is a National Treasure and several of the towers and gates are rated almost as highly. One of the towers functions as an art gallery and displays many art works and arms of the Ii family, the owners. (Tall people, watch your head on the beams!)

Two of the original three moats remain and their banks give good views of the walls and the castle itself. Cherry trees line the banks and during the cherry-blossom season (usually early to mid-April) the castle and grounds are one of the most beautiful places in Japan. Graceful swans swimming in the moat add a note of serene beauty.

A booklet in English is usually available (free) when entering the castle; it gives a good description of the various features of the castle and other attractions of Hikone. If the booklet *How to See Hikone in Japan* is not available at the castle or Genkyuen garden, ask at the *shi-yaku-sho* (city office).

Genkyuen Garden

Located just north of the castle moats is Genkyuen, a landscape garden patterned on the garden of the same name in China, dating from 1678. Although it is not as famous as the 'Big Three' gardens, I consider it far more attractive than any of the others and one of the loveliest in Japan. This view was shared by a Japanese garden lover I met while strolling around the central pond; according to her it is beautiful in all four seasons. If you take bread you can feed the colourful carp in the pond. The admission ticket for the castle also includes the garden.

Other

Other attractions in the Hikone area include *Taga-jinja* (shrine) and its garden; nearby *Konomiya* shrine and garden; *Ryotanji* temple and its highly regarded Zen-type rock garden; *Seiryoji* temple; *Daido Benzaiten* temple; and *Tenneiji* temple. These are all described in the city office publication mentioned earlier.

Festivals

Early April: Sakura-matsuri (Cherry Blossom Festival).

22 April: Taga-jinja matsuri.

1 August: Fireworks display.

8 August: Hikone Bayashi (dance) in the centre of the city.

Autumn: Shiro-matsuri (castle festival), a procession of children in costumes of feudal days.

Getting There

Hikone is on the main JNR line between Kyoto and Maibara, one stop before the latter, which is a major railway junction on the Shinkansen and Tokaido main line. It is about one hour from Kyoto.

WESTERN SHORE

OGOTO

Say 'Ogoto' to the average post-adolescent Japanese male and you are likely to receive a very knowing smile, as it ranks with Kawasaki and Gifu as one of the top Toruko (Soapland) towns in Japan. These thinly-disguised brothels are expensive (Y20,000 to Y40,000 is typical) and a foreigner alone, without some knowledge of Japanese, runs a strong risk of having difficulties in finding a place, making arrangements and avoiding misunderstandings. However, for those with the connections and wealth necessary to make such a visit possible, the reported services and variations could fill a book.

Hiei-san and Enryaku-ji temple

One of the four routes to the top of Mt Hiei and to Enryaku-ji, is via Sakamoto station of the Keihan line (from Kyoto; a change at Hama-otsu station is required) or from Eizan station of the JNR, both of which are close to the base station of a cable railway up the east side of Hiei-san. The mountain and temple are described in the Kyoto section.

GETTING AROUND – KINKI DISTRICT

The Kinki district, particularly between Nagoya and Osaka, is intensively blanketed by railway services. Since there are many destinations of interest to foreign visitors in this area and many places can be visited on a day trip (such as to Nara or Toba from Kyoto or Kyoto from Kobe etc), it is useful to have a general idea of the frequency of train services and the travel time between one place and another. The following is a summary of the lines likely to be of most interest to visitors. Other services, that go to specific tourist destinations have already been described in this chapter under their relevant locations as they are of no use for intercity travel. All descriptions are from east to west, north to south,

so look for the details of services between Nagoya and Osaka under Nagoya, not Osaka etc.

Nagoya-Kyoto-Osaka-Kobe-Himeji

JNR Shinkansen The fastest, most frequent and convenient service through these cities is the Shinkansen. Both Kodama and Hikari trains run between Nagoya and Osaka; the former make one extra stop (Gifu-Haneshima) and take 82 minutes over the distance – against 67 minutes for the Hikari. Charges are the same. Beyond Osaka, trains are mostly Hikari, but there are several different services (eg some only stop at Himeji and some even bypass Kobe) so it is necessary to check in advance to be sure of getting the right train beyond Osaka. The time and fare chart shows Hikari services that stop at all the above cities. Trains are very frequent – usually eight or more per hour through Nagoya.

JNR Tokaido line/Sanyo line

The former is the main JNR line from Tokyo to Osaka; the latter from Osaka to Okayama and both were the principal lines until the Shinkansen was built. Between Nagoya and Kyoto/Osaka there are only three direct expresses a day (just under two hours); for all the other trains (about 17 a day) it is necessary to change at Maibara, sometimes at Ogaki as well. This way the Nagoya – Kyoto trip can take 2½ hours with optimum connections if the trains are all locals; or 15 minutes less if one gets a Nagoya-Maibara express. From Osaka/Kyoto to Nagoya there is a similar number of trains also with changes at Maibara or Ogaki.

Alternative JNR service

There is another way from Nagoya to Kyoto/Osaka that might be of use to some travellers. From Nagoya, the trip begins by Kansai Honsen (Kansai main line) which passes through Nara en route to Osaka (14 a day), changing first at Kaneyama after about 1¼ hours, going to

Tsuge (about 35 minutes), then at Tsuge to the Kusatsu line to Kusatsu (45 minutes), then to the Tokaido line to Kyoto (25 minutes). (About eight trains a day go direct from Tsuge to Kyoto without the need to change at Kusatsu.) Depending on the connections, the trip can take 3½ to 4½ hours. The only exception is a single express between Nagoya-Kyoto that takes about three hours. There are about 20 sets of trains through the day in each direction that you can use for this route.

Note: In the majority of cases, railway connections in the Kinki district are more convenient, faster and cheaper by private railways. JNR services, like the one just described are listed mostly as a service for travellers using a Japanrail Pass.

Nagoya – Kyoto

Kintetsu The Kinki Nippon (Kintetsu) line offers a convenient service between Nagoya and Kyoto by a transfer at Yamato-Yagi between the Kyoto-Ise line and the Nagoya-Osaka line (both described below). Total travel time between Nagoya and Kyoto is about 2¾ hours and costs about Y2600.

JNR Another route to Kyoto from Nagoya is via JNR to Nara, then to Kyoto.

Nagoya – Osaka

Kintetsu The only direct service between these two cities is operated by the Kintetsu private railway. Every day on the hour, between 8 am and 7 pm, a train of the 'Non-stop tokkyu' service leaves Kintetsu-Nagoya and Kintetsu-Namba (Osaka) stations arriving at the other station 2¼ hours later. The fare is Y2590, including the express surcharge. Every hour on the half hour, from 7.30 am to 7.30 pm (from Nagoya) or 8.30 pm (from Osaka), there are similar expresses that make a few intermediate stops and take an extra 13 minutes. These are the trains to take for destinations between the cities, such as changing to go to Kyoto or Nara or to visit Iga-Ueno.

It is also possible to travel cheaper (and slower) between Nagoya and Osaka by non-express Kintetsu trains (same tracks) by using the Nagoya – Yamada, and Yamada – Osaka lines, with a change at Ise-Nakagawa. Time on the trains would be 3½ hours plus the wait for the connecting train. You could also go from one city to Ise/Toba for sightseeing and then proceed to the other city by this route. Refer to the later section on services to Ise for more details.

JNR There are no direct JNR Nagoya – Osaka trains; it is necessary to change trains at Nara. Refer to the sections Nagoya – Nara, and Nara – Osaka. There is normally a train at Nara for the transfer, so the wait is not more than a couple of minutes.

Nagoya – Nara

Kintetsu The quickest service from Nagoya to Nara is the Kintetsu Nagoya-Osaka line from Nagoya to Yamato-Yagi (just under two hours); changing there to the Kintetsu Kyoto-Ise line to Yamato-Saidaiji (20 minutes); and then taking the Osaka-Nara line to Nara (five minutes). The Nara – Nagoya trip is just the reverse. As described before, trains are scheduled for a minimum wait at Yamato-Yagi (about two minutes); and Nara – Yamato-Saidaiji trains run every five to 15 minutes.

JNR There are two expresses per day (about 2½ hours), one of which runs direct between the two cities, while the other requires a change of train at Kameyama. This change is required for all regular trains (12 a day); the delay at Kameyama for regular trains varies from three to 35 minutes. The trip usually takes 3½ hours.

Nagoya – Ise/Toba

Kintetsu The Kintetsu line offers convenient service between Nagoya (Kintetsu-Nagoya station) and Ise, Toba and Kashikojima (on the Shima-hanto peninsula). In both directions there are kyuko expresses every five to 30 minutes and futsu (regular) trains every 15 to 30 minutes; plus about 32 tokkyu special expresses (the fastest) daily. Tokkyu trains take about 1½ hours from Nagoya to Ise (Y1610), and 1¾ hours from Nagoya to Toba (Y1810), while ordinary kyuko and junkyu expresses take about 15 minutes longer and cost Y910 (Nagoya-Ise).

Note: the less expensive kyuko and junkyu trains can be used for travel between Nagoya and Osaka by taking a Nagoya-Ise train to Ise-Nakagawa and changing to an Ise-Osaka line train. This will be slower than the tokkyu Nagoya-Osaka trains (about three hours) but is cheaper. The route can also be used for a visit to Ise/ Toba en route between the two large cities.

JNR JNR services are much less convenient, requiring a minimum of one change of train. Five expresses run directly from Nagoya through to Taki, where a change must be made to a different train to Ise, Toba, etc. The expresses to Taki take from 1½ to two hours; and the local trains that connect with them take about 20 minutes to Ise and 50 minutes to Toba (depending on whether a change at Ise is required). Other than the expresses, no other trains leave from Nagoya; it is necessary to first go to Yokkaichi, change to a train to Tsu, change again to a Shingu-bound train and take it as a far as Taki, then change one last time to the local train to Ise and Toba. Nagoya-Yokkaichi takes about 45 minutes; Yokkaichi-Tsu about 45 minutes; Tsu-Yaki about an hour. This routing is obviously only of interest to holders of the Japanrail Pass.

Nagoya – Kii-Hanto Peninsula – Osaka

A JNR line runs around the periphery of the Kii-hanto peninsula. The links of this route are Nagoya (-Yokkaichi) – Shingu – Wakayama – Osaka.

Nara – Osaka

Kintetsu There are about 13 daily tokkyu expresses between Kintetsu-Nara and Kintetsu-Namba (Osaka) stations taking about 35 minutes (Y660), plus slower (five to 10 minutes) semi expresses every 15 minutes through the day (Y360).

JNR There are nearly 90 trains a day between Nara and Osaka (each direction) via two routes. Trains of the Kansai-honsen line take 49 minutes to each of the terminus stations in Osaka – Osaka station (in the north of the city, 27 a day) and Minato-machi station (in the south of the city, 31 a day). Trains of the Kata-machi-sen line take 51 minutes (30 a day) and also terminate at Minato-machi station. Fare for both is Y570.

Nara – Ise/Toba Area

Kintetsu There are no direct services from Nara but the trip can be made very conveniently by taking a local train from Kintetsu-Nara station to Yamato-Saidaiji (five minutes) and catching a Kyoto – Ise tokkyu train (described below); they leave Yamato-Saidaiji station 30 minutes after the times listed for leaving Kyoto.

JNR It is necessary to take the Kansai-honsen line (Nagoya bound) as far as Kameyama (about two hours), transfer to a Shingu-bound train as far as Taki, then take an Ise-bound train from there. There

are generally connecting trains at Kameyama and Taki for minimum wait, but these should be checked in advance.

Kyoto – Nara

Kintetsu The fastest Kyoto – Nara services are the 26 daily Kintetsu tokkyu expresses that run between Kyoto and Kintetsu-Nara stations with only a single stop (Yamato-Saidaiji). Most leave every 30 to 60 minutes, on the hour or half-hour, although there are also some jokers in the pack at odd times. The earliest is 6.22 am from Nara, 8 am from Kyoto. Travel time is 33 minutes and the fare is Y670.

Other expresses with the same fare but a few minutes slower and requiring a change at Yamato-Saidaiji are the Kyoto-Ise tokkyu expresses (detailed below) and tokkyu expresses bound for Kashihara-jingu-mae; these generally leave Kyoto on the quarter-hour and three-quarter-hour, respectively, through the day. Travel time to Yamato-Saidaiji is about 30 minutes; from that station, Kintetsu-Nara station is only a five-minute ride away.

Through the day at 10 to 30 minute intervals there are many kyuko expresses (somewhat slower) and futsu (local) trains that take 39 to 54 minutes but cost only Y370. With these it is generally necessary to change trains at Yamato-Saidaiji.

For the journey from Nara to Kyoto, the reverse trains can be used, so if there is no convenient train listed for Kyoto, you can take any train listed for anywhere (generally Osaka) and transfer at Yamato-Saidaiji to the first train passing through to Kyoto.

JNR Through the day there are about 24 trains running direct between Kyoto and Nara. One of these is an express train, taking 51 minutes; the rest are locals that take 68 minutes. The regular trains cost Y570; with a surcharge for the express.

Kyoto – Ise/Toba/Shima-hanto

Kintetsu The most convenient and fastest service between Kyoto and the Ise/Toba area is the Kintetsu tokkyu expresses that leave Kyoto hourly on the quarter-hour from 7.15 am to 6.15 pm, all of which run to Kashikojima (Shima-hanto) except the last two which terminate at Toba. In the return direction there are 11 trains a day every hour between 8.20 am and 6.20 pm, plus one train from Ise at 8.14 am. The fare from Kyoto to Ise is Y2220, from Kyoto to Toba is Y2410, and from Kyoto to Kashikojima is Y2700.

Less expensive but longer and more troublesome is to take a local train to Yamato-Saidaiji (35 to 50 minutes); change to a train originating there, bound for Kashihara-jingu-mae and take it as far as Yamato-Yagi (about 30 minutes); then change to the Osaka-Yamada line going toward the latter, which is one stop beyond Ise (1 hour 40 minutes). Waits between trains are variable and should be checked in advance. (From Ise to Kyoto (or Nara) the route would be the opposite.)

JNR To use JNR trains to the Ise/Toba area, a train from Kyoto bound for Nara can be used to connect with a train originating in Nara that will lead to the Ise area. (As detailed in the section Nara-Ise, this trip requires more than one change of train.) The quickest connection to the Nara – Ise train is generally made at Kizu, one stop out of Nara. (Many trains from Kyoto do not reach Nara in time for the earliest connection with a train to the Ise area.)

Kyoto – Osaka/Kobe

The least expensive way to travel between Kyoto and Osaka is on one of two private lines, Hankyu and Keihan. The fastest is by JNR. To Kobe, the less expensive Hankyu line may be used with a transfer at Osaka; the JNR service is direct and faster.

Hankyu Kyuko expresses of the Hankyu ('Osaka – Kyoto') line take 46 minutes, tokkyu expresses a little less, and ordinary (futsu) trains take 64 minutes between the two cities. Trains of the various services are interspersed through the day and can be identified on the timetable on the platforms by colour code: white on solid red for tokkyu (4 per hour), red in a red box is the next fastest, red for the next and black for futsu.

The four stations in Kyoto of the Hankyu line are conveniently located underground along Shijo-dori, and the line functions as an east-west subway line along this street, connecting with the north-south subway line at Karasuma station, although separate fares are charged. At Osaka, the terminus is Hankyu-Umeda, very close to JNR Osaka station, at the north of the city. The fare is Y280.

The Hankyu line can also be used for convenient transport to and from Kobe by taking it as far as Juso, one station from Osaka terminus (Hankyu-Umeda), and transferring to the Hankyu-Kobe line. (This line is detailed in the section Osaka–Kobe.)

Keihan Trains of the Keihan ('Kyoto – Osaka') line take longer than those of the Hankyu line and the main Kyoto station (Keihan-Sanjo) is less conveniently located a few blocks east of Karasuma-dori, the main street of Kyoto. (Trains of the Keihan line also go to Otsu, to the east.) The Osaka terminus is Yodoyabashi, somewhat closer to the centre of Osaka and the line intersects the JNR Osaka loop line at Kyobashi. (There is no convenient transfer to a Kobe-bound train.) The fare is Y280.

JNR Trains of the JNR line run a considerable distance beyond Kyoto and Osaka in each direction, so the Kyoto – Osaka segment of the JNR service will be covered in the following section.

Kusatsu – Kyoto – Osaka – Kobe – Himeji
In addition to the Shinkansen trains which pass through this area several times an hour there are regular trains that normally stop at every station, plus an express

service, the Shin-Kaisoku, that stops only at the cities listed in the heading, plus one other. Although the Shin-Kaisoku is a tokkyu express, there is no surcharge over the regular fare, so its price is reasonable and it is faster than any of the competing private lines.

The extremities of the Shin-Kaisoku are Kusatsu (east of Kyoto) and Himeji (west of Kobe), although not all trains serve all cities.

West from Kyoto: Trains leave Kyoto station every 15 minutes between 9.15 am and 4.30 pm and take 29 minutes to reach Osaka, 55 minutes to Kobe (Sannomiya and Kobe stations), 1 hour 23 minutes to Akashi and 1 hour 45 minutes to Himeji. Trains leaving on the quarter hour and three-quarter-hour from 10.15 am to 3.45 pm go through to Himeji, while those on the hour go only to Akashi.

West from Osaka: West-bound trains leave Osaka station (platform 5 and 6) 30 minutes after the times listed for departure from Kyoto.

East from Osaka: At 9.10 am and 9.39 am and every 15 minutes on the quarter-hour from 10 am to 4.45 pm, a Shin-Kaisiku train leaves Osaka station (platforms 7 and 8) for Kyoto and arrives (non-stop) 29 minutes later.

Some trains continue east from Kyoto as far as Kusatsu (25 minutes). From Osaka, between 10.45 am and 3.45 pm the trains on the three-quarter-hour, plus those at 9.39 am, 3.15 pm and 4.15pm continue to Kusatsu.

East from Himeji: Trains from Himeji are scheduled so they can leave Osaka on an exact hour or half hour (except 12 noon).

In addition many futsu trains that stop at every station also make the run, continuing beyond in both directions, to Okayama (west of Himeji) and to Maibara and Nagoya (east of Kyoto).

Osaka – Ise/Toba
Kintetsu From 6.50 am to 7.10 pm there is a tokkyu express train leaving Kami-

honmachi station at 10 to and 10 after the hour for Ise (1¾ hours), Uji-Yamada (one hour 50 minutes) and Toba (just over two hours). The '10 to' trains go through to Kashikojima (2½ hours). The last of these trains from Kami-honmachi is at 7.50 pm. There are also slightly faster trains leaving at 20 past the hour from 7.20 am to 4.20 pm that skip Ise but stop at the other three stations. The fares are: Ise – Y1890; Toba – 1280; and Kashikojima Y2470. As well as the expresses, there are cheaper local trains at five to 20 minute intervals through the day from Kami-honmachi. The fastest of these (tokkyu) takes just over two hours to Ise and costs Y1160.

JNR The situation for using JNR from Osaka to Ise/Toba is the same as that from Kyoto to Ise/Toba – you go to Nara first then through a succession of train changes from there.

Osaka – Kobe/Himeji
In addition to the JNR Shinkansen, Shin-Kaisoku and regular services already described there are also two private lines that can be used between Osaka and Kobe and one to Himeji.

Hankyu The Hankyu-Kobe line runs from Hankyu-Umeda station (near Osaka station) to Hankyu-Sannomiya (central Kobe). There are expresses and locals every 10 minutes (the latter takes about 40 minutes) and the fare is Y280. Juso, one stop out of Umeda, is the transfer point between the Kobe line and the Kyoto line, so Hankyu trains can be used between Kyoto and Kobe. Using a kyuko express from Kyoto to Juso (44 minutes) it should be possible to travel Kyoto – Kobe in less that 1½ hours for just under Y500. The Hankyu line can also be used beyond Kobe to Himeji; this is detailed in the section Kobe – Himeji.

Hanshin Also giving Osaka – Kobe service is the Hanshin line from Hanshin-Umeda station (also close to Osaka station) to Hanshin-Sannomiya and Hanshin-Motomachi stations, both in central Kobe. The fare to both is Y210 and it takes about one hour to Sannomiya.

Osaka – Himeji
The alternative to the JNR services detailed previously is the Hankyu line from Kobe. The first leg is Hankyu-Sannomiya to Nishi-Shiro (17 minutes, Y80), then the Sanjo-denki line to Dentetsu-Himeji station (one hour, Y560). Trains leave every 10 to 15 minutes.

LONG DISTANCE BUSES
Virtually the only long distance bus services in Japan run between Tokyo and Osaka, with the major stops at Nagoya and Kyoto. The buses run along the Tomei (Tokyo – Nagoya) and Meishin (Nagoya – Kobe) expressways. Buses do not go into the many cities along the road; they stop only at shelters by the expressway from where passengers can walk a short distance to transfer to local transport.

Buses run frequently through the day between Osaka/Kyoto and Nagoya, and between Nagoya and Tokyo. All passengers must change at Nagoya when travelling between Tokyo and Kyoto/Osaka during the day.

Buses that make every stop in the Nagoya – Kyoto run take nearly three hours, while the few super expresses take 2½ hours. Most buses stop at Kyoto; only seven a day go to Osaka and only one of these is an express. Travel time is about 3½ hours. Between Nagoya and Tokyo buses take about 6¼ hours. The fares are: Nagoya – Kyoto Y1800; Nagoya – Osaka Y2200; and Nagoya – Tokyo Y4500.

Night buses: every night buses run non-stop Tokyo – Nagoya; Tokyo – Kyoto; and Tokyo – Osaka (both directions). They leave late enough and drive slowly enough that they reach their destination at a reasonable hour in the morning. Seats recline so sleeping is relatively comfortable and if you're lucky you can get a seat at the back where there is slightly more leg room.

The advantages of taking the night bus are the saving of a night's accommodation and an enforced early start to the day's sightseeing.

The fare is reasonably low (same as for day service) but the buses are popular and heavily used so reservations are often a necessary evil, costing Y1500, which brings the fare close to two-thirds of the Shinkansen fare (Tokyo – Kyoto).

The departure/arrival times (reverse direction in parentheses) and fares are:
Tokyo – Nagoya: 11.20 pm/6.01 am (11.20 pm/6 am) Y4500

Tokyo – Kyoto: 11 pm/7.45 am (10 pm/6.43am) Y6300

Tokyo – Osaka: 10.20 pm/7.40 am (10.40 pm/8.15 am) Y6700

Chugoku Highway Bus

The only other expressway bus runs 189 km westward from Osaka into the Chugoku region. Most go as far as Tsuyama, almost due north of Okayama and about midway between the coasts.

Western Honshu

Chugoku

This section describes Chugoku, 'Middle Country', the western end of the main island, Honshu. The description begins at Himeji and follows a route clockwise along the south shore (*San-yo kaigan*), around the end of the island and back along the northern shore (*San-in kaigan*) almost to Kyoto.

The San-in coast is by far the more enjoyable for scenery and uncrowded and non-developed conditions. The route is excellent for cyclists as it is mostly flat and road traffic is reasonable.

The San-yo coast is very heavily developed through to Hiroshima and road traffic moves very slowly. However it has more specific places to visit.

The Chugoku expressway (Chuguko kosokudoro) runs from Osaka to Shimon-oseki at the west end and connects there, via the Kanmon-ohashi bridge, to the Kyushu expressway. This is the route for hitchhikers in a hurry, but the scenery is only pleasant not memorable.

Further details on road conditions and a summary of attractions along the way may be found in the section on Shimonoseki.

The name Chugoku implies that this was in the centre of Japanese civilisation in the past. Archaeological remains can be found near Okayama and other places and the nation's most venerated ancient shrine site is at Izumo (near Matsue, San-in coast).

Himeji properly belongs in this region but it was described in the Kinki section because it can easily be reached from Kyoto as a day trip and is most conveniently dealt with as part of the Kinki region.

In addition to road and rail connections from the Osaka area to the west, there are also daily ferry connections between Kobe and Kokura and between Osaka and Shin-Moji and Kanda; the latter are all in north-east Kyushu and easily accessible from Shimonoseki. Details are given in the general Getting Around section earlier in the book. There are also numerous connections from points in the Chugoku region to Shikoku and Kyushu. These connections are identified in the write-up on each place, although details of frequency, etc, are given only for the connecting locale in Shikoku and Kyushu.

Okayama-ken

BIZEN

The city of Bizen is famous in Japan for the pottery known as *Bizen-yaki*; numerous potteries and kilns can be found in and around the city. The pottery is of a very old (1200 years) and simple style, obtaining its characteristic finish and patterns from the firing rather than the glazing.

An interesting sidelight of the pottery craft is a reported reduction in the number of birds in the coastal area. So many pine trees have been cut down as fuel for the kilns that the roosts and sources of insects have been reduced.

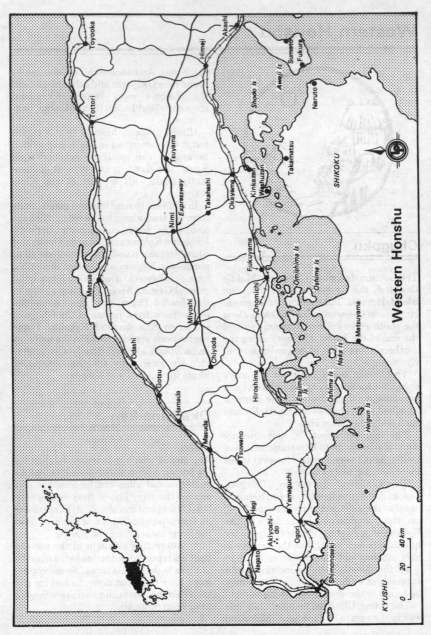

Western Honshu

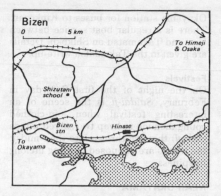

Shizutani School

This historical school may not be recognisable as such to westerners. It dates from 1666 and resembles classical schools of China and Korea. It was the first school in Japan for commoners. The white-walled buildings are roofed with Bizen-ware tiles and surrounded with a rock-covered earthen wall which is broken by small picturesque gates. It is located at the foot of a tree-covered hill that is colourful in autumn. The appearance of the school is very uncommon in a Japanese setting.

OKAYAMA

Okayama is the better known city of the pair Okayama-Kurashiki, but they can best be regarded as two parts of a whole. The city centres are only 16 km apart, so travel between them is convenient.

Tescort

Members of Tescort are willing to act as unpaid escorts for visitors to Okayama in return for the opportunity to speak English. To make arrangements phone 32-2751 (area code: 0862) and ask for the Tescort co-ordinator.

Things to See
Korako-en Park

This is the main attraction of Okayama and the Japanese rate it as one of the 'Big Three' gardens of Japan. The 'strolling' landscape garden was laid out more than 290 years ago. It has many of the features westerners associate with a Japanese garden such as the careful placement of rocks, ponds, miniature hills, etc, as well as flower beds, blossom trees and a teahouse. However, I was rather disappointed by it, as much of its expanse is open lawn similar to that found in any western park – a novelty to the Japanese, where space is at such a premium. To be sure, it is pretty, but do not expect too much of it. Near the garden is a museum (hakubutsukan).

A bus from Okayama station runs reasonably close to the garden; a taxi can also be used. The information centre at the station (well equipped with literature in English) can help you get the right bus.

Okayama-jo Castle

The original castle here was built in 1573, but subsequently destroyed. The present concrete reconstruction preserves the external appearance and adds a traditional note to the Korako-en, which it overlooks. It is black, which is a departure from the

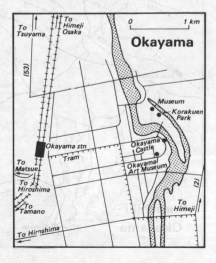

usual white of most castles, including Japan's finest at nearby Himeji. Okayama-jo's nickname, *Ujo* (crow) pokes fun at the name of Himeji's pride which translates as 'white egret'. *Ujo* is not far from Korako-en and is reached by a bridge across the river. Nearby is *Okayama Bijutsukan* (Art Museum).

Kinkozan

An excursion by bus from Okayama passes by Kojima Bay to Kinkozan hill. The bay is not spectacular, but is interesting for being the second largest man-made lake in the world (after one in Holland). It allowed the reclamation of a large area of farm land.

Kinkozan hill (403 metres) offers one of the best views of the Inland Sea. Check at

Okayama station for buses to Kinkozan. There is a regular boat service between Uno and Takamatsu on Shikoku. Details are given in the Takamatsu write-up.

Festivals

On the night of the first Saturday in February, *Saidai-ji* is the scene of an interesting festival when loin-clothed young men vie to keep two sacred wands (*shingi*) that are thrown into their midst; the wands are supposed to bring lifelong happiness.

NEAR OKAYAMA
Shibukawa-hama Beach

One of the best beaches (white sand, etc) is about eight km from Uno station, accessible by train from Okayama to Uno

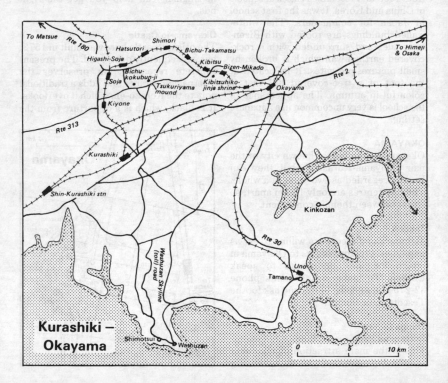

Kurashiki – Okayama

station, and by bus from there in 25 minutes.

Tsuyama

Inland, due north of Okayama, lies Tsuyama. In cherry-blossom season the site of the old castle (destroyed in 1873) is very beautiful, as the grounds (now Kazukan-koen) are planted with 8000 cherry trees. Of interest at any time to historians is the site of a Yayoi-era (pre-Yamato Japanese civilisation) pit dwelling that has been excavated. Little is known of the people of that era, but their pottery and the remnants of their dwellings of 2000 years ago have been found in many parts of Japan. About 2.5 km north-east of Numa station, one Yayoi-type dwelling has been reconstructed and is open to the public. (Refer to the section on Shizuoka for more information on pit dwellings.)

KURASHIKI

This is possibly the most charming town in Japan (well parts of it, at least). It was extremely prosperous in feudal days when rice from the very productive inland region was shipped through here. Merchants built large and elaborate storehouses of dark stone and contrasting white mortar, which still stand in one section of the town. A canal (also stonewalled and once used to transport rice to and from the storehouses) passes by the buildings and willows drop gracefully over the water. Although the architecture is Japanese, the mood of the area is almost that of old Europe. You can enjoy just walking around, absorbing the appearance and atmosphere and possibly taking a short rickshaw ride along the narrow streets. I first saw the area late in the afternoon when the sun was low, and was captivated; but I could never quite recapture that mood again. May every visitor have such an opportunity. The area is not large, so a stroll of half an hour or so down the back streets will probably be enough before returning to the attractions along the canal.

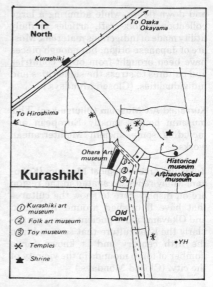

Kurashiki

① Kurashiki art museum
② Folk art museum
③ Toy museum
✳ Temples
★ Shrine

Information

The city has an information office near the Ohara Museum. If you are beginning your travels in Tokyo, you should pick up a copy of the photocopied information sheet on Kurashiki at the TIC.

Things to See

The Warehouses

Several of the 'kura' (or warehouses, hence the name Kurashiki) have been converted into museums and are worth visiting. They are described in the order that they are encountered along the canal bank.

Toy Museum (Kyodo gangu-kan) This houses a collection of toys from all over Japan, including many types no longer used, which are interesting for the simplicity of their designs, using local materials.

Folk-craft Museum (Mingei-kan) Several adjoining kura have been combined so you can walk back and forth within them, up and down floors, while admiring a large collection of folk-craft, articles of daily utility made of indigenous materials. Most are of Japanese origin, but enough pieces have been brought from other countries and cultures to stress the similarities and individualities. (Closed Mondays.)

Kurashiki Art Museum (Bijutsu-kan) This museum houses mostly European art, including some ancient Mediterranean works.

Kurashiki Archaeological Museum (Koko-kan) Many relics excavated in the region are on display here to show the cultures that have flourished around Kurashiki and Okayama since ancient times; particularly the Kibi culture that survived into the fifth century and is known for a number of tomb mounds in the vicinity of the city. (Closed Mondays.)

Ohara Art Museum (Ohara Bijutsu-kan) No, not founded by an errant Irishman, but a wealthy Japanese textile manufacturer, Magosaburo Ohara, who collected western art. To house his collection, he constructed a large Greek-style building complete with columns. The collection is interesting but not exciting, at least for those who have had access to the great western museums. In the grounds behind this building are other museums housing contemporary Japanese art, pottery, Chinese art and other assorted collections. Some regard these as more interesting than the main museum.

Kurashiki Historical Museum (Rekishi-kan) This museum is apart from the others and can be reached in 10 to 15 minutes on foot.

Ivy Square Built as a textile factory soon after the Meiji restoration in 1868, this ivy-covered red brick complex has been converted into a cluster of tourist attractions. It is of greatest interest to the Japanese (to whom such a brick structure is exotic), but there is a small museum of the Kurashiki textile industry which may interest foreign visitors, plus restaurants, coffee houses, an open square and a hotel.

Places to Stay
In addition to the hotel in Ivy Square, there are many hotels and ryokan of various price ranges, as well as a pleasant hilltop youth hostel. Assistance in finding a room is available from the railway station.

Getting There
Kurashiki is accessible by Shinkansen via Shin-Kurashiki station, but the connections make it simpler to transfer from Okayama station (also on the Shinkansen), which allows a visit to Okayama as well.

NEAR KURASHIKI
Just north of Kurashiki is the Kibi plain, which was settled long before recorded history; many historic and prehistoric remains may be found in the area. *Kibitsu-hiko-jinja* shrine at the foot of a forested hill (near Bizen-Mikado station) is one of the attractions; its main building is built in an unusual Kibitsu-zukuri style, and dates from 1425 (a national treasure).

Tsukuriyama Tomb Mound
In the same area is the Tsukuriyama tomb mound, the largest such burial site in the Kibi area, and the fourth largest in Japan. Similar mounds are found in Kyushu, near Osaka (including the largest) and near Tokyo. The practice of building such mounds was also prevalent in Korea, so the question remains whether these people were Korean in origin, or if they were only influenced by the culture across the water. It is a keyhole-shaped mound of earth 350 metres long, 238 metres wide at the greatest point, and 25 metres high. It is of limited interest to most people, however, because it simply looks like any other hill, even though man-made; its significance is more interesting.

Another attraction in the same area is *Bichu-Kokubunji* temple. It has a picturesque five-storey pagoda. To reach these attractions make enquiries locally.

WASHUZAN
An excellent view over the Inland Sea (*Seto Nai-Kai*) is available at Washuzan, almost due south of Kurashiki. Buses run many times a day from Kurashiki station, taking about 80 minutes. Buses also run regularly from Okayama station (90 minutes), so you can make a looping trip from one city to the other. It may be necessary to climb for a while from the bus stop, so be prepared with walking shoes.

There is a youth hostel near Washuzan; and a regular boat service between nearby Shimotsui and Marugame on Shikoku. (Details are given in the Marugame section.)

FUKUYAMA
This industrial city is of little interest, although it has a 1966 reproduction of its historic castle. It is best known for the nearby town of Tomo-no-ura, regarded as one of the most picturesque places in the Inland Sea area (and Japan). The town of Tomo-no-ura (port for Fukuyama) overlooks the islands of Sensui, Benten and Kogo.

There is a regular boat service between Fukuyama (Higashi-Fukuyama port) and Tadotsu and Takamatsu on Shikoku.

(Details given in the write-ups of those places.)

Abuto-Kannon Temple This temple to the Goddess of Mercy is built on a cape less than 30 metres above the water, and is noted for its superb view. It is only four km from Tomo-no-ura, and is accessible from there by bus or boat; or from Fukuyama by bus to Abuto-guchi, from where it's a 20 minute walk.

ONOMICHI
One of the best views of the Inland Sea may be had from the heights of *Senko-ji* temple. It is accessible in 20 minutes by direct bus, or by bus (five minutes) to Nagaeguchi, then by cable car to the top. The park at the top is noted for cherry blossoms in season, and picturesque rocks.

The city was not touched by the war, so many older houses and buildings have survived and a walk around may provide some of the mood of olden times. The city is noted for a number of temples, such as *Jodo-ji, Saigo-ji, Saikoku-ji* and *Tennei-ji* (there are many others). A map of the city, showing the temples, is available at the station and can be used as a guide while strolling around.

There is a regular boat service between Onomichi and Matsuyama and Imabari on Shikoku, the latter offering a service to Omishima island as well. (Details are given in the write-ups of those places.)

Mukai-shima
Located near Onomichi, and accessible by a bridge, Mukai-shima island has an observation post (tempodai) that features an excellent view of the Inland Sea and Onomichi.

MIHARA & IKUCHI ISLAND
The industrial city of Mihara is the gateway to the island of Ikuchi, 12 km to the south. Setoda, on Ikuchi, is noted for its interesting temple *Kosan-ji*. Dating from 1946, the temple has several build-

ings modelled on those of famous temples elsewhere in Japan (such as the Hall of Dreams in Nara) as well as a collection of cultural and religious objects.

Access is by ferry (50 minutes) or fast boat (20 minutes) from Mihara to Setoda; the temple is about 10 minutes walk east of the dock.

There is a regular boat service between Mihara and Matsuyama and Imabari on Shikoku. (Details are given in the sections on those places.) The terminal is close to the station.

KURE

Along the coast east of Hiroshima is the ship building centre of Kure. During the war, the giant battleship *Yamato* was built here. The largest of its day, carrying 18-inch guns, it was sunk by US aircraft without contributing to the Japanese war effort. In post-war days Kure has produced many of the world's super-tankers that would dwarf the *Yamato*. If you want to visit the shipyards, inquire in advance; the city has no other attractions, being a typical industrial port city.

There are regular boat services between Kure and Matsuyama on Shikoku (details in the section on Matsuyama); and between Niigata and Imabari on Shikoku (details in the section on Imabari).

Nikyu Gorge

About 15 km north-east of Kure lies this scenic gorge, most noted for many water-falls and Jacob's wells. It can be reached by bus from Kure in 40 minutes.

Takehara There is a regular boat service between Takehara and Imabari and Namikata on Shikoku, the former offering service en-route to Omishima island. (Details are given in the write-ups of those places.)

TAISHAKU-KYO GORGE

This scenic gorge stretches about 20 km upstream from Taishaku-mura village along the Taishaku river. About 2.4 km

from the village is *Oni-wa-iwaya* (Demon Cave), known for its stalactites. Further along there are two natural rock bridges. The gorge is in one part of Hiba-Taishaku Quasi National Park. Other attractions of the region include mountain, marsh and forest views. Taishaku-mura can be reached by bus in about one hour from Bingo-Shobara station.

MIYOSHI AREA

The inland areas of Chugoku have not gained a great name for tourist attractions but the scenery along the exressway from Miyoshi to Osaka is enjoyable.

Ukai (cormorant fishing) is carried out through June, July and August near the junction of three rivers, not far from Nishi-Miyoshi station.

SANDAN-KYO GORGE

A pleasant excursion from Hiroshima is north-west to Sandan-kyo. Its 16 km length, covered on foot, takes in a number of waterfalls and scenery ranging from pretty to spectacular. Access is by train to Sansan-kyo station (JNR) or by bus, both from Hiroshima.

Hiroshima-ken

HIROSHIMA

The city of Hiroshima is known to the inhabitants of every civilised country in the world because of an instant in 1945 when it was destroyed by an atom bomb. For this reason large numbers of tourists visit the city during a stay in Japan; but be warned that there is relatively little else in Hiroshima city itself as it is first and foremost an industrial city (which is why it was chosen as a target).

It is built on the flat estuary of the Ota river and has little natural beauty, although this is more than offset by the beauties of nearby Miyajima Island. However, the relics and exhibits related to the A-bomb do make Hiroshima a recommended

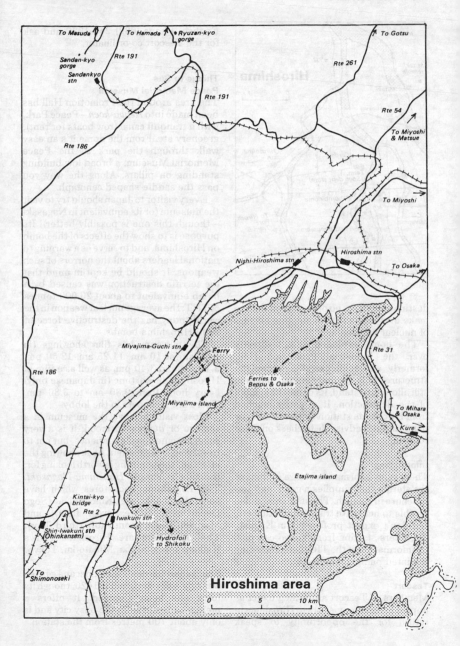

Hiroshima area

0   5   10 km

Hiroshima

0   1 km

destination – if for no other reason than to make everyone aware of the true horrors of nuclear warfare.

The bomb exploded almost directly over the Industrial Promotion Hall, formerly an architecturally noteworthy structure. It is the only ruined building still allowed to stand, its dome the symbol of the destruction. It is easily reached from Hiroshima station by tram 2 or 6, or bus 3 (but it is advisable to check on these routes).

Information

There is an information centre in front of the station that supplies a good map and brochure in English. The staff should also be able to help with tram information etc, but don't expect proficiency in English. Travellers starting from Tokyo can pick up information at the TIC there, including a printed pamphlet (MG-19).

Tescort

Members of Tescort are willing to act as unpaid escorts for visitors to Hiroshima in return for the opportunity to speak

English. Phone (082) 249-1920 and ask for the Tescort co-ordinator.

Things to See
Peace Memorial Museum

The area around the Promotion Hall has been made into *Heiwa-koen* – Peace Park, with a tranquil canal (row boats for rent), greenery etc. From the dome it's an easy walk through the park to the Peace Memorial Museum, a broad low building standing on pillars. Along the way you pass the saddle-shaped cenotaph.

Every visitor to Japan should try to visit the museum (or its equivalent in Nagasaki – though this one is possibly better). Its purpose is to show the effects of the bomb on Hiroshima, and to serve as a warning to national leaders about the horrors of such weapons. It should be kept in mind that the terrific destruction was caused by a bomb equivalent to about 20,000 tonnes of TNT; the average nuclear weapon in the world today has the destructive force of 2000 Hiroshima bombs.

The museum has film showings (in English) at 10 am, 11.25 am, 12.50 pm, 2.15 pm and 3.40 pm, as well as a film of Hiroshima in wartime (in Japanese only) every hour from 9.30 am to 3.30 pm. There are signposts in the lobby.

Most visitors leave the museum in a sombre or depressed mood; it is a very sobering emotional experience, but not to be missed. An excellent book showing the effects of the bombing is worth looking for; the title is simply *Hiroshima-Nagasaki*. Two Hiroshima bookstores which have sold the book are Kinokuniya (Sogo Department Store, sixth floor), and Maruzen Department Store (third floor). The publishers are Hiroshima Heiwa Kaikan, 1-4-9, Shiba, Minato-ku, Tokyo.

Shukkei-en Garden This landscape garden was originally designed in 1620, though its form has been changed. It offers a pleasant respite from the busy city and is only about 700 metres from the station.

Hiroshima Castle The original castle stood here from 1589 until it was destroyed by the bomb. It was rebuilt in concrete and preserves the external appearance of the former building. It is now a local museum and gives some idea of the appearance of old Hiroshima. The late afternoon offers the best light for photographs.

Places to Stay

There are many hotels etc in Hiroshima as well as a youth hostel. The information centre may have directions on how to get to the youth hostel; if not, walk towards the post office (to the right at the front of the station), cross the street and turn right. A short distance along should be a sign '50 metres to Hiroshima Youth Hostel bus stop'. More than one bus uses the same stop so ask the driver before boarding and get off at Ushita-shin-machi or Ushita I-chome; signs from there should be clear guides up the hill to the hostel. It is one of the best-marked hostels in Japan, and is one of the more pleasant (apart from the 6.30 am reveille); it is also an excellent source of travel information.

Another accommodation centre is the World Friendship Association; the information centre at the station should be able to help.

Getting There

Trains Hiroshima is one of the major stops on the JNR Shinkansen super express train that runs between Tokyo and Hakata (Kyushu). Tokyo is about five hours away (depending on the number of stops made), while Kyoto is two to three hours away. There are also slower, less expensive JNR services. Shinkansen services are detailed in the general Getting Around section early in the book.

Ferries There is a daily overnight ferry service between Hiroshima and Beppu (each way) making this a convenient and relatively inexpensive way of getting to Kyushu, saving the cost of one night's accommodation. Details of this service

are given in the general Getting Around section. There are also regular boats (including speedy hydrofoils) between Hiroshima and Matsuyama and Imabari, both on Shikoku. (Details are given in the write-ups of these places.) The dock area can be reached from Hiroshima station by tram or bus. The information centre can give assistance. There are also boats from nearby Iwakuni to Shikoku.

Hitching Hitching along the south coast is very slow and unpleasant, although unavoidable if you wish to go to Okayama, etc. Route 2 passes through the city and can be intercepted by a tram No 8 going south.

To use the Chugoku expressway to/ from Kyushu (west) or Osaka/Kyoto (east), the most convenient interchange is Hiroshima-kita, about 25 km out of the city. From Hiroshima it can be reached by taking Route 54 to Kami-ga-hara, then going left about seven km. The interchange is close to the west (far) end of the tunnel. The interchange can also be reached from Aki-Imuro, which is a little more than an hour out of Hiroshima station (some trains begin only at Yokogawa station through which all pass), but there are only about five trains a day. The interchange is about three km east of Aki-Imuro station.

Getting Around

The simplest way to get around Hiroshima is by tram; one goes to the A-bomb dome, and you can return by the same route or walk along Peace Boulevard (Heiwa Dori) and across the river, returning to the station by another line.

The reason for the weird and wonderful variety in the colour scheme of the trams is because Hiroshima (which wisely kept its tram tracks) bought up trams from other cities as they phased out tram services. The trams retain their original colours.

There are buses to Hiroshima station from various parts of the city. The bus station is in the Sogo Department Store; it serves both city buses and those to other cities. Any red or orange bus goes to the station; red-and-white striped ones pass by the castle.

MIYAJIMA

The major attraction of the Hiroshima area is Miyajima (Shrine Island). Its best known feature is one of the most famous symbols of all Japan, the huge off-shore torii gate that is seen in every travelogue and book on Japan. The island is ranked traditionally as one of the three most beautiful sights in Japan (along with Matsushima, near Sendai, and Amanohashidate, on the north coast). There are many beautiful scenes on and around the island and a visit is sure to be enjoyed – for the famous shrine, the torii, a walk through the heavy woods, tame deer and other attractions. A half-day will take in a good number of the features of the island, but an overnight stay would allow greater relaxation and time to absorb the mood.

The ferry from Miyajima-guchi on the mainland arrives at Miyajima-ko in 10 minutes. In front of the building at the entrance to the dock is a large three-dimensional information board for orientation. Most visitors set off immediately to the right, to the main attraction of the island, *Itsukushima-jinja* shrine.

Itsukushima-jinja

The shrine is unusual because the buildings are built on piles over the shallows at the water's edge and are joined by narrow galleries. One explanation of the unusual construction is that the island has been regarded as sacred from ancient times and Taira Kiyomori had the shrine built in this way in the 12th century so that it could be approached by boat without setting foot on land. (Earlier shrines had stood on the same spot since 593.)

The principal buildings of Itsukushima Shrine are the *honden* (main hall), *heiden* (offering hall), *haiden* (hall of worship) and *haraiden* (purification hall). In the *Asazaya* (morning prayer room), dance costumes and masks etc are displayed. The public is allowed only as far as the outer sanctuary of the honden; all these buildings, plus the corridors, are ranked as National Treasures.

The great torii gate in the water (accessible on foot at low tide for those who don't mind mud) dates from 1875 and is the largest wooden torii in Japan, 16.2 metres high and 23.3 metres wide. The large stone torii on the shore dates from 1905.

The first shrine structure seen when approaching from the ferry dock is *Marodo-jinja*, the largest shrine after Itsukushima-jinja itself.

Noh Theatre Most of the shrine buildings are of comparatively recent construction, but the Noh theatre dates from 1568, and was rebuilt in Edo times. It is the oldest Noh theatre in Japan, and one of the only stages in the world where the audience is unlikely to crowd around and block the view, especially at high tide.

Dances The shrine is noted for performances of *Bugaku* and *Kagura* dances on the takabutai stage at the end of the shrine nearest the channel; and every brochure on Japan is likely to feature a photo of a masked dancer with the torii in the background. However, performances do not seem to be regularly scheduled but are performed according to the payment of a suitable fee, so seeing one may be hit-or-miss, depending on the arrival of a tour group.

Treasure Hall On the shore near the shrine is the Treasure Hall (*homostu-kan*), which contains more than 3500 historical and cultural items including a number of national treasures. The building resembles a simple temple but was built specifically for its purpose to replace an older wooden building.

A folklore museum (*mingeikan*) is housed in an old, traditional-style house nearby.

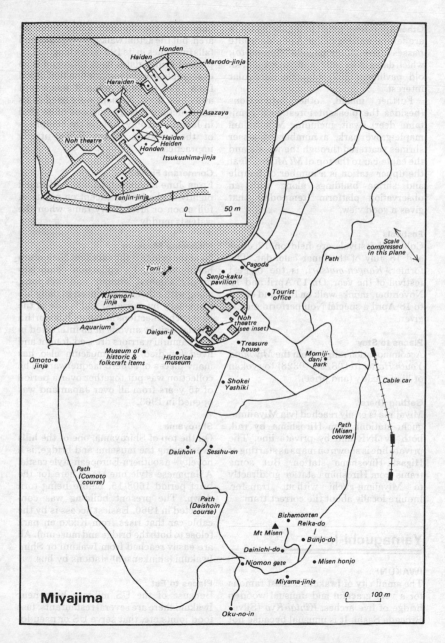

Miyajima

Inset labels:
Honden
Haiden
Marodo-jinja
Haraiden
Asazaya
Noh theatre
Haiden
Heiden
Honden
Itsukushima-jinja
Tenjin-jinja

0   50 m

Scale compressed in this plane

Torii
Pagoda
Senjo-kaku pavilion
Path
Kiyomori-jinja
Tourist office
Aquarium
Noh theatre (see inset)
Daigan-ji
Treasure house
Omoto-jinja
Museum of historic & folkcraft items
Historical museum
Momiji-dani park
Cable car
Shokei Yashiki
Path (Misen course)
Daishoin
Sesshu-en
Path (Comoto course)
Path (Daishoin course)
Bishamonten
Reika-do
Mt Misen
Bunjo-do
Dainichi-do
Misen honjo
Niomon gate
Miyama-jinja
Oku-no-in

0   100 m

Other Apart from a visit to the shrine there are several walking paths. A popular route passes a five-storey pagoda (*goju-no-to*), which dates from 1407, and *Senjokaku*, an old pavilion (1587) of little particular interest.

Further inland, other attractions (besides the pleasant forest and semi-tame deer) await, including Momijidani maple-grove park, a number of lesser shrines scattered through the woods and the cable-car to the top of *Mt Misen*. Near the upper station is a number of temple and shrine buildings along with an observation platform (tempodai) that gives a good view.

Festivals
Colourful festivals are held on 17 June and 18 July of the lunar calendar. The former, *Kangen-matsuri*, is the biggest festival of the year. On 15 April and 15 November, monks walk on fire; and on 16 to 18 April a special Noh performance is given.

Places to Stay
Accommodation ranges from the *Miyajima Youth Hostel* (tel 08294 40328) to ryokan of high quality (and price).

Getting There
Miyajima is easily reached (via Miyajima-guchi station) from Hiroshima by rail, both by JNR and by private line. The private line is shown on maps as starting at Higashi-Hiroshima station. But some trams from Hiroshima station go directly to Miyajima-guchi without transfer. Inquire locally about the correct tram.

Yamaguchi-ken

IWAKUNI
The small city of Iwakuni is most famous for a very graceful and unusual wooden bridge of five arches, *Kintai-Kyo* (Silver Brocade Sash). It is unusual because not only does the understructure form an arch, but the actual walkway also rises and falls five times in its 193 metre length. The present bridge dates from 1953 and is an exact replica of the historic one that stood from 1673 to 1950, when it was swept away by a flood. No nails were used in its construction. It is the only one of its kind in Japan, probably because the steepness of the walkway makes it so utterly impractical.

Cormorant Fishing
From June to August, *ukai* is performed nightly at the bridge except on nights of full moon or after heavy rains when the water is muddy.

Nishimura Museum
Near the bridge is the excellent Nishimura hakubutsukan. Its collection comprises mostly samurai armour and weapons, along with other objects used in daily life (especially by warriors) and is one of the best such collections in Japan. It is worth a special visit by anyone at all interested in how samurai warriors dressed, fought and lived (or died). The museum also has many pieces of superb lacquerware. The collection was put together over a period of 45 years from all over Japan and was opened in 1963.

Shiroyama
On the top of Shiroyama, one of the hills overlooking the museum and bridge, is a novelty – a southern-European-style castle! A Japanese-style one stood here for the brief period 1608-15, before being torn down. The present building was constructed in 1960. Easiest access is by the cable-car that rises from Kikko-en park (close to both the bridge and museum). All are easily reached from Iwakuni or Shin-Iwakuni (shinkansen) stations by bus.

Places to Eat
Because of the US military base near Iwakuni there are several restaurants, fast food joints etc, that serve US or pseudo-

US food, which may be of interest to those suffering advanced junk-food withdrawal symptoms.

HOFU

Located here is one of Japan's better-known shrines, *Hofu-Tenmangu (Matsugasaki)* shrine. The buildings are large, colourful and impressive.

TOKUYAMA

There is a regular boat service between Tokuyama (Shinnanyo port) and Taketazu, on the Kunisaki peninsula of Kyushu. Details are given under Taketazu.

YANAI

There is a regular boat service between Yanai and Matsuyama on Shikoku. More details are given in the section on Matsuyama.

OGORI

There are no notable tourist attractions at Ogori other than its summer steam-train excursions to and from Tsuwano. These are detailed in the general Getting Around section earlier in the book.

YAMAGUCHI

Formerly a castle town, this reached its zenith in the 1500s and declined when the *daimyo* found himself on the losing side in the civil war. Relics from those days include *Ruriko-ji* (from the 14th century) and its five-storey pagoda; a landscape garden by the famous designer Sesshu; *Joei-ji* temple; and the (modern) cathedral that commemorates the time spent in Yamaguchi by St Francis Xavier in 1551.

Chomon Gorge

About 20 km from Yamaguchi is the pretty gorge Chomon-kyo. It begins close to the station of the same name and extends for 12 km to Uzugahara. The Abu-kawa river has sculpted the rock into fanciful shapes, pools, falls and Jacob's wells.

AKIYOSHI

Clumps of limestone rocks dot this rolling tableland, looking like thousands of sheep or tombstones. Although the rocks look small from a distance, many are as tall as a man.

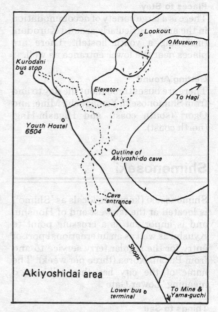

Akiyoshidai area

Akiyoshi Cave

Beneath the plateau is Akiyoshi-do, the largest cave in the Far East. It extends several km into the ground, of which about one km is accessible to visitors. Electric lights and walkways make the expedition simple, and you pass typical features of limestone caves, like stalagmites and stalactites (as children remember it, the mites go up and the tites go down), as well as other fantastic forms that the limestone takes as it precipitates out of solution.

Well into the cave there is a lift that rises near Kurodani (Black Valley), which is located among the rocks of the plateau. A path leads up to a lookout (tempodai) and a museum of specimens associated with the cave and plateau. Buses run between the Kurodani area and the terminal near the entrance to the cave, so you can return to one entrance from the other by bus or retrace your steps through the cave.

Places to Stay

There is a large variety of accommodation in the area, particularly around Kurodani (including a youth hostel). There are places near the lower entrance as well.

Getting Around

There are buses throughout the day to and from Shimonoseki, Yamaguchi, Mine, and Ogori (south coast) and Higashi-Hagi (north coast).

Shimonoseki

Shimonoseki (known to locals as 'Shimo') is located at the far west end of Honshu, and is important as a crossing point to Kyushu as well as an international port of entry for the regular ferry service to and from Pusan, Korea (three per week). The name of the city has the well-earned meaning 'Lower Gate'.

Things to See

If this is your first time in Japan, you can get a good idea of the prosperity of the country by a quick walk around either Daiei or Daimaru department stores on the square facing the station; the contrast with Korea will be quite striking (as will some of the prices).

One of the major attractions of Shimonoseki is *Akamon-jinja*, a large and colourful shrine. It's made of concrete, not the traditional wood, and is named for its red gate of uncommon Chinese shape. There are many shrines in Japan that are more exciting. The shrine can be reached by the same bus that goes to the hostel.

The other attraction is a view over the Kanmon Strait from *Hinoyama* (Fire Mountain). This can be enjoyed from the

youth hostel or take the cable-car to the top of Hinoyama. The base station can be reached by bus from the station, either the hourly one from stand 3 to 'Koku-minshuku-sha-mae', which goes right up to and past the station; or any bus going past 'Ropeway-mae', where you get off and walk up the hill.

You may also see a sign pointing to the site of the battle of Dan-no-ura in 1185, but most of the action took place in the water and whatever beach might have existed has disappeared under the tall pillars of the graceful Kanmon-ohashi suspension bridge.

Shimonoseki Aquarium

An attraction of Shimo is its aquarium, claimed to be the largest in the Orient. It has a collection of some truly weird and wonderful creatures of the deep; dolphin and seal shows are part of the entertainment. The aquarium (*suizukukan*) is easily reached from Shimo station or by bus; the name of the bus stop is Suizuku-kan-mae.

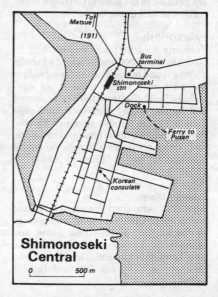

Shimonoseki Central

0   500 m

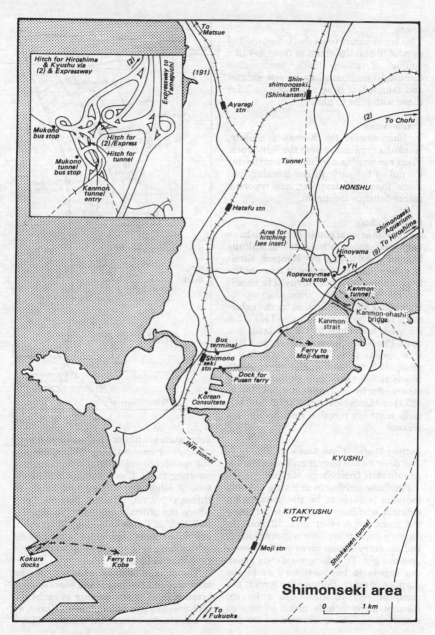

To Matsue

(191)

Ayaragi stn

Shin-shimonoseki stn
(Shinkansen)

(2) To Chofu

Inset:

Hitch for Hiroshima & Kyushu via (2) & Expressway

(2)

Expressway to Yamaguchi

Mukono bus stop

Hitch for (2)/Express

Hitch for (2)/Express

Hitch for tunnel

Mukono tunnel bus stop

Kanmon tunnel entry

Tunnel

HONSHU

Hatafu stn

Area for hitching (see inset)

Hinoyama

YH

Ropeway-mae bus stop

Shimonoseki Aquarium

To Hiroshima

Kanmon strait

Kanmon tunnel

Kanmon-ohashi bridge

Kanmon strait

Bus terminal

Shimono seki stn

Dock for Pusan ferry

Ferry to Moji-hama

Korean Consulate

JNR tunnel

KYUSHU

KITAKYUSHU CITY

Kokura docks

Ferry to Kobe

Moji stn

Shinkansen tunnel

Shimonoseki area

0   1 km

To Fukuoka

Chofu

This is a separate town that is included as part of Shimo. Its claim to fame lies in a couple of streets with earth-walled samurai-style houses, and a few shrines and temples. It is an enjoyable walk for those with time to pass.

Korean visas

In Shimonoseki the Korean consulate, Kankoku ryojikan, is near the ferry dock. Visas can be obtained here within the day if applied for early in the morning, but more than one traveller has reported rather brusque treatment.

Places to Stay

Along with several hotels, etc, Shimo has a very pleasant youth hostel beautifully located overlooking the Kanmon Strait and the suspension bridge. It is one of the best vantage points in the city. The view is second only to that from the top of Hinoyama; the base station for the cable-car is only 100 metres away and it's a 1.8 km walk (downhill) to the Mukono bus stop. The house parents are very nice (the wife speaks some English), and only a passport is required. If *Hinoyama Youth Hostel* is full there may be vacancies at others nearby at Toyota (tel (08376) 6-8271) or Akiyoshidai (tel (08376) 2-0341), or in northern Kyushu. See the Kyushu section.

Getting There – From Korea

The dock for the ferry from Korea is a 10-minute walk from Shimo station.

For those arriving from Korea, the only problem is likely to be the immigration officials, who have a reputation for being the most unpleasant and officious in Japan: passports are rigorously scrutinized, and an entry stamp given as if it was a precious gift. Travellers re-entering Japan can expect to be questioned as to the purpose of entry. Because the ferry is the cheapest way to and from a foreign country many people make to trip to renew visas. Those entitled to 90-day

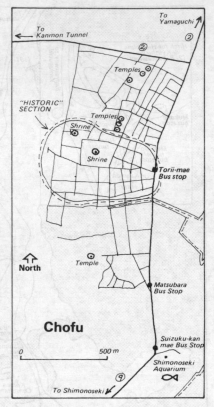

Chofu

entry status (without visa) will find it very difficult or impossible to obtain despite the existence of bilateral agreements covering them. If you anticipate difficulties, it might be simpler just to fly in through Narita, Osaka, Nagoya, etc, where the officials are more reasonable. (Officials at Fukuoka, nearby in Kyushu, are close runners-up, so there is no likely advantage going that way if you expect problems at Shimo).

There is a money changer in the terminus and the rate is the same as that given at local banks. Be sure to exchange all Korean money before leaving Korea, as it is worthless outside the country. There is an exchange office at the Pusan terminal.

Trains

Regular JNR services to points in Honshu and Kyushu leave from Shimonoseki station. The Shinkansen super-expresses (the fastest service to Hiroshima, Kyoto, Tokyo, etc) leave from Shin-Shimonoseki station, two stops away by local train and also accessible by bus from Shimo station; local trains are scheduled to reach Shin-Shimo station in time for each train. There is a schedule of all services posted in Shimo station in adequate English, and staff at the information centre should be able to give basic information. (As advised elsewhere, always speak slowly and clearly, avoid slang, and watch the person's face for signs of non-comprehension.) To cross to Kyushu, the simplest way is by train through the tunnel to Moji, Kitakyushu, etc.

Ferries

A convenient way to get from Shimonoseki to points further east on Honshu and to Shikoku is by overnight ferry from places in nearby northern Kyushu. From Kokura (part of Kitakyushu city) there are two daily boats to Kobe and one daily boat to Osaka (both destinations conveniently close to Kyoto), plus one boat every second day to Tokyo. There is a daily overnight ferry to Osaka from Shin Moji-ko, a short distance down the coast from Kitakyushu, and from Kanda-ko, just a little further down the coast. From Kokura there is also a daily overnight ferry to Matsuyama, on Shikoku.

Details on these ferries are given in the general Getting Around section earlier in the book.

From Shimonoseki there is a ferry crossing to Moji-ko, on Kyushu, every 15 to 30 minutes between 6.15 am and 10 pm (Y250). (Note that Moji-ko is near Moji city, and some distance from Shin Moji-ko.) There has been a local car ferry from Shimo that crossed to Kokura, very close to the ferry terminal. Ask at Shimo station if it still runs and if so which buses pass near the dock.

Road

By road eastward from Shimonoseki toward Osaka/Kyoto and Tokyo there are three main routes, north along the San-in kaigan coast (Route 191 out of Shimo), south along the San-yo kaigan coast (Route 2 out of Shimo), and the Chugoku expressway (kosoku-doro).

The San-in route has only a few specific places to visit, like Hagi and Matsue, but it is one of the most pleasant areas in Japan to travel through for seascapes, peaceful landscapes of farms, mountains (generally low), and even sand dunes. It is quite flat along the coast so can be particularly recommended for cyclists; traffic is not too heavy either. At the end of the San-in region it is easy to get to Kyoto and other attractions of central Honshu or you can take a ferry to Hokkaido.

The San-yo route is quite pleasant and scenic as far as Hiroshima, with many hilly roads, large farmhouses and some interesting side trips. East of Hiroshima is heavily populated and industrialised and road traffic moves at snail's pace most of the way to Kyoto. (I made the trip by motorcycle in less-crowded 1971 and the Hiroshima-Kyoto trip took 17 hours almost non-stop.) However, the attractions of Okayama, Kurashiki and Himeji are on this road and there are some views of the Inland Sea.

A 'compromise' route can be followed by travellers who do not have the option of going by one coast in one direction and returning via the other; and that is to cut across country one or more times using any of several road or rail links across the island. The width at the end of the island is approximately 70-110 km, as the crow flies.

The quickest road route eastward would be via the Chugoku expressway to Osaka; there it connects directly with the Meishin expressway past Kyoto to Nagoya, where you can continue (without stopping) via the Tomei expressway to Tokyo. The scenery along the expressway is attractive but not outstanding. For hitchhikers in a hurry it is the only way.

Buses

Buses are not used very much in Japan for long-distance inter-city travel (unlike Korea). They can be useful at Shimo for getting out of the city to start hitching. There is a direct bus service (seven per day) from Shimo station to the Akiyoshi area, described earlier.

Hitching

As described at the beginning of this book, hitching is easy in Japan and one of the best ways to travel, both for economy and for experiencing the kindness of the Japanese people. The following section details the starting points for hitching out of Shimo.

Eastbound – south shore The road along the south shore is labelled Route 9, but it runs only a few km before becoming Route 2 and doesn't resume a separate identity until Ogori, 60 km away. Route 2 to Osaka (where it ends) is more direct than Route 191, and takes in Hiroshima, Kirishima/ Okayama and Himeji, but travellers should be aware that this road, along with Route 1 from Osaka to Tokyo, is one of the busiest in Japan and is almost one continuous urban area from Ogori to Tokyo. The road does pass along much of the Inland Sea, but the few glimpses of it from the road are not memorable. All roads in Japan, except expressways, have an absurd maximum speed of 60 km/h, though actual averages are much lower than this because of an endless succession of red lights and urban areas. To make time, though without views, it is fastest to hitch at night with a truck.

Expressway/Route 2 The Chugoku Kosokudoro (expressway) runs from Shimo east to Osaka. The expressway from

Shimo also runs west to Kyushu across the graceful Kanmon-ohashi suspension bridge. Eastbound, Route 2 curves to meet the coast and generally runs parallel to it as far as Osaka, passing virtually the only non-built-up area of the entire road, with good views of countryside, farms, etc. The expressway, on the other hand, saves time in terms of distance covered. To hitch on the expressway or Route 2 toward Kyushu (via either bridge or tunnel), the best starting point is in a maze of interchanges – a map of which resembles the result of an explosion in a spaghetti factory. To reach it from Shimo station, take a bus from stand 2, but be sure that it is not an express: the destination is Mukuno-tunnel, where you get off and continue walking in the same direction. This should lead to a junction identified with directions signs to Kawatana (left) and Hiroshima/expressway/ tunnel (right): follow the road to the right and another set of signs will come into view. Traffic heading left to the expressway will subsequently split into streams going west to Kyushu and east toward Yama-guchi, while that to the right will branch off either towards the tunnel to Kyushu or to Hiroshima. Position yourself for the stream you want; there is one place that catches all traffic, but it is very busy so you must have a very large sign with the name of your destination in kanji, and there must be a clear place for a car to stop safely. It might be advisable to make a choice between the expressway or Route 2 tunnel, as the approach road to each offers better stopping places than the point where they divide. If you want only the tunnel, it would be better to stand near the entrance (quite close to Mukuno bus stop).

For those hitching to the Shimo area, a bus from Mukuno bus stop goes into the station, but quite infrequently during the day. If you are coming through the tunnel you should try to get out of the vehicle as soon as possible after clearing the tunnel exit. If crossing the bridge, get off at or before the Shimonoseki/Dannoura exit and scramble back to the road that leads back to the youth hostel.

SAN-IN COAST

The northern San-in Kaigan coast is relatively undeveloped, mostly lush green farms (in summer) and prosperous-looking farm houses, plus coastal scenery. It is a much more pleasant area to travel through than the heavily industrialised southern coast (San-yo Kaigan). Compared with the southern coast however, it has few specific attractions.

The area between Shimonoseki and Hagi was quite off the beaten track until comparatively recently. In the early '70s there were still many houses made of mud and wattle. Along the main road they have now all been replaced by wood or concrete buildings with aluminium doors and windows – vastly more practical and comfortable, but yet another Japanese tradition has gone.

There are several picturesque fishing villages along the way and many views of the sea.

NAGATO

Off the end of Omi-shima island, near Nagato-shi city, is a picturesque promontory of rocks, including twin pillars that jut more than 40 metres straight out of the sea. Access is by bus, and a cruise around the island is available.

The caves of Akiyoshi (described earlier) are accessible from Nagato. You can go by train to Mine and to Akiyoshi by bus, then carry on from there to Hagi (north coast) or Mine, Yamaguchi, etc, on the south coast.

HAGI

The city of Hagi is a very popular holiday destination for the Japanese, partly for what there is to see, but also for its historical associations, particularly those leading to the Meiji restoration. The latter is invisible to foreigners of course, so the importance of Hagi is a little less for non-Japanese, but it is worth a look around.

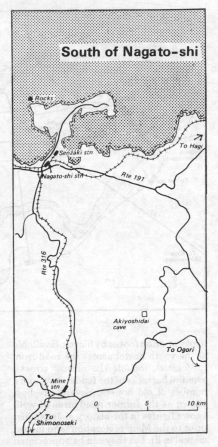

The attractions of Hagi result from its having been the castle town of the Mori clan. The castle stood from 1604 to 1871, when it was torn down – unfortunately, because the remaining walls and moats are quite picturesque.

Visitors will be most interested in the castle fortifications, the grounds (which now make up Shizuki-koen park, and house its historical museum as well as a shrine), and a lovely beach. Hagi is built on the delta of several rivers. The nearby attractions, good for an hour or two of

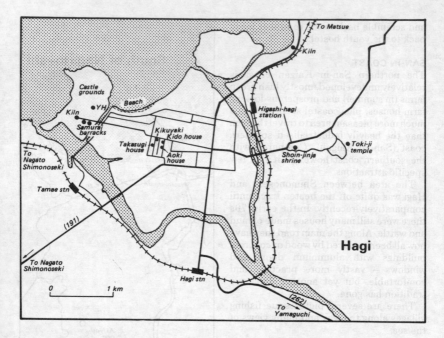

exploration on foot or by bicycle (available at the youth hostel across the road from the castle), include the narrow streets, samurai barracks of the feudal days, and a number of old houses. Several are best known as the former residences of well-known figures in the history of Japan just prior to the Meiji restoration (and instrumental in it), but they can be appreciated just for their appearance as well. There are three potteries near the castle, Shiroyama, Shogetsu, and Hagi-jo.

The castle area is closest to Tamae station, one stop beyond Hagi station. Buses are also available, the closest stop being Shizuku-bashi.

Shoin Shrine

In the grounds of Shoin-jinja is a building that served as the village school where Shoin Yoshida taught; he was loyal to the emperor and was executed by the Tokugawa government.

Near Shoin-jinja is *Toko-ji*, the family temple of the Mori family and famous for 494 stone lanterns erected by their subordinates over several generations.

The Shoin-jinja area is easily reached by bus from Higashi-Hagi station (Nakano-kuru stop).

Myojin-ike lake Built as a retreat by the Mori, this lake outside the city is connected to the ocean and follows its tides.

Potteries There are four potteries in the vicinity of Shoin-jinja: Miwa, Shodo, Renzokan and Hosen.

Other

Of lesser interest is a pretty little shrine to the right of the road when going into Hagi from Hagi station. I was interested in a stone turtle statue bearing a commemorative stone on its back, a common sight in Korea but almost unknown in Japan. It may have some relationship to the Korean potters who were brought here in the early 1600s by the Tokugawa following an invasion of Korea, or it may indicate earlier ties with that country.

Places to Stay

There are numerous hotels, ryokan, etc, in Hagi, as well as a youth hostel near the castle. Across the street from it is a Koku-minshu-kusha.

East from Hagi

From Hagi to Tottori the coast is quite scenic with a succession of towns and cities, some fishing villages, and many farms. It is one of the better areas for observing unpolluted rural Japan. Foreigners are quite rare so the people are even nicer than usual.

Shimane-ken

Masuda

In the somewhat industrial city of Masuda, the attractions are *Manpukuji* and *Iko-ji*, both of which have noted landscape gardens.

From Masuda, Route 9 and the train cross diagonally to Yamaguchi via Tsuwano, while Route 191 and rail continue along the coast to Hagi and Shimonoseki at the western tip of Honshu.

Tsuwano

The old castle town of Tsuwano has long been known for carp, and recently for steam as well. The former, come in a variety of beautiful colours, number in the tens of thousands, and measure up to a metre in length. They may been found in ponds of most business establishments, hotels, etc, and even in the channels passing beside the road in the Tonomachi district of the town.

Inari-jinja is the best known shrine in Tsuwano, and is noted for its huge, bright-orange torii gate. Near the shrine is a museum (Kyodo-kan) of historical items.

The other reason for fame is that Tsuwano is the north-east terminus of a steam train run from Ogori, Yamaguchi-ken, one of only two surviving in Japan. Further details are given in the section on rail transport in the introductory Getting Around chapter.

Mt Sanbe

The next major attraction is inland from Oda. The mountain can be climbed easily in an hour from Sanbe-onsen (hot-spring resort), which is accessible by bus (12 per day) from Oda. Nearby is a large lava field and a lake, Ukinu-no-ike.

Easily reached from the area is the Dangyo-kei ravine that stretches four km along the Yagami-kawa river. The ravine is six km from Imbara, on the railway line passing close to Sanbeonsen; a bus runs toward the ravine from Imbara.

MATSUE

Picturesquely located between a lake (Shinji) and a lagoon (Naka-umi), the city of Matsue is the proud owner of one of the few original castles surviving in Japan, a small but attractive structure dating from 1611.

Near the castle is *bukei yashiki*, an old samurai residence that has been well preserved and opened to the public. Nearby is the former residence of Lafcadio Hearn, an English writer who lived in Matsue during the 1890's and wrote a number of books about the Japan of that day, many of which are still readily available as reprints. Close to his old house is *Yakumo-kinenkan*, a museum of manuscripts and other memorabilia.

Kaga

A stretch of picturesque coast may be found at Kaga, north of Matsue. The most interesting part is the cave Kagano-kukedo, which is entered by boat; the opening is small but the interior is large. Access is by bus from Matsue, taking a little over an hour.

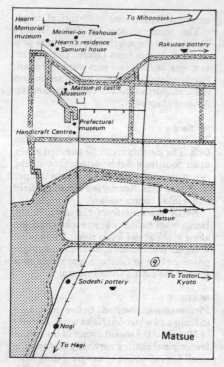

Matsue

Fudoki Hill

The Matsue area was one of the regions settled before the Yamato conquest of the Japanese islands. There is an archaeological site of an ancient village to the south of Matsue at Fudoki-no-oka, with a museum displaying artefacts of this old civilisation. Inquire locally for information on how to get to the museum.

Izumo-taisha

Not far from Matsue is the oldest Shinto shrine in Japan, Izumo, which ranks only behind the grand shrines of Ise in importance. It is most easily reached from Matsue by the Ichihata private railway line; the 40 km trip takes less than an hour, and 21 trains a day run from Matsue-onsen to Izumo-taisha-mae station. You can also go by JNR, transferring at Izumo-

shi (city) to Taisha. In either case, turn right when leaving the station of either line and walk up the hill. If travelling by the private line note the tall trees grown as windbreaks on the windswept flat peninsula.

Typical of shrines in Japan, although the site is ancient, the buildings are comparatively recent and date from 1874 (the main shrine from 1744). They are built in the oldest style of architecture known in Japan and are quite imposing. The grounds are covered with tall old trees and the shrine is backdropped by Yakumo hill. There is a museum in the grounds.

By the old (lunar) calendar, the month of October was the time when all the Shinto gods met at Izumo, so the month was known in the Izumo area as *Kamiarizuki* (month with gods) and as *Kaminazuki* (month without gods) everywhere else in Japan.

Hirata

Between Matsue-onsen and Izumo is Hirata, where *Gakuen-ji* temple is noted for the brilliant autumn colours of trees in its grounds.

Inasano-hama

This is a beach close to Izumo-taisha shrine, about two km from the stations; swimming is good. About 6.5 km northwest of the beach is Cape Hino-misaki, site of ancient Hinomisaki shrine and a lighthouse, and with very pretty coastal scenery.

Buses run to both the beach and the cape. It's about 35 minutes to the latter from the station.

Tachikue Gorge

Near Izumo-shi is the pretty one-km-long Tachikue-kyo, formed of cliffs, picturesquely eroded rock and basalt columns. It is easily reached from Izumi-shi station by train to Tachikue-kyo station in 30 minutes.

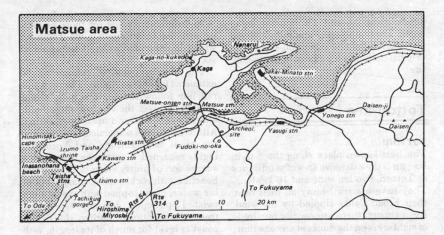

Festivals

Annual festivals at *Izumo-taisha* are on 14-16 May, 11-17 October (lunar calendar), and 22-3 November. October is also very popular for weddings at Izumo, so it may be possible to see brides in gorgeous kimonos; with the shrine as a backdrop, you should get some terrific photos.

At Matsue, festivals are held in the first half of April (Castle Festival), and the last third of July (Matsue-odori dance and fireworks display); there is also the summer festival of *Tenmangu jinja* shrine.

On 16 August (Toro-nagashi), many paper lanterns on tiny boats are released on Shinji-ko lake. In the middle of the month is the Obon festival, and *Takeuchi-jinja* shrine festival is at the end. There are also various festivals on 3, 5 and 6 November.

NEAR MATSUE

Oki Islands

These islands, almost due north of Matsue, are known for their high steep cliffs and generally wild scenery. Access is by boat from near Matsue (Sakaiminato and Nanarui) to Saigocho on the main island. There are two youth hostels on Dogo-shima, and one each on the three lesser islands.

Mt Daisen

For a considerable distance along the way the form of Mt Daisen is visible. It is interesting because although it presents a conical face from the west, it is seen as a succession of smaller peaks from the north or south. It may be climbed quite easily and offers a good view over the coast (including the Oki Islands) and nearby peaks. In clear weather it is possible to see Shikoku to the south. The climb begins at Daisen Temple, which is easily reached by bus from Daisenguchi station. The 5.5 km climb takes about 3½

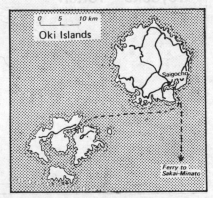

hours going up and 1½ hours coming down. The temple was founded in 718 and was once huge and powerful, but all its original buildings have been destroyed by fire.

Tottori-ken

TOTTORI

The best-known place along the San-in Kaigan is the extensive area of sand dunes at Tottori, two km wide and 16 km long. They have a stark beauty all their own, their broad flanks rippled by the wind. Even though there are usually hundreds of sightseers on the dunes at any one time, they are swallowed in its expanse and the energetic can walk beyond the area usually tromped by the hordes. In the heat of the summer it is advisable to have a canteen of water or some soft drinks as the air is very dehydrating. The dunes are slightly to the east of town; the entrance is easily reached by bus from Tottori.

In the city of Tottori itself, *Tottori Mingei-hakubutsukan* (Folk Art Museum) may be of interest, along with the garden of *Kannon-in* temple.

An alternative route for those headed toward the south coast is via Tsuyama which is described in the Okayama-ken section.

The San-in coast is considered to extend as far east as Amino. The road and rail line follow the coast closely, giving good views over the sea to contrast with spreads of farms and inland mountains. Although there is no particular attraction, the areas near Kasumi and Yoroi are highly regarded. Typical sea scenery is a succession of pretty views of small white beaches with rocks jutting sharply out of the water, many topped with one or more twisted 'patented Japanese-type' pine trees. As mentioned earlier, the San-in coast is level for much of its length, with relatively gentle grades where they do appear. Because of the sparse (by Japanese standards) traffic the area can be particularly recommended to cyclists.

TOYOOKA

In the vicinity of this small city in northern Hyogo-ken, are the well known basalt caves of Gembudo. Unlike limestone caves, these were not formed by water erosion that dissolved the rock, but by a lava flow that cooled on the surface. Some

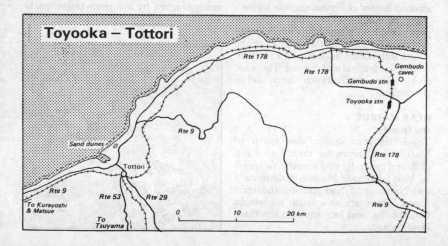

Toyooka – Tottori

still-liquid lava escaped, leaving caves or tunnels within the solid mass. Visible inside the caves are pillars six to nine metres in height, of five, six, seven and eight faces, some parallel, others growing at odd angles. There are five caves or grottoes, 23 to 30 metres or so in depth. They are located not far from Gembudo station, 5.3 km out of Toyooka.

AMANOHASHIDATE

About 30 km west of Maizuru, and almost due north of Kobe (in northern Kyoto-fu) lies one of the Japanese 'Big Three' scenic places traditionally regarded as the finest views in Japan. (The other two are Matsushima near Sendai and Miyajima near Hiroshima).

The cause of this excitement is a sand bar that stretches 3.6 km across peaceful Miyazu bay. It varies from 35 to 110 metres in width and has many twisted pine trees of the 'picturesque Japanese' variety.

The best view is obtained from Kasamutsu Park to the north-west, accessible by cable-car or from Ochitoge (pass) on a local road to Tango-Omiya. The former

can be reached by bus to Ichinomiya from Amanohashidate station (15 minutes), or ferry from Amanohashidate or Miyazu (15 and 25 minutes respectively). The traditional way to look at the scene is by bending over and looking at it through your legs!

It should be noted that the scenery is in fact, not terribly spectacular, and the modern generation of Japanese do not fall into raptures at the sight. It's worth a look for those passing through but not worth a special trip for itself alone.

OKU-TANGO PENINSULA

A route taken by few travellers leads around the Oku-tango (or Yosa) peninsula, which begins at Amanohashidate. Friends of mine described a very picturesque fishing village, Ine, about 20 km from Miyazu and built right to the water's edge around a semicircular bay.

WAKASA BAY

This area is north of Kyoto. The description begins just west of Tsuruga. (Tsuruga, like Maizuru, is a port for ferries to

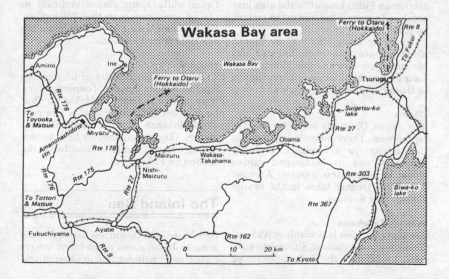

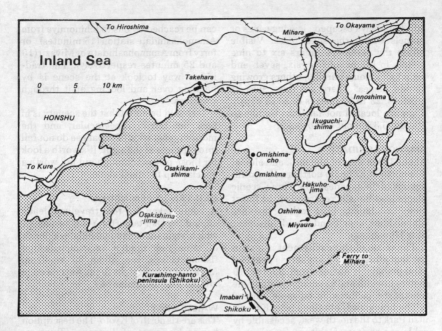

Hokkaido, and is described under the section on Fukui-ken; while the area just south of Tsuruga is covered in the section on Kyoto).

Travelling along Route 27 or by rail along the coast between Tsuruga and Maizuru, you can see the Mikata Five Lakes. They can all be viewed from the top of Baijo Hill near Lake Suigetsu.

Obama

The city of Obama is noted for Wakasa lacquerware. There are several old temples in the city; to a foreigner, probably *Mantokuji* and its landscaped garden would be of greatest interest. A cruise boat from Obama takes in the nearby scenic coast Sotomo.

Wakasa-Takahama

Another good view is available at Wakasa-Takahama, especially at Shiroyama-koen park, 1.6 km from the station. Stretching for two km north-west of the city are the Otomi cliffs, rising almost vertically in places, sometimes more than 250 metres. Boat cruises lasting about two hours are available from Takahama.

Maizuru

This is an industrial city of no touristic interest but it is the port of departure for a ferry service to Otaru on Hokkaido (four boats a week). The terminal is located a short distance north of Nishi-Maizuru station. (Details on another boat service to Otaru from Tsuruga is described in the section on Fukui-ken.)

The Inland Sea

Seto Naikai, the Inland Sea, is one of those areas in Japan about which travel writers have traditionally written in superlatives.

The fact is, that while there *are* many very lovely views around this body of water, it has changed greatly since it first came to the notice of western eyes. Many fishing villages have been replaced by modern industries – substituting 'progress' and pollution for once idyllic scenes. The waters are filled with large numbers of ships and the peace and serenity of 20 to 30 years ago has gone. Anyone arriving with the expectation of charming views at every turn is doomed to disappointment, but time spent seeking out some or all of the places mentioned below will be rewarded.

The book *The Inland Sea* by Japan expert Donald Richie gives a good description of the area and is beautifully illustrated (though it probably outdoes present reality).

Along the north shore of the sea, good views are available (from east to west) near Okayama/Kurashiki, Onomichi, Fukuyama and Itsukushima, as well as at Shimonoseki which marks the western end of the sea. (Each vantage point is described under the appropriate city.) The most beautiful maritime views are in the area bounded on the east by Shodo Island and on the west by Tono-no-ura (Honshu) and Tadotsu (Shikoku).

In addition to the numerous 'shuttle' ferries between Honshu and Shikoku that pass through various parts of the Inland Sea, the overnight ferry from Beppu to Kobe and Osaka (leaving Beppu at 9 pm) passes through some of the most scenic parts of the sea in the early morning. As the sky is light as early as 4.30 am, early risers can have a couple of hours of sightseeing before the boat docks at Takamatsu at 7.30 am (and more after it leaves). It reaches Kobe at 11.50 am and Osaka at 1.10 pm. The boat which leaves Osaka at 9 pm and Kobe at 10.30 pm reaches Imabari at 5.40 am, so this trip would provide some views of the western part of the Inland Sea by daylight although you would have passed through the 'best' part before sunrise.

There are a number of ferries and hydrofoils across the Inland Sea between Honshu and Shikoku. Terminals are shown on the map and the frequency and travel time information is given in the write-up for the places on Shikoku (not Honshu).

The best way to enjoy the mood of the Inland Sea (if you have time to spare) is to pick an island or two and spend some time there. Some have youth hostels and an island of any size is sure to have a minshuku; an isolated area is the best place to enjoy the homely pleasures of minshuku accommodation.

The islands described fall into three groups: Awaji-Shima; Shodo-Shima and nearby islands; and Innoshima and nearby islands.

AWAJI-SHIMA

This is the largest island in the Inland Sea and one of the most densely populated

islands in Japan. It is relatively flat and agricultural, holding no fantastic visual delights. It serves as a bridge between the Kobe area (via Akashi) and Shikoku.

Puppet Theatre

Awaji appears to be the home of the oldest puppet theatre in Japan; more ancient though less famous than the Bunraku of Osaka. Short (about 30 minutes) performances of puppet plays are given daily at *Ningyo-za*, the small puppet theatre by the ferry dock at Fukura at 11 am between 1 March and 30 November. At other times you must be content with a look at the large number of puppets on display around the walls.

It was feared that the puppetry tradition would die out completely, as the 15 performers at Fukura are the only ones left on Awaji and their average age is close to 70. However a renaissance seems to be in action, so there may be a return to the golden days of the start of the Meiji era, when there were 48 theatres on Awaji.

Naruto Whirlpools

The whirlpools are almost next door to Fukura. They are at their mightiest at high and low tide, when the water swirls into or out of the Inland Sea through the narrow (1.3 km) Naruto Strait between Awaji and Shikoku. The rapids run in one direction at high tide and in the opposite at full ebb. It is necessary to catch their either extreme to see the whirlpools at their greatest (over 20 metres across); tide tables are posted at touristed locales, and places of accommodation should also have information. There is a lookout over the strait, accessible by toll road, a little to the north of Fukura and near the pier of the giant bridge going across the strait. Cruise boats from Fukura travel very close to the whirlpools, though without danger.

Other

Other sightseeing on Awaji-shima includes the beaches and sea views of Goshikihama

and Kei-no-Matsubara. The former (meaning 'five-coloured beach') has multi-coloured pebbles. Each stretches several km and both are accessible by bus from Sumoto in less than an hour.

Places to Stay

There are several hotels, ryokan and minshuku around the island as well as a temple youth hostel at Sumoto, the major town.

Getting There

From Kobe, ferries cross to Sumoto; and from Akashi, ferries are available to Iwaya. At the south end ferries cross from Nandan to Naruto and from Anaga to Kame-ura (both destinations on Shikoku).

The graceful Naruto Ohashi suspension bridge stretches between Fukura (Awaji-shima) and Shikoku. It should be open in mid-1985. A bridge will eventually link Awaji with Honshu, near Kobe.

SHODO-SHIMA

Everyone who visits Shodo Island has a good word for it. It is sufficiently off the beaten track not to be over-run with tourists but it has adequate accommodation and travel facilities as well as lots of beautiful scenery.

The main attraction of the island is Kanka-kei Gorge, near the east end. A cable-car descends through the most scenic part. There are also many fine views of unspoilt countryside, tidy terraced paddies up hillsides, mountains, farmers and fishermen; as well as quarries that supplied the giant stones for Osaka Castle.

Other sights include groves of olive trees (in the south and central part of the island); a replica of a Greek temple (at Tayo-no-Oka Heiwa-koen) overlooking the sea and beautiful scenery; and a monkey park (friendly simians in the lower park, unfriendly higher up) where even a short-time visitor can get a feel for the social organisation within their community.

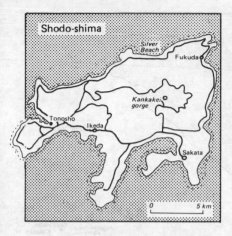

Shodo-shima

Silver Beach
Fukuda
Kankakei gorge
Tonosho
Ikeda
Sakata

0   5 km

Places to Stay

Accommodation is usually no problem as there are many ryokan plus two youth hostels. Assistance in finding a room is available at the information centre at both Tonosho and Sakata.

Getting Around

Getting around Shodo is no problem, as buses run regularly – both special and sightseeing coaches and scheduled public transport. The usual starting point is Tonosho, but tour buses also leave from Sakata and possibly from other ports served by ferries. Generally it seems there is a tour bus waiting for each ferry arrival. More than one person has liked the relaxed pace of Shodo life and stayed for several days. You can get a good idea of its attractions by taking a bus tour on arrival, then explore by public bus afterward.

Ferries connect the towns of Tonosho, Ikeda, Sakata and Fukudo (on Shodo) with Takamatsu, Ono, Okayama, Hinase, Himeji, Kobe and Osaka. Check the schedules in *Jikokuhyo*, or get help at an information centre or travel agency.

OTHER ISLANDS

From Shodo-shima you can island-hop via Toyo-shima to Uno, near Okayama. Other good, really out-of-the-way islands (some are described below) are situated between Imabari (Shikoku) and Mihara (Honshu) and are accessible (along with nearby islands) from both places. Anyone really interested in this type of exploring might try to obtain a copy of Nancy Phelan's book *A Pillow of Grass*.

Ikuguchi

The island offers views of orange groves, shrines, temples and most important, an atmosphere of rural Japan. Besides the youth hostel overlooking a quiet village there is also ryokan and minshuku.

Innoshima

This island is also worth a visit but has no youth hostel. Ikuguchi Island is 'next-door' however.

Omishima

Fifteen km off the north coast of the Kurushima-hanto Peninsula, Omishima is noted for the *Oyamazumi-jinja* shrine, dedicated to the guardian gods of sailors. In historic times it was visited by many warriors off to battle, and a large amount of the finest armour was donated in supplication for good fortune in battle. As a result, 80% of all the armour in Japan that has survived and been given the rating 'national treasure' or 'important cultural property' belongs to this shrine. Most of it is on display, unlike other museums which only show a small sample of their collections. The shrine is near Miyaura, the town where the ferries dock.

Getting to Korea

There are three sailings a week in each direction by the Kampu ferry *Pukwan* between Shimonoseki and Pusan in Korea. It leaves from Shimo on Mondays, Wednesdays and Fridays at 5 pm; and from Pusan on Tuesdays and Thursdays

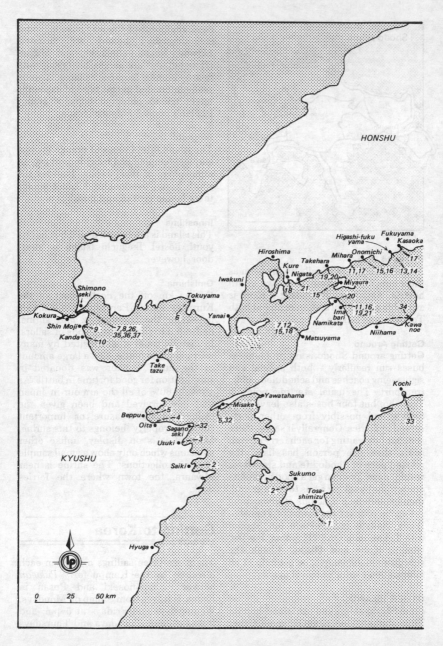

Ports with Ferry Services

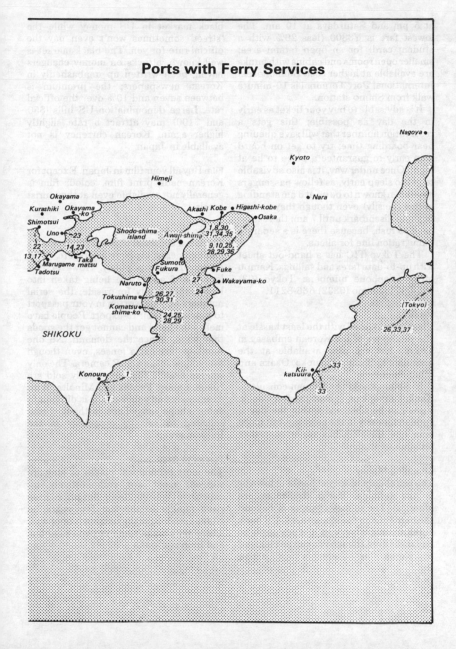

at 5 pm and Saturdays at 10 am. The lowest fare is Y8800 (less 20% with a student card) for an open tatami area; smaller open rooms and cabins with bunks are available at higher cost. Shimonoseki International Port Terminal is 10-minute walk from Shimo station.

It is advisable to buy your ticket as early in the day as possible; this gets a reservation number that will save queuing near boarding time; try to get on board ship early to guarantee a place to lie at night. Once under way, it is also advisable to get to sleep early, as fellow passengers have been known to be up at 3 am standing in line (noisily) even though they cannot begin to disembark until 7 am; there is no need to rush, because there is a separate immigration line for aliens.

The Tokyo TIC has a hand-out sheet with up-to-date fares and sailings. Kampu office telephone numbers: Tokyo (03) 567-0971; Shimo (0832) 666-8211.

Visas

Visas are obtained with the least hassle at the visa annex of the Korean embassy in Tokyo, but are also available at the consulate at Shimo, Fukuoka, Osaka and other cities.

In Shimonoseki the Korean consulate, Kankoku ryojikan, is near the ferry dock. Visas *can* be obtained within the day if applied for early in the morning, but more than one traveller has reported rather brusque treatment.

Changing Money

You can change money at banks in town or in the terminal itself; the rates are identical. The money changer is beyond the barrier from the lounge area. US bank notes are available, and it is advisable to buy these even though yen can be changed in Korea, as there is an active black market in US money while the 'street' sometimes won't even pay the official rate for yen. The black market is well known, attacks on money changers having been written up unabashedly in Korean newspapers; the premium is between seven and 10% over the official rate. Large denomination US bills ($50 and $100) may attract a rate slightly higher again. Korean currency is not available in Japan.

Film Buy all your film in Japan. Except for Korean-made print film, colour film is generally not available even at the tourist hotels.

Selling goods in Korea

There is a continual demand for Japanese-made cameras, tape-recorders, etc, (hair-dryers are also popular). However if it looks as if goods are being taken into Korea specifically for resale, the serial numbers may be written in your passport to guarantee their re-export. People have money to spend and cannot get the goods they want, hence the demand. No one wants to buy extra lenses, even though everyone wants an SLR camera. The only camera brands that are readily sold are Nikon, Canon, Pentax and Minolta. With a camera round your neck, it is difficult to enter shops anywhere without being solicited to sell it, especially in the Itaewon area.

Places to Stay

The most economical places to stay are *yogwon*; most are comparatively inexpensive (W1500-2000), but prices have risen rapidly in the last few years, so Korea is no longer the bargain it once was. There are always some yogwon near bus and train stations.

Top: Festival wagon (*yatai*) at Takayama Matsuri festival
Left: Furukawa Matsuri is famous for the procession of large drums through the streets at night
Right: Sharing

Top: Kintai-kyo (Bridge of the Brocade Sash), Iwakuni (Hiroshima-ken)
Bottom: Hakuro-jo (White Egret) Castle, Himeji, Japan's finest

Shikoku

Shikoku is the fourth main island of the Japanese group. It is generally rural and gets bypassed by most travellers, but it has a couple of unique attractions that could be of interest if you have a little extra time.

On Shikoku you are almost sure to see large numbers of people dressed in white, making pilgrimages to the 88 temples related to the priest Kobo-Daishi. It should not be difficult to locate the temples as they are marked by road signs (in Japanese only), but few are outstanding.

Kagawa-ken

NARUTO
The great whirlpools of the Naruto Strait have already been described in the section on Awaji-shima. From the Shikoku side an excellent view is available from Naruto Park on Oge-shima Island (eight km north-east of Naruto city); buses run from Naruto station. The park is also accessible from Awaji-shima by ferry from Anaga (a little above Fukura), and there is also a ferry service from Fukura.

TOKUSHIMA
This city is known for a crazy dance, puppets and a fine garden. One of the most famous festivals in Japan is the Awa-odori (15 to 18 August) when large numbers of celebrants dressed in traditional costume dance in the city streets through much of the night.

Puppet Theatre
Along with Awaji-shima and Osaka, Tokushima has a tradition of puppet theatre. Performances are usually given by farmers, so they are more likely to be seen after harvest time and before planting; make inquiries locally.

Tokushima Park
This park contains a garden that was part of the mansion associated with Tokushima Castle (now ruined) and dates from 1586. It is a landscape garden typical of the Momoyama period. The park is 400 metres east of the station.

Other
East from Tokushima you can go to Anabuki station and then take a bus (15 minutes) north-east to an interesting natural phenomenon. Pillars of earth have been formed by erosion and stand 12 to 18 metres high. They are similar to the Hoodoos in Alberta (Canada) and other formations in the Tyrol.

South from Tokushima lies Anan, beside Tachibana Bay. It offers a good view of many islands compared by locals to the famous Matsushima (near Sendai).

From a point one km south of Mugi, Yasakahama beach stretches for about 10 km.

Getting There
The ferry between Tokyo and Kokura (Kyushu), every two days stops at Tokushima en route each way. For details refer to the general Getting Around section earlier in the book.

Locally, ferries run to Kobe, Osaka and

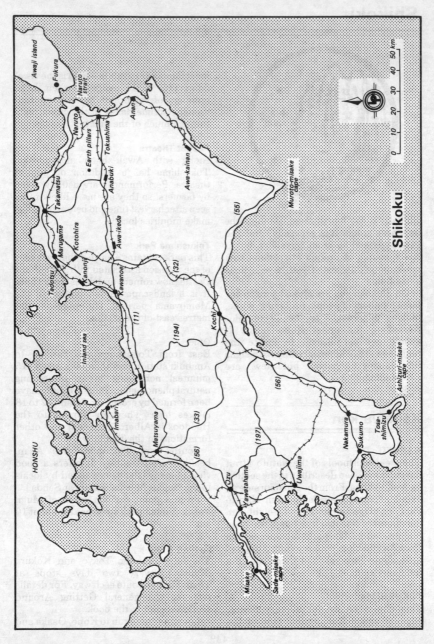

Shikoku

Fuke-ko (near Wakayama, south of Osaka). Between Tokushima and Fuke-ko there are 11 boats a day in each direction. The fare is Y1370 and the trip takes about 2½ hours. Between Tokushima and Osaka (Tempozan) there are six boats a day in each direction (Y4400, two hours); and between Tokushima and Osaka (Minato-ko ferry futo) there are three a day (Y1920, 3½ hours). Between Tokushima and Kobe (Higashi Kobe, Aoki port) there are five boats a day in each direction (Y1920 minimum, three hours); and between Tokushima and Kobe (Naka-tottei pier, central Kobe) there are four a day, both ways (Y4400, two hours).

Komatsushima Between Komatsushima-ko and Wakayama-ko there are 16 boats a day in each direction. The fare is Y3300 for the fastest service (1 hour 15 minutes), Y1650 minimum, for the slower (2 hours).

Between Komatsushima-ko and Osaka (Minato-ko ferry futo) there are two ferries a day in each direction (Y2000, 4 hours). Most departure and arrival times are very inconvenient.

From Komatsushima you can continue down to Cape Muroto at the far south-east tip of the island.

Konoura

The daily boat between Kobe and Tosa-Shimizu (south-west Shikoku) stops en route both ways at Konoura. Details are given in the general Getting Around section.

NORTH-WEST FROM NARUTO

From Naruto to Takamatsu, the main road runs parallel to the coast and offers several pretty views. (Lookouts are provided by the road.) The rafts visible in the water are used to grow edible seaweed not pearls.

TAKAMATSU

Probably the most enjoyable city on

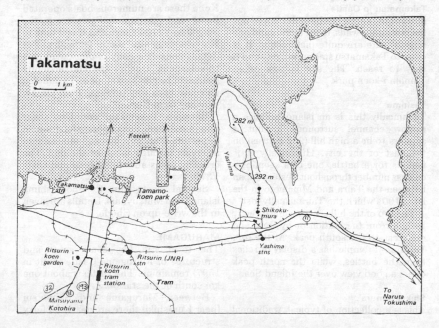

Shikoku, Takamatsu features one of the finest gardens in Japan as well as a number of other attractions.

Things to See
Ritsurin-koen Garden
This is one of the finest gardens in Japan, superior (in my eyes) to at least two of the 'Big Three' gardens – those at Mito and Okayama – and at least the equal of Kenroku-en in Kanazawa. It is built around an interconnected series of ponds and comprises a large variety of views, taking advantage of a large hill and natural forests in its plan. It dates from the mid-1600s.

A folk-craft museum in the park features an excellent collection of hand-crafted utensils, etc. It has two sections, one for Shikoku crafts, the other for those from other regions of Japan.

The garden is easily reached by tram; the stop is Ritsurin-koen.

Takamatsu-jo Castle
Most of the castle has been destroyed but the remaining walls, three turrets and one original gate are quite picturesque. It is close to Takamatsu station and pier and is easy to reach. The site is now called Tamamo-koen park.

Yashima
Technically this is an island because a narrow channel surrounds it, but it appears to be a high hill (292 metres) on the east of the city. Historically it is famous for a battle, one of a seemingly endless number throughout western Japan between the Taira and Minamoto in the late 1100s which the Taira usually lost.

The top of the hill is accessible directly by bus from the station or by tram and cable-car to the south peak. At the top, Yashima-ji temple has a display of relics from the battles, while the north peak offers a good view over the Inland Sea.

Shikoku-mura
This is a collection of typical, traditional buildings from various locations around the island and includes a vine suspension bridge of the type once common in isolated valleys. It is interesting if you have not visited such a village elsewhere, but could be a bit of a letdown if you have already been to Takayama.

Megishima Island
This tiny island (eight km in circumference) is famous in Japan through the children's story of Momotaro, a boy who cleaned out a pack of demons. It offers a good view of the Inland Sea; is only four km from the city, and easily reached by ferry.

Places to Stay
There are two youth hostels at Takamatsu, as well as ryokan, minshuku and hotels.

Getting There
Takamatsu is linked with several places on Honshu by ferry. Between Takamatsu (and Takamatsu higashi-ko) and Osaka/Kobe there are numerous boats operated by several companies. Fares are in the Y2000 to Y2700 range and travel time to Kobe is typically about 4½ hours. For details consult a copy of *Jikokuhyo* or a travel agent. One of the Osaka-Beppu overnight ferries also stops at Takamatsu en route each way (evening from Osaka, morning from Beppu).

Between Takamatsu and Uno (near Okayama) three lines operate ferries with departures at 20, 30 and 40 minute intervals through much of the day. The crossing takes about one hour and costs Y370.

Several boats run to Shodo-shima island from Matsuyama. Details are given in the write-up on Shodo.

MARUGAME
The town still has some gates and structures of Marugame Castle (built in 1597) remaining. The castle is about one km south of the station.

Between Marugame and Shimotsui (near Kurashiki) there are nearly 20 ferry crossings daily in each direction (Y630, 50 minutes). Between Marugame and Fukuyama there are four daily crossings each way (Y3000, 70 minutes).

TADOTSU

Tadotsu is interesting in *sakura* time when 10,000 trees in Toryo-koen park (1.5 km west of the station) are in bloom. The same park gives a good view over the sea and there is a good beach nearby.

Between Tadotsu and Fukuyama there are 15 boat crossings a day in each direction (Y1300, 1¾ hours). There is another route from Tadotsu to Honshu, landing at the port of Kasaoka but the boat hops to several islands en route; and of the several daily boats leaving in each direction only two permit through connections to the other side. The trip will take between 2½ hours and four hours, and costs Y1040.

KOTOHIRA & KOMPIRA-SAN

One of the best-known shrines in Japan is *Kotohira-gu*, on Kompira-san. It was, for a long time, the shrine for mariners who brought their boats nearby to be blessed. The shrine is on a high hill and is accessible only by a very long climb.

From the top there is a good view of the nearby countryside and there are several attractive shrine buildings, lanterns, etc, to see on the way up. These include paintings by Maruyama on the doors of the Shoin shrine (built 1659). However, this shrine is little different from a number of other old shrines in Japan, and the one km climb (it seems like 10) is not rewarded in proportion to the effort.

A single male wandering the back streets at night might get the impression that not all visitors to Kotohira come for religious experience. A woman in a dimly-lit window beckoned conspiringly to me and offered 'Korean women'. (Korean women are widely and mistakenly believed by many Japanese men to have no morals.)

Places to Stay

Of interest to anyone wanting to sample gracious ryokan living would be a small cluster of high-class (and price) inns at the foot of the hill where the path (and rows of souvenir stands) begins. Several have very ornate carved wooden panels, intimate gardens and other 'typical' Japanalia, that are in fact not often seen. Of minor interest, just a little to the south, is an old-style bridge with a decorative roof.

Getting There

Kotohira is easily reached from Takamatsu by Takamatsu-Kotohira Dentetsu railway, (the same line that can be taken from Takamatsu station to Ritsurin), or by bus, both taking about an hour.

KANONJI

An unusual sight here, visible from Kotohiki-koen park (1.5 km north of Kanonji station) is *Zenigata*, the huge outline of an ancient square-holed coin, with four kanji characters. It is made of a series of trenches in the ground and is 345 metres wide. It dates from the Kan-ei era (1624-44) and is explained by one source as having been made by the people as a reminder to their feudal lord that they would be careful not to waste money. (In view of the heavy taxes of those days, it was more likely a reminder to the lord not to waste *their* money.) A good view of the Inland Sea is available from *Kotohiki Hachiman* shrine.

KAWANOE

From here you can go east via Route 192 to Awa-Ikeda, to travel south by the following recommended route.

There is also a ferry service to Kobe (see the section on Nihama). You can also travel west, but the north coast of Shikoku is more industrialised and of little interest.

The following description follows a route south from Takamatsu.

NIHAMA

There is a regular ferry service between Nihama/Kawanoe and Kobe (Higashi-Kobe, Aoki port); one by day, one by night. Both boats from Kobe go first to Kawanoe, then to Nihama (7½, 9¾ hours respectively) same fare to both. In the return direction the day boat leaves Nihama, then goes to Kawanoe, while the night boat takes the opposite course before going to Kobe.

AWA-IKEDA TO KOCHI

South of Kompira-san lies some lovely inland scenery of the mountain and valley type. The starting point is Awa-Ikeda, not far below Kompira. You can either follow the main road (Route 32 and JNR), or branch inland for a while. Road and rail continue through the valley of the Yoshino river, passing the biggest gorge in Shikoku, which is particularly noteworthy for a 7.5 km stretch that includes two picturesque rock formations (Koboke and Oboke). There is a JNR station near each, both of which are accessible by train or bus from from Awa-Ikeda station. From a point two km north of Oboke, a boat is available for a descent of the river (30 to 40 minutes), ending about 3.5 km from Koboke station. A toll road links Oboke to Iyadani Gorge.

Iyadani-kei Gorge

This is a very lovely valley rather off the beaten track. The gorge extends from a point near Iyaguchi for about 45 km to Sugeoi. After only a few km a toll road branches west to rejoin Route 32. A short distance past the junction is the 45 metre-long Iya-no-kazura-bashi, the last surviving original vine suspension bridge of the type once common in the region. (They had the advantage of being easily cut to block the ingress of invaders.) The inhabitants of the valley are believed to be descendants of the Taira who survived the defeat at Yashima and retreated here, much as other Taira descendants are found in the Shirakawago area of Gifu-ken. (The

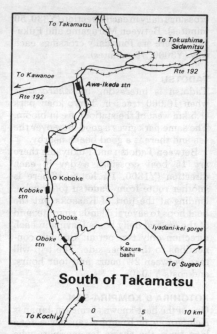

South of Takamatsu

0   5   10 km

bridge is of the same type as the one at Shikoku-mura in Takamatsu; those in a rush can be content with the latter.) There is a fee for crossing the bridge and the keeper becomes angry if you set foot on it without paying.

There are several buses daily running through the very pretty valley to Sugeoi. Beyond that the bus continues in a near-circle north to Sadamitsu station; an area where a foreigner is sure to be a rarity. From there it would be simple to return to Awa-Ikeda. Alternatively you can back-track to the toll road and out to Oboke to take the boat ride or just continue south toward Kochi.

Jofuki-ji

On the way to Kochi, Toyonaga station is the landmark for Jofuki-ji. Not a famous 'sight', it is a temple/youth hostel. The young priest speaks good English, is very friendly, well-travelled and happy to introduce guests to Zen, including meditation. Travellers have been known to stay here for weeks and it's easy to understand why – the surroundings are peaceful and beautiful. The temple is located high on the side of the valley among tall trees; it is 1.7 km from the station. Ask for directions on arrival.

Buraku-ji
Located one km north of Otaguchi station, this temple is noted for the architecture of its main hall *Yakushido*, which was built in 1151. It is a national treasure and a good example of Fujiwara architecture (897-1192 AD).

Ryugado Cave
Discovered in 1931, this cave contained clay dishes of a prehistoric people. It features stalagmites and stalactites and other sights of a typical limestone cave. It is accessible in 20 minutes by bus from Tosa-Yamada station.

Oshino
The Kochi area is noted historically for the raising of roosters with incredible tail plumage, sometimes more than six metres in length. The village of Oshino is the centre where such birds are raised (said to be a fading interest). Oshino is a district in the city of Nangoku, accessible from Gomen station. Local inquiries in the city (or possibly in Kochi) would be required to track down these birds.

KOCHI
The main attraction of Kochi is its five-storey castle, the present buildings dating from 1748. It gives an open view of the city and surrounding hills (which I found to be of quite limited interest).

Getting There
There is a daily overnight ferry in each direction between Kochi and Osaka and every second day between Kochi and Tokyo. The latter stops at Kii-Katsuura

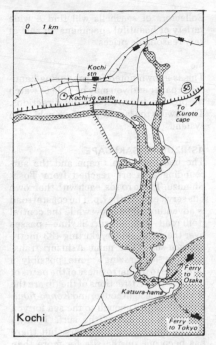

Kochi

(each direction) on the Kii-hanto peninsula south of Osaka and Nagoya. Details are given in the general Getting Around section earlier in the book.

Cape Muroto
From Kochi you can make a side-trip to Cape Muroto in the south-east (also accessible from Tokushima). The five km tip is known for its lighthouse and generally wild atmosphere. About 10 buses a day run to the cape from Kochi or nearby Harimaya-bashi. Close to the tip is *Higashi-dera* temple; it is worth a visit and is also a youth hostel.

Katsurahama Beach
Located 13 km south-east of Kochi, this beach offers white sand, good swimming and scenic rock formations. It is accessible in 35 minutes by bus from Kochi station.

Collectors of seashells will find a wide variety of beautiful specimens on sale at very reasonable prices.

Ino

This is a town noted for producing handmade paper and you may be able to watch the process. Inquire locally for directions. The town is the last stop of the Kochi tram system.

ASHIZURI-MISAKI CAPE

The beauties of this cape and the surrounding area are reached from Tosa-Shimizu. Three roads, each with their own bus service run to the tip. The coastal road is adventurously narrow while the central (toll) road – the Ashizuri Skyline – passes over the central ridge, skirting 433-metre *Shiraou-san*. (The name Ashizuri translates as 'leg grazing', quite possibly a reference to the narrowness of the paths of olden times.) Attractions of the tip are the wildness, the lighthouse, and *Kongo-fuku-ji* temple, close enough to the sea for you to hear the crash of the surf. Today's temple dates back 300 years, but there has been one on the site for more than 1100 years. The vegetation verges on tropical, with palms and banyan trees, and there are coral reefs to contrast with granite cliffs.

Ashizuri-misaki cape

Tosa-Shimizu

There is a daily boat between Tosa-Shimizu and Kobe, stopping en route (both ways) at Konoura on the south-east coast of Shikoku. Details are given in the general Getting Around section earlier in the book.

MINOKOSHI AREA

Continuing west from Tosa-Shimizu takes you to the coastal area of Minokoshi which contains some of the most beautiful views of all. Glass-bottom boats can be hired to see the colourful fish of the coral reefs. Beside the road are eroded limestone cliffs of wondrous shapes, which lead up to another strange rock formation at Tatsukushi. Tatsukushi means 'dragon skewers', a name taken from the number of slim cylinders of stone.

The Hall of Shells At Tatsukushi town there is a very interesting museum that displays nothing but seashells – about 50,000 of them including many rare and beautiful types. The building is modern and the displays are well planned. Many typhoons pass through this area and stir up the sea bottom, bringing large numbers of sea shells onto the shore.

NORTH FROM MINOKOSHI

The coast north from the Minokoshi area is also very scenic, although of the rias type (submerged fingers of land). There are views of the sea and the coast to the west and orange groves and other greenery to the east.

Sukumo

Ferries run between Sukumo and Saiki (Kyushu) usually six times a day (three hours, Y1600 minimum).

UWAJIMA

Uwajima has several other attractions including Uwajima Castle, which dates from 1665, and Atago-koen Park on a hill high enough to give a good view of the city and sea. The impressions of this city and the entire coast is of unusually lush foliage. There is a fine landscape garden,

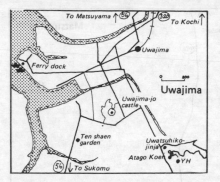

('Heavenly Forgiveness Garden'), two km south of the city.

World War II buffs might be interested in looking for the remains of the Shiden-kai fighter aircraft that was raised from the bottom of Kure Bay in 1979, where it had lain since being shot down in July 1945. It was to be put on display in a local park, without restoration, and is believed to be the only example of its type in Japan.

Bull Fights

Uwajima is famous for its *togyu* bull fights. These are not the kind that pit matador against animal with the result of hundreds of kg of beef, but are contests between two animals that lock horns and try to push the other backwards. Generally there is a fight every month but, with the exception of Wareisai summer festival (23-4 July), dates vary from year to year. Information offices such as the TIC in Tokyo or Kyoto, as well as travel agencies, should be able to provide details. The fights are held at *Togyu-jo* at the foot of *Tenman-yama*, a 30 minute walk from Uwajima station.

OZU

There is *ukai* (cormorant fishing) on the river at Ozu from 1 June to 20 September.

YAWATAHAMA

The hillsides behind this port city are noted for the scenic appearance of their terraces as well as the many orange groves. *Kinzan Shusseki* temple, at the top of Kinzan, gives an excellent view of the Inland Sea and as far away as Kyushu. Yawatahama is a convenient port for ferries to Usuki and Beppu – both in Kyushu.

There are five boats in each direction for Beppu (three hours, about Y2000); and nine a day each way for Usuki (three hours, Y1270).

SADAMISAKI CAPE

This cape, more than 50 km long, projects toward Kyushu. Reports indicate however, that there is nothing of exceptional interest to be found there.

Misaki

There are three ferries a day (each direction) between Misaki and Saganoseki on Kyushu (70 minutes, Y400).

MATSUYAMA

The main attraction in Matsuyama is its castle. *Matsuyama-jo* is a three-storey building dating from 1602, one of the best-preserved castles in Japan. It also functions as a museum. It is atop Shiroyama hill, which is accessible by climbing, or by cable-car (gondola) from the east side (remote from the station).

Dogo-onsen

Matsuyama is famous among the Japanese for its nearby hot-spring resort, Dogo-onsen, which is known for the traditional architecture of its municipal bathhouse (*Shinrokaku*) and the variety of waters available there. However Japanese sources continually overstress hotsprings in tourist literature, so this one will be of limited interest to most foreign visitors.

Ishite Temple Near the hot spring, this is the only temple of note in the area. It dates back to 1318 and illustrates the Kamakura style of architecture.

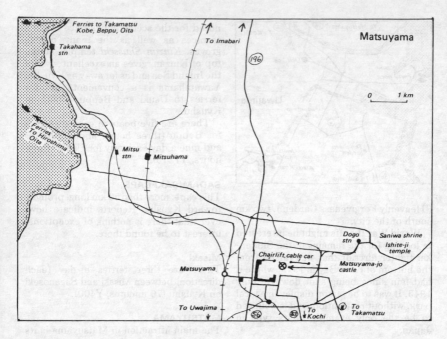

Getting There & Getting Around

Matsuyama is connected by a number of ferries to ports on Honshu and Kyushu. Overnight ferries between Beppu (Kyushu) and Osaka, and between Oita (Kyushu) and Kobe, stop at Matsuyama. Schedule and fare information on these is given in the general Getting Around chapter earlier in the book.

In addition, there are numerous ferries to nearby points on Honshu. Between Hiroshima and Matsuyama there are about 20 daily crossings each way; typically 12 hydrofoils using Matsuyama kanko-ko port (one hour, Y4800), and eight conventional ferries using both Matsuyama kanko-ko port (2 hours 45 minutes, Y1800) and Mitsuhama port (three hours, Y1800). Between Yanai and Mitsuhama there are also hydrofoils – six a day (one hour, Y4800) and ferries – 21 per day (2½ hours). Between Iwakuni and Mitsuhama there are six daily ferries (2½ hours direct

Y1800; or three hours that stop at Inoda on Oshima). Between Mihara and Matsuyama kanko-ko there are eight hydrofoil crossings in each direction (1½ hours, Y4800). Between Kure and Horie-ko port there are 16 daily crossings in each direction (two hour, Y1200).

Between Kokura (northern Kyushu) and Matsuyama kanko-ko there is one overnight ferry (in each direction) departing mid-evening and arriving at 5 am at each destination (Y3400 minimum).

Between Matsuyama kanko-ko and Onomichi there are five daily high speed boats in each direction, stopping at one or two islands en route. The trip takes 1 hour 25 minutes with one stop and costs Y4800.

IMABARI

This industrial port city at the top of the Kurashima-hanto peninsula has very little of interest. The nearby strait between Imabari and Oshima Island is famous for its whirlpools that form at high and low tide like those at Naruto.

Getting There

Imabari has several ferry connections with Honshu. Between Imabari and Mihara there are two types of ferry service, fast and slow. The 'slow' ones take 1¾ hours and leave on the hour (both directions) through most of the day; the fare is Y1270. The 'fast' boats also run throughout the day but don't have such evenly spaced departures. They take one hour and cost Y2880.

Between Imabari and Onomichi there are six high speed boats in each direction daily (1½ hours, Y3800). In addition 14 slower boats (each direction) run only between Imabari and Miyaura on Omishima Island (connected to the mainland near Onomichi by bridge); these take about two hours and cost Y1040. (The high speed boats also stop here going both ways; to/from this stop the fare is Y2190 and take just under one hour). Yet another service runs between Imabari and Onomichi, with stops at two islands en route. The six daily boats (each way) take 1½ hours between the two end points (Y3180).

Between Imabari and Takehara there are three boats a day (each way). With a stop at Miyaura (Omishima island) en route, the trip takes an hour (Y2230). To Miyaura from Imabari takes 40 minutes. The same company operates 12 boats a day between just Imabari and Miyaura (1¾ hours, Y700).

Between Imabari and Niigata there are four high speed boats daily each way (1½ hours, Y2980).

Between Imabari and Hiroshima there are five daily hydrofoils (each way) which take about 90 minutes and cost Y4800.

Between Imabari and Kobe (Higashi-Kobe, Aoki port) there are two boats (one overnight) in each direction. Sailing time is about eight hours and the fare is Y3500 (minimum). The daytime sailing from Kobe would pass through much of the scenic part of the Inland Sea area by daylight.

Between Namikata and Takehara there are 16 boats a day, both ways, (70 minutes, Y860). In addition there are four a day that stop en route at Miyaura on Omishima island. From Namikata to Miyaura takes 55 minutes (Y640); to Takehara is 1¾ hours (Takehara to Miyaura is 45 minutes/Y420.)

GETTING THERE – SHIKOKU

Apart from the connections for the variety of ship services between Honshu and Kyushu already mentioned, there are also air services from the principal cities in each of the four prefectures that give Shikoku its name of Four Districts. In March 1984 the graceful 1629 metre-long Naruto Ohashi suspension bridge was completed between Awaji-shima and Naruto, across the Naruto Strait. It is the longest suspension bridge in the Orient and is scheduled to be open to traffic in June 1985. Another bridge will eventually link Awaji Island with the Kobe area; and two other sets of bridges are under construction to link Honshu and Shikoku – one in the area below Okayama and one in the Mihara area where the Inland Sea is the narrowest.

Kyushu

Kyushu, the southern-most of the four main islands of Japan, is regarded as the 'cradle of Japanese civilisation', and has many places of interest. It was from here that the Yamato tribe (possibly of continental origin) spread to the Kobe-Osaka-Ise area before subjugating the peoples already occupying other parts of the country. However because of the antiquity of these events (dating from about 600 BC) only archaeological remains are left, mostly in the Usuki and Miyazaki areas. Kyushu has also been substantially influenced by Chinese and Korean civilisations because it is the part of Japan closest to those countries.

The main attractions of Kyushu are Mt Aso, the Yamanami Highway, Kagoshima/ Sakurajima, Kirishima, various islands off the coasts, some interesting hot springs, temples, shrines, Nagasaki, the anti-Mongol wall and many gardens. The people of Kyushu also have a reputation for being more friendly than in most parts of Japan (though there can be no complaints about other Japanese).

Even if you have studied Japanese and speak it well, you can expect great difficulties in speaking to people in Kyushu, especially around Kagoshima, as the local dialect is quite different from standard Japanese. The old dialect of Kagoshima, *Satsuma-ben*, now spoken only by older generations, is totally incomprehensible to other Japanese. The story given (and apparently believed by most Japanese) is that a local feudal lord commanded that the people change their way of speaking so that spies from Honshu could be detected. (But as any school teacher can certify, correcting even one grammatical error like 'I seen' can be a hopeless task, so this explanation can be taken 'cum grano salis'.) The most likely answer is that the accent is a carry-over from languages spoken by early inhabitants from other areas; in the same way that accents in England reflect intonations brought by the various tribes and groups from the continent. The dialect of Okinawa, for example, only a relatively short distance to the south, is virtually a separate language.

The description begins at Kitakyushu in the north and follows an anti-clockwise route back. I also suggest some side-trips and shortcuts that will assist travellers with limited time, or those who begin their Kyushu travels at a different point.

Fukuoka-ken

KITAKYUSHU

When crossing from Shimonoseki (on western Honshu) to Kyushu, the first city encountered is Kitakyushu, a composite of five formerly separate cities (Moji, Kokura, Tobata, Yahata and Wakamatsu) that stretches a considerable distance along the northern shore of the island. Few people visit this city for its tourist attractions, unless they are enamoured of steel mills, smoke stacks and other appurtenances of a modern industrial city. Fortunately it is the only major city of this kind on Kyushu; most of the island is still green and natural attractions abound.

If you do have a reason for staying in the

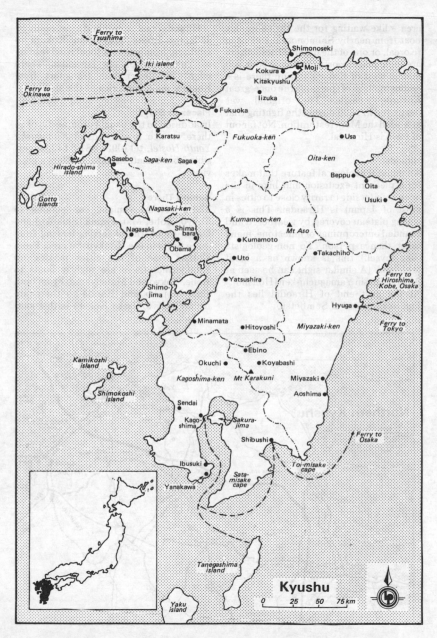

Kyushu

0   25   50   75 km

area – like waiting for the thrice-weekly boat from nearby Shimonoseki to Pusan (Korea), or one of the other ferries – there are some places worth visiting. About 500 metres west of Kokura station there is a reconstruction of (parts of) the once-great *Kokura-jo* castle. The original was destroyed in 1866 during the fighting that attended the Meiji restoration. Not far out of town is Hiraodai.

Hiraodai

An unusual geological feature that makes for a pleasant excursion and hike in the open countryside (a rarity close to cities in most of Japan) is Hiraodai. This is a rolling plateau covered by weathered and rounded outcroppings of limestone, many taller than a person. To non-geologists (like myself) this is known as a karst tableland. (A similar sight can be seen at Akiyoshidai in Yamaguchi-ken (Honshu).) At the east end of Hiraodai lies the limestone grotto of Sembetsu.

Hiraodai can be reached most easily by JNR (or Route 322) from Kokura to Ishihara, from where a local road leading to Yukuhashi passes Hiraodai. There might be direct bus transport from Kokura; make inquiries at the station.

Places to Stay

In addition to the usual hotels and ryokan there is also a nice hostel *Kitakyushu Youth Hostel*, tel (093) 681-8142, accessible from Yahata station. It offers a good view.

Getting There

There are convenient connections to Tokyo, Kobe, Matsuyama (Shikoku) and Osaka by overnight ferries leaving from three ports in the Kitakyushu area. From Kokura (one of the cities making up Kitakyushu) there are nightly boats to Kobe, Tokyo and Matsuyama. From both Shin Moji-ko and Kanda-ko there are nightly boats to Osaka. Kokura-ko (harbour)

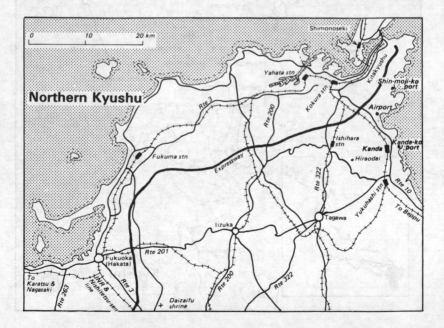

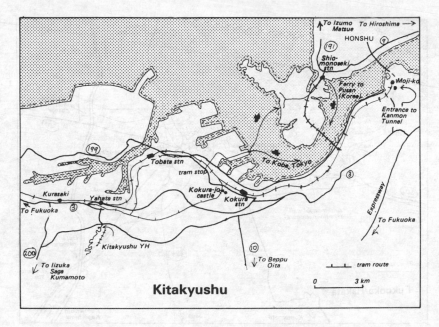

Kitakyushu

To Izumo Matsue To Hiroshima →
HONSHU
(191)
Shio-
monoseki
stn
Ferry to
Pusan
(Korea)
Moji-ko
Entrance to
Kanmon
Tunnel
To Kobe, Tokyo
Tobata stn
tram stop
(199)
Kurasaki
Yahata stn
Kokura-jo
castle
Kokura
stn
(3)
Expressway
To Fukuoka
(3)
To Fukuoka
Kitakyushu YH
(200)
To Iizuka
Saga
Kumamoto
(10)
↓To Beppu
Oita
tram route
0   3 km

dock is not far from Kokura station; there should be a bus. Kanda-ko can be reached from JNR Kanda station (connections from Kokura station), while there is likely to be a bus from JNR Moji station to Shin Moji-ko, but it will be necessary to check on the spot. Fare and schedule information on these boats is given in the general Getting Around chapter earlier in the book.

The simplest way of getting to and from Shimonoseki, on the other side of the Kanmon Strait, is by JNR train which goes through a tunnel. Shimonoseki is the station on the other side and any of the several stations on the Kyushu side can be used, such as Moji, Kokura etc. (Moji is the first after exiting the tunnel.)

Hitching from central Kitakyushu to the other side is not exactly simple, as the city is the seventh largest in Japan and is very spread out. To Honshu, I would recommend taking the train across and following the instructions in the Shimonoseki write-

up for hitching from there. Likewise it is simpler to take a train or a bus some distance out of Kitakyushu before trying to hitch elsewhere in Kyushu. For the adventurous who would nevertheless like to try to hitch out of Kitakyushu, the entrance to the Kanmon tunnel for cars (where it should be possible to get a lift in either direction, to Shimonoseki or into Kyushu) is not far from the Moji station (the final stop of the tram line that passes through the city) or JNR Moji-ko station. As for the expressway across Kanmon-ohashi bridge and on to Hiroshima, Osaka and Tokyo or through Kyushu to Kumamoto, etc, the nearest interchange is some distance from the centre of the city and quite difficult to reach; local help would be required to find out how to get to it.

FUKUOKA/HAKATA
The largest city of Kyushu, Fukuoka has a limited number of attractions worth

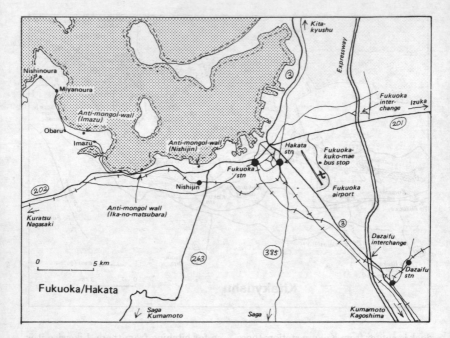

Fukuoka/Hakata

looking at. It is also an international port of entry.

Information

If setting out from Hakata station, first stop at the Travel Centre and pick up a copy of their map of the Fukuoka area. Everything is marked in both Japanese and English, so it can be useful for finding your way almost anywhere. There are other information centres in the same station but they don't have much useful info, so be sure to get the right one.

There is a Korean consulate in Fukuoka, making it a convenient place to obtain a visa.

If you need film, Doi camera shop, near the station, has good prices.

Things to See

Sumiyoshi-jinja (shrine)

This shrine, less than one km from Hakata station, has buildings dating from 400

years ago. Its annual festival is held on 12-14 October.

Shofuku-ji temple

Also located not far from Hakata station, this temple was the first centre of Zen teachings in Japan, from 1195.

Potteries

There are several pottery making centres in northern Kyushu. Some, if not all, are the legacy of Korean potters who came to Japan about 200 years ago. Within Fukuoka are the well-known towns of Agano and Koishiwara; less famous is the town of Onta, near Koishiwara, the last village of Japanese potters who work as a cooperative. There is usually no pottery for sale, because the climbing kilns are fired only occasionally and the production is generally spoken for in advance, but the methods used are traditional as is some of the equipment. Of the 14 houses in the village, 10 produce pottery. On the Fukuoka city map is another pottery, indicated as 'Takatori Kiln (Famous Folk Pottery)'.

Festival

10-12 July: The *Daiko (drum) matsuri*, when over 100 floats carrying drums and drummers parade through the city. Japanese drumming is both complex and unexpectedly primitive, so such a festival is interesting.

Places to Eat

For those who are arriving from Korea after a long time in South-East Asia and may be suffering acute junk food withdrawal symptoms, there is a Shakey's Pizza Parlour in Fukuoka. It is in the central business district; ask for directions at the travel centre.

Places to Stay

There are many hotels, business hotels and ryokan in Fukuoka, as well as in nearby hot-spring resorts. Assistance is available at the information centre at Hakata station. *Jodoji Youth Hostel* is a temple, and temples are usually the nicest kind of hostel in Japan, but it has only 16 beds (tel(092) 751-3377). *Daizaifu Youth Hostel* is an alternative but it has only 24 beds (tel(09292) 28740). Other hostels in the area include *Kongo-kaku* (45 beds, tel (09405) 20009) at Tsuyazaki (toward Kitakyushu); or *Kitakyushu Youth Hostel* (96 beds, tel (093) 681-8142). Both can easily be reached by JNR, the former from Fukuma station, the latter from Yahata.

Getting There – International

Fukuoka is connected by air with Hong Kong, Honolulu, Manila, Taipei, Seoul and Pusan – the latter being the cheapest flight from Korea. It is a convenient gateway to Japan because it allows a circling route through Kyushu (if desired) without back-tracking before carrying on east and northward to the heart of Japan. Fukuoka airport is – with one caveat – a delight to use because it is only a short distance out of town and connections are easily made by frequent bus service from the main JNR station (which is called Hakata, not Fukuoka).

The warning is that budget travellers, especially those who have been in and out of Japan on a seemingly regular basis (as if working illegally and prolonging their stay in this manner) may have a rougher time here than at the larger, more cosmopolitan ports of entry. For those who are entitled to a 90-day period of stay by bilateral agreement (refer to the Immigration section for details), the bad news is that the officials here, like those at Shimonoseki, have been very reluctant to put a 90-day stamp in the passport of a traveller entitled to it and one is often forced to accept a much less desirable 60-day 'tourist' status.

Getting There – Domestic

In addition to several flights a day to various points within Japan, there is a good train service. Hakata is the western terminus of the Shinkansen and the trip to or from Tokyo takes less than seven hours with the fastest trains.

SOUTH OF FUKUOKA

Daizaifu-Temmangu shrine

Less than an hour south of Fukuoka by train is the famous shrine Daizaifu-Temmangu, one of the highest ranking shrines in Japan. The grounds and picturesque bright-orange buildings (dating from 1590) are attractive and include an arched stone bridge. From the 7th to the 14th century, Daizaifu was the residence of the Kyushu governor. The shrine's annual festival takes place on 23-25 September and features a procession.

The shrine is easily reached by the Nishitetsu line that leaves from Nishitetsu-Fukuoka station. At Nishitetsu-Futsukaichi it is necessary to change trains and go one stop to Daizaifu station, from which the shrine is about 500 metres. If you are beginning at Hakata station it is simpler to go by JNR to Kokutetsu-Futsukaichi station then take a bus to the other station, Nishitetsu-Futsukaichi. Buses run every 10 minutes. Daizaifu Youth Hostel is near the shrine.

Close to Daizaifu-jinja are *Komyo-ji* and *Kanzeon-ji* temples, as well as the *Fukuoka-ken Rekishi Hakubutsukan* (historical museum). Komyo-ji has a very pretty Zen-style garden. Kanzeon-ji has a number of valued Buddhist images on display.

Pottery

If you are interested in pottery it is worth visiting the kilns and potters in the towns of Koishiwara, Hoju and Ichinose, all in the vicinity of Kurume.

Hot Springs

Two hot-spring resort towns, Harazura (in southern Fukuoka-ken) and Hita (just across the boundary in Oita-ken) feature *ukai* (cormorant fishing) on the nearby river; May to September in Harazuru and until the end of October in Hita.

WEST OF FUKUOKA

The major route westward from Fukuoka takes you along the coast towards Nagasaki.

Anti-Mongol wall

To combine a swim on a white-sand beach with a bit of history, visit the remnants of the 20 km wall built around Hakata Bay to prevent the landing of the Mongol hordes in 1281. It was feared that the next wave of invaders would overpower the defenders, but a typhoon sank the Mongol fleet, thus saving Japan from the last attempted invasion until 1945 (which explains the great shock felt at the end of the last war). Because this wind saved Japan, it was named 'Kamikaze' (wind of the gods), a word revived in the last war but with less effective results.

Only traces of the walls (originally three metres high) remain. Near Imazu, one stretch of 100 metres or so has been excavated from the sand. Once you see this remnant (still nearly two metres high), you realise that the traces of rocks just below the sand through the groves of picturesque, twisted pine trees near the shore, are the top of the wall. From here it is only a short walk to the beach. To take the bus from Hakata station, ask for the Nishi-no-ura yuki bus, which probably leaves from gate 3 on the second floor. The location is shown on the handout map in Japanese as well as English. The wall is marked as 'Genko Fort', but ask for 'boheki', which is its local name. The bus trip takes about two hours.

GENKAI PARK

The anti-Mongol wall at Imazu, and others (shown on the handout map, but said to be in much poorer condition), are part of Genkai Quasi-National Park that extends about 90 km along the north coast of Kyushu into Saga-ken. Other features are more white sand beaches and more groves of gnarled pine trees, the best-known of which is at Niji-no-matsubara.

Keya-no-Ota

The main attraction of the park is 'the Great Cave of Keya', a rocky promontory at the western end of Itoshima Peninsula. It juts 60 metres out of the sea, and is formed of groups of parallel columns of basalt projecting at different angles (probably created as lava cooled in a large mass and formed giant crystals). The sea has eroded a cave nine metres high and 18 metres wide, that extends more than 50 metres into the rock. (Like most attractions in Japan it will have many tourists and tour buses.)

Keya-no-Ota can be reached by bus from either Chikuzen-Maibara station (40 minutes) or directly from Hakata station (95 minutes).

Saga-ken

There are three famous pottery towns in

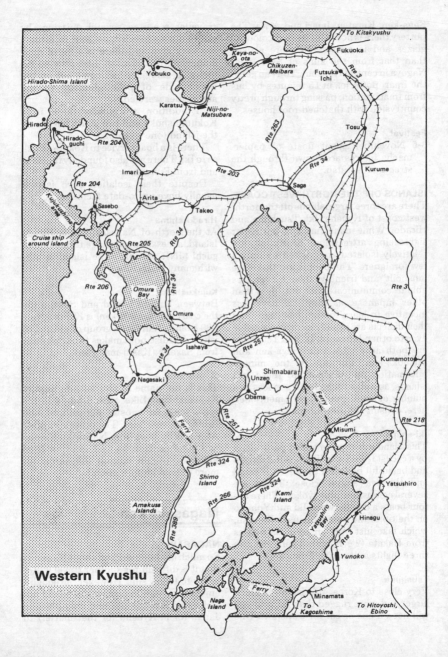

Western Kyushu

Saga-ken: Karatsu, Imari and Arita. The pottery there is noted for its very colourful glazes and is considered more artistic than that from the kilns of Seto (near Nagoya in central Honshu). You can get to the Imari potteries in 15 minutes by bus from Imari station, passing through pretty countryside with thatched-roof houses.

Festival
3-5 November: giant floats of papier-mache figures are drawn through the streets of Karatsu.

ISLANDS OFF THE NORTH-WEST COAST
There are three large islands off the north-west coast of Kyushu: Iki, Tsushima and Hirado. While none has any particular sightseeing attractions, nearly all are relatively isolated and visited by only a few foreigners. The people are therefore 'unspoilt' and friendly, though even less able to communicate with outsiders than other Japanese, as they still have less incentive to learn foreign languages and their dialects are usually incomprehensible even to other Japanese. Iki and Tsushima are both accessible from Saga-ken and Fukuoka-ken. For up to the minute information on transport to these two islands, as well as scheduled services to a number of smaller islands not mentioned here, consult the *Jikokuhyo*.

Iki-shima
This island was recommended particularly by a cyclist friend who liked its flat terrain and beautiful beaches; the island is small and the sea always close. There are several campsites, plus ryokan. There are four boats a day between Iki and Yobuko on the tip of the peninsula near Karatsu, which take just over an hour, as well as from Hakata (2½ hours). There are also three flights a day from Fukuoka.

Tsushima
Very close to Korea, this island is much larger and more rugged than Iki, and you will need a bus or car for transport. One

traveller reported several quizzings by police during his visit, because foreigners are very rare and there is a lot of drug smuggling from Korea. Just prior to his arrival a smuggler had come out on the wrong side of police bullets, so the authorities were edgy.

In addition to ryokan there is a Kokuminshuku and two youth hostels on the island (one a temple).

There is a boat service to Kokura as well as to Iki. There are also four daily flights to and from Fukuoka.

Despite their isolation such islands usually have up-to-date facilities.

Hirado-shima
At the north of Nagasaki-ken is Hirado Island, accessible by bridge from Hirado-guchi (JNR station). The island is hilly with many high cliffs.

Kujukushima
Between Hirado Island and Sasebo (on the coast of Nagasaki-ken) is Kujukushima ('99 islands'), in fact a group of about 170 islets. A cruise boat makes two trips daily from Sasebo (Kashi-mae pier).

Goto-shima
This is the name of five islands west of Kujukushima. Like other islands in the area, they are mostly agricultural and fishing communities. The coast is rugged. Access is by boat from Nagasaki, Sasebo and other centres, as well as by air from Fukuoka. (Again consult *Jikokuhyo* for more detailed information.)

Nagasaki-ken

NAGASAKI
So much has been written about Nagasaki that it is difficult for another travel writer to try to follow suit. However, although I enjoyed my visit to Nagasaki, I would not claim that it is the one and only place in Japan (or in Kyushu for that matter) to

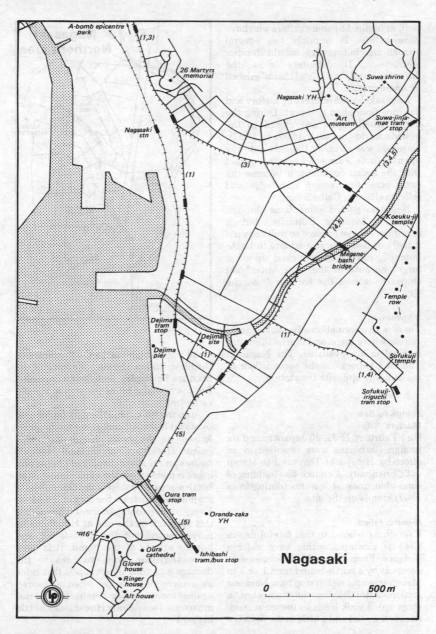

Nagasaki

0   500 m

visit, as implied by some writers who have gone before. It certainly has several attractions, but reality should temper enthusiasm. It definitely lacks the 'haunting beauty' and 'fatal charm' gushed by one writer.

Nagasaki has an interesting history and has long flourished as a port. During the period when Japan was closed to the outside world (the early 1600s to 1867), Nagasaki was virtually the only gateway open for trade. Formerly a point of contact with the Asian continent, it became the entry point for western knowledge and religion (Roman Catholicism).

Nagasaki gained some fame through Puccini's 'Madame Butterfly', but it might never have become so well known if it had not been the second city to be A-bombed, having been picked up as a target because of the huge Mitsubishi shipyards across the harbour from the city.

Information

There is an information office at Nagasaki station where maps and tourist literature in English are available. The Nagasaki Tourist Centre is on the second floor of the building opposite the station.

Things to See
Martyrs' Site

On 5 February 1597, 20 Japanese and six foreign Christians were crucified in an effort by Hideyoshi Toyotomi to stamp out Christianity. A church-like building of somewhat unusual features (dating from 1962) stands on the site.

A-bomb relics

Everything related to that fateful day in 1945 is clustered within easy walking distance. From Nagasaki station, easiest access is by a north-bound tram 1 or 3 to Matsuyama-cho, eighth stop from Nagasaki station. After leaving the tram stop, a short uphill walk leads to the main road. Across the road and a little to the right is a

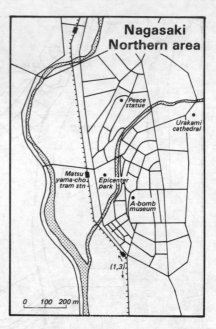

small park which marks the epicentre of the blast. Relics showing the force of the blast are on display, including a crumpled fire-tower and a bit of the wall of the old cathedral.

Atop the hill behind the park (accessible by stairs) is the A-bomb museum, properly known as *Nagasaki Kokusai Bunka-kaikan* (International Cultural Hall). It houses an excellent display of photos and other remains from the explosion; melted bottles, scorched stones and other objects graphically illustrate the fury of the blast. Every visitor to Japan should see either this museum or the one at Hiroshima to fully comprehend the devastating and horrific effects of the bomb. It is even more terrifying when you realise the damage was done by a weapon that rates as a mere fire cracker when measured against today's super-bombs. (Of the two museums, I would rate Hiroshima's a little higher.)

North of the park and museum is Peace Park (Heiwa-koen), with ponds, fountains and a statue said to symbolize peace. The statue is a little grotesque, the head being too small for the body, and is scarcely worth going to see.

Urakami Catholic Cathedral

The original church on this site was finished in 1914 after 32 years of work. It was the largest church in the Orient till it was destroyed by the bomb. Part of one of its pillars stands in the epicentre park. The present building was finished in 1959. Nagasaki has been the centre of Roman Catholicism in Japan since the 16th century; it is ironic that this city and Hiroshima (which was the centre of Protestant Christianity) were the two targets A-bombed.

Sofuku-ji temple

From the A-bomb area, a tram No 1 back to the end of the line deposits you at the foot of the street leading up to Sofuku-ji. This temple dates back to 1629 and is noted for its Chinese architecture, particularly the second gate and main hall (Hondo) which were built in late Ming-dynasty style. From the temple, the athletic can walk along the row of temples shown on the map (the best known of which is Kofuku-ji) via Megane-bashi bridge to Suwa-jinja shrine. An alternative route is tram 4 to Suwa-jinja-mae.

Megane-bashi bridge

'Spectacles Bridge' has two steep arches, and when the river level is high enough the reflection forms two ovals that look like eyeglasses. The original bridge was built in 1634 with the help of Chinese Buddhist priests but was swept away in a flood caused by a typhoon in 1983. The bridge was rebuilt in three months in its original form.

Suwa-jinja

Although there is no particular 'sight' here the buildings are attractive and typical of large shrines throughout Japan. There is a good view over the city from the hill on which Suwa-jinja stands. The grounds are heavily wooded and offer a haven from city buildings. Okunchi is the shrine's annual festival (7-9 October) and its dragon dance dates from the days of trade with China.

Glover House

From the shrine area, tram 5 (southbound) leads to Glover House. Get off at the first stop after the tram turns left to run beside a canal. A nearby bridge leads to the house.

One of the best-known landmarks of Nagasaki, Glover House is a large English-style mansion that was the home of a remarkable Englishman named (what else?) Glover. He supervised the construction of railways and the opening of mines and introduced a tremendous amount of modern technology to Japan after it was opened to the world in the latter part of the 19th century.

The house has a lovely garden and the view from the porch out over the harbour is probably the finest in the city. The interior of the house is well preserved. Attesting to the numbers of visitors is an outdoor escalator which lifts people up the hill on which the house is perched.

In the grounds, observe (for humour's sake) the statue of Madame Butterfly. Whether there ever was such a person is not really known (some say 'yes' and some say 'no') but there is certainly no connection with this house. However local tourist authorities are pushing the story for all it's worth.

Nearby are three other houses of the same era, two of which are also known for their former residents, Alt and Ringer. The third house ('No 16') has considerable quantities of Victorian bric-a-brac. In the bottom of the building is a museum of portable shrines, costumes and a dragon—all of which are carried in the annual Okunchi festival. A videotape shows scenes from the celebrations.

Oura Tenshu-do Catholic Cathedral

This is the oldest Gothic-style structure in Japan, dating from 1865. It was built in memory of the 26 Christian martyrs. A museum in front of the cathedral (*shiryokan*) has exhibits showing the history of the persecution of the Christians under the Tokugawa.

From this area, tram 5 returns to Dejima Pier area.

Koshibyo-tojinkan

This building is in very traditional Chinese style with red pillars and walls and a yellow roof with dragons cavorting on the peaks. The original temple was destroyed by the A-bomb. It is now a museum of traditional Chinese art.

Dejima

The pier where visiting cruise ships dock is named after Dejima Island, a small body of land to which Dutch traders were restricted during the 'closed' years when Japan's only connection with the rest of the world was through Nagasaki. The island no longer exists, as the harbour was filled in to make the pier and the dock area is now further out than the island used to be. A garden and reproduction of an old warehouse now stand on the site of the former island.

Nagasaki Aquarium

There is an aquarium about 12 km from the city; access is by bus or taxi from Nagasaki station.

Prins Willem

In mid 1984 the tourist firm Nagasaki Dutch Village announced they had ordered a full scale replica of the Dutch warship 'Prins Willem' which was launched in 1650. It was one of the many ships which sailed between the Netherlands and Asia providing sea trade which brought great riches and power to the small European country. The replica will serve as a seafaring museum and will be moored at Omura Bay.

Views of the city

The best view of the city is from the top of *Mt Inasa* (332 metres). A cable-car runs from a point about one km from Nagasaki station. The view at night is especially attractive, somewhat resembling Hong Kong, although the lights are not so numerous nor so bright.

Places to Stay

As can be expected at a very popular destination for domestic travel there is plenty of accommodation available, with many hotels and ryokan clustered around the station. As in any city of reasonable size in Japan assistance in finding a place to stay can be obtained from the station or the tourist centre. There are three youth hostels: two are in town, the third is quite far away.

Nagasaki-kenritsu Youth Hostel, (tel (0958) 23-5032) is a 12 minute walk from Nagasaki station. Go up the little street opposite the station, to the end, then turn right and cross seven intersections of various sizes. It is a little to the left from there. *Nagasaki Oranda-zaka Youth Hostel*, (tel (0958) 22-2730) is further away. Staff at the information office could help.

Getting There

Internationally Nagasaki has an air link with Shanghai, a city with historic trade ties. Domestically Nagasaki is served by JNR lines as well as air links with several other cities. The airport is 10 minutes from Omura station by bus and 90 minutes from Nagasaki by bus. The train passes briefly along the shore of Omura Bay en route to Nagasaki; the main highway goes inland most of the way. Northward to Sasebo, both pass along the shore for most of the distance, giving pleasant views including the rafts of pearl farms. This is the second largest pearl-producing area in Japan after Ise. Inter-city buses leave from the terminal across from Nagasaki station.

If travelling by aid of the thumb, you will

find it simplest to take a train or bus to Isahaya and start hitching from there.

Getting Around

The easiest way to get around the city is by tram, as the five lines pass near all points of interest and are clearly numbered. (The lines and their turning points are shown on the map.) City buses cover much more extensive routes but they are difficult to use because they are identified only in Japanese.

FROM NAGASAKI TO KUMAMOTO

From Nagasaki, one of the most popular routes is via Obama and Unzen to Shimabara, from where frequent ferries ply to and from Misumi on the Uto Peninsula. From Misumi it is only a short distance north to Kumamoto or south to Kagoshima.

Unzen

In the days of the British Empire, Unzen was a favourite resort for colonial officials and old China hands, breeds now vanished. There are still some attractions, though most travellers stop only for a look around before continuing. Unzen has golf courses and other recreational facilities but its raison d'etre is the hot-spring waters. These boil up – violently in places – in a steaming, desolate but colourful area near town. The waters are conducted to the various hotels for the baths. The claims of curative properties would get hotels in plenty of hot water of another kind if made in countries with strong consumer-protection laws. During the days of Christian persecution, these boiling waters were put to another use – disposing of those who refused to renounce their faith.

Another attraction of Unzen is the Roman Catholic church, a Y130 million brick-clad building which is a bit of a curiosity as there were only eight known catholics in the area when it was built in 1982. This anomaly makes a little more sense with the knowledge that the area's relics, remains and evidence of the exotic Christian history and tradition constitute one of the mainstays of what had been a declining tourist industry.

A toll road loops up between Nodake and Myoken mountains. The view from the road itself is not spectacular but from the top cable-car station there is a beautiful view of the ocean and offshore islands. Wildflowers are pretty in spring and summer while leaves are the attraction in autumn. The youth hostel at Unzen is unusually large.

Shimabara

Another place of interest on the Shimabara Peninsula is Shimabara with its reconstructed castle. The original was destroyed in 1637 in an episode during the government's effort to eradicate Christianity. About 30,000 of the faithful captured the castle but it was later retaken by the authorities and the defenders were slaughtered. The castle was ruined at that time but the large reproduction, built in 1964, recreates the beautiful appearance of the white original and serves as a museum. Among the exhibits are *fumi-e* ('trampling images'), images of Christian significance upon which people had to tread in order to prove that they were not Christians. The castle is about 400 metres west of the station. Ferries to Misumi are frequent.

Misumi

From Misumi it is 27 km to the main north-south road (Route 3) at Uto, from where it is only 15 km to Kumamoto. An alternative is a visit to the Amakusa Islands.

Kumamoto-ken

KUMAMOTO

Kumamoto is the third largest city on Kyushu and was one of the major military centres of Japan until the last century. It is best described as rather provincial;

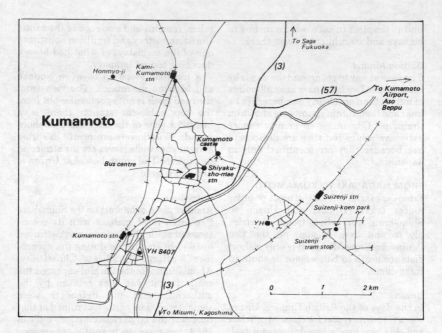

Kumamoto

(On map: To Saga Fukuoka; (3); (57); To Kumamoto Airport, Aso Beppu; Honmyo-ji; Kami-Kumamoto stn; Kumamoto castle; Bus centre; Shiyaku-sho-mae stn; Suizenji stn; Suizenji-koen park; YH; Suizenji tram stop; Kumamoto stn; YH 8407; (3); To Misumi, Kagoshima; 0 1 2 km)

although it has modern buildings, shops etc, it is not a metropolis. Some sections of the city are delightfully seedy and are worth seeing for that reason before they are conquered by the aluminium-and-glass that has transformed the traditional appearance of nearly all Japan.

The two major attractions of Kumamoto are Suizenji-koen garden and Kumamoto-jo castle, plus a shrine or two.

Information
A small handout map with tram lines and major sightseeing spots is available at the station. It has sufficient English to be useful.

Things to See
Suizenji-koen park
This is a very attractive landscape garden, larger than most in Japan. I would rate it ahead of two of the 'Big Three' gardens, behind only Kenroku-en in Kanazawa. The hills and water have been arranged to

resemble famous natural features such as Mt Fuji and Lake Biwa, and there is a teahouse identical in every feature to one of the most famous of such buildings in Kyoto. The garden dates from 1632 so it is much older than the more celebrated ones mentioned above. It was part of a villa of the Hosokawa clan who once commanded the region.

The park is easily reached by tram from Kumamoto station; the stop is Suizenji.

Kumamoto-jo
Kumamoto was once one of the principal castle towns of Japan, ranking only behind Osaka and Nagoya. The original castle was finished in 1607 and stood until 1867, when most of it was burned in a siege during the civil war period at the time of the Meiji restoration. In 1960 the structure was reproduced in concrete and now houses a good museum. I usually down play such reproductions for their lack of authenticity but this one is so large and set

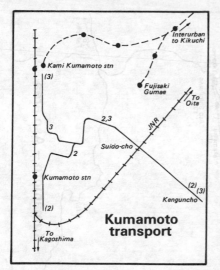

Kumamoto transport

(Map labels: Interurban to Kikuchi; Kami Kumamoto stn (3); Fujisaki Gumae; To Oita; 2,3; JNR; 3; Suido-cho; 2; Kumamoto stn; (2); (2)(3); Kenguncho; To Kagoshima)

in such attractive surroundings of tall trees and stone walls that it is worth at least a look if you are passing through.

The castle is easily reached on foot or by tram from the station; the stop is 'Shi-yaku-sho mae' (town hall).

Other

Other attractions that can be singled out are *Hommyo-ji* temple and Tatsuta-koen park. The latter houses a folk-art museum (*mingei hakubutsukan*) as well as an attractive garden and teahouse from 350 years ago.

Undefinable attractions include several streets of shops that appear to have survived from pre-war times and preserve the appearance of the Japan of those days. The buildings are all wood with features such as sliding doors of wood and small panes of glass, and canopies that overhang and shelter the sidewalk.

The other intangible feature of the city is an impression of 'raunchiness'. Other writers have reported being taken to shows in bars and clubs that left absolutely nothing to the imagination sexually, and

this is the only city in Japan where I encountered a 'pink light' area. Along the riverside road leading to Youth Hostel 8407, I passed several small buildings, each open doorway illuminated by a single pink fluorescent tube. Inside could be seen a small bar in one room and a bed in the adjacent one; there was a woman standing near the doorway. Yes, Kumamoto is a little out of the ordinary.

Festivals

15 September: At Fujisaki Hachi-mangu shrine, there is an annual procession of 'warriors' on horseback, who wear ancient armour to escort three portable shrines.

Places to Stay

There are several hotels, minshuku etc, in Kumamoto. Assistance in finding a room can be obtained at information centres at the airport, station or travel agencies. There are also three youth hostels: *Ryokan Shokaku* (8407, tel (0963) 52-1468), a delightfully seedy old ryokan close to the station; *Suizenji YH* (8406, tel (0963) 71-9193), accessible in 25 minutes by tram from the station; and *Kumamoto-Shiritsu YH* (8408, tel (0963) 52-2441), a municipal hostel that is more difficult to reach. Details on hostels in the Aso area are given in that section; they can be considered as alternatives because of the short travelling time from Kumamoto (100 minutes by train).

Getting There

Kumamoto recently joined the list of international ports of entry for air travellers. Although the connections are limited to Seoul it is a step forward and offers an alternative to Fukuoka. The airport is near the road/rail route to Mt Aso, so on arrival you have the option of taking the bus into Kumamoto or proceeding directly to the Aso area. From the airport there may be a direct bus to Aso or it might be necessary to go to Higo-Otsu station and take a train or bus from there.

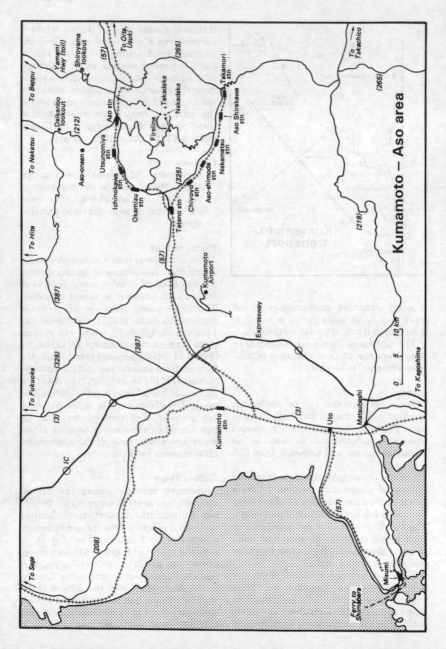

Kumamoto – Aso area

To Beppu

To Nakatsu

To Hita

To Fukuoka

To Saga

To Takachico

To Kagoshima

To Olta, Usuki

Shiroyama lookout

Yamami Hwy (toll)

(57)

(265)

Daikanbo lookout

(212)

Takadake stn

Aso stn

Takadake

Nakadake

Fireline

Aso-onsen

Aso Shirakawa stn

Utsunomiya stn

Nakamatsu stn

Ichinokawa stn

Aso-himoda stn

Okamizu stn

Chiyoyo stn

(325)

Tateno stn

(57)

Kumamoto Airport

(265)

(218)

Kumamoto Transport

Expressway

(387)

(387)

(325)

(3)

Kumamoto stn

IC

(208)

Uto

Matsubashi

Misumi

To Shimabara

Ferry to Shimabara

(57)

0   5   10 km

The Aso Region

Aso-zan

The present Aso-zan sits in the midst of the largest volcanic crater on earth, and is still fuming after 80 million years of activity. Several routes go to the top if you have your own vehicle, but for most travellers the simplest way is by one of the frequent buses from Aso station (JNR). From here, one route goes to the west side of the crater (Kako-nishi), the other to the east side (Kako-higashi) via Miyaji. You can go up either way and then take a bus at the top to reach the other. There are also buses from Takamori and Akamizu stations, but the services are few. (Complete schedules are printed in *Jikokuhyo*.)

En route to the western peak, the road twists and turns up the flank of the mountain (passing Aso Youth Hostel just before the toll gate). At the lush meadows you may see Japanese tourists jumping out of their cars to photograph an exotic species of animal life – a cow. Clearly visible in the green are fingers of lava from prehistoric flows. The road also passes a smallish cone, *Komezuka*, an 'after thought' of a later mini eruption.

Eventually the road reaches the flattened top of Aso-zan. From the first lookout near the crest of the uphill road, you can finally see (on a clear day, at least) the enormity of the crater. The cliffs several km away are in fact the walls of the original hole. Its dimensions are given variously as 23 or 32 km north-south, 16 km east-west, and 80 or 128 km in circumference. Any way you measure it, it's huge and the mind boggles at the amount of energy released from this place. Although the volcano has been active for about 30 million years, the present form probably dates back a little more than 120 millennia.

The road circles around a lake before the bus reaches the base station of the Kako-nishi cable-car (four minutes to the top). A toll road also continues the short distance to the same place. The view from here is one of great desolation, mostly black ash thrown out over the centuries. A path leads to the very rim of the main crater (no guard rail – caution!) in the side of *Nakadake*, on the far side of which can be seen layers of ash and lava – mostly black, but with colorful streaks of dark red. In its own sombre way it is very picturesque.

Far below, down in the deep black cavity, steam billows forth continuously, sometimes diminishing only to burst forth in greater volume. Is it safe? Generally yes, as a constant watch is kept and visitors are barred from the rim area when it is active. However, in September 1979, while access was barred, a particularly violent explosion hurled head-sized rocks nearly a km away into an area thought safe, killing three sightseers. Prior to this, the last eruption had been in November 1977. These eruptions explain the presence of the numerous concrete domes near the rim, built as emergency shelters after an unexpected eruption in 1958 when 12 people were killed.

Close to the base station of the cable-car, buses depart for the circling route to Kako-higashi via the 'Fireline' road. The view from 'High Line' looking out along the way takes in the entire crater, and gives a better idea of its magnitude. A cable-car from Kako-higashi runs down to the terminal at Aso-zan-higashi from where a bus runs back to Aso (or Miyaji) station.

At the bottom, a short distance from Miyaji station, lies *Aso-jinja* shrine. This is one of those attractions that can be described as 'nice if you haven't seen one before'. There are some attractive carvings on the buildings.

Places to Stay

In addition to hotels, ryokan and minshuku, there are three youth hostels around the base of the mountain. I stayed at *Aso Youth Hostel* (8402, tel (09673) 4-0804) and found it pleasant; it can be reached by

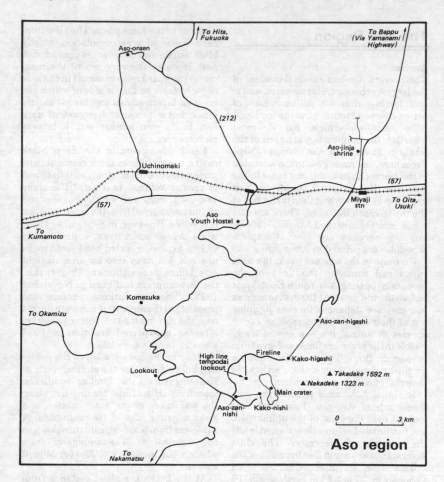

Aso region

the bus to Kako-nishi and is just a short distance before the toll gate. The others are *Aso YMCA Camp Youth Hostel* (tel (09673) 5-0124), and *Murataya-Ryokan* (tel (09676) 2-0066), though one traveller gave a low rating to the latter.

Views of Aso-zan

Another good overall view of the crater can be had from *Takadake* ('High Peak'), an easy hike to the east from the upper station at Kako-higashi. There are also two places on the northern rim that offer excellent views of the present mountain and the valley floor, with its patchwork of small fields. One is Daikanbo, a little distance above Aso-onsen (also known as Uchinomaki-onsen) and accessible from Uchinomaki station. The other is Shiroyama-tempodai, at the rim of the old crater where the Yamanami Highway climbs out of the valley – the view from almost any point here is memorable.

Yamanami Highway

Aso lies partway along the highway that links Beppu with Nagasaki. Between Aso and Beppu it traverses some of the nicest countryside in Kyushu, and some of the most unusual in Japan. It is a rolling highland plateau that passes a number of mountain peaks, like *Kuju-san*, 1788 metres, the highest in Kyushu. The overall effect is memorable in all seasons: in spring it is made colourful by wildflowers; in summer it is a lush green; and the autumn has its own beauty, for even though all is reduced to shades of brown, the tall pampas grass moves gracefully with the wind.

There are several buses each day that make the run between Aso and Beppu along the Yamanami Highway. Depending on the number of stops, the trip takes three to four hours. An alternative route northward from Aso (for those in a rush) is via Hita, but the attractions of the Yamanami Highway make it preferable.

From Aso, another route is south-east through Takachiho Gorge, a very pleasant place to visit. Like Beppu however, it lies in Miyazaki-ken and is described in that section.

KUMAMOTO TO KAGOSHIMA

Yatsushiro

This is an industrial city of little interest except for pottery addicts; it is the place of origin for *Koda-yaki* (or *Yatsushiro-yaki*) pottery, carrying on a tradition started by Korean potters who came here in the 16th century.

In late August-early September strange lights can be seen in the sea late at night. Known as *shiranui*, it is caused by phosphorescence from a kind of marine life. It is described in Japanese literature as occurring in late summer/early autumn.

Hinagu

The view from the shore near this hot-spring resort is regarded as particularly appealing, taking in the Amakusa islands and the bay in front of them.

Minamata

This is another industrial city of no touristic merit but it was brought to world attention in the early 1970s because of the illness caused by mercury poisoning, now known as Minamata disease.

Yunoko

The swimming is good here.

Hitoyoshi

Travellers descending from the Kumamoto area bound for Kagoshima could do far worse than to turn inland at Yatsushiro and travel through the pretty, wooded valley to Hitoyoshi by rail or road (Route 219). The Kuma River, flowing through the valley, is intensely green. At Hitoyoshi, both rail and road turn southward; the road (Route 221) to Ebino and Kobayashi, rail to Yoshimatsu and Kagoshima. A branch from Yoshimatsu goes to Ebino and Kobayashi.

From Hitoyoshi, you can shoot the rapids in a 2½ hour trip on the Kuma river for 18 km to Osakahama (on the JNR). The starting point is 1.5 km south-east of Hitoyoshi station, opposite the grounds of the former castle, *Hitoyoshi-jo*. The rapids are rated among the three swiftest in Japan, but there is no risk involved.

I was struck by the strange appearance of one town along routes 219-221 (possibly Hitoyoshi itself – memory fails), which looked as if every building along the main street had been built from the same pre-fab components (of non-Japanese style) with only the colours varying. It's nothing special, just a curiosity to look out for.

Kobayashi

This is one entry point for a trip through the very scenic Kirishima National Park. Several buses a day leave for Ebino-kogen, the changing point for the most scenic parts. (This same trip can be made in reverse from Kagoshima.) There are also buses to Kobayashi from Miyazaki many times a day. The trips takes 1½ to two hours.

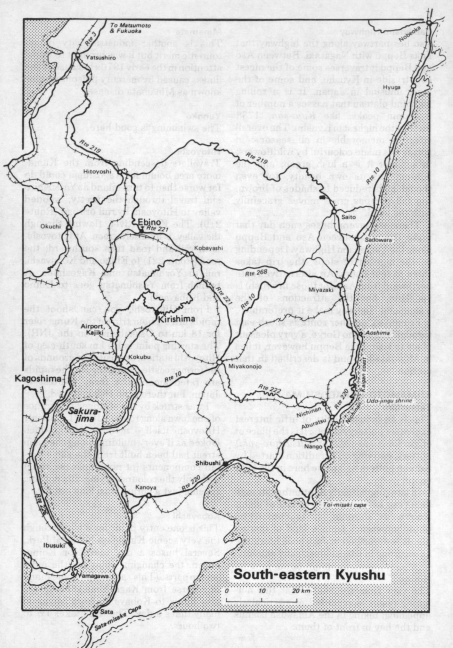

South-eastern Kyushu

0   10   20 km

Top: Cherry blossoms and evergreens at Heian-jingu shrine, Kyoto
Left: Entrance of Sanzen-in temple, Chara (near Kyoto)
Right: Kinkaku ('gold pavilion') of Kinkaku-ji temple, Kyoto

Top: Blood-red waters of Chi-no-ike jigoku, near Beppu (Kyushu)
Bottom: Carved stone Buddha heads, Usuki (Kyushu)

Kagoshima-ken

KIRISHIMA AREA

The Kirishima area is very scenic and well known for the two peaks *Karakuni-dake* (1700 metres), and *Takachiho-no-mine* (1574 metres) which are 16 km apart; between them stand 21 lesser peaks. Easily visible from the Kirishima Skyline toll road (along which the bus passes) are colourful caldera lakes, craters and much other evidence of volcanic activity. It is unusual scenery and definitely worth seeing.

Ebino-kogen

From Kobayashi, the local road passes under the freeway, twists along to the entrance of the toll road, then twists a great deal more up to Ebino-kogen (Ebino highland plateau). This is the terminus of the bus and the transfer point for another bus bound for Kagoshima.

At Ebino-kogen there are three small lakes, or rather 'ponds'. They are volcano calderas, and quite round; all are of different colours, including one of the most intense green I have encountered. (Use a polarising filter to photograph them, otherwise reflection from the water will wash out the colour.) There are several paths to follow for different views. Karakuni-dake is visible from here as well.

From Ebino-kogen south along the toll road to Shinyu-onsen, various views of Karakuni-dake unfold to the east. A short distance later is Onami-ike, a caldera lake even more circular than the others mentioned above. (Shinsho lookout gives a good view.) Here and there along the road steam pours out of the ground, sometimes beside the road (or even through the cracks in the pavement) – evidence of the potential geological forces underfoot.

A fork east at the junction of the toll roads (Shinyu-onsen) leads to Takachiho-kawara. From here, there is a good view of

Takachiho-no-mine, an ugly, scenic, still-active volcano. Its rim is red-brown, heat-discoloured rock; the conical top vanished in prehistoric eruptions. The gaping crater, backdropped by yet more craters and peaks, gives an other-worldly look to the area. Takachiho-kawara is the starting point for hiking to the picturesque cratered cone.

Kirishima

Kirishima-jingu shrine (in Kirishima town, which is 15 minutes from the JNR Kirishima-jingu station) is colourful with wood carvings and set amidst tall cedars. There is a youth hostel in the town as well as ryokan and hotels.

There are several bus services through the Ebino – Kirishima area. The main routes are: Miyazaki – Kobayashi – Ebino-kogen – Hayashida-onsen, and Ebino-onsen – Hayashida-onsen – Kirishima-jingu – Nishi-Kagoshima station. Unfortunately there is no service listed to Takachiho-kawara, but it is less than eight km, so it should be easy to hitch. Schedules change seasonally, so check if there is a local service by inquiring locally.

KAGOSHIMA

The largest city in southern Kyushu, Kagoshima is an international airport as well as a seaport for regular boats to and from Okinawa and other southern islands. It is also a stop-over point for some cruise ships.

There are some things to see in Kagoshima itself and enough attractions nearby that two or three days can be profitably spent looking around.

Kagoshima is one of the few cities in the world where an umbrella is useful, rain or shine. The reason is Kagoshima's most spectacular feature – the massive smoking cone of *Sakurajima*, across the bay. Sakurajima has an awesome history of eruptions and its south peak is still active, regularly spewing fine black ash into the air. With an unfavourable wind it blows over Kagoshima and covers the streets with a thin layer, or drifts into shallow piles. A good view of Sakurajima may be had from the top of *Shiroyama*, the hill behind the city. Bus 25 runs close to the top and you can also walk up from Shiroyama tram stop. The park was formerly the site of a castle.

The main attractions of the city are located a little to the north, and are associated (like most history of Kagoshima up to the time of the Meiji restoration in 1868) with the Shimazu family who controlled the area for only five years short of seven centuries.

Information

There is an excellent information centre at the station. The person on duty when I was there spoke excellent English and was very helpful. The office keeps generous hours (6 am to 10 pm), has literature in English and can give any information required for further travel connections, access to boat docks for Okinawa, etc.

Home visit

At the information centre at Nishi-Kagoshima station you can arrange a visit to a private home. Families who speak English or other foreign languages have been selected for this programme. Arrangements can also be made by phone (tel 24-1111).

Things to See

Iso-tei-en

This is a large landscape garden over 300 years old, one of the nicest in Japan, employing ponds and plants in artistic arrangement. It stretches along the coast, overlooking the magnificence of Sakurajima and overlooked by nearby *Isoyama* (which has a cable-car). In the midst of the garden stands a 13-room villa (traditional Japanese style) and there is a good beach nearby. Iso-tei-en can be reached by city bus No 1 in 20 minutes.

Shoko-Shuseikan Museum

This building was formerly a factory, built in the second quarter of the 19th century by Nariakira Shimazu, an exceptionally enlightened *diamyo* of the area. He introduced his people to a number of western skills, like photography, telegraphy, cotton-spinning, glass and armaments making, etc. The museum displays items from 700 years of the Shimazu family, and is located beside Iso-tei-en garden.

Ijinkan

A short distance back toward the city from the museum is Ijinkan ('foreigners residence'), built for overseas advisors in the last century. It is a large wooden house of distinctively foreign architecture – probably early Victorian – and is an anomaly in Japan, especially when contrasted with the lovely and traditional villa in Iso-tei-en garden.

Other

Another (lesser) attraction of Kagoshima is the foundation stones and walls of the

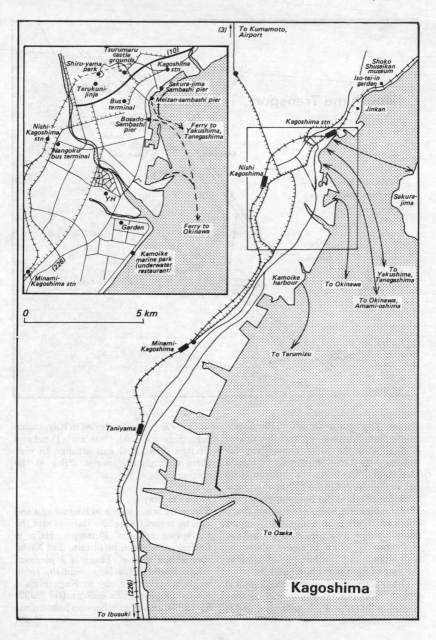

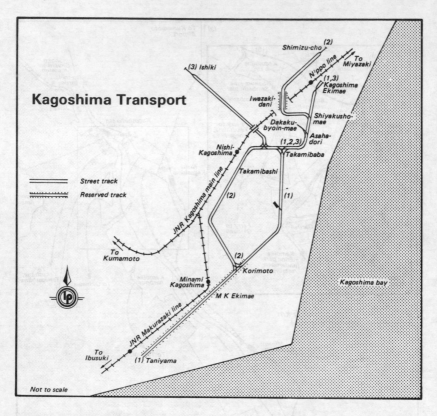

Kagoshima Transport

Shimizu-cho (2)

(3) Ishiki

N'ippo line

To Miyazaki

(1,3) Kagoshima Ekimae

Iwazaki-dani

Shiyakusho-mae

Dakaku-byoin-mae

(1,2,3)

Asaha-dori

Nishi-Kagoshima

Takamibaba

Takamibashi

(2)

(1)

Street track

Reserved track

JNR Kagoshima main line

To Kumamoto

(2)

Korimoto

Kagoshima bay

Minami Kagoshima

M K Ekimae

JNR Makurazaki line

To Ibusuki

(1) Taniyama

Not to scale

former *Tsurumaru Castle*. The north-bound tram line passes it and the closest stop is also the most convenient for walking up to *Shiroyama* ('Castle Mountain'). The castle was built in 1602 but was destroyed in the 1870s when local Satsuma rebels under Saigo opposed the Meiji restoration. Saigo's battle was futile and ended when he committed *sepuku* (ritual suicide) in a cave near the castle. His name is found in many places in Kagoshima, and *Terukuni-jinja* shrine at the foot of Shiroyama honours him.

Other attractions include the Tropical Plants Botanical Garden, and nearby Kamoike Marine Park with its under water restaurant.

There are three potteries in Kagoshima area: Satsuma Toki, Urushima-Togei and Chotaro-Yaki. You can arrange to visit them through the tourist office at the station.

Places to Stay

There are many hotels in Kagoshima and nearby resort towns like Ibusuki and the hot-spring town of Furusato. Help in finding a room can be obtained at Nishi-Kagoshima station. There is a pleasant youth hostel (in a large, oldish, semi-western style building) in Kagoshima – *Kagoshima-ken Fujin-kaikan*, (tel (0992) 51-1087); as well as others on Sakurajima across the harbour – *Sakurajima Youth*

Hostel, (tel (099293) 2150); at Ibusuki – *Ibusuki Youth Hostel* (tel (09932) 2-2758); and *Tamaya Youth Hostel* (tel (09932) 2-3553). *Fujin-kaikan Youth Hostel* is easily reached from Nishi-Kagoshima station by tram 1 (north-bound for Kagoshima station). One line branches off to the left after crossing a bridge; shortly afterward another branches off to the right. (If your tram doesn't make this right turn, get off at the next stop and catch a tram 1 going in the opposite direction; it will make the turn.) Get off at the fourth stop after the turn (the second after crossing the large Takeno bridge). Buses 16 and 25 also pass close by.

Getting There & Getting Around

Kagoshima is linked with Hong Kong, Guam and Nauru (South Pacific) by regular flights, which makes it a convenient port of entry for travellers from those areas who wish to start their Japan travels in the south. The airport is north of the city and connections are convenient by bus. Departures are every 20 minutes and the trip takes about an hour. If you want to make your way immediately to the Kirishima area, try to get to Kajiki station, from where seven trains a day run directly to Kirishima-jingu station. Information can be obtained at the airport about schedules.

Airport buses make more than one stop in Kagoshima; the best place to get off is Nishi-Kagoshima station (West Kagoshima), which is close to the post office and the central business district. (Nishi-Kagoshima is the main station of the city; Kagoshima station is rather minor in importance.)

There is an overnight boat to Osaka every day and a regular service to Okinawa. For details refer to the general Getting Around chapter early in the book.

SAKURAJIMA

The cone of Sakurajima dominates the skyline of Kagoshima. The city is some-

Sakura-jima

To Kagoshima

Kurokami buried torii

Yunohira observatory (Tempodai)

Sakura-jima ko

▲ *Kita-dake 1118 m*

▲ *Minami-dake 1059 m*

Lava observatory (Tempodai)

Kaigata onsen ttn

0   5 km

times compared with Naples, and this is one time that the comparison is not far-fetched (as it often is elsewhere in Japan). Sakurajima was an island until 1914 when an immense eruption poured out an estimated 3000 million tons of lava and ash, and bridged the gap to the mainland on the side facing away from Kagoshima. The peninsula is virtually one lava and ash field and it is interesting to spend some time looking around the huge and jagged masses of ugly but fascinating black rock. You can take a sightseeing bus from the Sakurajima ferry dock; the trip takes 1¾ hours. The lava field begins about 10 minutes walk away from the dock. Only *Minami-dake* (south peak) is still active; it occasionally ejects rock, so climbing is prohibited. Large clouds of smoke and fine ash are also common.

One of the interesting sights on the island is the torii (gate) of a shrine at Kurokami. It was once four metres tall, but the eruption buried so much of it that only the top metre still shows above the ground.

There is a lava observatory (tempodai) on the south side of the island, giving a good view of the great expanse of lava hurled out during the 20 or so known eruptions during recorded history. On the peninsula are farms that produce the largest radishes in the world – some 50 cm in diameter and 45 kg in weight!

Ferries to Sakurajima leave the Kagoshima side regularly; the dock (Sakurajima-sambashi) is close to Kagoshima station.

CHIRAN

This little town, a bit over an hour from Kagoshima by bus, preserves one corner much as it was two centuries ago. Several samurai houses are open to the public and a worth visiting to see the lovely gardens and large residences of this formerly privileged class. Buses to Chiran leave Kagoshima from Yama-gataya bus terminal (Yamagataya department store), and make trips in each direction 11 times a day.

IBUSUKI

About an hour south of Kagoshima by train or bus (from Nishi-Kagoshima station), Ibusuki is a pleasant hot-spring resort town. Unlike most such towns, this one can be readily enjoyed by westerners as well as Japanese, because it isn't necessary to stay at a ryokan or to be familiar with Japanese customs.

Information

At Ibusuki station, your first stop should be the tourist information office to pick up a map of the area; it has enough English to be useful. The girls at the office probably won't speak English but they are friendly and helpful.

For the day's nibbles you could try to find the Lotteria coffee shop near the station; a shop in the building sells a variety of tempura, good for a picnic lunch.

Sand Bath (Sunamushi)

One of the most enjoyably unusual sensations of Japan is to be buried up to

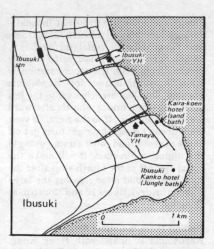

Ibusuki

the neck in hot sand. This is possible where a hot spring surfaces near a beach, permeating the sand and heating it to a high but still bearable temperature. Go to the Kairo-kuen Hotel and ask for a sunamushi; you'll be directed to a small area on the beach behind the hotel next to the sea-wall, where the attendant will dig a hole and shovel you in. The experience is wonderfully relaxing, probably better left for the end of a day's explorations lest all your energy be sapped at the start!

Jungle Bath (Junguro-furo)

After lying in the sand, move down the road a km or so to the huge Ibusuki Kanko Hotel, a very popular destination for Japanese honeymooners and recommended to anyone travelling on a non-budget basis. Its facilities are quite luxurious and on a grand scale.

The Jungle Bath is a building the size of an aircraft hangar, to the left of the main hotel building. It contains over 15 pools of hot-spring water of different temperatures, size, shape and mineral content. Luxuriant growths of tropical plants decorate the room. Depending on the season it may be crowded or you may have the place almost to yourself. The sensation of luxuriating in the various pools is marvellous, but it is best to go with a friend because the experience can become boring without someone to talk to. It doesn't matter whether the friend is male or female as this is one of the few easily-found mixed baths in Japan. There is a ladies-only section, but it has only two or three pools. If you would like to try it, but are shy, remember that a towel can hide everything worth hiding, and the novelty wears off so that the whole experience seems quite natural. The baths are open from 7 am to 1 am and entry costs about Y500.

There is also a sand bath adjacent to the pools but it is indoors and the water is piped, so the sunamushi at the beach would be more 'authentic'.

Kaimon-dake
Another attraction of the Ibusuki area is the graceful conical shape of Kaimon-dake. Buses run from Yamagawa (near the Kanko Hotel) past the mountain to Makurazaki; from there buses run to Kagoshima via Chiran, allowing a circular route around the bottom of the peninsula. Kaimon-dake can be climbed in about two hours, starting from Kaimon-dake bus stop. Another nearby feature is the round caldera lake, Ikeda-ko; and projecting below the body of the peninsula is the spit Nagasaki-bana (Long Cape Harbour) which offers an excellent view of Kaimon-dake and the sea.

Bus tours
Several bus tours begin at Ibusuki station and make sightseeing in the area very easy. All but one begin in the morning; some return to Ibusuki and some terminate in Kagoshima. The basic tours take in Kaimon-dake and Ikeda-ko; others take in destinations such as Ibusuki Skyline Highway, Chiran and Sakurajima; while others cross the bay to Sata-misaki cape ending at Kagoshima. Info on these tours and others from Kagoshima, is available from the information centres at Nishi-Kagoshima or Ibusuki stations.

SATA-MISAKI CAPE
Sata-Misaki, across Kagoshima Bay, is the southern-most point of the main islands of Japan. Rugged rocks projecting out of the sea, blue water and the first lighthouse in the country (built under the supervision of an Englishman soon after the country was opened to foreigners) are the attractions. The area is a park with lush semi-tropical vegetation. The cape can be reached easily by tour bus from Nishi-Kagoshima station or by ferry and bus from the Ibusuki area. (The ferry crosses from Yamagawa to Sata.)

Miyazaki-ken

TOI-MISAKI CAPE
This is another scenic cape, north-east of Cape Sata, famed for small herds of wild horses that are allowed to roam free. It is most easily reached by bus from Aburatsu or Miyazaki; a sightseeing bus travels from the latter along the picturesque Nichinan coast.

NICHINAN-KAIGAN COAST
This is a very pretty stretch of coast extending about 100 km from Shibushi Bay to Miyazaki city. It has been compared with the Amalfi coast of Italy, and one cyclist friend said he was tempted to turn around and return the way he had come because he found it so good. Because the climate is so mild, semi-tropical plants such as palms flourish.

Along the way is *Udo-jingu* shrine, perched on cliffs at the edge of the sea, partly in a cave.

Aoshima
Aoshima is a small island, now connected to the mainland by a causeway. It is covered with betel-nut palms and the surrounding beach has many tiny sea shells mixed with the sand. It is famous for the Ogres' Washboard, formed over the ages when sedimentary rock became up-

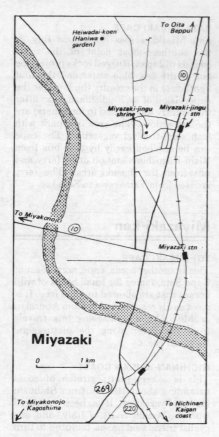

To Oita
Beppu!

Heiwadai-koen
(Haniwa
garden)

To Miyakonojō

Miyazaki-jingu
shrine

Miyazaki-jingu
stn

Miyazaki stn

Miyazaki

0   1 km

To Miyakonojo
Kagoshima

To Nichinan
Kaigan
coast

ended and eroded to form a series of parallel ridges of rock a metre or so apart. It is quite interesting at low tide.

There is good swimming at Aoshima; and other places to visit are the Cactus Park (with a reputed million plants) and the Sub-tropical Plant Garden. Because it is a popular tourist destination there are many hotels etc. There is also a youth hostel close by.

MIYAZAKI

The city of Miyazaki sits in the middle of the area that was the centre of early

Japanese civilisation (as we know it). Because this period predates written history, much of its story is mythical and no structures survive. However some interesting remains have been excavated and are worth visiting. The name Miyazaki means 'shrine promontory'.

Things to See
Heiwadai Park

The city of Miyazaki is quite ordinary but you can spend your time profitably by visiting Heiwadai-koen park. Heiwa means 'peace', so it is somewhat ironic that the 36-metre tower was built in 1940. The tower is of little interest unless you look for the marker on the path leading to the main staircase. Standing there, clapping your hands loudly results in a strange groaning echo. The main attraction of the park, other than the many flowers that bloom during the first five months, is Haniwa-niwa.

Haniwa-niwa

Haniwa are charming and attractive clay figures that have been excavated from the many burial mounds found in the vicinity. Reproductions of many of these have been artistically located around the park, surrounded by flowers, under shrubs, beside trees. Most of the figures are about a metre high, so the details are clearly discernible and they have very charming and humorous expressions. There are knights with horses, court ladies, even a vacant-faced village idiot – I found it an excellent introduction to archaeology. Miniature reproductions of many of the figures are on sale at the administrative building near the garden. They can also be bought in Tokyo and other centres, but finding them elsewhere can be a problem without time to look around and the selection may not be as great.

Miyazaki-jingu shrine

The first emperor of Japan was Jimmu, a man known more from myths than actual fact. He was the ruler of this area of

Kyushu about 600 BC; his descendants – the Yamato tribe – went on to conquer all of Japan, thus determining its culture. He is enshrined in Miyazaki-jingu, and in the grounds there is a museum of items excavated from nearby tombs.

Both Heiwadai and Miyazaki-jingu are accessible from Miyazaki station by bus; the first station north of Miyazaki (called Miyazaki-jingu) is also close to the shrine.

Saitobaru

The early settlers of this area brought with them the practice of building tomb mounds (kofun), which was carried on into at least the 7th century – culminating in the largest at Sakai, near Osaka. Similar mound building customs existed in Korea, especially in the Kyongju area, not too far from the coast facing Japan.

Other evidence suggesting continental ties are haniwa funerary clay figures of horses and horsemen found in the tombs; horses were not known in Japan until the 3rd century AD. The figures were buried with important people, in place of live humans, in the same way as was the practice in China.

This is intended as an introduction to Saitobaru, where about 300 tomb mounds dot the flat countryside. They will probably be of limited interest to most visitors because they are little more than grassy mounds of earth. Some are only a metre or so in height, others are large enough to be mistaken for hills; they will be of greater interest to archaeologists. Items excavated from the tombs are interesting and are displayed at the museums in Saito and at Miyazaki-jingu; the figures at Haniwa-niwa are reproductions of funerary items from this area.

The tomb area is close to Saito on Route 219, which leads to Hitoyoshi; the closest railway station is Tsuki, reached by branching off the main line at Sadowara.

HYUGA

The city of Hyuga is not special tourist-ically but it is connected, by ferries, with Kobe, Osaka and Kawasaki (near Tokyo). Details of schedules and fares are given in the general Getting Around chapter early in the book.

TAKACHIHO-KYO GORGE

Inland from Nobeoka by road (Route 218) or JNR, or south-east from the Aso area by Routes 325 or 265/218, is the lovely Takachiho-kyo gorge. The cliffs are formed by columnar basalt, lava that has cooled into parallel pillars of rock up to 80 metres high. The green water of the Gokase river passes through the narrow valley, and waterfalls splash down here and there.

Also of interest is *Takachiho-jinja* shrine. This sacred site is said to be the 'Cradle of Japan', so the shrine is quite important. Of special interest is the sacred dance, *Iwato Kagura*, which is performed every day.

Places to Stay

In addition to other accommodation in the area, there are three youth hostels. One traveller had nothing but the highest praise for the food at *Yamatoya Youth Hostel*; however I tried three times to obtain accommodation there without success.

Oita-ken

SAIKI

There is a regular boat service between Saiki and Sukumo on Shikoku. Details are given in the Sukumo write-up.

USUKI AREA

The attraction of the Usuki area is a number of statues of Buddha dating from the 10th and 12th centuries. The most artistic and numerous of these are located near Usuki; several are largely intact, while elsewhere only the heads have survived (but these heads are well formed and some of the original colouring remains).

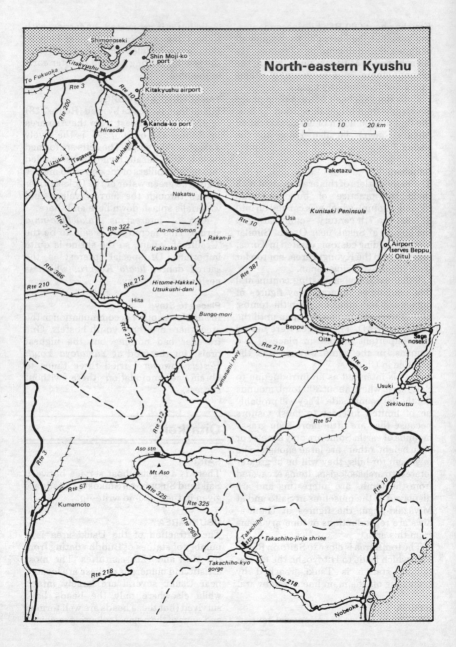

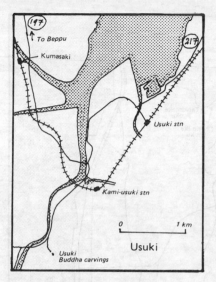

Usuki

The Usuki images, *Seki-butsu*, are displayed in a small ravine not far from Kami-Usuki station (JNR). A good descriptive pamphlet in English is given out when you enter.

Other rock sculptures are scattered through the valleys of the Oita and Ono rivers at Motomachi, Takase, Sugao, Ogata and Fukoji, as well as on the Kunisake Peninsula to the north. Motomachi has some of the best preserved images, those at Magari are badly weathered and those at Takase are so-so.

Saganoseki

There is a ferry service between Saganoseki and Misaki on Shikoku. Details are given in the Misaki write-up.

Takeda

Ogata and Fukoji are quite close to Takeda (Bungo-Takeda station) where *Oka-jo* castle once stood. The castle was destroyed in the late 19th century and only its foundation stones and walls still stand, rising high up a hillside. It inspired the very famous composition *Kojo-no-tsuki* ('Moon over Castle Ruins'), a hauntingly beautiful piece of music, especially when played on the intended *koto* and *shakuhachi*. Its composer, Rentaro Taki, was influenced by western music so western ears will find it very pleasing. (A record including this composition would make a good souvenir of Japan.) Also in this area is Harajiki-yaki waterfall.

OITA

There are two daily ferry services each way between Oita and Kobe with a stop at Matsuyama (Shikoku). One of the Kobe-bound boats passes through much of the scenic area of the Inland Sea in daylight. For details refer to the general Getting Around chapter.

BEPPU

Beppu is one of the best-known hot-spring resorts in Japan, ideal for sybaritic delights and interesting sightseeing. There are eight 'towns ' with hot-springs within the bounds of Beppu; the total water outflow exceeds 100 million litres per day.

Information

There is an information centre at the station that gives out maps and other literature, some in English. As usual with Japanese maps, some may only have a superficial resemblance to true scale and actual locations.

Things to See
The hells (Jigoku)

For those not particularly interested in hot-spring bathing, there is another attraction – the jigoku or 'hells'. In several places around the city, subterranean water of boiling temperature comes to the surface, sometimes violently, sometimes quietly but colourfully – would you believe a pond of naturally red water? Other malevolent emanations include geysers and dark, malodorous, bubbling pools of mud.

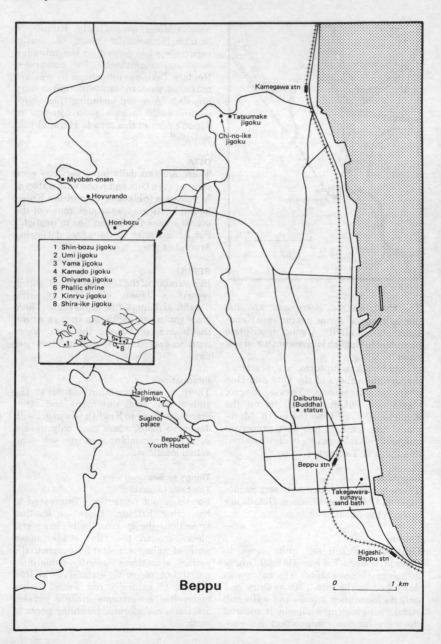

Kamegawa stn

Tatsumake jigoku

Chi-no-ike jigoku

Myoban-onsen

Hoyurando

Hon-bozu

1 Shin-bozu jigoku
2 Umi jigoku
3 Yama jigoku
4 Kamado jigoku
5 Oniyama jigoku
6 Phallic shrine
7 Kinryu jigoku
8 Shira-ike jigoku

Hachiman jigoku

Suginoi palace

Beppu Youth Hostel

Daibutsu (Buddha) statue

Beppu stn

Takegawara-sunayu sand bath

Higashi-Beppu stn

Beppu

0   1 km

The hells are located in two areas of Beppu. Several are clustered close together at Kannawa, about six km from Beppu station, and the other two are a couple of km further away. The first cluster can be reached from Beppu station by bus 16, 17, 24, 25 or 27, getting off at Kannawa. A ticket for entry to most of the nine hells is available for the price of five. (In fact only about five of them are really worth visiting.) The following list describes the hells from west to east, and then the separate ones.

Hon Bozu jigoku Not included on the multiple ticket, and some distance up a long hill (accessible from Hon Bozu bus stop, the second after Kannawa), this hell features a number of grey mud pools that plurp and plop in a humorous manner. Recommended more to those who will not have any other opportunity to see such boiling mud.

Umi jigoku *Umi* means sea, and the water here is a very picturesque green. It is hot enough to boil eggs, as demonstrated by a basket of them suspended in the water. Around the grounds are torii gates. There is a second pond, also green, but cooler.

Yama jigoku This is of minimal proportions and wild animals on display are the attraction. Their living conditions demonstrate an unfortunate Japanese trait of not caring for the comfort of animals. Not recommended.

Garden The garden on the corner between the hells is pleasant, but not particularly noteworthy. Admission is separate.

Oniyama jigoku The hell content here is negligible; the attraction is a number of crocodiles.

Phallic shrine Amidst the hells is this strange little shrine with a sizeable collection of carved phalluses. For those with an earthy sense of humour, very

recommendable; for those easily shocked, to be avoided.

Kinryu jigoku The name means 'golden dragon'. There is nothing to see except clouds of steam and gaudy, faded Buddhist images. A waste of time.

Shiroike jigoku The attraction is a cloudy-white pond and several small aquaria of fish not native to Japan, including large ungainly pirarucu from the Amazon. The pond is similar to that at Hoyurando (described later) but of minor interest. The name means 'white pond'.

Kamado jigoku One of the main attractions here is the noise, as steam jets non-stop out of the ground with a great roar. Also interesting is red-brown bubbling mud. If one dares to believe signs, the precipitated minerals on sale are good for the following collection of ailments: 'chronic mascular rheumatism, mascular rigidity, neuralgia, arthritis, gout, swelling of gland and syphilis, anaemia, weakness after illness, chronic gastroenteric catarrhs and fatigue, evidation after getting a wind, haemorrhoids, scabies, honeycomb ringworm, scaly tetter, moist tetter, leucodermia and other chronic skin diseases and ulcers'.

Chi-no-ike jigoku The name means 'blood hell' and comes from the surprising red of the water (due to ferrous oxide). It is worth seeing for its unusual colour. To reach this and the following jigoku, it is necessary to take a bus or taxi to Chinoike stop. The two hells are a short walk back up the hill.

Tatsumaki jigoku This is the only geyser of the Beppu hells. The name means 'waterspout hell' and it erupts frequently enough to be worth waiting for.

Tsurumi jigoku Not on the 'regular' route, this jigoku is close to the Suginoi Hotel. It also has a number of Buddha statues, said to be 'in good taste'.

Takasagi-yama

One of the other sightseeing 'targets', this mountain is known for its semi-wild monkeys (tame enough to have no fear of humans, but wild enough not to trust). The mountain is most easily reached by bus from Beppu station; ask at the information centre for directions.

Daibutsu

This large concrete figure of Buddha is a rather unusual sight in Beppu, mostly of curiosity value. Unlike the usual benevolent visage, this Buddha scowls and looks generally unpleasant. Mixed into the concrete are the ashes of thousands of cremated Buddhists.

Hoyurando Hot-spring Baths

The best (perhaps only) outdoor hot-spring pools around Beppu are located at Hoyurando, a hotel-style resort; the name translates as either 'Recreation land' or 'Recuperation land'. Behind the hotel building are two outdoor pools of bluish-white water, strongly sulphurous to the nose. Bathing here is mixed but there are segregated pools inside the buildings.

To use the baths, you enter the hotel lobby, pay the fee, then leave by the rear and follow the long covered walkway downhill to the baths. After disrobing and washing you then enter the chosen bath or pool. (Hints for proper decorum in mixed nude baths is given in the section on Noboribetsu-onsen, Hokkaido.) The outdoor pools are most enjoyable in warm, sunny weather although the warm water guarantees comfort in any season while submerged. There are also two kinds of mud baths. (A friend amused himself by building an eight cm nose; the Japanese didn't know what to make of him.)

Behind the hotel and to the left is the source of the hot water, marked by the bright colours of chemicals precipitated from the subterranean water as it cools.

Hoyurando is a couple of km beyond the jigoku of the Kannawa area, on the road that forks off to the right. There is a bus

service (en route to Ajimu); the stop is Hoyurando. On the way the bus passes through another of the eight active hot-spring areas, Myoban. Numbers of little tent-like grass huts have been built over the sources of underground steam and heat to form natural steam baths.

Suginoi Hotel

The huge Suginoi Hotel can be recommended for its annex, Suginoi Palace. Along with arcade games, it has a large stage with a nightly production of a play, mini-circus or other act. In the same complex are two gigantic bath rooms, both the size of an aircraft hangar, one each for men and women (no mixed section). In each are several pools of different size and temperature; from two-people size to gigantic, from frigid to *very* hot. Decorations on the men's side include a waterfall, a slide, torii gate and a Chinese-style temple with heated marble floor. The ladies side has a large and benevolent Buddha and equally lush greenery.

Oishi-so Bath

This smaller-scale bath is open to the public. It has tastefully decorated pools with rock walls and floors. It is located a short distance down from the cluster of jigoku on the main road. (It also offers accommodation.) A sand bath is included in the amenities.

Hot-Sand Baths

Another activity to enjoy in Beppu is a sand bath, where one is buried to the neck in naturally hot, steaming sand. Public sand baths (suna) are found both on the beach and indoors at Takegawara. The latter is a large, oldish, wooden building where you pay at the entrance, put your clothes in a locker, rinse at the small concrete tub, pick up your towel (or one of the many lying around) and follow one of the ladies to the hole she has dug for you in the sand. Lie down, put the towel where it will do the most good, and relax while she piles more hot sand over your body. A feeling of infinite relaxation will overtake you as the warmth permeates. When your time is up, rinse off the sand, soap, rinse again and it's all over. (Take your own soap and towel.) Definitely worthwhile and it only costs a few hundred yen.

It's quite common to have your picture taken in the sand bath; pre-set your camera, and use sign language to explain to the 'burier' what you want. It is best to keep your camera in a plastic bag until it is time to take the picture, otherwise the lens will steam up.

There is also an open-air sand bath on the beach near Kamegawa station; ask for 'sunayu'.

Other activities: 'Onsen', or hot-spring resort is virtually synonymous in Japan with 'sex'. It is said that no man with Y10,000 in his pocket need spend the night in Beppu alone as it is one of the most famous places in Japan for play-for-pay. With the right guidance one can also locate interesting live shows.

Places to Stay
In addition to countless hotels, ryokan and minshuku, there is also a *Beppu Youth Hostel*. The information centre should have instructions on how to get there. It is very close to the Suginoi Hotel.

Getting There
In addition to train services and flights from nearby Oita airport (which is actually north of Beppu, on the Kunisake Peninsula), there are also ferries to points on Shikoku. The dock is 10 minutes from the station by bus. There are regular overnight ferries between Beppu and Hiroshima and Osaka as well as between nearby Oita and Kobe. Some of these stop at ports in Shikoku en route and some pass through the most scenic parts of the Inland Sea in daylight. For details refer to the general Getting Around chapter.

YUFUIN-ONSEN
This is another hot-spring resort town, not

too far from Beppu. Accommodation is in the Y10,000 a night range, so not for budget travellers, but if you are not worried about money you would enjoy staying at one of the thatched-roof farmhouses that serve as inns. The town reputedly has the only free public bath in Japan. The setting is very scenic, with a mountain in the background. It can be reached by bus directly from Beppu or indirectly via Oita by train.

YAMANAMI HIGHWAY
Beppu is the eastern terminus of this highway that crosses Kyushu via Mt Aso and Kumamoto, ending in Nagasaki. It passes through some of the prettiest countryside in Kyushu and can be recommended. Four buses leave Beppu daily, one of which goes non-stop to Nagasaki, the others finishing at Kumamoto.

USA
To the north of Beppu lies the shrine city of Usa. The bright-orange shrine buildings are decorated with carvings; the style of the buildings is of the Heian era (1000-1100) but the shrine was founded earlier (725). The hill on which the shrine is built is an old burial mound.

Usa was once the political, economic and cultural centre of Kyushu. At one time there were 65 temples in the area but through the years they have disappeared— only the carved Buddha heads and tombstones scattered around nearby Kunisake-hanto peninsula testify to its former importance and strong Buddhist influence.

A story, probably dubious, reported that interest in Usa picked up in the immediate post-war occupation period because of companies who wanted to be able to mark their manufactures MADE IN USA.

Kunisake Peninsula
There are nine ferries a day in each direction between Taketazu (Kunisake peninsula) and Tokuyama (western

Honshu). Sailings are scheduled through the day, around the clock (Y300, 2 hours).

YABAKEI GORGE

Attractive scenery may be found along the Yamakuni-kawa river in Yabakei Gorge. It is 'pleasant' rather than 'spectacular', as the cliffs on either side of the river (along which the road passes) are often too far apart and do not soar skyward as do those of some other gorges in Japan.

The gorge is easily seen by bus from Nakatsu. The starting point of the main gorge is near Ao-no-Domon, about 16 km out of Nakatsu and continues for about 10 km to Kakizaka. Apart from the main gorge (Hon-Yabakei), there are several gorges that branch off from it, the most attractive of which is Shin-Yabakei ('deep Yabakei'), beginning at Kakizaka. The main attractions begin about eight km into the valley and include Hitome-Hakkei ('one look – eight views') and Utsukushi-dani ('beautiful valley'). However, despite the fame and reputation of the valley, I was somewhat underwhelmed and would suggest it mostly for those with a little extra time.

From Nakatsu station, buses run at least as far as Kakizaka (23 a day); of these, three a day turn and go through Shin-Yabakei (with another four a day that originate at Kakizaka) as far as Bungo-Mori (on Route 210 and JNR). There are six buses a day returning from Bungo-mori to Kakizaka and a much greater number from there back to Nakatsu (or on to Hita), so a one-day excursion out of Nakatsu is possible.

Kanda & Moji

There is a nightly ferry, to and from Osaka, from both these places. Information for getting to the docks is given at the beginning of the chapter (Kitakyushu write-up) and schedule details are given in the general Getting Around chapter at the start of the book.

GETTING THERE – KYUSHU

There are several ways to enter Kyushu.

International The cities of Fukuoka, Nagasaki, Kumamoto and Kagoshima are international air ports of entry. The overseas cities connected to them are listed in the write-up on those cities. Check with a travel agent if you are travelling from Asia to Japan and wish to land in Kyushu, because new services seem to be added yearly.

Domestic All-the major cities are linked to other cities around Japan by air; many flights pass through Fukuoka, the regional air transport centre.

Rail The Shinkansen super express train links Fukuoka (northern Kyushu) to all the major cities of Honshu, such as Hiroshima, Kyoto and Tokyo, in a few hours; Tokyo is about seven hours away. Fukuoka and Kokura are the only stops on Kyushu. There are also ordinary train services to Honshu (at lower cost) via Shimonoseki.

Road Road links include a tunnel and bridge from Shimonoseki, and there are overnight ferries that carry passengers and vehicles to Tokyo, Kawasaki, Osaka, Kobe, Hiroshima and ports on Shikoku.

Ferries Ferries leave from the Kyushu ports of Kokura (Kitakyushu city), Kanda, Moji, Beppu, Oita, Hyuga and Kagoshima as well as some less frequent services to Okinawa and some of the other southern islands of Japan from Kagoshima and Fukuoka. In addition there are several ferries across the relatively narrow Hoyo Straits to/from Shikoku and Honshu. These 'local' ferries connect the following cities: Beppu – Yawatahama and Misaki (Shikoku); Saganoseki – Misaki; Usuki – Yawatahama; Saiki – Sukumo (Shikoku); Taketazu – Shinnanyo (near Tokuyama, western Honshu). There are generally several sailings every day for each of these.

Southern Islands

There are two chains of islands to the south of the main islands of Japan: the Nansei-shoto group, stretching south and east from southern Kyushu; and the Ogasawara-shoto group (the Bonin islands) more-or-less due south of Tokyo, a continuation of the Izu islands.

Nansei Islands

Below Kyushu and stretching to Taiwan are the Nansei (south-west) Islands. Some are mere atolls, while others support sizeable populations.

The islands as far as Yoron-to are part of Kagoshima-ken, while Okinawa and all the islands south of it make up Okinawa-ken. Close to Kagoshima are Tanegashima and Yaku-shima, and further south is the Amami-shoto group (which includes Amami-oshima, Tokuno-shima, Okino-erabu-jima and Yoron-to). Below them is the Ryukyu group (made up of Okinawa and the islands around it); the Saki group (around Miyako); and the Yaeyama group (Ishigaki, Iriomote and Yonaguni).

All offer a semi-tropical flavour not found in the main islands of Japan.

The culture of the Nansei Islands is basically Japanese but there is also a Chinese element. The islands closest to Kagoshima were most strongly influenced by the Satsuma culture, while the islands closest to Taiwan had the greatest Chinese influence. The unfortunate islanders had the misfortune of being squeezed between two powers, and had to pay tribute to both, causing much misery in olden times. Until quite recently there was a distinct Okinawan language, related to Japanese but quite incomprehensible to the people on the main islands, even those of the Satsuma area. Many place names use unique local pronunciation of kanji; these are used in this book as much as possible and may differ from other sources that use standard Japanese (but incorrect pronunciation).

Snake Warning
Nearly all islands except Miyako are inhabited by a venomous snake – the habu. Every year about 300 people are bitten, four or five of whom die. (Prompt medical treatment from special clinics keeps the toll this low.) The snakes are nocturnal, so be especially careful at night. Carry a bright light (which they dislike) and make lots of noise, particularly walking heavily, as although snakes are deaf they can feel the vibrations. They are always found in pineapple plantations.

TANEGASHIMA
Both this island and Yaku-shima are close to southern Kyushu and are easily reached by boat (two or more sailings a day to each island), or air from Kagoshima.

There is no special attraction on Tanegashima other than its relative remoteness; the island is flat and agricultural. There are campsites, and a bus service several times a day between the north and south.

The main city and boat landing point is Nishino-omote.

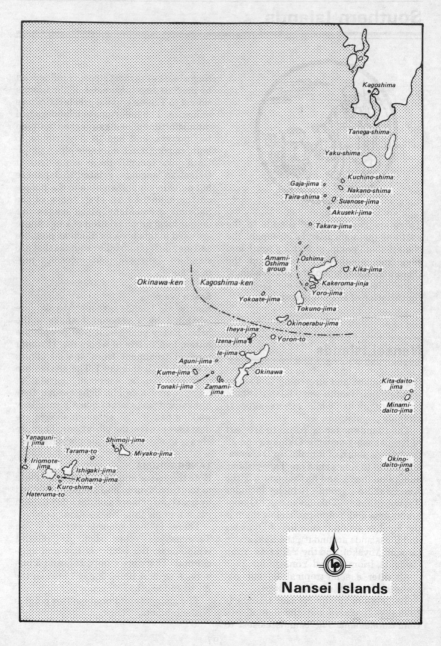

Nansei Islands

YAKU-SHIMA

Whereas Tanegashima is quite flat, Yaku-shima has the highest mountain in Kyushu, *Miyano-ura-dake* (1935 metres), plus a number of lesser peaks. The island is well-known for huge centuries-old cedar trees (*yaku-sugi*).

Boats from Kagoshima dock at Miyano-ura and there are several buses daily covering three-quarters of the distance around the island.

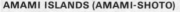

Tanegashima & Yaku-shima

AMAMI ISLANDS (AMAMI-SHOTO)

The Amami group comprises the main islands of Amami-oshima, Kikai-jima, Tokuno-shima, Okino-erabu-jima and Yoron-to. While there are no single attractions (the islands are basically agricultural, producing crops like sugar, bananas and pineapples), there are many good beaches ideal for just relaxing on.

The scenery of Amami-oshima and the other islands is beautiful. There are buses or you can rent a bicycle or motorcycle. Camping is good. In contrast with the emerald of the coral sea around Okinawa, the water here is deep blue.

Okinawa

The largest of the south-west islands is Okinawa. From the 14th to the 19th century, this was a nominally independent kingdom with its own language and culture, related to Japanese but with a strong Chinese influence. Japan and China maintained suzerainty of the islands and the people were kept poor by having to provide tribute to both governments. In the last century the Japanese connection became dominant, but the people have generally been regarded as somewhat second class citizens. After World War II the American military occupation continued, making travel there difficult until 1972 when it reverted to Japanese control.

Okinawa and the other islands of the Ryukyu group (south and west to Taiwan) are still economically disadvantaged in comparison to the main islands of Japan, and depend mainly on agriculture tourism. All the islands offer a warm to hot climate similar to the tropics and most have good beaches and clear water, so they have become popular

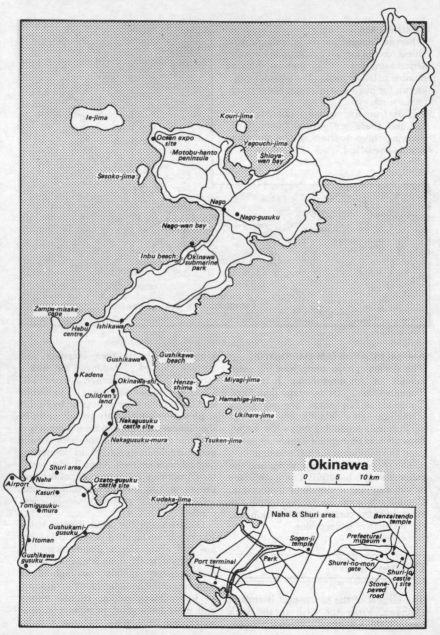

Okinawa

0   5   10 km

destinations for the main-island Japanese, especially in winter.

Information

A good first stop is the tourist information office, located on the city side of the harbour and river near the end of Meiji-bashi bridge. It is near the bus terminal and can be recognised by its red roof tiles. Staff there can provide information for getting around and make hotel bookings.

Additional information on Okinawa is available from the TIC in Tokyo, including the booklet *Okinawa Japan*, and the photocopied sheets *How to Get to Keelung* (No. 20), and *Okinawa* (No. 54) which give updated information on ships to Naha, hotels, etc. Information can also be obtained from the Okinawa-ken office in the Kokusai-kanko-kaikan building in Marunouchi (Tokyo). It might be worthwhile ringing them first (tel 231-0848) to see if they speak English.

NAHA

Today the administrative centre of Okinawa-ken, Naha was the capital of the Ryukyu kingdom for about 400 years. Remnants of three major castles and several lesser ones still stand from those days, along with some historic gates and other relics of Ryukyu design. Although the design of some of these structures appears Chinese, the architecture is an authentically Ryukyuan style that evolved through the centuries.

Things to See
The Boulevards

The main area of Naha is the 1.6 km Kok'sai-dori (International Boulevard). It has several large department stores, as well many shops catering for tourists, with well-known Okinawa products like Bingata textiles, and shell and coral products. Near the end of Kok'sai-dori is *Sogen-ji* temple, known for the stone gates on two sides. Heavily damaged during the war, they were restored afterward. A uniquely Okinawan programme of classical and folk dances and music is performed weekly at Oki-e theatre (near Mitsukoshi department store) and would be worth seeing.

Heiwa-dori (Peace Boulevard) runs off Kok'sai-dori and is the area of a typical Okinawa-style market. Women sit by their baskets of produce in a scene more like South-East Asia than Japan.

Shuri

Shuri is the former location of the castle of the kings of Okinawa during the zenith of the Ryukyu civilisation. The centrepiece, and symbol of this civilisation, is *Shurei-no-mon* gate. The original, dating from the founding of the castle, was destroyed during the war and faithfully rebuilt afterward. Much of the original castle wall still stands but a university now occupies the site of the castle itself.

Nearby is attractive Ryutan-ike pond and surrounding park and not far away is *Benzaitendo* temple. The original was built in 1502, but it too was destroyed during the war and was rebuilt in 1968. On the north side of the pond is the very good prefectural museum, *Kenritsu hakubutsu-kan*, which is housed in the large and traditional residence of the Osho family.

A charming walk goes along the stone-paved street of Kinjo ('silver castle') town. It leads down from the castle site to the harbour and is lined with many fine traditional houses.

Other attractions of the area are Sone hiyan-utaki stone gate, Kankaimon gate of typical Ryukyu style (first built in the early 1500s and rebuilt after the war), and *Enkaku-ji somon* temple (pre-1500s and also rebuilt after the war).

The Shuri area can be reached by bus 25 or 26 from the bus centre.

Arts and Crafts

A little further away, you can find a workshop where Bingata textiles are produced. The dyes and patterns are very bright, quite different from the more subdued and restrained colours used on the main islands.

Another craft to look for is pottery. Tsuboya ware (named for the area where it is made) is quite simple and intended mainly for use as storage vessels for water etc. The forms and finishes owe more to Chinese and southern areas than to Japanese influences. The workshops are open to the public.

Tomigusuku

A castle once stood at Tomigusuku, south of Naha, but today only depressions in the ground indicate its site. More interesting, at least to those concerned with events of World War II, is the nearby headquarters of the Imperial Navy, easily reached on foot. The entire building was located underground and was so well concealed that it was not discovered by the victorious American forces until three weeks after the landing. To their horror, they found that 4000 men and officers had committed suicide in the underground tunnels rather than surrender. The tunnels and rooms are now open for inspection, with no hint of that grisly occurrence in 1945. Buses to Tomigusuku leave from Naha bus centre.

Places to Stay

As well as hotels and ryokan, there are three youth hostels in Naha. The *Harumiso* (tel 67-3218) has the best reputation; the *Tamazano* (tel 67-5377) is rated as OK; and the *Maeda-Misaki* (tel 098964 – 2497), 70 minutes north by bus, is also spoken of well.

AROUND THE COAST

As you travel south of Naha along town and country roads, a common sight is Okinawan houses with tiled roofs. All the tiles are firmly cemented to guard against wind storms, and surmounted by a fierce *shiisaa*, the guardian lion that keeps evil spirits from the house. (Very similar tiling can be seen in India.) In former times the tiles were shaped and fired on site and the shiisaa was sculpted from the same clay; but these days most are made in factories and lack individuality.

The south coast was the scene of the heaviest fighting of the landings of World War II – at Mabuni hill alone, 200,000 people died. If you are interested in the various memorial sites, visit the tourist information office for more details. (*Note:* Residents still find live ordnance on the battlefields, and if you discover any you should notify the police or contact the USAF Kadena base.)

Gyokusendo

This is a limestone cave with a claimed 460,000 stalactites and other limestone configurations, many of which have interesting and lovely colours. About 800 metres of the cave is open for inspection.

Kasuri

If you are interested in weaving, visit the village of Kasuri (comprising Kiyan, Motobo and Teruya) where the hand-woven, vegetable-dyed Kasuri fabrics (mostly silk) are made.

Coastal Views

Continuing around the south coast and up the east, you are constantly in view of the deep-emerald sea. Along this coast and others you are likely to see uniquely Okinawan tombs – large structures with a surrounding semicircular wall, set into hillsides overlooking the coast. There is nothing like them elsewhere in Japan.

Nakagusuku Castle Site

Possibly the finest of such sites on Okinawa; the length and height of the remaining walls and three citadels give a good idea of the scale of the former buildings. From the ramparts you can see the Pacific Ocean in one direction and the East China Sea in the other. It is quite close to Nakagusuku-mura ('Central Castle Village').

Nakumuru House (Nakumuru-ke)

In the same area as Nakagusuku Castle, this is probably the finest residence on Okinawa. It was built in the mid-1700s by a wealthy farmer, and the five structures embody the best of traditional Okinawan building and decorative techniques.

OKINAWA-SHI

Much of this city is aimed at providing recreation for the US airmen of nearby Kadena Airforce Base. With its many clubs and bars, it bears little resemblance to anything typically Okinawan or Japanese (other than an ability to make money). The mood is American, or at least the Japanese impression of American.

Of great interest to the Japanese is Plaza House shopping centre complete with large car park (an unaffordable luxury in most of Japan because of land costs). The Tuttle Bookshop stocks a large number of books on Okinawa.

Things to See
Okinawa Children's Land (Kodomo-no-Kuni)

To the south-east of the city, this aquarium raises more than 60 kinds of reptiles, and has exhibitions of more than 200 kinds of tropical freshwater fish.

The Municipal Colosseum

At Gushikawa, near Children's Land, this is the venue of Sunday bullfights. These are not like the Spanish variety, but are 'bull sumo' – two bulls trying to force each other out of the ring by locking horns and pushing. Similar fights are found on several other islands of Japan and as far south as Indonesia.

The South-east Botanical Garden

This has a large variety and huge number of tropical plants, 600 kinds of flowers, and 200 types of tropical fruit trees intended to emphasize the island's nearly-tropical climate. A small lake and boats are also attractive.

HEDO-MISAKI CAPE

The view from this, the northern tip of Okinawa, is very pretty and on a clear day you can see Yoron Island on the horizon.

The view is definitely worth the trip, which passes a number of attractive villages along the way.

THE WEST COAST

Much of the west coast has been set aside as Okinawa Coast Quasi-National Park, which takes in the area from Hedo-misaki to the northern side of Motobu-hanto Peninsula, and resumes from the south side almost an equal distance to Zampa-misaki. The main attraction is the view of the coast and the beautiful colours of the water.

Motobu-hanto Peninsula

At the north-east neck of the peninsula, there is a beautiful view overlooking Yagachi and Okubo islands (large and small respectively).

Ocean Expo In 1975 a mini World Expo was held near the north-west tip of the peninsula, based on the theme of using oceans. Although the exhibition lasted only six months, sufficient attractions have been carried over or added to give you an enjoyable day's outing.

The Okinawa Village Pavilion demonstrates the old culture of Okinawa and has examples of houses in both traditional and modern styles. The Oceanic Culture Pavilion shows the rich variety of cultures found among the races and ethnic groups of the South Pacific. On the same site is the largest aquarium in the world, featuring three display areas that show tropical, ocean and deep sea fish as well as nine performing dolphins (at Okichan Theatre). Floating City is a science-fiction writer's delight, a large steel multi-columned structure in the water that supposedly represents the way we will live in the future, with appropriate phrases like 'new era' and 'producing harmony between science and nature'. It's interesting but not to be taken seriously. All attractions are close on Mondays.

At the northern end of the site is the graceful arc of beautiful Expo beach.

Accommodation in the vicinity of the Expo site is generally not inexpensive. Okinawa Resort Station is a resort village for young people and uses retired JNR sleeping cars for accommodation. They had to be brought to Okinawa, along with an idled steam engine, for there are no railways on the island.

NAGO

Located at the southern neck of the peninsula, Nago was little damaged during the war so you can still see several houses in the traditional Okinawan style. There are also tall *gajyumaru* trees, 300 years old, on the south-east approaches to the city. In late January and early February, the cherry blossoms are beautiful on the site of former *Nago-gusuku* castle, reached via a long stone staircase. At the top, you can enjoy an excellent view of the surrounding sea and land.

Okinawa Marine Park

A long walkway extends beyond the shallows of a reef here, to a column with underwater glass-windows, so visitors may look out from beneath sea-level. Depending on conditions the number of fish in view may be rather limited; visitors generally tend to visit Ocean Expo instead.

In addition to the 'reverse aquarium' where fish can come to look at people, there is a museum showing many of the seashells found around the island. Glass-bottomed boats may be rented as well.

A short distance to the south are three fine beaches, beginning with Inbu Beach.

Habu Centre

Here you can see the venomous habu snake in perfect safety. A feature is a fight between a habu and a mongoose; the agile animal wins about 99% of the time, particularly because the nocturnal snake is at a disadvantage. The fights are staged relatively frequently, probably a reflection of the plentiful supply. Recent research has shown that mature snakes can survive

two to three years without any food whatsoever.

Places to Stay

In addition to several hotels of good quality, there are also many ryokan. Bookings may be made at the information centre.

Getting There

International: There are flights between Naha and Seoul, Taipai, Manila, Hong Kong, Guam, Saipan and Nauru.

Arimura Sangyo shipping company operates a weekly boat to and from Keelung, in northern Taiwan. The ship leaves Naha at 7 pm Friday and reaches Keelung at about 5 pm Saturday. En route it stops at Ishigaki island, from 7 am to 9.20 am Saturday. It leaves Keelung Monday at 8 am and sails direct to Naha, arriving Tuesday at 7.20 am. The lowest fare (shared, open tatami mat area) is Y15600. Reservations are recommended. The phone numbers of Arimura Sangyo offices are: Tokyo 562-2091; Osaka 345-7421; Naha 68-2191.

Travellers en route to Taiwan must obtain a visa in advance (unless exempt) from the representative of the government of Taiwan, the Association of East Asia Relations in Tokyo. The address and access information are given earlier in the book in the chapter on Facts for the Visitor.

Domestic: There are boat services to Naha from Tokyo, Osaka/Kobe, Hakata (Fukuoka), and Kagoshima. Because several of these stop at islands between Kagoshima and Naha, island hopping is feasible. The various services are detailed in the general Getting Around section early in the book.

There are also flights from Sendai, Tokyo, Osaka, Nagoya, Fukuoka, Nagasaki, Kumamoto, Kagoshima, Miyazaki, and the more important small Nansei islands nearby. (Nearly all the main small islands are accessible by air.)

Getting Around

There are several bus tours (in Japanese only) to different destinations on Okinawa lasting 4½ to 9½ hours. There are also many local buses for the adventurous.

Other Ryukyu Islands

Ie-jima

Off the Motobu-hanto Peninsula, Ie island is easily traversed in a short time. There are many lovely views of the deep-blue sea. The Travel Village (on the side nearest Okinawa) is especially aimed at young travellers.

Minni-jima

This island is claimed to offer the most beautiful sunsets in Okinawa.

Kohama-jima

Once bypassed by tourists, Kohama now has full-scale recreational facilities (Japanese-style) and is attracting more visitors to its fine beaches of white sand and the coral reefs offshore.

Kudaka-jima

The 'Island of the Gods', just off Okinawa, is quite sacred to Okinawans. There are many burials here and funerary practices in the past were rather unusual. Many bodies were exposed to the elements in special places, and only after decomposition were the bones cleaned and buried. (This practice may still be found in mountain villages on the island of Bali in Indonesia.)

Especially on Kudaka, but true everywhere on Okinawa, foreigners are ill-advised to enter cemeteries. It will upset many of the local people, who believe that the presence of an outsider (especially a foreigner) will disturb the spirits of the dead, with bad results for the living. It is worth reading up in advance of a visit to Kudaka to avoid any misunderstanding. Try the Tuttle bookstore in Naha.

Others

Okinawa are Iheya, Izena, Kerama (a group of about 20), and Kume. Information on how to get there can be obtained from the information centre in Okinawa or from travel agents.

MIYAKO-JIMA

There are many beautiful views on Miyako, as well as fine beaches. Miyako-jima was not damaged during the war, so its appearance is more traditional than Okinawa. Most houses are surrounded by walls of coral as protection against the frequent typhoons. Unfortunately it can be a little difficult actually seeing the houses because screens of wood and rock usually block the view through the gateway. The purpose of the screen is to keep out evil spirits as it is believed these little demons can only hop in straight lines. Such superstitions are still strong here and a talisman will often be seen on a wall opposite the road that ends in a T-junction.

Miyako-jima is one of the few islands free of the deadly habu snake.

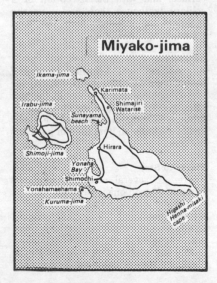

Things to See

Ohonoyama-mura

Miyako Tropical Botanical Garden near here occupies 226 hectares of land, and boasts 40,000 trees and more than 1200 kinds of flowering plants from Central and South America, Africa and the Philippines.

The 'poll stone' near Ohonoyama is a relic of harsh times in the past, when the islanders were little more than slaves, being taxed by both Chinese and Satsuma authorities. A person was compelled to pay taxes when his or her height equalled that of this stone. Its name is *Jintozeizeki* or *Bubakarüsu*, depending on the dialect.

Yonahamae Beach

Four km of white sand stretch along the blue waters and offer excellent swimming.

Sunayama (Sand Mountain) Beach

Swimming is also good here, and nearby Miyako-jinja shrine is worth a visit.

Agari-henna Misaki Cape

The view over the sea here is beautiful. Cliffs drop to the sea, rocks jut above its surface, and with the exception of a solitary lighthouse, there are no nearby buildings to interfere with the wild atmosphere

Jofu fabric

A common sight following the rainy season is great lengths of yarn draped over any available support to dry in the sun after dyeing. It is then woven into Jofu fabric, a well-known product of the island and historically an item used in payment of taxes.

Places to Stay

There are several minshuku near the harbour. A good one is *Ueno-so*.

Getting There

In addition to regular air services, there are scheduled boats between Okinawa (Naha) and Ishigaki. Two lines operate the ships and they largely complement each other; so there is a Naha-Miyako boat every one to four days, and an Ishigaki – Miyako boat every two to seven days. In addition to these there are some sailings that skip Miyako, cutting a few hours off the trip between Naha and Ishigaki. If you want to go to Miyako, make sure you get the right one. Ships from Naha that make the stop depart at 6 pm or 8 pm (depending on the line), and depart Ishigaki at 11 am for both lines. Sailing times are: Naha – Miyako: 13½ to 14½ hours; Naha – Ishigaki (non-stop): 13 to 14 hours; Miyako – Ishigaki: 5½ hours; Ishigaki – Miyako: 8 hours; Ishigaki – Naha (non-stop): 12 to 14 hours; Miyako – Naha: 12½ to 13 hours.

Getting Around

The best way to get around is by bicycle or motorcycle rented from one of the shops near the harbour of the main city, Hirara.

Yaeyama Islands

The Yaeyama group of islands extends from Ishigaki to Yonaguni in a south-westerly arc.

ISHIGAKI-JIMA

The most important of the group, Ishigaki, is famed for its many beautiful beaches. The main city and port is Ishigaki.

Things to See

Miyara Dunchi

This is the house of a noble of the old Ryukyu kingdom, dating from 1819. It follows the plan of houses for people of equal rank that were built around the castle at Shuri on Okinawa; here it is unique, the island's most valued cultural asset. (It may be described as a samurai house, but there were no true samurai in this region.) It houses a small museum of the period, and is also noted for its garden and stone wall.

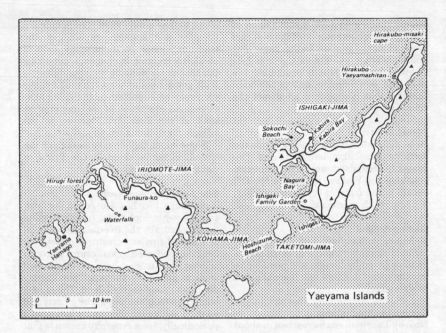

Yaeyama Islands

Yaeyama Shiritsu Museum

Exhibits relating to the culture of the Yaeyama islands are on display at this very interesting museum. Labels, unfortunately, are only in Japanese, but most displays can be understood.

Chorin-ji

This temple has some beautiful old Buddhist sculptures.

Chinese Cemetery

The very Chinese-looking monument here commemorates 128 Chinese who were killed in a fight on a British ship in the last century, and is considered a general monument to peace.

Kabira-wan Bay

Most visitors consider this the most beautiful place on the island. Pearls are cultivated here, and are of an unusual (and thus very costly) black hue. They take the

name of the island group, Yaeyama. The bay can be reached by bus.

The Beaches

Most visitors will want to enjoy the fine beaches of Ishigaki; skin-diving and scuba gear are available for rent. Since there are many types of incredible and beautiful tropical fish in the waters around this (and all the other) islands, diving can be recommended. Water-skiing and fishing are other potential activities.

At the time of revising this book there were still good coral reefs around much of the island, with the usual complement of colourful fish, clear water, etc; they have been one of the main attractions of Ishigaki. However, this has to be written tentatively because, in the name of 'progress' (and bringing in more tourists) an extension to the airport runway has been planned. This project would require extension into the sea, with consequent landfill that would destroy much or all of the reefs near Shiraho; one of the best reef areas of all the islands. Let us hope that common sense overcomes the greed or political ambition that is promoting the plan that would destroy one of the main features that is supposed to attract the tourists.

Places to Stay
Accommodation is plentiful, mostly in the form of minshuku, but there are two camping grounds as well. There are two youth hostels, *Yashima Ryokan* (tel (09808) 2-3157), and *Ishigaki-shi-tei* (tel (09808) 2-2720), both in Ishigaki.

Getting Around
Bicycles, motorcycles and cars can be rented from several shops near the centre of town (even by bicycle it is possible to see the island in a day) and there is also a bus service.

Getting to Other Islands
Nearby Taketomi can be reached in about 20 minutes (Y300, eight trips a day): and Iriomote is accessible by regular boat or hovercraft.

There is a regular Naha – Miyako – Ishigaki (and return) boat service; and the weekly boat to Keelung (Taiwan) from Naha also stops at Ishigaki (but not the return sailing). The former is detailed in the section on Miyako-jima; and the latter in the Naha section. There is air service to and from Naha on Okinawa as well as to Yonaguni, Tarama and Hateruma islands.

TAKETOMI-JIMA
Just a short distance west of Ishigaki, tiny Taketomi (11 km in circumference) can be explored easily in a day on bicycle (available near the boat dock). The island is very popular with day-trippers from Ishigaki, as its magnificent beaches virtually surround the island.

Because it was an untouristed backwater until only a decade or so ago, the pace of life and traditions on Taketomi are much as they always were. The people are friendly and houses are still of the traditional style, surrounded by walls of coral. It is common to see people preparing the thread for weaving minsaori fabric, a craft going back to the 17th century; the yarn may be stretched by the side of the street. An exhibition of weaving may be seen at the Folk Art Museum in the village; small items are on sale.

Some water-buffalo may be seen on the island, either working in the fields or pulling carts for tourists.

Star Sand (hoshi-no-sun)
Taketomi's beaches are noted for 'star sand' – what looks like ordinary white sand is actually the five-pointed skeletal remains of tiny sea creatures. Most of it has been collected by visitors (or souvenir sellers), but it may be possible to find some in pockets in the coral, particularly on the south side of the island. The sand is stirred up from the depths by storms and washed ashore, so the supply is renewed periodically. (Not generally known is that this sand is found on all the Yaeyama islands.) If you find a 'deposit', remember the motto: 'Take a little and it will bring lots of happiness; take a lot and it will bring little happiness'. Leave some for the next person.

Places to Stay
There are minshuku and a youth hostel, *Takana Ryokan*, (tel (098094) 2151) in Taketomi.

IRIOMOTE
More than 80% of this island (plus nearby Kohama, Taketomi, Kuroshima and Aragusuku islands) forms Iriomote National Park, habitat of the primitive Iriomote wildcat. Thought to have remained unchanged in five to 10 million years, this 'living fossil' is the size of a domestic cat and nocturnal, so it is seldom seen, even by residents. It is believed there are only 30 to 40 still living. Star sand is found on the island but you are not

allowed to collect it because Iriomote is a national park. The island also has habu snakes, so take care.

Things to See
Ura-uchi-kawa
The best single excursion on the island is up the Ura-uchi river. Beginning at the mouth of the river, the boat usually carries about 12 people. There is no trouble making up a party, because many day-trippers cross from Ishigaki. After half an hour or so, you disembark and walk for about 40 minutes through canopied near-jungle to two pretty waterfalls, Mariyudo and Kampira. The first has three drops totaling 33 metres, ending in a deep pool; the latter is a long incline with numerous Jacob's wells ('pot holes' formed by small rocks swirling around in depressions and grinding the holes larger).

Skin-diving
As on many of the other islands, skin-diving in the colourful coral beds among equally colourful fish is to be recommended. A barrier reef surrounds the island.

Places to Stay
There are several minshuku as well as two youth hostels at Funaura-ko. Of the latter, *Irumote-so* is the better, with pleasant staff and a nice view over the countryside.

Getting There & Getting Around
The boat, and possibly a hydrofoil, from Ishigaki (60 to 90 minutes) docks at Ohara, from where a bus leaves soon afterward for the other side of the island and the trip up the Ura-uchi river. You can rent bicycles and motorcycles at a shop two minutes from Irumote-so Youth Hostel.

YONAGUNI-JIMA
This is the western-most part of Japan, and on a clear day you can see Taiwan from Irizaki (West Cape). The main attraction is scenery, beaches, warm water and the largest moths in the world.

A beautiful view waits at the top of the 231-metre hill overlooking the village of Sonae.

Kubura-wari
One curiosity is this natural hole in the ground near Kubura. Legend has it that anyone able to jump over it won't have to pay taxes, will have a long life and women will give birth easily. It is wide enough that few are known to test the legend. It is surrounded by interesting rock formations and is situated behind Kubura school.

Places to Stay
There are only minshuku, no youth hostels.

Getting Around
Bicycles and motorcycles may be rented for convenient transport.

HATERUMA-JIMA
This small island is the southern-most part of Japan and a pleasant place to visit. One good place to stay is a room adjacent to the Ishino-ume Restaurant.

GETTING THERE – Nansei Islands
There are boat services from Tokyo, Osaka/Kobe, Hakata, Fukuoka (northern Kyushu), and Kagoshima (southern Kyushu) to Naha on Okinawa. Many of these ships stop at some of the smaller islands between Kagoshima and Okinawa (the Amami-shoto group of islands, a group beginning just north of Okinawa), and there are separate services from Kagoshima to just this group as well as to the two closer islands of Tanega-shima and Yaku-shima. All these services are detailed in the general Getting Around chapter at the start of the book.

There are also air services to Tanegashima, Yakushima, Amami-oshima, Kikai-jima, Tokuno-jima, Kume-jima, Kita Daito-jima, Minami Daito-jima, Miyako-jima, Shimoji-jima, Tarama-to, Ishigaki-jima, Yonaguni-jima and Hateruma-to. Information on flights to these places can be obtained from any travel agent in Japan.

Ogasawara Islands

South of the Izu Islands is another group, the Ogasawara-shoto Islands. These are part of the Tokyo-to administrative district and extend to latitudes as far south as Okinawa.

The islands are ideal for really getting away from it all; access is only by ship from Tokyo (about twice a week), and they are beyond TV and regular radio range. The climate is semi-tropical, slightly cooler than Okinawa, small palm trees grow and there are frequent rain showers. While the Izu Islands (see the end of the Near Tokyo chapter) offer a good weekend excursion for swimming and meeting people, the Ogasawara Islands are better for quiet exploration and adventure.

The main islands are named after family members such as Chichi-jima (father), Haha-jima (mother), and Ani-jima (elder brother). The first two are the main islands; Ani is a small island just above Chichi-jima. Muko-jima is a cluster of small islands to the north. To the south are the Kazan (Volcano) islands, which include Io-jima (better known in English as Iwo-jima), famed as a battle site in World War II and memorialized in the photo of Marines raising the US flag atop 185-metre *Suribachi-san* (a posed shot, by the way). Tourists are not allowed on Io-jima because large areas still have live ordnance from the fighting, and the remains of many Japanese soldiers lie entombed in the caves where they died. Chichi and Haha are the only populated islands.

CHICHI-JIMA

This, the largest island, has peaks up to 600 metres and also has beaches and good swimming. It is small enough to walk across in two hours, or around in a day; roads are good and there is a bus service. Bougainvillea and hibiscus give a tropical air.

There are three beaches, one of which is sandy while another has some coral. Skin-diving can be recommended at many places around the island, especially between Chichi-jima and Ani-jima because of the many fantastically coloured tropical fish; they are not afraid of people and come close. There are also turtles and rays. Scuba and less complex diving equipment is available for hire. You can also rent a boat and circle the island, stopping to dive where desired. It is reminiscent of Australia's Great Barrier Reef. Throwing bread on the water from shore results in 'instant fish'. The water is a darker blue than that of the Okinawa area and is not as clear.

On the west side, the rusting hull of a small ship is a relic of the war. There are also caves around the shore that were used for defence purposes; some are now used by fishermen for storage and others are blocked by gates.

There are minshuku on the island, but they tend to be crowded and generally do not serve meals, so you have to eat at restaurants or buy food at a local store. The few shops close by 6.30 pm; and the hottest nightspot, a coffee shop, is closed by 10 pm.

Because the island was under US control for a long time, many people can communicate in English, and there are several US-style buildings, a curiosity to the Japanese.

Getting There

Access is from Tokyo to Futami-ura. There are one or two sailings a week in each direction (depending on season); the trip takes a little over a day. Further information is available at the Tourist Information Centre, Tokyo.

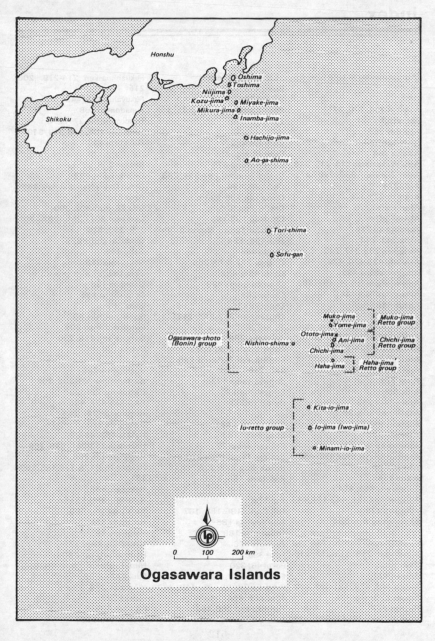

Ogasawara Islands

Index